SQL Server 2008
Transact-SQL Recipes

Joseph Sack

Apress®

SQL Server 2008 Transact-SQL Recipes

Copyright © 2008 by Joseph Sack

ISBN-13 (pbk): 978-1-59059-980-8

ISBN-10 (pbk): 1-59059-980-2

ISBN-13 (electronic): 978-1-4302-0626-2

Printed and bound in the United States of America 9 8 7 6 5 4 3 2 1

Lead Editor: Jonathan Gennick
Technical Reviewer: Evan Terry
Editorial Board: Clay Andres, Steve Anglin, Ewan Buckingham, Tony Campbell, Gary Cornell,
    Jonathan Gennick, Matthew Moodie, Joseph Ottinger, Jeffrey Pepper, Frank Pohlmann,
    Ben Renow-Clarke, Dominic Shakeshaft, Matt Wade, Tom Welsh
Project Manager: Susannah Davidson Pfalzer
Copy Editor: Ami Knox
Associate Production Director: Kari Brooks-Copony
Production Editor: Laura Cheu
Compositor: Dina Quan
Proofreader: Liz Welch
Indexer: Brenda Miller
Artist: April Milne
Cover Designer: Kurt Krames
Manufacturing Director: Tom Debolski

Distributed to the book trade worldwide by Springer-Verlag New York, Inc., 233 Spring Street, 6th Floor, New York, NY 10013. Phone 1-800-SPRINGER, fax 201-348-4505, e-mail orders-ny@springer-sbm.com, or visit http://www.springeronline.com.

For information on translations, please contact Apress directly at 2855 Telegraph Avenue, Suite 600, Berkeley, CA 94705. Phone 510-549-5930, fax 510-549-5939, e-mail info@apress.com, or visit http://www.apress.com.

Apress and friends of ED books may be purchased in bulk for academic, corporate, or promotional use. eBook versions and licenses are also available for most titles. For more information, reference our Special Bulk Sales—eBook Licensing web page at http://www.apress.com/info/bulksales.

Contents at a Glance

Contents

About the Author

JOSEPH SACK is a dedicated support engineer in the Microsoft Premier Field Engineering organization and has worked with SQL Server since 1997. He is the author of *SQL Server 2005 T-SQL Recipes* (Apress, 2005) and *SQL Server 2000 Fast Answers for DBAs and Developers* (Apress, 2005). He coauthored *Pro SQL Server 2005* (Apress, 2005) and *Beginning SQL Server 2000 DBA: From Novice to Professional* (Apress, 2004). Joseph graduated with an associate's degree in arts from Bard College at Simon's Rock and earned a bachelor's degree in psychology from the University of Minnesota. You can reach Joseph on his blog, www.joesack.com.

About the Technical Reviewer

 **EVAN TERRY** is the chief technical consultant for The Clegg Company, specializing in data management and information architecture. His past and current clients include the State of Idaho, Albertsons, American Honda Motors, Toyota Motor Sales, The Polk Company, and General Motors. He is the coauthor of Apress's *Beginning Relational Data Modeling*, has published articles in *DM Review*, and has presented at the IAIDQ and DAMA International conferences. For questions or consulting needs, Evan can be contacted at evan_terry@cleggcompany.com.

Acknowledgments

This book is dedicated to David Hatch, and to the family members, friends, and coworkers who helped us get through a very challenging year. From Guillain-Barré syndrome to a broken foot—you were there for us, and we are very lucky to have you in our lives.

During the 9-month writing process, the Apress team helped facilitate a very positive and smooth experience. I want to thank the lead editor, Jonathan Gennick, who was responsive, collaborative, and an all-around great guy to work with. I also appreciate Evan Terry's astute and detailed technical editing—thanks for coming back for a second round!

I also want to thank the amazing Susannah Davidson Pfalzer for her excellent project management skills and positive voice. Thank you also to the keen-eyed Ami Knox, who put the critical finishing touches on this work, and also to Laura Cheu, for the production editing and patience with my last-minute changes.

Lastly—thank you to the rest of the behind-the-scenes Apress team who I may not have met over e-mail or the phone, but who still deserve credit for bringing this book to the market.

Introduction

The purpose of this book is to quickly provide you with the skills you need to solve problems and perform tasks using the Transact-SQL language. I wrote this book in a problem/solution format in order to establish an immediate understanding of a task and its associated Transact-SQL solution. You can use this book to look up the task you want to perform, read how to do it, and then perform the task on your own system. While writing this book, I followed a few key tenets:

- Keep it brief, providing just enough information needed to get the job done.

- Allow recipes and chapters to stand alone—keeping cross-references and distractions to a tolerable minimum.

- Focus on features that are typically implemented entirely using Transact-SQL. For example, I cover the new Resource Governor feature because it will typically be deployed by DBAs using Transact-SQL—whereas I do not cover Policy-Based Management due to its underlying dependencies on SQL Server Agent, SQL Server Management Objects (SMO), and SQL Server Management Studio. Fortunately, most of the new SQL Server engine improvements *are* entirely Transact-SQL based, and therefore are included in this book.

- Write recipes that help a range of skill sets, from novice to professional. I begin each chapter with basic recipes and progressively work up to more advanced topics.

Regarding new SQL Server 2008 features, I have interwoven them throughout the book in the chapters where they apply. If you are just looking for a refresh on new Transact-SQL features, I specifically call them out at the beginning of each chapter in which they exist.

Although a key tenet of this book is to keep things brief, you'll notice that this book is still quite large. This is a consequence of the continually expanding SQL Server feature set; however, rest assured that the recipes contained within are still succinct and constructed in such a way as to quickly give you the answers you need to get the job done.

I've written this book for SQL Server developers, administrators, application developers, and IT generalists who are tasked with developing databases or administering a SQL Server environment. You can read this book from start to finish or jump around to topics that interest you. You can use this book to brush up on topics before a job interview or an exam. Even for the more experienced SQL Server professionals, memory fades—and this book can help quickly refresh your memory on the usage of a command or technique.

Thanks for reading!

CHAPTER 1

■■■

SELECT

In this chapter, I include recipes for returning data from a SQL Server database using the SELECT statement. At the beginning of each chapter, you'll notice that most of the basic concepts are covered first. This is for those of you who are new to the SQL Server 2008 Transact-SQL query language. In addition to the basics, I'll also provide recipes that can be used in your day-to-day development and administration. These recipes will also help you learn about the new functionality introduced in SQL Server 2008.

A majority of the examples in this book use the AdventureWorks database (SQL Server 2008 OLTP version), which can be downloaded online from the CodePlex site (www.codeplex.com), under the "Microsoft SQL Server Product Samples: Database" project. Look for the file named AdventureWorks2008.msi. Also, if you do decide to follow along with the recipe examples, I strongly recommend that you do so with a non-production learning environment. This will give you the freedom to experiment without negative consequences.

Brevity and simplicity is a key tenet of this book, so when initially describing a new T-SQL concept, I'll distill syntax blocks down to only the applicable code required. If an example doesn't require a syntax block in order to illustrate a concept or task, I won't include one. For full syntax, you can always reference Books Online, so instead of rehashing what you'll already have access to, I'll focus only on the syntax that applies to the recipe. Regarding the result sets returned from the recipes in this book, I'll often pare down the returned columns and rows shown on the page.

SQL Server 2008 new features will be interwoven throughout the book. For those more significant improvements, I'll call them out at the beginning of the chapter so that you know to look out for them. The new SQL Server 2008 features I cover in this chapter include

- New extensions to the GROUP BY clause that allow you to generate multiple grouping result sets within the same query without having to use UNION ALL

- A new method of initializing a variable on declaration, allowing you to reduce the code needed to set a variable's value

You can read the recipes in this book in almost any order. You can skip to the topics that interest you or read it through sequentially. If you see something that is useful to you, perhaps a code chunk or example that you can modify for your own purposes or integrate into a stored procedure or function, then this book has been successful.

The Basic SELECT Statement

The SELECT command is the cornerstone of the Transact-SQL language, allowing you to retrieve data from a SQL Server database (and more specifically from database objects within a SQL Server database). Although the full syntax of the SELECT statement is enormous, the basic syntax can be presented in a more boiled-down form:

```
SELECT select_list
FROM table_list
```

The select_list argument shown in the previous code listing is the list of columns that you wish to return in the results of the query. The table_list arguments are the actual tables and or views that the data will be retrieved from.

The next few recipes will demonstrate how to use a basic SELECT statement.

Selecting Specific Columns from a Table

This example demonstrates a very simple SELECT query against the AdventureWorks database, whereby three columns are returned, along with several rows from the HumanResources.Employee table. Explicit column naming is used in the query:

```
USE AdventureWorks
GO

SELECT NationalIDNumber,
       LoginID,
       JobTitle
FROM HumanResources.Employee
```

The query returns the following abridged results:

NationalIDNumber	LoginID	JobTitle
295847284	adventure-works\ken0	Chief Executive Officer
245797967	adventure-works\terri0	Vice President of Engineering
509647174	adventure-works\roberto0	Engineering Manager
112457891	adventure-works\rob0	Senior Tool Designer
...		
954276278	adventure-works\rachel0	Sales Representative
668991357	adventure-works\jae0	Sales Representative
134219713	adventure-works\ranjit0	Sales Representative

```
(290 row(s) affected)
```

How It Works

The first line of code sets the context database context of the query. Your initial database context, when you first log in to SQL Server Management Studio (SSMS), is defined by your login's default database. USE followed by the database name changes your connection context:

```
USE AdventureWorks
GO
```

The SELECT query was used next. The few lines of code define which columns to display in the query results:

```
SELECT NationalIDNumber,
       LoginID,
       JobTitle
```

The next line of code is the FROM clause:

```
FROM    HumanResources.Employee
```

The FROM clause is used to specify the data source, which in this example is a table. Notice the two-part name of HumanResources.Employee. The first part (the part before the period) is the *schema*, and the second part (after the period) is the actual table name. A schema contains the object, and that schema is then owned by a user. Because users own a schema, and the schema contains the object, you can change the owner of the schema without having to modify object ownership.

Selecting Every Column for Every Row

If you wish to show *all* columns from the data sources in the FROM clause, you can use the following query:

```
USE AdventureWorks
GO
SELECT   *
FROM   HumanResources.Employee
```

The abridged column and row output is shown here:

BusinessEntityID	NationalIDNumber	LoginID	OrganizationNode
1	295847284	adventure-works\ken0	0x
2	245797967	adventure-works\terri0	0x58
3	509647174	adventure-works\roberto0	0x5AC0
4	112457891	adventure-works\rob0	0x5AD6
...			

How It Works

The asterisk symbol (*) returns all columns for every row of the table or view you are querying. All other details are as explained in the previous recipe.

Please remember that, as good practice, it is better to explicitly reference the columns you want to retrieve instead of using SELECT *. If you write an application that uses SELECT *, your application may expect the same columns (in the same order) from the query. If later on you add a new column to the underlying table or view, or if you reorder the table columns, you could break the calling application, because the new column in your result set is unexpected. Using SELECT * can also negatively impact performance, as you may be returning more data than you need over the network, increasing the result set size and data retrieval operations on the SQL Server instance. For applications requiring thousands of transactions per second, the number of columns returned in the result set can have a non-trivial impact.

Selective Querying Using a Basic WHERE Clause

In a SELECT query, the WHERE clause is used to restrict rows returned in the query result set. The simplified syntax for including the WHERE clause is as follows:

```
SELECT select_list
FROM table_list
[WHERE search_conditions]
```

The WHERE clause uses search conditions that determine the rows returned by the query. Search conditions use predicates, which are expressions that evaluate to TRUE, FALSE, or UNKNOWN.

UNKNOWN values can make their appearance when NULL data is accessed in the search condition. A NULL value doesn't mean that the value is blank or zero—only that the value is unknown. Also, two NULL values are *not* equal and cannot be compared without producing an UNKNOWN result.

The next few recipes will demonstrate how to use the WHERE clause to specify which rows are and aren't returned in the result set.

Using the WHERE Clause to Specify Rows Returned in the Result Set

This basic example demonstrates how to select which rows are returned in the query results:

```
SELECT    Title,
    FirstName,
    LastName
FROM    Person.Person
WHERE Title = 'Ms.'
```

This example returns the following (abridged) results:

```
Title    FirstName    LastName
Ms.      Gail         Erickson
Ms.      Janice       Galvin
Ms.      Jill         Williams
Ms.      Catherine    Abel
...
Ms.      Abigail      Coleman
Ms.      Angel        Gray
Ms.      Amy          Li

(415 row(s) affected)
```

How It Works

In this example, you can see that only rows where the person's title was equal to Ms. were returned. This search condition was defined in the WHERE clause of the query:

```
WHERE Title = 'Ms.'
```

Only one search condition was used in this case; however, an almost unlimited number of search conditions can be used in a single query, as you'll see in the next recipe.

Combining Search Conditions

This recipe will demonstrate connecting multiple search conditions by utilizing the AND, OR, and NOT logical operators. The AND logical operator joins two or more search conditions and returns the row or rows only when each of the search conditions is true. The OR logical operator joins two or more search conditions and returns the row or rows in the result set when *any* of the conditions are true.

In this first example, two search conditions are used in the WHERE clause, separated by the AND operator. The AND means that for a given row, both search conditions must be true for that row to be returned in the result set:

```
SELECT    Title,
        FirstName,
        LastName
```

```
FROM    Person.Person
WHERE Title = 'Ms.' AND
      LastName = 'Antrim'
```

This returns the following results:

```
Title    FirstName    LastName
Ms.      Ramona       Antrim

(1 row(s) affected)
```

In this second example, an OR operator is used for the two search conditions instead of an AND, meaning that if *either* search condition evaluates to TRUE for a row, that row will be returned:

```
SELECT    Title,
          FirstName,
          LastName
FROM    Person.Person
WHERE Title = 'Ms.' OR
      LastName = 'Antrim'
```

This returns the following (abridged) results:

```
Title    FirstName    LastName
Ms.      Gail         Erickson
Ms.      Janice       Galvin
...
Ms.      Ramona       Antrim
...
Ms.      Abigail      Coleman
Ms.      Angel        Gray
Ms.      Amy          Li

(415 row(s) affected)
```

How It Works

In the first example, two search conditions were joined using the AND operator:

```
WHERE Title = 'Ms.' AND
      LastName = 'Antrim'
```

As you add search conditions to your query, you join them by the logical operators AND and OR. For example, if both the Title equals Ms. *and* the LastName equals Antrim, any matching row or rows will be returned. The AND operator dictates that *both* joined search conditions must be true in order for the row to be returned.

The OR operator, on the other hand, returns rows if *either* search condition is TRUE, as the third example demonstrated:

```
WHERE Title = 'Ms.' OR
      LastName = 'Antrim'
```

So instead of a single row as the previous query returned, rows with a Title of Ms. or a LastName of Antrim were returned.

Negating a Search Condition

The NOT logical operator, unlike AND and OR, isn't used to combine search conditions, but instead is used to negate the expression that follows it.

This next example demonstrates using the NOT operator for reversing the result of the following search condition and qualifying the Title to be equal to Ms. (reversing it to anything *but* Ms.):

```
SELECT   Title,
         FirstName,
         LastName
FROM   Person.Person
WHERE NOT Title = 'Ms.'
```

This returns the following (abridged) results:

Title	FirstName	LastName
Mr.	Jossef	Goldberg
Mr.	Hung-Fu	Ting
Mr.	Brian	Welcker
Mr.	Tete	Mensa-Annan
Mr.	Syed	Abbas
Mr.	Gustavo	Achong
Sr.	Humberto	Acevedo
Sra.	Pilar	Ackerman
...		

How It Works

This example demonstrated the NOT operator:

```
WHERE NOT Title = 'Ms.'
```

NOT specifies the reverse of a search condition, in this case specifying that only rows that *don't* have the Title equal to Ms. be returned.

Keeping Your WHERE Clause Unambiguous

You can use multiple operators (AND, OR, NOT) in a single WHERE clause, but it is important to make your intentions clear by properly embedding your ANDs and ORs in parentheses. The AND operator limits the result set, and the OR operator expands the conditions for which rows will be returned. When multiple operators are used in the same WHERE clause, operator precedence is used to determine how the search conditions are evaluated (similar to order of operations used in arithmetic and algebra). For example, the NOT operator takes precedence (is evaluated first) before AND. The AND operator takes precedence over the OR operator. Using both AND and OR operators in the same WHERE clause without using parentheses can return unexpected results.

For example, the following query may return unintended results:

```
SELECT   Title,
    FirstName,
    LastName
FROM   Person.Person
WHERE   Title = 'Ms.' AND
    FirstName = 'Catherine' OR
    LastName = 'Adams'
```

This returns the following (abridged) results:

```
Title    FirstName    LastName
NULL     Jay          Adams
Ms.      Catherine    Abel
Ms.      Frances      Adams
Ms.      Carla        Adams
Mr.      Jay          Adams
Mr.      Ben          Adams
Ms.      Catherine    Whitney
...
```

Was the intention of this query to return results for all rows with a Title of Ms., and of those rows, only include those with a FirstName of Catherine or a LastName of Adams? Or did the query author wish to search for all people named Ms. with a FirstName of Catherine, *as well as* anyone with a LastName of Adams?

A query that uses both AND and OR should always use parentheses to clarify exactly what rows should be returned. For example, this next query returns anyone with a Title of Ms. *and* a FirstName equal to Catherine. It also returns anyone else with a LastName of Adams—regardless of Title and FirstName:

```
SELECT  Title,
        FirstName,
        MiddleName,
        LastName
FROM    Person.Person
WHERE   (Title = 'Ms.' AND
        FirstName = 'Catherine') OR
        LastName = 'Adams'
```

How It Works

Use parentheses to clarify multiple operator WHERE clauses. Parentheses assist in clarifying a query as they help SQL Server identify the order that expressions should be evaluated. Search conditions enclosed in parentheses are evaluated in an inner-to-outer order, so in the example from this recipe, the following search conditions were evaluated first:

```
(Title = 'Ms.' AND
FirstName = 'Catherine')
```

before evaluating the outside OR search expression:

```
LastName = 'Adams'
```

Using Operators and Expressions

So far, this chapter has used the = (equals) operator to designate what the value of a column in the result set should be. The = comparison operator tests the equality of two expressions. An *expression* is a combination of values, identifiers, and operators evaluated by SQL Server in order to return a result (for example, return TRUE or FALSE or UNKNOWN).

Table 1-1 lists some of the operators you can use in a search condition.

Table 1-1. *Operators*

Operator	Description
!=	Tests two expressions not being equal to each other.
!>	Tests that the left condition is not greater than the expression to the right.
!<	Tests that the right condition is not greater than the expression to the right.
<	Tests the left condition as less than the right condition.
<=	Tests the left condition as less than or equal to the right condition.
<>	Tests two expressions not being equal to each other.
=	Tests equality between two expressions.
>	Tests the left condition being greater than the expression to the right.
>=	Tests the left condition being greater than or equal to the expression to the right.
ALL	When used with a comparison operator and subquery, retrieves rows if all retrieved values satisfy the search condition.
ANY	When used with a comparison operator and subquery, retrieves rows if any retrieved values satisfy the search condition.
BETWEEN	Designates an inclusive range of values. Used with the AND clause between the beginning and ending values. This operator is useful for data comparisons.
CONTAINS	Does a fuzzy search for words and phrases.
ESCAPE	Allows you to designate that a wildcard character be interpreted as a literal value instead. This is used in conjunction with the LIKE operator. For example, the percentage (%), underscore (_), and square brackets ([]) all have wildcard meanings within the context of a pattern search using LIKE. If you would like to find the actual percentage character explicitly, you must define the ESCAPE character that will precede the wildcard value, indicating that it is a literal character.
EXISTS	When used with a subquery, tests for the existence of rows in the subquery.
FREETEXT	Searches character-based data for words using meaning, rather than literal values.
IN	Provides an inclusive list of values for the search condition.
IS NOT NULL	Evaluates whether the value is NOT NULL.
IS NULL	Evaluates whether the value is NULL.
LIKE	Tests character string for pattern matching.
NOT BETWEEN	Specifies a range of values NOT to include. Used with the AND clause between the beginning and ending values.
NOT IN	Provides a list of values for which NOT to return rows.
NOT LIKE	Tests character string, excluding those with pattern matches.
SOME	When used with a comparison operator and subquery, retrieves rows if any retrieved values satisfy the search condition.

As you can see from Table 1-1, SQL Server 2008 includes several operators that can be used within query expressions. Specifically, in the context of a WHERE clause, operators can be used to compare two expressions, and also check whether a condition is TRUE, FALSE, or UNKNOWN.

■**Note** SQL Server 2008 also introduces new assignment operators, which I'll discuss in Chapter 2.

The next few recipes will demonstrate how the different operators are used within search expressions.

Using BETWEEN for Date Range Searches

This example demonstrates the BETWEEN operator, used to designate sales orders that occurred between the dates 7/28/2002 and 7/29/2002:

```
SELECT   SalesOrderID,
      ShipDate
FROM Sales.SalesOrderHeader
WHERE ShipDate BETWEEN  '7/28/2002 00:00:00' AND '7/29/2002 23:59:59'
```

The query returns the following results:

```
SalesOrderID    ShipDate
46845           2002-07-28 00:00:00.000
46846           2002-07-28 00:00:00.000
46847           2002-07-28 00:00:00.000
46848           2002-07-28 00:00:00.000
46849           2002-07-28 00:00:00.000
46850           2002-07-28 00:00:00.000
46851           2002-07-28 00:00:00.000
46852           2002-07-28 00:00:00.000
46853           2002-07-28 00:00:00.000
46854           2002-07-28 00:00:00.000
46855           2002-07-29 00:00:00.000
46856           2002-07-29 00:00:00.000
46857           2002-07-29 00:00:00.000
46858           2002-07-29 00:00:00.000
46859           2002-07-29 00:00:00.000
46860           2002-07-29 00:00:00.000
46861           2002-07-29 00:00:00.000

(17 row(s) affected)
```

How It Works

The exercise demonstrated the BETWEEN operator, which tested whether or not a column's ShipDate value fell between two dates:

```
WHERE ShipDate BETWEEN  '7/28/2002 00:00:00' AND '7/29/2002 23:59:59'
```

Notice that I designated the specific time in hours, minutes, and seconds as well. Had I just designated 7/29/2002, I would have only included 00:00:00 in the range.

Using Comparisons

This next example demonstrates the < (less than) operator, which is used in this query to show only products with a standard cost below $110.00:

```
SELECT   ProductID,
         Name,
         StandardCost
FROM    Production.Product
WHERE    StandardCost < 110.0000
```

This query returns the following (abridged) results:

```
ProductID   Name                    StandardCost
1           Adjustable Race         0.00
2           Bearing Ball            0.00
3           BB Ball Bearing         0.00
4           Headset Ball Bearings   0.00
...
994         LL Bottom Bracket       23.9716
995         ML Bottom Bracket       44.9506
996         HL Bottom Bracket       53.9416

(317 row(s) affected)
```

How It Works

This example demonstrated the < operator, returning all rows with a StandardCost less than 110.0000:

```
WHERE     StandardCost < 110.0000
```

Checking for NULL Values

This next query tests for the NULL value of a specific column. A NULL value does *not* mean that the value is blank or zero—only that the value is *unknown*. This query returns any rows where the value of the product's weight is unknown:

```
SELECT   ProductID,
         Name,
         Weight
FROM     Production.Product
WHERE    Weight IS NULL
```

This query returns the following (abridged) results:

```
ProductID   Name                    Weight
1           Adjustable Race         NULL
2           Bearing Ball            NULL
3           BB Ball Bearing         NULL
4           Headset Ball Bearings   NULL
...
(299 row(s) affected)
```

How It Works

This example demonstrated the IS NULL operator, returning any rows where the Weight value was unknown:

```
WHERE     Weight IS NULL
```

Returning Rows Based on a List of Values

In this example, the IN operator validates the equality of the Color column to a list of expressions:

```
SELECT    ProductID,
      Name,
      Color
FROM Production.Product
WHERE Color IN ('Silver', 'Black', 'Red')
```

This returns the following (abridged) results:

```
ProductID   Name                                Color
317         LL Crankarm                         Black
318         ML Crankarm                         Black
319         HL Crankarm                         Black
...
725         LL Road Frame - Red, 44             Red
739         HL Mountain Frame - Silver, 42      Silver
(174 row(s) affected)
```

How It Works

This example demonstrated the IN operator, returning all products that had a Silver, Black, or Red color:

```
WHERE Color IN ('Silver', 'Black', 'Red')
```

Using Wildcards with LIKE

Wildcards are used in search expressions to find pattern matches within strings. In SQL Server 2008, you have the wildcard options described in Table 1-2.

Table 1-2. *Wildcards*

Wildcard	Usage
%	Represents a string of zero or more characters
_	Represents a single character
[]	Specifies a single character, from a selected range or list
[^]	Specifies a single character not within the specified range

This example demonstrates using the LIKE operation with the % wildcard, searching for any product with a name starting with the letter B:

```
SELECT    ProductID,
      Name
FROM    Production.Product
WHERE Name LIKE 'B%'
```

This returns the following results:

ProductID	Name
3	BB Ball Bearing
2	Bearing Ball
877	Bike Wash - Dissolver
316	Blade

(4 row(s) affected)

What if you want to search for the literal value of the % (percentage sign) or an _ (underscore) in your character column? For this, you can use the ESCAPE operator (first described earlier in Table 1-1).

This next query searches for any product name with a literal _ underscore value in it. The ESCAPE operator allows you to search for the wildcard symbol as an actual character. I'll first modify a row in the Production.ProductDescription table, adding a percentage sign to the Description column:

```
UPDATE Production.ProductDescription
SET Description = 'Chromoly steel. High % of defects'
WHERE ProductDescriptionID = 3
```

Next, I'll query the table, searching for any descriptions containing the literal value of the percentage sign:

```
SELECT ProductDescriptionID,Description
FROM Production.ProductDescription
WHERE Description LIKE '%/%%' ESCAPE '/'
```

This returns

ProductDescriptionID	Description
3	Chromoly steel. High % of defects

How It Works

Wildcards allow you to search for patterns in character-based columns. In the example from this recipe, the % percentage sign was used to represent a string of zero or more characters:

```
WHERE Name LIKE 'B%'
```

If searching for a literal value that would otherwise be interpreted by SQL Server as a wildcard, you can use the ESCAPE keyword. The example from this recipe searched for a literal percentage sign in the Description column:

```
WHERE Description LIKE '%/%%' ESCAPE '/'
```

A backslash embedded in single quotes was put after the ESCAPE command. This designates the backslash symbol as the escape character for the preceding LIKE expression string. If an escape character precedes the underscore within a search condition, it is treated as a literal value instead of a wildcard.

Declaring and Assigning Values to Variables

Throughout the book, you'll see examples of variables being used within queries and module-based SQL Server objects (stored procedures, triggers, and more). Variables are objects you can create to temporarily contain data. Variables can be defined across several different data types and then referenced within the allowable context of that type.

In this recipe, I'll demonstrate using a variable to hold a search string. You'll see two different methods for creating and assigning the value of the variable. The first query demonstrates the pre–SQL Server 2008 method:

```
DECLARE @AddressLine1 nvarchar(60)
SET @AddressLine1 = 'Heiderplatz'

SELECT AddressID, AddressLine1
FROM Person.Address
WHERE AddressLine1 LIKE '%' + @AddressLine1 + '%'
```

The query in this example returns all rows with an address containing the search string value:

```
AddressID    AddressLine1
20333        Heiderplatz 268
17062        Heiderplatz 268
24962        Heiderplatz 662
...
19857        Heiderplatz 948
25583        Heiderplatz 948
28939        Heiderplatz 948
16799        Heiderplatz 978

(18 row(s) affected)
```

Now in SQL Server 2008, you can reduce the required T-SQL code by removing the SET instruction and instead just assigning the value within the DECLARE statement:

```
DECLARE @AddressLine1 nvarchar(60) = 'Heiderplatz'

SELECT AddressID, AddressLine1
FROM Person.Address
WHERE AddressLine1 LIKE '%' + @AddressLine1 + '%'
```

At face value, this enhancement doesn't seem groundbreaking; however, if you are declaring and setting hundreds of variables, the amount of code you'll be saved from having to write could be significant.

How It Works

The first query began by declaring a new variable that is prefixed by the @ symbol and followed by the defining data type that will be used to contain the search string:

```
DECLARE @AddressLine1 nvarchar(60)
```

After declaring the variable, a value could be assigned to it by using the SET command (this could have been done with SELECT as well):

```
SET @AddressLine1 = 'Heiderplatz'
```

After that, the populated search value could be used in the WHERE clause of a SELECT query, embedding it between the % wildcards to find any row with an address containing the search string:

```
WHERE AddressLine1 LIKE '%' + @AddressLine1 + '%'
```

In the next query, I issued the same query, only this time taking advantage of the SQL Server 2008 ability to assign a variable within the DECLARE statement:

```
DECLARE @AddressLine1 nvarchar(60) = 'Heiderplatz'
```

■**Note** In Chapter 2, I'll show you how this assignment can be coupled with new assignment operators added to SQL Server 2008, which allows for an inline data value modification.

Grouping Data

The GROUP BY clause is used in a SELECT query to determine the groups that rows should be put in. The simplified syntax is as follows:

```
SELECT select_list
FROM table_list
[WHERE search_conditions]
[GROUP BY group_by_list]
```

GROUP BY follows the optional WHERE clause and is most often used when aggregate functions are referenced in the SELECT statement (aggregate functions are reviewed in more detail in Chapter 8).

Using the GROUP BY Clause

This example uses the GROUP BY clause to summarize total amount due by order date from the Sales.SalesOrderHeader table:

```
SELECT   OrderDate,
    SUM(TotalDue) TotalDueByOrderDate
FROM    Sales.SalesOrderHeader
WHERE OrderDate BETWEEN '7/1/2001' AND '7/31/2001'
GROUP BY OrderDate
```

This returns the following (abridged) results:

```
OrderDate                    TotalDueByOrderDate
2001-07-01 00:00:00.000      665262.9599
2001-07-02 00:00:00.000      15394.3298
2001-07-03 00:00:00.000      16588.4572
...
2001-07-30 00:00:00.000      15914.584
2001-07-31 00:00:00.000      16588.4572

(31 row(s) affected)
```

How It Works

In this recipe's example, the GROUP BY clause was used in a SELECT query to determine the groups that rows should be put in. Stepping through the first line of the query, the SELECT clause designated that the OrderDate should be returned, as well as the SUM total of values in the TotalDue column. SUM is an aggregate function. An aggregate function performs a calculation against a set of values (in this case TotalDue), returning a single value (the total of TotalDue by OrderDate):

```
SELECT   OrderDate,
   SUM(TotalDue) TotalDueByOrderDate
```

Notice that a *column alias* for the SUM(TotalDue) aggregation was used. A column alias returns a different name for a calculated, aggregated, or regular column. In the next part of the query, the Sales.SalesOrderHeader table was referenced in the FROM clause:

```
FROM   Sales.SalesOrderHeader
```

Next, the OrderDate was qualified to return rows for the month of July and the year 2001:

```
WHERE OrderDate BETWEEN '7/1/2001' AND '7/31/2001'
```

The result set was grouped by OrderDate (note that grouping can occur against one or more combined columns):

```
GROUP BY OrderDate
```

Had the GROUP BY clause been left out of the query, using an aggregate function in the SELECT clause would have raised the following error:

```
Msg 8120, Level 16, State 1, Line 1
Column 'Sales.SalesOrderHeader.OrderDate' is invalid in the select list because
it is not contained in either an aggregate function or the GROUP BY clause.
```

This error is raised because any column that is *not* used in an aggregate function in the SELECT list must be listed in the GROUP BY clause.

Using GROUP BY ALL

By adding the ALL keyword after GROUP BY, all row values are used in the grouping, even if they were not qualified to appear via the WHERE clause.

This example executes the same query as the previous recipe's example, except it includes the ALL clause:

```
SELECT   OrderDate,
         SUM(TotalDue) TotalDueByOrderDate
FROM   Sales.SalesOrderHeader
WHERE OrderDate BETWEEN '7/1/2001' AND '7/31/2001'
GROUP BY ALL OrderDate
```

This returns the following (abridged) results:

```
OrderDate                    TotalDueByOrderDate
2002-08-12 00:00:00.000      NULL
2003-07-25 00:00:00.000      NULL
2004-06-21 00:00:00.000      NULL
2001-07-22 00:00:00.000      42256.626
Warning: Null value is eliminated by an aggregate or other SET operation.

(1124 row(s) affected)
```

How It Works

In the results returned by the GROUP BY ALL example, notice that TotalDueByOrderDate was NULL for those order dates not included in the WHERE clause. This does not mean they have zero rows, but instead, that data is not returned for them.

This query also returned a warning along with the results:

```
Warning: Null value is eliminated by an aggregate or other SET operation.
```

This means the SUM aggregate encountered NULL values and didn't include them in the total. For the SUM aggregate function, this was okay; however, NULL values in other aggregate functions can cause undesired results. For example, the AVG aggregate function ignores NULL values, but the COUNT function does not. If your query uses both these functions, you may think that the NULL value included in COUNT helps make up the AVG results—but it doesn't.

Selectively Querying Grouped Data Using HAVING

The HAVING clause of the SELECT statement allows you to specify a search condition on a query using GROUP BY and/or an aggregated value. The syntax is as follows:

```
SELECT select_list
FROM table_list
[ WHERE search_conditions ]
[ GROUP BY group_by_list ]
[ HAVING search_conditions ]
```

The HAVING clause is used to qualify the results after the GROUP BY has been applied. The WHERE clause, in contrast, is used to qualify the rows that are returned *before* the data is aggregated or grouped. HAVING qualifies the aggregated data *after* the data has been grouped or aggregated.

This example queries two tables, Production.ScrapReason and Production.WorkOrder. The Production.ScrapReason is a lookup table that contains manufacturing failure reasons, while the Production.WorkOrder table contains the manufacturing work orders that control which products are manufactured in the quantity and time period, in order to meet inventory and sales needs.

This example reports to management which "failure reasons" have occurred 50 or more times:

```
SELECT  s.Name,
    COUNT(w.WorkOrderID) Cnt
FROM Production.ScrapReason s
INNER JOIN Production.WorkOrder w ON
    s.ScrapReasonID = w.ScrapReasonID
GROUP BY s.Name
HAVING COUNT(*)>50
```

This query returns

```
Name                            Cnt
Gouge in metal                  54
Stress test failed              52
Thermoform temperature too low  63
Trim length too long            52
Wheel misaligned                51
(5 row(s) affected)
```

How It Works

In this recipe, the SELECT clause requested a count of WorkOrderIDs by failure name:

```
SELECT   s.Name,
      COUNT(w.WorkOrderID)
```

Two tables were joined by the ScrapReasonID column:

```
FROM Production.ScrapReason s
INNER JOIN Production.WorkOrder w ON
   s.ScrapReasonID = w.ScrapReasonID
```

Since an aggregate function was used in the SELECT clause, the non-aggregated columns must appear in the GROUP BY clause:

```
GROUP BY s.Name
```

Lastly, using the HAVING query determines that, *of the selected and grouped data*, only those rows in the result set with a count of 50 or higher will be returned:

```
HAVING COUNT(*)>50
```

Ordering Results

The ORDER BY clause orders the results of a query based on designated columns or expressions. The basic syntax for ORDER BY is as follows:

```
SELECT select_list
FROM table_list
[WHERE search_conditions]
[GROUP BY group_by_list]
[HAVING search_conditions]
[ORDER BY order_list [ASC | DESC] ]
```

ORDER BY must appear after the required FROM clause, as well as the optional WHERE, GROUP BY, and HAVING clauses.

Using the ORDER BY Clause

This example demonstrates ordering the query results by columns ProductID and EndDate:

```
SELECT   p.Name,
      h.EndDate,
      h.ListPrice
FROM    Production.Product p
INNER JOIN Production.ProductListPriceHistory h ON
   p.ProductID = h.ProductID
ORDER BY p.Name, h.EndDate
```

This query returns

Name	EndDate	ListPrice
All-Purpose Bike Stand	NULL	159.00
AWC Logo Cap	NULL	8.99
AWC Logo Cap	2002-06-30 00:00:00.000	8.6442
AWC Logo Cap	2003-06-30 00:00:00.000	8.6442
Bike Wash - Dissolver	NULL	7.95

```
Cable Lock                 2003-06-30 00:00:00.000   25.00
Chain                      NULL                       20.24
...
(395 row(s) affected)
```

The default sorting order of ORDER BY is ascending order, which can be explicitly designated as ASC too. The NULL values for each EndDate are sorted to the top for each change in the name.

In this next example, DESC is used to return the results in reverse (descending) order:

```
SELECT    p.Name,
          h.EndDate,
          h.ListPrice
FROM    Production.Product p
INNER JOIN Production.ProductListPriceHistory h ON
    p.ProductID = h.ProductID
ORDER BY p.Name DESC, h.EndDate DESC
```

This returns the following abridged results:

```
Name                     EndDate                    ListPrice
Women's Tights, S        2003-06-30 00:00:00.000    74.99
Women's Tights, M        2003-06-30 00:00:00.000    74.99
...
AWC Logo Cap             2002-06-30 00:00:00.000    8.6442
AWC Logo Cap             NULL                       8.99
All-Purpose Bike Stand   NULL                       159.00

(395 row(s) affected)
```

This third example demonstrates ordering results based on a column that is not used in the SELECT clause:

```
SELECT    p.Name
FROM    Production.Product p
ORDER BY p.Color
```

This returns the following abridged results:

```
name
Guide Pulley
LL Grip Tape
ML Grip Tape
HL Grip Tape
Thin-Jam Hex Nut 9
...
```

How It Works

Although queries sometimes appear to return data properly without an ORDER BY clause, the natural ordering of results is determined by the physical key column order in the clustered index (see Chapter 5 for more information on clustered indexes). If the row order of your result sets is critical, you should *never* depend on the implicit physical order. Always use an ORDER BY if result set ordering is required.

In the first example, the `Production.Product` and `Production.ProductListPriceHistory` tables were queried to view the history of product prices over time.

Note The full details of `INNER JOIN` are provided later in the chapter in the section "Using INNER Joins."

The following line of code sorted the results first alphabetically by product name, and then by the end date:

```
ORDER BY p.Name, h.EndDate
```

You can designate one or more columns in your `ORDER BY` clause, so long as the columns do not exceed 8,060 bytes in total.

The second example demonstrated returning results in descending order (ascending is the default order). The `DESC` keyword was referenced behind each column that required the descending sort:

```
ORDER BY p.Name DESC, h.EndDate DESC
```

The third example demonstrated ordering the results by a column that was not used in the `SELECT` statement:

```
ORDER BY p.Color
```

One caveat when ordering by unselected columns is that `ORDER BY` items must appear in the select list if `SELECT DISTINCT` is specified.

Using the TOP Keyword with Ordered Results

The `TOP` keyword allows you to return the first *n* number of rows from a query based on the number of rows or percentage of rows that you define. The first rows returned are also impacted by how your query is ordered.

Note SQL Server also provides ranking functions, which can be used to rank each row within the partition of a result set. For a review of ranking functions, see Chapter 8.

In this example, the top ten rows are retrieved from the `Purchasing.Vendor` table for those rows with the highest value in the `CreditRating` column:

```
SELECT TOP 10 v.Name,
    v.CreditRating
FROM Purchasing.Vendor v
ORDER BY v.CreditRating DESC, v.Name
```

This returns

Name	CreditRating
Merit Bikes	5
Victory Bikes	5
Proseware, Inc.	4
Recreation Place	4
Consumer Cycles	3
Continental Pro Cycles	3

```
Federal Sport            3
Inner City Bikes         3
Northern Bike Travel     3
Trey Research            3

(10 row(s) affected)
```

The next example demonstrates limiting the *percentage* of rows returned in a query using a local variable:

```
DECLARE @Percentage float

SET @Percentage = 1

SELECT TOP (@Percentage) PERCENT
      Name
FROM Production.Product
ORDER BY Name
```

This returns the top 1 percent of rows from the Production.Product table, ordered by product name:

```
Name
Adjustable Race
All-Purpose Bike Stand
AWC Logo Cap
BB Ball Bearing
Bearing Ball
Bike Wash - Dissolver
(6 row(s) affected)
```

How It Works

In previous versions of SQL Server, developers used SET ROWCOUNT to limit how many rows the query would return or impact. In SQL Server 2005 and 2008, you should use the TOP keyword instead of SET ROWCOUNT, as the TOP will usually perform faster. Also, *not* having the ability to use local variables in the TOP clause was a major reason why people still used SET ROWCOUNT over TOP in previous versions of SQL Server. With these functionality barriers removed, there is no reason not to start using TOP.

■**Tip** The TOP keyword can also now be used with INSERT, UPDATE, and DELETE statements—something that will not be supported with SET ROWCOUNT in future versions of SQL Server. For more information about TOP used in conjunction with data modifications, see Chapter 2.

The key to the first example was the TOP keyword, followed by the number of rows to be returned:

```
SELECT TOP 10 v.Name
```

Also important was the ORDER BY clause, which ordered the results prior to the TOP *n* rows being returned:

```
ORDER BY v.CreditRating DESC, v.Name
```

The second example demonstrated how to use the new local variable assignment functionality with TOP PERCENT:

```
DECLARE @Percentage float

SET @Percentage = 1

SELECT TOP (@Percentage) PERCENT
```

The new local variable functionality allows you to create scripts, functions, or procedures that can determine the number of rows returned by a query based on the value set by the caller, instead of having to hard-code a set TOP number or percentage of rows.

SELECT Clause Techniques

The SELECT clause is primarily used to define which columns are returned in the result set, but its functionality isn't limited to just that. This next set of queries will detail a number of SELECT clause techniques, including the following:

- Using the DISTINCT keyword to remove duplicate values
- Renaming columns using column aliases
- Concatenating string values into a single column
- Creating a SELECT statement that itself creates an executable Transact-SQL script
- Creating a comma-delimited array list of values

Using DISTINCT to Remove Duplicate Values

The default behavior of a SELECT statement is to use the ALL keyword (although because it is the default, you'll rarely see this being used in a query), meaning that all rows will be retrieved and displayed if they exist. Using the DISTINCT keyword instead of ALL allows you to return only unique rows (across columns selected) in your results.

This example shows you how to use the DISTINCT keyword to remove duplicate values from a set of selected columns, so that only unique rows appear:

```
SELECT   DISTINCT HireDate
FROM   HumanResources.Employee
```

The results show all unique hire dates from the HumanResources.Employee table:

```
HireDate
1996-07-31 00:00:00.000
1997-02-26 00:00:00.000
1997-12-12 00:00:00.000
1998-01-05 00:00:00.000
...
2002-11-01 00:00:00.000
2003-04-15 00:00:00.000
2003-07-01 00:00:00.000

(164 row(s) affected)
```

How It Works

Use the DISTINCT keyword to return distinct values in the result set. In this recipe, DISTINCT was used to return unique HireDate column values.

■Caution Be sure to use DISTINCT only when actually needed or necessary, as it can slow the query down on larger result sets.

Using DISTINCT in Aggregate Functions

You can also use DISTINCT for a column that is used within an aggregate function (aggregate functions are reviewed in more detail in Chapter 8). You may wish to do this in order to perform aggregations on only the unique values of a column.

For example, if you wanted to calculate the average product list price, you could use the following query:

```
SELECT   AVG(ListPrice)
FROM Production.Product
```

This returns

438.6662

But the previous query calculated the average list price across *all* products. What if some product types are more numerous than others? What if you are only interested in the average price of *unique* price points?

In this case, you would write the query as follows:

```
SELECT   AVG(DISTINCT ListPrice)
FROM Production.Product
```

This returns the unique set of price points first, *and then* averages them (although the difference doesn't end up being that large):

437.4042

How It Works

DISTINCT can be used to return unique rows from a result set, as well as force unique column values within an aggregate function. In this example, the DISTINCT keyword was put within the parentheses of the aggregate function.

Using Column Aliases

For column computations or aggregate functions, you can use a column alias to explicitly name the columns of your query output. You can also use column aliases to rename columns that already *have* a name, which helps obscure the underlying column from the calling application (allowing you to swap out underlying columns without changing the returned column name). You can designate a column alias by using the AS keyword, or by simply following the column or expression with the column alias name.

This example demonstrates producing column aliases using two different techniques:

```
SELECT   Color AS 'Grouped Color',
      AVG(DISTINCT ListPrice) AS 'Average Distinct List Price',
      AVG(ListPrice) 'Average List Price'
FROM Production.Product
GROUP BY Color
```

This returns the following abridged results:

```
Grouped Color     Average Distinct List Price     Average List Price
NULL              65.9275                         16.8641
Black             527.5882                        725.121
Blue              825.2985                        923.6792
Grey              125.00                          125.00
Multi             49.6566                         59.865
Red               1332.6425                       1401.95
Silver            726.2907                        850.3053
Silver/Black      61.19                           64.0185
White             9.245                           9.245
Yellow            991.7562                        959.0913
(10 row(s) affected)
```

How It Works

This recipe shows three examples of using column aliasing. The first example demonstrated how to rename an *existing* column using the AS clause. The AS clause is used to change a column name in the results, or add a name to a derived (calculated or aggregated) column:

```
SELECT Color AS 'Grouped Color',
```

The second example demonstrated how to add a column name to an aggregate function:

```
AVG(DISTINCT ListPrice) AS 'Average Distinct List Price',
```

The third example demonstrated how to add a column alias without using the AS keyword (it can simply be omitted):

```
AVG(ListPrice) 'Average List Price'
```

Using SELECT to Create a Script

As a DBA or developer, you sometimes need a Transact-SQL script to run against several objects within a database or against several databases across a SQL Server instance. For example, you may want to show how many rows exist in every user table in the database. Or perhaps you have a very large table with several columns, which you need to validate in search conditions, but you don't want to have to manually type each column.

This next recipe offers a time-saving technique, using SELECT to write out Transact-SQL for you. You can adapt this recipe to all sorts of purposes.

In this example, assume that you wish to check for rows in a table where all values are NULL. There are many columns in the table, and you want to avoid hand-coding them. Instead, you can create a script to do the work for you:

```
SELECT column_name + ' IS NULL AND '
FROM INFORMATION_SCHEMA.columns
WHERE table_name = 'Employee'
ORDER BY ORDINAL_POSITION
```

This returns code that you can integrate into a WHERE clause (after you remove the trailing AND at the last WHERE condition):

```
EmployeeID IS NULL AND
NationalIDNumber IS NULL AND
ContactID IS NULL AND
LoginID IS NULL AND
ManagerID IS NULL AND
Title IS NULL AND
BirthDate IS NULL AND
MaritalStatus IS NULL AND
Gender IS NULL AND
HireDate IS NULL AND
SalariedFlag IS NULL AND
VacationHours IS NULL AND
SickLeaveHours IS NULL AND
CurrentFlag IS NULL AND
rowguid IS NULL AND
ModifiedDate IS NULL AND

(16 row(s) affected)
```

How It Works

The example used string concatenation and the INFORMATION_SCHEMA.columns system view to generate a list of columns from the Employee table. For each column, IS NULL AND was concatenated to its name. The results can then be copied to the WHERE clause of a query, allowing you to query for rows where each column has a NULL value.

This general technique of concatenating SQL commands to various system data columns can be used in numerous ways, including for creating scripts against tables or other database objects.

Caution Do be careful when scripting an action against multiple objects or databases—make sure that the change is what you intended, and that you are fully aware of the script's outcome.

Performing String Concatenation

String concatenation is performed by using the + operator to join two expressions, as this example demonstrates:

```
SELECT   'The ' +
       p.name +
       ' is only ' +
       CONVERT(varchar(25),p.ListPrice) +
       '!'
FROM   Production.Product p
WHERE  p.ListPrice between 100 AND 120
ORDER BY p.ListPrice
```

This returns

```
The ML Bottom Bracket is only 101.24!
The ML Headset is only 102.29!
The Rear Brakes is only 106.50!
The Front Brakes is only 106.50!
The LL Road Rear Wheel is only 112.57!
The Hitch Rack - 4-Bike is only 120.00!
```

How It Works

When used with character data types, the + operator is used to concatenate expressions together. In this example, literal values were concatenated to columns from the Production.Product table. Each row formed a sentence celebrating the low price of each row's product. You can also concatenate dates, so long as these are converted to a character or variable character data type using CAST or CONVERT.

String concatenation is often used when generating end-user reports that require denormalization (such as displaying the first and last name in a single column) or when you need to combine multiple data columns into a single column (as you'll see in the next recipe).

Creating a Comma-Delimited List Using SELECT

This next recipe demonstrates how to create a comma-delimited list using a SELECT query. You can use this recipe in several ways. For example, you could integrate it into a user-defined function that returns a comma-delimited list of the regions that a salesperson sells to into a single column (see Chapter 11).

This example demonstrates returning one-to-many table data into a single presentable string:

```
DECLARE @Shifts varchar(20) = ''

SELECT   @Shifts = @Shifts + s.Name + ','
FROM    HumanResources.Shift s
ORDER BY s.EndTime

SELECT @Shifts
```

This query returns

```
Night,Day,Evening,

(1 row(s) affected)
```

How It Works

In the first part of this script, a local variable was created to hold a comma-delimited list. Because you cannot concatenate NULL values with strings, the variable should be set to an initial blank value instead, as was done in the recipe:

```
DECLARE @Shifts varchar(20) = ''
```

In the query itself, a list of shifts are gathered from the HumanResources.Shift table, ordered by EndTime. At the core of this example, you see that the local variable is assigned to the value of itself concatenated to the shift name, and then concatenated to a comma. The query loops through each value ordered by EndTime, appending each one to the local variable:

```
SELECT    @Shifts = @Shifts + s.Name + ','
FROM    HumanResources.Shift s
ORDER BY s.EndTime
```

SELECT is then used to display the final contents of the local variable:

```
SELECT @Shifts
```

Using the INTO Clause

The INTO clause of the SELECT statement allows you to create a new table based on the columns and rows of the query results. Ideally you should be creating your tables using the CREATE TABLE command: however, using INTO provides a quick method of creating a new table without having to explicitly define the column names and data types.

The INTO clause allows you to create a table in a SELECT statement based on the columns and rows the query returns. The syntax for INTO is as follows:

```
SELECT select_list
[INTO new_table_name]
FROM table_list
```

The INTO clause comes after the SELECT clause but before the FROM clause, as the next recipe will demonstrate.

In this first example, a new table is created based on the results of a query:

```
SELECT    BusinessEntityID,
          Name,
          SalesPersonID,
          Demographics
INTO    Store_Archive
FROM    Sales.Store
```

The query returns the number of rows inserted into the new Store_Archive table, but does not return query results:

```
(701 row(s) affected)
```

In the second example, a table is created without inserting rows into it:

```
SELECT    BusinessEntityID,
          Name,
          SalesPersonID,
          Demographics
INTO    Store_Archive_2
FROM    Sales.Store
WHERE    1=0
```

This returns the number of rows inserted into your new Store_Archive_2 table (which in this case is zero):

```
(0 row(s) affected)
```

How It Works

This recipe's example looked like a regular SELECT query, only between the SELECT and FROM clauses the following instructions were inserted:

```
INTO    Store_Archive
```

The INTO clause is followed by the new table name (which must not already exist). This can be a permanent, temporary, or global temporary table (see Chapter 4 for more information on these object types). The columns you select determine the structure of the table.

This is a great technique for quickly "copying" the base table structure and data of an existing table. Using INTO, you are not required to predefine the new table's structure explicitly (for example, you do not need to issue a CREATE TABLE statement).

■**Caution** Although the structure of the selected columns is reproduced, the constraints, indexes, and other separate objects dependent on the source table are *not* copied.

In the second example, a new table was created without also populating it with rows. This was achieved by using a WHERE clause condition that always evaluates to FALSE:

```
WHERE    1=0
```

Since the number 1 will never equal the number 0, no rows will evaluate to TRUE, and therefore no rows will be inserted into the new table. However, the new table is created anyway.

Subqueries

A subquery is a SELECT query that is nested within another SELECT, INSERT, UPDATE, or DELETE statement. A subquery can also be nested inside another subquery. Subqueries can often be rewritten into regular JOINs; however, sometimes an existence subquery (demonstrated in this recipe) can perform better than equivalent non-subquery methods.

A *correlated* subquery is a subquery whose results depend on the values of the outer query.

Using Subqueries to Check for Matches

This first example demonstrates checking for the existence of matching rows within a correlated subquery:

```
SELECT DISTINCT s.PurchaseOrderNumber
FROM Sales.SalesOrderHeader s
WHERE EXISTS (   SELECT SalesOrderID
        FROM Sales.SalesOrderDetail
        WHERE UnitPrice BETWEEN 1000 AND 2000 AND
            SalesOrderID = s.SalesOrderID)
```

This returns the following abridged results:

```
PurchaseOrderNumber
PO8410140860
PO12325137381
PO1160166903
PO1073122178
...
```

```
PO15486173227
PO14268145224
```

```
(1989 row(s) affected)
```

This second example demonstrates a regular non-correlated subquery:

```
SELECT    BusinessEntityID,
          SalesQuota CurrentSalesQuota
FROM      Sales.SalesPerson
WHERE      SalesQuota =
              (SELECT MAX(SalesQuota)
               FROM Sales.SalesPerson)
```

This returns the three salespeople who had the maximum sales quota of 300,000:

```
BusinessEntityID    CurrentSalesQuota
275                 300000.00
279                 300000.00
287                 300000.00
Warning: Null value is eliminated by an aggregate or other SET operation.
```

```
(3 row(s) affected)
```

How It Works

The critical piece of the first example was the subquery in the WHERE clause, which checked for the existence of SalesOrderIDs that had products with a UnitPrice between 1000 and 2000. A JOIN was used in the WHERE clause of the subquery, between the outer query and the inner query, by stating SalesOrderID = s.SalesOrderID. The subquery used the SalesOrderID from each returned row in the outer query.

In the second example, there is no WHERE clause in the subquery used to join to the outer table. It is not a correlated subquery. Instead, a value is retrieved from the query to evaluate against in the = operator of the WHERE clause.

Querying from More Than One Data Source

The JOIN keyword allows you to combine data from multiple tables and/or views into a single result set. It joins a column or columns from one table to another table, evaluating whether there is a match.

With the JOIN keyword, you join two tables based on a join condition. Most often you'll see a join condition testing the equality of one column in one table compared to another column in the second table (joined columns do not need to have the same name, only compatible data types).

■**Tip** As a query performance best practice, try to avoid having to convert data types of the columns in your join clause (using CONVERT or CAST, for example). Opt instead for modifying the underlying schema to match data types (or convert the data beforehand in a separate table, temp table, table variable, or Common Table Expression [CTE]). Also, allowing implicit data type conversions to occur for frequently executed queries can cause significant performance issues (for example, converting nchar to char).

SQL Server 2005 join types fall into three categories: inner, outer, and cross. Inner joins use the INNER JOIN keywords. INNER JOIN operates by matching common values between two tables. Only table rows satisfying the join conditions are used to construct the result set. INNER JOINs are the default JOIN type, so if you wish, you can use just the JOIN keyword in your INNER JOIN operations.

Outer joins have three different join types: LEFT OUTER, RIGHT OUTER, and FULL OUTER joins. LEFT OUTER and RIGHT OUTER JOINs, like INNER JOINs, return rows that match the conditions of the join condition. *Unlike* INNER JOINs, LEFT OUTER JOINs return unmatched rows from the first table of the join pair, and RIGHT OUTER JOINs return unmatched rows from the second table of the join pair. The FULL OUTER JOIN clause returns unmatched rows on both the left *and* right tables.

An infrequently used join type is CROSS JOIN. A CROSS JOIN returns a *Cartesian product* when a WHERE clause isn't used. A Cartesian product produces a result set based on every possible combination of rows from the left table, multiplied against the rows in the right table. For example, if the Stores table has 7 rows, and the Sales table has 22 rows, you would receive 154 rows (or 7 times 22) in the query results (each possible combination of row displayed).

The next few recipes will demonstrate the different join types.

Using INNER Joins

This inner join joins three tables in order to return discount information on a specific product:

```
SELECT    p.Name,
          s.DiscountPct
FROM Sales.SpecialOffer s
INNER JOIN Sales.SpecialOfferProduct o ON
          s.SpecialOfferID = o.SpecialOfferID
INNER JOIN Production.Product p ON
          o.ProductID = p.ProductID
WHERE p.Name = 'All-Purpose Bike Stand'
```

The results of this query are as follows:

```
Name                     DiscountPct
All-Purpose Bike Stand   0.00

(1 row(s) affected)
```

How It Works

A join starts after the first table in the FROM clause. In this example, three tables were joined together: Sales.SpecialOffer, Sales.SpecialOfferProduct, and Production.Product. Sales.SpecialOffer, the first table referenced in the FROM clause, contains a lookup of sales discounts:

```
FROM Sales.SpecialOffer s
```

Notice the letter s which trails the table name. This is a *table alias*. Once you begin using more than one table in a query, it is important to explicitly identify the data source of the individual columns. If the same column names exist in two different tables, you could get an error from the SQL compiler asking you to clarify which column you really wanted to return.

As a best practice, it is a good idea to use aliases whenever column names are specified in a query. For each of the referenced tables, a character was used to symbolize the table name—saving you the trouble of spelling it out each time. This query used a single character as a table alias, but you can use any valid identifier. A table alias, aside from allowing you to shorten or clarify the original table name, allows you to swap out the base table name if you ever have to replace it with a different table or view, or if you need to self-join the tables. Table aliases are optional, but recommended when your query has more than one table. A table alias follows the table name in the statement FROM clause. Because table aliases are optional, you could specify the entire table name every time you refer to the column in that table.

Getting back to the example . . . the INNER JOIN keywords followed the first table reference, and then the table being joined to it, followed by its alias:

```
INNER JOIN Sales.SpecialOfferProduct o
```

After that, the ON keyword prefaces the column joins:

```
ON
```

This particular INNER JOIN is based on the equality of two columns—one from the first table and another from the second:

```
s.SpecialOfferID = o.SpecialOfferID
```

Next, the Production.Product table is INNER JOINed too:

```
INNER JOIN Production.Product p ON
    o.ProductID = p.ProductID
```

Lastly, a WHERE clause is used to filter rows returned in the final result set:

```
WHERE Name = 'All-Purpose Bike Stand'
```

Using OUTER Joins

This recipe compares the results of an INNER JOIN versus a LEFT OUTER JOIN. This first query displays the tax rates states and provinces using the Person.StateProvince table and the Sales.SalesTaxRate table. The following query uses an INNER JOIN:

```
SELECT    s.CountryRegionCode,
          s.StateProvinceCode,
          t.TaxType,
          t.TaxRate
FROM Person.StateProvince s
INNER JOIN Sales.SalesTaxRate t ON
    s.StateProvinceID = t.StateProvinceID
```

This returns the following (abridged) results:

CountryRegionCode	StateProvinceCode	TaxType	TaxRate
CA	AB	1	14.00
CA	ON	1	14.25
CA	QC	1	14.25
...			
FR	FR	3	19.60
GB	ENG	3	17.50

```
(29 row(s) affected)
```

But with the INNER JOIN, you are only seeing those records from Person.StateProvince that *have* rows in the Sales.SalesTaxRate table. In order to see *all* rows from Person.StateProvince, whether or not they have associated tax rates, LEFT OUTER JOIN is used:

```
SELECT   s.CountryRegionCode,
         s.StateProvinceCode,
         t.TaxType,
         t.TaxRate
FROM Person.StateProvince s
LEFT OUTER JOIN Sales.SalesTaxRate t ON
    s.StateProvinceID = t.StateProvinceID
```

This returns the following (abridged) results:

CountryRegionCode	StateProvinceCode	TaxType	TaxRate
CA	AB	1	14.00
CA	AB	2	7.00
US	AK	NULL	NULL
US	AL	NULL	NULL
US	AR	NULL	NULL
AS	AS	NULL	NULL
US	AZ	1	7.75
...			
FR	94	NULL	NULL
FR	95	NULL	NULL

(184 row(s) affected)

How It Works

This recipe's example demonstrated an INNER JOIN query versus a LEFT OUTER JOIN query. The LEFT OUTER JOIN query returned unmatched rows from the first table of the join pair. Notice how this query returned NULL values for those rows from Person.StateProvince that didn't have associated rows in the Sales.SalesTaxRate table.

Using CROSS Joins

In this example, the Person.StateProvince and Sales.SalesTaxRate tables are CROSS JOINed:

```
SELECT   s.CountryRegionCode,
         s.StateProvinceCode,
         t.TaxType,
         t.TaxRate
FROM Person.StateProvince s
CROSS JOIN Sales.SalesTaxRate t
```

This returns the following (abridged) results:

CountryRegionCode	StateProvinceCode	TaxType	TaxRate
CA	AB	1	14.00
US	AK	1	14.00
US	AL	1	14.00
US	AR	1	14.00
AS	AS	1	14.00
...			
FR	94	3	17.50
FR	95	3	17.50

(5249 row(s) affected)

How It Works

A CROSS JOIN without a WHERE clause returns a Cartesian product. The results of this CROSS JOIN show StateProvince and SalesTaxRate information that doesn't logically go together. Since the Person.StateProvince table had 181 rows, and the Sales.SalesTaxRate had 29 rows, the query returned 5249 rows.

Referencing a Single Table Multiple Times in the Same Query

Sometimes you may need to treat the same table as two separate tables. This may be because the table contains nested hierarchies of data (for example, a table containing employee records has a manager ID that is a foreign key reference to the employee ID), or perhaps you wish to reference the same table based on different time periods (comparing sales records from the year 2007 versus the year 2008).

You can achieve this joining of a table with itself through the use of table aliases.

In this example, the Sales.SalesPersonQuotaHistory table is referenced twice in the FROM clause, with one referencing 2004 sales quota data and the other 2003 sales quota data:

```
SELECT s.BusinessEntityID,
          SUM(s2004.SalesQuota) Total_2004_SQ,
       SUM(s2003.SalesQuota) Total_2003_SQ
FROM Sales.SalesPerson s
LEFT OUTER JOIN Sales.SalesPersonQuotaHistory s2004 ON
       s.BusinessEntityID = s2004.BusinessEntityID AND
       YEAR(s2004.QuotaDate)= 2004
LEFT OUTER JOIN Sales.SalesPersonQuotaHistory s2003 ON
       s.BusinessEntityID = s2003.BusinessEntityID AND
       YEAR(s2003.QuotaDate)= 2003
GROUP BY s.BusinessEntityID
```

This returns the following (abridged) results:

BusinessEntityID	Total_2004_SQ	Total_2003_SQ
274	1084000.00	1088000.00
275	6872000.00	9432000.00
276	8072000.00	9364000.00
...		
289	8848000.00	10284000.00
290	6460000.00	5880000.00

(17 row(s) affected)

How It Works

This recipe queried the year 2004 and year 2003 sales quota results. The FROM clause included an anchor to all salesperson identifiers:

```
...
FROM Sales.SalesPerson s
```

I then left outer joined the first reference to the sales quota data, giving it an alias of s2004:

```
LEFT OUTER JOIN Sales.SalesPersonQuotaHistory s2004 ON
       s.BusinessEntityID = s2004.BusinessEntityID AND
       YEAR(s2004.QuotaDate)= 2004
```

Next, another reference was created to the same sales quota table—however, this time aliasing the table as s2003:

```
LEFT OUTER JOIN Sales.SalesPersonQuotaHistory s2003 ON
    s.BusinessEntityID = s2003.BusinessEntityID AND
    YEAR(s2003.QuotaDate)= 2003
GROUP BY s.BusinessEntityID
```

As demonstrated here, you can reference the same table multiple times in the same query so long as that table has a unique table alias to differentiate it from other referenced objects.

Using Derived Tables

Derived tables are SELECT statements that act as tables in the FROM clause. Derived tables can sometimes provide better performance than using temporary tables (see Chapter 4 for more on temporary tables). Unlike temporary tables, derived tables don't require persisted data to be populated beforehand.

This example demonstrates how to use a derived table in the FROM clause of a SELECT statement:

```
SELECT DISTINCT s.PurchaseOrderNumber
FROM Sales.SalesOrderHeader s
INNER JOIN (SELECT SalesOrderID
        FROM Sales.SalesOrderDetail
        WHERE UnitPrice BETWEEN 1000 AND 2000) d ON
    s.SalesOrderID = d.SalesOrderID
```

This returns the following abridged results:

```
PurchaseOrderNumber
PO8410140860
PO12325137381
PO1160166903
PO1073122178
...
PO15486173227
PO14268145224

(1989 row(s) affected)
```

How It Works

This example's query searches for the PurchaseOrderNumber from the Sales.SalesOrderHeader table for any order containing products with a UnitPrice between 1000 and 2000.

The query joins a table to a derived table using INNER JOIN. The derived table query is encapsulated in parentheses and followed by a table alias. The derived table is a separate query in itself, and doesn't require the use of a temporary table to store the results. Thus, queries that use derived tables can sometimes perform significantly better than temporary tables, as you eliminate the steps needed for SQL Server to create and allocate the temporary table prior to use.

Combining Result Sets with UNION

The UNION operator is used to append the results of two or more SELECT statements into a single result set. Each SELECT statement being merged must have the same number of columns, with the same or compatible data types in the same order, as this example demonstrates:

```
SELECT    BusinessEntityID, GETDATE() QuotaDate, SalesQuota
FROM        Sales.SalesPerson
WHERE       SalesQuota > 0
      UNION
SELECT    BusinessEntityID, QuotaDate, SalesQuota
FROM        Sales.SalesPersonQuotaHistory
WHERE       SalesQuota > 0
ORDER BY    BusinessEntityID  DESC, QuotaDate DESC
```

This returns the following (abridged) results:

```
SalesPersonID    QuotaDate                       SalesQuota
290              2007-09-01 14:26:28.870         250000.00
290              2004-04-01 00:00:00.000         421000.00
290              2004-01-01 00:00:00.000         399000.00
290              2003-10-01 00:00:00.000         389000.00
...
268              2001-10-01 00:00:00.000         7000.00
268              2001-07-01 00:00:00.000         28000.00
(177 row(s) affected)
```

How It Works

This query appended two result sets into a single result set. The first result set returned the BusinessEntityID, the current date function (see Chapter 8 for more information on this), and the SalesQuota. Since GETDATE() is a function, it doesn't naturally return a column name—so a QuotaDate column alias was used in its place:

```
SELECT    BusinessEntityID, GETDATE() QuotaDate, SalesQuota
FROM        Sales.SalesPerson
```

The WHERE clause filtered data for those salespeople with a SalesQuota greater than zero:

```
WHERE       SalesQuota > 0
```

The next part of the query was the UNION operator, which appended the *distinct* results with the second query:

```
UNION
```

The second query pulled data from the Sales.SalesPersonQuotaHistory, which keeps history for a salesperson's sales quota as it changes through time:

```
SELECT    BusinessEntityID, QuotaDate, SalesQuota
FROM        Sales.SalesPersonQuotaHistory
WHERE       SalesQuota > 0
```

The ORDER BY clause sorted the result set by BusinessEntityID and QuotaDate, both in descending order. The ORDER BY clause, when needed, must appear at the bottom of the query and cannot appear after queries prior to the final UNIONed query. The ORDER BY clause should also only refer to column names from the *first* result set:

```
ORDER BY BusinessEntityID DESC, QuotaDate DESC
```

Looking at the results again, for a single salesperson, you can see that the current QuotaDate of 2005-02-27 is sorted at the top. This was the date retrieved by the GETDATE() function. The other rows for SalesPersonID 290 are from the Sales.SalesPersonQuotaHistory table:

SalesPersonID	QuotaDate	SalesQuota
290	2005-02-27 10:10:12.587	250000.00
290	2004-04-01 00:00:00.000	421000.00
290	2004-01-01 00:00:00.000	399000.00
290	2003-10-01 00:00:00.000	389000.00

Keep in mind that the default behavior of the UNION operator is to remove *all duplicate rows* and display column names based on the first result set. For large result sets, this can be a very costly operation, so if you don't need to de-duplicate the data, or if the data is naturally distinct, you can add the ALL keyword to the UNION:

```
UNION ALL
```

With the ALL clause added, duplicate rows are NOT removed.

■**Caution** Similar to using DISTINCT—using UNION instead of UNION ALL can lead to additional query resource overhead. If you do not need to remove duplicate rows, use UNION ALL.

Using APPLY to Invoke a Table-Valued Function for Each Row

APPLY is used to invoke a table-valued function for each row of an outer query. A table-valued function returns a result set based on one or more parameters. Using APPLY, the input of these parameters are the columns of the left referencing table. This is useful if the left table contains columns and rows that must be evaluated by the table-valued function and to which the results from the function should be attached.

CROSS APPLY works like an INNER JOIN in that unmatched rows between the left table and the table-valued function don't appear in the result set. OUTER APPLY is like an OUTER JOIN, in that non-matched rows are still returned in the result set with NULL values in the function results.

The next two recipes will demonstrate both CROSS APPLY and OUTER APPLY.

■**Note** This next example covers both the FROM and JOIN examples and user-defined table-valued functions. Table-valued functions are reviewed in more detail in Chapter 11.

Using CROSS APPLY

In this recipe, a table-valued function is created that returns work order routing information based on the WorkOrderID passed to it:

```
CREATE FUNCTION dbo.fn_WorkOrderRouting
  (@WorkOrderID int) RETURNS TABLE
AS
RETURN
  SELECT WorkOrderID,
       ProductID,
       OperationSequence,
       LocationID
```

```
    FROM Production.WorkOrderRouting
    WHERE WorkOrderID = @WorkOrderID
GO
```

Next, the WorkOrderID is passed from the Production.WorkOrder table to the new function:

```
SELECT   w.WorkOrderID,
        w.OrderQty,
        r.ProductID,
        r.OperationSequence
FROM Production.WorkOrder w
  CROSS APPLY dbo.fn_WorkOrderRouting
  (w.WorkOrderID) AS r
ORDER BY   w.WorkOrderID,
        w.OrderQty,
        r.ProductID
```

This returns the following (abridged) results:

WorkOrderID	OrderQty	ProductID	OperationSequence
13	4	747	1
13	4	747	2
13	4	747	3
13	4	747	4
13	4	747	6
...			
72586	1	803	6
72587	19	804	1
72587	19	804	6

(67131 row(s) affected)

How It Works

The first part of this recipe was the creation of a table-valued function. The function accepts a single parameter, @WorkOrderID, and when executed, returns the WorkOrderID, ProductID, OperationSequence, and LocationID from the Production.WorkOrderRouting table for the specified WorkOrderID.

The next query in the example returned the WorkOrderID and OrderQty from the Production.WorkOrder table. In addition to this, two columns from the table-valued function were selected:

```
SELECT   w.WorkOrderID,
        w.OrderQty,
        r.ProductID,
        r.OperationSequence
```

The key piece of this recipe comes next. Notice that in the FROM clause, the Production.WorkOrder table is joined to the new table-valued function using CROSS APPLY, only unlike a JOIN clause, there isn't an ON followed by join conditions. Instead, in the parentheses after the function name, the w.WorkOrderID is passed to the table-valued function from the left Production.WorkOrder table:

```
FROM Production.WorkOrder w
  CROSS APPLY dbo.fn_WorkOrderRouting
  (w.WorkOrderID) AS r
```

The function was aliased like a regular table, with the letter r.

Lastly, the results were sorted:

```
ORDER BY    w.WorkOrderID,
            w.OrderQty,
            r.ProductID
```

In the results for WorkOrderID 13, each associated WorkOrderRouting row was returned next to the calling tables WorkOrderID and OrderQty. Each row of the WorkOrder table was duplicated for each row returned from fn_WorkOrderRouting—all were based on the WorkOrderID.

Using OUTER APPLY

In order to demonstrate OUTER APPLY, I'll insert a new row into Production.WorkOrder (see Chapter 2 for a review of the INSERT command):

```
INSERT INTO [AdventureWorks].[Production].[WorkOrder]
            ([ProductID]
            ,[OrderQty]
            ,[ScrappedQty]
            ,[StartDate]
            ,[EndDate]
            ,[DueDate]
            ,[ScrapReasonID]
            ,[ModifiedDate])
     VALUES
            (1,
            1,
            1,
            GETDATE(),
            GETDATE(),
            GETDATE(),
            1,
            GETDATE())
```

Because this is a new row, and because Production.WorkOrder has an IDENTITY column for the WorkOrderID, the new row will have the maximum WorkOrderID in the table. Also, this new row will *not* have an associated value in the Production.WorkOrderRouting table, because it was just added.

Next, a CROSS APPLY query is executed, this time qualifying it to only return data for the newly inserted row:

```
SELECT    w.WorkOrderID,
          w.OrderQty,
          r.ProductID,
          r.OperationSequence
FROM Production.WorkOrder AS w
  CROSS APPLY dbo.fn_WorkOrderRouting
  (w.WorkOrderID) AS r
WHERE w.WorkOrderID IN
        (SELECT MAX(WorkOrderID)
         FROM Production.WorkOrder)
```

This returns nothing, because the left table's new row is unmatched:

```
WorkOrderID   OrderQty   ProductID   OperationSequence

(0 row(s) affected)
```

Now an OUTER APPLY is tried instead, which then returns the row from WorkOrder in spite of there being no associated value in the table-valued function:

```
SELECT   w.WorkOrderID,
      w.OrderQty,
      r.ProductID,
      r.OperationSequence
FROM Production.WorkOrder AS w
  OUTER APPLY dbo.fn_WorkOrderRouting
  (w.WorkOrderID) AS r
WHERE w.WorkOrderID IN
      (SELECT MAX(WorkOrderID)
       FROM Production.WorkOrder)
```

This returns

WorkOrderID	OrderQty	ProductID	OperationSequence
72592	1	NULL	NULL

(1 row(s) affected)

How It Works

CROSS and OUTER APPLY provide a method for applying lookups against columns using a table-valued function. CROSS APPLY was demonstrated against a row *without* a match in the table-valued function results. Since CROSS APPLY works like an INNER JOIN, no rows were returned. In the second query of this example, OUTER APPLY was used instead, this time returning unmatched NULL rows from the table-valued function, similar to an OUTER JOIN.

Advanced Techniques for Data Sources

This next set of recipes shows you a few advanced techniques for sampling, manipulating, and comparing data sources (a data source being any valid data source reference in a FROM clause), including the following:

- Returning a sampling of rows using TABLESAMPLE
- Using PIVOT to convert values into columns, and using an aggregation to group the data by the new columns
- Using UNPIVOT to normalize repeating column groups
- Using INTERSECT and EXCEPT operands to return distinct rows that only exist in either the left query (using EXCEPT), or only distinct rows that exist in both the left and right queries (using INTERSECT)

Using the TABLESAMPLE to Return Random Rows

TABLESAMPLE allows you to extract a sampling of rows from a table in the FROM clause. This sampling can be based on a percentage of number of rows. You can use TABLESAMPLE when only a sampling of rows is necessary for the application instead of a full result set. TABLESAMPLE also provides you with a somewhat randomized result set.

This example demonstrates a query that returns a percentage of random rows from a specific data source using TABLESAMPLE:

```
SELECT FirstName,LastName
FROM Person.Person
TABLESAMPLE SYSTEM (2 PERCENT)
```

This returns the following (abridged) results:

```
FirstName    LastName
Andre        Suri
Adam         Turner
Eric         Turner
Jackson      Turner
Meghan       Rowe
...
(232 row(s) affected)
```

Executing it again returns a new set of (abridged) results:

```
FirstName    LastName
Robert       King
Ricardo      Raje
Jose         King
Ricardo      Chande
...
Martin       Perez
Carlos       Collins

(198 row(s) affected)
```

How It Works

TABLESAMPLE works by extracting a sample of rows from the query result set. In this example, 2 percent of rows were sampled from the Person.Person table. However, don't let the "percent" fool you. That percentage is the *percentage of the table's data pages*. Once the sample pages are selected, all rows for the selected pages are returned. Since the fill state of pages can vary, the number of rows returned will also vary—you'll notice that the first time the query is executed in this example there were 232 rows, and the second time there were 198 rows. If you designate the number of rows, this is actually converted by SQL Server into a percentage, and then the same method used by SQL Server to identify the percentage of data pages is used.

Using PIVOT to Convert Single Column Values into Multiple Columns and Aggregate Data

The PIVOT operator allows you to create cross-tab queries that convert values into columns, using an aggregation to group the data by the new columns.

PIVOT uses the following syntax:

```
FROM  table_source
PIVOT      ( aggregate_function ( value_column )
        FOR pivot_column
        IN ( <column_list>)
    ) table_alias
```

The arguments of PIVOT are described in Table 1-3.

Table 1-3. *PIVOT Arguments*

Argument	Description
table_source	The table where the data will be pivoted
aggregate_function (value_column)	The aggregate function that will be used against the specified column
pivot_column	The column that will be used to create the column headers
column_list	The values to pivot from the pivot column
table_alias	The table alias of the pivoted result set

This next example shows you how to PIVOT and aggregate data similar to the pivot features in Microsoft Excel—shifting values in a single column into multiple columns, with aggregated data shown in the results.

The first part of the example displays the data prepivoted. The query results show employee shifts, as well as the departments that they are in:

```
SELECT    s.Name ShiftName,
        h.BusinessEntityID,
        d.Name DepartmentName
FROM    HumanResources.EmployeeDepartmentHistory h
INNER JOIN HumanResources.Department d ON
        h.DepartmentID = d.DepartmentID
INNER JOIN HumanResources.Shift s ON
        h.ShiftID = s.ShiftID
WHERE    EndDate IS NULL AND
        d.Name IN ('Production', 'Engineering', 'Marketing')
ORDER BY ShiftName
```

Notice that the varying departments are all listed in a single column:

```
ShiftName    BusinessEntityID    DepartmentName
Day          3                   Engineering
Day          9                   Engineering
...
Day          2                   Marketing
Day          6                   Marketing
...
Evening      25                  Production
Evening      18                  Production
Night        14                  Production
Night        27                  Production
...
Night        252.                Production

(194 row(s) affected)
```

The next query pivots the department values into columns, along with a count of employees by shift:

```
SELECT    ShiftName,
        Production,
        Engineering,
        Marketing
FROM
(SELECT    s.Name ShiftName,
        h.BusinessEntityID,
        d.Name DepartmentName
FROM    HumanResources.EmployeeDepartmentHistory h
INNER JOIN HumanResources.Department d ON
        h.DepartmentID = d.DepartmentID
INNER JOIN HumanResources.Shift s ON
        h.ShiftID = s.ShiftID
WHERE    EndDate IS NULL AND
        d.Name IN ('Production', 'Engineering', 'Marketing')) AS a
PIVOT
(
        COUNT(BusinessEntityID)
        FOR DepartmentName IN ([Production], [Engineering], [Marketing])
) AS b
ORDER BY ShiftName
```

This returns

```
ShiftName    Production    Engineering    Marketing
Day          79            6              9
Evening      54            0              0
Night        46            0              0

(3 row(s) affected)
```

How It Works

The result of the PIVOT query returned employee counts by shift and department. The query began by naming the fields to return:

```
SELECT    ShiftName,
        Production,
        Engineering,
        Marketing
```

Notice that these fields were actually the converted rows, but turned into column names.

The FROM clause referenced the subquery (the query used at the beginning of this example). The subquery was aliased with an arbitrary name of a:

```
FROM
(SELECT    s.Name ShiftName,
        h. BusinessEntityID,
        d.Name DepartmentName
FROM    HumanResources.EmployeeDepartmentHistory h
INNER JOIN HumanResources.Department d ON
        h.DepartmentID = d.DepartmentID
INNER JOIN HumanResources.Shift s ON
        h.ShiftID = s.ShiftID
WHERE    EndDate IS NULL AND
        d.Name IN ('Production', 'Engineering', 'Marketing')) AS a
```

Inside the parentheses, the query designated which columns would be aggregated (and how). In this case, the number of employees would be counted:

```
PIVOT
(COUNT(BusinessEntityID)
```

After the aggregation section, the FOR statement determined which row values would be converted into columns. Unlike regular IN clauses, single quotes aren't used around each string character, instead using square brackets. DepartmentName was the data column where values are converted into pivoted columns:

```
FOR DepartmentName IN ([Production], [Engineering], [Marketing]))
```

■**Note** The list of pivoted column names cannot already exist in the base table or view query columns being pivoted.

Lastly, a closed parenthesis closed off the PIVOT operation. The PIVOT operation was then aliased like a table with an arbitrary name (in this case b):

```
AS b
```

The results were then ordered by ShiftName:

```
ORDER BY ShiftName
```

The results took the three columns fixed in the FOR part of the PIVOT operation and aggregated counts of employees by ShiftName.

Normalizing Data with UNPIVOT

The UNPIVOT command does *almost* the opposite of PIVOT by changing columns into rows. It also uses the same syntax as PIVOT, only UNPIVOT is designated instead.

This example demonstrates how UNPIVOT can be used to remove column-repeating groups often seen in denormalized tables. For the first part of this recipe, a denormalized table is created with repeating, incrementing phone number columns:

```
CREATE TABLE dbo.Contact
   (EmployeeID int NOT NULL,
    PhoneNumber1 bigint,
    PhoneNumber2 bigint,
    PhoneNumber3 bigint)
GO

INSERT dbo.Contact
(EmployeeID, PhoneNumber1, PhoneNumber2, PhoneNumber3)
VALUES(   1, 2718353881, 3385531980, 5324571342)

INSERT dbo.Contact
(EmployeeID, PhoneNumber1, PhoneNumber2, PhoneNumber3)
VALUES(   2, 6007163571, 6875099415, 7756620787)

INSERT dbo.Contact
(EmployeeID, PhoneNumber1, PhoneNumber2, PhoneNumber3)
VALUES(   3, 9439250939, NULL, NULL)
```

Now using UNPIVOT, the repeating phone numbers are converted into a more normalized form (reusing a single PhoneValue field instead of repeating the phone column multiple times):

```
SELECT    EmployeeID,
        PhoneType,
        PhoneValue
FROM
(SELECT    EmployeeID, PhoneNumber1, PhoneNumber2, PhoneNumber3
FROM dbo.Contact) c
UNPIVOT
    (PhoneValue FOR PhoneType IN ([PhoneNumber1], [PhoneNumber2], [PhoneNumber3])
) AS p
```

This returns

EmployeeID	PhoneType	PhoneValue
1	PhoneNumber1	2718353881
1	PhoneNumber2	3385531980
1	PhoneNumber3	5324571342
2	PhoneNumber1	6007163571
2	PhoneNumber2	6875099415
2	PhoneNumber3	7756620787
3	PhoneNumber1	9439250939

```
(7 row(s) affected)
```

How It Works

This UNPIVOT example began by selecting three columns. The EmployeeID came from the subquery. The other two columns, PhoneType and PhoneValue, were defined later on in the UNPIVOT statement:

```
SELECT    EmployeeID,
        PhoneType,
        PhoneValue
```

Next, the FROM clause referenced a subquery. The subquery selected all four columns from the contact table. The table was aliased with the letter c (table alias name was arbitrary):

```
FROM
(SELECT    EmployeeID, PhoneNumber1, PhoneNumber2, PhoneNumber3
FROM dbo.Contact) c
```

A new column called PhoneValue (referenced in the SELECT) holds the individual phone numbers across the three denormalized phone columns:

```
UNPIVOT
(PhoneValue FOR PhoneType IN ([PhoneNumber1], [PhoneNumber2], [PhoneNumber3])
```

FOR references the name of the pivot column, PhoneType, which holds the column names of the denormalized table. The IN clause following PhoneType lists the columns from the original table to be narrowed into a single column.

Lastly, a closing parenthesis is used, and then aliased with an arbitrary name, in this case p:

```
) AS p
```

This query returned the phone data merged into two columns, one to describe the phone type, and another to hold the actual phone numbers. Also notice that there are seven rows, instead of nine. This is because for EmployeeID 3, only non-NULL values were returned. UNPIVOT does not return NULL values from the pivoted result set.

Returning Distinct or Matching Rows Using EXCEPT and INTERSECT

The INTERSECT and EXCEPT operands allow you to return either distinct rows that exist only in the left query (using EXCEPT) or distinct rows that exist in both the left and right queries (using INTERSECT).

INTERSECT and EXCEPT are useful in dataset comparison scenarios; for example, if you need to compare rows between test and production tables, you can use EXCEPT to easily identify and populate rows that existed in one table and not the other. These operands are also useful for data recovery, because you could restore a database from a period prior to a data loss, compare data with the current production table, and then recover the deleted rows accordingly.

For this recipe, demonstration tables are created that are partially populated from the Production.Product table:

```
-- First two new tables based on ProductionProduct will be
-- created, in order to demonstrate EXCEPT and INTERSECT.
-- See Chapter 8 for more on ROW_NUMBER

-- Create TableA
SELECT    prod.ProductID,
       prod.Name
INTO dbo.TableA
FROM
(SELECT ProductID,
       Name,
       ROW_NUMBER() OVER (ORDER BY ProductID) RowNum
FROM Production.Product) prod
WHERE RowNum BETWEEN 1 and 20

-- Create TableB
SELECT    prod.ProductID,
       prod.Name
INTO dbo.TableB
FROM
(SELECT ProductID,
       Name,
       ROW_NUMBER() OVER (ORDER BY ProductID) RowNum
FROM Production.Product) prod
WHERE RowNum BETWEEN 10 and 29
```

This returns

```
(20 row(s) affected)

(20 row(s) affected)
```

Now the EXCEPT operator will be used to determine which rows exist *only* in the left table of the query, TableA, and not in TableB:

```
SELECT    ProductID,
       Name
FROM    dbo.TableA
EXCEPT
```

```
SELECT   ProductID,
       Name
FROM   dbo.TableB
```

This returns

```
ProductID   Name
1           Adjustable Race
2           Bearing Ball
3           BB Ball Bearing
4           Headset Ball Bearings
316         Blade
317         LL Crankarm
318         ML Crankarm
319         HL Crankarm
320         Chainring Bolts

(9 row(s) affected)
```

To show distinct values from *both* result sets that match, use the INTERSECT operator:

```
SELECT   ProductID,
       Name
FROM   dbo.TableA
INTERSECT
SELECT   ProductID,
       Name
FROM   dbo.TableB
```

This returns

```
ProductID   Name
321         Chainring Nut
322         Chainring
323         Crown Race
324         Chain Stays
325         Decal 1
326         Decal 2
327         Down Tube
328         Mountain End Caps
329         Road End Caps
330         Touring End Caps
331         Fork End

(11 row(s) affected)
```

How It Works

The example started off by creating two tables (using INTO) that contain overlapping sets of rows.

■**Note** The ROW_NUMBER function used to populate the tables in this recipe is described in more detail in Chapter 8.

The first table, TableA, contained the first 20 rows (ordered by ProductID) from the Production.
Product table. The second table, TableB, also received another 20 rows, half of which overlapped
with TableA's rows.

To determine which rows exist *only* in TableA, the EXCEPT operand was placed after the FROM
clause of the first query and before the second query:

```
SELECT    ProductID,
       Name
FROM    dbo.TableA
EXCEPT
SELECT    ProductID,
       Name
FROM    dbo.TableB
```

In order for EXCEPT to be used, both queries must have the same number of columns. Those
columns also need to have compatible data types (it's not necessary that the column names from
each query match). The advantages of EXCEPT is that *all* columns are evaluated to determine
whether there is a match, which is much more efficient than using INNER JOIN (which would
require explicitly joining the tables on each column in both data sources).

The results of the EXCEPT query show the first nine rows from TableA that were not also populated into TableB.

In the second example, INTERSECT was used to show rows that *overlap* between the two tables.
Like EXCEPT, INTERSECT is placed between the two queries:

```
SELECT    ProductID,
       Name
FROM    dbo.TableA
INTERSECT
SELECT    ProductID,
       Name
FROM    dbo.TableB
```

The query returned the 11 rows that overlapped between both tables. The same rules about
compatible data types and number of columns apply to INTERSECT as for EXCEPT.

Summarizing Data

In these next three recipes, I will demonstrate summarizing data within the result set using the following operators:

- Use CUBE to add summarizing total values to a result set based on columns in the GROUP BY
  clause.

- Use ROLLUP with GROUP BY to add hierarchical data summaries based on the ordering of
  columns in the GROUP BY clause.

- Use the GROUPING SETS operator to define custom aggregates in a single result set without
  having to use UNION ALL.

I'll start this section off by demonstrating how to summarize data with CUBE.

Summarizing Data Using CUBE

CUBE adds rows to your result set, summarizing total values based on the columns in the GROUP BY
clause.

This example demonstrates a query that returns the total quantity of a product, grouped by the shelf the product is kept on:

```
SELECT   i.Shelf,
       SUM(i.Quantity) Total
FROM    Production.ProductInventory i
GROUP BY CUBE (i.Shelf)
```

This returns the following results:

Shelf	Total
A	26833
B	12672
C	19868
D	17353
E	31979
F	21249
G	40195
H	20055
J	12154
K	16311
L	13553
M	3567
N	5254
N/A	30582
R	23123
S	5912
T	10634
U	18700
V	2635
W	2908
Y	437
NULL	335974

```
(22 row(s) affected)
```

In this next query, I'll modify the SELECT and GROUP BY clauses by adding LocationID:

```
SELECT   i.Shelf,
     i.LocationID,
     SUM(i.Quantity) Total
FROM    Production.ProductInventory i
GROUP BY CUBE (i.Shelf,i.LocationID)
```

This returns a few levels of totals, the first being by location (abridged):

Shelf	LocationID	Total
A	1	2727
C	1	13777
D	1	6551
...		
K	1	6751
L	1	7537
NULL	1	72899

In the same result set, later on you also see totals by shelf, and then across all shelves and locations:

```
Shelf   LocationID   Total
...
T        NULL         10634
U        NULL         18700
V        NULL         2635
W        NULL         2908
Y        NULL         437
NULL     NULL         335974
```

How It Works

Because the first query groups by shelf, and because I used GROUP BY CUBE, an extra row was added to the bottom of the result set that shows the total for all shelves:

```
GROUP BY CUBE (i.Shelf)
```

■**Caution** When using CUBE, you must be careful not to accidentally double-count your aggregated values.

This is slightly different syntax from previous versions of SQL Server. In SQL Server 2008, CUBE is after the GROUP BY, instead of trailing the GROUP BY clause with a WITH CUBE. Notice also that the column lists are contained within parentheses:

```
GROUP BY CUBE (i.Shelf,i.LocationID)
```

Adding additional columns to the query, included in the GROUP BY CUBE clause, you saw aggregate values for each grouping combination. CUBE is often used for reporting purposes, providing a simple way to return totals by grouped column.

■**Note** In earlier versions of SQL Server, you may have used COMPUTE BY to also provide similar aggregations for your query. Microsoft has deprecated COMPUTE BY functionality for backward compatibility. Unlike WITH CUBE, COMPUTE BY created an entirely new summarized result set after the original query results, which were often difficult for calling applications to consume.

Summarizing Data Using ROLLUP

GROUP BY ROLLUP is used to add hierarchical data summaries based on the ordering of columns in the GROUP BY clause.

This example retrieves the shelf, product name, and total quantity of the product:

```
SELECT   i.Shelf,
         p.Name,
         SUM(i.Quantity) Total
FROM   Production.ProductInventory i
INNER JOIN Production.Product p ON
     i.ProductID = p.ProductID
GROUP BY ROLLUP (i.Shelf, p.Name)
```

This returns the following (abridged) results:

```
Shelf    Name                   Total
A        Adjustable Race        761
A        BB Ball Bearing        909
...
A        NULL                   26833
B        Adjustable Race        324
B        BB Ball Bearing        443
B        Bearing Ball           318
...
B        Touring Front Wheel    304
B        NULL                   12672
C        Chain                  236
C        Chain Stays            585
Y        LL Spindle/Axle        209
Y        NULL                   437
NULL     NULL                   335974
```

How It Works

The order you place the columns in the GROUP BY ROLLUP impacts how data is aggregated. ROLLUP in this query aggregated total quantity for each change in Shelf. Notice the row with shelf A and the NULL name; this holds the total quantity for shelf A. Also notice that the final row was the grand total of all product quantities. Whereas CUBE creates a result set that aggregates all combinations for the selected columns, ROLLUP generates the aggregates for a hierarchy of values.

```
GROUP BY ROLLUP (i.Shelf, p.Name)
```

ROLLUP aggregated a grand total and totals by shelf. Totals were *not* generated for the product name but would have been had I designated CUBE instead.

Just like CUBE, ROLLUP uses slightly different syntax from previous versions of SQL Server. In SQL Server 2008, ROLLUP is after the GROUP BY, instead of trailing the GROUP BY clause with a WITH ROLLUP. Notice also that the column lists are contained within parentheses.

Creating Custom Summaries Using Grouping Sets

SQL Server 2008 introduces the ability to define your own grouping sets within a single query result set without having to resort to multiple UNION ALLs. Grouping sets also provides you with more control over what is aggregated, compared to the previously demonstrated CUBE and ROLLUP operations. This is performed by using the GROUPING SETS operator.

First, I'll demonstrate by defining an example business requirement for a query. Let's assume I want a single result set to contain three different aggregate quantity summaries. Specifically, I would like to see quantity totals by shelf, quantity totals by shelf *and* product name, and then also quantity totals by location *and* name.

To achieve this in previous versions of SQL Server, you would need to have used UNION ALL:

```
SELECT
     NULL,
     i.LocationID,
     p.Name,
     SUM(i.Quantity) Total
FROM   Production.ProductInventory i
```

```
INNER JOIN Production.Product p ON
    i.ProductID = p.ProductID
WHERE Shelf IN ('A','C') AND
    Name IN ('Chain', 'Decal', 'Head Tube')
GROUP BY i.LocationID, p.Name
UNION ALL
SELECT
     i.Shelf,
         NULL,
         NULL,
     SUM(i.Quantity) Total
FROM   Production.ProductInventory i
INNER JOIN Production.Product p ON
    i.ProductID = p.ProductID
WHERE Shelf IN ('A','C') AND
    Name IN ('Chain', 'Decal', 'Head Tube')
GROUP BY i.Shelf
UNION ALL
SELECT
     i.Shelf,
     NULL,
     p.Name,
     SUM(i.Quantity) Total
FROM   Production.ProductInventory i
INNER JOIN Production.Product p ON
    i.ProductID = p.ProductID
WHERE Shelf IN ('A','C') AND
    Name IN ('Chain', 'Decal', 'Head Tube')
GROUP BY i.Shelf, p.Name
```

This returns

LocationID	Name	Total	
NULL	1	Chain	236
NULL	5	Chain	192
NULL	50	Chain	161
NULL	20	Head Tube	544
A	NULL	NULL	897
C	NULL	NULL	236
A	NULL	Chain	353
C	NULL	Chain	236
A	NULL	Head Tube	544

```
(9 row(s) affected)
```

In SQL Server 2008, you can save yourself all that extra code by using the GROUPING SETS operator instead to define the various aggregations you would like to have returned in a single result set:

```
SELECT
     i.Shelf,
     i.LocationID,
     p.Name,
     SUM(i.Quantity) Total
FROM   Production.ProductInventory i
INNER JOIN Production.Product p ON
    i.ProductID = p.ProductID
WHERE Shelf IN ('A','C') AND
```

```
    Name IN ('Chain', 'Decal', 'Head Tube')
GROUP BY GROUPING SETS
    ((i.Shelf), (i.Shelf, p.Name), (i.LocationID, p.Name))
```

This returns the same result set as the previous query (only ordered a little differently):

Shelf	LocationID	Name	Total
NULL	1	Chain	236
NULL	5	Chain	192
NULL	50	Chain	161
NULL	20	Head Tube	544
A	NULL	Chain	353
A	NULL	Head Tube	544
A	NULL	NULL	897
C	NULL	Chain	236
C	NULL	NULL	236

(9 row(s) affected)

How It Works

The new GROUPING SETS operator allows you to define varying aggregate groups in a single query, while avoiding the use of multiple queries attached together using UNION ALL. The core of this recipe's example is the following two lines of code:

```
GROUP BY GROUPING SETS
    ((i.Shelf), (i.Shelf, p.Name), (i.LocationID, p.Name))
```

Notice that unlike a regular aggregated query, the GROUP BY clause is not followed by a list of columns. Instead, it is followed by GROUPING SETS. GROUPING SETS is then followed by parentheses and the groupings of column names, each also encapsulated in parentheses.

Revealing Rows Generated by GROUPING

You may have noticed that those rows that were grouped in the previous recipes had NULL values in the columns that weren't participating in the aggregate totals. For example, when shelf C was totaled up, the location and product name columns were NULL:

```
C    NULL    NULL    236
```

The NULL values are acceptable if your data doesn't explicitly contain NULLs—however, what if it does? How can you differentiate "stored" NULLs from those generated in the rollups, cubes, and grouping sets?

In order to address this issue, you can use the GROUPING and GROUPING_ID functions. I'll discuss GROUPING in this recipe and GROUPING_ID in the next. GROUPING was available in previous versions of SQL Server, and it allowed simple evaluation of whether or not a row is a product of aggregation. For example, the following query uses a CASE statement to evaluate whether each row is a total by shelf, total by location, grand total, or regular non-cubed row:

```
SELECT
    i.Shelf,
    i.LocationID,
    CASE
      WHEN GROUPING(i.Shelf) = 0 AND
```

```
            GROUPING(i.LocationID) = 1 THEN 'Shelf Total'
        WHEN GROUPING(i.Shelf) = 1 AND
            GROUPING(i.LocationID) = 0 THEN 'Location Total'
        WHEN GROUPING(i.Shelf) = 1 AND
            GROUPING(i.LocationID) = 1 THEN 'Grand Total'
        ELSE 'Regular Row'
    END RowType,
    SUM(i.Quantity) Total
FROM    Production.ProductInventory i
WHERE LocationID = 2
GROUP BY CUBE (i.Shelf,i.LocationID)
```

This returns

Shelf	LocationID	RowType	Total
B	2	Regular Row	900
C	2	Regular Row	1557
D	2	Regular Row	3092
NULL	2	Location Total	5549
NULL	NULL	Grand Total	5549
B	NULL	Shelf Total	900
C	NULL	Shelf Total	1557
D	NULL	Shelf Total	3092

(8 row(s) affected)

How It Works

The GROUPING function allows you to differentiate and act upon those rows that are generated automatically for aggregates using CUBE, ROLLUP, and GROUPING SETS. In this example, I started off the SELECT statement as normal, with the Shelf and Location columns:

```
SELECT
    i.Shelf,
    i.LocationID,
```

Following this, I then began a CASE statement that would evaluate the combinations of return values for the GROUPING statement.

■**Tip** For more on CASE, see Chapter 9.

When GROUPING returns a 1 value (true), it means the column NULL is not an actual data value, but is a result of the aggregate operation, standing in for the value "all". So for example, if the shelf value is not NULL and the location ID is null due to the CUBE aggregation process and not the data itself, the string Shelf Total is returned:

```
CASE
    WHEN GROUPING(i.Shelf) = 0 AND
        GROUPING(i.LocationID) = 1 THEN 'Shelf Total'
```

This continues with similar logic, only this time if the shelf value is NULL due to the CUBE aggregation process, but the location is not null, a location total is provided:

```
    WHEN GROUPING(i.Shelf) = 1 AND
        GROUPING(i.LocationID) = 0 THEN 'Location Total'
```

The last WHEN defines when both shelf and location are NULL due to the CUBE aggregation process, which means the row contains the grand total for the result set:

```
WHEN GROUPING(i.Shelf) = 1 AND
     GROUPING(i.LocationID) = 1 THEN 'Grand Total'
```

GROUPING only returns a 1 or a 0; however, in SQL Server 2008, you also have the option of using GROUPING_ID to compute grouping at a finer grain, as I'll demonstrate in the next recipe.

Advanced Group-Level Identification with GROUPING_ID

■**Note** This recipe assumes an understanding of the binary/base-2 number system.

Identifying which rows belong to which type of aggregate becomes progressively more difficult for each new column you add to GROUP BY and each unique data value that can be grouped and aggregated. For example, assume that I have a non-aggregated report showing the quantity of products that exist in location 3 within bins 1 and 2:

```
SELECT
    i.Shelf,
    i.LocationID,
    i.Bin,
    i.Quantity
FROM    Production.ProductInventory i
WHERE i.LocationID IN (3) AND
      i.Bin IN (1,2)
```

This query returns only two rows:

Shelf	LocationID	Bin	Quantity
A	3	2	41
A	3	1	49

Now what if I wanted to report aggregations based on the various combinations of shelf, location, and bin? I could use CUBE to give summaries of all these potential combinations:

```
SELECT
    i.Shelf,
    i.LocationID,
    i.Bin,
    SUM(i.Quantity) Total
FROM    Production.ProductInventory i
WHERE i.LocationID IN (3) AND
      i.Bin IN (1,2)
GROUP BY CUBE (i.Shelf,i.LocationID, i.Bin)
ORDER BY i.Shelf, i.LocationID, i.Bin
```

Although the query returns the various aggregations expected from CUBE, the results are difficult to decipher:

Shelf	LocationID	Bin	Total
NULL	NULL	NULL	90
NULL	NULL	1	49
NULL	NULL	2	41

NULL	3	NULL	90
NULL	3	1	49
NULL	3	2	41
A	NULL	NULL	90
A	NULL	1	49
A	NULL	2	41
A	3	NULL	90
A	3	1	49
A	3	2	41

(12 row(s) affected)

This is where GROUPING_ID comes in handy. Using this function, I can determine the level of grouping for the row. This function is more complicated than GROUPING, however, because GROUPING_ID takes one or more columns as its input and then returns the integer equivalent of the base-2 (binary) number calculation on the columns.

This is best described by example, so I'll demonstrate taking the previous query and adding CASE logic to return proper row descriptors:

```
SELECT
    i.Shelf,
    i.LocationID,
    i.Bin,
    CASE GROUPING_ID(i.Shelf,i.LocationID, i.Bin)
        WHEN 1 THEN 'Shelf/Location Total'
        WHEN 2 THEN 'Shelf/Bin Total'
        WHEN 3 THEN 'Shelf Total'
        WHEN 4 THEN 'Location/Bin Total'
        WHEN 5 THEN 'Location Total'
        WHEN 6 THEN 'Bin Total'
        WHEN 7 THEN 'Grand Total'
    ELSE 'Regular Row'
    END,
    SUM(i.Quantity) Total
FROM    Production.ProductInventory i
WHERE i.LocationID IN (3) AND
      i.Bin IN (1,2)
GROUP BY CUBE (i.Shelf,i.LocationID, i.Bin)
ORDER BY i.Shelf, i.LocationID, i.Bin
```

I'll explain what each of the integer values mean in the "How It Works" section. The results returned from this query give descriptions of the various aggregations CUBE resulted in:

Shelf	LocationID	Bin		Total	
NULL	NULL	NULL	Grand Total	90	
NULL	NULL	1	Bin Total	49	
NULL	NULL	2	Bin Total	41	
NULL	3	NULL	Location Total		90
NULL	3	1	Location/Bin Total	49	
NULL	3	2	Location/Bin Total	41	
A	NULL	NULL	Shelf Total	90	
A	NULL	1	Shelf/Bin Total	49	
A	NULL	2	Shelf/Bin Total	41	
A	3	NULL	Shelf/Location Total	90	
A	3	1	Regular Row	49	

```
A        3         2       Regular Row            41
(12 row(s) affected)
```

How It Works

GROUPING_ID takes a column list and returns the integer value of the base-2 binary column list calculation (I'll step through this).

The query started off with the list of the three non-aggregated columns to be returned in the result set:

```
SELECT
    i.Shelf,
    i.LocationID,
    i.Bin,
```

Next, I defined a CASE statement that evaluated the return value of GROUPING_ID for the list of the three columns:

```
CASE GROUPING_ID(i.Shelf,i.LocationID, i.Bin)
```

In order to illustrate the base-2 conversion to integer concept, I'll focus on a single row, the row that shows the grand total for shelf A generated automatically by CUBE:

Shelf	LocationID	Bin	Total
A	NULL	NULL	90

Now envision another row beneath it that shows the bit values being enabled or disabled based on whether the column is not a grouping column. Both Location and Bin from GROUPING_ID's perspective have a bit value of 1 because neither of them are a grouping column for this specific row. For this row, Shelf is the grouping column:

Shelf	LocationID	Bin
A	NULL	NULL
0	1	1

Converting the binary 011 to integer, I'll add another row that shows the integer value beneath the flipped bits:

Shelf	LocationID	Bin
A	NULL	NULL
0	1	1
4	2	1

Because only location and bin have enabled bits, I add 1 and 2 to get a summarized value of 3, which is the value returned for this row by GROUPING_ID. So the various combinations of grouping are calculated from binary to integer. In the CASE statement that follows, 3 translates to a shelf total.

Since I have three columns, the various potential aggregations are represented in the following WHEN/THENs:

```
CASE GROUPING_ID(i.Shelf,i.LocationID, i.Bin)
    WHEN 1 THEN 'Shelf/Location Total'
    WHEN 2 THEN 'Shelf/Bin Total'
    WHEN 3 THEN 'Shelf Total'
```

```
      WHEN 4 THEN 'Location/Bin Total'
      WHEN 5 THEN 'Location Total'
      WHEN 6 THEN 'Bin Total'
      WHEN 7 THEN 'Grand Total'
   ELSE 'Regular Row'
END,
```

Each potential combination of aggregations is handled in the CASE statement. The rest of the query involves using an aggregate function on quantity, and then using CUBE to find the various aggregation combinations for shelf, location, and bin:

```
   SUM(i.Quantity) Total
FROM    Production.ProductInventory i
WHERE i.LocationID IN (3) AND
      i.Bin IN (1,2)
GROUP BY CUBE (i.Shelf,i.LocationID, i.Bin)
ORDER BYi.Shelf, i.LocationID, i.Bin
```

Common Table Expressions

A Common Table Expression, or CTE, is similar to a view or derived query, allowing you to create a temporary query that can be referenced within the scope of a SELECT, INSERT, UPDATE, or DELETE query. Unlike a derived query, you don't need to copy the query definition multiple times each time it is used. You can also use local variables within a CTE definition—something you can't do in a view definition.

The basic syntax for a CTE is as follows:

```
WITH expression_name [ ( column_name [ ,...n ] ) ]
AS ( CTE_query_definition )
```

The arguments of a CTE are described in the Table 1-4.

Table 1-4. *CTE Arguments*

Argument	Description
expression_name	The name of the common table expression
column_name [,...n]	The unique column names of the expression
CTE_query_definition	The SELECT query that defines the common table expression

A *non-recursive* CTE is one that is used within a query without referencing itself. It serves as a temporary result set for the query. A *recursive* CTE is defined similarly to a non-recursive CTE, only a recursive CTE returns hierarchical self-relating data. Using a CTE to represent recursive data can minimize the amount of code needed compared to other methods.

The next two recipes will demonstrate both non-recursive and recursive CTEs.

Using a Non-Recursive Common Table Expression

This example of a common table expression demonstrates returning vendors in the Purchasing.Vendor table—returning the first five and last five results ordered by name:

```
WITH VendorSearch (RowNumber, VendorName, AccountNumber)
AS
(
SELECT ROW_NUMBER() OVER (ORDER BY Name) RowNum,
       Name,
       AccountNumber
FROM Purchasing.Vendor
)

SELECT   RowNumber,
       VendorName,
       AccountNumber
FROM VendorSearch
WHERE RowNumber BETWEEN 1 AND 5
UNION
SELECT   RowNumber,
       VendorName,
       AccountNumber
FROM VendorSearch
WHERE RowNumber BETWEEN 100 AND 104
```

This returns

RowNumber	VendorName	AccountNumber
1	A. Datum Corporation	ADATUM0001
2	Advanced Bicycles	ADVANCED0001
3	Allenson Cycles	ALLENSON0001
4	American Bicycles and Wheels	AMERICAN0001
5	American Bikes	AMERICAN0002
100	Vista Road Bikes	VISTARO0001
101	West Junction Cycles	WESTJUN0001
102	WestAmerica Bicycle Co.	WESTAMER0001
103	Wide World Importers	WIDEWOR0001
104	Wood Fitness	WOODFIT0001

(10 row(s) affected)

The previous example used UNION; however, non-recursive CTEs can be used like any other SELECT query too:

```
WITH VendorSearch (VendorID, VendorName)
AS
(
SELECT BusinessEntityID,
       Name
FROM Purchasing.Vendor
)

SELECT   v.VendorID,
       v.VendorName,
       p.ProductID,
       p.StandardPrice
FROM VendorSearch v
INNER JOIN Purchasing.ProductVendor p ON
   v.VendorID = p.VendorID
ORDER BY v.VendorName
```

This returns the following (abridged) results:

VendorID	VendorName	ProductID	StandardPrice
32	Advanced Bicycles	359	45.41
32	Advanced Bicycles	360	43.41
32	Advanced Bicycles	361	47.48
32	Advanced Bicycles	362	43.41
32	Advanced Bicycles	363	41.41
...			

(460 row(s) affected)

How It Works

In the first example of the recipe, WITH defined the CTE name and the columns it returned. This was a non-recursive CTE because CTE data wasn't being joined to itself. The CTE in this example was only using a query that UNIONed two data sets:

```
WITH VendorSearch (RowNumber, VendorName, AccountNumber)
```

The column names defined in the CTE can match the actual names of the query within—or you can create your own alias names. For example, here the Purchasing.Vendor column Name has been referenced as VendorName in the CTE.

Next in the recipe, AS marked the beginning of the CTE query definition:

```
AS
(
```

Inside the parentheses, the query used a function that returned the sequential row number of the result set—ordered by the vendor name (see Chapter 8 for a review of ROW_NUMBER):

```
SELECT ROW_NUMBER() OVER (ORDER BY Name) RowNum,
       Name,
       AccountNumber
FROM Purchasing.Vendor
)
```

The vendor name and AccountNumber from the Purchasing.Vendor table were also returned. The CTE definition finished after marking the closing parentheses.

Following the CTE definition was the query that used the CTE. Keep in mind that a SELECT, INSERT, UPDATE, or DELETE statement that references some or all the CTE columns *must* follow the definition of the CTE:

```
SELECT   RowNumber,
    VendorName,
    AccountNumber
FROM VendorSearch
WHERE RowNumber BETWEEN 1 AND 5
```

The SELECT column names were used from the new VendorSearch CTE. In the WHERE clause, the first query returns rows 1 through 5. Next the UNION operator was used prior to the second query:

```
UNION
```

This second query displayed the last five rows. The VendorSearch CTE was referenced twice—but the full query definition only had to be defined a single time (unlike using derived queries)—thus reducing code.

In the second example of the recipe, a simple CTE was defined without using any functions, just `BusinessEntityID` and `VendorName` from the `Purchasing.Vendor` table:

```
WITH VendorSearch (VendorID, VendorName)
AS
(
SELECT BusinessEntityID,
       Name
FROM Purchasing.Vendor
)
```

In the query following this CTE definition, the CTE `VendorSearch` was joined just like a regular table (only without specifying the owning schema):

```
SELECT   v.VendorID,
       v.VendorName,
       p.ProductID,
       p.StandardPrice
FROM VendorSearch v
INNER JOIN Purchasing.ProductVendor p ON
   v.VendorID = p.BusinessEntityID
ORDER BY v.VendorName
```

■**Caution** If the CTE is part of a batch of statements, the statement before its definition must be followed by a semicolon.

■**Note** You can use a semicolon as a SQL Server statement terminator. Doing so isn't mandatory in most areas, but it is ANSI compliant, and you'll see it being used in some of the documentation coming from Microsoft.

Using a Recursive Common Table Expression

In this example, the new `Company` table will define the companies in a hypothetical giant mega con-glomerate. Each company has a `CompanyID` and an optional `ParentCompanyID`. The example will demonstrate how to display the company hierarchy in the results using a recursive CTE. First, the table is created:

```
CREATE TABLE dbo.Company
   (CompanyID int NOT NULL PRIMARY KEY,
    ParentCompanyID int NULL,
    CompanyName varchar(25) NOT NULL)
```

Next, rows are inserted into the new table (using new SQL Server 2008 syntax that I'll be demonstrating in Chapter 2):

```
INSERT dbo.Company (CompanyID, ParentCompanyID, CompanyName)
VALUES
   (1, NULL, 'Mega-Corp'),
   (2, 1, 'Mediamus-Corp'),
   (3, 1, 'KindaBigus-Corp'),
   (4, 3, 'GettinSmaller-Corp'),
   (5, 4, 'Smallest-Corp'),
   (6, 5, 'Puny-Corp'),
   (7, 5, 'Small2-Corp')
```

Now the actual example:

```
WITH CompanyTree(ParentCompanyID, CompanyID, CompanyName, CompanyLevel)
AS
(
    SELECT    ParentCompanyID,
      CompanyID,
      CompanyName,
      0 AS CompanyLevel
    FROM dbo.Company
    WHERE ParentCompanyID IS NULL
    UNION ALL
    SELECT    c.ParentCompanyID,
      c.CompanyID,
      c.CompanyName,
      p.CompanyLevel + 1
    FROM dbo.Company c
        INNER JOIN CompanyTree p
        ON c.ParentCompanyID = p.CompanyID
)
SELECT ParentCompanyID, CompanyID, CompanyName, CompanyLevel
FROM CompanyTree
```

This returns

```
ParentCompanyID   CompanyID   CompanyName          CompanyLevel
NULL              1           Mega-Corp            0
1                 2           Mediamus-Corp        1
1                 3           KindaBigus-Corp      1
3                 4           GettinSmaller-Corp   2
4                 5           Smallest-Corp        3
5                 6           Puny-Corp            4
5                 7           Small2-Corp          4

(7 row(s) affected)
```

How It Works

In this example, the CTE name and columns are defined first:

```
WITH CompanyTree(ParentCompanyID, CompanyID, CompanyName, CompanyLevel)
```

The CTE query definition began with AS and an open parenthesis:

```
AS
(
```

The SELECT clause began with the "anchor" SELECT statement. The anchor definition has to be defined first. When using recursive CTEs, "anchor" refers to the fact that it defines the base of the recursion—in this case the top level of the corporate hierarchy (the parentless Mega-Corp). This SELECT also includes a CompanyLevel column alias, preceded with the number zero. This column will be used in the recursion to display how many levels deep a particular company is in the company hierarchy:

```
SELECT ParentCompanyID,
  CompanyID,
  CompanyName,
  0 AS CompanyLevel
FROM dbo.Company
WHERE ParentCompanyID IS NULL
```

Next was the UNION ALL, to join the second, recursive query to the anchor member (UNION ALL, and not just UNION, is required for the last anchor member and the first recursive member in a recursive CTE):

```
UNION ALL
```

After that was the recursive query. Like the anchor, the SELECT clause references the ParentCompanyID, CompanyID, and CompanyName from the dbo.Company table. Unlike the anchor, the CTE column references p.CompanyLevel (from the anchor query), adding 1 to its total at each level of the hierarchy:

```
SELECT    c.ParentCompanyID,
  c.CompanyID,
  c.CompanyName,
  p.CompanyLevel + 1
```

The dbo.Company table was joined to the CompanyTree CTE, joining the CTE's recursive query's ParentCompanyID to the CTE's CompanyID:

```
FROM dbo.Company c
    INNER JOIN CompanyTree p
    ON c.ParentCompanyID = p.CompanyID
)
```

After the closing of the CTE's definition, the query selected from the CTE based on the columns defined in the CTE definition.

```
SELECT ParentCompanyID, CompanyID, CompanyName, CompanyLevel
FROM CompanyTree
```

In the results, for each level in the company hierarchy, the CTE increased the CompanyLevel column.

With this useful new feature come some cautions, however. If you create your recursive CTE incorrectly, you could cause an infinite loop. While testing, to avoid infinite loops, use the MAXRECURSION hint mentioned earlier in the chapter.

For example, you can stop the previous example from going further than two levels by adding the OPTION clause with MAXRECURSION at the end of the query:

```
WITH CompanyTree(ParentCompanyID, CompanyID, CompanyName, CompanyLevel) AS
(
    SELECT ParentCompanyID, CompanyID, CompanyName, 0 AS CompanyLevel
    FROM dbo.Company
    WHERE ParentCompanyID IS NULL
    UNION ALL
    SELECT c.ParentCompanyID, c.CompanyID, c.CompanyName, p.CompanyLevel + 1
    FROM dbo.Company c
        INNER JOIN CompanyTree p
        ON c.ParentCompanyID = p.CompanyID
)
SELECT ParentCompanyID, CompanyID, CompanyName, CompanyLevel
FROM CompanyTree
OPTION (MAXRECURSION 2)
```

This returns

```
ParentCompanyID    CompanyID    CompanyName           CompanyLevel
NULL               1            Mega-Corp             0
1                  2            Mediamus-Corp         1
1                  3            KindaBigus-Corp       1
3                  4            GettinSmaller-Corp    2
Msg 530, Level 16, State 1, Line 2
The statement terminated. The maximum recursion 2 has
been exhausted before statement completion.
```

As a best practice, set the MAXRECURSION based on your understanding of the data. If you know that the hierarchy cannot go more than ten levels deep, for example, then set MAXRECURSION to that value.

■**Tip** You can also use the new HierarchyID data type to more easily traverse data hierarchies. For more information on this new SQL Server 2008 data type, see Chapter 14.

CHAPTER 2

■ ■ ■

Perform, Capture, and Track Data Modifications

In this chapter, I review how to modify data using the Transact-SQL INSERT, UPDATE, and DELETE commands. I'll review the basics of each command and cover specific techniques such as inserting data from a stored procedure and importing an image file into a table using OPENROWSET BULK functionality.

The new SQL Server 2008 features I cover in this chapter include the following:

- Inserting multiple rows from a single INSERT statement. I'll also demonstrate using the multiple-row technique to create a query data source in a SELECT clause (without having to create a permanent or temporary table).

- New assignment operators that allow you to modify a passed data value with minimal coding.

- The new MERGE command, which allows you to consolidate and apply data modification commands using a single block of code.

- Storing unstructured data on the file system while maintaining SQL Server transactional control using the new FILESTREAM attribute.

- Two new options for tracking table data changes using Change Data Capture (CDC) and Change Tracking built-in functionality.

Before going into the new features, however, I'll start the chapter off by reviewing basic INSERT concepts.

INSERT

The simplified syntax for the INSERT command is as follows:

```
INSERT
    [ INTO]
    table_or_view_name
    [ ( column_list ) ]
    VALUES (({DEFAULT | NULL | expression } [ ,...n ]) [ ,...n ])
```

The arguments of this command are described in Table 2-1.

Table 2-1. *INSERT Command Arguments*

Argument	Description
table_or_view_name	The name of the table or updateable view that you are inserting a row into.
column_list	The explicit comma-separated list of columns on the insert table that will be populated with values.
(DEFAULT | NULL | expression }[,...n])	The comma-separated list of values to be inserted as a row into the table. In SQL Server 2008, you can insert multiple rows in a single statement. Each value can be an expression, NULL value, or DEFAULT value (if a default was defined for the column).

Inserting a Row into a Table

In this recipe, I demonstrate the use of INSERT to add new rows into a table (as specified by table_name), specifying a column_list of columns into which the data should be inserted, and a corresponding comma-separated list of values to be inserted, [,....n], in the VALUES clause. Specifically, here I demonstrate inserting a single row into the AdventureWorks Production.Location table:

```
USE AdventureWorks
GO

INSERT Production.Location
(Name, CostRate, Availability)
VALUES ('Wheel Storage', 11.25, 80.00)
```

This returns

```
(1 row(s) affected)
```

This next query then searches for any row with the name Wheel Storage:

```
SELECT  Name,
    CostRate,
    Availability
FROM Production.Location
WHERE Name = 'Wheel Storage'
```

This returns

```
Name            CostRate    Availability
Wheel Storage   11.25       80.00

(1 row(s) affected)
```

How It Works

In this recipe, a new row was inserted into the Production.Location table.

The query began with the INSERT command and the name of the table that will receive the inserted data (the INTO keyword is optional):

```
INSERT Production.Location
```

The next line of code explicitly listed the columns of the destination table that I wish to insert the data into:

```
(Name, CostRate, Availability)
```

A comma must separate each column. Columns don't need to be listed in the same order as they appear in the base table—as long as the values in the VALUES clause exactly match the order of the column list. Column lists are not necessary if the values are all provided and are in the same order. However, using column lists should be required for your production code, particularly if the base schema undergoes periodic changes. This is because explicitly listing columns allows you to add new columns to the base table without changing the referencing code (assuming the new column has a default value).

The next line of code was the VALUES clause and a comma-separated list of values (expressions) to insert:

```
VALUES ('Wheel Storage', 11.25, 80.00)
```

As I've noted previously, the values in this list must be provided in the same order as the listed columns or, if no columns are listed, the same order of the columns in the table.

Inserting a Row Using Default Values

In this recipe, I'll show you how to load a row into a table such that it takes a default value for a certain column (or columns), using the DEFAULT keyword. In the previous recipe, the Production.Location table had a row inserted into it. The Production.Location table has two other columns that were not explicitly referenced in the INSERT statement. If you look at the column definition of Table 2-2, you'll see that there is also a LocationID and a ModifiedDate column that were not included in the previous example's INSERT.

Table 2-2. *Production.Location Table Definition*

Column Name	Data Type	Nullability	Default Value	Identity Column?
LocationID	smallint	NOT NULL		Yes
Name	dbo.Name (user-defined data type)	NOT NULL		No
CostRate	smallmoney	NOT NULL	0.00	No
Availability	decimal(8,2)	NOT NULL	0.00	No
ModifiedDate	datetime	NOT NULL	GETDATE() (function to return the current date and time)	No

■**Note** See Chapter 4 for more information on the CREATE TABLE command, IDENTITY columns, and DEFAULT values.

The ModifiedDate column has a default value that populates the current date and time for new rows if the column value wasn't explicitly inserted. The INSERT could have been written to update this column too. For example:

```
INSERT Production.Location
(Name, CostRate, Availability, ModifiedDate)
VALUES ('Wheel Storage 2', 11.25, 80.00, '1/1/2005')
```

When a column has a default value specified in a table, you can use the DEFAULT keyword in the VALUES clause, in order to explicitly trigger the default value.

For example:

```
INSERT Production.Location
(Name, CostRate, Availability, ModifiedDate)
VALUES ('Wheel Storage 3', 11.25, 80.00, DEFAULT)
```

If each column in the table uses defaults for all columns, you can trigger an insert that inserts a row using only the defaults by including the DEFAULT VALUES option. For example:

```
INSERT dbo.ExampleTable
DEFAULT VALUES
```

How It Works

The DEFAULT keyword allows you to explicitly set a column's default value in an INSERT statement. The DEFAULT VALUES keywords can be used in your INSERT statement to explicitly set all the column's default values (assuming the table is defined with a default on each column).

The LocationID column from the Production.Location table, however, is an IDENTITY column (not a defaulted column). An IDENTITY property on a column causes the value in that column to automatically populate with an incrementing numeric value. Because LocationID is an IDENTITY column, the database manages inserting the values for this row, so an INSERT statement cannot normally specify a value for an IDENTITY column. If you want to specify a certain value for an IDENTITY column, you need to follow the procedure outlined in the next recipe.

Explicitly Inserting a Value into an IDENTITY Column

In this recipe, I'll demonstrate how to explicitly insert values into an IDENTITY property column. A column using an IDENTITY property automatically increments based on a numeric seed value and incrementing value for every row inserted into the table. IDENTITY columns are often used as surrogate keys (a *surrogate key* is a unique primary key generated by the database that holds no business-level significance other than to ensure uniqueness within the table).

In data load or recovery scenarios, you may find that you need to manually insert explicit values into an IDENTITY column. For example, if a row with the key value of 4 were deleted accidentally, and you needed to manually reconstruct that row, preserving the original value of 4 with the old business information, you would need to be able to explicitly insert this value into the table.

To explicitly insert a numeric value into a column using an IDENTITY property, you must use the SET IDENTITY_INSERT command. The syntax is as follows:

```
SET IDENTITY_INSERT [ database_name . [ schema_name ] . ] table { ON | OFF }
```

The arguments of this command are described in Table 2-3.

Table 2-3. *SET IDENTITY_INSERT Command*

Argument	Description
[database_name . [schema_name] .]	These specify the optional database name, optional schema name, and required table name for which explicit values will be allowed to be inserted into table an IDENTITY property column.
ON | OFF	When set ON, explicit value inserts are allowed. When OFF, explicit value inserts are *not* allowed.

In this recipe, I'll demonstrate how to explicitly insert the value of an IDENTITY column into a table. The following query first demonstrates what happens if you try to do an explicit insert into an identity column without first using IDENTITY_INSERT:

```
INSERT HumanResources.Department
(DepartmentID,  Name,  GroupName)
VALUES (17,  'Database Services',  'Information Technology')
```

This returns an error, keeping you from inserting an explicit value for the identity column:

```
Msg 544, Level 16, State 1, Line 2
Cannot insert explicit value for identity column in table 'Department' when
IDENTITY_INSERT is set to OFF.
```

Using SET IDENTITY_INSERT removes this barrier, as this next example demonstrates:

```
SET IDENTITY_INSERT HumanResources.Department ON

INSERT HumanResources.Department
(DepartmentID,  Name,  GroupName)
VALUES (17,  'Database Services',  'Information Technology')

SET IDENTITY_INSERT HumanResources.Department OFF
```

How It Works

In the recipe, this property was set ON prior to the insert:

```
SET IDENTITY_INSERT HumanResources.Department ON
```

The INSERT was then performed using a value of 17. When inserting into an identity column, you must also explicitly list the column names after the INSERT table_name clause:

```
INSERT HumanResources.D epartment
(DepartmentID,  Name,  GroupName)
VALUES (17,  'Database Services',  'Information Technology')
```

For inserted values greater than the current identity value, new inserts to the table will automatically use the new value as the identity seed.

IDENTITY_INSERT should be set OFF once you are finished explicitly inserting values:

```
SET IDENTITY_INSERT HumanResources.Department OFF
```

You should set this OFF once you are finished, as only one table in the session (your database connection session) can have IDENTITY_INSERT ON at the same time (assuming that you wish to insert explicit values for multiple tables). Closing your session will remove the ON property, setting it back to OFF.

Inserting a Row into a Table with a uniqueidentifier Column

In this recipe, I'll show you how to insert data into a table that uses a uniqueidentifier column. This data type is useful in scenarios where your identifier *must* be unique across several SQL Server instances. For example, if you have ten remote SQL Server instances generating records that are then consolidated on a single SQL Server instance, using an IDENTITY value generates the risk of primary key conflicts. Using a uniqueidentifier data type would allow you to avoid this.

A uniqueidentifier data type stores a 16-byte globally unique identifier (GUID) that is often used to ensure uniqueness across tables within the same or a different database. GUIDs offer an alternative to integer value keys, although their width compared to integer values can sometimes result in slower query performance for bigger tables.

To generate this value for a new INSERT, the NEWID system function is used. NEWID generates a unique uniqueidentifier data type value, as this recipe demonstrates:

```
INSERT Purchasing.ShipMethod
(Name,  ShipBase,  ShipRate,  rowguid)
VALUES('MIDDLETON CARGO TS1',  8.99,  1.22,  NEWID())


SELECT rowguid,  name
FROM Purchasing.ShipMethod
WHERE Name = 'MIDDLETON CARGO TS1'
```

This returns the following (if you are following along, note that your Rowguid value will be different from mine):

Rowguid	name
174BE850-FDEA-4E64-8D17-C019521C6C07	MIDDLETON CARGO TS1

How It Works

The rowguid column in the Purchasing.ShipMethod table is a uniqueidentifier data type column. Here is an excerpt from the table definition:

```
rowguid uniqueidentifier ROWGUIDCOL  NOT NULL DEFAULT (newid()),
```

To generate a new uniqueidentifier data type value for this inserted row, the NEWID() function was used in the VALUES clause:

```
VALUES('MIDDLETON CARGO TS1',  8.9 9,  1.2 2,  NEWID())
```

Selecting the new row that was just created, the rowguid was given a uniqueidentifier value of 174BE850-FDEA-4E64-8D17-C019521C6C07 (although when you test it yourself, you'll get a different value because NEWID creates a new value each time it is executed).

Inserting Rows Using an INSERT...SELECT Statement

The previous recipes showed you how to insert a single row of data. In this recipe, I'll show you how to insert multiple rows into a table using INSERT..SELECT. The syntax for performing an INSERT..SELECT operation is as follows:

```
INSERT
    [ INTO]
    table_or_view_name
    [ ( column_list ) ]
    SELECT column_list FROM data_source
```

The syntax for using INSERT...SELECT is almost identical to inserting a single row, only instead of using the VALUES clause, you designate a SELECT query that will populate the columns and rows into the table or updateable view. The SELECT query can be based on one or more data sources, so long as the column list conforms to the expected data types of the destination table.

For the purposes of this example, a new table will be created for storing the rows. The example populates values from the HumanResources.Shift table into the new dbo.Shift_Archive table:

```
CREATE TABLE [dbo]. [Shift_Archive](
  [ShiftID] [tinyint]  NOT NULL,
  [Name] [dbo]. [Name]  NOT NULL,
  [StartTime] [datetime]  NOT NULL,
  [EndTime] [datetime]  NOT NULL,
  [ModifiedDate] [datetime]  NOT NULL DEFAULT (getdate()),
 CONSTRAINT [PK_Shift_ShiftID]  PRIMARY KEY CLUSTERED
([ShiftID]  ASC)
)
GO
```

Next, an INSERT..SELECT is performed:

```
INSERT dbo.Shift_Archive
(ShiftID, Name,  StartTime, EndTime, ModifiedDate)
SELECT ShiftID, Name, StartTime, EndTime, ModifiedDate
FROM HumanResources.Shift
ORDER BY ShiftID
```

The results show that three rows were inserted:

```
(3 row(s)  affected)
```

Next, a query is executed to confirm the inserted rows in the Shift_Archive table:

```
SELECT ShiftID,  Name
FROM Shift_Archive
```

This returns

```
ShiftID       Name
1             Day
2             Evening
3             Night

(3 row(s) affected)
```

How It Works

Using the INSERT...SELECT statement, you can insert multiple rows into a table based on a SELECT query. Just like regular, single-value INSERTs, you begin by using INSERT table_name and the list of columns to be inserted into the table (in parentheses):

```
INSERT Shift_Archive
(ShiftID, Name,  StartTime, EndTime, ModifiedDate)
```

Following this is the query used to populate the table. The SELECT statement must return columns in the same order as the columns appear in the INSERT column list. The columns list must also have data type compatibility with the associated INSERT column list:

```
SELECT ShiftID, Name,  StartTime, EndTime, ModifiedDate
FROM HumanResources.Shift
ORDER BY ShiftID
```

When the column lists aren't designated, the SELECT statement must provide values for *all* the columns of the table into which the data is being inserted.

Inserting Data from a Stored Procedure Call

In this recipe, I demonstrate how to insert table data by using a stored procedure. A *stored procedure* groups one or more Transact-SQL statements into a logical unit and stores it as an object in a SQL Server database. Stored procedures allow for more sophisticated result set creation (for example, you can use several intermediate result sets built in temporary tables before returning the final result set). Reporting system stored procedures that return a result set can also be used for INSERT...EXEC, which is useful if you wish to retain SQL Server information in tables.

This recipe also teaches you how to add rows to a table based on the output of a stored procedure. A stored procedure can only be used in this manner if it returns data via a SELECT command from within the procedure definition and the result set (or even multiple result sets) match the required number of supplied values to the INSERT.

■**Note** For more information on stored procedures, see Chapter 10.

The syntax for inserting data from a stored procedure is as follows:

```
INSERT
    [ INTO]
    table_or_view_name
    [ ( column_list ) ]
    EXEC stored_procedure_name
```

The syntax is almost identical to the previously demonstrated INSERT examples, only this time the data is populated via an executed stored procedure.

In this example, a stored procedure is created that returns rows from the Production. TransactionHistory table based on the begin and end dates passed to the stored procedure. These results returned by the procedure also only return rows that don't exist in the Production. TransactionHistoryArchive:

```
CREATE PROCEDURE dbo.usp_SEL_Production_TransactionHistory
    @ModifiedStartDT datetime,
    @ModifiedEndDT datetime
AS

SELECT TransactionID, ProductID, ReferenceOrderID, ReferenceOrderLineID,
 TransactionDate, TransactionType, Quantity, ActualCost, ModifiedDate
FROM Production.TransactionHistory
WHERE ModifiedDate BETWEEN @ModifiedStartDT AND @ModifiedEndDT AND
    TransactionID NOT IN
      (SELECT TransactionID
        FROM Production.TransactionHistoryArchive)

GO
```

Next, this example tests the stored procedures to precheck which rows will be inserted:

```
EXEC dbo.usp_SEL_Production_TransactionHistory '6/2/04', '6/3/04'
```

This returns 568 rows based on the date range passed to the procedure. In the next example, this stored procedure is used to insert the 568 rows into the Production.TransactionHistoryArchive table:

```
INSERT Production.TransactionHistoryArchive
(TransactionID, ProductID, ReferenceOrderID, ReferenceOrderLineID, TransactionDate,
TransactionType, Quantity, ActualCost, ModifiedDate)
EXEC dbo.usp_SEL_Production_TransactionHistory '6/2/04', '6/3/04'
```

How It Works

This example demonstrated using a stored procedure to populate a table using INSERT and EXEC. The INSERT began with the name of the table to be inserted into:

```
INSERT Production.TransactionHistoryArchive
```

Next was the list of columns to be inserted into:

```
(TransactionID, ProductID, ReferenceOrderID, ReferenceOrderLineID,
TransactionDate, TransactionType, Quantity, ActualCost, ModifiedDate)
```

Last was the EXEC statement, which executed the stored procedures. Any parameters the stored procedure expects follow the stored procedure name:

```
EXEC usp_SEL_Production_TransactionHistory '6/2/04', '6/3/04'
```

Inserting Multiple Rows with VALUES

SQL Server 2008 introduces the ability to insert multiple rows using a single INSERT command without having to issue a subquery or stored procedure call. This allows the application to reduce the code required to add multiple rows and also reduce the number of individual commands executed. Essentially, you use the VALUES to group and specify one or more rows and their associated column values, as the following recipe demonstrates:

```
-- Create a lookup table
CREATE TABLE HumanResources.Degree
    (DegreeID int NOT NULL IDENTITY(1,1) PRIMARY KEY,
    DegreeNM varchar(30) NOT NULL,
    DegreeCD varchar(5) NOT NULL,
    ModifiedDate datetime NOT NULL)
GO

INSERT HumanResources.Degree
(DegreeNM, DegreeCD, ModifiedDate)
VALUES
  ('Bachelor of Arts', 'B.A.', GETDATE()),
  ('Bachelor of Science', 'B.S.', GETDATE()),
  ('Master of Arts', 'M.A.', GETDATE()),
  ('Master of Science', 'M.S.', GETDATE()),
  ('Associate''s Degree', 'A.A.', GETDATE())
GO
```

This returns the following query output:

```
(5 row(s) affected)
```

How It Works

In this recipe, I demonstrated inserting multiple rows from a single INSERT statement. I started off by creating a new table to hold information on college degree types. I then used the INSERT in a typical fashion, showing the column names that would have values passed to it for each row:

```
INSERT HumanResources.Degree
(DegreeNM, DegreeCD, ModifiedDate)
```

Next, in the VALUES clause, I designated a new row for each degree type. Each row had three columns, and these columns were encapsulated in parentheses:

```
VALUES
 ('Bachelor of Arts', 'B.A.', GETDATE()),
 ('Bachelor of Science', 'B.S.', GETDATE()),
 ('Master of Arts', 'M.A.', GETDATE()),
 ('Master of Science', 'M.S.', GETDATE()),
 ('Associate''s Degree', 'A.A.', GETDATE())
GO
```

This new feature allowed me to insert multiple rows without having to retype the initial INSERT table name and column list. An example of where this may be useful would be for custom applications that include a database schema along with a set of associated lookup values. Rather than hand-code 50 INSERT statements in your setup script, you can create a single INSERT with multiple rows designated. This also allows you to bypass importing a rowset from an external source.

Using VALUES As a Table Source

The previous recipe demonstrated how to insert multiple rows without having to retype the initial INSERT table name and column list. Using this same new feature in SQL Server 2008, you can also reference the VALUES list in the FROM clause of a SELECT statement.

This recipe will demonstrate how to reference a result set without having to use a permanent or temporary table. The following query demonstrates listing various college degrees in a five-row result set—without having to persist the rows in a table or reference in a subquery:

```
SELECT DegreeNM, DegreeCD, ModifiedDT
FROM
(VALUES
 ('Bachelor of Arts', 'B.A.', GETDATE()),
 ('Bachelor of Science', 'B.S.', GETDATE()),
 ('Master of Arts', 'M.A.', GETDATE()),
 ('Master of Science', 'M.S.', GETDATE()),
 ('Associate''s Degree', 'A.A.', GETDATE()))
Degree (DegreeNM, DegreeCD, ModifiedDT)
```

This returns

DegreeNM	DegreeCD	ModifiedDT
Bachelor of Arts	B.A.	2007-08-21 19:10:34.667
Bachelor of Science	B.S.	2007-08-21 19:10:34.667
Master of Arts	M.A.	2007-08-21 19:10:34.667
Master of Science	M.S.	2007-08-21 19:10:34.667
Associate's Degree	A.A.	2007-08-21 19:10:34.667

```
(5 row(s) affected)
```

How It Works

This recipe demonstrated using a new SQL Server 2008 technique for returning a result set to persist the rows in storage. Breaking down the query, the first row in the SELECT clause listed the column names:

```
SELECT DegreeNM, DegreeCD, ModifiedDT
```

These are not actual column names from a referenced table—but instead are aliased names I defined later on in the query itself.

The next line defined the FROM clause for the data source, followed by a parenthesis encapsulating the VALUES keyword:

```
FROM
(VALUES
```

The next few lines of code listed rows I wished to return from this query (similar to how I inserted multiple rows in a single INSERT in the previous recipe):

```
('Bachelor of Arts', 'B.A.', GETDATE()),
('Bachelor of Science', 'B.S.', GETDATE()),
('Master of Arts', 'M.A.', GETDATE()),
('Master of Science', 'M.S.', GETDATE()),
('Associate''s Degree', 'A.A.', GETDATE())
)
```

Lastly, after the final closing parenthesis for the row list, I defined a name for this data source and the associated column names to be returned for each column (and to be referenced in the SELECT clause):

```
Degree (DegreeNM, DegreeCD, ModifiedDT)
```

This new technique allowed me to specify rows of a table source without having to actually create a temporary or permanent table.

UPDATE

The following is basic syntax for the UPDATE statement:

```
UPDATE <table_or_view_name>
SET column_name = {expression | DEFAULT | NULL} [ ,...n ]
WHERE <search_condition>
```

The arguments of this command are described in Table 2-4.

Table 2-4. *UPDATE Command Arguments*

Argument	Description
table_or_view_name	The table or updateable view containing data to be updated.
column_name = {expression	DEFAULT	NULL}	The name of the column or columns to be updated. The column can be set to an expression, the DEFAULT value of the column, or a NULL.
search_condition	The search condition that defines *what* rows are modified. If this isn't included, all rows from the table or updateable view will be modified.

Updating a Single Row

In this recipe, I'll demonstrate how to use the UPDATE statement to modify data. With the UPDATE statement, you can apply changes to single or multiple columns, as well as to single or multiple rows.

In this example, a single row is updated by designating the SpecialOfferID, which is the primary key of the table (for more on primary keys, see Chapter 4). Before performing the update, I'll first query the specific row that I plan on modifying:

```
SELECT DiscountPct
FROM Sales.SpecialOffer
WHERE SpecialOfferID = 10
```

This returns

```
DiscountPct
0.50
```

Now I'll perform the modification:

```
UPDATE Sales.SpecialOffer
SET DiscountPct = 0.15
WHERE SpecialOfferID = 10
```

Querying that specific row after the update confirms that the value of DiscountPct was indeed modified:

```
SELECT DiscountPct
FROM Sales.SpecialOffer
WHERE SpecialOfferID = 10
```

This returns

```
DiscountPct
0.15
```

How It Works

In this example, the query started off with UPDATE and the table name Sales.SpecialOffer:

```
UPDATE Sales.SpecialOffer
```

Next, SET was used, followed by the column name to be modified, and an equality operator to modify the DiscountPct to a value of 0.15. Relating back to the syntax at the beginning of the recipe, this example is setting the column to an expression value, and not a DEFAULT or NULL value:

```
SET DiscountPct = 0.15
```

Had this been the end of the query, *all* rows in the Sales.SpecialOffer table would have been modified, because the UPDATE clause works at the table level, not the row level. But the intention of this query was to only update the discount percentage for a specific product. The WHERE clause was used in order to achieve this:

```
WHERE SpecialOfferID = 10
```

After executing this query, only one row is modified. Had there been multiple rows that met the search condition in the WHERE clause, those rows would have been modified too.

■**Tip** Performing a SELECT query with the FROM and WHERE clauses of an UPDATE, prior to the UPDATE, allows you to see what rows you will be updating (an extra validation that you are updating the proper rows). This is also a good opportunity to use a transaction to allow for rollbacks in the event that your modifications are undesired. For more on transactions, see Chapter 3.

Updating Rows Based on a FROM and WHERE Clause

In this recipe, I'll show you how to use the UPDATE statement to modify rows based on a FROM clause and associated WHERE clause search conditions. The basic syntax, elaborating from the last example, is as follows:

```
UPDATE <table_or_view_name>
SET column_name = {expression | DEFAULT | NULL}  [ ,...n ]
FROM <table_source>
WHERE <search_condition>
```

The FROM and WHERE clauses are not mandatory; however, you will find that they are almost always implemented in order to specify exactly which rows are to be modified, based on joins against one or more tables.

In this example, assume that a specific product, "Full-Finger Gloves, M," from the Production. Product table has a customer purchase limit of two units per customer. For this query's requirement, any shopping cart with a quantity of more than two units for this product should immediately be adjusted back to the required limit:

```
UPDATE Sales.ShoppingCartItem
SET   Quantity =2,
  ModifiedDate = GETDATE()
FROM Sales.ShoppingCartItem c
INNER JOIN Production.Product p ON
  c.ProductID = p.ProductID
WHERE p.Name = 'Full-Finger Gloves,  M ' AND
  c.Quantity > 2
```

How It Works

Stepping through the code, the first line showed the table to be updated:

```
UPDATE Sales.ShoppingCartItem
```

Next, the columns to be updated were designated in the SET clause:

```
SET   Quantity =2,
  ModifiedDate = GETDATE()
```

Next came the optional FROM clause where the Sales.ShoppingCartItem and Production. Product tables were joined by ProductID. As you can see, the object being updated can also be referenced in the FROM clause. The reference in the UPDATE and in the FROM were treated as the same table:

```
FROM Sales.ShoppingCartItem c
INNER JOIN Production.Product p ON
  c.ProductID = p.P roductID
```

Using the updated table in the FROM clause allows you to join to other tables. Presumably, those other joined tables will be used to filter the updated rows or to provide values for the updated rows.

If you are self-joining to more than one reference of the updated table in the FROM clause, at least one reference to the object *cannot* specify a table alias. All the other object references, however, would have to use an alias.

The WHERE clause specified that only the "Full-Finger Gloves, M" product in the Sales. ShoppingCartItem should be modified, and only if the Quantity is greater than 2 units:

```
WHERE p.Name = 'Full-Finger Gloves,  M ' AND
   c.Quantity > 2
```

Updating Large Value Data Type Columns

In this recipe, I'll show you how to modify large-value data type column values. SQL Server introduced new large-value data types in the previous version, which were intended to replace the deprecated text, ntext, and image data types. These data types include

- varchar(max), which holds non-Unicode variable-length data

- nvarchar(max), which holds Unicode variable-length data

- varbinary(max), which holds variable-length binary data

These data types can store up to $2^{31}-1$ bytes of data (for more information on data types, see Chapter 4).

One of the major drawbacks of the old text and image data types is that they required you to use separate functions such as WRITETEXT and UPDATETEXT in order to manipulate the image/text data. Using the new large-value data types, you can now use regular INSERT and UPDATEs instead.

The syntax for inserting a large-value data type is no different from a regular insert. For updating large-value data types, however, the UPDATE command now includes the .WRITE method:

```
UPDATE <table_or_view_name>
SET column_name = .WRITE ( expression , @Offset , @Length )
FROM <table_source>
WHERE <search_condition>
```

The parameters of the .WRITE method are described in Table 2-5.

Table 2-5. *UPDATE Command with .WRITE Clause*

Argument	Description
expression	The expression defines the chunk of text to be placed in the column.
@Offset	@Offset determines the starting position in the existing data the new text should be placed. If @Offset is NULL, it means the new expression will be appended to the end of the column (also ignoring the second @Length parameter).
@Length	@Length determines the length of the section to overlay.

This example starts off by creating a table called RecipeChapter:

```
CREATE TABLE dbo.RecipeChapter
   (ChapterID int NOT NULL,
    Chapter varchar(max)  NOT NULL)
GO
```

Next, a row is inserted into the table. Notice that there is nothing special about the string being inserted into the Chapter varchar(max) column:

```
INSERT dbo.RecipeChapter
(ChapterID,  Chapter)
VALUES
(1,  'At the beginning of each chapter you will notice
that basic concepts are covered first.' )
```

This next example updates the newly inserted row, adding a sentence to the end of the existing sentence:

```
UPDATE RecipeChapter
SET Chapter .WRITE ('  In addition to the basics,  this chapter will also provide
recipes that can be used in your day to day development and administration.' ,
NULL,  NULL)
WHERE ChapterID = 1
```

Next, for that same row, the phrase "day to day" is replaced with the single word "daily":

```
UPDATE RecipeChapter
SET Chapter .WRITE('daily',  181,  10)
WHERE ChapterID = 1
```

Lastly, the results are returned for that row:

```
SELECT Chapter
FROM RecipeChapter
WHERE ChapterID = 1
```

This returns

```
Chapter
At the beginning of each chapter you will notice that basic concepts
are covered first.
In addition to the basics,  this chapter will also provide recipes
 that can be used in your daily development and administration.
```

How It Works

The recipe began by creating a table where book chapter descriptions would be held. The Chapter column used a varchar(max) data type:

```
CREATE TABLE RecipeChapter
  (ChapterID int NOT NULL,
   Chapter varchar(max)  NOT NULL)
```

Next, a new row was inserted. Notice that the syntax for inserting a large-object data type doesn't differ from inserting data into a regular non-large-value data type:

```
 INSERT RecipeChapter
(ChapterID,  Chapter)
VALUES
(1,  'At the beginning of each chapter you will
notice that basic concepts are covered first.' )
```

Next, an UPDATE was performed against the RecipeChapter table to add a second sentence after the end of the first sentence:

```
UPDATE RecipeChapter
```

The SET command was followed by the name of the column to be updated (Chapter) and the new .WRITE command. The .WRITE command was followed by an open parenthesis, a single quote, and the sentence to be appended to the end of the column:

```
SET Chapter .WRITE(' In addition to the basics,
this chapter will also provide recipes that can be
used in your day to day development and administration.' ,
NULL, NULL)
```

The WHERE clause specified that the Chapter column for a single row matching ChapterID = 1 be modified:

```
WHERE ChapterID = 1
```

The next example of .WRITE demonstrated replacing data within the body of the column. In the example, the expression day to day was replaced with daily. The bigint value of @Offset and @Length are measured in bytes for varbinary(max) and varchar(max) data types. For nvarchar(max), these parameters measure the actual number of characters. For the example, the .WRITE had a value for @Offset (181 bytes into the text) and @Length (10 bytes long):

```
UPDATE RecipeChapter
SET Chapter .WRITE('daily', 181, 10)
WHERE ChapterID = 1
```

Inserting or Updating an Image File Using OPENROWSET and BULK

In this recipe, I demonstrate how to insert or update an image file from the file system into a SQL Server table. Adding images to a table in earlier versions of SQL Server usually required the use of external application tools or scripts. There was no elegant way to insert images using just Transact-SQL.

As of SQL Server 2005 and 2008, UPDATE and OPENROWSET can be used together to import an image into a table. OPENROWSET can be used to import a file into a single-row, single-column value. The basic syntax for OPENROWSET as it applies to this recipe is as follows:

```
OPENROWSET
( BULK 'data_file' ,
        SINGLE_BLOB | SINGLE_CLOB | SINGLE_NCLOB )
```

The parameters for this command are described in Table 2-6.

Table 2-6. *The OPENROWSET Command Arguments*

Parameter	Description
data_file	This specifies the name and path of the file to read.
SINGLE_BLOB |SINGLE_CLOB	SINGLE_NCLOB	Designate the SINGLE_BLOB object for importing into a varbinary(max) data type. Designate SINGLE_CLOB for ASCII data into a varchar(max) data type and SINGLE_NCLOB for importing into a nvarchar(max) Unicode data type.

■**Note** See Chapter 27 for a detailed review of the syntax of OPENROWSET.

The first part of the recipe creates a new table that will be used to store image files:

```
CREATE TABLE dbo.StockBmps
  (StockBmpID int NOT NULL,
   bmp varbinary(max)  NOT NULL)
GO
```

Next, a row containing the image file will be inserted into the table:

```
INSERT dbo.StockBmps
(StockBmpID,  bmp)
SELECT  1,
     BulkColumn
FROM OPENROWSET(BULK
'C:\Apress\StockPhotoOne.bmp', SINGLE_BLOB) AS x
```

This next query selects the row from the table:

```
SELECT bmp
FROM StockBmps
WHERE StockBmpID = 1
```

This returns the following (abridged) results:

```
bmp
0x424D3656000000000000360400002800000007D000000A4000000010008000000000000052000000000
000000000000000010000001000001B71900057575E00EFEFEF000F0B0C0023A7D30028D2FF001A5B7
1005473A1008C8C8C00B3B3B300208BB00031303100D1D1D1005896B20018425600112C3500777D
7B00474F9100A089660078CDDD0071AFC6009D9D9D0045444A00686B6F00728FAD0077998C001
C1D1E000904050008030400050100026C4FF
```

The last example in this recipe updates an existing BMP file, changing it to a different BMP file:

```
UPDATE dbo.StockBmps
SET bmp =
(SELECT BulkColumn
FROM OPENROWSET(BULK 'C:\Apress\StockPhotoTwo.bmp', SINGLE_BLOB) AS x)
WHERE StockBmpID =1
```

How It Works

In this recipe, I've demonstrated using OPENROWSET with the BULK option to insert a row containing a BMP image file, and then the way to update it to a different GIF file.

First, a table was created to hold the GIF files using a varbinary(max) data type:

```
CREATE TABLE dbo.StockBmps
  (StockBmpID int NOT NULL,
   bmp varbinary(max)  NOT NULL)
```

Next, a new row was inserted using INSERT:

```
INSERT dbo.StockBmps
(StockBmpID,  bmp)
```

The INSERT was populated using a SELECT query against the OPENROWSET function to bring in the file data. The BulkColumn referenced in the query represents the varbinary value to be inserted into the varbinary(max) row from the OPENROWSET data source:

```
SELECT  1,
     BulkColumn
```

In the FROM clause, OPENROWSET was called. OPENROWSET allows you to access remote data from a data source:

```
FROM OPENROWSET(BULK
'C:\Apress\StockPhotoOne.bmp', SINGLE_BLOB) AS x
```

The BULK option was used inside the function, followed by the file name and the SINGLE_BLOB keyword. The BULK option within OPENROWSET means that data will be read from a file (in this case, the BMP file specified after BULK). The SINGLE_BLOB switch tells OPENROWSET to return the contents of the data file as a single-row, single-column varbinary(max) rowset.

This recipe also demonstrates an UPDATE of the varbinary(max) column from an external file. The UPDATE designated the StockBmps table and used SET to update the bmp column:

```
UPDATE StockBmps
SET bmp =
```

The expression to set the new image to StockPhotoTwo.bmp from the previous StockPhotoOne.bmp occurred in a subquery. It used almost the same syntax as the previous INSERT; only this time the only value returned in the SELECT is the BulkColumn column:

```
(SELECT BulkColumn
FROM OPENROWSET(BULK 'C:\Apress\StockPhotoTwo.bmp', SINGLE_BLOB) AS x)
```

The image file on the machine was then stored in the column value for that row as varbinary(max) data.

Storing Unstructured Data on the File System While Maintaining SQL Server Transactional Control

SQL Server 2008 introduces the new FILESTREAM attribute, which can be applied to the varbinary(max) data type. Using FILESTREAM, you can exceed the 2GB limit on stored values and take advantage of relational handling of files via SQL Server, while actually storing the files on the file system. BACKUP and RESTORE operations maintain both the database data as well as the files saved on the file system, thus handling end-to-end data recoverability for applications that store both structured and unstructured data. FILESTREAM marries the transactional consistency capabilities of SQL Server with the performance advantages of NT file system streaming.

T-SQL is used to define the FILESTREAM attribute and can be used to handle the data; however, Win32 streaming APIs are the preferred method from the application perspective when performing actual read and write operations (specifically using the OpenSqlFilestream API). Although demonstrating Win32 and the implementation of applicable APIs is outside of the scope of this book, I will use this recipe to walk you through how to set up a database and table with the FILESTREAM attribute, INSERT a new row, and use a query to pull path and transaction token information that is necessary for the OpenSqlFilestream API call.

■**Tip** FILESTREAM must be configured at both the Windows and SQL Server scope. To enable FILESTREAM for the Windows scope and define the associated file share, use SQL Server Configuration Manager. To enable FILESTREAM at the SQL Server instance level, use sp_configure with the filestream_access_level option.

To confirm whether FILESTREAM is configured for the SQL Server instance, I can validate the setting using the SERVERPROPERTY function and three different properties that describe the file share name of the filestream share and the associated effective and actual configured values:

```
SELECT SERVERPROPERTY('FilestreamShareName') ShareName,
       SERVERPROPERTY('FilestreamEffectiveLevel') EffectiveLevel,
       SERVERPROPERTY('FilestreamConfiguredLevel') ConfiguredLevel
```

This returns

ShareName	EffectiveLevel	ConfiguredLevel
AUGUSTUS	3	3

Next, I will create a new database that will have a filegroup containing FILESTREAM data.

■**Tip** See Chapter 22 for more on the CREATE DATABASE command.

Unlike regular file/filegroup assignments in CREATE DATABASE, I will associate a filegroup with a specific path, and also designate the name of the folder that will be created by SQL Server on the file system and will contain all FILESTREAM files associated with the database:

```
USE master
GO

CREATE DATABASE PhotoRepository ON  PRIMARY
( NAME = N'PhotoRepository',
  FILENAME = N'C:\Apress\MDF\PhotoRepository.mdf' ,
  SIZE = 3048KB ,
  FILEGROWTH = 1024KB ),
  FILEGROUP FS_PhotoRepository CONTAINS FILESTREAM
  (NAME = 'FG_PhotoRepository',
   FILENAME = N'C:\Apress\FILESTREAM')
 LOG ON
( NAME = N'PhotoRepository_log',
  FILENAME = N'C:\Apress\LDF\PhotoRepository_log.ldf' ,
  SIZE = 1024KB ,
  FILEGROWTH = 10%)
GO
```

Now I can create a new table that will be used to store photos for book covers. I will designate the BookPhotoFile column as a varbinary(max) data type, followed by the FILESTREAM attribute:

```
USE PhotoRepository
GO

CREATE TABLE dbo.BookPhoto
   (BookPhotoID uniqueidentifier ROWGUIDCOL NOT NULL  PRIMARY KEY,
    BookPhotoNM varchar(50) NOT NULL,
    BookPhotoFile varbinary(max) FILESTREAM)
GO
```

Now that the table is created, I can INSERT a new row using the regular INSERT command and importing a file using OPENROWSET (demonstrated in the previous recipe):

```
INSERT dbo.BookPhoto
(BookPhotoID, BookPhotoNM, BookPhotoFile)
SELECT  NEWID(),
        'SQL Server 2008 Transact-SQL Recipes cover',
```

```
        BulkColumn
FROM OPENROWSET(BULK
'C:\Apress\TSQL2008Recipes.bmp', SINGLE_BLOB) AS x
```

If I look under the `C:\Apress\FILESTREAM` directory, I will see a new subdirectory and a new file. In this case, on my server, I see a new file called `00000012-000000e1-0002` under the path `C:\Apress\FILESTREAM\33486315-2ca1-43ea-a50e-0f84ad8c3fa6\e2f310f3-cd21-4f29-acd1-a0a3ffb1a681`. Files created using `FILESTREAM` should only be accessed within the context of T-SQL and the associated Win32 APIs.

After inserting the value, I will now issue a `SELECT` to view the contents of the table:

```
SELECT BookPhotoID, BookPhotoNM, BookPhotoFile
FROM dbo.BookPhoto
```

This returns

BookPhotoID	BookPhotoNM	BookPhotoFile
236E5A69-53B3-4CB6-9F11-EF056082F542	SQL Server 2008 T-SQL Recipes cover	0x424D36560000000000003604000028000 0007D000000A4000000010008000000000 0052000000000000000000000000100000001 0000276B8E0026B0ED005B5D6900EEEEEE00 528CA2000E0A0B001C597900B3B3B3008B8A 8D00D1D1D1002AC6FF002394C7002280AB00 2C2A2B00193F560066ADBD0025A4DC001128 34005E

Now assuming I have an application that uses OLEDB to query the SQL Server instance, I need to now collect the appropriate information about the file system file in order to stream it using my application.

I'll begin by opening up a transaction and using the new `PathName()` method of the varbinary column to retrieve the logical path name of the file:

```
BEGIN TRAN

SELECT BookPhotoFile.PathName()
FROM dbo.BookPhoto
WHERE BookPhotoNM = 'SQL Server 2008 Transact-SQL Recipes cover'
```

This returns

```
\\CAESAR\AUGUSTUS\v1\PhotoRepository\dbo\BookPhoto\BookPhotoFile\
236E5A69-53B3-4CB6-9F11-EF056082F542
```

Next, I need to retrieve the transaction token, which is also needed by the Win 32 API:

```
SELECT GET_FILESTREAM_TRANSACTION_CONTEXT()
```

This returns

```
0x57773034AFA62746966EE30DAE70B344
```

After I have retrieved this information, the application can use the `OpenSQLFileStream` API with the path and transaction token to perform functions such as `ReadFile` and `WriteFile` and then close the handle to the file.

After the application is finished with its work, I can either roll back or commit the transaction:

```
COMMIT TRAN
```

If I wish to delete the file, I can set the column value to NULL:

```
UPDATE dbo.BookPhoto
SET BookPhotoFile = NULL
WHERE BookPhotoNM = 'SQL Server 2008 T-SQL Recipes cover'
```

You may not see the underlying file on the file system removed right away; however, it will be removed eventually by the garage collector process.

How It Works

In this recipe, I demonstrated how to use the new SQL Server 2008 FILESYSTEM attribute of the varbinary(max) data type to store unstructured data on the file system. This enables SQL Server functionality to control transactions within SQL Server and recoverability (files get backed up with BACKUP and restored with RESTORE), while also being able to take advantage of high-speed streaming performance using Win 32 APIs.

In this recipe, I started off by checking whether FILESTREAM was enabled on the SQL Server instance. After that, I created a new database, designating the location of the FILESTREAM filegroup and file name (which is actually a path and not a file):

```
...
  FILEGROUP FS_PhotoRepository CONTAINS FILESTREAM
  (NAME = 'FG_PhotoRepository',
   FILENAME = N'C:\Apress\FILESTREAM')
...
```

Keep in mind that the path up to the last folder has to exist, but the last folder referenced cannot exist. For example, C:\Apress\ existed on my server; however, FILESTREAM can't exist prior to the database creation.

After creating the database, I then created a new table to store book cover images. For the BookPhotoFile column, I designated the varbinary(max) type followed by the FILESTREAM attribute:

```
...
    BookPhotoFile varbinary(max) FILESTREAM)
...
```

Had I left off the FILESTREAM attribute, any varbinary data stored would have been contained within the database data file, and not stored on the file system. The column maximum size would also have been capped at 2GB.

Next, I inserted a new row into the table that held the BMP file of the *SQL Server 2008 Transact-SQL Recipes* book cover. The varbinary(max) value was generated using the OPENROWSET technique I demonstrated in the previous recipe:

```
INSERT dbo.BookPhoto
(BookPhotoID, BookPhotoNM, BookPhotoFile)
SELECT  NEWID(),
        'SQL Server 2008 Transact-SQL Recipes cover',
        BulkColumn
FROM OPENROWSET(BULK
'C:\Apress\TSQL2008Recipes.bmp', SINGLE_BLOB) AS x
```

From an application perspective, I needed a couple of pieces of information in order to take advantage of streaming capabilities using Win 32 APIs. I started off by opening up a new transaction:

```
BEGIN TRAN
```

After that, I referenced the path name of the stored file using the PathName() method:

```
SELECT BookPhotoFile.PathName()
...
```

This function returned a path as a token, which the application can then use to grab a Win32 handle and perform operations against the value.

Next, I called the GET_FILESTREAM_TRANSACTION_CONTEXT function to return a token representing the current session's transaction context:

```
SELECT GET_FILESTREAM_TRANSACTION_CONTEXT()
```

This was a token used by the application to bind file system operations to an actual transaction.

After that, I committed the transaction and then demonstrated how to "delete" the file by updating the BookPhotoFile column to NULL for the specific row I had added earlier. Keep in mind that deleting the actual row would serve the same purpose (deleting the file on the file system).

Assigning and Modifying Database Values "in Place"

SQL Server 2008 introduces new compound assignment operators beyond the standard equality (=) operator that allow you to both assign and modify the outgoing data value. These operators are similar to what you would see in the C and Java languages. New assignment operators include the following:

- += (add, assign)
- -= (subtract, assign)
- *= (multiply, assign)
- /= (divide, assign)
- |= (bitwise |, assign)
- ^= (bitwise exclusive OR, assign)
- &= (bitwise &, assign)
- %= (modulo, assign)

This recipe will demonstrate modifying base pay amounts using assignment operators. I'll start by creating a new table and populating it with a few values:

```
USE AdventureWorks
GO

CREATE TABLE HumanResources.EmployeePayScale
    (EmployeePayScaleID int NOT NULL PRIMARY KEY IDENTITY(1,1),
    BasePayAMT numeric(9,2) NOT NULL,
    ModifiedDate datetime NOT NULL DEFAULT GETDATE())
GO

-- Using new multiple-row insert functionality
INSERT HumanResources.EmployeePayScale
(BasePayAMT)
VALUES
        (30000.00),
        (40000.00),
        (50000.00),
        (60000.00)
```

Next, I'll double-check the initial value of a specific pay scale row:

```
SELECT  BasePayAMT
FROM    HumanResources.EmployeePayScale
WHERE   EmployeePayScaleID = 4
```

This returns

```
BasePayAMT
60000.00
```

Before SQL Server 2008, if I wanted to modify a value within an UPDATE based on the row's existing value, I would need to do something like the following:

```
UPDATE  HumanResources.EmployeePayScale
SET BasePayAMT  =  BasePayAMT + 10000
WHERE   EmployeePayScaleID = 4
```

Querying that row, I see that the base pay amount has increased by 10,000:

```
SELECT  BasePayAMT
FROM    HumanResources.EmployeePayScale
WHERE   EmployeePayScaleID = 4
```

This returns

```
BasePayAMT
70000.00
```

Now I'll start experimenting with the assignment operators. This new feature allows me to simplify my code—assigning values in place without having to include another column reference in the value expression.

In this example, the base pay amount is increased by another 10,000 dollars:

```
UPDATE  HumanResources.EmployeePayScale
SET BasePayAMT += 10000
WHERE   EmployeePayScaleID = 4

SELECT  BasePayAMT
FROM    HumanResources.EmployeePayScale
WHERE   EmployeePayScaleID = 4
```

This returns

```
BasePayAMT
80000.00
```

Next, the base pay amount is multiplied by 2:

```
UPDATE  HumanResources.EmployeePayScale
SET BasePayAMT *= 2
WHERE   EmployeePayScaleID = 4

SELECT  BasePayAMT
FROM    HumanResources.EmployeePayScale
WHERE   EmployeePayScaleID = 4
```

This returns

```
BasePayAMT
160000.00
```

How It Works

Assignment operators help you modify values with a minimal amount of coding. In this recipe, I demonstrated using the add/assign operator:

```
SET BasePayAMT += 10000
```

and the multiply/assign operator:

```
SET BasePayAMT *= 2
```

The expressions designated the column name to be modified on the left, followed by the assignment operator, and then associated data value to be used with the operator. Keep in mind that this functionality isn't limited to UPDATE statements; you can use this new functionality when assigning values to variables.

DELETE

The simple syntax for DELETE is as follows:

```
DELETE [FROM] table_or_view_name
WHERE search_condition
```

The arguments of this command are described in Table 2-7.

Table 2-7. *The DELETE Command Arguments*

Argument	Description
table_or_view_name	This specifies the name of the table or updateable view that you are deleting rows from.
search_condition	The search condition(s) in the WHERE clause defines which rows will be deleted from the table or updateable view.

Deleting Rows

In this recipe, I show you how to use the DELETE statement to remove one or more rows from a table. First, take an example table that is populated with rows:

```
SELECT *
INTO Production.Example_ProductProductPhoto
FROM Production.ProductProductPhoto
```

This returns

```
(504 row(s) affected)
```

Next, *all* rows are deleted from the table:

```
DELETE Production.Example_ProductProductPhoto
```

This returns

```
(504 row(s) affected)
```

This next example demonstrates using DELETE with a WHERE clause. Let's say that the relationship of keys between two tables gets dropped, and the users were able to delete data from the primary key table and not the referencing foreign key tables (see Chapter 4 for a review of primary and foreign keys). Only rows missing a corresponding entry in the Product table are deleted from the example product photo table. In this example, no rows meet this criteria:

```
-- Repopulate the Example_ProductProductPhoto table
INSERT Production.Example_ProductProductPhoto
SELECT *
FROM Production.ProductProductPhoto

DELETE Production.Example_ProductProductPhoto
WHERE ProductID NOT IN
     (SELECT ProductID
      FROM Production.Product)
```

This third example demonstrates the same functionality of the previous example, only the DELETE has been rewritten to use a FROM clause instead of a subquery:

```
DELETE Production.ProductProductPhoto
FROM Production.Example_ProductProductPhoto ppp
LEFT OUTER JOIN Production.Product p ON
  ppp.ProductID = p.ProductID
WHERE p.ProductID IS NULL
```

How It Works

In the first example of the recipe, all rows were deleted from the Example_ProductProductPhoto table:

```
DELETE Production.Example_ProductProductPhoto
```

This is because there was no WHERE clause to specify which rows would be deleted.

In the second example, the WHERE clause was used to specify rows to be deleted based on a subquery lookup to another table:

```
WHERE ProductID NOT IN
     (SELECT ProductID
      FROM Production.Product)
```

The third example used a LEFT OUTER JOIN instead of a subquery, joining the ProductID of the two tables:

```
FROM Production.Example_ProductProductPhoto ppp
LEFT OUTER JOIN Production.Product p ON
  ppp.ProductID = p.ProductID
```

Because the same object that is being deleted from Production.ProductProductPhoto is also the same object in the FROM clause, and since there is only *one* reference to that table in the FROM clause, it is assumed that rows identified in the FROM and WHERE clause will be one and the same—it will be associated to the rows deleted from the Production.ProductProductPhoto table.

Because a LEFT OUTER JOIN was used, if any rows did *not* match between the left and right tables, the fields selected from the right table would be represented by NULL values. Thus, to show rows in Production.Example_ProductProductPhoto that don't have a matching ProductID in the Production.Product table, you can qualify the Production.Product as follows:

```
WHERE p.ProductID IS NULL
```

Any rows without a match to the Production.Product table will be deleted from the Production.Example_ProductProductPhoto table.

Truncating a Table

In this recipe, I show you how to delete rows from a table in a minimally logged fashion (hence, much quicker if you have very large tables). Generally, you should use DELETE for operations that should be fully logged; however, for test or throwaway data, this is a fast technique for removing the data. "Minimal logging" references how much recoverability information is written to the database's transaction log (see Chapter 22). To achieve this, use the TRUNCATE command.

The syntax is as follows:

```
TRUNCATE TABLE table_name
```

This command takes just the table name to truncate. Since it always removes *all* rows from a table, there is no FROM or WHERE clause, as this recipe demonstrates:

```
-- First populating the example
SELECT *
INTO Sales.Example_Store
FROM Sales.Store

-- Next, truncating ALL rows from the example table
TRUNCATE TABLE Sales.Example_Store
```

Next, the table's row count is queried:

```
SELECT COUNT(*)
FROM Sales.Example_Store
```

This returns

```
0
```

How It Works

The TRUNCATE TABLE statement, like the DELETE statement, can delete rows from a table. TRUNCATE TABLE deletes rows faster than DELETE, because it is minimally logged. Unlike DELETE however, the TRUNCATE TABLE removes ALL rows in the table (no WHERE clause).

Although TRUNCATE TABLE is a faster way to delete rows, you can't use it if the table columns are referenced by a foreign key constraint (see Chapter 4 for more information on foreign keys), if the table is published using transactional or merge replication, or if the table participates in an indexed view (see Chapter 7 for more information). Also, if the table has an IDENTITY column, keep in mind that the column will be reset to the seed value defined for the column (if no seed was explicitly set, it is set to 1).

Advanced Data Modification Techniques

These next two recipes will demonstrate more advanced data modification techniques. Specifically, I'll demonstrate how to improve the throughput of data modifications by "chunking" them into smaller sets.

I'll also demonstrate the new SQL Server 2008 MERGE command, which you can use to efficiently apply changes to a target table based on the data in a table source without having to designate multiple DML statements.

Chunking Data Modifications with TOP

I demonstrated using TOP in Chapter 1. TOP can also be used in DELETE, INSERT, or UPDATE statements as well. This recipe further demonstrates using TOP to "chunk" data modifications, meaning instead of executing a very large operation in a single statement call, you can break the modification into smaller pieces, potentially increasing performance and improving database concurrency for larger, frequently accessed tables. This technique is often used for large data loads to reporting or data warehouse applications.

Large, single-set updates can cause the database transaction log to grow considerably. When processing in chunks, each chunk is committed after completion, allowing SQL Server to potentially reuse that transaction log space. In addition to transaction log space, on a very large data update, if the query must be cancelled, you may have to wait a long time while the transaction rolls back. With smaller chunks, you can continue with your update more quickly. Also, chunking allows more concurrency against the modified table, allowing user queries to jump in, instead of waiting several minutes for a large modification to complete.

In this recipe, I show you how to modify data in blocks of rows in multiple executions, instead of an entire result set in one large transaction. First, I create an example deletion table for this recipe:

```
USE AdventureWorks
GO

SELECT *
INTO Production.Example_BillOfMaterials
FROM Production.BillOfMaterials
```

Next, all rows will be deleted from the table in 500-row chunks:

```
WHILE (SELECT COUNT(*)FROM Production.Example_BillOfMaterials)>  0
BEGIN

  DELETE TOP(500)
  FROM Production.Example_BillOfMaterials

END
```

This returns

```
(500 row(s) affected)
(500 row(s) affected)
(500 row(s) affected)
(500 row(s) affected)
(500 row(s) affected)
(179 row(s)  affected)
```

How It Works

In this example, I used a WHILE condition to keep executing the DELETE while the count of rows in the table was greater than zero (see Chapter 9 for more information on WHILE):

```
WHILE (SELECT COUNT(*)FROM Production.Example_BillOfMaterials)> 0
BEGIN
```

Next was the DELETE, followed by the TOP clause, and the row limitation in parentheses:

```
DELETE TOP(500)
FROM Production.BillOfMaterials
```

This recipe didn't use a WHERE clause, so no filtering was applied, and *all* rows were deleted from the table—but only in 500-row chunks. Once the WHILE condition no longer evaluated to TRUE, the loop ended. After executing, the row counts affected in each batch were displayed. The first five batches deleted 500 rows, and the last batch deleted the remaining 179 rows.

This "chunking" method can be used with INSERTs and UPDATEs too. For INSERT and UPDATE, the TOP clause follows right after the INSERT and UPDATE keyword, for example:

```
INSERT TOP(100)
...
```

```
UPDATE TOP(25)
...
```

The expanded functionality of TOP (beyond just SELECT) adds a new technique for managing large data modifications against a table. By reducing the size of large modifications, you can improve database concurrency by reducing the time that locks are held during the operation (leaving small windows for other sessions), and also help manage the size of the transaction log (more commits, instead of one single commit for a gigantic transaction).

Executing INSERTs, UPDATEs, and DELETEs in a Single Statement

SQL Server 2008 introduces the MERGE command to efficiently apply changes to a target table based on the data in a table source. If you've ever had to load and incrementally modify relational data warehouses or operational data stores based on incoming data from external data sources, you'll find this technique to be a big improvement over previous methods.

Rather than create multiple data modification statements, you can instead point MERGE to your target and source tables, defining what actions to take when search conditions find a match, when the target table does not have a match, or when the source table does not have a match. Based on these matching conditions, you can designate whether or not a DELETE, INSERT, or UPDATE operation takes place (again, within the same statement).

This recipe will demonstrate applying changes to a production table based on data that exists in a staging table (presumably staged data from an external data source). I'll start off by creating a production table that tells me whether or not a corporate housing unit is available for renting. If the IsRentedIND is 0, the unit is not available. If it is 1, it is available:

```
CREATE TABLE HumanResources.CorporateHousing
    (CorporateHousingID int NOT NULL PRIMARY KEY IDENTITY(1,1),
     UnitNBR int NOT NULL,
     IsRentedIND bit NOT NULL,
     ModifiedDate datetime NOT NULL DEFAULT GETDATE())
GO
```

```
-- Insert existing units
INSERT HumanResources.CorporateHousing
(UnitNBR, IsRentedIND)
VALUES
(1, 0),
(24, 1),
(39, 0),
(54, 1)
```

In this scenario, I receive periodic data feeds that inform me of rental status changes for corporate units. Units can shift from rented to not rented. New units can be added based on contracts signed, and existing units can be removed due to contract modifications or renovation requirements. So for this recipe, I'll create a staging table that will receive the current snapshot of corporate housing units from the external data source. I'll also populate it with the most current information:

```
CREATE TABLE dbo.StagingCorporateHousing
     (UnitNBR int NOT NULL,
      IsRentedIND bit NOT NULL)
GO

INSERT dbo.StagingCorporateHousing
(UnitNBR, IsRentedIND)
VALUES
-- UnitNBR "1" no longer exists
(24, 0), -- UnitNBR 24 has a changed rental status
(39, 1), -- UnitNBR 39 is the same
(54, 0), -- UnitNBR 54 has a change status
(92, 1) -- UnitNBR 92 is a new unit, and isn't in production yet
```

Now my objective is to modify the target production table so that it reflects the most current data from our data source. If a new unit exists in the staging table, I want to add it. If a unit number exists in the production table but not the staging table, I want to delete the row. If a unit number exists in both the staging and production tables, but the rented status is different, I want to update the production (target) table to reflect the changes.

I'll start by looking at the values of production before the modification:

```
-- Before the MERGE
SELECT CorporateHousingID, UnitNBR, IsRentedIND
FROM HumanResources.CorporateHousing
```

This returns

CorporateHousingID	UnitNBR	IsRentedIND
1	1	0
2	24	1
3	39	0
4	54	1

Next, I'll modify the production table per my business requirements:

```
MERGE INTO HumanResources.CorporateHousing p
USING dbo.StagingCorporateHousing s
ON p.UnitNBR = s.UnitNBR
WHEN MATCHED AND s.IsRentedIND <> p.IsRentedIND THEN
    UPDATE SET IsRentedIND = s.IsRentedIND
WHEN TARGET NOT MATCHED THEN
```

```
   INSERT (UnitNBR, IsRentedIND) VALUES (s.UnitNBR, s.IsRentedIND)
WHEN SOURCE NOT MATCHED THEN
   DELETE;
```

This returns

```
(5 row(s) affected)
```

Next, I'll check the "after" results of the production table:

```
-- After the MERGE
SELECT CorporateHousingID, UnitNBR, IsRentedIND
FROM HumanResources.CorporateHousing
```

This returns

CorporateHousingID	UnitNBR	IsRentedIND
2	24	0
3	39	1
4	54	0
5	92	1

How It Works

In this recipe, I demonstrated how to apply INSERT/UPDATE/DELETE modifications using a MERGE statement. The MERGE command allowed me to modify a target table based on the expression validated against a source staging table.

In the first line of the MERGE command, I designated the target table where I will be applying the data modifications:

```
MERGE INTO HumanResources.CorporateHousing p
```

On the second line, I identified the data source that will be used to compare the data against the target table. This source could have also been based on a derived or linked server table:

```
USING dbo.StagingCorporateHousing s
```

Next, I defined how I am joining these two data sources. In this case, I am using what is essentially a natural key of the data. This natural key is what uniquely identifies the row both in the source and target tables:

```
ON p.UnitNBR = s.UnitNBR
```

Next, I defined what happens when there is a match between the unit numbers by designating WHEN MATCHED. I also added an addition search condition, which indicates that if the rental indicator doesn't match, the rental indicator should be changed to match the staging data:

```
WHEN MATCHED AND s.IsRentedIND <> p.IsRentedIND THEN
   UPDATE SET IsRentedIND = s.IsRentedIND
```

Next, I evaluated what happens when there is not a match from the source to the target table—for example, if the source table has a value of 92 for the unit number, but the target table does not have such a row. When this occurs, I directed this command to add the missing row to the target table:

```
WHEN TARGET NOT MATCHED THEN
   INSERT (UnitNBR, IsRentedIND) VALUES (s.UnitNBR, s.IsRentedIND)
```

Lastly, if there are rows in the target table that aren't in the source staging table, I directed the command to remove the row from the target production table:

```
WHEN SOURCE NOT MATCHED THEN
    DELETE;
```

Notice that this is one of those commands that require termination with a semicolon. You should also note that not every MERGE command requires an associated INSERT/UPDATE/DELETE. You may decide that you wish to only add new rows and update existing ones. Or you may decide that, rather than remove a row from production, you want to "logically" delete it instead by updating a flag.

Using MERGE will allow you to apply data modifications to target tables with less code than in previous versions, as well as realize some performance benefits when applying data modifications incrementally, as you'll be making a single pass over the source and target data rather than multiple passes for each modification type.

Capturing and Tracking Data Modification Changes

The last few recipes in this chapter will demonstrate how to capture and track data modification activity.

In the first recipe, I'll show you how to use the OUTPUT clause to show impacted rows from an INSERT, UPDATE, or DELETE operation. After that, I'll demonstrate two new features introduced in SQL Server 2008: Change Data Capture (CDC) and Change Tracking.

Change Data Capture (CDC for short) has minimal performance overhead and can be used for incremental updates of other data sources, for example, migrating changes made in the OLTP database to your data warehouse database.

While CDC was intended to be used for asynchronous tracking of incremental data changes for data stores and warehouses and also provides the ability to detect intermediate changes to data, *Change Tracking* is a synchronous process that is part of the transaction of a DML operation itself (INSERT/UPDATE/DELETE) and is intended to be used for detecting net row changes with minimal disk storage overhead.

Returning Rows Affected by a Data Modification Statement

In this recipe, I show you how to return information about rows that are impacted by an INSERT, UPDATE, or DELETE operation using the OUTPUT clause (MERGE can also be captured). In this first example, an UPDATE statement modifies the name of a specific product. OUTPUT is then used to return information on the original and updated column names:

```
DECLARE @ProductChanges TABLE
  (DeletedName nvarchar(50),
   InsertedName nvarchar(50))

UPDATE Production.Product
SET Name = 'HL Spindle/Axle XYZ'
OUTPUT DELETED.Name,
       INSERTED.Name
 INTO @ProductChanges
WHERE ProductID = 524
```

```
SELECT DeletedName,
    InsertedName
FROM @ProductChanges
```

This query returns

```
DeletedName       InsertedName
HL Spindle/Axle  HL Spindle/Axle XYZ
```

This next example uses OUTPUT for a DELETE operation. First, I'll create a demonstration table to hold the data:

```
SELECT *
INTO Sales.Example_SalesTaxRate
FROM Sales.SalesTaxRate
```

Next, I create a table variable to hold the data, delete rows from the table, and then select from the table variable to see which rows were deleted:

```
DECLARE @SalesTaxRate TABLE(
  [SalesTaxRateID]  [int]  NOT NULL,
  [StateProvinceID]  [int]  NOT NULL,
  [TaxType]  [tinyint]  NOT NULL,
  [TaxRate]  [smallmoney]  NOT NULL,
  [Name]  [dbo]. [Name]  NOT NULL,
  [rowguid]  [uniqueidentifier]  ,
  [ModifiedDate]  [datetime]  NOT NULL )

DELETE Sales.Example_SalesTaxRate
OUTPUT DELETED.*
INTO @SalesTaxRate

SELECT  SalesTaxRateID,
    Name
FROM @SalesTaxRate
```

This returns the following abridged results:

```
SalesTaxRateID     Name
1                  Canadian GST + Alberta Provincial Tax
2                  Canadian GST + Ontario Provincial Tax
3                  Canadian GST + Quebec Provincial Tax
4                  Canadian GST
...
27                 Washington State Sales Tax
28                 Taxable Supply
29                 Germany Output Tax
30                 France Output Tax
31                 United Kingdom Output Tax

(29 row(s) affected)
```

In the third example, I'll demonstrate using an INSERT with OUTPUT. A new row is inserted into a table, and the operation is captured to a table variable table:

```
DECLARE @NewDepartment TABLE
  (DepartmentID smallint NOT NULL,
   Name nvarchar(50)  NOT NULL,
   GroupName nvarchar(50)  NOT NULL,
   ModifiedDate datetime NOT NULL)

INSERT HumanResources.Department
(Name,  GroupName)
OUTPUT INSERTED.*
INTO @NewDepartment
VALUES ('Accounts Receivable',  'Accounting')

SELECT  DepartmentID,
    ModifiedDate
FROM  @NewDepartment
```

This returns

```
DepartmentID    ModifiedDate
18              2007-09-15 08:38:28.833
```

How It Works

The first example used a temporary table variable to hold the OUTPUT results (see Chapter 4 for more information on temporary table variables):

```
DECLARE @ProductChanges TABLE
  (DeletedName nvarchar(50),
   InsertedName nvarchar(50))
```

Next, the first part of the UPDATE changed the product name to HL Spindle/Axle XYZ:

```
UPDATE Production.Product
SET Name = 'HL Spindle/Axle XYZ'
```

After the SET clause, but *before* the WHERE clause, the OUTPUT defined which columns to return:

```
OUTPUT DELETED.Name,
       INSERTED.Name
```

Like DML triggers (covered in Chapter 12), two "virtual" tables exist for the OUTPUT to use—INSERTED and DELETED—both of which hold the original and modified values for the updated table. The INSERTED and DELETED virtual tables share the same column names of the modified table—in this case returning the original name (DELETED.Name) and the new name (INSERTED.Name).

The values of this OUTPUT were placed into the temporary table variable by using INTO, followed by the table name:

```
 INTO @ProductChanges
```

The UPDATE query qualified that only ProductID 524 would be modified to the new name:

```
WHERE ProductID = 524
```

After the update, a query was executed against the @ProductChanges temporary table variable to show the before/after changes:

```
SELECT DeletedName,
   InsertedName
FROM @ProductChanges
```

The DELETE and INSERT examples using OUTPUT were variations on the first example, where OUTPUT pushes the deleted rows (for DELETE) or the inserted rows (for INSERT) into a table variable.

Asynchronously Capturing Table Data Modifications

SQL Server 2008 provides a built-in method for asynchronously tracking all data modifications that occur against your user tables without your having to code your own custom triggers or queries. Change Data Capture has minimal performance overhead and can be used for incremental updates of other data sources, for example, migrating changes made in the OLTP database to your data warehouse database. The next set of recipes will demonstrate how to use this new functionality.

To begin with, I'll create a new database that will be used to demonstrate this functionality:

```
IF NOT EXISTS (SELECT name
               FROM sys.databases
               WHERE name = 'TSQLRecipe_CDC_Demo')
BEGIN
    CREATE DATABASE TSQLRecipe_CDC_Demo
END
GO
```

In this first recipe, I'll demonstrate adding CDC to a table in the TSQLRecipe_CDC_Demo database. The first step is to validate whether the database is enabled for Change Data Capture:

```
SELECT is_cdc_enabled
FROM sys.databases
WHERE name = 'TSQLRecipe_CDC_Demo'
```

This returns

```
is_cdc_enabled
0
```

Change Data Capture is configured and managed using various stored procedures. In order to enable the database, I'll execute the sys.dp_cdc_enable_db stored procedure in the context of the TSQLRecipe_CDC_Demo database:

```
USE TSQLRecipe_CDC_Demo
GO

EXEC sys.sp_cdc_enable_db
GO
```

This returns

```
Command(s) completed successfully.
```

Next, I'll revalidate that Change Data Capture is enabled:

```
SELECT is_cdc_enabled
FROM sys.databases
WHERE name = 'TSQLRecipe_CDC_Demo'
```

This returns

```
is_cdc_enabled
1
```

Now that Change Data Capture is enabled, I can proceed with capturing changes for tables in the database by using the `sys.sp_cdc_enable_table` system stored procedure. The parameters of this stored procedure are described in Table 2-8.

Table 2-8. *sp_cdc_enable_table Parameters*

Parameter	Description
@source_schema	This parameter defines the schema of the object.
@source_name	This parameter specifies the table name.
@role_name	This option allows you to select the name of the user-defined role that will have permissions to access the CDC data.
@capture_instance	You can designate up to *two* capture instances for a single table. This comes in handy if you plan on altering the schema of a table already captured by CDC. You can alter the schema without affecting the original CDC (unless it is a data type change), create a new capture instance, track changes in two tables, and then drop the original capture instance once you are sure the new schema capture fits your requirements. If you don't designate the name, the default value is schema_source.
@supports_net_changes	When enabled, this option allows you to show just the latest change to the data within the LSN range selected. This option requires a primary key be defined on the table. If no primary key is defined, you can also designate a unique key in the @index_name option.
@index_name	This parameter allows you to designate the unique key on the table to be used by CDC if a primary key doesn't exist.
@captured_column_list	If you aren't interested in tracking all column changes, this option allows you to narrow down the list.
@filegroup_name	This option allows you to designate where the CDC data will be stored. For very large data sets, isolation on a separate filegroup may yield better manageability and performance.
@partition_switch	This parameter takes a TRUE or FALSE value designating whether or not a ALTER TABLE...SWITCH PARTITION command will be allowed against the CDC table (default is FALSE).

In this recipe, I would like to track all changes against the following new table:

```
USE TSQLRecipe_CDC_Demo
GO

CREATE TABLE dbo.Equipment
   (EquipmentID int NOT NULL PRIMARY KEY IDENTITY(1,1),
    EquipmentDESC varchar(100) NOT NULL,
    LocationID int NOT NULL)
GO
```

I would like to be able to capture all changes made to rows, as well as return just the net changes for a row. For other options, I'll be going with the default:

```
EXEC sys.sp_cdc_enable_table
   @source_schema = 'dbo',
   @source_name = 'Equipment',
   @role_name = NULL,
   @capture_instance = NULL,
   @supports_net_changes = 1,
```

```
@index_name = NULL,
@captured_column_list = NULL,
@filegroup_name = default,
@partition_switch = FALSE
```

The results of this procedure call indicate that two SQL Server Agent jobs were created (SQL Server Agent has to be running):

```
Job 'cdc.TSQLRecipe_CDC_Demo_capture' started successfully.
Job 'cdc.TSQLRecipe_CDC_Demo_cleanup' started successfully.
```

Two jobs, a capture and a cleanup, are created for each database that has CDC enabled for tables.

■**Tip** Had CDC already been enabled for a table in the same database, the jobs would not have been re-created.

I can confirm that this table is now tracked by executing the following query:

```
SELECT is_tracked_by_cdc
FROM sys.tables
WHERE name = 'Equipment' and
    schema_id = SCHEMA_ID('dbo')
```

This returns

```
is_tracked_by_cdc
1
```

I can also validate the settings of your newly configured capture instance using the sys.sp_cdc_help_change_data_capture stored procedure:

```
EXEC sys.sp_cdc_help_change_data_capture 'dbo', 'Equipment'
```

This returns the following result set (presented in name/value pairs for formatting purposes):

```
source_schema            dbo
source_table             Equipment
capture_instance         dbo_ Equipment
object_id                357576312
source_object_id         293576084
start_lsn                NULL
end_lsn                  NULL
supports_net_changes     1
has_drop_pending         NULL
role_name                NULL
index_name               PK__Equipmen__344745994707859D
filegroup_name           NULL
create_date               2008-03-16 09:27:52.990
index_column_list        [EquipmentID]
captured_column_list     [EquipmentID], [EquipmentDESC], [LocationID]
```

How It Works

In this recipe, I started off by enabling CDC capabilities for the database using sp_cdc_enable_db. Behind the scenes, enabling CDC for the database creates a new schema called cdc and a few new tables in the database, detailed in Table 2-9. You shouldn't need to query these tables directly, as there are system stored procedures and functions that can return the same data in a cleaner format.

Table 2-9. *CDC System Tables*

Table	Description
cdc.captured_columns	Returns the columns tracked for a specific capture instance.
cdc.change_tables	Returns tables created when CDC is enabled for a table. Use sys.sp_cdc_help_change_data_capture to query this information rather than query this table directly.
cdc.ddl_history	Returns rows for each DDL change made to the table, once CDE is enabled. Use sys.sp_cdc_get_ddl_history instead of querying this table directly.
cdc.index_columns	Returns index columns associated with the CDC-enabled table. Query sys.sp_cdc_help_change_data_capture to retrieve this information rather than querying this table directly.
cdc.lsn_time_mapping	Helps you map the log sequence number to transaction begin and end times. Again, avoid querying the table directly, and instead use the functions sys.fn_cdc_map_lsn_to_time and sys.fn_cdc_map_time_to_lsn.

I'll review how some of the more commonly used functions and procedures are used in upcoming recipes.

After enabling the database for CDC, I then added CDC tracking to a user table in the database using the sp_cdc_enable_table procedure. I designated the schema, name, and the net changes flag. All other options were left to the default values.

Once sp_cdc_enable_table was executed, because this was the first source table to be enabled in the database, two new SQL Agent jobs were created. One job was called cdc.TSQLRecipe_CDC_Demo_capture. This job is responsible for capturing changes made using replication log reader technology and is scheduled to start automatically when SQL Server starts and run continuously. The second job, cdc.TSQLRecipe_CDC_Demo_cleanup, is scheduled by default to run daily at 2 a.m. and cleans up data older than three days (72 hours) by default.

Executing sys.sp_cdc_help_change_data_capture allowed me to validate various settings of the capture instance, including the support of net changes, tracking columns, creation date, and primary key used to determine uniqueness of the rows.

Enabling CDC for a table also causes a new table to be created in the CDC schema. In this case, a new table called cdc.dbo_Equipment_CT was created automatically. This table has the same columns as the base table, along with five additional columns added to track LSN, operation, and updated column information. You shouldn't query this directly, but instead use functions as I'll demonstrate in the next recipe.

Querying All Changes from CDC Tables

Now that CDC is enabled for the database and a change capture instance is created for a table, I'll go ahead and start making changes to the table in order to demonstrate the functionality:

```
USE TSQLRecipe_CDC_Demo
GO

INSERT dbo.Equipment
(EquipmentDESC, LocationID)
VALUES ('Projector A', 22)

INSERT dbo.Equipment
(EquipmentDESC, LocationID)
VALUES ('HR File Cabinet', 3)

UPDATE dbo.Equipment
SET EquipmentDESC = 'HR File Cabinet 1'
WHERE EquipmentID = 2

DELETE dbo.Equipment
WHERE EquipmentID = 1
```

After making the changes, I can now view a history of what was changed using the CDC functions. Data changes are tracked at the log sequence number (LSN) level. An LSN is a record in the transaction log that uniquely identifies activity.

I will now pull the minimum and maximum LSN values based on the time range I wish to pull changes for. To determine LSN, I'll use the sys.fn_cdc_map_time_to_lsn function, which takes two input parameters, the relational operator, and the tracking time (there are other ways to do this, which I demonstrate later on in the chapter). The relational operators are as follows:

- Smallest greater than

- Smallest greater than or equal

- Largest less than

- Largest less than or equal

These operators are used in conjunction with the Change Tracking time period you specify to help determine the associated LSN value. For this recipe, I want the minimum and maximum LSN values between two time periods:

```
SELECT sys.fn_cdc_map_time_to_lsn
( 'smallest greater than or equal' , '2008-03-16 09:34:11') as BeginLSN

SELECT sys.fn_cdc_map_time_to_lsn
( 'largest less than or equal' , '2008-03-16 23:59:59') as EndLSN
```

This returns the following results (your actual LSN if you are following along will be different):

```
BeginLSN
0x0000001C000001020001

(1 row(s) affected)

EndLSN
0x0000001C000001570001

(1 row(s) affected)
```

I now have my LSN boundaries to detect changes that occurred during the desired time range.

My next decision is whether or not I wish to see all changes or just net changes. I can call the same functions demonstrated in the previous query in order to generate the LSN boundaries and populate them into variables for use in the cdc.fn_cdc_get_all_changes_dbo_Equipment function. As the name of that function suggests, I'll demonstrate showing *all* changes first:

```
DECLARE @FromLSN varbinary(10) =
  sys.fn_cdc_map_time_to_lsn
    ( 'smallest greater than or equal' , '2008-03-16 09:34:11')

DECLARE @ToLSN varbinary(10) =
  sys.fn_cdc_map_time_to_lsn
    ( 'largest less than or equal' , '2008-03-16 23:59:59')

SELECT
    __$operation,
    __$update_mask,
    EquipmentID,
    EquipmentDESC,
    LocationID
FROM cdc.fn_cdc_get_all_changes_dbo_Equipment
    (@FromLSN, @ToLSN, 'all')
```

This returns the following result set:

__$operation	__$update_mask	EquipmentID	EquipmentDESC	LocationID
2	0x07	1	Projector A	22
2	0x07	2	HR File Cabinet	3
4	0x02	2	HR File Cabinet 1	3
1	0x07	1	Projector A	22

This result set revealed all modifications made to the table. Notice that the function name, cdc.fn_cdc_get_all_changes_dbo_Equipment, was based on my CDC instance capture name for the source table. Also notice the values of __$operation and __$update_mask. The __$operation values are interpreted as follows:

- 1 is a delete.

- 2 is an insert.

- 3 is the "prior" version of an updated row (use all update old option to see—I didn't use this in the prior query).

- 4 is the "after" version of an updated row.

The update mask uses bits to correspond to the capture column modified for an operation. I'll demonstrate how to translate these values in a separate recipe.

Moving forward in this current recipe, I could have also used the all update old option to show previous values of an updated row prior to the modification. I can also add logic to translate the values seen in the result set for the operation type. For example:

```
DECLARE @FromLSN varbinary(10) =
  sys.fn_cdc_map_time_to_lsn
    ( 'smallest greater than or equal' , '2008-03-16 09:34:11')

DECLARE @ToLSN varbinary(10) =
  sys.fn_cdc_map_time_to_lsn
    ( 'largest less than or equal' , '2008-03-16 23:59:59')
```

```
SELECT
    CASE __$operation
        WHEN 1 THEN 'DELETE'
        WHEN 2 THEN 'INSERT'
        WHEN 3 THEN 'Before UPDATE'
        WHEN 4 THEN 'After UPDATE'
    END Operation,
    __$update_mask,
    EquipmentID,
    EquipmentDESC,
    LocationID
FROM cdc.fn_cdc_get_all_changes_dbo_Equipment
    (@FromLSN, @ToLSN, 'all update old')
```

This returns

Operation	__$update_mask	EquipmentID	EquipmentDESC	LocationID
INSERT	0x07	1	Projector A	22
INSERT	0x07	2	HR File Cabinet	3
Before UPDATE	0x02	2	HR File Cabinet	3
After UPDATE	0x02	2	HR File Cabinet 1	3
DELETE	0x07	1	Projector A	22

How It Works

In this recipe, modifications were made against the CDC tracked table. Because the underlying CDC data is actually tracked by LSN, I needed to translate my min/max time range to the minimum and maximum LSNs that would include the data changes I was looking for. This was achieved using sys.fn_cdc_map_time_to_lsn.

■**Tip** There is also a sys.fn_cdc_map_lsn_to_time function available to convert your tracked LSNs to temporal values.

Next, I executed the cdc.fn_cdc_get_all_changes_dbo_Equipment function, which allowed me to return all changes made for the LSN range I passed:

```
SELECT
    __$operation,
    __$update_mask,
    EquipmentID,
    EquipmentDESC,
    LocationID
FROM cdc.fn_cdc_get_all_changes_dbo_Equipment
    (@FromLSN, @ToLSN, 'all')
```

For an ongoing incremental load, it may also make sense to store the beginning and ending LSN values for each load, and then use the sys.fn_cdc_increment_lsn function to increment the old upper bound LSN value to be your future lower bound LSN value for the next load (I'll demonstrate this in a later recipe).

In the last example of this recipe, I used the all update old parameter to return both before and after versions of rows from UPDATE statements, and also encapsulated the operation column in a CASE statement for better readability.

Querying Net Changes from CDC Tables

In the original CDC setup recipe, `sp_cdc_enable_table_change_data_capture` was executed with `@supports_net_changes = 1` for the source table. This means that I also have the option of executing the *net* changes version of the CDC procedure. The `fn_cdc_get_net_changes_` version of the stored procedure also takes a beginning and ending LSN value; however, the third parameter differs in the row filter options:

- `all`, which returns the last version of a row without showing values in the update mask.

- `all with mask`, which returns the last version of the row along with the update mask value (the next recipe details how to interpret this mask).

- `all with merge`, which returns the final version of the row as either a delete or a merge operation (either an insert or update). Inserts and updates are not broken out.

The following recipe demonstrates showing net changes without displaying the update mask. I'll start by issuing a few new data modifications:

```
INSERT dbo.Equipment
(EquipmentDESC, LocationID)
VALUES
('Portable White Board', 18)

UPDATE dbo.Equipment
SET LocationID = 1
WHERE EquipmentID = 3
```

Next, I track the net effect of my changes using the following query:

```
DECLARE @FromLSN varbinary(10) =
  sys.fn_cdc_map_time_to_lsn
  ( 'smallest greater than or equal' , '2008-03-16 09:45:00')

DECLARE @ToLSN varbinary(10) =
  sys.fn_cdc_map_time_to_lsn
  ( 'largest less than or equal' , '2008-03-16 23:59:59')

SELECT
   CASE __$operation
      WHEN 1 THEN 'DELETE'
      WHEN 2 THEN 'INSERT'
      WHEN 3 THEN 'Before UPDATE'
      WHEN 4 THEN 'After UPDATE'
      WHEN 5 THEN 'MERGE'
   END Operation,
   __$update_mask,
   EquipmentID,
   EquipmentDESC,
   LocationID
FROM cdc.fn_cdc_get_net_changes_dbo_Equipment
   (@FromLSN, @ToLSN, 'all with mask')
```

This returns

Operation	__$update_mask	EquipmentID	EquipmentDESC	LocationID
INSERT	NULL	3	Portable White Board	1

How It Works

In this recipe, I used cdc.fn_cdc_get_net_changes_dbo_Equipment to return the net changes of rows between the specific LSN range. I first inserted a new row and then updated it. I queried cdc.fn_cdc_get_net_changes_dbo_Equipment to show the net change based on the LSN range. Although two changes were made, only one row was returned to reflect the final change needed, an INSERT operation that would produce the final state of the row.

Translating the CDC Update Mask

The update mask returned by the cdc.fn_cdc_get_all_changes_ and cdc.fn_cdc_get_net_changes_ functions allows you to determine which columns were affected by a particular operation. In order to interpret this value, however, you need the help of a couple of other CDC functions:

- sys.fn_cdc_is_bit_set is used to check whether a specific bit is set within the mask. Its first parameter is the ordinal position of the bit to check, and the second parameter is the update mask itself.

- sys.fn_cdc_get_column_ordinal is the function you can use in conjunction with sys.fn_cdc_is_bit_set to determine the ordinal position of the column for the table. This function's first parameter is the name of the capture instance. The second parameter is the name of the column.

In this recipe, I'll use both of these functions to help identify which columns were updated within the specific LSN boundary. First, I'll make two updates against two different rows:

```
UPDATE dbo.Equipment
SET EquipmentDESC = 'HR File Cabinet A1'
WHERE EquipmentID = 2

UPDATE dbo.Equipment
SET LocationID = 35
WHERE EquipmentID = 3
```

Now I'll issue a query to determine which columns have been changed using the update mask:

```
DECLARE @FromLSN varbinary(10) =
  sys.fn_cdc_map_time_to_lsn
   ( 'smallest greater than or equal' , '2008-03-16 10:02:00')

DECLARE @ToLSN varbinary(10) =
  sys.fn_cdc_map_time_to_lsn
   ( 'largest less than or equal' , '2008-03-16 23:59:59')

SELECT
   sys.fn_cdc_is_bit_set (
     sys.fn_cdc_get_column_ordinal (
         'dbo_Equipment' , 'EquipmentDESC' ),
             __$update_mask) EquipmentDESC_Updated,
   sys.fn_cdc_is_bit_set (
     sys.fn_cdc_get_column_ordinal (
         'dbo_Equipment' , 'LocationID' ),
             __$update_mask) LocationID_Updated,
   EquipmentID,
   EquipmentDESC,
   LocationID
```

```
FROM cdc.fn_cdc_get_all_changes_dbo_Equipment
    (@FromLSN, @ToLSN, 'all')
WHERE __$operation = 4
```

This returns

EquipmentDESC_Updated	LocationID_Updated	EquipmentID	EquipmentDESC	LocationID
1	0	2	HR File Cabinet A1	3
0	1	3	Portable White Board	35

How It Works

In this recipe, I updated two rows. One update involved changing only the equipment description, and the second update involved changing the location ID.

In order to identify whether or not a bit is set, I used the following function call:

```
SELECT  sys.fn_cdc_is_bit_set (
```

The first parameter of this function call is the ordinal position of the column I wish to check. In order to return this information, I used the following function call:

```
sys.fn_cdc_get_column_ordinal ( 'dbo_Equipment' , 'EquipmentDESC' )
```

The second parameter of sys.fn_cdc_is_bit_set is the update mask column name to be probed. I referenced this, along with an aliased name of the column in the query:

```
, __$update_mask) EquipmentDESC_Updated,
```

I repeated this code for the LocationID in the next line of the query:

```
sys.fn_cdc_is_bit_set (sys.fn_cdc_get_column_ordinal
( 'dbo_Equipment' , 'LocationID' ), __$update_mask) LocationID_Updated,
```

The rest of the query was standard, returning the change column values and querying the "all changes" CDC function:

```
DepartmentID,
Name,
GroupName
FROM cdc.fn_cdc_get_all_changes_dbo_Department
    (@FromLSN, @ToLSN, 'all')
```

Lastly, I qualified the query to only return type 4 rows, which are after versions of rows for an update operation:

```
WHERE __$operation = 4
```

Working with LSN Boundaries

I've demonstrated how to determine the minimum and maximum LSN boundaries using sys.fn_cdc_map_time_to_lsn. However, you aren't limited to just using this function to define your boundaries. The following functions in this recipe can also be used to generate LSN values:

- sys.fn_cdc_increment_lsn allows you to return the next LSN number based on the input LSN number. So, for example, you could use this function to convert your last loaded upper bound LSN into your next lower bound LSN.

- sys.fn_cdc_decrement_lsn returns the prior LSN based on the input LSN number.
- sys.fn_cdc_get_max_lsn returns the largest LSN from the CDC data collected for your capture instance.
- sys.fn_cdc_get_min_lsn returns the oldest LSN from the CDC data collected for your capture instance.

The following recipe demonstrates retrieving LSN values from the CDC data collected for the dbo.Equipment table:

```
SELECT sys.fn_cdc_get_min_lsn ('dbo_Equipment') Min_LSN

SELECT sys.fn_cdc_get_max_lsn () Max_LSN

SELECT sys.fn_cdc_increment_lsn (sys.fn_cdc_get_max_lsn()) New_Lower_Bound_LSN

SELECT sys.fn_cdc_decrement_lsn (sys.fn_cdc_get_max_lsn())
New_Lower_Bound_Minus_one_LSN
```

This returns the following (note that your results will be different):

```
Min_LSN
0x0000001C000001040014

(1 row(s) affected)

Max_LSN
0x0000001E0000008B0001

(1 row(s) affected)

New_Lower_Bound_LSN
0x0000001E0000008B0002

(1 row(s) affected)

New_Lower_Bound_Minus_one_LSN
0x0000001E0000008B0000

(1 row(s) affected)
```

How It Works

The new CDC functionality provides built-in methods for tracking changes to target tables in your database; however, you must still consider what logic you will use to capture time ranges for your Change Tracking. This recipe demonstrated methods you can use to retrieve the minimum and maximum available LSNs from the CDC database.

The sys.fn_cdc_get_min_lsn function takes the capture instance name as its input parameter, whereas sys.fn_cdc_get_max_lsn returns the maximum LSN at the database scope. The sys.fn_cdc_increment_lsn and sys.fn_cdc_decrement_lsn functions are used to increase and decrease the LSN based on the LSN you pass it. These functions allow you to create new boundaries for queries against the CDC data.

Disabling Change Data Capture from Tables and the Database

This recipe demonstrates how to remove Change Data Capture from a table. To do so, I'll execute the sys.sp_cdc_disable_table stored procedure. In this example, I will disable all Change Tracking from the table that may exist:

```
EXEC sys.sp_cdc_disable_table
    'dbo', 'Equipment', 'all'
```

I can then validate that the table is truly disabled by executing the following query:

```
SELECT is_tracked_by_cdc
FROM sys.tables
WHERE name = 'Equipment' and
    schema_id = SCHEMA_ID('dbo')
```

This returns

```
is_tracked_by_cdc
0

(1 row(s) affected)
```

To disable CDC for the database itself, I execute the following stored procedure:

```
EXEC sys.sp_cdc_disable_db
```

This returns

```
Command(s) completed successfully.
```

How It Works

The stored procedure sys.sp_cdc_disable_table is used to remove CDC from a table. The first parameter of this stored procedure designates the schema name, and the second parameter designates the table name. The last parameter designates whether you wish to remove all Change Tracking by designating all or instead specify the name of the capture instance.

To entirely remove CDC abilities from the database itself, I executed the sys.sp_cdc_disable_db procedure, which also removes the CDC schema and associated SQL Agent jobs.

Tracking Net Data Changes with Minimal Disk Overhead

CDC was intended to be used for asynchronous tracking of incremental data changes for data stores and warehouses and also provides the ability to detect intermediate changes to data. Unlike CDC, *Change Tracking* is a synchronous process that is part of the transaction of a DML operation itself (INSERT/UPDATE/DELETE) and is intended to be used for detecting net row changes with minimal disk storage overhead.

The synchronous behavior of Change Tracking allows for a transactionally consistent view of modified data, as well as the ability to detect data conflicts. Applications can use this functionality with minimal performance overhead and without the need to add supporting database object modifications (no custom change-detection triggers or table timestamps needed).

In this recipe, I'll walk through how to use the new Change Tracking functionality to detect DML operations. To begin with, I'll create a new database that will be used to demonstrate this functionality:

```
IF NOT EXISTS (SELECT name
                FROM sys.databases
                WHERE name = 'TSQLRecipeChangeTrackDemo')
BEGIN
    CREATE DATABASE TSQLRecipeChangeTrackDemo
END
GO
```

To enable Change Tracking functionality for the database, I have to configure the CHANGE_ TRACKING database option. I also can configure how long changes are retained in the database and whether or not automatic cleanup is enabled. Configuring your retention period will impact how much Change Tracking is maintained for the database. Setting this value too high can impact storage. Setting it too low could cause synchronization issues with the other application databases if the remote applications do not synchronize often enough:

```
ALTER DATABASE TSQLRecipeChangeTrackDemo
SET CHANGE_TRACKING = ON
(CHANGE_RETENTION = 36 HOURS,
 AUTO_CLEANUP = ON)
```

A best practice when using Change Tracking is to enable the database for Snapshot Isolation. For databases and tables with significant DML activity, it will be important that you capture Change Tracking information in a consistent fashion—grabbing the latest version and using that version number to pull the appropriate data.

■**Caution** Enabling Snapshot Isolation will result in additional space usage in tempdb due to row versioning generation. This can also increase overall I/O overhead.

Not using Snapshot Isolation can result in transactionally inconsistent change information:

```
ALTER DATABASE TSQLRecipeChangeTrackDemo
SET  ALLOW_SNAPSHOT_ISOLATION ON
GO
```

I can confirm that I have properly enabled the database for Change Tracking by querying sys.change_tracking_databases:

```
SELECT DB_NAME(database_id) DBNM,is_auto_cleanup_on,
       retention_period,retention_period_units_desc
FROM sys.change_tracking_databases
```

This returns

DBNM	is_auto_cleanup_on	retention_period	retention_period_units_desc
TSQLRecipeChangeTrackDemo	1	36	HOURS

Now I will create a new table that will be used to demonstrate Change Tracking:

```
USE TSQLRecipeChangeTrackDemo
GO

CREATE TABLE dbo.BookStore
(BookStoreID int NOT NULL IDENTITY(1,1) PRIMARY KEY CLUSTERED,
 BookStoreNM varchar(30) NOT NULL,
 TechBookSection bit NOT NULL)
GO
```

Next, for each table that I wish to track changes for, I need to use the ALTER TABLE command with the CHANGE_TRACKING option. If I also want to track which columns were updated, I need to enable the TRACK_COLUMNS_UPDATED option, as demonstrated next:

```
ALTER TABLE dbo.BookStore
ENABLE CHANGE_TRACKING
WITH (TRACK_COLUMNS_UPDATED = ON)
```

I can validate which tables are enabled for Change Tracking by querying the sys.change_tracking_tables catalog view:

```
SELECT OBJECT_NAME(object_id) ObjNM,is_track_columns_updated_on
FROM sys.change_tracking_tables
```

This returns

ObjNM	is_track_columns_updated_on
BookStore	1

Now I will demonstrate Change Tracking by doing an initial population of the table with three new rows:

```
INSERT dbo.BookStore
(BookStoreNM, TechBookSection)
VALUES
('McGarnicles and Bailys', 1),
('Smith Book Store', 0),
('University Book Store',1)
```

One new function I can use for ongoing synchronization is the CHANGE_TRACKING_CURRENT_VERSION function, which returns the version number from the last committed transaction for the table. Each DML operation that occurs against a change-tracked table will cause the version number to increment. I'll be using this version number later on to determine changes:

```
SELECT CHANGE_TRACKING_CURRENT_VERSION ()
```

This returns

```
1
```

Also, I can use the CHANGE_TRACKING_MIN_VALID_VERSION function to check the minimum version available for the change-tracked table. If a disconnected application is not synchronized for a period of time exceeding the Change Tracking retention period, a full refresh of the application data would be necessary:

```
SELECT CHANGE_TRACKING_MIN_VALID_VERSION
( OBJECT_ID('dbo.BookStore') )
```

This returns

```
0
```

To detect changes, I can use the CHANGETABLE function. This function has two varieties of usage, using the CHANGES keyword to detect changes as of a specific synchronization version and using the VERSION keyword to return the latest Change Tracking version for a row.

I'll start off by demonstrating how CHANGES works. The following query demonstrates returning the latest changes to the BookStore table as of version 0. The first parameter is the name of the Change Tracking table, and the second parameter is the version number:

```
SELECT BookStoreID,SYS_CHANGE_OPERATION,
       SYS_CHANGE_VERSION
FROM CHANGETABLE
 (CHANGES dbo.BookStore, 0) AS CT
```

This returns the primary key of the table, followed by the DML operation type (I for INSERT, U for UPDATE, and D for DELETE), and the associated row version number (since all three rows were added for a single INSERT, they all share the same version number):

BookStoreID	SYS_CHANGE_OPERATION	SYS_CHANGE_VERSION
1	I	1
2	I	1
3	I	1

■**Caution** When gathering synchronization information, use SET TRANSACTION ISOLATION LEVEL SNAPSHOT and BEGIN TRAN...COMMIT TRAN to encapsulate gathering of change information and associated current Change Tracking versions and minimum valid versions. Using Snapshot Isolation will allow for a transactionally consistent view of the Change Tracking data.

Now I'll modify the data a few more times in order to demonstrate Change Tracking further:

```
UPDATE dbo.BookStore
SET BookStoreNM = 'King Book Store'
WHERE BookStoreID = 1

UPDATE dbo.BookStore
SET TechBookSection = 1
WHERE BookStoreID = 2

DELETE dbo.BookStore
WHERE BookStoreID = 3
```

I'll check the latest version number:

```
SELECT CHANGE_TRACKING_CURRENT_VERSION ()
```

This is now incremented by three (there were three operations that acted against the data):

```
4
```

Now let's assume that an external application gathered information as of version 1 of the data. The following query demonstrates how to detect any changes that have occurred since version 1:

```
SELECT BookStoreID,
       SYS_CHANGE_VERSION,
       SYS_CHANGE_OPERATION,
       SYS_CHANGE_COLUMNS
FROM CHANGETABLE
 (CHANGES dbo.BookStore, 1) AS CT
```

This returns information on the rows that were modified since version 1, displaying the primary keys for the two updates I performed earlier and the primary key for the row I deleted:

BookStoreID	SYS_CHANGE_VERSION	SYS_CHANGE_OPERATION	SYS_CHANGE_COLUMNS
1	2	U	0x0000000002000000
2	3	U	0x0000000003000000
3	4	D	NULL

The SYS_CHANGE_COLUMNS column is a varbinary value that contains the columns that changed since the last version. To interpret this, I can use the CHANGE_TRACKING_IS_COLUMN_IN_MASK function, as I'll demonstrate next. This function takes two arguments, the column ID of the table column and the varbinary value to be evaluated. The following query uses this function to check whether the columns BookStoreNM and TechBookSection were modified:

```
SELECT BookStoreID,
 CHANGE_TRACKING_IS_COLUMN_IN_MASK(
      COLUMNPROPERTY(
        OBJECT_ID('dbo.BookStore'),'BookStoreNM', 'ColumnId') ,
        SYS_CHANGE_COLUMNS) IsChanged_BookStoreNM,
 CHANGE_TRACKING_IS_COLUMN_IN_MASK(
      COLUMNPROPERTY(
        OBJECT_ID('dbo.BookStore'), 'TechBookSection', 'ColumnId') ,
        SYS_CHANGE_COLUMNS) IsChanged_TechBookSection
FROM CHANGETABLE
 (CHANGES dbo.BookStore, 1) AS CT
WHERE SYS_CHANGE_OPERATION = 'U'
```

This returns bit values of 1 for true and 0 for false regarding what columns were modified:

BookStoreID	IsChanged_BookStoreNM	IsChanged_TechBookSection
1	1	0
2	0	1

Next, I'll demonstrate that the VERSION argument of CHANGETABLE can be used to return the latest change version for each row. This version value can be stored and tracked by the application in order to facilitate Change Tracking synchronization:

```
SELECT bs.BookStoreID, bs.BookStoreNM, bs.TechBookSection,
        ct.SYS_CHANGE_VERSION
FROM dbo.BookStore bs
CROSS APPLY CHANGETABLE
 (VERSION dbo.BookStore, (BookStoreID), (bs.BookStoreID)) as ct
```

This returns the SYS_CHANGE_VERSION column along with the current column values for each row:

BookStoreID	BookStoreNM	TechBookSection	SYS_CHANGE_VERSION
1	King Book Store	1	2
2	Smith Book Store	1	3

Now I'll perform another UPDATE to demonstrate the version differences:

```
UPDATE dbo.BookStore
SET BookStoreNM = 'Kingsly Book Store',
    TechBookSection = 0
WHERE BookStoreID = 1
```

Next, I'll execute another query using CHANGETABLE:

```
SELECT bs.BookStoreID, bs.BookStoreNM, bs.TechBookSection,
       ct.SYS_CHANGE_VERSION
FROM dbo.BookStore bs
CROSS APPLY CHANGETABLE
 (VERSION BookStore, (BookStoreID), (bs.BookStoreID)) as ct
```

This shows that the row version of the row I just modified is now incremented to 5—but the other row that I did not modify remains at a version number of 2:

BookStoreID	BookStoreNM	TechBookSection	SYS_CHANGE_VERSION
1	Kingsly Book Store	0	5
2	Smith Book Store	1	3

I'll now check the current version number:

```
SELECT  CHANGE_TRACKING_CURRENT_VERSION ()
```

This returns

```
5
```

The version number matches the latest change made to the table for the last committed transaction.

For the final part of this recipe, I will also demonstrate how to provide Change Tracking application context information with your DML operations. This will allow you to track which application made data modifications to which rows—which is useful information if you are synchronizing data across several data sources. In order to apply this data lineage, I can use the CHANGE_TRACKING_CONTEXT function. This function takes a single input parameter of context, which is a varbinary data type value representing the calling application.

I start off by declaring a variable to hold the application context information. I then use the variable within the CHANGE_TRACKING_CONTEXT function prior to an INSERT of a new row to the change-tracked table:

```
DECLARE @context varbinary(128) = CAST('Apress_XYZ' as varbinary(128));

WITH CHANGE_TRACKING_CONTEXT (@context)
INSERT dbo.BookStore
(BookStoreNM, TechBookSection)
VALUES
('Capers Book Store', 1)
```

Next, I will check for any changes that were made since version 5 (what I retrieved earlier on using CHANGE_TRACKING_CURRENT_VERSION):

```
SELECT BookStoreID,
       SYS_CHANGE_OPERATION,
       SYS_CHANGE_VERSION,
       CAST(SYS_CHANGE_CONTEXT as varchar) ApplicationContext
FROM CHANGETABLE
 (CHANGES dbo.BookStore, 5) AS CT
```

This returns the new row value that was inserted, along with the application context information that I converted from the SYS_CHANGE_CONTEXT column:

BookStoreID	SYS_CHANGE_OPERATION	SYS_CHANGE_VERSION	ApplicationContext
4	I	6	Apress_XYZ

How It Works

In this recipe, I demonstrated how to use Change Tracking in order to detect net row changes with minimal disk storage overhead. I started off by creating a new database and then using ALTER DATABASE...SET CHANGE_TRACKING to enable Change Tracking in the database. I also designated a 36-hour Change Tracking retention using the CHANGE_RETENTION and AUTO_CLEANUP options. I used the sys.change_tracking_databases catalog view to check the status of the change-tracked database.

I also enabled Snapshot Isolation for the database. This is a best practice, as you'll want to use Snapshot Isolation–level transactions when retrieving row change versions and the associated data from the change-tracked table.

Next, I created a new table and then used ALTER TABLE...ENABLE CHANGE_TRACKING. I designated that column-level changes also be tracked by enabling TRACK_COLUMNS_UPDATED. I validated the change-tracked status of the table by querying the sys.change_tracking_tables catalog view.

After that, I demonstrated several different functions that are used to retrieve Change Tracking data, including

- CHANGE_TRACKING_CURRENT_VERSION, which returns the version number from the last committed transaction for the table

- CHANGE_TRACKING_MIN_VALID_VERSION, which returns the minimum version available for the change-tracked table

- CHANGETABLE with CHANGES, to detect changes as of a specific synchronization version

- CHANGE_TRACKING_IS_COLUMN_IN_MASK, to detect which columns were updated from a change-tracked table

- CHANGETABLE with VERSION, to return the latest change version for a row

- CHANGE_TRACKING_CONTEXT, to store change context with a DML operation so you can track which application modified what data

Change Tracking as a feature set allows you to avoid having to custom-code your own net Change Tracking solution. This feature has minimal overhead and doesn't require schema modification in order to implement (no triggers or timestamps).

CHAPTER 3

■■■

Transactions, Locking, Blocking, and Deadlocking

In the last two chapters, I covered Data Modification Language and provided recipes for SELECT, INSERT, UPDATE, and DELETE statements. Before moving on to Data Definition Language (creating/altering/dropping tables, indexes, views, and more), in this chapter I'll review recipes for handling transactions, lock monitoring, blocking, and deadlocking. I'll review the new SQL Server 2008 table option that allows you to disable lock escalation or enable it for a partitioned table. I'll demonstrate the snapshot isolation level, as well as Dynamic Management Views that are used to monitor and troubleshoot blocking and locking.

Transaction Control

Transactions are an integral part of a relational database system, and they help define a single unit of work. This unit of work can include one or more Transact-SQL statements, which are either committed or rolled back as a group. This all-or-none functionality helps prevent partial updates or inconsistent data states. A partial update occurs when one part of an interrelated process is rolled back or cancelled without rolling back or reversing all of the other parts of the interrelated processes.

A transaction is bound by the four properties of the ACID test. ACID stands for Atomicity, Consistency, Isolation (or Independence), and Durability:

- *Atomicity* means that the transactions are an all-or-nothing entity—carrying out all steps or none at all.

- *Consistency* ensures that the data is valid both before and after the transaction. Data integrity must be maintained (foreign key references, for example), and internal data structures need to be in a valid state.

- *Isolation* is a requirement that transactions not be dependent on other transactions that may be taking place concurrently (either at the same time or overlapping). One transaction can't see another transaction's data that is in an intermediate state, but instead sees the data as it was either before the transaction began or after the transaction completes.

- *Durability* means that the transaction's effects are fixed after the transaction has committed, and any changes will be recoverable after system failures.

In this chapter, I'll demonstrate and review the SQL Server mechanisms and functionality that are used to ensure ACID test compliance, namely locking and transactions.

There are three possible transaction types in SQL Server: autocommit, explicit, or implicit.

Autocommit is the default behavior for SQL Server, where each separate Transact-SQL statement you execute is automatically committed after it is finished. For example, if you have two INSERT statements, with the first one failing and the second one succeeding, the second change is maintained because each INSERT is automatically contained in its own transaction. Although this mode frees the developer from having to worry about explicit transactions, depending on this mode for transactional activity can be a mistake. For example, if you have two transactions, one that credits an account and another that debits it, and the first transaction failed, you'll have a debit without the credit. This may make the bank happy, but not necessarily the customer, who had his account debited. Autocommit is even a bit dangerous for ad hoc administrative changes—for example, if you accidentally delete all rows from a table, you don't have the option of rolling back the transaction after you've realized the mistake.

Implicit transactions occur when the SQL Server session automatically opens a new transaction when one of the following statements is first executed: ALTER TABLE, FETCH, REVOKE, CREATE, GRANT, SELECT, DELETE, INSERT, TRUNCATE TABLE, DROP, OPEN, and UPDATE.

A new transaction is automatically created (opened) once any of the aforementioned statements are executed, and remains open until either a ROLLBACK or COMMIT statement is issued. The initiating command is included in the open transaction. Implicit mode is activated by executing the following command in your query session:

SET IMPLICIT_TRANSACTIONS ON

To turn this off (back to explicit mode), execute the following:

SET IMPLICIT_TRANSACTIONS OFF

Implicit mode can be *very* troublesome in a production environment, as application designers and end users could forget to commit transactions, leaving them open to block other connections (more on blocking later in the chapter).

Explicit transactions are those that you define yourself. This is by far the recommended mode of operation when performing data modifications for your database application. This is because you explicitly control which modifications belong to a single transaction, as well as the actions that are performed if an error occurs. Modifications that must be grouped together are done using your own instruction.

Explicit transactions use the Transact-SQL commands and keywords described in Table 3-1.

Table 3-1. *Explicit Transaction Commands*

Command	Description
BEGIN TRANSACTION	Sets the starting point of an explicit transaction.
ROLLBACK TRANSACTION	Restores original data modified by a transaction and brings data back to the state it was in at the start of the transaction. Resources held by the transaction are freed.
COMMIT TRANSACTION	Ends the transaction if no errors were encountered and makes changes permanent. Resources held by the transaction are freed.
BEGIN DISTRIBUTED TRANSACTION	Allows you to define the beginning of a distributed transaction to be managed by Microsoft Distributed Transaction Coordinator (MS DTC). MS DTC must be running locally and remotely.
SAVE TRANSACTION	Issues a savepoint within a transaction, which allows one to define a location to which a transaction can return if part of the transaction is cancelled. A transaction must be rolled back or committed immediately after rolling back to a savepoint.

Command	Description
@@TRANCOUNT	Returns the number of active transactions for the connection. BEGIN TRANSACTION increments @@TRANCOUNT by 1, and ROLLBACK TRANSACTION and COMMIT TRANSACTION decrements @@TRANCOUNT by 1. ROLLBACK TRANSACTION to a savepoint has no impact.

Using Explicit Transactions

This recipe's example demonstrates how to use explicit transactions to commit or roll back a data modification depending on the return of an error in a batch of statements:

```
USE AdventureWorks
GO

-- Before count
SELECT COUNT(*) BeforeCount FROM HumanResources.Department

-- Variable to hold the latest error integer value
DECLARE @Error int

BEGIN TRANSACTION

INSERT HumanResources.Department
(Name, GroupName)
VALUES ('Accounts Payable', 'Accounting')

SET @Error = @@ERROR
IF (@Error<> 0) GOTO Error_Handler

INSERT HumanResources.Department
(Name, GroupName)
VALUES ('Engineering', 'Research and Development')

SET @Error = @@ERROR
IF (@Error <> 0) GOTO Error_Handler

COMMIT TRAN

Error_Handler:
IF @Error <> 0
BEGIN
    ROLLBACK TRANSACTION
END

-- After count
SELECT COUNT(*) AfterCount FROM HumanResources.Department
```

This returns

```
BeforeCount
16

(1 row(s) affected)
```

```
(1 row(s) affected)

Msg 2601, Level 14, State 1, Line 14
Cannot insert duplicate key row in object 'HumanResources.Department'
with unique index 'AK_Department_Name'.
The statement has been terminated.

AfterCount
16

(1 row(s) affected)
```

How It Works

The first statement in this example validated the count of rows in the HumanResources.Department table, returning 16 rows:

```
-- Before count
SELECT COUNT(*) BeforeCount FROM HumanResources.Department
```

A local variable was created to hold the value of the @@ERROR function (which captures the latest error state of a SQL statement):

```
-- Variable to hold the latest error integer value
DECLARE @Error int
```

Next, an explicit transaction was started:

```
BEGIN TRANSACTION
```

The next statement attempted an INSERT into the HumanResources.Department table. There was a unique key on the department name, but because the department name didn't already exist in the table, the insert succeeded:

```
INSERT HumanResources.Department
(Name, GroupName)
VALUES ('Accounts Payable', 'Accounting')
```

Next was an error handler for the INSERT:

```
SET @Error = @@ERROR
IF (@Error <> 0) GOTO Error_Handler
```

This line of code evaluates the @@ERROR function. The @@ERROR system function returns the last error number value for the last executed statement within the scope of the current connection. The IF statement says that *if* an error occurs, the code should jump to the Error_Handler section of the code (using GOTO).

Note For a review of GOTO, see Chapter 9. For a review of @@Error, see Chapter 16. Chapter 16 also introduces a new error handling command, TRY...CATCH.

GOTO is a keyword that helps you control the flow of statement execution. The identifier after GOTO, Error_Handler, is a user-defined code section.

Next, another insert is attempted, this time for a department that already exists in the table. Because the table has a unique constraint on the Name column, this insert will fail:

```
INSERT HumanResources.Department
(Name, GroupName)
VALUES ('Engineering', 'Research and Development')
```

The failure will cause the @@ERROR following this INSERT to be set to a non-zero value. The IF statement will then evaluate to TRUE, which will invoke the GOTO, thus skipping over the COMMIT TRAN to the Error_Handler section:

```
SET @Error = @@ERROR
IF (@Error <> 0) GOTO Error_Handler          ·

COMMIT TRAN
```

Following the Error_Handler section is a ROLLBACK TRANSACTION:

```
Error_Handler:
IF @Error <> 0
BEGIN
    ROLLBACK TRANSACTION
END
```

Another count is performed after the rollback, and again, there are only 16 rows in the database. This is because both INSERTs were in the same transaction, and one of the INSERTs failed. Since a transaction is all-or-nothing, no rows were inserted:

```
-- After count
SELECT COUNT(*) AfterCount FROM HumanResources.Department
```

Some final thoughts and recommendations regarding how to handle transactions in your Transact-SQL code or through your application:

- Keep transaction time as short as possible for the business process at hand. Transactions that remain open can hold locks on resources for an extended period of time, which can block other users from performing work or reading data.

- Minimize resources locked by the transaction. For example, update only tables that are related to the transaction at hand. If the data modifications are logically dependent on each other, they belong in the same transaction. If not, the unrelated updates belong in their own transaction.

- Add only *relevant* Transact-SQL statements to a transaction. Don't add extra lookups or updates that are not germane to the specific transaction. Executing a SELECT statement within a transaction can create locks on the referenced tables, which can in turn block other users/sessions from performing work or reading data.

- Do not open new transactions that require user or external feedback within the transaction. Open transactions can hold locks on resources, and user feedback can take an indefinite amount of time to receive. Instead, gather user feedback *before* issuing an explicit transaction.

Displaying the Oldest Active Transaction with DBCC OPENTRAN

If a transaction remains open in the database, whether intentionally or not, this transaction can block other processes from performing activity against the modified data. Also, backups of the transaction log can only truncate the inactive portion of a transaction log, so open transactions can cause the log to grow (or reach the physical limit) until that transaction is committed or rolled back.

In order to identify the oldest active transactions in a database, you can use the DBCC OPENTRAN command. This example demonstrates using DBCC OPENTRAN to identify the oldest active transaction in the database:

```
BEGIN TRANSACTION

DELETE Production.ProductProductPhoto
WHERE ProductID = 317

DBCC OPENTRAN('AdventureWorks')

ROLLBACK TRAN
```

This returns

```
(1 row(s) affected)
Transaction information for database 'AdventureWorks'.

Oldest active transaction:
    SPID (server process ID): 54
    UID (user ID)  : -1
    Name           : user_transaction
    LSN            : (41:1021:39)
    Start time     : Sep 15 2008 10:45:53:780AM
    SID            : 0x0105000000000000515000000a065cf7e784b9b5fe77c8770375a2900
DBCC execution completed. If DBCC printed error messages,
contact your system administrator.
```

How It Works

The recipe started off by opening up a new transaction, and then deleting a specific row from the Production.ProductProductPhoto table. Next, the DBCC OPENTRAN was executed, with the database name in parentheses:

```
DBCC OPENTRAN(AdventureWorks)
```

These results showed information regarding the oldest active transaction, including the server process ID, user ID, and start time of the transaction. The key pieces of information from the results are the SPID (server process ID) and Start time.

Once you have this information, you can validate the Transact-SQL being executed using Dynamic Management Views, figure out how long the process has been running for, and if necessary, shut down the process. DBCC OPENTRAN is useful for troubleshooting orphaned connections (connections still open in the database but disconnected from the application or client), and the identification of transactions missing a COMMIT or ROLLBACK.

This command also returns the oldest distributed and undistributed replicated transactions, if any exist within the database. If there are no active transactions, no session-level data will be returned.

Querying Transaction Information by Session

This recipe demonstrates how to find out more information about an active transaction. To demonstrate, I'll describe a common scenario: your application is encountering a significant number of blocks with a high duration. You've been told that this application always opens up an explicit transaction prior to each query.

To illustrate this scenario, I'll execute the following SQL (representing the application code causing the concurrency issue):

```
SET TRANSACTION ISOLATION LEVEL SERIALIZABLE

BEGIN TRAN

SELECT *
FROM HumanResources.Department

INSERT HumanResources.Department
(Name, GroupName)
VALUES ('Test', 'QA')
```

In a separate/new SQL Server Management Studio query window, I would like to identify all open transactions by querying the sys.dm_tran_session_transactions Dynamic Management View (DMV):

```
SELECT session_id, transaction_id, is_user_transaction, is_local
FROM sys.dm_tran_session_transactions
WHERE is_user_transaction = 1
```

This returns the following (your actual session IDs and transaction IDs will vary):

session_id	transaction_id	is_user_transaction	is_local
54	145866	1	1

Now that I have a session ID to work with, I can dig into the details about the most recent query executed by querying sys.dm_exec_connections and sys.dm_exec_sql_text:

```
SELECT s.text
FROM sys.dm_exec_connections c
CROSS APPLY sys.dm_exec_sql_text(c.most_recent_sql_handle)  s
WHERE session_id = 54
```

This returns the last statement executed. (I could have also used the sys.dm_exec_requests DMV for an ongoing and active session; however, nothing was currently executing for my example transaction, so no data would have been returned.)

```
text
SET TRANSACTION ISOLATION LEVEL SERIALIZABLE

BEGIN TRAN

SELECT *
FROM HumanResources.Department

INSERT HumanResources.Department
(Name, GroupName)
VALUES ('Test', 'QA')
```

Since I also have the transaction ID from the first query against sys.dm_tran_session_transactions, I can use the sys.dm_tran_active_transactions to learn more about the transaction itself:

```
SELECT transaction_begin_time,
       CASE transaction_type
           WHEN 1 THEN 'Read/write transaction'
           WHEN 2 THEN 'Read-only transaction'
           WHEN 3 THEN 'System transaction'
           WHEN 4 THEN 'Distributed transaction'
       END tran_type,
       CASE transaction_state
           WHEN 0 THEN 'not been completely initialized yet'
           WHEN 1 THEN 'initialized but has not started'
           WHEN 2 THEN 'active'
           WHEN 3 THEN 'ended (read-only transaction)'
           WHEN 4 THEN 'commit initiated for distributed transaction'
           WHEN 5 THEN 'transaction prepared and waiting resolution'
           WHEN 6 THEN 'committed'
           WHEN 7 THEN 'being rolled back'
           WHEN 8 THEN 'been rolled back'
       END tran_state
FROM sys.dm_tran_active_transactions
WHERE transaction_id = 145866
```

This returns information about the transaction begin time, the type of transaction, and the state of the transaction:

transaction_begin_time	tran_type	tran_state
2008-08-26 10:03:26.520	Read/write transaction	active

How It Works

This recipe demonstrated how to use various DMVs to troubleshoot and investigate a long-running, active transaction. The columns you decide to use depend on the issue you are trying to trouble-shoot. In this scenario, I used the following troubleshooting path:

- I queried sys.dm_tran_session_transactions in order to display a mapping between the session ID and the transaction ID (identifier of the individual transaction).

- I queried sys.dm_exec_connections and sys.dm_exec_sql_text in order to find the latest command executed by the session (referencing the most_recent_sql_handle column).

- Lastly, I queried sys.dm_tran_active_transactions in order to determine how long the transaction was opened, the type of transaction, and the state of the transaction.

Using this troubleshooting technique allows you to go back to the application and pinpoint query calls for abandoned transactions (opened but never committed), and transactions that are inappropriate because they run too long or are unnecessary from the perspective of the application.

Locking

Locking is a normal and necessary part of a relational database system, ensuring the integrity of the data by not allowing concurrent updates to the same data or viewing of data that is in the middle of being updated. Locking can also prevent users from reading data while it is being updated. SQL Server manages locking dynamically; however, it is still important to understand how Transact-SQL queries impact locking in SQL Server. Before proceeding on to the recipe, I'll briefly describe SQL Server locking fundamentals.

Locks help prevent concurrency problems from occurring. Concurrency problems (discussed in detail in the next section, "Transaction, Locking, and Concurrency") can happen when one user attempts to read data that another is modifying, modify data that another is reading, or modify data that another transaction is trying to modify.

Locks are placed against SQL Server resources. How a resource is locked is called its *lock mode*. Table 3-2 reviews the main lock modes that SQL Server has at its disposal.

Table 3-2. *SQL Server Lock Modes*

Name	Description
Shared lock	Shared locks are issued during read-only, non-modifying queries. They allow data to be read, but not updated by other processes while being held.
Intent lock	Intent locks effectively create a lock queue, designating the order of connections and their associated right to update or read resources. SQL Server uses intent locks to show future intention of acquiring locks on a specific resource.
Update lock	Update locks are acquired prior to modifying the data. When the row is modified, this lock is escalated to an exclusive lock. If not modified, it is downgraded to a shared lock. This lock type prevents deadlocks if two connections hold a shared lock on a resource and attempt to convert to an exclusive lock, but cannot because they are each waiting for the other transaction to release the shared lock.
Exclusive lock	This type of lock issues a lock on the resource that bars any kind of access (reads or writes). It is issued during INSERT, UPDATE, or DELETE statements.
Schema modification	This type of lock is issued when a DDL statement is executed.
Schema stability	This type of lock is issued when a query is being compiled. It keeps DDL operations from being performed on the table.
Bulk update	This type of lock is issued during a bulk-copy operation. Performance is increased for the bulk copy operation, but table concurrency is reduced.
Key-range	Key-range locks protect a range of rows (based on the index key)—for example, protecting rows in an UPDATE statement with a range of dates from 1/1/2005 to 12/31/2005. Protecting the range of data prevents row inserts into the date range that would be missed by the current data modification.

You can lock all manner of objects in SQL Server, from a single row in a database, to a table, to the database itself. Lockable resources vary in granularity, from small (at the row level) to large (the entire database). Small-grain locks allow for greater database concurrency, because users can execute queries against specified unlocked rows. Each lock placed by SQL Server requires memory, however, so thousands of individual row locks can also affect SQL Server performance. Larger-grained locks reduce concurrency, but take up fewer resources. Table 3-3 details the resources SQL Server can apply locks to.

Table 3-3. *SQL Server Lock Resources*

Resource Name	Description
Allocation unit	A set of related pages grouped by data type, for example, data rows, index rows, and large object data rows.
Application	An application-specified resource.
DB	An entire database lock.
Extent	Allocation unit of eight 8KB data or index pages.
File	The database file.
HOBT	A heap (table without a clustered index) or B-tree.
Metadata	System metadata.
Key	Index row lock, helping prevent phantom reads. Also called a key-range lock, this lock type uses both a range and a row component. The range represents the range of index keys between two consecutive index keys. The row component represents the lock type on the index entry.
Object	A database object (for example a view, stored procedure, function).
Page	An 8KB data or index page.
RID	Row identifier, designating a single table row.
Table	A resource that locks entire table, data, and indexes.

Not all lock types are compatible with each other. For example, no other locks can be placed on a resource that has already been locked by an exclusive lock. The other transaction must wait or time out until the exclusive lock is released. A resource locked by an update lock can only have a shared lock placed on it by another transaction. A resource locked by a shared lock can have other shared or update locks placed on it.

Locks are allocated and escalated automatically by SQL Server. Escalation means that finer-grain locks (row or page locks) are converted into coarse-grain table locks. SQL Server will attempt to initialize escalation when a single Transact-SQL statement has more than 5,000 locks on a single table or index, or if the number of locks on the SQL Server instance exceeds the available memory threshold. Locks take up system memory, so converting many locks into one larger lock can free up memory resources. The drawback to freeing up the memory resources, however, is reduced concurrency.

■**Note** SQL Server 2008 has a new table option that allows you to disable lock escalation or enable lock escalation at the partition (instead of table) scope. I'll demonstrate this in the "Controlling a Table's Lock Escalation Behavior" recipe.

Viewing Lock Activity

This recipe shows you how to monitor locking activity in the database using the SQL Server sys.dm_tran_locks Dynamic Management View. The example query being monitored by this DMV will use a table locking hint.

In the first part of this recipe, a new query editor window is opened, and the following command is executed:

```
USE AdventureWorks

BEGIN TRAN
SELECT ProductID, ModifiedDate
FROM Production.ProductDocument
WITH (TABLOCKX)
```

In a second query editor window, the following query is executed:

```
SELECT request_session_id sessionid,
       resource_type type,
       resource_database_id dbid,
       OBJECT_NAME(resource_associated_entity_id, resource_database_id) objectname,
       request_mode rmode,
       request_status rstatus
FROM sys.dm_tran_locks
WHERE resource_type IN ('DATABASE', 'OBJECT')
```

■**Tip** This recipe narrows down the result set to two SQL Server resource types of DATABASE and OBJECT for clarity. Typically, you'll monitor several types of resources. The resource type determines the meaning of the resource_associated_entity_id column, as I'll explain in the "How It Works" section.

The query returned information about the locking session identifier (server process ID, or SPID), the resource being locked, the database, object, resource mode, and lock status:

sessionid	type	dbid	objectname	rmode	rstatus
53	DATABASE	8	NULL	S	GRANT
52	DATABASE	8	NULL	S	GRANT
52	OBJECT	8	ProductDocument	X	GRANT

How It Works

The example began by starting a new transaction and executing a query against the Production. ProductDocument table using a TABLOCKX locking hint (this hint places an exclusive lock on the table). In order to monitor what locks are open for the current SQL Server instance, the sys.dm_tran_locks Dynamic Management View was queried. It returned a list of active locks in the AdventureWorks database. The exclusive lock on the ProductDocument table could be seen in the last row of the results.

The first three columns define the session lock, resource type, and database ID:

```
SELECT request_session_id sessionid,
       resource_type type,
       resource_database_id dbid,
```

The next column uses the OBJECT_NAME function. Notice that it uses two parameters (object ID and database ID) in order to specify which name to access (this second database ID parameter was introduced in SP2 of SQL Server 2005 to allow you to specify which database you are using in order to translate the object name):

```
       OBJECT_NAME(resource_associated_entity_id, resource_database_id) objectname,
```

I also query the locking request mode and status:

```
request_mode rmode,
request_status rstatus
```

Lastly, the FROM clause references the DMV, and the WHERE clause designates two resource types:

```
FROM sys.dm_tran_locks
WHERE resource_type IN ('DATABASE', 'OBJECT')
```

The resource_type column designates what the locked resource represents (for example, DATABASE, OBJECT, FILE, PAGE, KEY, RID, EXTENT, METADATA, APPLICATION, ALLOCATION_UNIT, or HOBT type). The resource_associated_entity_id depends on the resource type, determining whether the ID is an object ID, allocation unit ID, or Hobt ID:

- If the resource_associated_entity_id column contains an object ID (for a resource type of OBJECT), you can translate the name using the sys.objects catalog view.

- If the resource_associated_entity_id column contains an allocation unit ID (for a resource type of ALLOCATION_UNIT), you can reference sys.allocation_units and reference the container_id. Container_id can then be joined to sys.partitions where you can then determine the object ID.

- If the resource_associated_entity_id column contains a Hobt ID (for a resource type of KEY, PAGE, ROW, or HOBT), you can directly reference sys.partitions and look up the associated object ID.

- For resource types such as DATABASE, EXTENT, APPLICATION, or METADATA, the resource_associated_entity_id column will be 0.

Use sys.dm_tran_locks to troubleshoot unexpected concurrency issues, such as a query session that may be holding locks longer than desired, or issuing a lock resource granularity or lock mode that you hadn't expected (perhaps a table lock instead of a finer-grained row or page lock). Understanding what is happening at the locking level can help you troubleshoot query concurrency more effectively.

Controlling a Table's Lock Escalation Behavior

Each lock that is created in SQL Server consumes memory resources. When the number of locks increases, memory decreases. If the percentage of memory being used for locks exceeds a certain threshold, SQL Server can convert fine-grained locks (page or row) into coarse-grained locks (table locks). This process is called *lock escalation*. Lock escalation reduces the overall number of locks being held on the SQL Server instance, reducing lock memory usage.

While finer-grained locks do consume more memory, they also can improve concurrency, as multiple queries can access unlocked rows. Introducing table locks may reduce memory consumption, but they also introduce blocking, because a single query holds an entire table. Depending on the application using the database, this behavior may not be desired, and you may wish to exert more control over when SQL Server performs lock escalations.

SQL Server 2008 introduces the ability to control lock escalation at the table level using the ALTER TABLE command. You are now able to choose from the following three settings:

- TABLE, which is the default behavior used in SQL Server 2005. When configured, lock escalation is enabled at the table level for both partitioned and non-partitioned tables.

- AUTO enables lock escalation at the partition level (heap or B-tree) if the table is partitioned. If it is not partitioned, escalation will occur at the table level.

- DISABLE removes lock escalation at the table level. Note that you still may see table locks due to TABLOCK hints or for queries against heaps using a serializable isolation level.

This recipe demonstrates modifying a table across the two new SQL Server 2008 settings:

```
ALTER TABLE Person.Address
SET ( LOCK_ESCALATION = AUTO )

SELECT lock_escalation,lock_escalation_desc
FROM sys.tables
WHERE name='Address'
```

This returns

lock_escalation	lock_escalation_desc
2	AUTO

Next, I'll disable escalation:

```
ALTER TABLE Person.Address
SET ( LOCK_ESCALATION = DISABLE)

SELECT lock_escalation,lock_escalation_desc
FROM sys.tables
WHERE name='Address'
```

This returns

lock_escalation	lock_escalation_desc
1	DISABLE

How It Works

This recipe demonstrated enabling two new SQL Server 2008 table options that control locking escalation. The command began with a standard ALTER TABLE designating the table name to modify:

```
ALTER TABLE Person.Address
```

The second line designated the SET command along with the LOCK_ESCALATION configuration to be used:

```
SET ( LOCK_ESCALATION = AUTO )
```

After changing the configuration, I was able to validate the option by querying the lock_escalation_desc column from the sys.tables catalog view.

Once the AUTO option is enabled, if the table is partitioned, lock escalation will occur at the partitioned level, which improves concurrency if there are multiple sessions acting against separate partitions.

■Note For further information on partitioning, see Chapter 4.

If the table is not partitioned, table-level escalation will occur as usual. If you designate the DISABLE option, table-level lock escalation will not occur. This can help improve concurrency, but could result in increased memory consumption if your requests are accessing a large number of rows or pages.

Transaction, Locking, and Concurrency

One of the listed ACID properties was *Isolation*. Transaction isolation refers to the extent to which changes made by one transaction can be seen by other transactions occurring in the database (i.e., under conditions of concurrent database access). At the highest possible degree of isolation, each transaction occurs as if it were the only transaction taking place at that time. No changes made by other transactions are visible to it. At the lowest level, anything done in one transaction, whether committed or not, can been seen by another transaction.

The ANSI/ISO SQL standard defines four types of interactions between concurrent transactions. These are

- *Dirty reads*: These occur while a transaction is updating a row, and a second transaction reads the row before the first transaction is committed. If the original update rolls back, the uncommitted changes will be read by the second transaction, even though they are never committed to the database. This is the definition of a dirty read.

- *Non-repeatable reads*: These occur when one transaction is updating data, and a second is reading the same data while the update is in progress. The data retrieved before the update will not match data retrieved after the update.

- *Phantom reads*: These occur when a transaction issues two reads, and between the two reads the underlying data is updated with data being inserted or deleted. This causes the results of each query to differ. Rows returned in one query that do not appear in the other are called *phantom rows*.

- *Lost updates*: This occurs when two transactions update a row's value, and the transaction to last update the row "wins." Thus the first update is lost.

SQL Server uses locking mechanisms to control the competing activity of simultaneous transactions. In order to avoid the concurrency issues such as dirty reads, non-repeatable reads, and so on, it implements locking to control access to database resources and to impose a certain level of transaction isolation. Table 3-4 describes the available isolation levels in SQL Server.

Table 3-4. *SQL Server Isolation Levels*

Isolation Level	Description
READ COMMITTED (this is the default behavior of SQL Server)	While READ COMMITTED is used, uncommitted data modifications can't be read. Shared locks are used during a query, and data cannot be modified by other processes while the query is retrieving the data. Data inserts and modifications to the same table are allowed by other transactions, so long as the rows involved are not locked by the first transaction.
READ UNCOMMITTED	This is the least restrictive isolation level, issuing no locks on the data selected by the transaction. This provides the highest concurrency but the lowest amount of data integrity, as the data that you read can be changed while you read it (as mentioned previously, these reads are known as dirty reads), or new data can be added or removed that would change your original query results. This option allows you to read data without blocking others but with the danger of reading data "in flux" that could be modified during the read itself (including reading data changes from a transaction that ends up getting rolled back). For relatively static and unchanging data, this isolation level can potentially improve performance by instructing SQL Server not to issue unnecessary locking on the accessed resources.

Isolation Level	Description
REPEATABLE READ	When enabled, dirty and non-repeatable reads are not allowed. This is achieved by placing shared locks on all read resources. New rows that may fall into the range of data returned by your query can, however, still be inserted by other transactions.
SERIALIZABLE	When enabled, this is the most restrictive setting. Range locks are placed on the data based on the search criteria used to produce the result set. This ensures that actions such as insertion of new rows, modification of values, or deletion of existing rows that would have been returned within the original query and search criteria are not allowed.
SNAPSHOT	This isolation level allows you to read a transactionally consistent version of the data as it existed at the *beginning* of a transaction. Data reads do not block data modifications— however, the SNAPSHOT session will not detect changes being made.

Transactions and locking go hand in hand. Depending on your application design, your transactions can significantly impact database concurrency and performance. Concurrency refers to how many people can query and modify the database and database objects at the same time. For example, the READ UNCOMMITTED isolation level allows the greatest amount of concurrency since it issues no locks—with the drawback that you can encounter a host of data isolation anomalies (dirty reads, for example). The SERIALIZABLE mode, however, offers very little concurrency with other processes when querying a larger range of data.

Configuring a Session's Transaction Locking Behavior

This recipe demonstrates how to use the SET TRANSACTION ISOLATION LEVEL command to set the default transaction locking behavior for Transact-SQL statements used in a connection. You can have only one isolation level set at a time, and the isolation level does not change unless explicitly set. SET TRANSACTION ISOLATION LEVEL allows you to change the locking behavior for a specific database connection. The syntax for this command is as follows:

```
SET TRANSACTION ISOLATION LEVEL
    { READ UNCOMMITTED
    | READ COMMITTED
    | REPEATABLE READ
    | SNAPSHOT
    | SERIALIZABLE
    }
```

In this first example, SERIALIZABLE isolation is used to query the contents of a table. In the *first query editor window*, the following code is executed:

```
USE AdventureWorks
GO

SET TRANSACTION ISOLATION LEVEL SERIALIZABLE
GO

BEGIN TRAN
```

```
SELECT    AddressTypeID, Name
FROM Person.AddressType
WHERE AddressTypeID BETWEEN 1 AND 6
```

This returns the following results (while still leaving a transaction open for the query session):

AddressTypeID	Name
1	Billing
2	Home
3	Main Office
4	Primary
5	Shipping
6	Archive

In a *second query editor*, the following query is executed to view the kinds of locks generated by the SERIALIZABLE isolation level:

```
SELECT resource_associated_entity_id, resource_type,
       request_mode, request_session_id
FROM sys.dm_tran_locks
```

This shows several key locks being held for request_session_id 52 (which is the other session's ID):

resource_associated_entity_id	resource_type	request_mode	request_session_id
0	DATABASE	S	52
0	DATABASE	S	53
72057594043039744	PAGE	IS	52
101575400	OBJECT	IS	52
72057594043039744	KEY	RangeS-S	52
72057594043039744	KEY	RangeS-S	52
72057594043039744	KEY	RangeS-S	52
72057594043039744	KEY	RangeS-S	52
72057594043039744	KEY	RangeS-S	52
72057594043039744	KEY	RangeS-S	52
72057594043039744	KEY	RangeS-S	52

Back in the first query editor window, execute the following code to end the transaction and remove the locks:

```
COMMIT TRAN
```

In contrast, the same query is executed again in the first query editor window, this time using the READ UNCOMMITTED isolation level to read the range of rows:

```
SET TRANSACTION ISOLATION LEVEL READ UNCOMMITTED
GO

BEGIN TRAN

SELECT    AddressTypeID, Name
FROM Person.AddressType
WHERE AddressTypeID BETWEEN 1 AND 6
```

In a second query editor, the following query is executed to view the kinds of locks generated by the READ UNCOMMITTED isolation level:

```
SELECT resource_associated_entity_id, resource_type,
request_mode, request_session_id
FROM sys.dm_tran_locks
```

This returns (abridged results)

resource_associated_entity_id	resource_type	request_mode	request_session_id
0	DATABASE	S	52
0	DATABASE	S	53

Unlike SERIALIZABLE, the READ UNCOMMITTED isolation level creates no additional locks on the keys of the Person.AddressType table.

Returning back to the first query editor with the READ UNCOMMITTED query, the transaction is ended for cleanup purposes:

```
COMMIT TRAN
```

I'll demonstrate the SNAPSHOT isolation level next. In the first query editor window, the following code is executed:

```
ALTER DATABASE AdventureWorks
SET ALLOW_SNAPSHOT_ISOLATION ON
GO

USE AdventureWorks
GO

SET TRANSACTION ISOLATION LEVEL SNAPSHOT
GO

BEGIN TRAN

SELECT   CurrencyRateID,
     EndOfDayRate
FROM Sales.CurrencyRate
WHERE CurrencyRateID = 8317
```

This returns

CurrencyRateID	EndOfDayRate
8317	0.6862

In a second query editor window, the following query is executed:

```
USE AdventureWorks
GO

UPDATE Sales.CurrencyRate
SET EndOfDayRate = 1.00
WHERE CurrencyRateID = 8317
```

Now back to the first query editor, the following query is reexecuted:

```
SELECT   CurrencyRateID,
   EndOfDayRate
FROM Sales.CurrencyRate
WHERE CurrencyRateID = 8317
```

This returns

```
CurrencyRateID    EndOfDayRate
8317              0.6862
```

The same results are returned as before, even though the row was updated by the second query editor query. The SELECT was not blocked from reading the row, nor was the UPDATE blocked from making the modification.

Now I am going to commit the transaction and reissue the query:

```
COMMIT TRAN

SELECT   CurrencyRateID,
    EndOfDayRate
FROM Sales.CurrencyRate
WHERE CurrencyRateID = 8317
```

This returns the updated value:

```
CurrencyRateID    EndOfDayRate
8317              1.00
```

How It Works

In this recipe, I demonstrated how to change the locking isolation level of a query session by using the SET TRANSACTION ISOLATION LEVEL. Executing this command isn't necessary if you wish to use the default SQL Server isolation level, which is READ COMMITTED. Otherwise, once you set an isolation level, it remains in effect for the connection until explicitly changed again.

The first example in the recipe demonstrated using the SERIALIZABLE isolation level:

```
SET TRANSACTION ISOLATION LEVEL SERIALIZABLE
GO
```

An explicit transaction was then started, and a query was executed against the Person. AddressType table for all rows that fell between a specific range of AddressTypeID values:

```
BEGIN TRAN

SELECT   AddressTypeID, Name
FROM Person.AddressType
WHERE AddressTypeID BETWEEN 1 AND 6
```

In a separate connection, a query was then executed against the sys.dm_tran_locks Dynamic Management View, which returned information about active locks being held for the SQL Server instance. In this case, we saw a number of key range locks, which served the purpose of prohibiting other connections from inserting, updating, or deleting data that would cause different results in the query's search condition (WHERE AddressTypeID BETWEEN 1 AND 6).

In the second example, the isolation level was set to READ UNCOMMITTED:

```
SET TRANSACTION ISOLATION LEVEL READ UNCOMMITTED
GO
```

Querying sys.dm_tran_locks again, we saw that this time no row, key, or page locks were held at all on the table, allowing the potential for other transactions to modify the queried rows while the original transaction remained open. With this isolation level, the query performs dirty reads, meaning that the query could read data with in-progress modifications, whether or not the actual modification is committed or rolled back later on.

In the third example from the recipe, the database setting ALLOW_SNAPSHOT_ISOLATION was enabled for the database (see Chapter 22 for more information on ALTER DATABASE):

```
ALTER DATABASE AdventureWorks
SET ALLOW_SNAPSHOT_ISOLATION ON
GO
```

This option had to be ON in order to start a snapshot transaction. In the next line of code, the database context was changed, and SET TRANSACTION ISOLATION LEVEL was set to SNAPSHOT:

```
USE AdventureWorks
GO
```

```
SET TRANSACTION ISOLATION LEVEL SNAPSHOT
GO
```

A transaction was then opened and a query against Sales.CurrencyRate was performed:

```
BEGIN TRAN
```

```
SELECT   CurrencyRateID,
         EndOfDayRate
FROM Sales.CurrencyRate
WHERE CurrencyRateID = 8317
```

In the second query editor session, the same Sales.CurrencyRate row being selected in the first session query was modified:

```
USE AdventureWorks
GO
```

```
UPDATE Sales.CurrencyRate
SET EndOfDayRate = 1.00
WHERE CurrencyRateID = 8317
```

Back at the first query editor session, although the EndOfDayRate was changed to 1.0 in the second session, executing the query again in the SNAPSHOT isolation level shows that the value of that column was still 0.6862. This new isolation level provided a consistent view of the data as of the beginning of the transaction. After committing the transaction, reissuing the query against Sales.CurrencyRate revealed the latest value.

What if you decide to UPDATE a row in the snapshot session that was updated in a separate session? Had the snapshot session attempted an UPDATE against CurrencyRateID 8317 instead of a SELECT, an error would have been raised, warning you that an update was made against the original row while in snapshot isolation mode:

```
Msg 3960, Level 16, State 1, Line 2
Cannot use snapshot isolation to access table 'Sales.CurrencyRate'
directly or indirectly in database 'AdventureWorks'.
Snapshot transaction aborted due to update conflict.
Retry transaction.
```

Blocking

Blocking occurs when one transaction in a database session is locking resources that one or more other session transactions wants to read or modify. Short-term blocking is usually OK and expected for busy applications. However, poorly designed applications can cause long-term blocking, unnecessarily keeping locks on resources and blocking other sessions from reading or updating them.

In SQL Server, a blocked process remains blocked indefinitely or until it times out (based on SET LOCK_TIMEOUT), the server goes down, the process is killed, the connection finishes its updates, or something happens to the original transaction to cause it to release its locks on the resource.

Some reasons why long-term blocking can happen:

- Excessive row locks on a table without an index can cause SQL Server to acquire a table lock, blocking out other transactions.

- Applications open a transaction and then request user feedback or interaction while the transaction stays open. This is usually when an end user is allowed to enter data in a GUI while a transaction remains open. While open, any resources referenced by the transaction may be held with locks.

- Transactions BEGIN and then look up data that could have been referenced prior to the transaction starting.

- Queries use locking hints inappropriately, for example, if the application uses only a few rows, but uses a table lock hint instead (for an overview of locking hints, see the recipes in the section "Using Table Hints" in Chapter 15, which include a list of the available locking hints).

- The application uses long-running transactions that update many rows or many tables within one transaction (chunking large updates into smaller update transactions can help improve concurrency).

Identifying and Resolving Blocking Issues

In this recipe, I'll demonstrate how to identify a blocking process, view the Transact-SQL being executed by the process, and then forcibly shut down the active session's connection (thus rolling back any open work not yet committed by the blocking session). First, however, let's go to a quick background on the commands used in this example.

This recipe demonstrates how to identify blocking processes with the SQL Server Dynamic Management View sys.dm_os_waiting_tasks. This view is intended to be used instead of the sp_who system stored procedure, which was used in previous versions of SQL Server.

After identifying the blocking process, this recipe will then use the sys.dm_exec_sql_text dynamic management function and sys.dm_exec_connections DMV used earlier in the chapter to identify the SQL text of the query that is being executed—and then as a last resort, forcefully end the process.

To forcefully shut down a wayward active query session, the KILL command is used. KILL should only be used if other methods are not available, including waiting for the process to stop on its own or shutting down or canceling the operation via the calling application. The syntax for KILL is as follows:

```
KILL {spid | UOW} [WITH STATUSONLY]
```

The arguments for this command are described in Table 3-5.

Table 3-5. *KILL Command Arguments*

Argument	Description
spid	This indicates the session ID associated with the active database connection to be shut down.
UOW	This is the unit-of-work identifier for a distributed transaction, which is the unique identifier of a specific distributed transaction process.
WITH STATUSONLY	Some KILL statements take longer to roll back a transaction than others (depending on the scope of updates being performed by the session). In order to check the status of a rollback, you can use WITH STATUSONLY to get an estimate of rollback time.

Beginning the example, the following query is executed in the first query editor session in order to set up a blocking process:

```
BEGIN TRAN

UPDATE Production.ProductInventory
SET Quantity = 400
WHERE ProductID = 1 AND
LocationID = 1
```

Next, in a second query editor window, the following query is executed:

```
BEGIN TRAN

UPDATE Production.ProductInventory
SET Quantity = 406
WHERE ProductID = 1 AND
LocationID = 1
```

Now in a third query editor window, I'll execute the following query:

```
SELECT blocking_session_id, wait_duration_ms, session_id
FROM  sys.dm_os_waiting_tasks
WHERE blocking_session_id IS NOT NULL
```

This returns

blocking_session_id	wait_duration_ms	session_id
54	27371	55

This query identified that session 54 is blocking session 55.

To see what session 54 is doing, I execute the following query in the same window as the previous query:

```
SELECT t.text
FROM sys.dm_exec_connections c
CROSS APPLY sys.dm_exec_sql_text (c.most_recent_sql_handle) t
WHERE c.session_id = 54
```

This returns

```
text
BEGIN TRAN
```

```
UPDATE Production.ProductInventory
SET Quantity = 400
WHERE ProductID = 1 AND
LocationID = 1
```

Next, to forcibly shut down the session, execute this query:

```
KILL 54
```

This returns

```
Command(s) completed successfully.
```

The second session's UPDATE is then allowed to proceed once the other session's connection is removed.

How It Works

The recipe demonstrated blocking by executing an UPDATE against the Production.ProductInventory table with a transaction that was opened but *not* committed. In a different session, a similar query was executed against the same table and the same row. Because the other connection's transaction never committed, the second connection must wait in line indefinitely before it has a chance to update the record.

In a third Query Editor window, the sys.dm_os_waiting_tasks Dynamic Management View was queried, returning information on the session being blocked by another session.

When troubleshooting blocks, you'll want to see exactly what the blocking session_id is doing. To view this, the recipe used a query against sys.dm_exec_connections and sys.dm_exec_sql_text. The sys.dm_exec_connections DMV was used to retrieve the most_recent_sql_handle column for session_id 53. This is a pointer to the SQL text in memory, and was used as an input parameter for the sys.dm_exec_sql_text dynamic management function. The text column is returned from sys.dm_exec_sql_text displaying the SQL text of the blocking process.

■**Note** Often blocks *chain*, and you must work your way through each blocked process up to the original blocking process using the blocking_session_id and session_id columns.

KILL was then used to forcibly end the blocking process, but in a production scenario, you'll want to see whether the process is valid, and if so, whether it should be allowed to complete or if it can be shut down or cancelled using the application (by the application end user, for example). Prior to stopping the process, be sure that you are not stopping a long-running transaction that is critical to the business, like a payroll update, for example. If there is no way to stop the transaction (for example, the application that spawned it cannot commit the transaction), you can use the KILL command (followed by the SPID to terminate).

Configuring How Long a Statement Will Wait for a Lock to Be Released

When a transaction or statement is being *blocked*, this means it is waiting for a lock on a resource to be released. This recipe demonstrates the SET LOCK_TIMEOUT option, which specifies how long the blocked statement should wait for a lock to be released before returning an error.

The syntax is as follows:

```
SET LOCK_TIMEOUT timeout_period
```

The timeout period is the number of milliseconds before a locking error will be returned. In order to set up this recipe's demonstration, I will execute the following batch:

```
BEGIN TRAN

UPDATE Production.ProductInventory
SET Quantity = 400
WHERE ProductID = 1 AND
LocationID = 1
```

In a second query window, this example demonstrates setting up a lock timeout period of one second (1000 milliseconds):

```
SET LOCK_TIMEOUT 1000

UPDATE Production.ProductInventory
SET Quantity = 406
WHERE ProductID = 1 AND
LocationID = 1
```

After one second (1000 milliseconds), I receive the following error message:

```
Msg 1222, Level 16, State 51, Line 3
Lock request time out period exceeded.
The statement has been terminated.
```

How It Works

In this recipe, the lock timeout is set to 1000 milliseconds (1 second). This setting doesn't impact how long a resource can be *held* by a process, only how long it has to wait for another process to release access to the resource.

Deadlocking

Deadlocking occurs when one user session (let's call it Session 1) has locks on a resource that another user session (let's call it Session 2) wants to modify, and Session 2 has locks on resources that Session 1 needs to modify. Neither Session 1 nor Session 2 can continue until the other releases the locks, so SQL Server chooses one of the sessions in the deadlock as the *deadlock victim*.

■**Note** A deadlock victim has its session killed and transactions rolled back.

Some reasons why deadlocks can happen:

- The application accesses tables in different order. For example, Session 1 updates Customers and then Orders, whereas Session 2 updates Orders and then Customers. This increases the chance of two processes deadlocking, rather than them accessing and updating a table in a serialized (in order) fashion.

- The application uses long-running transactions, updating many rows or many tables within one transaction. This increases the surface area of rows that can cause deadlock conflicts.

- In some situations, SQL Server issues several row locks, which it later decides must be escalated to a table lock. If these rows exist on the same data pages, and two sessions are both trying to escalate the lock granularity on the same page, a deadlock can occur.

Identifying Deadlocks with a Trace Flag

If you are having deadlock trouble in your SQL Server instance, this recipe demonstrates how to make sure deadlocks are logged to the SQL Server Management Studio SQL log appropriately using the DBCC TRACEON, DBCC TRACEOFF, and DBCC TRACESTATUS commands. These functions enable, disable, and check the status of trace flags.

■Tip There are other methods in SQL Server for troubleshooting deadlocks, such as using SQL Profiler, but since this book is Transact-SQL focused, I don't cover them here.

Trace flags are used within SQL Server to enable or disable specific behaviors for the SQL Server instance. By default, SQL Server doesn't return significant logging when a deadlock event occurs. Using trace flag 1222, information about locked resources and types participating in a deadlock are returned in an XML format, helping you troubleshoot the event.

The DBCC TRACEON command enables trace flags. The syntax is as follows:

```
DBCC TRACEON ( trace# [ ,...n ][ ,-1 ] ) [ WITH NO_INFOMSGS ]
```

The arguments for this command are described in Table 3-6.

Table 3-6. *DBCC TRACEON Command Arguments*

Argument	Description
trace#	This specifies one or more trace flag numbers to enable.
-1	When -1 is designated, the specified trace flags are enabled globally.
WITH NO_INFOMSGS	When included in the command, WITH NO_INFOMSGS suppresses informational messages from the DBCC output.

The DBCC TRACESTATUS command is used to check on the status (enabled or disabled) for a specific flag or flags. The syntax is as follows:

```
DBCC TRACESTATUS ( [ [ trace# [ ,...n ] ] [ , ] [ -1 ] ] ) [ WITH NO_INFOMSGS ]
```

The arguments for this command are described in Table 3-7.

Table 3-7. *DBCC TRACESTATUS Command Arguments*

Argument	Description
trace#	This specifies one or more trace flag numbers to check the status of.
-1	This shows globally enabled flags.
WITH NO_INFOMSGS	When included in the command, WITH NO_INFOMSGS suppresses informational messages from the DBCC output.

The DBCC TRACEOFF command disables trace flags. The syntax is as follows:

```
DBCC TRACEOFF ( trace# [ ,...n ] [ , -1 ] ) [ WITH NO_INFOMSGS ]
```

The arguments for this command are described in Table 3-8.

Table 3-8. *DBCC TRACEOFF Command Arguments*

Argument	Description
trace#	This indicates one or more trace flag numbers to disable.
-1	This disables the globally set flags.
WITH NO_INFOMSGS	When included in the command, WITH NO_INFOMSGS suppresses informational messages from the DBCC output.

In order to demonstrate this recipe, a deadlock will be simulated. In a new query editor window, the following query is executed:

```
SET NOCOUNT ON
SET TRANSACTION ISOLATION LEVEL SERIALIZABLE

WHILE 1=1
BEGIN
BEGIN TRAN

    UPDATE Purchasing.Vendor
    SET CreditRating = 1
    WHERE BusinessEntityID = 1494

    UPDATE Purchasing.Vendor
    SET CreditRating = 2
    WHERE BusinessEntityID = 1492

COMMIT TRAN
END
```

In a second query editor window, the following query is executed:

```
SET NOCOUNT ON
SET TRANSACTION ISOLATION LEVEL SERIALIZABLE

WHILE 1=1
BEGIN
BEGIN TRAN

    UPDATE Purchasing.Vendor
    SET CreditRating = 2
    WHERE BusinessEntityID = 1492

    UPDATE Purchasing.Vendor
    SET CreditRating = 1
    WHERE BusinessEntityID = 1494

COMMIT TRAN
END
```

After a few seconds, check each query editor window until the following error message appears on one of the query editors:

```
Msg 1205, Level 13, State 51, Line 9
Transaction (Process ID 53) was deadlocked on lock resources
with another process and has been chosen as the deadlock victim.
Rerun the transaction.
```

Looking at the SQL log in SQL Server Management Studio, the deadlock event was not logged. I'll now open a third query editor window and execute the following command:

```
DBCC TRACEON (1222, -1)
GO
DBCC TRACESTATUS
```

DBCC TRACESTATUS shows the active traces running for both the local session and globally:

```
TraceFlag   Status   Global   Session
1222        1        1        0
```

To simulate another deadlock, I'll restart the "winning" connection query (the one that wasn't killed in the deadlock), and then the deadlock losing session, causing another deadlock after a few seconds.

After the deadlock has occurred, I stop the other executing query. Now the SQL log in SQL Server Management Studio contains a detailed error message from the deadlock event, including the database and object involved, the lock mode, and the Transact-SQL statements involved in the deadlock.

For example, when deadlocks occur, you'll want to make sure to find out the queries that are involved in the deadlock, so you can troubleshoot them accordingly. The following excerpt from the log shows a deadlocked query:

```
09/15/2008 20:20:00,spid15s,Unknown,
UPDATE [Purchasing].[Vendor] set [CreditRating] = @1
WHERE [BusinessEntityID]=@2
```

From this we can tell which query was involved in the deadlocking, which is often enough to get started with a solution. Other important information you can retrieve by using trace 1222 includes the login name of the deadlocked process, the client application used to submit the query, and the isolation level used for its connection (letting you know whether that connection is using an isolation level that doesn't allow for much concurrency):

```
... clientapp=Microsoft SQL Server Management Studio - Query hostname=CAESAR
hostpid=2388 loginname=CAESAR\Administrator isolationlevel=serializable (4)
xactid=1147351 currentdb=8 lockTimeout=4294967295
clientoption1=673187936 clientoption2=390200
```

After examining the SQL log, disable the trace flag in the query editor:

```
DBCC TRACEOFF (1222, -1)
GO
DBCC TRACESTATUS
```

How It Works

In this recipe, I simulated a deadlock using two separate queries that updated the same rows repeatedly: updating two rows in the opposite order. When a deadlock occurred, the error message was logged to the query editor window, but nothing was written to the SQL log.

To enable deadlock logging to the SQL log, the recipe enabled the trace flag 1222. Trace 1222 returns detailed deadlock information to the SQL log. The -1 flag indicated that trace flag 1222 should be enabled globally for all SQL Server connections. To turn on a trace flag, DBCC TRACEON was used, with the 1222 flag in parentheses:

```
DBCC TRACEON (1222, -1)
```

To verify that the flag was enabled, DBCC TRACESTATUS was executed:

```
DBCC TRACESTATUS
```

After encountering another deadlock, the deadlock information was logged in the SQL log. The flag was then disabled using DBCC TRACEOFF:

```
DBCC TRACEOFF (1222, -1)
```

Setting Deadlock Priority

You can increase a query session's chance of being chosen as a deadlock victim by using the SET DEADLOCK_PRIORITY command. The syntax for this command is as follows:

```
SET DEADLOCK_PRIORITY { LOW | NORMAL | HIGH | <numeric-priority> }
```

The arguments for this command are described in Table 3-9.

Table 3-9. *SET DEADLOCK_PRIORITY Command Arguments*

Argument	Description
LOW	LOW makes the current connection the likely deadlock victim.
NORMAL	NORMAL lets SQL Server decide based on which connection seems least expensive to roll back.
HIGH	HIGH lessens the chances of the connection being chosen as the victim, unless the other connection is also HIGH or has a numeric priority greater than 5.
<numeric-priority>	The numeric priority allows you to use a range of values from -10 to 10, where -10 is the most likely deadlock victim, up to 10 being the least likely to be chosen as a victim. The higher number between two participants in a deadlock wins.

For example, had the first query from the previous recipe used the following deadlock priority command, it would almost certainly have been chosen as the victim (normally, the default deadlock victim is the connection SQL Server deems least expensive to cancel and roll back):

```
SET NOCOUNT ON
SET TRANSACTION ISOLATION LEVEL SERIALIZABLE
SET DEADLOCK_PRIORITY LOW

BEGIN TRAN
```

```
UPDATE Purchasing.Vendor
SET CreditRating = 1
WHERE BusinessEntityID  = 2

UPDATE Purchasing.Vendor
SET CreditRating = 2
WHERE BusinessEntityID  = 1

COMMIT TRAN
```

How It Works

You can also set the deadlock priority to HIGH and NORMAL. HIGH means that unless the other session is of the same priority, it will not be chosen as the victim. NORMAL is the default behavior and will be chosen if the other session is HIGH, but not chosen if the other session is LOW. If both sessions have the same priority, the least expensive transaction to roll back will be chosen.

CHAPTER 4

■ ■ ■

Tables

In this chapter, I'll present recipes that demonstrate table creation and manipulation. Tables are used to store data in the database and make up the central unit upon which most SQL Server database objects depend. Tables are uniquely named within a database and schema and contain one or more columns. Each column has an associated data type that defines the kind of data that can be stored within it.

■**Tip** SQL Server 2008 includes new date types for handling date and time, hierarchy, space (geography and geometry), and the FILESTREAM attribute. I'll discuss the hierarchical and spatial data types in Chapter 14 and cover the FILESTREAM attribute in this chapter.

As I've done in the previous chapters, I'll provide basic table recipes throughout, and break them up with walkthroughs of more complex functionality. Regarding new features introduced in SQL Server 2008, I'll demonstrate the sparse column improvement in the "Reducing Storage for Null Columns" recipe. Also, in the "Manageability for Very Large Tables" section, I'll introduce the new data compression functionality available in the Enterprise Edition and Developer Edition of SQL Server 2008.

■**Caution** If you decide to follow along with some of these recipes, consider backing up the AdventureWorks database beforehand, so that you can restore it to a clean version once you are finished.

Table Basics

You can create a table using the CREATE TABLE command. The full syntax is quite extensive, so this chapter will build upon the different areas of the command as the chapter progresses. The simplified syntax is as follows:

```
CREATE TABLE
    [ database_name . [ schema_name ] . | schema_name . ] table_name
        ( column_name <data_type> [ NULL | NOT NULL ] [ ,...n ] )
```

The arguments of this command are described in Table 4-1.

Table 4-1. *CREATE TABLE Arguments*

Argument	Description
`[ database_name . [ schema_name ] .` `| schema_name . ] table_name`	This argument indicates that you can qualify the new table name using the database, schema, and table name, or just the schema and table name.
`column_name`	This argument defines the name of the column.
`data_type`	This argument specifies the column's data type (data types are described next).
`NULL | NOT NULL`	The `NULL | NOT NULL` option refers to the column nullability. *Nullability* defines whether a column can contain a `NULL` value. A `NULL` value means that the value is unknown. It does not mean that the column is zero, blank, or empty.

Each column requires a defined data type. The data type defines and restricts the type of data the column can hold.

Table 4-2 details the system data types available in SQL Server.

Table 4-2. *SQL Server Data Types*

Data Type	Value Range
`bigint`	This specifies a whole number from -2^{63} ($-9,223,372,036,854,775,808$) through $2^{63} - 1$ ($9,223,372,036,854,775,807$).
`binary`	This specifies fixed-length binary data with a maximum of 8000 bytes.
`bit`	This specifies a whole number, either 0 or 1.
`char`	This specifies fixed-length character data with maximum length of 8000 characters.
`date`	This stores dates to an accuracy of 1 day, ranging from 1-01-01 through 9999-12-31.
`datetime`	This provides date and time storage with an accuracy of 0.333 seconds, ranging from January 1, 1753, through December 31, 9999. (1753 was the year following the adoption of the Gregorian calendar, which produced a difference in days to the previous calendar of 12 days. Beginning with the year 1753 sidesteps all sorts of calculation problems.)
`datetime2`	This stores date and time to an accuracy of 100 nanoseconds, ranging from 1-01-01 00:00:00.0000000 through 9999-12-31 23:59:59.9999999.
`datetimeoffset`	The time zone offset is the difference in time between a specific time zone and Coordinated Universal Time (UTC). You can use this new data type with the `SYSDATETIMEOFFSET` system function to store the current system timestamp along with the database time zone. You can also use this data type with the `SWITCHOFFSET` function to change the time zone offset by a specific increment/decrement. This data type is stored within an accuracy of 100 nanoseconds, ranging from 1-01-01 00:00:00.0000000 through 9999-12-31 23:59:59.9999999.

Data Type	Value Range
decimal or numeric (no difference between the two)	This stores data ranging from –10^38 +1 through 10^38 –1. decimal uses precision and scale. Precision determines maximum total number of decimal digits, both left and right of the decimal point. Scale determines maximum decimal digits to the right of the decimal point.
float	This specifies a floating-precision number from –1.79E + 308 to –2.23E – 308, 0, and 2.23E – 308 to 1.79E + 308.
geography and geometry	These specify native storage of spatial data. The geometry data type represents flat-earth (Euclidean) coordinate spatial data and also allows for storage of points, polygons, curves, and collections. The geography data type is used for round-earth spatial storage, allowing for latitude and longitude coordinates and storage of points, polygons, curves, and collections. These data types are new to SQL Server 2008 and are discussed in Chapter 14.
hierarchyid	This natively stores a position within a tree hierarchy. This data type is new to SQL Server 2008 and is discussed in Chapter 14.
int	This specifies a whole number from –2^31 (–2,147,483,648) through 2^31–1 (2,147,483,647).
money	This specifies a monetary value between –2^63 (–922,377,203,685,477.5808) through 2^63–1 (+922,337,203,685,477.5807).
nchar	This specifies a fixed-length Unicode character data with a maximum length of 4000 characters.
nvarchar	This specifies variable-length Unicode character data with a maximum length of 4000 characters. SQL Server also has the max option, which allows you to store up to 2^31–1bytes. This option allows you to use the regular data types instead of SQL Server 2000's text, ntext, and image.
real	This specifies a floating-precision number from –3.40E + 38 to –1.18E – 38, 0, and 1.18E – 38 to 3.40E + 38.
smalldatetime	This indicates the date and time from January 1, 1900, through June 6, 2079.
smallint	This specifies a whole number from –32,768 through 32,767.
smallmoney	This specifies a monetary value between –214,748.3648 through +214,748.3647.
sql_variant	This data type can store all data types except text, ntext, timestamp, varchar(max), nvarchar(max), varbinary(max), xml, image, user-defined types, and another sql_variant.
table	The table data type can't be used in CREATE TABLE as a column type. Instead, it is used for table variables or for storage of rows for a table-valued function.
time	This stores the time to an accuracy of 100 nanoseconds, ranging from 00:00:00.0000000 to 23:59:59.9999999.
timestamp	This specifies a database-wide unique number that is updated when a row is modified.
tinyint	This specifies a whole number from 0 through 255.

Continued

Table 4-2. *Continued*

Data Type	Value Range
uniqueidentifier	This stores a 16-byte globally unique identifier (GUID).
varbinary	This specifies variable-length data with a maximum of 8000 bytes. SQL Server also has the max value, which allows you to store up to 2^31 –1bytes. This option allows you to use the regular data types instead of SQL Server 2000's text, ntext, and image.
varchar	This specifies variable-length character data with a maximum length of 8,000 characters. SQL Server also has the max value, which allows you to store up to 2^31 –1bytes. This option allows you to use the regular data types instead of SQL Server 2000's text, ntext, and image.
xml	This data type stores native XML data.

Following are some basic guidelines when selecting data types for your columns:

- Store character data types in character type columns (char, nchar, varchar, nvarcht), numeric data in numeric type columns (int, bigint, tinyint, smallmoney, money, decimal\numeric, float), and date and/or time data in smalldate, date, datetime2, time, datetimeoffset, or datetime data types. For example, although you *can* store numeric and datetime information in character-based fields, doing so may slow down your performance when attempting to utilize the column values within mathematical or other Transact-SQL functions.

- If your character data type columns use the same or a similar number of characters consistently, use fixed-length data types (char, nchar). Fixed-length columns consume the same amount of storage for each row, whether or not they are fully utilized. If, however, you expect that your character column's length will vary significantly from row to row, use variable-length data types (varchar, nvarchar). Variable-length columns have some storage overhead tacked on; however, they will only consume storage for characters used. Only use char or nchar if you are sure that you will have consistent lengths in your strings, and that most of your string values will be present.

- Choose the smallest numeric or character data type required to store the data. You may be tempted to select data types for columns that use more storage than is necessary, resulting in wasted storage. Conserving column space, particularly for very large tables, can increase the number of rows that can fit on an 8KB data page, reduce total storage needed in the database, and potentially improve index performance (smaller index keys).

A table can have up to 1024 columns (with the exception of sparse columns as of SQL Server 2008 RTM), but can't exceed a total of 8060 actual used bytes per row. A data page size is 8KB, including the header, which stores information about the page. This byte limit is not applied to the large object data types varchar(max), nvarchar(max), varbinary(max), text, image, or xml.

Another exception to the 8060-byte limit rule is SQL Server's *row overflow* functionality for regular varchar, nvarchar, varbinary, and sql_variant data types. If the lengths of these individual data types do not exceed 8,000 bytes, but the combined width of more than one of these columns together in a table exceeds the 8060-byte row limit, the column with the largest width will be dynamically moved to another 8KB page and replaced in the original table with a 24-byte pointer. Row overflow provides extra flexibility for managing large row sizes, but you should still limit your potential maximum variable data type length in your table definition when possible, as reliance on page overflow may decrease query performance, as more data pages need to be retrieved by a single query.

Creating a Table

In this recipe, I will create a simple table called EducationType owned by the Person schema:

```
USE AdventureWorks
GO

CREATE TABLE Person.EducationType
    (EducationTypeID int NOT NULL,
    EducationTypeNM varchar(40) NOT NULL)
```

How It Works

In this example, a very simple, two-column table was created within the AdventureWorks database using the Person schema. The first line of code shows the schema and table name:

```
CREATE TABLE Person.EducationType
```

The column definition follows on the second line of code within the parentheses:

```
(EducationTypeID int NOT NULL,
    EducationTypeNM varchar(40) NOT NULL)
```

The first column name, EducationTypeID, was defined with an integer data type and NOT NULL specified (meaning that NULL values are not allowed for this column). The second column was the EducationTypeNM column name with a data type of varchar(40) and the NOT NULL option.

In the next recipe, you'll learn how to add additional columns to an existing table.

Adding a Column to an Existing Table

After a table is created, you can modify it using the ALTER TABLE command. Like CREATE TABLE, this chapter will demonstrate the ALTER TABLE and CREATE TABLE functionality in task-based parts. In this recipe, I demonstrate how to add a column to an existing table.

The specific syntax for adding a column is as follows:

```
ALTER TABLE table_name
ADD { column_name data_type } NULL
```

Table 4-3 details the arguments of this command.

Table 4-3. *ALTER TABLE ADD Column Arguments*

Argument	Description
table_name	The table name you are adding the column to
column_name	The name of the column
data_type	The column's data type

This example demonstrates adding a column to an existing table (note that using this method adds the column to the last column position in the table definition):

```
ALTER TABLE HumanResources.Employee
ADD Latest_EducationTypeID int NULL
```

How It Works

ALTER TABLE was used to make modifications to an existing table. The first line of code designated the table to have the column added to:

```
ALTER TABLE HumanResources.Employee
```

The second line of code defined the new column and data type:

```
ADD Latest_EducationTypeID int NULL
```

When adding columns to a table that already has data in it, you will be required to add the column with NULL values allowed. You can't specify that the column be NOT NULL, because you cannot add the column to the table and simultaneously assign values to the new column. By default, the value of the new column will be NULL for every row in the table.

Changing an Existing Column Definition

In addition to adding new columns to a table, you can also use ALTER TABLE to modify an existing column's definition.

The syntax for doing this is as follows:

```
ALTER TABLE table_name
ALTER COLUMN column_name
[type_name] [NULL | NOT NULL] [COLLATE collation_name]
```

Table 4-4 details the arguments of this command.

Table 4-4. *ALTER TABLE...ALTER COLUMN Arguments*

Argument	Description
table_name	The table name containing the column to be modified.
column_name	The name of the column to modify.
type_name	The column's data type to modify.
NULL | NOT NULL	The nullability option to modify.
COLLATE collation_name	The column collation (for character-based data types) to modify. Collations define three settings: a code page used to store non-Unicode character data types, the sort order for non-Unicode character data types, and the sort order for Unicode data types. Collations are reviewed later on in the chapter in the section "Collation Basics."

This example demonstrates how to change an existing table column's nullability and data type. The Gender column in the HumanResources.Employee table is originally NOT NULL, and the original data type of the LoginID column is nvarchar(256):

```
-- Make it Nullable
ALTER TABLE HumanResources.Employee
ALTER COLUMN Gender nchar(1) NULL

-- Expanded nvarchar(256) to nvarchar(300)
ALTER TABLE HumanResources.Employee
ALTER COLUMN LoginID nvarchar(300) NOT NULL
```

How It Works

In this recipe, two columns were modified in the `HumanResources.Employee` table. The `ALTER COLUMN` modified the `Gender` column to allow `NULL` values, although the data type remained the same:

```
ALTER COLUMN Gender nchar(1) NULL
```

In the second `ALTER TABLE`, the `LoginID` column's data type of `nvarchar(256)` was expanded to `nvarchar(300)`:

```
ALTER COLUMN LoginID nvarchar(300) NOT NULL
```

There are limitations to the kind of column changes that can be made. For example, you can't alter a column that is used in an index unless the column data type is `varchar`, `nvarchar`, or `varbinary`—and even then, the new size of that data type must be *larger* than the original size. You also can't use `ALTER COLUMN` on columns referenced in a primary key or foreign key constraint. The full list of other column modification limitations (and there are quite a few) are documented in SQL Server Books Online.

Creating a Computed Column

A column defined within a `CREATE TABLE` or `ALTER TABLE` statement can be derived from a freestanding or column-based calculation. Computed columns are sometimes useful when a calculation must be recomputed on the same data repeatedly in referencing queries. A computed column is based on an expression defined when you create or alter the table, and is not physically stored in the table unless you use the `PERSISTED` keyword.

In this recipe, I'll give a demonstration of creating a computed column, as well as presenting ways to take advantage of SQL Server 2005's `PERSISTED` option. The syntax for adding a computed column either by `CREATE` or `ALTER TABLE` is as follows:

```
column_name AS computed_column_expression
[ PERSISTED ]
```

The `column_name` is the name of the new column. The `computed_column_expression` is the calculation you wish to be performed in order to derive the column's value. Adding the `PERSISTED` keyword actually causes the results of the calculation to be physically stored.

In this example, a new, calculated column is added to an existing table:

```
ALTER TABLE Production.TransactionHistory
ADD CostPerUnit AS (ActualCost/Quantity)
```

The previous example created a calculated column called `CostPerUnit`. This next query takes advantage of it, returning the highest `CostPerUnit` for quantities over 10:

```
SELECT TOP 1 CostPerUnit, Quantity, ActualCost
FROM Production.TransactionHistory
WHERE Quantity > 10
ORDER BY ActualCost DESC
```

This returns

CostPerUnit	Quantity	ActualCost
132.0408	13	1716.5304

The next example creates a `PERSISTED` calculated column, which means the calculated data will actually be physically stored in the database (but still automatically calculated by SQL Server):

```
CREATE TABLE HumanResources.CompanyStatistic
(CompanyID int NOT NULL,
 StockTicker char(4) NOT NULL,
 SharesOutstanding int NOT NULL,
 Shareholders int NOT NULL,
 AvgSharesPerShareholder AS (SharesOutStanding/Shareholders) PERSISTED)
```

How It Works

The first example added a new, non-persisted column called `CostPerUnit` to the `Production.TransactionHistory` table, allowing it to be referenced in `SELECT` queries like a regular table column:

```
ADD CostPerUnit AS (ActualCost/Quantity)
```

Computed columns can't be used within a `DEFAULT` or `FOREIGN KEY` constraint. A calculated column can't be explicitly updated or inserted into (since its value is always derived).

Computed columns can be used within indexes, but must meet certain requirements, such as being deterministic (always returning the same result for a given set of inputs) and precise (not containing float values).

The second example demonstrated using a computed column in a `CREATE TABLE` command:

```
AvgSharesPerShareholder AS (SharesOutStanding/Shareholders) PERSISTED
```

Unlike the first example, adding the `PERSISTED` keyword means that the data is actually physically stored in the database. Any changes made to columns that are used in the computation will cause the stored value to be updated again. The stored data still can't be modified directly—the data is still computed. Storing the data does mean, however, that the column can be used to partition a table (see the "Implementing Table Partitioning" recipe later in the chapter), or can be used in an index with an imprecise (float-based) value—unlike its non-persisted version.

Reducing Storage for Null Columns

SQL Server 2008 introduces *sparse columns*, a storage optimization improvement that enables zero-byte storage of `NULL` values. Consequently, this allows a large number of sparse columns to be defined for a table (as of this writing, 30,000 sparse columns are allowed). This improvement is ideal for database designs and applications requiring a high number of infrequently populated columns or for tables having sets of columns related only with a subset of the data stored in the table.

To define a sparse column, you need only add the `SPARSE` storage attribute after the column definition within a `CREATE` or `ALTER TABLE` command, as the following query demonstrates:

```
CREATE TABLE dbo.WebsiteProduct
(WebsiteProductID int NOT NULL PRIMARY KEY IDENTITY(1,1),
 ProductNM varchar(255) NOT NULL,
 PublisherNM varchar(255) SPARSE NULL,
 ArtistNM varchar(150) SPARSE NULL,
 ISBNNBR varchar(30) SPARSE NULL,
 DiscsNBR int SPARSE NULL,
 MusicLabelNM varchar(255) SPARSE NULL)
```

The previous table takes a somewhat denormalized approach to creating columns that apply only to specific product types. For example, the `PublisherNM` and `ISBNNBR` columns apply to a book product, whereas `DiscsNBR`, `ArtistNM`, and `MusicLabelNM` will more often apply to a music product. When a product row is stored, the sparse columns that do not apply to it will *not* incur a storage cost for each `NULL` value.

Continuing the demonstration, I'll insert two new rows into the table (one representing a book and one a music album):

```
INSERT dbo.WebsiteProduct
(ProductNM, PublisherNM, ISBNNBR)
VALUES
('SQL Server 2008 Transact-SQL Recipes',
 'Apress',
 '1590599802')

INSERT dbo.WebsiteProduct
(ProductNM, ArtistNM, DiscsNBR, MusicLabelNM)
VALUES
('Etiquette',
 'Casiotone for the Painfully Alone',
 1,
 'Tomlab')
```

Sparse columns can be queried using a couple of methods. The following is an example of using a standard method of querying:

```
SELECT ProductNM, PublisherNM,ISBNNBR
  FROM dbo.WebsiteProduct
  WHERE ISBNNBR IS NOT NULL
```

This returns

ProductNM	PublisherNM	ISBNNBR
SQL Server 2008 Transact-SQL Recipes	Apress	1590599802

The second method is to use a column set. A *column set* allows you to logically group all sparse columns defined for the table. This xml data type calculated column allows for SELECTs and data modification and is defined by designating COLUMN_SET FOR ALL_SPARSE_COLUMNS after the column definition. You can only have one column set for a single table, and you also can't add one to a table that already has sparse columns defined in it. In this next example, I'll re-create the previous table with a column set included:

```
DROP TABLE dbo.WebsiteProduct

CREATE TABLE dbo.WebsiteProduct
(WebsiteProductID int NOT NULL PRIMARY KEY IDENTITY(1,1),
 ProductNM varchar(255) NOT NULL,
 PublisherNM varchar(255) SPARSE NULL,
 ArtistNM varchar(150) SPARSE NULL,
 ISBNNBR varchar(30) SPARSE NULL,
 DiscsNBR int SPARSE NULL,
 MusicLabelNM varchar(255) SPARSE NULL,
 ProductAttributeCS xml COLUMN_SET FOR ALL_SPARSE_COLUMNS)

-- Re-insert data
INSERT dbo.WebsiteProduct
(ProductNM, PublisherNM, ISBNNBR)
VALUES
('SQL Server 2008 Transact-SQL Recipes',
 'Apress',
 '1590599802')
```

```
INSERT dbo.WebsiteProduct
(ProductNM, ArtistNM, DiscsNBR, MusicLabelNM)
VALUES
('Etiquette',
 'Casiotone for the Painfully Alone',
 1,
 'Tomlab')
```

Now that the column set is defined, I can reference it instead of the individual sparse columns:

```
SELECT ProductNM, ProductAttributeCS
  FROM dbo.WebsiteProduct
  WHERE ProductNM IS NOT NULL
```

This returns

ProductNM	ProductAttributeCS
SQL Server 2008 Transact-SQL Recipes	`<PublisherNM>Apress</PublisherNM><ISBNNBR>` `1590599802</ISBNNBR>`

Etiquette	`<ArtistNM>Casiotone for the Painfully Alone`
	`</ArtistNM><DiscsNBR>1</DiscsNBR>< MusicLabelNM>`
	`Tomlab</ MusicLabelNM>`

As you can see from the previous results, each row shows untyped XML data that displays elements for each non-NULL column value.

I can use both an INSERT and UPDATE to modify the values across all sparse columns. The following query demonstrates adding a new row:

```
INSERT dbo.WebsiteProduct
  (ProductNM,ProductAttributeCS)
  VALUES
  ('Roots & Echoes',
   '<ArtistNM>The Coral</ArtistNM>
   <DiscsNBR>1</DiscsNBR>
   <MusicLabelNM>Deltasonic</ MusicLabelNM>')
```

Any sparse columns not referenced in my DML operation will be set to a NULL value. Once a column set is defined for a table, performing a SELECT * query no longer returns each individual sparse column, as the following query demonstrates (only non-sparse columns and then the column set):

```
SELECT *
FROM dbo.WebsiteProduct
```

WebsiteProductID	ProductNM	ProductAttributeCS

1	SQL Server 2008 Transact-SQL Recipes	`<PublisherNM>Apress`
		`</PublisherNM><ISBNNBR>`
		`1590599802</ISBNNBR>`

2	Etiquette	`<ArtistNM>Casiotone for the`
		`Painfully Alone</ArtistNM>`
		`<DiscsNBR>1</DiscsNBR>`
		`<MusicLabelNBR>Tomlab`
		`</MusicLabelNBR>`

3	Roots & Echoes	`<ArtistNM>The Coral</ArtistNM>`
		`<DiscsNBR>1</DiscsNBR>`
		`<MusicLabelNM>Deltasonic`
		`</MusicLabelNNM>`

You still, however, have the option of explicitly naming each sparse column you wish to see, rather than viewing the entire sparse column:

```
SELECT ProductNM, ArtistNM
FROM dbo.WebsiteProduct
WHERE ArtistNM IS NOT NULL
```

This returns

ProductNM	ArtistNM
Etiquette	Casiotone for the Painfully Alone
Roots & Echoes	The Coral

How It Works

The sparse column storage attribute allows you to store up to 30,000 infrequently populated columns on a single table. As demonstrated in this recipe, defining a column as SPARSE is as simple as adding the name within the column definition:

```
CREATE TABLE dbo.WebsiteProduct
...
ArtistNM varchar(150) SPARSE NULL,
...
```

Most data types are allowed for a sparse column, with the exception of the image, ntext, text, timestamp, geometry, geography, or user-defined data types.

■**Caution** Sparse columns also add *more* required space for non-null values than for regular non-sparse, non-null columns.

This recipe also demonstrated the use of a column set, which was defined within the column definition during the CREATE TABLE (but can also be added using ALTER TABLE if no other column set or sparse columns exist):

```
CREATE TABLE dbo.WebsiteProduct
...
ProductAttributeCS xml COLUMN_SET FOR ALL_SPARSE_COLUMNS)
```

The column set becomes particularly useful when a table has thousands of sparse tables, as it allows you to avoid directly referencing each sparse column name in your query. The column set allows querying and DML operations. When performing an INSERT or UPDATE, all unreferenced sparse columns are set to NULL and have zero-byte storage.

Dropping a Table Column

You can use ALTER TABLE to drop a column from an existing table.

The syntax for doing so is as follows:

```
ALTER TABLE table_name
DROP COLUMN column_name
```

Table 4-5 details the arguments of this command.

Table 4-5. *ALTER TABLE...DROP COLUMN Arguments*

Argument	Description
table_name	The table name containing the column to be dropped
column_name	The name of the column to drop from the table

This recipe demonstrates how to drop a column from an existing table:

```
ALTER TABLE HumanResources.Employee
DROP COLUMN Latest_EducationTypeID
```

How It Works

The first line of code designated the table for which the column would be dropped:

```
ALTER TABLE HumanResources.Employee
```

The second line designated the column to be dropped from the table (along with any data stored in it):

```
DROP COLUMN Latest_EducationTypeID
```

You can drop a column only if it isn't being used in a PRIMARY KEY, FOREIGN KEY, UNIQUE, or CHECK CONSTRAINT (these constraint types are all covered in this chapter). You also can't drop a column being used in an index or that has a DEFAULT value bound to it.

Reporting Table Information

The system stored procedure sp_help returns information about the specified table, including the column definitions, IDENTITY column, ROWGUIDCOL, filegroup location, indexes (and keys), CHECK, DEFAULT, and FOREIGN KEY constraints, and referencing views.

The syntax for this system stored procedure is as follows:

```
sp_help [ [ @objname = ] ' name ' ]
```

This example demonstrates how to report detailed information about the object or table (the results aren't shown here as they include several columns and multiple result sets):

```
EXEC sp_help 'HumanResources.Employee'
```

How It Works

The sp_help system stored procedure returns several different result sets with useful information regarding the specific object (in this example, it returns data about the table HumanResources. Employee). This system stored procedure can be used to gather information regarding other database object types as well.

Dropping a Table

In this recipe, I'll demonstrate how to drop a table. The DROP command uses the following syntax:

```
DROP TABLE schema.tablename
```

The DROP TABLE takes a single argument, the name of the table. In this example, the Person. EducationType table is dropped:

```
DROP TABLE Person.EducationType
```

How It Works

The DROP command removes the table definition and its data permanently from the database. In this example, the DROP command would have failed had another table been referencing the table's primary key in a foreign key constraint. If there are foreign key references, you must drop them first before dropping the primary key table.

Collation Basics

If your database requires international or multilingual data storage, your default SQL Server instance settings may not be sufficient for the task. This recipe describes how to view and manipulate code pages and sort order settings using collations. SQL Server collations determine how data is sorted, compared, presented, and stored.

SQL Server allows two types of collations: Windows or SQL. Windows collations are the preferred selection, as they offer more options and match the same support provided with Microsoft Windows locales. SQL collations are used in earlier versions of SQL Server and are maintained for backward compatibility.

In addition to SQL Server and database-level collation settings, you can also configure individual columns with their own collation settings. If you need to store character data in a column that uses a different default collation than your database or server-level collation, you use the COLLATE command within the column definition.

The Windows or SQL collation can be explicitly defined during a CREATE TABLE or ALTER TABLE operation for columns that use the varchar, char, nchar, and nvarchar data types.

Collations define three settings:

- A code page used to store non-Unicode character data types
- The sort order for non-Unicode character data types
- The sort order for Unicode data types

Your SQL Server instance's default collation was determined during the install, where you either used the default-selected collation or explicitly changed it. The next two recipes will demonstrate how to view information about the collations on your SQL Server instance, as well as define an explicit collation for a table column.

Viewing Collation Metadata

You can determine your SQL Server instance's default collation by using the SERVERPROPERTY function and the Collation option. For example:

```
SELECT SERVERPROPERTY('Collation')
```

This returns (for this example's SQL Server instance)

```
SQL_Latin1_General_CP1_CI_AS
```

In addition to the SQL Server instance's default collation settings, your database can also have a default collation defined for it. You can use the DATABASEPROPERTYEX system function to determine a database's default collation. For example, this next query determines the default database collation for the AdventureWorks database (first parameter is database name, second is the Collation option to be viewed):

```
SELECT DATABASEPROPERTYEX ( 'AdventureWorks' , 'Collation' )
```

This returns the following collation information for the database (which in this example is going to be the same as the SQL Server instance default until explicitly changed):

```
SQL_Latin1_General_CP1_CI_AS
```

■**Note** See Chapter 8 for more information on the SERVERPROPERTY and DATABASEPROPERTYEX functions.

But what do the results of these collation functions mean? To determine the actual settings that a collation applies to the SQL Server instance or database, you can query the table function fn_helpcollations for a more user-friendly description. In this example, the collation description is returned from the SQL_Latin1_General_CP1_CI_AS collation:

```
SELECT description
FROM sys.fn_helpcollations()
WHERE name = 'SQL_Latin1_General_CP1_CI_AS'
```

This returns the collation description:

```
description
Latin1-General, case-insensitive, accent-sensitive, kanatype-insensitive, width-
insensitive for Unicode Data, SQL Server Sort Order 52 on Code Page 1252 for non-
Unicode Data
```

The results show a more descriptive breakdown of the collation's code page, case sensitivity, sorting, and Unicode options.

How It Works

This recipe demonstrated how to view the default collation for a SQL Server instance and for specific databases. You also saw how to list the collation's code page, case sensitivity, sorting, and Unicode options using fn_helpcollations. Once you know what settings your current database environment is using, you may decide to apply different collations to table columns when internationalization is required. This is demonstrated in the next recipe.

Designating a Column's Collation

In this recipe, I'll demonstrate how to designate the collation of a table column using the ALTER TABLE command:

```
ALTER TABLE Production.Product
ADD IcelandicProductName nvarchar(50) COLLATE Icelandic_CI_AI,
UkrainianProductName nvarchar(50) COLLATE Ukrainian_CI_AS
```

How It Works

In this recipe, two new columns were added to the `Production.Product` table. The query began by using `ALTER TABLE` and the table name:

```
ALTER TABLE Production.Product
```

After that, `ADD` was used, followed by the new column name, data type, `COLLATE` keyword, and collation name (for a list of collation names, use the `fn_helpcollations` function described earlier):

```
ADD IcelandicProductName nvarchar(50) COLLATE Icelandic_CI_AI,
UkrainianProductName nvarchar(50) COLLATE Ukrainian_CI_AS
```

Be aware that when you define different collations within the same database or across databases in the same SQL Server instance, you can sometimes encounter compatibility issues. Cross-collation joins don't always work, and data transfers can result in lost or misinterpreted data.

Keys

A *primary key* is a special type of constraint that identifies a single column or set of columns, which in turn uniquely identifies all rows in the table.

Constraints place limitations on the data that can be entered into a column or columns. A primary key enforces *entity integrity*, meaning that rows are guaranteed to be unambiguous and unique. Best practices for database normalization dictate that every table should have a primary key. A primary key provides a way to access the record and ensures that the key is unique. A primary key column can't contain `NULL` values.

Only one primary key is allowed for a table, and when a primary key is designated, an underlying table *index* is automatically created, defaulting to a clustered index (index types are reviewed in Chapter 5). You can also explicitly designate a nonclustered index be created when the primary key is created instead, if you have a better use for the single clustered index allowed for a table. An index created on primary key counts against the total indexes allowed for a table.

To designate a primary key on a single column, use the following syntax in the column definition:

```
( column_name <data_type> [ NULL | NOT NULL ] PRIMARY KEY  )
```

The key words `PRIMARY KEY` are included at the end of the column definition.

A *composite primary key* is the unique combination of *more* than one column in the table. In order to define a composite primary key, you must use a *table constraint* instead of a *column constraint*. Setting a single column as the primary key within the column definition is called a column constraint. Defining the primary key (single or composite) outside of the column definition is referred to as a table constraint.

The syntax for a table constraint for a primary key is as follows:

```
CONSTRAINT constraint_name  PRIMARY KEY
(column [ ASC | DESC ] [ ,...n ] )
```

Table 4-6 details the arguments of this command.

Table 4-6. *Table Constraint, Primary Key Arguments*

Argument	Description
constraint_name	This specifies the unique name of the constraint to be added.
column [ASC | DESC] [,...n]	The column or columns that make up the primary key must uniquely identify a single row in the table (no two rows can have the same values for all the specified columns). The ASC (ascending) and DESC (descending) options define the sorting order of the columns within the clustered or nonclustered index.

Foreign key constraints establish and enforce relationships between tables and help maintain referential integrity, which means that every value in the foreign key column must exist in the corresponding column for the referenced table. Foreign key constraints also help define domain integrity, in that they define the range of potential and allowed values for a specific column or columns. Domain integrity defines the validity of values in a column.

The basic syntax for a foreign key constraint is as follows:

```
CONSTRAINT constraint_name
FOREIGN KEY (column_name)
REFERENCES [ schema_name.] referenced_table_name [ ( ref_column ) ]
```

Table 4-7 details the arguments of this command.

Table 4-7. *Foreign Key Constraint Arguments*

Argument	Description
constraint_name	The name of the foreign key constraint
column_name	The column in the current table referencing the primary key column of the primary key table
[schema_name.] referenced_table_name	The table name containing the primary key being referenced by the current table
ref_column	The primary key column being referenced

The next few recipes will demonstrate primary and foreign key usage in action.

Creating a Table with a Primary Key

In this recipe, I'll create a table with a single column primary key:

```
CREATE TABLE Person.CreditRating(
   CreditRatingID int NOT NULL PRIMARY KEY,
   CreditRatingNM varchar(40) NOT NULL)
GO
```

In the previous example, a primary key was defined on a single column. You can, however, create a composite primary key.

In this example, a new table is created with a PRIMARY KEY table constraint formed from two columns:

```
CREATE TABLE Person.EmployeeEducationType (
    EmployeeID int NOT NULL,
    EducationTypeID int NOT NULL,
    CONSTRAINT PK_EmployeeEducationType
    PRIMARY KEY (EmployeeID, EducationTypeID))
```

How It Works

In the first example of the recipe, I created the Person.CreditRating table with a single-column primary key. The column definition had the PRIMARY KEY keywords following the column definition:

```
CreditRatingID int NOT NULL PRIMARY KEY,
```

The primary key column was defined at the column level, whereas the second example defines the primary key at the table level:

```
CONSTRAINT PK_EmployeeEducationType
    PRIMARY KEY (EmployeeID, EducationTypeID))
```

The constraint definition followed the column definitions. The constraint was named, and then followed by the constraint type (PRIMARY KEY) and the columns forming the primary key in parentheses.

Adding a Primary Key Constraint to an Existing Table

In this recipe, I'll demonstrate how to add a primary key to an existing table using ALTER TABLE and ADD CONSTRAINT:

```
CREATE TABLE Person.EducationType
    (EducationTypeID int NOT NULL,
    EducationTypeNM varchar(40) NOT NULL)

ALTER TABLE Person.EducationType
ADD CONSTRAINT PK_EducationType
PRIMARY KEY (EducationTypeID)
```

How It Works

In this recipe, ALTER TABLE was used to add a new primary key to an existing table that doesn't already have one defined. The first line of code defined the table to add the primary key to:

```
ALTER TABLE Person.EducationType
```

The second line of code defined the constraint name:

```
ADD CONSTRAINT PK_EducationType
```

On the last line of code in the previous example, the constraint type PRIMARY KEY was declared, followed by the column defining the key column in parentheses:

```
PRIMARY KEY (EducationTypeID)
```

Creating a Table with a Foreign Key Reference

In this recipe, I'll demonstrate how to create a table with a foreign key. In this example, I define two foreign key references within the definition of a CREATE TABLE statement:

```
CREATE TABLE Person.EmployeeCreditRating(
    EmployeeCreditRating int NOT NULL PRIMARY KEY,
    BusinessEntityID int NOT NULL,
    CreditRatingID int NOT NULL,
    CONSTRAINT FK_EmployeeCreditRating_Employee
    FOREIGN KEY(BusinessEntityID)
    REFERENCES HumanResources.Employee(BusinessEntityID),
    CONSTRAINT FK_EmployeeCreditRating_CreditRating
    FOREIGN KEY(CreditRatingID)
    REFERENCES Person.CreditRating(CreditRatingID)
)
```

How It Works

In this example, a table was created with two foreign key references. The first four lines of code defined the table name and its three columns:

```
CREATE TABLE Person.EmployeeCreditRating(
    EmployeeCreditRating int NOT NULL PRIMARY KEY,
    BusinessEntityID int NOT NULL,
    CreditRatingID int NOT NULL,
```

On the next line, the name of the first foreign key constraint is defined (must be a unique name in the current database):

```
CONSTRAINT FK_EmployeeCreditRating_Employee
```

The constraint type is defined, followed by the table's column (which will be referencing an outside primary key table):

```
FOREIGN KEY(BusinessEntityID)
```

The referenced table is defined, with that table's primary key column defined in parentheses:

```
REFERENCES HumanResources.Employee(BusinessEntityID),
```

A second foreign key is then created for the CreditRatingID column, which references the primary key of the Person.CreditRating table:

```
CONSTRAINT FK_EmployeeCreditRating_CreditRating
FOREIGN KEY(CreditRatingID)
REFERENCES Person.CreditRating(CreditRatingID)
)
```

As I demonstrated in this example, a table can have multiple foreign keys—and each foreign key can be based on a single or multiple (composite) key that references more than one column (referencing composite primary keys or unique indexes). Also, although the column names needn't be the same between a foreign key reference and a primary key, the primary key/unique columns must have the same data type. You also can't define foreign key constraints that reference tables across databases or servers.

Adding a Foreign Key to an Existing Table

Using ALTER TABLE and ADD CONSTRAINT, you can add a foreign key to an existing table. The syntax for doing so is as follows:

```
ALTER TABLE table_name
ADD CONSTRAINT  constraint_name
FOREIGN KEY (column_name)
REFERENCES [ schema_name.] referenced_table_name [ ( ref_column ) ]
```

Table 4-8 details the arguments of this command.

Table 4-8. *ALTER TABLE...ADD CONSTRAINT Arguments*

Argument	Description
table_name	The name of the table receiving the new foreign key constraint
constraint_name	The name of the foreign key constraint
column_name	The column in the current table referencing the primary key column of the primary key table
[schema_name.] referenced_table_name	The table name containing the primary key being referenced by the current table
ref_column	The primary key column being referenced

This example adds a foreign key constraint to an existing table:

```
CREATE TABLE Person.EmergencyContact (
   EmergencyContactID int NOT NULL PRIMARY KEY,
   BusinessEntityID int NOT NULL,
   ContactFirstNM varchar(50) NOT NULL,
   ContactLastNM varchar(50) NOT NULL,
   ContactPhoneNBR varchar(25) NOT NULL)

ALTER TABLE Person.EmergencyContact
ADD CONSTRAINT FK_EmergencyContact_Employee
FOREIGN KEY (BusinessEntityID)
REFERENCES HumanResources.Employee (BusinessEntityID)
```

How It Works

This example demonstrated adding a foreign key constraint to an existing table. The first line of code defined the table where the foreign key would be added:

```
ALTER TABLE Person.EmergencyContact
```

The second line defined the constraint name:

```
ADD CONSTRAINT FK_EmergencyContact_Employee
```

The third line defined the column from the table that will reference the primary key of the primary key table:

```
FOREIGN KEY (BusinessEntityID)
```

The last line of code defined the primary key table and primary key column name:

```
REFERENCES HumanResources.Employee (BusinessEntityID)
```

Creating Recursive Foreign Key References

A foreign key column in a table can be defined to reference its own primary/unique key. This technique is often used to represent recursive relationships, as I'll demonstrate. In this example, a table is created with a foreign key reference to its own primary key:

```
CREATE TABLE HumanResources.Company
    (CompanyID int NOT NULL PRIMARY KEY,
     ParentCompanyID int NULL,
     CompanyName varchar(25) NOT NULL,
     CONSTRAINT FK_Company_Company
     FOREIGN KEY (ParentCompanyID)
     REFERENCES HumanResources.Company(CompanyID))
```

A row specifying `CompanyID` and `CompanyName` is added to the table:

```
INSERT HumanResources.Company
(CompanyID, CompanyName)
VALUES(1, 'MegaCorp')
```

A second row is added, this time referencing the `ParentCompanyID`, which is equal to the previously inserted row:

```
INSERT HumanResources.Company
(CompanyID, ParentCompanyID, CompanyName)
VALUES(2, 1, 'Medi-Corp')
```

A third row insert is attempted, this time specifying a `ParentCompanyID` for a `CompanyID` that does *not* exist in the table:

```
INSERT HumanResources.Company
(CompanyID, ParentCompanyID, CompanyName)
VALUES(3, 8, 'Tiny-Corp')
```

The following error message is returned:

```
Msg 547, Level 16, State 0, Line 1
The INSERT statement conflicted with the FOREIGN KEY SAME TABLE constraint
 "FK_Company_Company". The conflict occurred in database "AdventureWorks", table
"Company", column 'CompanyID'.
The statement has been terminated.
```

How It Works

In this example, the `HumanResources.Company` table was created with the `CompanyID` column defined as the primary key, and with a foreign key column defined on `ParentCompanyID` that references `CompanyID`:

```
CONSTRAINT FK_Company_Company
    FOREIGN KEY (ParentCompanyID)
    REFERENCES HumanResources.Company(CompanyID)
```

The foreign key column ParentCompanyID must be nullable in order to handle a parent-child hierarchy. A company with a NULL parent is at the top of the company hierarchy (which means it doesn't have a parent company). After the table was created, three new rows were inserted.

The first row inserted a company without designating the ParentCompanyID (which means the value for the ParentCompanyID column for this company is NULL):

```
INSERT HumanResources.Company
(CompanyID, CompanyName)
VALUES(1, 'MegaCorp')
```

The second insert created a company that references the first company, MegaCorp, defined in the previous INSERT statement. The value of 1 was valid in the ParentCompanyID column, as it refers to the previously inserted row:

```
INSERT HumanResources.Company
(CompanyID, ParentCompanyID, CompanyName)
VALUES(2, 1, 'Medi-Corp')
```

The third insert tries to create a new company with a ParentCompanyID of 8, which does not exist in the table:

```
INSERT HumanResources.Company
(CompanyID, ParentCompanyID, CompanyName)
VALUES(3, 8, 'Tiny-Corp')
```

Because there is no company with a CompanyID of 8 in the table, the foreign key constraint prevents the row from being inserted and reports an error. The row is not inserted.

Allowing Cascading Changes in Foreign Keys

Foreign keys restrict the values that can be placed within the foreign key column or columns. If the associated primary key or unique value does not exist in the reference table, the INSERT or UPDATE to the table row fails. This restriction is bidirectional in that if an attempt is made to delete a primary key, but a row referencing that specific key exists in the foreign key table, an error will be returned. All referencing foreign key rows must be deleted prior to deleting the targeted primary key or unique value; otherwise, an error will be raised.

SQL Server provides an automatic mechanism for handling changes in the primary key/unique key column, called *cascading changes*. In previous recipes, cascading options weren't used. You can allow cascading changes for deletions or updates using ON DELETE and ON UPDATE. The basic syntax for cascading options is as follows:

```
[ ON DELETE { NO ACTION | CASCADE | SET NULL | SET DEFAULT } ]
[ ON UPDATE { NO ACTION | CASCADE | SET NULL | SET DEFAULT } ]
[ NOT FOR REPLICATION ]
```

Table 4-9 details the arguments of this command.

Table 4-9. *Cascading Change Arguments*

Argument	Description
NO ACTION	The default setting for a new foreign key is NO ACTION, meaning if an attempt to delete a row on the primary key/unique column occurs when there is a referencing value in a foreign key table, the attempt will raise an error and prevent the statement from executing.
CASCADE	For ON DELETE, if CASCADE is chosen, foreign key rows referencing the deleted primary key are also deleted. For ON UPDATE, foreign key rows referencing the updated primary key are also updated.

Continued

Table 4-9. *Continued*

Argument	Description
SET NULL	If the primary key row is deleted, the foreign key referencing row(s) can also be set to NULL (assuming NULL values are allowed for that foreign key column).
SET DEFAULT	If the primary key row is deleted, the foreign key referencing row(s) can also be set to a DEFAULT value. The new cascade SET DEFAULT option assumes the column has a default value set for a column. If not, and the column is nullable, a NULL value is set.
NOT FOR REPLICATION	The NOT FOR REPLICATION option is used to prevent foreign key constraints from being enforced by SQL Server Replication Agent processes (allowing data to arrive via replication potentially out-of-order from the primary key data).

In this example, a table is created using cascading options:

```
-- Drop old version of table
DROP TABLE Person.EmployeeEducationType

CREATE TABLE Person.EmployeeEducationType(
   EmployeeEducationTypeID int NOT NULL PRIMARY KEY,
   BusinessEntityID int NOT NULL,
   EducationTypeID int NULL,
   CONSTRAINT FK_EmployeeEducationType_Employee
   FOREIGN KEY(BusinessEntityID)
   REFERENCES HumanResources.Employee(BusinessEntityID)
   ON DELETE CASCADE,
   CONSTRAINT FK_EmployeeEducationType_EducationType
   FOREIGN KEY(EducationTypeID)
   REFERENCES Person.EducationType(EducationTypeID)
   ON UPDATE SET NULL)
```

How It Works

In this recipe, one of the foreign key constraints uses ON DELETE CASCADE in a CREATE TABLE definition:

```
CONSTRAINT FK_EmployeeEducationType_Employee
   FOREIGN KEY(BusinessEntityID)
   REFERENCES HumanResources.Employee(BusinessEntityID)
   ON DELETE CASCADE
```

Using this cascade option, if a row is deleted on the HumanResources.Employee table, any referencing BusinessEntityID in the Person.EmployeeEducationType table will also be deleted.

A second foreign key constraint was also defined in the CREATE TABLE using ON UPDATE:

```
CONSTRAINT FK_EmployeeEducationType_EducationType
   FOREIGN KEY(EducationTypeID)
   REFERENCES Person.EducationType(EducationTypeID)
   ON UPDATE SET NULL
```

If an update is made to the primary key of the Person.EducationType table, the EducationTypeID column in the referencing Person.EmployeeEducationType table will be set to NULL.

Surrogate Keys

Surrogate keys, also called *artificial keys,* can be used as primary keys and have no inherent business/data meaning. Surrogate keys are independent of the data itself and are used to provide a single unique record locator in the table. A big advantage to surrogate primary keys is that they don't need to change. If you use business data to define your key (natural key), such as first name and last name, these values can change over time and change arbitrarily. Surrogate keys don't have to change, as their only meaning is within the context of the table itself.

The next few recipes will demonstrate methods for generating and managing surrogate keys using IDENTITY property columns and uniqueidentifier data type columns.

The IDENTITY column property allows you to define an automatically incrementing numeric value for a single column in a table. An IDENTITY column is most often used for surrogate primary key columns, as they are more compact than non-numeric data type natural keys. When a new row is inserted into a table with an IDENTITY column property, the column is inserted with a unique incremented value. The data type for an IDENTITY column can be int, tinyint, smallint, bigint, decimal, or numeric. Tables may only have one identity column defined, and the defined IDENTITY column can't have a DEFAULT or rule settings associated with it.

The basic syntax for an IDENTITY property column is as follows:

```
[ IDENTITY [ ( seed ,increment ) ] [NOT FOR REPLICATION] ]
```

The IDENTITY property takes two values: seed and increment. seed defines the starting number for the IDENTITY column, and increment defines the value added to the previous IDENTITY column value to get the value for the next row added to the table. The default for both seed and increment is 1. The NOT FOR REPLICATION option preserves the original values of the publisher IDENTITY column data when replicated to the subscriber, retaining any values referenced by foreign key constraints (preventing the break of relationships between tables that may use the IDENTITY column as a primary key and foreign key reference).

Unlike the IDENTITY column, which guarantees uniqueness within the defined table, the ROWGUIDCOL property ensures a very high level of uniqueness (Microsoft claims that it can be unique for every database *networked* in the world). This is important for those applications that merge data from multiple sources, where the unique values cannot be duplicated across tables. This unique ID is stored in a uniqueidentifier data type and is generated by the NEWID system function. The ROWGUIDCOL is a marker designated in a column definition, allowing you to query a table not only by the column's name, but also by the ROWGUIDCOL designator, as this recipe demonstrates.

Which surrogate key data type is preferred? Although using a uniqueidentifier data type with a NEWID value for a primary key may be more unique, it takes up more space than an integer-based IDENTITY column. If you only care about unique values within the table, you may be better off using an integer surrogate key, particularly for very large tables. However, if uniqueness is an absolute requirement, with the expectation that you may be merging data sources in the future, uniqueidentifier with NEWID may be your best choice.

The next set of recipes will demonstrate IDENTITY and ROWGUIDCOL properties in action.

Using the IDENTITY Property During Table Creation

In this example, I'll demonstrate how to create a new table with a primary key IDENTITY column. The IDENTITY keyword is placed after the nullability option but before the PRIMARY KEY keywords:

```
CREATE TABLE HumanResources.CompanyAuditHistory
   (CompanyAuditHistory int NOT NULL IDENTITY(1,1) PRIMARY KEY,
   CompanyID int NOT NULL ,
   AuditReasonDESC varchar(50) NOT NULL,
   AuditDT datetime NOT NULL DEFAULT GETDATE())
```

Two rows are inserted into the new table:

```
INSERT HumanResources.CompanyAuditHistory
(CompanyID, AuditReasonDESC, AuditDT)
VALUES
(1, 'Bad 1099 numbers.', '6/1/2009')

INSERT HumanResources.CompanyAuditHistory
(CompanyID, AuditReasonDESC, AuditDT)
VALUES
(1, 'Missing financial statement.', '7/1/2009')
```

Even though the `CompanyAuditHistory` column wasn't explicitly populated with the two inserts, querying the table shows that the `IDENTITY` property on the column caused the values to be populated:

```
SELECT CompanyAuditHistory, AuditReasonDESC
FROM HumanResources.CompanyAuditHistory
```

This returns

```
CompanyAuditHistory    AuditReasonDESC
1                      Bad 1099 numbers.
2                      Missing financial statement.
```

How It Works

In this example, an `IDENTITY` column was defined for a new table. The `IDENTITY` property was designated after the column definition, but before the `PRIMARY KEY` definition:

```
CompanyAuditHistory int NOT NULL IDENTITY(1,1) PRIMARY KEY
```

After creating the table, two rows were inserted without explicitly inserting the `CompanyAuditHistory` column value. After selecting from the table, these two rows were automatically assigned values based on the `IDENTITY` property, beginning with a seed value of 1, and incrementing by 1 for each new row.

Using DBCC CHECKIDENT to View and Correct IDENTITY Seed Values

In this recipe, I'll show you how to check the current `IDENTITY` value of a column for a table by using the `DBCC CHECKIDENT` command. `DBCC CHECKIDENT` checks the current maximum value for the specified table. The syntax for this command is as follows:

```
DBCC CHECKIDENT
( 'table_name' [ , {NORESEED | { RESEED [ , new_reseed_value ] }}])
[ WITH NO_INFOMSGS ]
```

Table 4-10 details the arguments of this command.

Table 4-10. *CHECKIDENT Arguments*

Argument	Description
table_name	This indicates the name of the table to check IDENTITY values for.
NORESEED | RESEED	NORESEED means that no action is taken other than to report the maximum identity value. RESEED specifies what the current IDENTITY value should be.
new_reseed_value	This specifies the new current IDENTITY value.
WITH NO_INFOMSGS	When included in the command, WITH NO_INFOMSGS suppresses informational messages from the DBCC output.

In this example, the current table IDENTITY value is checked:

```
DBCC CHECKIDENT('HumanResources.CompanyAuditHistory', NORESEED)
```

This returns

```
Checking identity information: current identity value '2',
current column value '2'.
DBCC execution completed. If DBCC printed error messages,
contact your system administrator.
```

This second example resets the seed value to a higher number:

```
DBCC CHECKIDENT ('HumanResources.CompanyAuditHistory', RESEED, 50)
```

This returns

```
Checking identity information: current identity value '2',
current column value '50'.
DBCC execution completed. If DBCC printed error messages,
contact your system administrator.
```

How It Works

The first example demonstrated checking the current IDENTITY value using the DBCC CHECKIDENT and the NORESEED option. The second example demonstrated actually resetting the IDENTITY value to a higher value. Any future inserts will begin from that value.

Why make such a change? DBCC CHECKIDENT with RESEED is often used to fill primary key gaps. If you deleted rows from the table that had the highest value for the IDENTITY column, the used identity values will not be reused the next time records are inserted into the table. For example, if the last row inserted had a value of 22, and you deleted that row, the next inserted row would be 23. Just because the value is deleted doesn't mean the SQL Server will backfill the gap. If you need to reuse key values (which is generally OK to do in the test phase of your database—in production you really shouldn't reuse primary key values), you can use DBCC CHECKIDENT to reuse numbers after a large row deletion.

Using the ROWGUIDCOL Property

First, a table is created using ROWGUIDCOL, identified after the column data type definition but before the default definition (populated via the NEWID system function):

```
CREATE TABLE HumanResources.BuildingAccess
 (   BuildingEntryExitID uniqueidentifier ROWGUIDCOL DEFAULT NEWID(),
   EmployeeID int NOT NULL,
   AccessTime datetime NOT NULL,
   DoorID int NOT NULL)
```

Next, a row is inserted into the table:

```
INSERT HumanResources.BuildingAccess
(EmployeeID, AccessTime, DoorID)
VALUES (32, GETDATE(), 2)
```

The table is then queried, using the ROWGUIDCOL designator instead of the original BuildingEntryExitID column name (although the original name can be used too—ROWGUIDCOL just offers a more generic means of pulling out the identifier in a query):

```
SELECT   ROWGUIDCOL,
      EmployeeID,
      AccessTime,
      DoorID
FROM   HumanResources.BuildingAccess
```

This returns

BuildingEntryExitID	EmployeeID	AccessTime	DoorID
92ED29C7-6CE4-479B-8E47-30F6D7B2AD4F	32	2008-09-15 16:45:04.553	2

How It Works

The recipe started by creating a new table with a uniqueidentifier data type column:

```
BuildingEntryExitID uniqueidentifier ROWGUIDCOL DEFAULT NEWID(),
```

The column was bound to a default of the function NEWID—which returns a uniqueidentifier data type value. In addition to this, the ROWGUIDCOL property was assigned. Only one ROWGUIDCOL column can be defined for a table. You can still, however, have multiple uniqueidentifier columns in the table.

A SELECT query then used ROWGUIDCOL to return the uniqueidentifier column, although the column name could have been used instead.

Constraints

Constraints are used by SQL Server to enforce column data integrity. Both primary and foreign keys are forms of constraints. Other forms of constraints used for a column include the following:

- UNIQUE constraints, which enforce uniqueness within a table on non-primary key columns

- DEFAULT constraints, which can be used when you don't know the value of a column in a row when it is first inserted into a table, but still wish to populate that column with an anticipated value

- CHECK constraints, which are used to define the data format and values allowed for a column

The next few recipes will discuss how to create and manage these constraint types.

Creating a Unique Constraint

You can only have a single primary key defined on a table. If you wish to enforce uniqueness on other non-primary key columns, you can use a UNIQUE constraint. A unique constraint, by definition, creates an alternate key. Unlike a PRIMARY KEY constraint, you can create multiple UNIQUE constraints for a single table and are also allowed to designate a UNIQUE constraint for columns that allow NULL values (although only one NULL value is allowed for a single-column key per table). Like primary keys, UNIQUE constraints enforce entity integrity by ensuring that rows can be uniquely identified.

The UNIQUE constraint creates an underlying table index when it is created. This index can be CLUSTERED or NONCLUSTERED, although you can't create the index as CLUSTERED if a clustered index already exists for the table.

As with PRIMARY KEY constraints, you can define a UNIQUE constraint when a table is created either on the column definition or at the table constraint level. The syntax for defining a UNIQUE constraint during a table's creation is as follows:

```
( column_name <data_type> [ NULL | NOT NULL ] UNIQUE  )
```

This example demonstrates creating a table with both a PRIMARY KEY and UNIQUE key defined:

```
CREATE TABLE HumanResources.EmployeeAnnualReview(
    EmployeeAnnualReviewID int NOT NULL PRIMARY KEY,
    EmployeeID int NOT NULL,
    AnnualReviewSummaryDESC varchar(900) NOT NULL UNIQUE)
```

You can apply a unique constraint across multiple columns by creating a table constraint:

```
CONSTRAINT constraint_name  UNIQUE
(column [ ASC | DESC ] [ ,...n ] )
```

Table 4-11 details the arguments of this command.

Table 4-11. *UNIQUE Constraint Arguments*

Argument	Description
constraint_name	This specifies the unique name of the constraint to be added.
column [ASC	DESC] [,...n]	The values stored in the column(s) must uniquely identify a single row in the table (i.e., no two rows can have the same values for all the specified columns). The ASC (ascending) and DESC (descending) options define the sorting order of the columns within the clustered or nonclustered index.

In this example, a new table is created with a UNIQUE constraint based on three table columns:

```
-- Drop the old version of the table
DROP TABLE Person.EmergencyContact

CREATE TABLE Person.EmergencyContact (
    EmergencyContactID int NOT NULL PRIMARY KEY,
    EmployeeID int NOT NULL,
    ContactFirstNM varchar(50) NOT NULL,
    ContactLastNM varchar(50) NOT NULL,
```

```
ContactPhoneNBR varchar(25) NOT NULL,
CONSTRAINT UNQ_EmergencyContact_FirstNM_LastNM_PhoneNBR
UNIQUE (ContactFirstNM, ContactLastNM, ContactPhoneNBR))
```

How It Works

In the first example, a UNIQUE constraint was defined in the CREATE TABLE for a specific column:

```
AnnualReviewSummaryDESC varchar(900) NOT NULL UNIQUE
```

The UNIQUE keyword follows the column definition and indicates that a UNIQUE constraint is to be created on the column AnnualReviewSummaryDESC.

In the second example, a UNIQUE constraint is created based on three table columns defined in CREATE TABLE. The constraint is defined after the column definitions. The first line of code defines the constraint name:

```
CONSTRAINT UNQ_EmergencyContact_FirstNM_LastNM_PhoneNBR
```

The second line of code defines the constraint type (UNIQUE) and a list of columns that make up the constraint in parentheses:

```
UNIQUE (ContactFirstNM, ContactLastNM, ContactPhoneNBR)
```

Adding a UNIQUE Constraint to an Existing Table

Using ALTER TABLE, you can add a UNIQUE constraint to an existing table. The syntax is as follows:

```
ALTER TABLE table_name
ADD CONSTRAINT  constraint_name
UNIQUE  (column [ ASC | DESC ] [ ,...n ] )
```

Table 4-12 details the arguments of this command.

Table 4-12. *ALTER TABLE...ADD CONSTRAINT (Unique) Arguments*

Argument	Description
table_name	This specifies the name of the table receiving the new unique key index.
constraint_name	This indicates the unique name of the constraint to be added.
column [ASC | DESC] [,...n]	The values stored in the column(s) must uniquely identify a single row in the table (i.e., no two rows can have the same values for all the specified columns). The ASC (ascending) and DESC (descending) options define the sorting order of the columns within the clustered or nonclustered index.

This example demonstrates adding a UNIQUE key to the Production.Culture table:

```
ALTER TABLE Production.Culture
ADD CONSTRAINT UNQ_Culture_Name
UNIQUE (Name)
```

How It Works

In this example, the first line of code defined the table to be modified:

```
ALTER TABLE Production.Culture
```

The second line of code defined the name of the constraint:

```
ADD CONSTRAINT UNQ_Culture_Name
```

The third line of code defined the constraint type, followed by the column name it will apply to:

```
UNIQUE (Name)
```

The columns specified in the UNIQUE constraint definition can't have duplicate values occurring in the table; otherwise, the operation will fail with an error that a duplicate key value was found.

Using CHECK Constraints

The CHECK constraint is used to define what format and values are allowed for a column. The syntax of the CHECK constraint is as follows:

```
CHECK ( logical_expression )
```

If the logical expression of CHECK evaluates to TRUE, the row will be inserted. If the CHECK constraint expression evaluates to FALSE, the row insert will fail. This example demonstrates adding a CHECK constraint to a CREATE TABLE definition. The GPA column's values will be restricted to a specific numeric range:

```
-- Drop old version of the table
DROP TABLE Person.EmployeeEducationType

CREATE TABLE Person.EmployeeEducationType(
   EmployeeEducationTypeID int NOT NULL PRIMARY KEY,
   EmployeeID int NOT NULL,
   EducationTypeID int NULL,
   GPA numeric(4,3) NOT NULL CHECK (GPA > 2.5 AND GPA <=4.0))
```

In the previous example, the CHECK constraint expression was defined at the column constraint level. A CHECK constraint can also be defined at the table constraint level—where you are allowed to reference multiple columns in the expression, as this next example demonstrates:

```
-- Drop old version of the table
DROP TABLE Person.EmployeeEducationType

CREATE TABLE Person.EmployeeEducationType(
   EmployeeEducationTypeID int NOT NULL PRIMARY KEY,
   EmployeeID int NOT NULL,
   EducationTypeID int NULL,
   GPA numeric(4,3) NOT NULL,
   CONSTRAINT CK_EmployeeEducationType
   CHECK (EducationTypeID > 1 AND GPA > 2.5 AND GPA <=4.0))
```

How It Works

In the first example, a CHECK column constraint was placed against the GPA column in the Person. EmployeeEducationType table:

```
GPA numeric(4,3) NOT NULL CHECK (GPA > 2.5 AND GPA <=4.0)
```

Only a GPA column value greater than 2.5 or less than/equal to 4.0 is allowed in the table—anything else out of that range will cause any INSERT or UPDATE to fail.

In the second example, the CHECK table constraint evaluated two table columns:

```
CHECK (EducationTypeID > 1 AND GPA > 2.5 AND GPA <=4.0)
```

This CHECK constraint requires that the EducationTypeID value be greater than 1, in addition to the GPA requirements.

Adding a CHECK Constraint to an Existing Table

Like other constraint types, you can add a CHECK constraint to an existing table using ALTER TABLE and ADD CONSTRAINT. The syntax is as follows:

```
ALTER TABLE table_name
WITH CHECK | WITH NOCHECK
ADD CONSTRAINT  constraint_name
CHECK ( logical_expression )
```

Table 4-13 details the arguments of this command.

Table 4-13. *ALTER TABLE...ADD CONSTRAINT (Check) Arguments*

Argument	Description
table_name	This specifies the name of the table receiving the new CHECK constraint.
CHECK | WITH NOCHECK	With the CHECK option (the default), existing data is validated against the new CHECK constraint. NOCHECK skips validation of new data, limiting the constraint to validation of new values (inserted or updated).
constraint_name	This defines the name of the CHECK constraint.
logical_expression	This specifies the logical expression to use to restrict values that are allowed in the column.

In this example, a new CHECK request is added to the Person.ContactType table:

```
ALTER TABLE Person.ContactType WITH NOCHECK
ADD CONSTRAINT  CK_ContactType
CHECK (Name NOT LIKE '%assistant%')
```

How It Works

A new constraint was added to the Person.ContactType table to not allow any name like "assistant." The first part of the ALTER TABLE statement included WITH NOCHECK:

```
ALTER TABLE Person.ContactType WITH NOCHECK
```

Had this statement been executed without WITH NOCHECK, it would have failed because there are already rows in the table with "assistant" in the name. Adding WITH NOCHECK means that existing values are ignored going forward, and only new values are validated against the CHECK constraint.

▪Caution Using WITH NOCHECK may cause problems later on, as you cannot depend on the data in the table conforming to the constraint.

The next part of the statement defined the new constraint name:

```
ADD CONSTRAINT  CK_ContactType
```

The constraint type CHECK was used followed by the logical expression to limit the Name column's contents:

```
CHECK (Name NOT LIKE '%assistant%')
```

Disabling and Enabling a Constraint

The previous exercise demonstrated using NOCHECK to ignore existing values that disobey the new constraints rule when adding a new constraint to the table. Constraints are used to maintain data integrity, although sometimes you may need to relax the rules while performing a one-off data import or non-standard business operation. NOCHECK can also be used to disable a CHECK or FOREIGN KEY constraint, allowing you to insert rows that disobey the constraints rules.

In the setup of this example, an insert is attempted to the Sales.PersonCreditCard table:

```
INSERT Sales.PersonCreditCard
(BusinessEntityID, CreditCardID)
VALUES (14425, 924533)
```

The insert fails, returning the following error message:

```
Msg 547, Level 16, State 0, Line 1
The INSERT statement conflicted with the FOREIGN KEY constraint
"FK_PersonCreditCard_CreditCard_CreditCardID". The conflict occurred in database
"AdventureWorks", table "Sales.CreditCard", column 'CreditCardID'.
The statement has been terminated.
```

Next, the foreign key constraint that caused the previous error message will be disabled using NOCHECK:

```
ALTER TABLE Sales.PersonCreditCard
NOCHECK CONSTRAINT FK_PersonCreditCard_CreditCard_CreditCardID
```

The insert is then attempted again:

```
INSERT Sales.PersonCreditCard
(BusinessEntityID, CreditCardID)
VALUES (14425, 924533)
```

This time it succeeds:

```
(1 row(s) affected)
```

I can then DELETE the newly inserted row, so as not to leave data integrity issues once the constraint is reenabled:

```
DELETE Sales.PersonCreditCard
WHERE BusinessEntityID = 14425 AND
      CreditCardID = 924533
```

To reenable checking of the foreign key constraint, CHECK is used in an ALTER TABLE statement:

```
ALTER TABLE Sales.PersonCreditCard
CHECK CONSTRAINT FK_PersonCreditCard_CreditCard_CreditCardID
```

To disable or enable all CHECK and FOREIGN KEY constraints for the table, you should use the ALL keyword, as this example demonstrates:

```
-- disable checking on all constraints
ALTER TABLE Sales.PersonCreditCard
NOCHECK CONSTRAINT ALL

-- enable checking on all constraints
ALTER TABLE Sales.PersonCreditCard
CHECK CONSTRAINT ALL
```

■**Caution** Disabling all CHECK and FOREIGN KEY constraints for a table should only be performed when absolutely necessary. Reenable all constraints when you are finished.

How It Works

In this recipe, an insert was attempted against Sales.PersonCreditCard with a CreditCardID that didn't exist in the primary key table. The insert causes a conflict with the FK_PersonCreditCard_CreditCard_CreditCardID foreign key constraint.

To disable the constraint from validating new values, ALTER TABLE and NOCHECK CONSTRAINT were used. After disabling the constraint with NOCHECK, the CreditCardID value was then allowed to be inserted, even though it doesn't exist in the primary key table. The scenario was completed by reenabling the constraint again and deleting the value just inserted.

The next example demonstrated disabling all foreign key and check constraints on a table using the ALL keyword:

```
NOCHECK CONSTRAINT ALL
```

All constraints for the table were then reenabled using the following code:

```
CHECK CONSTRAINT ALL
```

Using a DEFAULT Constraint During Table Creation

If you don't know the value of a column in a row when it is first inserted into a table, you can use a DEFAULT constraint to populate that column with an anticipated or non-NULL value. The syntax for designating the default value in the column definition of a CREATE TABLE is as follows:

```
DEFAULT constant_expression
```

The constant_expression is the default value you wish to populate into the column when the column's value isn't explicitly specified in an INSERT. This example demonstrates setting the default value of the EducationTypeID column to 1:

```
-- Drop old table
DROP TABLE Person.EmployeeEducationType

CREATE TABLE Person.EmployeeEducationType(
    EmployeeEducationTypeID int NOT NULL PRIMARY KEY,
    EmployeeID int NOT NULL,
    EducationTypeID int NOT NULL DEFAULT 1,
    GPA numeric(4,3) NOT NULL )
```

How It Works

In this example, the default value of EducationTypeID was set to a default of 1. The keyword DEFAULT was placed after the column definition and followed by the default value (which must match the data type of the column):

```
EducationTypeID int NOT NULL DEFAULT 1
```

Since this column has a DEFAULT value, if the value isn't explicitly inserted with an INSERT statement, the value 1 will be inserted instead of a NULL value.

Adding a DEFAULT Constraint to an Existing Table

Like other constraint types, you can add a default constraint to an existing table column using ALTER TABLE and ADD CONSTRAINT. The syntax for doing this is as follows:

```
ALTER TABLE table_name
ADD CONSTRAINT  constraint_name
DEFAULT default_value
FOR column_name
```

Table 4-14 details the arguments of this command.

Table 4-14. *ALTER TABLE...ADD CONSTRAINT (Default) Arguments*

Argument	Description
table_name	The name of the table receiving the new DEFAULT constraint
constraint_name	The name of the DEFAULT constraint
default_value	The default value to be used for the column
column_name	The name of the column the default is being applied to

This example demonstrates adding a default to an existing table column:

```
ALTER TABLE HumanResources.Company
ADD CONSTRAINT DF_Company_ParentCompanyID
DEFAULT 1 FOR ParentCompanyID
```

How It Works

In this example, a new default was applied to an existing table column. The first line of ALTER TABLE defined the impacted table:

```
ALTER TABLE HumanResources.Company
```

The second line of the statement added a constraint and defined the constraint name:

```
ADD CONSTRAINT DF_Company_ParentCompanyID
```

The third line of code defined the constraint type, DEFAULT, followed by the value to use for the default:

```
DEFAULT 1
```

Lastly, the column that the default was applied to was used in the FOR clause:

```
FOR ParentCompanyID
```

Dropping a Constraint from a Table

Now that I've reviewed several constraints that can be added to a table, in this recipe I'll demonstrate how to now *drop* a constraint using ALTER TABLE and DROP CONSTRAINT. The basic syntax for dropping a constraint is as follows:

```
ALTER TABLE table_name
DROP CONSTRAINT constraint_name
```

The table_name designates the table you are dropping the constraint from, and the constraint_name designates the name of the constraint to be dropped. In this example, a default constraint is dropped from the HumanResources.Company table:

```
ALTER TABLE HumanResources.Company
DROP CONSTRAINT DF_Company_ParentCompanyID
```

How It Works

In the first line of code in this example, the table to drop the constraint from was designated:

```
ALTER TABLE HumanResources.Company
```

In the second line of code, the name of the constraint to drop was designated:

```
DROP CONSTRAINT DF_Company_ParentCompanyID
```

Notice that the constraint type wasn't needed, and that only the constraint name was used. To find out the constraints present on a table, use the sp_help system stored procedure.

Temporary Tables and Table Variables

Temporary tables are defined just like regular tables, only they are automatically stored in the tempdb database (no matter which database context you create them in). Temporary tables are often used in the following scenarios:

- *As an alternative to cursors*: For example, instead of using a Transact-SQL cursor to loop through a result set, performing tasks based on each row, you can populate a temporary table instead. Using a WHILE loop, you can loop through each row in the table, perform the action for the specified row, and then delete the row from the temp table.

- *As an incremental storage of result sets*: For example, let's say you have a single SELECT query that performs a join against ten tables. Sometimes queries with several joins can perform badly. One technique to try is to break down the large query into smaller, incremental queries. Using temporary tables, you can create intermediate result sets based on smaller queries, instead of trying to execute a single, very large, multi-joined query.

- *As a temporary, low-overhead lookup table*: For example, imagine that you are using a query that takes several seconds to execute but only returns a small result set. You wish to use the small result set in several areas of your stored procedure, but each time you reference it, you incur the query execution time overhead. To resolve this, you can execute the query just once within the procedure, populating the temporary table. Then you can reference the temporary table in multiple places in your code, without incurring the extra overhead.

There are two different temporary table types: *global* and *local*. Local temporary tables are prefixed with a single # sign, and global temporary tables with a double ## sign.

Local temporary tables are available for use by the current user connection that created them. Multiple connections can create the same-named temporary table for local temporary tables without encountering conflicts. The internal representation of the local table is given a unique name, so as not to conflict with other temporary tables with the same name created by other connections in the tempdb database. Local temporary tables are dropped by using the DROP statement or are automatically removed from memory when the user connection is closed.

Global temporary tables have a different scope from local temporary tables. Once a connection creates a global temporary table, any user with proper permissions to the current database he is in can access the table. Unlike local temporary tables, you can't create simultaneous versions of a global temporary table, as this will generate a naming conflict. Global temporary tables are removed from SQL Server if explicitly dropped by DROP TABLE. They are also automatically removed after the connection that created it disconnects and the global temporary table is no longer referenced by other connections. As an aside, I rarely see global temporary tables used in the field. When a table must be shared across connections, a real table is created, instead of a global temporary table. Nonetheless, SQL Server offers this as a choice.

Temporary tables are much maligned by the DBA community due to performance issues— some of these complaints are valid, and some aren't. It is true that temporary tables may cause unwanted disk overhead in tempdb, locking of tempdb during their creation, as well as stored procedure recompilations, when included within a stored procedure's definition (a *recompilation* is when an execution plan of the stored procedure is re-created instead of reused).

A *table variable* is a data type that can be used within a Transact-SQL batch, stored procedure, or function—and is created and defined similarly to a table, only with a strictly defined lifetime scope. Table variables are often good replacements of temporary tables when the data set is small. Statistics are not maintained for table variables like they are for regular or temporary tables, so using too large a table variable may cause query optimization issues. Unlike regular tables or temporary tables, table variables can't have indexes or FOREIGN KEY constraints added to them. Table variables do allow some constraints to be used in the table definition (PRIMARY KEY, UNIQUE, CHECK).

Reasons to use table variables include the following:

- Well scoped. The lifetime of the table variable only lasts for the duration of the batch, function, or stored procedure.

- Shorter locking periods (because of the tighter scope).

- Less recompilation when used in stored procedures.

As stated earlier, there are drawbacks to using table variables. Table variable performance suffers when the result set becomes too large or when column data cardinality is critical to the query optimization process. When encountering performance issues, be sure to test all alternative solutions, and don't necessarily assume that one option (temporary tables) is less desirable than others (table variables).

Using a Temporary Table for Multiple Lookups Within a Batch

In this example, I'll demonstrate creating a local temporary table that is then referenced multiple times in a batch of queries. This technique can be helpful if the query used to generate the lookup values takes several seconds to execute. Rather than execute the SELECT query multiple times, I can query the pre-aggregated temp table instead:

```
CREATE TABLE #ProductCostStatistics
( ProductID int NOT NULL PRIMARY KEY,
  AvgStandardCost money NOT NULL,
  ProductCount int NOT NULL)
```

```
INSERT #ProductCostStatistics
(ProductID, AvgStandardCost, ProductCount)
SELECT ProductID,
       AVG(StandardCost) AvgStandardCost,
       COUNT(ProductID) Rowcnt
FROM Production.ProductCostHistory
GROUP BY ProductID

SELECT TOP 3 *
FROM #ProductCostStatistics
ORDER BY AvgStandardCost ASC

SELECT TOP 3 *
FROM #ProductCostStatistics
ORDER BY AvgStandardCost DESC

SELECT AVG(AvgStandardCost) Average_of_AvgStandardCost
FROM #ProductCostStatistics

DROP TABLE #ProductCostStatistics
```

This returns three result sets from the temporary table:

ProductID	AvgStandardCost	ProductCount
873	0.8565	1
922	1.4923	1
870	1.8663	1

ProductID	AvgStandardCost	ProductCount
749	2171.2942	1
750	2171.2942	1
751	2171.2942	1

Average_of_AvgStandardCost
423.0001

How It Works

In this recipe, a temporary table called #ProductCostStatistics was created. The table had rows inserted into it like a regular table, and then the temporary table was queried three times (again, just like a regular table), and then dropped. The table was created and queried with the same syntax as a regular table, only the temporary table name was prefixed with a # sign. In situations where the initial population query execution time takes too long to execute, this is one technique to consider.

Creating a Table Variable to Hold a Temporary Result Set

Table variables were first demonstrated in Chapter 2, in the "Returning Rows Affected by a Data Modification Statement" recipe. There you learned to use them to hold the results of the OUTPUT command.

■Note SQL Server 2008 introduces table-valued parameters and user-defined types, which you can use to pass temporary result sets between modules. These topics are covered in Chapter 11.

The syntax to creating a table variable is similar to creating a table, only the DECLARE keyword is used and the table name is prefixed with an @ symbol:

```
DECLARE @TableName TABLE
    (column_name <data_type> [ NULL | NOT NULL ] [ ,...n ]  )
```

In this example, a table variable is used in a similar fashion to the temporary table of the previous recipe. This example demonstrates how the implementation differs (including how you don't explicitly DROP the table):

```
DECLARE @ProductCostStatistics TABLE
( ProductID int NOT NULL PRIMARY KEY,
  AvgStandardCost money NOT NULL,
  ProductCount int NOT NULL)

INSERT @ProductCostStatistics
(ProductID, AvgStandardCost, ProductCount)
SELECT ProductID,
     AVG(StandardCost) AvgStandardCost,
     COUNT(ProductID) Rowcnt
FROM Production.ProductCostHistory
GROUP BY ProductID

SELECT TOP 3 *
FROM @ProductCostStatistics
ORDER BY ProductCount
```

This returns

ProductID	AvgStandardCost	ProductCount
710	3.3963	1
709	3.3963	1
731	352.1394	1

How It Works

This recipe used a table variable in much the same way as the previous recipe did with temporary tables. There are important distinctions between the two recipes, however.

First, this time a table variable was defined using DECLARE @Tablename TABLE instead of CREATE TABLE. Secondly, unlike the temporary table recipe, there isn't a GO after each statement, as temporary tables can only be scoped within the batch, procedure, or function.

In the next part of the recipe, I used inserts and selects from the table variable as you would a regular table, only this time using the @tablename format:

```
INSERT @ProductCostStatistics
...

SELECT TOP 3 *
FROM @ProductCostStatistics
...
```

No DROP TABLE was necessary at the end of the example, as the table variable is eliminated from memory after the end of the batch/procedure/function execution.

Manageability for Very Large Tables

These next few recipes will demonstrate methods for managing very large tables (with millions of rows, for example). Specifically, I'll discuss SQL Server table-partitioning functionality, and then filegroup placement.

Table partitioning provides you with a built-in method of horizontally partitioning data within a table and/or index while still maintaining a single logical object. *Horizontal partitioning* involves keeping the same number of columns in each partition, but reducing the number of rows. Partitioning can ease management of very large tables and/or indexes, decrease load time, improve query time, and allow smaller maintenance windows. These next few recipes in this section will demonstrate how to use Transact-SQL commands to create, modify, and manage partitions and partition database objects.

■**Tip** SQL Server 2008 introduces partitioned table query processing improvements, including partition-aware seek operations, better visibility of accessed partitions in the execution plan, and the new trace flag 2440, which enables the assignment of multiple threads of execution per partition in a parallel query plan.

I'll also cover *filegroup* placement. Database data files belong to filegroups. Every database has a primary filegroup, and you can add additional filegroups as needed. Adding new filegroups to a database is often used for *very large databases (VLDB)*, as they can ease backup administration and potentially improve performance by distributing data over multiple arrays. I'll demonstrate placing a table on a specific filegroup in the last recipe of this chapter.

Before diving into the partitioning-related recipes, I'll discuss the two new commands CREATE PARTITION FUNCTION and CREATE PARTITION SCHEME. The CREATE PARTITION FUNCTION maps columns to partitions based on the value of a specified column. For example, if you are evaluating a column with a datetime data type, you can partition data to separate filegroups based on the year or month.

The basic syntax for CREATE PARTITION FUNCTION is as follows:

```
CREATE PARTITION FUNCTION partition_function_name(input_parameter_type)
AS RANGE [ LEFT | RIGHT ]
FOR VALUES ( [ boundary_value [ ,...n ] ] )
```

Table 4-15 details the arguments of this command.

Table 4-15. *CREATE PARTITION FUNCTION Arguments*

Argument	Description
partition_function_name	This specifies the partition function name.
input_parameter_type	This indicates the data type of the partitioning column. You cannot use large value data types (text, ntext, image, xml, timestamp, varchar(max), varbinary(max), nvarchar(max)), CLR user-defined data types, or aliased data types. If you wished to partition table data by a datetime column, you would designate datetime for the input_parameter_type.
LEFT | RIGHT	You also have a choice of LEFT or RIGHT, which defines which boundary the defined values in the boundary_value argument belong to (see the upcoming "How It Works" section for a review of LEFT versus RIGHT).

Argument	Description
`[ boundary_value [ ,...n ] ]`	This argument defines the range of values in each partition. You can define up to 999 partitions (however, that many isn't recommended due to potential performance concerns). The number of values you choose in this argument amounts to a total of $n + 1$ partitions (again, see the upcoming "How It Works" section for a more in-depth explanation).

Once a partition function is created, it can be used with one or more partition schemes. A *partition scheme* maps partitions defined in a partition function to actual filegroups.

The basic syntax for `CREATE PARTITION SCHEME` is as follows:

```
CREATE PARTITION SCHEME partition_scheme_name
AS PARTITION partition_function_name
[ ALL ] TO ( { file_group_name | [PRIMARY] } [ ,...n] )
```

Table 4-16 details the arguments of this command.

Table 4-16. *CREATE PARTITION SCHEME Arguments*

Argument	Description
`partition_scheme_name`	This specifies the name of the partition scheme.
`partition_function_name`	This indicates the name of the partition function that the scheme will bind to.
`ALL`	If `ALL` is designated, all partitions will map to the filegroup designated in the `file_group_name` argument.
`{ file_group_name	[PRIMARY] } [,...n]`	This defines the filegroup or filegroups assigned to each partition. When `PRIMARY` is designated, the partition will be stored on the primary filegroup.

Implementing Table Partitioning

In this recipe, I'll demonstrate how to

- Create a filegroup or filegroups to hold the partitions.

- Add files to each filegroup used in the partitioning.

- Use the `CREATE PARTITION FUNCTION` command to determine how the table's data will be partitioned.

- Use the `CREATE PARTITION SCHEME` command to bind the `PARTITION FUNCTION` to the specified filegroups.

- Create the table, binding a specific partitioning column to a `PARTITION SCHEME`.

The recipe creates a table called `Sales.WebSiteHits`, which is used to track each hit to a hypothetical web site. In this scenario, the table is expected to grow large quickly. Because of the potential size, queries may not perform as well as they could, and backup operations against the entire database take longer than the current maintenance window allows.

To address this application scenario, the data from this table will be partitioned horizontally, which means that groups of rows based on a selected column (in this case `HitDate`) will be mapped into separate underlying physical files on the disk. The first part of this example demonstrates adding the new filegroups to the AdventureWorks database:

```
ALTER DATABASE AdventureWorks
ADD FILEGROUP hitfg1

ALTER DATABASE AdventureWorks
ADD FILEGROUP hitfg2

ALTER DATABASE AdventureWorks
ADD FILEGROUP hitfg3

ALTER DATABASE AdventureWorks
ADD FILEGROUP hitfg4
```

Next, for each new filegroup created, a new database file is added to it:

```
ALTER DATABASE AdventureWorks
ADD FILE
(    NAME = awhitfg1,
     FILENAME = 'c:\Apress\aw_hitfg1.ndf',
     SIZE = 1MB
)
TO FILEGROUP hitfg1
GO

ALTER DATABASE AdventureWorks
ADD FILE
(    NAME = awhitfg2,
     FILENAME = 'c:\Apress\aw_hitfg2.ndf',
     SIZE = 1MB
)
TO FILEGROUP hitfg2
GO

ALTER DATABASE AdventureWorks
ADD FILE
(    NAME = awhitfg3,
     FILENAME = 'c:\Apress\aw_hitfg3.ndf',
     SIZE = 1MB
)
TO FILEGROUP hitfg3
GO

ALTER DATABASE AdventureWorks
ADD FILE
(    NAME = awhitfg4,
     FILENAME = 'c:\Apress\aw_hitfg4.ndf',
     SIZE = 1MB
)
TO FILEGROUP hitfg4
GO
```

Now that the filegroups are ready for their partitioned data, the partition function will be created, which determines how the table will have its data horizontally partitioned (in this case, by date range):

```
CREATE PARTITION FUNCTION HitDateRange (datetime)
AS RANGE LEFT FOR VALUES ('1/1/2006', '1/1/2007', '1/1/2008')
GO
```

After creating the partition function, I create the partition scheme in order to bind the partition function to the new filegroups:

```
CREATE PARTITION SCHEME HitDateRangeScheme
AS PARTITION HitDateRange
TO ( hitfg1, hitfg2, hitfg3, hitfg4 )
```

Lastly, I create a table that uses the partition scheme on the HitDate column in the ON clause of the CREATE TABLE statement:

```
CREATE TABLE Sales.WebSiteHits
(WebSiteHitID bigint NOT NULL IDENTITY(1,1),
 WebSitePage varchar(255) NOT NULL,
 HitDate datetime NOT NULL,
 CONSTRAINT PK_WebSiteHits
 PRIMARY KEY (WebSiteHitID, HitDate))
ON [HitDateRangeScheme] (HitDate)
```

How It Works

In the first part of the recipe, four new filegroups were added to the AdventureWorks database. After that, a database file was added to each filegroup.

Next, a partition function was created that defined the partition boundaries for the partition function and the expected partition column data type. On the first line of the CREATE PARTITION FUNCTION command, the datetime data type was selected:

```
CREATE PARTITION FUNCTION HitDateRange (datetime)
```

The next line defined the ranges for values for the partition function, creating partitions by year:

```
AS RANGE LEFT FOR VALUES ('1/1/2006', '1/1/2007', '1/1/2008')
```

You can define up to 999 partitions (however, that many isn't recommended due to potential performance concerns). The number of values you choose amounts to a total of $n + 1$ partitions. You also have a choice of LEFT or RIGHT, which defines the boundary that the defined values belong to. In this recipe, LEFT was chosen. Table 4-17 shows the partition boundaries (or partitions where rows will be placed) in this case.

Table 4-17. *LEFT Boundaries*

Partition #	Lower Bound datetime	Upper Bound datetime
1	Lowest allowed datetime	1/1/2006 00:00:00
2	1/1/2006 00:00:01	1/1/2007 00:00:00
3	1/1/2007 00:00:01	1/1/2008 00:00:00
4	1/1/2008 00:00:01	Highest allowed datetime

Had RIGHT been chosen instead, the partition boundaries would have been as shown in Table 4-18.

Table 4-18. *RIGHT Boundaries*

Partition #	Lower Bound datetime	Upper Bound datetime
1	Lowest allowed datetime	12/31/2005 12:59:59
2	1/1/2006 00:00:00	12/31/2006 12:59:59
3	1/1/2007 00:00:00	12/31/2007 12:59:59
4	1/1/2008 00:00:00	Highest allowed datetime

Once a partition function is created, it can be used with one or more partition schemes. A partition scheme maps the partitions defined in a partition function to actual filegroups. The first line of the new partition scheme defined the partition scheme name:

```
CREATE PARTITION SCHEME HitDateRangeScheme
```

The second line of code defined the partition function of the partition scheme it is bound to (the function created in the previous step):

```
AS PARTITION HitDateRange
```

The TO clause defines which filegroups map to the four partitions defined in the partition function, in order of partition sequence:

```
TO ( hitfg1, hitfg2, hitfg3, hitfg4 )
```

After a partition scheme is created, it can then be bound to a table. In the CREATE TABLE statement's ON clause (last row of the table definition), the partition scheme is designated with the column to partition in parentheses:

```
CREATE TABLE Sales.WebSiteHits
(WebSiteHitID bigint NOT NULL IDENTITY(1,1),
 WebSitePage varchar(255) NOT NULL,
 HitDate datetime NOT NULL,
 CONSTRAINT PK_WebSiteHits
 PRIMARY KEY (WebSiteHitID, HitDate))
ON [HitDateRangeScheme] (HitDate)
```

Notice that the primary key is made up of both the WebSiteHitID and HitDate. The partitioned key column (HitDate) must be part of the primary key.

The Sales.WebSiteHits table is now partitioned—and can be worked with just like a single regular table. You needn't do anything special to your SELECT, INSERT, UPDATE, or DELETE statements. In the background, as data is added, rows are inserted into the appropriate filegroups based on the partition function and scheme.

Determining the Location of Data in a Partition

Because partitioning happens in the background, you don't actually query the individual partitions directly. In order to determine which partition a row belongs to, you can use the $PARTITION function.

The syntax for $PARTITION is as follows:

```
$PARTITION.partition_function_name(expression)
```

Table 4-19 details the arguments of this command.

Table 4-19. *$PARTITION Function Arguments*

Argument	Description
partition_function_name	The name of the partition function used to partition the table
expression	The column used as the partitioning key

This example demonstrates how to use this function. To begin with, four rows are inserted into the Sales.WebSiteHits partitioned table:

```
INSERT Sales.WebSiteHits
(WebSitePage, HitDate)
VALUES ('Home Page', '10/22/2007')

INSERT Sales.WebSiteHits
(WebSitePage, HitDate)
VALUES ('Home Page', '10/2/2006')

INSERT Sales.WebSiteHits
(WebSitePage, HitDate)
VALUES ('Sales Page', '5/9/2008')

INSERT Sales.WebSiteHits
(WebSitePage, HitDate)
VALUES ('Sales Page', '3/4/2000')
```

The table is then queried using SELECT and the $PARTITION function:

```
SELECT  HitDate,
   $PARTITION.HitDateRange (HitDate) Partition
FROM  Sales.WebSiteHits
```

This returns

```
HitDate                        Partition
2000-03-04 00:00:00.000        1
2006-10-02 00:00:00.000        2
2007-10-22 00:00:00.000        3
2008-05-09 00:00:00.000        4
```

How It Works

The recipe started out by inserting four rows into the partitioned Sales.WebSiteHits table. Each insert is for a row with a different HitDate year (in order to demonstrate the function).

Next, a query was executed against the table using the $PARTITION function:

```
SELECT  HitDate,
   $PARTITION.HitDateRange (HitDate) Partition
FROM  Sales.WebSiteHits
```

The partition_function_name is the name of the function created in the last recipe. The expression in parentheses is the HitDate, which is the column used to partition the data.

The $PARTITION function evaluates each HitDate and determines what partition it is stored in based on the partition function. This allows you to see how data is distributed across the different partitions. If one partition is uneven with the rest, you can explore creating or removing existing partitions—both functions of which are demonstrated next.

Adding a New Partition

Over time, you may decide that your partitioned table needs additional partitions (for example, you can create a new partition for each new year). To add a new partition, the ALTER PARTITION SCHEME and ALTER PARTITION FUNCTION commands are used.

Before a new partition can be created on an existing partition function, you must first prepare a filegroup for use in holding the new partition data (a new or already used filegroup can be used). The first step is designating the next partition filegroup to use with ALTER PARTITION SCHEME.

The syntax for ALTER PARTITION SCHEME is as follows:

```
ALTER PARTITION SCHEME partition_scheme_name
NEXT USED [ filegroup_name ]
```

Table 4-20 details the arguments of this command.

Table 4-20. *ALTER PARTITION SCHEME Arguments*

Argument	Description
partition_scheme_name	This specifies the name of the partition scheme to modify.
NEXT USED [filegroup_name]	The NEXT USED keywords queues the next filegroup to be used by any new partition.

After adding a reference to the next filegroup, ALTER PARTITION FUNCTION is used to create (split) the new partition (and also remove/merge a partition). The syntax for ALTER PARTITION FUNCTION is as follows:

```
ALTER PARTITION FUNCTION partition_function_name()
{
    SPLIT RANGE ( boundary_value )
  | MERGE RANGE ( boundary_value )
}
```

Table 4-21 details the arguments of this command.

Table 4-21. *ALTER PARTITION FUNCTION Arguments*

Argument	Description
partition_function_name	This specifies the name of the partition function to add or remove a partition from.
SPLIT RANGE (boundary_value) | MERGE RANGE (boundary_value)	SPLIT RANGE is used to create a new partition by defining a new boundary value. MERGE RANGE is used to remove an existing partition.

This example demonstrates how to create (split) a new partition. The first step is creating a new filegroup to be used by the new partition. In this example, the PRIMARY filegroup is used:

```
ALTER PARTITION SCHEME HitDateRangeScheme
NEXT USED [PRIMARY]
```

Next, the partition function is modified to create a new partition, defining a boundary of January 1, 2009:

```
ALTER PARTITION FUNCTION HitDateRange ()
SPLIT RANGE ('1/1/2009')
```

After the new partition is created, a new row is inserted to test the new partition:

```
INSERT Sales.WebSiteHits
(WebSitePage, HitDate)
VALUES ('Sales Page', '3/4/2009')
```

The table is queried using $PARTITION:

```
SELECT   HitDate,
$PARTITION.HitDateRange (HitDate) Partition
FROM   Sales.WebSiteHits
```

This shows the newly inserted row has been stored in the new partition (partition number 5):

```
HitDate                         Partition
2000-03-04 00:00:00.000         1
2006-10-02 00:00:00.000         2
2007-10-22 00:00:00.000         3
2008-05-09 00:00:00.000         4
2009-03-04 00:00:00.000         5
```

How It Works

In this recipe's example, the HitDateRangeScheme was altered using ALTER PARTITION SCHEME and the NEXT USED keywords. The NEXT USED keywords queue the next filegroup to be used by any new partition. In this example, the default PRIMARY filegroup was selected as the destination for the new partition:

```
ALTER PARTITION SCHEME HitDateRangeScheme
NEXT USED [PRIMARY]
```

ALTER PARTITION FUNCTION was then used with SPLIT RANGE in order to add a new partition boundary:

```
ALTER PARTITION FUNCTION HitDateRange ()
SPLIT RANGE ('1/1/2006')
```

Only one value was used to add the new partition, which essentially splits an existing partition range into two, using the original boundary type (LEFT or RIGHT). You can only use SPLIT RANGE for a single split at a time—and you can't add multiple partitions in a statement.

This example's split added a new partition, partition 5, as shown in Table 4-22.

Table 4-22. *New Partition Layout*

Partition #	Lower Bound datetime	Upper Bound datetime
1	Lowest allowed datetime	1/1/2006 00:00:00
2	1/1/2006 00:00:01	1/1/2007 00:00:00
3	1/1/2007 00:00:01	1/1/2008 00:00:00
4	1/1/2008 00:00:01	1/1/2009 00:00:00
5	1/1/2009 00:00:01	Highest allowed datetime

A new row was inserted into the Sales.WebSiteHits table, which used the partition function. A query was executed to view the partitions that each row belongs in, and it is confirmed that the new row was inserted into the fifth partition.

Removing a Partition

The previous recipe showed the syntax for ALTER PARTITION FUNCTION, including a description of the MERGE RANGE functionality, which is used to remove an existing partition. Removing a partition essentially merges two partitions into one, with rows relocating to the resulting merged partition.

This example demonstrates removing the 1/1/2007 partition from the HitDateRange partition function:

```
ALTER PARTITION FUNCTION HitDateRange ()
MERGE RANGE ('1/1/2007')
```

Next, the partitioned table is queried using the $PARTITION function:

```
SELECT   HitDate,
    $PARTITION.HitDateRange (HitDate) Partition
FROM  Sales.WebSiteHits
```

This returns the following results:

```
HitDate                      Partition
2000-03-04 00:00:00.000      1
2007-10-22 00:00:00.000      2
2006-10-02 00:00:00.000      2
2008-05-09 00:00:00.000      3
2009-03-04 00:00:00.000      4
```

How It Works

ALTER PARTITION FUNCTION is used for both splitting and merging partitions. In this case, the MERGE RANGE keywords were used to eliminate the 1/1/2007 partition boundary:

```
ALTER PARTITION FUNCTION HitDateRange ()
MERGE RANGE ('1/1/2007')
```

A query was executed to view which rows belong to which partitions. Table 4-23 lists the boundaries after the MERGE.

Table 4-23. *New Partition Layout*

Partition #	Lower Bound datetime	Upper Bound datetime
1	Lowest allowed datetime	1/1/2006 00:00:00
2	1/1/2006 00:00:01	1/1/2008 00:00:00
3	1/1/2008 00:00:01	1/1/2009 00:00:00
4	1/1/2009 00:00:01	Highest allowed datetime

Partition 2 now encompasses the data for two years instead of one. You can only merge one partition per ALTER PARTITION FUNCTION execution, and you can't convert a partitioned table into a non-partitioned table using ALTER PARTITION FUNCTION—you can only reduce the number of partitions down to a single partition.

Moving a Partition to a Different Table

With SQL Server's partitioning functionality, you can transfer partitions between different tables with a minimum of effort or overhead. You can transfer partitions between tables using ALTER TABLE... SWITCH. Transfers can take place in three different ways: switching a partition from a partitioned table to another partitioned table (both needing to be partitioned on the same column), transferring an entire table from a non-partitioned table to a partitioned table, or moving a partition from a partitioned table to a non-partitioned table.

■**Tip** In SQL Server 2005, partitioned tables couldn't be referenced in a view with schema binding, a restriction that prevented the use of indexed views. SQL Server 2008 now supports schema binding and partition-aligned indexed views.

The basic syntax for switching partitions between tables is as follows:

```
ALTER TABLE tablename
SWITCH [ PARTITION source_partition_number_expression ]
TO [ schema_name. ] target_table
[ PARTITION target_partition_number_expression ]
```

Table 4-24 details the arguments of this command.

Table 4-24. *ALTER TABLE...SWITCH Arguments*

Argument	Description
tablename	The source table to move the partition from
source_partition_number_expression	The partition number being relocated
[schema_name.] target_table	The target table to receive the partition
partition.target_partition_number_expression	The destination partition number

This example demonstrates moving a partition between Sales.WebSiteHits and a new table called Sales.WebSiteHitsHistory. In the first step, a new table is created to hold historical web site hit information:

```
CREATE TABLE Sales.WebSiteHitsHistory
(WebSiteHitID bigint NOT NULL IDENTITY(1,1),
 WebSitePage varchar(255) NOT NULL,
 HitDate datetime NOT NULL,
 CONSTRAINT PK_WebSiteHitsHistory
 PRIMARY KEY (WebSiteHitID, HitDate))
ON [HitDateRangeScheme] (HitDate)
```

Next, ALTER TABLE is used to move partition 3 from Sales.WebSiteHits to partition 3 of the new Sales.WebSiteHitsHistory table:

```
ALTER TABLE Sales.WebSiteHits SWITCH PARTITION 3
TO Sales.WebSiteHitsHistory PARTITION 3
```

Next, a query is executed using $PARTITION to view the transferred data in the new table:

```
SELECT   HitDate,
$PARTITION.HitDateRange (HitDate) Partition
FROM  Sales.WebSiteHitsHistory
```

This returns

HitDate	Partition
2008-05-09 00:00:00.000	3

How It Works

The first part of the recipe created a new table called Sales.WebSiteHitsHistory and used the same partition scheme as the Sales.WebSiteHits table.

The source table and partition number to transfer was referenced in the first line of the ALTER TABLE command:

```
ALTER TABLE Sales.WebSiteHits SWITCH PARTITION 3
```

The TO keyword designated the destination table and partition to move the data to:

```
TO Sales.WebSiteHitsHistory PARTITION 3
```

Moving partitions between tables is much faster than performing a manual row operation (INSERT..SELECT, for example) because you aren't actually moving physical data. Instead, you are only changing the metadata regarding where the partition is currently stored. Also, keep in mind that the target partition of any existing table needs to be empty for the destination partition. If it is a non-partitioned table, it must also be empty.

Removing Partition Functions and Schemes

If you try to drop a partition function or scheme while it is still bound to an existing table or index, you'll get an error message. You also can't directly remove a partition scheme or function while it is bound to a table (unless you drop the entire table as will be done in this recipe). If you had originally created the table as a heap (a table without a clustered index), and then created a clustered index bound to a partition scheme, you can use the CREATE INDEX DROP_EXISTING option (see Chapter 5) to rebuild the index without the partition scheme reference.

Dropping a partition scheme uses the following syntax:

```
DROP PARTITION SCHEME partition_scheme_name
```

This command takes the name of the partition scheme to drop.

Dropping a partition function uses the following syntax:

```
DROP PARTITION FUNCTION partition_function_name
```

Again, this command only takes the partition function name that should be dropped.

This example demonstrates how to drop a partition function and scheme, assuming that it is okay in this scenario to drop the source tables (which oftentimes in a production scenario will *not* be acceptable!):

```
DROP TABLE Sales.WebSiteHitsHistory
DROP TABLE Sales.WebSiteHits

-- Dropping the partition scheme and function
DROP PARTITION SCHEME HitDateRangeScheme
DROP PARTITION FUNCTION HitDateRange
```

How It Works

This example demonstrated dropping a partition scheme and function; for this example, this required that the source tables be dropped beforehand. One alternative solution is to copy out the results to an external table, drop the tables, drop the partition scheme and partition function, and then rename the tables that you copied the data to. If your goal is just to get the table down to a single partition, you can merge all partitions, while still keeping the partition scheme and function. A single partitioned table is functionally equivalent to a regular, non-partitioned table.

Easing VLDB Manageability with Filegroups

Filegroups are often used for very large databases because they can ease backup administration and potentially improve performance by distributing data over disk LUNs or arrays. When creating a table, you can specify that it be created on a specific filegroup. For example, if you have a table that you know will become very large, you can designate that it be created on a specific filegroup.

■**Note** This recipe includes filegroup techniques and concepts covered in more detail in Chapter 22.

The basic syntax for designating a table's filegroup is as follows:

```
CREATE TABLE ...
    [ ON {filegroup | "default" }]
[ { TEXTIMAGE_ON { filegroup | "default" } ]
```

Table 4-25 details the arguments of this command.

Table 4-25. *Arguments for Creating a Table on a Filegroup*

Argument	Description
filegroup	This specifies the name of the filegroup on which the table will be created.
"DEFAULT"	This sets the table to be created on the default filegroup defined for the database.
TEXTIMAGE_ON { filegroup	"DEFAULT" }	This option stores in a separate filegroup the data from text, ntext, image, xml, varchar(max), nvarchar(max), and varbinary(max) data types.

This example demonstrates how to place a table on a non-default, user-created filegroup. The first step involves creating a new filegroup in the AdventureWorks database:

```
ALTER DATABASE AdventureWorks
ADD FILEGROUP AW_FG2
GO
```

Next, a new file is added to the filegroup:

```
ALTER DATABASE AdventureWorks
ADD FILE
(   NAME = AW_F2,
    FILENAME = 'C:\Apress\aw_f2.ndf',
    SIZE = 1MB
)
TO FILEGROUP AW_FG2
GO
```

I'll then create a new table on the new filegroup (causing its data to be stored in the new file, contained within the filegroup):

```
CREATE TABLE HumanResources.AWCompany(
   AWCompanyID int IDENTITY(1,1) NOT NULL PRIMARY KEY,
   ParentAWCompanyID int NULL,
   AWCompanyNM varchar(25) NOT NULL,
   CreateDT datetime NOT NULL DEFAULT (getdate())
) ON AW_FG2
```

In the second example, a table is created by specifying that large object data columns be stored on a separate filegroup (AW_FG2) from the regular data (on the PRIMARY filegroup):

```
CREATE TABLE HumanResources.EWCompany(
   EWCompanyID int IDENTITY(1,1) NOT NULL PRIMARY KEY,
   ParentEWCompanyID int NULL,
   EWCompanyName varchar(25) NOT NULL,
   HeadQuartersImage varbinary(max) NULL,
   CreateDT datetime NOT NULL DEFAULT (getdate())
) ON [PRIMARY]
TEXTIMAGE_ON AW_FG2
```

How It Works

The recipe started by creating a new filegroup called AW_FG2. This was done using the ALTER DATABASE command. After that, a new database file was added to the AdventureWorks database, which was placed into the new filegroup.

CREATE TABLE was then executed normally, only in the last part of the table definition ON AW_FG2 was used in order to place it into the AW_FG2 filegroup:

```
ON AW_FG2
```

If an ON filegroup clause isn't used in a CREATE TABLE, it's assumed that the table will be placed on the default filegroup (which, if you haven't changed it, is called PRIMARY).

If this table becomes very large, and you've placed it on its own filegroup, a filegroup backup can be used to specifically back up the table and any other tables or indexes that are placed in it (see Chapter 5 for more on placing an index into a filegroup and Chapter 29 for a review of filegroup backups).

For the second example, a table was created with filegroup options placing regular data on the PRIMARY filegroup and text/image data on the AW_FG2 filegroup (doing so requires that your table actually *have* a large value data type):

```
ON [PRIMARY]
TEXTIMAGE_ON AW_FG2
```

Separating out large object data may ease database maintenance and improve performance, depending on your database design and physical hardware, the types of queries accessing it, and the location of the file(s) in the filegroup.

Reducing Disk Space Usage with Data Compression

SQL Server 2008 Enterprise Edition and Developer Edition introduce row- and page-level compression for tables, indexes, and associated partitions.

Row compression applies variable-length storage to numeric data types (for example, int, bigint, and decimal) and fixed-length types such as money and datetime. Row compression also applies variable-length format to fixed-character strings and doesn't store trailing blank characters, NULL, and 0 values.

Page compression includes row compression, and also adds prefix and dictionary compression. Prefix compression involves the storage of column prefix values that are stored multiple times in a column across rows and replaces the redundant prefixes with references to the single value. Dictionary compression occurs after prefix compression and involves finding repeated data values anywhere on the data page (not just prefixes) and then replacing the redundancies with a pointer to the single value.

■**Tip** Chapter 5 reviews how to use CREATE INDEX and ALTER INDEX to enable compression for nonclustered indexes.

This recipe will show how to use CREATE TABLE and ALTER TABLE to enable row and page compression. In the first example, I will enable row compression for a new table. To do so, I designate the DATA_COMPRESSION table option and select either NONE, ROW, or PAGE:

```
CREATE TABLE dbo.ArchiveJobPosting
(JobPostingID int NOT NULL IDENTITY(1,1) PRIMARY KEY CLUSTERED,
 CandidateID int NOT NULL,
 JobDESC char(2000) NOT NULL
)
WITH (DATA_COMPRESSION = ROW)
```

To reconfigure compression on an existing table, I can execute ALTER TABLE...REBUILD WITH with the DATA_COMPRESSION table option. For example, the following command turns off compression for the table I just created:

```
ALTER TABLE dbo.ArchiveJobPosting
REBUILD WITH
(DATA_COMPRESSION = NONE)
```

Next, I will populate the table with garbage data in order to demonstrate the benefits of compression. The following query inserts a row, choosing a random integer value for the CandidateID, and then repeating the letter "a" 50 times for the JobDESC. The GO command followed by 100000 means that the INSERT will execute 100,000 times, resulting in 100,000 new rows into this table (this may take a few minutes for you to execute if you are following along on your own test SQL Server instance):

```
INSERT dbo.ArchiveJobPosting
(CandidateID, JobDESC)
VALUES (CAST(RAND() * 10 as int),
        REPLICATE('a',50))
GO 100000
```

Now that the data is populated, I can execute the sp_estimate_data_compression_savings system stored procedure to get an estimate of how much disk savings I can expect to see when using either row or page compression. The sp_estimate_data_compression_savings stored procedure takes five arguments: the schema name of the table to be compressed, object name, index ID, partition number, and data compression method (NONE, ROW, or PAGE). In the following example, I will first check to see how much space can be saved by using row compression:

```
EXEC sys.sp_estimate_data_compression_savings
     @schema_name =  'dbo',
     @object_name =  'ArchiveJobPosting',
```

```
        @index_id = NULL,
        @partition_number = NULL,
        @data_compression = 'ROW'
```

This returns the following information (reformatted for readability):

object_name	ArchiveJobPosting
schema_name	dbo
index_id	1
partition_number	1
size_with_current_compression_setting(KB)	200752
size_with_requested_compression_setting(KB)	6536
sample_size_with_current_compression_setting(KB)	39776
sample_size_with_requested_compression_setting(KB)	1296

As you can see from the stored procedure results, adding row compression would save 194,216KB with the current data set. The sample size data is based on the stored procedure loading sample data into a cloned table in tempdb and validating the compression ratio accordingly.

Now I will test to see whether there are benefits to using page-level compression:

```
EXEC sys.sp_estimate_data_compression_savings
        @schema_name =  'dbo',
        @object_name =  'ArchiveJobPosting',
        @index_id = NULL,
        @partition_number = NULL,
        @data_compression = 'PAGE'
```

This returns

object_name	ArchiveJobPosting
schema_name	dbo
index_id	1
partition_number	1
size_with_current_compression_setting(KB)	200752
size_with_requested_compression_setting(KB)	1200
sample_size_with_current_compression_setting(KB)	40144
sample_size_with_requested_compression_setting(KB)	240

Sure enough, the page-level compression shows additional benefits beyond just row-level compression.

■**Caution** The trade-off for compression is some increased CPU utilization. You must consider and test your current application to determine whether the trade-off of disk space to ongoing CPU overhead is beneficial.

Next, I will go ahead and turn on page-level compression for the table using ALTER TABLE:

```
ALTER TABLE dbo.ArchiveJobPosting
REBUILD WITH
(DATA_COMPRESSION = PAGE)
```

Compression can also be configured at the partition level. In the next set of commands, I will create a new partitioning function and scheme, and apply it to a new table. The table will use varying compression levels based on the partition. I first start off by creating the partition function and scheme:

```
CREATE PARTITION FUNCTION pfn_ArchivePart(int)
AS RANGE LEFT FOR VALUES (50000, 100000, 150000)
GO

-- This command assumes your db has these filegroups
CREATE PARTITION SCHEME psc_ArchivePart
AS PARTITION pfn_ArchivePart
TO (hitfg1, hitfg2, hitfg3, hitfg4) ;
GO
```

Next, I create the table referencing the partition scheme on the JobPostingID integer column. I also designate which partitions will have PAGE compression and which partitions will have row compression:

```
CREATE TABLE dbo.ArchiveJobPosting_V2
(JobPostingID int NOT NULL IDENTITY(1,1) PRIMARY KEY CLUSTERED,
 CandidateID int NOT NULL,
 JobDESC char(2000) NOT NULL)
ON psc_ArchivePart(JobPostingID)
WITH (DATA_COMPRESSION = PAGE ON PARTITIONS (1 TO 3),
      DATA_COMPRESSION = ROW ON PARTITIONS (4))
```

If I want to change the compression level for any of the partitions, I can use ALTER TABLE, as demonstrated next, by changing partition 4 from row to page compression:

```
ALTER TABLE dbo.ArchiveJobPosting_V2
REBUILD PARTITION = 4
WITH (DATA_COMPRESSION = PAGE)
```

How It Works

This recipe demonstrated how to apply page- and row-level compression to a table by using CREATE TABLE and ALTER TABLE. SQL Server 2008 Enterprise Edition and Developer Edition introduce the compression feature, which is used to reduce overall disk usage for database tables. Depending on the type of data stored in your table, overall compression ratios will vary in significance. Also note that the benefit of compression comes with an overall CPU cost, which you'll want to thoroughly test prior to deploying in a production environment.

Enabling compression only involves using the DATA_COMPRESSION clause in conjunction with the CREATE TABLE or ALTER TABLE command (I'll demonstrate nonclustered index compression in Chapter 5). This compression can take place against a heap (no clustered index), clustered index, nonclustered index, indexed view, or specific partitions on a table or index. To validate the benefits of adding row or page compression, use the sp_estimate_data_compression_savings system stored procedure as was demonstrated in this recipe.

CHAPTER 5

■■■

Indexes

Indexes assist with query processing by speeding up access to the data stored in tables and views. Indexes allow for ordered access to data based on an ordering of data rows. These rows are ordered based upon the values stored in certain columns. These columns comprise the index key columns, and their values (for any given row) are a row's index key.

This chapter contains recipes for creating, altering, and dropping different types of indexes. I'll demonstrate how indexes can be created, including a syntax for index options, support for partition schemes, the INCLUDE command, page and row lock disabling, index disabling, and the ability to perform online operations.

I'll also cover a couple of new features in SQL Server 2008, including filtered indexes and index compression. For exercises performed in this chapter, you may wish to back up the AdventureWorks database beforehand, so that you can restore it to its original state after going through the recipes.

Note For coverage of index maintenance, reindexing, and rebuilding (ALTER INDEX), see Chapter 23. Indexed views are covered in Chapter 7. For coverage of index performance troubleshooting and fragmentation, see Chapter 28.

Index Overview

An index is a database object that, when created on a table, can provide faster access paths to data and can facilitate faster query execution. Indexes are used to provide SQL Server with a more efficient method of accessing the data. Instead of always searching every data page in a table, an index facilitates retrieving specific rows without having to read a table's entire content.

By default, rows in a regular unindexed table aren't stored in any particular order. A table in an orderless state is called a *heap*. In order to retrieve rows from a heap based on a matching set of search conditions, SQL Server would have to read through all the rows in the table. Even if only one row matched the search criteria and that row just happened to be the first row the SQL Server database engine read, SQL Server would still need to evaluate every single table row since there is no other way for it to know if other matching rows exist. Such a scan for information is known as a *full table scan*. For a large table, that might mean reading hundreds or thousands or millions and billions of rows just to retrieve a single row. However, if SQL Server knows that there is an index on a column (or columns) of a table, then it may be able to use that index to search for matching records more efficiently.

In SQL Server, a table is contained in one or more *partitions*. A partition is a unit of organization that allows you to horizontally separate allocation of data within a table and/or index, while still maintaining a single logical object. When a table is created, by default, all of its data is contained within a single partition. A partition contains heaps, or, when indexes are created, *B-tree structures.*

When an index is created, its index key data is stored in a B-tree structure. A B-tree structure starts with a root node, which is the beginning of the index. This *root node* has index data that contains a range of index key values that point to the next level of index nodes, called the *intermediate leaf level.* The bottom level of the node is called the *leaf level.* The leaf level differs based on whether the actual index type is *clustered* or *nonclustered.* If it is a clustered index, the leaf level is the actual data pages itself. If a nonclustered index, the leaf level contains pointers to the heap or clustered index data pages.

A clustered index determines how the actual table data is physically stored. You can only designate *one* clustered index. This index type stores the data according to the designated index key column or columns. Figure 5-1 demonstrates the B-tree structure of the clustered index. Notice that the leaf level consists of the actual data pages.

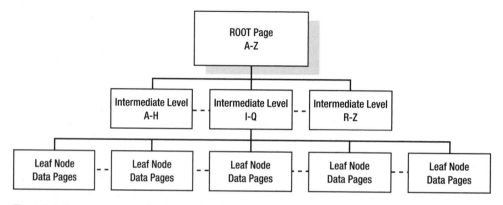

Figure 5-1. *B-tree structure of a clustered index*

Clustered index selection is a critical choice, as you can only have one clustered index for a single table. In general, good candidates for clustered indexes include columns that are queried often in range queries because the data is then physically organized in a particular order. Range queries use the BETWEEN keyword and the greater than (>) and less than (<) operators. Other columns to consider are those used to order large result sets, those used in aggregate functions, and those that contain entirely unique values. Frequently updated columns and non-unique columns are usually *not* a good choice for a clustered index key, because the clustered index key is contained in the leaf level of all dependent nonclustered indexes, causing excessive reordering and modifications. For this same reason, you should also avoid creating a clustered index with too many or very wide (many bytes) index keys.

Nonclustered indexes store index pages separately from the physical data, with pointers to the physical data located in the index pages and nodes. Nonclustered index columns are stored in the order of the index key column values. You can have up to 249 nonclustered indexes on a table or indexed view. For nonclustered indexes, the leaf node level is the index key coupled to a row locater that points to either the row of a heap or the clustered index row key, as shown in Figure 5-2.

When selecting columns to be used for nonclustered indexes, look for those columns that are frequently referenced in WHERE, JOIN, and ORDER BY clauses. Search for highly selective columns that would return smaller result sets (less than 20 percent of all rows in a table). *Selectivity* refers to how many rows exist for each unique index key value. If a column has poor selectivity, for example, only containing zeros or ones, it is unlikely that SQL Server will take advantage of that query when creating the query execution plan, because of its poor selectivity.

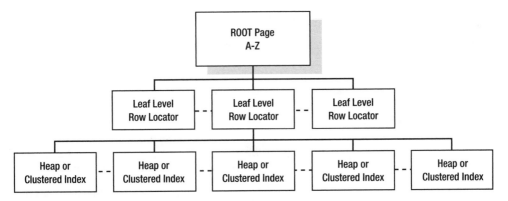

Figure 5-2. *B-tree structure of a nonclustered index*

An index, either clustered or nonclustered, is based on one or more key values. The index key refers to columns used to define the index itself. SQL Server also has a feature that allows the addition of non-key columns to the leaf level of the index by using the new INCLUDE clause demonstrated later on in the chapter. This feature allows more of your query's selected columns to be returned or "covered" by a single nonclustered index, thus reducing total I/O, as SQL Server doesn't have to access the clustered leaf level data pages at all.

You can use up to 16 key columns in a single index, so long as you don't exceed 900 bytes of all index key columns combined. You can't use large object data types within the index key, including varchar(max), nvarchar(max), varbinary(max), xml, ntext, text, and the image data types.

A clustered or nonclustered index can either be specified as unique or non-unique. Choosing a unique index makes sure that the data values inserted into the key column or columns are unique. For unique indexes using multiple keys (called a *composite index*), the combination of the key values have to be unique for every row in the table.

As noted earlier, indexes can be massively beneficial in terms of your query performance, but there are also costs associated with them. You should only add indexes based on expected query activity, and you should continually monitor whether or not indexes are still being used over time. If not, they should be removed. Too many indexes on a table can cause performance overhead whenever data modifications are performed to the table, as SQL Server must maintain the index changes alongside the data changes. Ongoing maintenance activities such as index rebuilding and reorganizations will also be prolonged with excessive indexing.

These next few recipes will demonstrate how to create, modify, disable, view, and drop indexes.

■**Note** See Chapter 28 to learn how to view which indexes are being used for a query. This chapter also covers how to view index fragmentation and identify whether or not an index is being used over time. To learn how to rebuild or reorganize indexes, see Chapter 23.

Creating a Table Index

In this recipe, I'll show you how to create two types of indexes, one clustered and the other nonclustered. An index is created by using the CREATE INDEX command. This chapter will review the many facets of this command; however, the basic syntax used in this upcoming example is as follows:

```
CREATE [ UNIQUE ] [ CLUSTERED | NONCLUSTERED ] INDEX index_name
    ON {
    [ database_name. [ schema_name ] . | schema_name. ]
        table_or_view_name}
( column [ ASC | DESC ] [ ,...n ] )
```

The arguments of this command are described in Table 5-1.

Table 5-1. *CREATE INDEX Command Arguments*

Argument	Description
[UNIQUE]	You can only have one primary key on each table. However, if you wish to enforce uniqueness in other non-key columns, you can designate that the index be created with the UNIQUE constraint. You can create multiple UNIQUE indexes for a single table and can include columns that contain NULL values (although only one NULL value is allowed per column combo).
[CLUSTERED	NONCLUSTERED]	This specifies the index type, either CLUSTERED or NONCLUSTERED. You can only have one CLUSTERED index, but up to 249 NONCLUSTERED indexes.
index_name	This defines the name of the new index.
[database_name. [schema_name] .	schema_name.] table_or_view_name}	This indicates the table or view to be indexed.
Column	This specifies the column or columns to be used as part of the index key.
[ASC	DESC]	This defines specific column order of indexing, either ASC for ascending order or DESC for descending order.

I'll also show you a few examples of modifying an existing index using the ALTER INDEX command:

```
ALTER INDEX index_name
ON object_name
...
```

This command includes many of the same options of CREATE INDEX, only you cannot use it to change which columns are used and their ordering. This command is also used to rebuild or reorganize an index (which is covered in Chapter 23).

Starting off the recipe, I'll create a new table in the AdventureWorks database for demonstration purposes. I will intentionally leave off a PRIMARY KEY in the table definition:

```
USE AdventureWorks
GO

CREATE TABLE HumanResources.TerminationReason(
   TerminationReasonID smallint IDENTITY(1,1) NOT NULL,
    TerminationReason varchar(50) NOT NULL,
   DepartmentID smallint NOT NULL,
 CONSTRAINT FK_TerminationReason_DepartmentID
   FOREIGN KEY (DepartmentID) REFERENCES
   HumanResources.Department(DepartmentID)
)
GO
```

Before I demonstrate how to use CREATE INDEX, it is important to remember that when a primary key is created on a column using CREATE TABLE or ALTER TABLE, that primary key also creates an index. Instead of defining this up front, in this example, I will create a CLUSTERED index on the TerminationReasonID using ALTER TABLE with ADD CONSTRAINT:

```
ALTER TABLE HumanResources.TerminationReason
ADD CONSTRAINT PK_TerminationReason PRIMARY KEY CLUSTERED (TerminationReasonID)
```

Next, I'll create a nonclustered index on the DepartmentID column:

```
CREATE NONCLUSTERED INDEX NCI_TerminationReason_DepartmentID ON
HumanResources.TerminationReason (DepartmentID)
```

How It Works

In this exercise, the TerminationReason table was created without a primary key defined, meaning that initially, the table was a "heap." The primary key was then added afterward using ALTER TABLE. The word CLUSTERED follows the PRIMARY KEY statement, thus designating a clustered index with the new constraint:

```
ALTER TABLE HumanResources.TerminationReason
ADD CONSTRAINT PK_TerminationReason PRIMARY KEY CLUSTERED (TerminationReasonID)
```

Had the TerminationReasonID column not been chosen as the primary key, you could have still defined a clustered index on it by using CREATE INDEX:

```
CREATE CLUSTERED INDEX CI_TerminationReason_TerminationReasonID ON
HumanResources.TerminationReason (TerminationReasonID)
```

Had a nonclustered index already existed for the table, the creation of the new clustered index would have caused the nonclustered index to be rebuilt, in order to swap the nonclustered leaf level row identifier with the clustered key.

The nonclustered index in the example was created as follows:

```
CREATE NONCLUSTERED INDEX NCI_TerminationReason_DepartmentID ON
HumanResources.TerminationReason (DepartmentID)
```

The only difference in syntax between the two index types was that the word NONCLUSTERED is designated between CREATE and INDEX.

Enforcing Uniqueness on Non-Key Columns

In this recipe, I'll show you how to enforce uniqueness for non-key table columns. The syntax for CREATE INDEX in the previous recipe showed the UNIQUE keyword. This example shows you how to create a unique index on the HumanResources.TerminationReason table's TerminationReason column:

```
CREATE UNIQUE NONCLUSTERED INDEX UNI_TerminationReason ON
HumanResources.TerminationReason (TerminationReason)
```

Now, I'll insert two new rows into the table with success:

```
INSERT HumanResources.TerminationReason
(DepartmentID, TerminationReason)
VALUES (1, 'Bad Engineering Skills')

INSERT HumanResources.TerminationReason
(DepartmentID, TerminationReason)
VALUES (2, 'Breaks Expensive Tools')
```

If I attempt to insert a row with a duplicate TerminationReason value, an error will be raised:

```
INSERT HumanResources.TerminationReason
(DepartmentID, TerminationReason)
VALUES (2, 'Bad Engineering Skills')
```

This returns

```
Msg 2601, Level 14, State 1, Line 9
Cannot insert duplicate key row in object 'HumanResources.TerminationReason'
with unique index 'UNI_TerminationReason'.
The statement has been terminated.
```

Selecting the current rows from the table shows that only the first two rows were inserted:

```
SELECT TerminationReasonID, TerminationReason, DepartmentID
FROM HumanResources.TerminationReason
```

This returns

TerminationReasonID	TerminationReason	DepartmentID
1	Bad Engineering Skills	1
2	Breaks Expensive Tools	2

How It Works

A unique index was created on the TerminationReason column, which means that each row must have a unique value. You can choose multiple unique constraints for a single table. NULL values are permitted in a unique index; however, they must only occur once. Like a primary key, unique indexes enforce entity integrity by ensuring that rows can be uniquely identified.

Creating an Index on Multiple Columns

In this recipe, I'll show you how to create a multiple-column index. In previous recipes, I've shown you how to create an index on a single column; however, many times you will want more than one column to be used in a single index. Use composite indexes when two or more columns are often searched within the same query, or are often used in conjunction with one another.

In this example, we're assuming that TerminationReason and the DepartmentID will often be used in the same WHERE clause of a SELECT query. With that in mind, I'll create the following multi-column NONCLUSTERED INDEX:

```
CREATE NONCLUSTERED INDEX NI_TerminationReason_TerminationReason_DepartmentID
ON HumanResources.TerminationReason(TerminationReason, DepartmentID)
```

How It Works

Choosing which columns to index is a bit of an art. You'll want to add indexes to columns that you know will be commonly queried; however, you must always keep a column's selectivity in mind. If a column has poor selectivity, for example, only containing a few unique values across thousands of rows, it is unlikely that SQL Server will take advantage of that query when creating the query execution plan. One general rule of thumb when creating a composite index is to put the most selective columns at the beginning, followed by the other less-selective columns. In this recipe's example, the

TerminationReason was chosen as the first column, followed by the DepartmentID. Both are guaranteed to be totally unique in the table, and therefore are equally selective.

■**Tip** Use the Database Tuning Advisor to help make index suggestions for you based on a query or batch of queries. See Chapter 28 for more information on index usage and performance.

Defining Index Column Sort Direction

In this recipe, I'll show you how to set the sort direction of an index column. The default sort for an indexed column is ascending order. You can explicitly set the ordering using ASC or DESC in the column definition of CREATE INDEX:

```
( column [ ASC | DESC ] [ ,...n ] )
```

In this example, I'll add a new column to a table and then index the column using a descending order:

```
ALTER TABLE HumanResources.TerminationReason
ADD ViolationSeverityLevel smallint
GO

CREATE NONCLUSTERED INDEX NI_TerminationReason_ViolationSeverityLevel
ON HumanResources.TerminationReason (ViolationSeverityLevel DESC)
```

How It Works

In this recipe's example, a new column, ViolationSeverityLevel, was added to the TerminationReason table:

```
ALTER TABLE HumanResources.TerminationReason
ADD ViolationSeverityLevel smallint
GO
```

Query authors may want to most commonly sort on this value, showing ViolationSeverityLevel from highest to lowest. Matching index order to how you think users will use ORDER BY in the query can improve query performance, as SQL Server isn't then required to re-sort the data when the query is processed. The index is created with the DESC instruction after the column name:

```
(ViolationSeverityLevel DESC)
```

If you have multiple key columns in your index, each can have its own separate sort order.

Viewing Index Meta Data

In this recipe, I'll show you how to view helpful information about indexes. Once you've created indexes on your tables, you'll need some mechanism for tracking where they are, what their names are, types, and the columns that define them. For this, use the sp_helpindex system stored procedure to view the index names, descriptions, and keys for indexes on a specific table. This system stored procedure only takes a single argument, the name of the table whose indexes you want to view.

This example demonstrates viewing all indexes on the Employee table:

```
EXEC sp_helpindex 'HumanResources.Employee'
```

This returns the following results:

index_name	index_description	index_keys
AK_Employee_LoginID	nonclustered, unique located on PRIMARY	LoginID
AK_Employee_NationalIDNumber	nonclustered, unique located on PRIMARY	NationalIDNumber
AK_Employee_rowguid	nonclustered, unique located on PRIMARY	rowguid
IX_Employee_ManagerID	nonclustered located on PRIMARY	ManagerID
PK_Employee_EmployeeID	clustered, unique, primary key located on PRIMARY	EmployeeID

For more in-depth index analysis of indexes, you can use the sys.indexes system catalog view. For example, the following query shows index options (which will be discussed later in the chapter) for the HumanResources.Employee table:

```
SELECT SUBSTRING(name, 1,30) index_name,
       allow_row_locks,
       allow_page_locks,
       is_disabled,
       fill_factor,
       has_filter
FROM sys.indexes
WHERE object_id = OBJECT_ID('HumanResources.Employee')
```

This returns

index_name	allow_row_locks	allow_page_locks	is_disabled	fill_factor	has_filter
PK_Employee_EmployeeID	1	1	0	0	0
AK_Employee_LoginID	1	1	0	0	0
AK_Employee_NationalIDNumber	1	1	0	0	0
AK_Employee_rowguid	1	1	0	0	0
IX_Employee_ManagerID	1	1	0	0	0

How It Works

You can use the system stored procedure sp_helpindex call to list the indexes on a specific table. The output also returns a description of the indexes, including the type and filegroup location. The key columns defined for the index are also listed.

The sys.indexes system catalog view can also be used to find out more about the configured settings of a specific index.

■ **Tip** For related index keys and included columns, use the sys.index_columns catalog view.

Several of the options shown in this system catalog view haven't been covered yet, but some of them that I've discussed are described in Table 5-2.

Table 5-2. *A Subset of the sys.indexes System Catalog Columns*

Column	Description
object_id	This is the object identifier of the table or view for which the index belongs. You can use the OBJECT_NAME function to show the table or view name, or OBJECT_ID to convert a table or view name into its database object identifier.
name	This indicates the index name.
index_id	When index_id is 0, the index is a heap. When index_id is 1, the index is a clustered index. When index_id is greater than 1, it is a nonclustered index.
type	This specifies the index type, which can be 0 for heap, 1 for clustered index, 2 for nonclustered, 3 for an XML index, and 4 for spatial.
type_desc	This defines the index type description.
is_unique	When is_unique is 1, the index is a unique index.
is_primary_key	When is_primary_key is 1, the index is the result of a primary key constraint.
is_unique_constraint	When is_unique_constraint is 1, the index is the result of a unique constraint.

Disabling an Index

In this recipe, I'll show you how to disable an index from being used in SQL Server queries. Disabling an index retains the metadata definition data in SQL Server but makes the index unavailable for use. Consider disabling an index as an index troubleshooting technique or if a disk error has occurred and you would like to defer the index's re-creation.

▓**Caution** If you disable a clustered index, keep in mind that the table index data will no longer be accessible. This is because the leaf level of a clustered index is the actual table data itself. Also, reenabling the index means either re-creating or rebuilding it (see the "How It Works" section for more information).

An index is disabled by using the ALTER INDEX command. The syntax is as follows:

```
ALTER INDEX index_name ON
table_or_view_name DISABLE
```

The command takes two arguments, the name of the index, and the name of the table or view that the index is created on.

In this example, I will disable the UNI_TerminationReason index on the TerminationReason table:

```
ALTER INDEX UNI_TerminationReason ON
HumanResources.TerminationReason DISABLE
```

How It Works

This recipe demonstrated how to disable an index. If an index is disabled, the index definition remains in the system tables, although the user can no longer use the index. For nonclustered indexes on a table, the index data is actually removed from the database. For a clustered index on a table, the data remains on disk, but because the index is disabled, you can't query it. For a clustered or nonclustered index on the view, the index data is removed from the database.

To reenable the index, you can use either the CREATE INDEX with DROP_EXISTING command (see later in this chapter) or ALTER INDEX REBUILD (described in Chapter 23). Rebuilding a disabled nonclustered index reuses the existing space used by the original index.

Dropping Indexes

In this recipe, I'll show you how to drop an index from a table or view. When you drop an index, it is physically removed from the database. If this is a clustered index, the table's data remains in an unordered (heap) form. You can remove an index entirely from a database by using the DROP INDEX command. The basic syntax is as follows:

```
DROP INDEX <table_or_view_name>.<index_name> [ ,...n ]
```

In this example, I'll demonstrate dropping a single index from a table:

```
DROP INDEX HumanResources.TerminationReason.UNI_TerminationReason
```

How It Works

You can drop one or more indexes for a table using the DROP INDEX command. Dropping an index frees up the space taken up by the index and removes the index definition from the database. You can't use DROP INDEX to remove indexes that result from the creation of a PRIMARY KEY or UNIQUE CONSTRAINT. If you drop a clustered index that has nonclustered indexes on it, those nonclustered indexes will also be rebuilt in order to swap the clustered index key for a row identifier of the heap.

Changing an Existing Index with DROP_EXISTING

In this recipe, I'll show you how to drop and re-create an index within a single execution, as well as change the key column definition of an existing index. The ALTER INDEX can be used to change index options, rebuild and reorganize indexes (reviewed in Chapter 23), and disable an index, but it is not used to actually add, delete, or rearrange columns in the index.

You can, however, change the column definition of an existing index by using CREATE INDEX...DROP_EXISTING. This option also has the advantage of dropping and re-creating an index within a single command (instead of using both DROP INDEX and CREATE INDEX). Also, using DROP_EXISTING on a clustered index will not cause existing nonclustered indexes to be automatically rebuilt, unless the index column definition has changed.

This first example demonstrates just rebuilding an existing nonclustered index (no change in the column definition):

```
CREATE NONCLUSTERED INDEX NCI_TerminationReason_DepartmentID ON
HumanResources.TerminationReason
(DepartmentID ASC)
WITH (DROP_EXISTING = ON)
GO
```

Next, a new column is added to the existing nonclustered index:

```
CREATE NONCLUSTERED INDEX NCI_TerminationReason_DepartmentID ON
HumanResources.TerminationReason
(ViolationSeverityLevel, DepartmentID DESC)
WITH (DROP_EXISTING = ON)
GO
```

How It Works

In the first example, the CREATE INDEX didn't change anything about the existing index definition, but instead just rebuilds it by using the DROP_EXISTING clause. Rebuilding an index can help defragment the data, something which is discussed in more detail in Chapter 23.

In the second statement, a new column was added to the existing index and placed right before the DepartmentID. The index was re-created with the new index key column, making it a composite index.

You can't use DROP_EXISTING to change the name of the index, however. For that, use DROP INDEX and CREATE INDEX with the new index name.

Controlling Index Build Performance and Concurrency

So far in this chapter, I've reviewed how an index is defined, but note that you can also determine under what circumstances an index is built. For example, when creating an index in SQL Server, in order to improve the performance, you can designate that a parallel plan of execution is used, instantiating multiple processors to help complete a time-consuming build. In addition to this, you could also direct SQL Server to create the index in tempdb, instead of causing file growth operations in the index's home database. If you are using Enterprise Edition, you can also allow concurrent user query access to the underlying table during the index creation by using the ONLINE option.

The next three recipes will demonstrate methods for improving the performance of the index build, as well as improving user concurrency during the operation.

Intermediate Index Creation in Tempdb

In this recipe, I'll show you how to push index creation processing to the tempdb system database. The tempdb system database is used to manage user connections, temporary tables, temporary stored procedures, or temporary work tables needed to process queries on the SQL Server instance. Depending on the database activity on your SQL Server instance, you can sometimes reap performance benefits by isolating the tempdb database on its own disk array, separate from other databases. If index creation times are taking too long for what you expect, you can try to use the index option SORT_IN_TEMPDB to improve index build performance (for larger tables). This option pushes the intermediate index build results to the tempdb database instead of using the user database where the index is housed.

The syntax for this option, which can be used in both CREATE INDEX and ALTER INDEX, is as follows:

```
WITH (SORT_IN_TEMPDB = { ON | OFF })
```

The default for this option is OFF. In this example, I'll create a new nonclustered index with the SORT_IN_TEMPDB option enabled:

```
CREATE NONCLUSTERED INDEX NI_Address_PostalCode ON
Person.Address (PostalCode)
WITH (SORT_IN_TEMPDB = ON)
```

How It Works

The SORT_IN_TEMPDB option enables the use of the tempdb database for intermediate index results. This option may decrease the amount of time it takes to create the index for a large table, but with the trade-off that the `tempdb` system database will need additional space to participate in this operation.

Controlling Parallel Plan Execution for Index Creation

In this recipe, I'll show you how to control the number of processors used to process a single query. If using SQL Server Enterprise Edition with a multiprocessor server, you can control/limit the number of processors potentially used in an index creation operation by using the `MAXDOP` index option. *Parallelism*, which in this context is the use of two or more processors to fulfill a single query statement, can potentially improve the performance of the index creation operation.

The syntax for this option, which can be used in both `CREATE INDEX` and `ALTER INDEX`, is as follows:

```
MAXDOP = max_degree_of_parallelism
```

The default value for this option is 0, which means that SQL Server can choose any or all of the available processors for the operation. A `MAXDOP` value of 1 disables parallelism on the index creation.

■**Tip** Limiting parallelism for index creation may improve concurrency for user activity running during the build, but may also increase the time it takes for the index to be created.

This example demonstrates how to control the number of processors used in parallel plan execution (parallelism) during an index creation:

```
CREATE NONCLUSTERED INDEX NI_Address_AddressLine1 ON
Person.Address (AddressLine1)
WITH (MAXDOP = 4)
```

How It Works

In this recipe, the index creation was limited to 4 processors:

```
WITH (MAXDOP = 4)
```

Just because you set `MAXDOP` doesn't make any guarantee that SQL Server will actually *use* the number of processors that you designate. It only ensures that SQL Server will not exceed the `MAXDOP` threshold.

Allowing User Table Access During Index Creation

In this recipe, I'll show you how to allow query activity to continue to access the index even while an index creation process is executing. If you are using SQL Server Enterprise Edition, you can allow concurrent user query access to the underlying table during the index creation by using the new `ONLINE` option, which is demonstrated in this next recipe:

```
CREATE NONCLUSTERED INDEX NCI_ProductVendor_MinOrderQty ON
Purchasing.ProductVendor(MinOrderQty)
WITH (ONLINE = ON)
```

How It Works

With the new ONLINE option in the WITH clause of the index creation, long-term table locks are not held during the index creation. This can provide better concurrency on larger indexes that contain frequently accessed data. When the ONLINE option is set ON, only intent share locks are held on the source table for the duration of the index creation, instead of the default behavior of a longer-term table lock held for the duration of the index creation.

Index Options

The next three recipes cover options that impact performance, although each in their own different ways. For example, the INCLUDE keyword allows you to add non-key columns to a nonclustered index. This allows you to create a covering index that can be used to return data to the user without having to access the clustered index data.

The second recipe will discuss how the PAD_INDEX and FILLFACTOR options determine how to set the initial percentage of rows to fill the index leaf level pages and intermediate levels of an index. The recipe will discuss how the fill factor impacts the performance of not only queries, but also insert, update, and delete operations.

The third recipe will cover how to disable certain locking types for a specific index. As will be discussed in the recipe, using these options allows you to control both concurrency and resource usage when queries access the index.

Using an Index INCLUDE

In this recipe, I'll show you how to include non-key columns within a nonclustered index. A *covering query* is a query whose referenced columns are found entirely within a nonclustered index. This scenario often results in better query performance, as SQL Server does not have to retrieve the actual data from the clustered index or heap—it only needs to read the data stored in the non-clustered index. The drawback, however, is that you can only include up to 16 columns or up to 900 bytes for an index key.

One solution to this problem is the INCLUDE keyword, which allows you to add up to 1023 *non-key* columns to the nonclustered index, helping you improve query performance by creating a covered index. These non-key columns are not stored at each level of the index, but instead are only found in the leaf level of the nonclustered index. The syntax for using INCLUDE with CREATE NONCLUSTERED INDEX is as follows:

```
CREATE NONCLUSTERED INDEX index_name
    ON table_or_view_name ( column [ ASC | DESC ] [ ,...n ] )
INCLUDE ( column [ ,... n ] )
```

Whereas the first column list is for key index columns, the column list after INCLUDE is for non-key columns. In this example, I'll create a new large object data type column to the TerminationReason table. I'll drop the existing index on DepartmentID and re-create it with the new non-key value in the index:

```
ALTER TABLE HumanResources.TerminationReason
ADD LegalDescription varchar(max)

DROP INDEX
HumanResources.TerminationReason.NI_TerminationReason_TerminationReason_DepartmentID

CREATE NONCLUSTERED INDEX NI_TerminationReason_TerminationReason_DepartmentID
ON HumanResources.TerminationReason (TerminationReason, DepartmentID)
INCLUDE (LegalDescription)
```

How It Works

This recipe demonstrated a technique for enhancing a nonclustered index's usefulness. The example started off by creating a new varchar(max) data type column. Because of its data type, it cannot be used as a key value in the index; however, using it within the INCLUDE keyword will allow you to reference the new large object data types. The existing index on the TerminationReason table was then dropped and re-created using INCLUDE with the new non-key column.

You can use INCLUDE only with a nonclustered index (where a covered query comes in handy), and you still can't include the deprecated image, ntext, and text data types. Also, if the index size increases too significantly because of the additional non-key values, you may lose some of the query benefits that a covering query can give you, so be sure to test comparative before/after performance.

Using PAD_INDEX and FILLFACTOR

In this recipe, I'll show you how to set the initial percentage of rows to fill the index leaf level pages and intermediate levels of an index. The fill factor percentage of an index refers to how full the leaf level of the index pages should be when the index is first created. The default fill factor, if not explicitly set, is 0, which equates to filling the pages as full as possible (SQL Server does leave *some* space available—enough for a single index row). Leaving some space available, however, allows new rows to be inserted without resorting to page splits. A page split occurs when a new row is added to a full index page. In order to make room, half the rows are moved from the existing full page to a new page. Numerous page splits can slow down INSERT operations. On the other hand, however, fully packed data pages allow for faster read activity, as the database engine can retrieve more rows from less data pages.

The PAD_INDEX option, used only in conjunction with FILLFACTOR, specifies that the specified percentage of free space be left open on the intermediate level pages of an index.

These options are set in the WITH clause of the CREATE INDEX and ALTER INDEX commands. The syntax is as follows:

```
WITH (PAD_INDEX  = { ON | OFF }
  | FILLFACTOR = fillfactor)
```

In this example, an index is dropped and re-created with a 50% fill factor and PAD_INDEX enabled:

```
DROP INDEX
HumanResources.TerminationReason.NI_TerminationReason_TerminationReason_DepartmentID

CREATE NONCLUSTERED INDEX NI_TerminationReason_TerminationReason_DepartmentID
ON HumanResources.TerminationReason
(TerminationReason ASC, DepartmentID ASC)
WITH (PAD_INDEX=ON, FILLFACTOR=50)
```

How It Works

In this recipe, the fill factor was configured to 50%, leaving 50% of the index pages free for new rows. PAD_INDEX was also enabled, so the intermediate index pages will also be left half free. Both options are used in the WITH clause of the CREATE INDEX syntax:

```
WITH (PAD_INDEX=ON, FILLFACTOR=50)
```

Using FILLFACTOR can be a balancing act between reads and writes. For example, a 100% fill factor can improve reads, but slow down write activity, causing frequent page splitting as the database engine must continually shift row locations in order to make space in the data pages. Having too *low* of a fill factor can benefit row inserts, but it can also slow down read operations, as more data pages must be accessed in order to retrieve all required rows. If you're looking for a general rule of thumb, use a 100% fill factor for tables with almost no data modification activity, 80–90% for low activity, 60–70% for medium activity, and 50% or lower for high activity on the index key.

Disabling Page and/or Row Index Locking

In this recipe, I'll show you how to change the lock resource types that can be locked for a specific index. In Chapter 3, I discussed various lock types and resources within SQL Server. Specifically, various resources can be locked by SQL Server from small (row and key locks) to medium (page locks, extents) to large (table, database). Multiple, smaller-grained locks help with query concurrency, assuming there are a significant number of queries simultaneously requesting data from the same table and associated indexes. Numerous locks take up memory, however, and can lower performance for the SQL Server instance as a whole. The trade-off is larger-grained locks, which increase memory resource availability but also reduce query concurrency.

You can create an index that restricts certain locking types when it is queried. Specifically, you can designate whether page or row locks are allowed.

In general you should allow SQL Server to automatically decide which locking type is best; however, there may be a situation where you wish to temporarily restrict certain resource locking types, for troubleshooting or a severe performance issue.

The syntax for configuring these options for both CREATE INDEX and ALTER INDEX is as follows:

```
WITH ( ALLOW_ROW_LOCKS = { ON | OFF }
  | ALLOW_PAGE_LOCKS = { ON | OFF })
```

This recipe shows you how to disable the database engine's ability to place row or page locks on an index, forcing it to use table locking instead:

```
-- Disable page locks. Table and row locks can still be used.
CREATE INDEX NI_EmployeePayHistory_Rate ON
HumanResources.EmployeePayHistory (Rate)
WITH (ALLOW_PAGE_LOCKS=OFF)

-- Disable page and row locks. Only table locks can be used.
ALTER INDEX NI_EmployeePayHistory_Rate ON
HumanResources.EmployeePayHistory
SET (ALLOW_PAGE_LOCKS=OFF,ALLOW_ROW_LOCKS=OFF )

-- Allow page and row locks.
ALTER INDEX NI_EmployeePayHistory_Rate ON
HumanResources.EmployeePayHistory
SET (ALLOW_PAGE_LOCKS=ON,ALLOW_ROW_LOCKS=ON )
```

How It Works

This recipe demonstrated three variations. The first query created a new index on the table, configured so that the database engine couldn't issue page locks against the index:

```
WITH (ALLOW_PAGE_LOCKS=OFF)
```

In the next statement, both page and row locks were turned OFF (the default for an index is for both to be set to ON):

```
ALTER INDEX NI_EmployeePayHistory_Rate ON
HumanResources.EmployeePayHistory
SET (ALLOW_PAGE_LOCKS=OFF,ALLOW_ROW_LOCKS=OFF )
```

In the last statement, page and row locking is reenabled:

```
SET (ALLOW_PAGE_LOCKS=ON,ALLOW_ROW_LOCKS=ON )
```

Removing locking options should only be done if you have a good reason to do so—for example, you may have activity that causes too many row locks, which can eat up memory resources. Instead of row locks, you may wish to have SQL Server use larger-grained page or table locks instead.

Managing Very Large Indexes

This next set of recipes for this chapter cover methods for managing very large indexes; however, the features demonstrated here can be applied to smaller and medium-sized indexes as well. For example, you can designate that an index is created on a separate filegroup. Doing so can provide benefits from both the manageability and performance sides, as you can then perform separate backups by filegroup, as well as improving I/O performance of a query if the filegroup has files that exist on a separate array.

As was initially reviewed in Chapter 4, you can also implement index partitioning. Partitioning allows you to break down the index data set into smaller subsets of data. As will be discussed in the recipe, if large indexes are separated onto separate partitions, this can positively impact the performance of a query (particularly for very large indexes).

SQL Server 2008 also introduces the filtered index feature and the ability to compress data at the page and row level. The filtered index feature allows you to create an index and associated statistics for a subset of values. If incoming queries only hit a small percentage of values within a column, for example, you can create a filtered index that will only target those common values—thus reducing the overall index size compared to a full table index, and also improving the accuracy of the underlying statistics.

As for the new compression feature, available in the Enterprise and Developer Editions, you can now designate row or page compression for an index or specified partitions. I originally demonstrated this feature for `CREATE TABLE` and `ALTER TABLE` in Chapter 4. In this chapter, I'll continue this discussion with how to enable compression using `CREATE INDEX` and `ALTER INDEX`.

Creating an Index on a Filegroup

In this recipe, I'll show you how to create an index on a specific filegroup. If not explicitly designated, an index is created on the same filegroup as the underlying table. This is accomplished using the `ON` clause of the `CREATE INDEX` command:

```
ON filegroup_name | default
```

This option can take an explicit filegroup name or the database default filegroup (for more information on filegroups, see Chapter 22).

This example demonstrates how to explicitly define which filegroup an index is stored on. First, I'll create a new filegroup on the `AdventureWorks` database:

```
ALTER DATABASE AdventureWorks
ADD FILEGROUP FG2
```

Next, I'll add a new file to the database and the newly created filegroup:

```
ALTER DATABASE AdventureWorks
ADD FILE
(   NAME = AW2,
    FILENAME = 'c:\Apress\aw2.ndf',
```

```
    SIZE = 1MB
)
TO FILEGROUP FG2
```

Lastly, I'll create a new index, designating that it be stored on the newly created filegroup:

```
CREATE INDEX NI_ProductPhoto_ThumnailPhotoFileName ON
Production.ProductPhoto (ThumbnailPhotoFileName)
ON [FG2]
```

How It Works

The first part of the recipe creates a new filegroup in the AdventureWorks database called FG2 using the ALTER DATABASE command. After that, a new database data file is created on the new filegroup. Lastly, a new index is created on the FG2 filegroup. The ON clause designated the filegroup name for the index in square brackets:

```
ON [FG2]
```

Filegroups can be used to help manage very large databases, both by allowing separate backups by filegroup, as well as improving I/O performance if the filegroup has files that exist on a separate array.

Implementing Index Partitioning

In this recipe, I'll show you how to apply partitioning to a nonclustered index. In Chapter 4, I demonstrated table partitioning. Partitioning can provide manageability, scalability, and performance benefits for large tables. This is because partitioning allows you to break down the data set into smaller subsets of data. Depending on the index key(s), an index on a table can also be quite large. Applying the partitioning concept to indexes, if large indexes are separated onto separate partitions, this can positively impact the performance of a query. Queries that target data from just one partition will benefit because SQL Server will target just the selected partition, instead of accessing all partitions for the index.

This recipe will now demonstrate index partitioning using the HitDateRangeScheme partition scheme that was created in Chapter 4 on the Sales.WebSiteHits table:

```
CREATE NONCLUSTERED INDEX NI_WebSiteHits_WebSitePage ON
Sales.WebSiteHits (WebSitePage)
ON [HitDateRangeScheme] (HitDate)
```

How It Works

The partition scheme is applied using the ON clause.

```
ON [HitDateRangeScheme] (HitDate)
```

Notice that although the HitDate column wasn't a nonclustered index key, it was included in the partition scheme, matching that of the table. When the index and table use the same partition scheme, they are said to be "aligned."

You can choose to use a different partitioning scheme for the index than the table; however, that scheme must use the same data type argument, number of partitions, and boundary values. Unaligned indexes can be used to take advantage of collocated joins—meaning if you have two columns from two tables that are frequently joined that also use the same partition function, same data type, number of partitions, and boundaries, you can potentially improve query join performance. However, the common approach will most probably be to use aligned partition schemes between the index and table, for administration and performance reasons.

Indexing a Subset of Rows

SQL Server 2008 introduces the ability to create filtered, nonclustered indexes in support of queries that require only a small percentage of table rows. The CREATE INDEX command now includes a filter predicate that can be used to reduce index size by indexing only rows that meet certain conditions. That reduced index size saves on disk space and potentially improves the performance of queries that now need only read a fraction of the index entries that they would otherwise have to process.

The filter predicate allows for several comparison operators to be used, including IS, IS NOT, =, <>, >, <, and more. In this recipe, I will demonstrate how to add filtered indexes to one of the larger tables in the AdventureWorks database, Sales.SalesOrderDetail. To set up my example, let's assume that I have the following common query against the UnitPrice column:

```
SELECT SalesOrderID
FROM Sales.SalesOrderDetail
WHERE UnitPrice BETWEEN 150.00 AND 175.00
```

Let's also assume that the person executing this query is the only one who typically uses the UnitPrice column in the search predicate, and when she does query it, she is only concerned with values between $150 and $175. Creating a full index on this column may be considered to be wasteful. If this query is executed often, and a full clustered index scan is performed against the base table each time, this may cause performance issues.

I have just described an ideal scenario for a filtered index on the UnitPrice column. You can create that filtered index as follows:

```
CREATE NONCLUSTERED INDEX NCI_UnitPrice_SalesOrderDetail
ON Sales.SalesOrderDetail(UnitPrice)
WHERE UnitPrice  >= 150.00 AND UnitPrice  <= 175.00
```

Queries that search against UnitPrice that also search in the defined filter predicate range will likely use the filtered index instead of performing a full index scan or using full-table index alternatives.

In this second example, let's assume that it is common to query products with two distinct IDs. In this case, I am also querying anything with an order quantity greater than ten; however, this is not my desired filtering scenario—just the product ID filtering:

```
SELECT SalesOrderDetailID
FROM Sales.SalesOrderDetail
WHERE ProductID IN (776, 777) AND
      OrderQty > 10
```

This query performs a clustered index scan. I can improve performance of the query by adding a filtered index, which will result in an index seek against that nonclustered index instead of the clustered index scan. Here's how to create that filtered index:

```
CREATE NONCLUSTERED INDEX NCI_ProductID_SalesOrderDetail
ON Sales.SalesOrderDetail(ProductID,OrderQty)
WHERE ProductID IN (776, 777)
```

The result will be less I/O, as the query can operate against the much smaller, filtered index.

How It Works

This recipe demonstrates how to use the filtered index feature to create a fine-tuned index that requires less storage than the full-table index alternative. Filtered indexes require that you understand the nature of incoming queries against the tables in your database. If you have a high percentage of queries that consistently query a small percentage of data in a set of tables, filtered indexes will allow you to improve I/O performance while also minimizing on-disk storage.

The CREATE INDEX statement isn't modified much from its original format. In order to implement the filter, I used a WHERE clause after the ON clause (if using an INCLUDE, the WHERE should appear after it):

```
CREATE NONCLUSTERED INDEX NCI_UnitPrice_SalesOrderDetail
ON Sales.SalesOrderDetail(UnitPrice)
WHERE UnitPrice  >= 150.00 AND UnitPrice  <= 175.00
```

The filter predicate allows for simple logic using operators such as IN, IS, IS NOT, =, <>, >, >=, !>, <, <=, and !<. You should also be aware that filtered indexes have filtered statistics created along with them. These statistics use the same filter predicate and can result in more accurate results because the sampling is against a smaller rowset.

Reducing Index Size

As I covered in Chapter 4, the SQL Server 2008 Enterprise and Developer Editions introduce page- and row-level compression for tables, indexes, and the associated partitions. In that chapter, I demonstrated how to enable compression using the DATA_COMPRESSION clause in conjunction with the CREATE TABLE and ALTER TABLE commands. That covered how you compress clustered indexes and heaps. For nonclustered indexes, you use CREATE INDEX and ALTER INDEX to implement compression. The syntax remains the same, designating the DATA_COMPRESSION option along with a value of either NONE, ROW, or PAGE. The following example demonstrates adding a nonclustered index with PAGE-level compression (based on the example table ArchiveJobPosting that I created in Chapter 4):

```
CREATE NONCLUSTERED INDEX NCI_SalesOrderDetail_CarrierTrackingNumber
ON Sales.SalesOrderDetail (CarrierTrackingNumber)
WITH (DATA_COMPRESSION = PAGE)
```

I can modify the compression level after the fact by using ALTER INDEX. In this example, I use ALTER INDEX to change the compression level to row-level compression:

```
ALTER INDEX NCI_SalesOrderDetail_CarrierTrackingNumber
ON Sales.SalesOrderDetail
REBUILD
WITH (DATA_COMPRESSION = ROW)
```

How It Works

This recipe demonstrated enabling row and page compression for a nonclustered index. The process for adding compression is almost identical to that of adding compression for the clustered index or heap, using the DATA_COMPRESSION index option. When creating a new index, the WITH clause follows the index key definition. When modifying an existing index, the WITH clause follows the REBUILD keyword.

CHAPTER 6

■ ■ ■

Full-Text Search

Full-text search functionality allows you to issue intelligent word—and phrase—searches against character and binary data, using full-text enabled operators, which can perform significantly better than a regular LIKE operator search.

With SQL Server 2008, full-text search functionality is now integrated into the database. Full-text catalogs are no longer stored separately on the file system and are now integrated with the database itself. Full-text indexing and querying support functionality is also no longer dependent on the separate MSFTESQL service as it was in earlier versions of SQL Server.

Tip SQL Server 2008 also fully integrates *stopwords* (formerly called noise words) into the database, allowing you to create your own stoplists and associated stopwords. The previous version used noise-word files external to the database. I'll review this functionality in the "Discarding Common Strings from a Full-Text Index" recipe.

In the first part of this chapter, I'll present recipes that teach you how to enable full-text search capabilities in your database using Transact-SQL. In the second half of this chapter, I'll demonstrate how to query the full-text indexes using basic and advanced Transact-SQL predicates.

Full-Text Indexes and Catalogs

Full-text indexes allow you to search against unstructured textual data using more sophisticated functions and a higher level of performance than using just the LIKE operator. Unlike regular B-tree clustered or nonclustered indexes, full-text indexes are compressed index structures comprised of *tokens* from the indexed textual data. Tokens are words or character strings that SQL Server has identified in the indexing process. Using special full-text functions, you can extend word or phrase searches beyond the character pattern, and search based on inflection, synonyms, wildcards, and proximity to other words.

Full-text catalogs are used to contain zero or more full-text indexes and, starting with SQL Server 2008, are stored within the database. (In previous versions, they were stored on the local hard drive of the SQL Server instance server.) A full-text catalog can contain full-text indexes that index one or more tables in a single database.

SQL Server uses a number of Transact-SQL commands to create, modify, and remove full-text catalog and full-text index objects, which the next set of recipes will demonstrate.

Creating a Full-Text Catalog

In its simplest form, you can create a new catalog just by defining its name. There are other options however, and the extended syntax for CREATE FULLTEXT CATALOG is as follows:

```
CREATE FULLTEXT CATALOG catalog_name
    [ON FILEGROUP 'filegroup']
    [IN PATH 'rootpath']
    [WITH ACCENT_SENSITIVITY = {ON|OFF}]
    [AS DEFAULT]
    [AUTHORIZATION owner_name ]
```

The arguments of this command are described in Table 6-1.

Table 6-1. *CREATE FULLTEXT CATALOG Arguments*

Argument	Description
catalog_name	This option specifies the name of the new full-text catalog.
filegroup	This argument designates that the catalog will be placed on a specific filegroup. If this isn't designated, the default filegroup for the database is used.
rootpath	This is a deprecated option as of SQL Server 2008 and is no longer used.
ACCENT_SENSITIVITY = {ON|OFF}	This option allows you to choose whether the indexes will be created within the catalog as accent sensitive or accent insensitive. *Accent sensitivity* defines whether or not SQL Server will distinguish between accented and unaccented characters.
AS DEFAULT	This option sets the catalog as the default catalog for all full-text indexes that are created in the database without explicitly defining an owning full-text catalog.
owner_name	The AUTHORIZATION option determines the owner of the new full-text catalog, allowing you to choose either a database user or a role.

In this first example, a new full-text catalog is created in the AdventureWorks database (note that a full-text catalog only belongs to a *single* database):

```
USE AdventureWorks
GO
CREATE FULLTEXT CATALOG cat_Production_Document
```

In the second example, a new full-text catalog is created with accent sensitivity enabled:

```
USE AdventureWorks
GO
CREATE FULLTEXT CATALOG cat_Production_Document_EX2
WITH ACCENT_SENSITIVITY = ON
```

How It Works

In this recipe, I demonstrated how to create a new full-text catalog using the CREATE FULLTEXT CATALOG command. This command creates an instance logical entity that can be used to group one or more full-text indexes.

Once a full-text catalog is created, you can then proceed with full-text indexes, which are reviewed in the next recipe.

Creating a Full-Text Index

In this recipe, I'll demonstrate how to create a full-text index on columns in a table, so that you can then take advantage of the more sophisticated search capabilities shown later on in the chapter.

The command for creating a full-text index is CREATE FULLTEXT INDEX. The abridged syntax is as follows:

```
CREATE FULLTEXT INDEX ON table_name
    [ ( { column_name
            [ TYPE COLUMN type_column_name ]
            [ LANGUAGE language_term ]
        } [ ,...n]
        ) ]
    KEY INDEX index_name
        [ ON fulltext_catalog_name]
        [ WITH [ ( ] <with_option> [ ,...n] [ ) ] ]
[;]

<with_option>::=
  {
    CHANGE_TRACKING [ = ] { MANUAL | AUTO | OFF [, NO POPULATION ] }
    | STOPLIST [ = ] { OFF | SYSTEM | stoplist_name }
  }
```

The arguments of this command are described in Table 6-2.

Table 6-2. *CREATE FULLTEXT INDEX Arguments*

Argument	Description
table_name	This specifies the name of the table that you are creating the full-text index on. There can only be one full-text index on a single table.
column_name	This indicates the listed column or columns to be indexed, which can be of the data types varchar, nvarchar, char, nchar, xml, varbinary, text, ntext, and image.
type_column_name	The TYPE COLUMN keyword token is used to designate a column in the table that tells the full-text index what type of data is held in the varbinary(max) or image data type column. SQL Server can interpret different file types, but must know exactly how to do so.
language_term	The optional LANGUAGE keyword can also be used within the column list to indicate the language of the data stored in the column. Specifying the language will help SQL Server determine how the data is parsed in the full-text indexing process and how it will be linguistically interpreted. For a list of available languages, query the sys.fulltext_languages table.
index_name	In order for the full-text index to be created on a table, that table must have a single-key, unique, non-nullable column. This can be, for example, a single column primary key or a column defined with a UNIQUE constraint that is also non-nullable. The KEY INDEX clause in the CREATE FULLTEXT INDEX command identifies the required unique key column on the specified table.

Continued

Table 6-2. *Continued*

Argument	Description
`fulltext_catalog_name`	The ON clause designates the catalog where the full-text index will be stored. If a default catalog was identified before creation of the index, and this option isn't used, the index will be stored on the default catalog. However, if no default was defined, the index creation will fail.
`CHANGE_TRACKING {MANUAL	AUTO	OFF [, NO POPULATION]}`	This argument determines how user data changes will be detected by the full-text service. Based on this configuration, indexes can be automatically updated as data is changed in the table. You also have the option of only manually repopulating the indexes at a time or on a schedule of your choosing. The AUTO option is designated to automatically update the full-text index as table data is modified. The MANUAL option means that changes will be either propagated manually by the user or initiated via a SQL Server Agent schedule. The OFF option means that SQL Server will not keep a list of user changes. Using OFF with NO POPULATION means that SQL Server will not populate the index after it is created. Under this option, full-text index population will only occur after someone executes ALTER FULLTEXT INDEX, which is reviewed in the next recipe.
`STOPLIST [=] { OFF	SYSTEM	stoplist_name }`	Stoplists contain a list of stopwords, which are strings that should be ignored by the search. The default option is SYSTEM, meaning that the default system stoplist will be used. When this option is set to OFF, no stoplist is used. Otherwise, designating stoplist_name allows you to use a user-defined stoplist.

In this recipe's example, a new full-text index is created on the AdventureWorks database's Production.Document table (I'll demonstrate how to query the index in future recipes). DocumentSummary is the column to be indexed, and FileExtension is the column that contains a pointer to the column's document type:

```
USE AdventureWorks
GO

CREATE FULLTEXT INDEX ON Production.Document
(DocumentSummary, Document TYPE COLUMN FileExtension)
KEY INDEX PK_Document_DocumentNode
ON cat_Production_Document
WITH CHANGE_TRACKING AUTO,
     STOPLIST = SYSTEM
```

How It Works

In this recipe, I created a new full-text index for the Production.Document table, on the DocumentSummary column (which has a varchar(max) data type) and Document column (which has a varbinary(max) data type). Stepping through the code, the first line designated the table the full-text index would be based on:

```
CREATE FULLTEXT INDEX ON Production.Document
```

The second line of code designated the column or columns to be indexed, and then a pointer to the column that tells SQL Server what document type is stored in the column. In this case, I am indexing both the DocumentSummary and Document columns. Since Document is varbinary(max), I designate the column that will contain the file type contained within the Document column:

```
(DocumentSummary, Document TYPE COLUMN FileExtension)
```

Keep in mind that the TYPE COLUMN clause is only necessary if you are indexing a varbinary(max) or image type column, as you'll be assisting SQL Server with interpreting the stored data. Regular text data types such as char, varchar, nchar, nvarchar, text, ntext, and xml don't require the TYPE COLUMN clause.

Next, the name of the key, non-null, unique column for the table was identified:

```
KEY INDEX PK_Document_DocumentNode
```

The ON clause designates which full-text catalog the full-text index will be stored in (created in the previous recipe):

```
ON cat_Production_Document
```

Next, the method of ongoing index population was designated for the index:

```
WITH CHANGE_TRACKING AUTO
```

Lastly, the option for the STOPLIST was designated—using the system default stoplist:

```
STOPLIST = SYSTEM
```

Once the full-text index is created, you can begin querying it. Before you get to this, however, there are other commands used for modifying or removing indexes and catalogs you should be aware of.

Modifying a Full-Text Catalog

In this recipe, I'll demonstrate ALTER FULLTEXT CATALOG, which you can use to do the following:

- Change accent-sensitive settings. Accent sensitivity defines whether or not SQL Server will distinguish between accented and unaccented characters, or treat them as equivalent characters in the search.

- Set the catalog as the default database catalog.

- REBUILD the entire catalog with all indexes in it.

- REORGANIZE the catalog, which optimizes internal index and catalog full-text structures. This process is called a *master merge*, which means that smaller indexes are physically processed (not logically, however) into one large index in order to improve performance.

The syntax for ALTER FULLTEXT CATALOG is as follows:

```
ALTER FULLTEXT CATALOG catalog_name
{ REBUILD [WITH ACCENT_SENSITIVITY = {ON|OFF} ]
    | REORGANIZE
    | AS DEFAULT
}
```

The arguments for this command are described in Table 6-3.

Table 6-3. *ALTER FULLTEXT CATALOG Arguments*

Argument	Description
REBUILD	The REBUILD option rebuilds the catalog.
[WITH ACCENT_SENSITIVITY = {ON|OFF}]	The ACCENT_SENSITIVITY option can only be configured when used in conjunction with a REBUILD.
REORGANIZE	This option causes SQL Server to optimize catalog structures and internal indexes.
AS DEFAULT	This option sets the catalog as the default database catalog.

In this first example in the recipe, a full-text catalog is optimized using the REORGANIZE keyword:

```
ALTER FULLTEXT CATALOG cat_Production_Document
REORGANIZE
```

In this second example, a full-text catalog is set to be the default full-text catalog for the database:

```
ALTER FULLTEXT CATALOG cat_Production_Document
AS DEFAULT
```

In this example, a full-text catalog (and all indexes within) is rebuilt along with disabling accent sensitivity:

```
ALTER FULLTEXT CATALOG cat_Production_Document
REBUILD WITH ACCENT_SENSITIVITY = OFF
```

How It Works

In this recipe, ALTER FULLTEXT CATALOG was used to optimize the indexes and internal data structures, set the catalog to the default database, and rebuild the catalog and indexes within. This command is used to maintain existing catalogs and keep them performing at their best as data modifications are made to the underlying indexed tables.

Modifying a Full-Text Index

The ALTER FULLTEXT INDEX command can be used both to change the properties of an index and to control/initiate index population. The syntax is as follows:

```
ALTER FULLTEXT INDEX ON table_name
    { ENABLE
    | DISABLE
    | SET CHANGE_TRACKING { MANUAL | AUTO | OFF }
    | ADD ( column_name
      [ TYPE COLUMN type_column_name ]
      [ LANGUAGE language_term ] [,...n] )
      [ WITH NO POPULATION ]
    | DROP ( column_name [,...n] )
      [WITH NO POPULATION ]
    | START { FULL | INCREMENTAL | UPDATE } POPULATION
    | {STOP | PAUSE | RESUME } POPULATION
    | SET STOPLIST { OFF| SYSTEM | stoplist_name }
      [WITH NO POPULATION] }
```

The arguments of this command are described in Table 6-4.

Table 6-4. *ALTER FULLTEXT INDEX Arguments*

Argument	Description
table_name	This argument specifies the name of the table of the index to be modified.
ENABLE | DISABLE	The ENABLE option activates the full-text index. DISABLE deactivates a full-text index. Deactivating a full-text index means that changes to the table columns are no longer tracked and moved to the full-text index (however, full-text search conditions are still allowed against the index).
SET CHANGE TRACKING {MANUAL|AUTO|OFF}	MANUAL specifies that change tracking on the source indexed data will be enabled on a schedule or manually executed basis. AUTO specifies that the full-text index is modified automatically when the indexed column(s) values are modified. OFF disables change tracking from occurring on the full-text index.
ADD (column_name [,...n])	This argument indicates the name of the column or columns to add to the existing full-text index.
type_column_name	This option specifies the column used to designate the full-text index file type of the data stored in the varbinary(max) or image data type column.
language_term	This indicates the optional LANGUAGE keyword used within the column list to indicate the language of the data stored in the column.
WITH NO POPULATION	When designated, the full-text index isn't populated after the addition or removal of a table column.
DROP (column_name [,...n])	This argument gives the name of the column or columns to remove from the existing full-text index.
START {FULL|INCREMENTAL|UPDATE} POPULATION	This option initiates the population of the full-text index based on the option of FULL, INCREMENTAL, and UPDATE. FULL refreshes every row from the table into the index. INCREMENTAL only refreshes the index for those rows that were modified since the last population, and in order for INCREMENTAL to be used, the indexed table requires a column with a timestamp data type. The UPDATE token refreshes the index for any rows that were inserted, updated, or deleted since the last index update.
{STOP | PAUSE | RESUME} POPULATION	For very large tables, full-text index population can consume significant system resources. Because of this, you may need to stop a population process while it is in progress. For indexes created with the MANUAL or OFF change tracking setting, you can use the STOP POPULATION option. PAUSE and RESUME are used when full populations are underway.
SET STOPLIST { OFF| SYSTEM | stoplist_name }	Designating SYSTEM means that the default system stoplist will be used. When this option is set to OFF, no stoplist is used. Otherwise, designating stoplist_name allows you to use a user-defined stoplist.

In this first example, a new column is added to the existing full-text index on the
Production.Document table:

```
ALTER FULLTEXT INDEX ON Production.Document
ADD (Title)
```

Next, a full-text index population is initiated:

```
ALTER FULLTEXT INDEX ON Production.Document
START FULL POPULATION
```

This returns a warning because the full-text index population was already underway for the
table (I didn't designate the WITH NO POPULATION option when adding the new column to the full-
text index):

```
Warning: Request to start a full-text index population on table or indexed view
'Production.Document' is ignored because a population is currently active for
this table or indexed view.
```

This next example demonstrates disabling change tracking for the table's full-text index:

```
ALTER FULLTEXT INDEX ON Production.Document
SET CHANGE_TRACKING OFF
```

This returns the following warning:

```
Warning: Request to stop change tracking has deleted all changes tracked on table or
indexed view 'Production'.
```

In this last example for the recipe, the Title column is dropped from the full-text index:

```
ALTER FULLTEXT INDEX ON Production.Document
DROP (Title)
```

How It Works

In this recipe, ALTER FULLTEXT INDEX was used to perform the following actions:

- Add a new column to an existing full-text index. This is useful if you wish to add additional
  columns to the full-text index that would benefit from more advanced searching
  functionality.

- Start a full-text index population (which works if the population isn't already set to automatically update). For very large tables, you may wish to manually control when the full-text
  index is populated, instead of allowing SQL Server to manually populate the index over time.

- Disable change tracking. This removes a log of any changes that have occurred to the
  indexed data.

- Drop a column from a full-text index. For example, if you have a column that isn't benefitting
  from the full-text index functionality, it is best to remove it in order to conserve space (from
  the stored indexing results) and resources (from the effort it takes SQL Server to update the
  data).

Other actions ALTER FULLTEXT INDEX can perform include disabling an enabled index using the
DISABLE option, thus making it unavailable for us (but keeping the metadata in the system tables).
You can then enable a disabled index using the ENABLE keyword.

Retrieving Full-Text Catalog and Index Metadata

This recipe shows you how to retrieve useful information regarding the full-text catalogs and indexes in your database by using system catalog views.

The sys.fulltext_catalogs system catalog view returns information on all full-text catalogs in the current database. For example:

```
SELECT name, path, is_default, is_accent_sensitivity_on
FROM sys.fulltext_catalogs
```

This returns

name	path	is_default	is_accent_sensitivity_on
cat_Production_Document	NULL	1	0
cat_Production_Document_EX2	NULL	0	1

The sys.fulltext_indexes system catalog view lists all full-text indexes in the database. For example:

```
SELECT object_name(object_id) table_name,
       change_tracking_state_desc, stoplist_id
FROM sys.fulltext_indexes
```

This returns

table_name	change_tracking_state_desc	stoplist_id
Document	OFF	0

The sys.fulltext_index_columns system catalog view lists all full-text indexed columns in the database. For example:

```
SELECT object_name(ic.object_id) tblname, c.name
FROM sys.fulltext_index_columns ic
INNER JOIN sys.columns c ON
    ic.object_id = c.object_id AND
    ic.column_id = c.column_id
```

This returns the table name and the indexed column names:

tblname	name
Document	DocumentSummary
Document	Document

Also, the FULLTEXTCATALOGPROPERTY system function can be used to return information about a specific catalog. The syntax is as follows:

```
FULLTEXTCATALOGPROPERTY ('catalog_name' ,'property')
```

The function takes two arguments, the name of the catalog and the name of the property to evaluate. Some of the more useful options for the property option are described in Table 6-5.

Table 6-5. *FULLTEXTCATALOGPROPERTY Property Options (Abridged)*

Property	Description
AccentSensitivity	Returns 1 for accent sensitive, 0 for insensitive
IndexSize	Returns the size of the full-text catalog in megabytes
MergeStatus	Returns 1 when a reorganization is in process, and 0 when it is not
PopulateStatus	Returns a numeric value representing the current population status of a catalog—for example, 0 for idle, 1 for an in-progress population, 2 for paused, 7 for building an index, and 8 for a full disk

In this example, the full-text catalog population status is returned:

```
SELECT FULLTEXTCATALOGPROPERTY ('cat_Production_Document','PopulateStatus')
PopulationStatus
```

This returns 0 for idle:

```
PopulationStatus
0
```

How It Works

This recipe used three different catalog views and a system function to return information about full-text catalogs and indexes in the current database. You'll need this information in order to keep track of their existence, as well as to track the current state of activity and settings.

Discarding Common Strings from a Full-Text Index

SQL Server 2008 introduces the ability to identify common strings that are unhelpful for a full-text index search. These unhelpful strings are called stopwords (called noise words in previous versions of SQL Server) and are contained within stoplists. A stoplist contains one or more stopwords and is used in conjunction with a full-text index. SQL Server includes a system default stoplist containing common stopwords across all supported languages.

To create your own custom stoplist, you use the CREATE FULLTEXT STOPLIST command. The syntax is as follows:

```
CREATE FULLTEXT STOPLIST stoplist_name
[ FROM { [ database_name. ] source_stoplist_name } | SYSTEM STOPLIST ]
[ AUTHORIZATION owner_name ];
```

The arguments of this command are described in Table 6-6.

Table 6-6. *CREATE FULLTEXT STOPLIST Arguments*

Argument	Description
stoplist_name	Supplies the name of the new user-defined stoplist
{ [database_name.] source_stoplist_name }	Allows you to reference the database name and source stoplist name from which to copy an already existing stoplist
SYSTEM STOPLIST	Allows you to copy the system default stoplist
AUTHORIZATION owner_name	Defines the database principal stoplist owner

In this example, I will create a new stoplist that is not copied from a preexisting stoplist (note that a full-text stoplist statement must be terminated by a semicolon [;]):

```
CREATE FULLTEXT STOPLIST TSQLRecipes;
```

To confirm the details of my new stoplist, I can query the sys.full_text_stoplists system catalog view:

```
SELECT stoplist_id,name,principal_id
FROM sys.fulltext_stoplists
```

This returns

stoplist_id	name	principal_id
5	TSQLRecipes	1

Once I have created the stoplist, I can now start populating it with stopwords by using the ALTER FULLTEXT STOPLIST command. The syntax for this command is as follows:

```
ALTER FULLTEXT STOPLIST stoplist_name
{    ADD 'stopword' LANGUAGE language_term
  | DROP
    {
                'stopword' LANGUAGE language_term
      | ALL LANGUAGE language_term
          | ALL };
```

The arguments of this command are described in Table 6-7.

Table 6-7. *ALTER FULLTEXT STOPLIST Arguments*

Argument	Description
stoplist_name	Specifies the name of the new user-defined stoplist.
ADD 'stopword'	Defines the string value of the stopword. Up to 64 characters can be added.
LANGUAGE language_term	Defines the language term associated with the stopword—which can be the string (alias from sys.syslanguages), integer (LCID), or hexadecimal representation (hex value of LCID).
DROP 'stopword' LANGUAGE language_term	Specifies that a specific stopword for a specific language should be dropped.
DROP ALL LANGUAGE language_term	Removes all stopwords for a language.
DROP ALL	Specifies that all stopwords be removed from the stoplist.

In this example, assume that I am indexing tables containing references to SQL Server documentation. In this case, the terms "SQL" and "Server" are not very helpful in the context of a search (almost every entry would contain it). So in this example, I will add two new stopwords to my stoplist created earlier:

```
ALTER FULLTEXT STOPLIST TSQLRecipes
ADD 'SQL' LANGUAGE 'English';

ALTER FULLTEXT STOPLIST TSQLRecipes
ADD 'Server' LANGUAGE 'English';
```

After adding the two new stopwords to my stoplist, I can validate the list by querying the sys.fulltext_stopwords system catalog view:

```
SELECT stoplist_id,stopword,language
FROM sys.fulltext_stopwords
```

This returns

stoplist_id	stopword	language
5	SQL	English
5	Server	English

In the next query, I'll demonstrate binding my new stoplist to a full-text index:

```
--Example table
CREATE TABLE dbo.SQLTopic
  (SQLTopic int IDENTITY PRIMARY KEY,
   SQLTopicHeaderNM varchar(255) NOT NULL,
   SQLTopicBody varchar(max) NOT NULL)
GO

-- Create example catalog
CREATE FULLTEXT CATALOG ftcat_SQLDocumentation
AS DEFAULT
GO

-- Create full-text index binding to our new stoplist
-- Look up your actual PK constraint name using sp_help 'dbo.sqltopic'
CREATE FULLTEXT INDEX ON dbo.SQLTopic(SQLTopicBody)
   KEY INDEX PK__SQLTopic__AD5554EC442B18F2
   WITH STOPLIST = TSQLRecipes
GO
```

I can confirm the stoplist binding using the sys.fulltext_indexes system catalog view:

```
SELECT stoplist_id
FROM sys.fulltext_indexes
WHERE object_id = object_id('dbo.SQLTopic')
```

This returns

stoplist_id
5

I can test whether or not my new stop words are recognized by the Full-Text Engine by using the sys.dm_fts_parser Dynamic Management View. The syntax for this DMV is as follows:

```
sys.dm_fts_parser('query_string', lcid, stoplist_id, accent_sensitivity)
```

The first parameter, query_string, is the query string you may use within a full-text index search. The lcid is the locale identifier, and stoplist_id is the unique ID for the stoplist (which you can retrieve from sys.fulltext_stoplists). The accent_sensitivity argument has a 1 or 0 value, indicating whether your search should be accent sensitive or insensitive. To demonstrate using this DMV, the following query tests searching on the phase SQL Server 2008 Transact-SQL Recipes using the stoplist created earlier:

```
 SELECT display_term, special_term
FROM sys.dm_fts_parser
('"SQL Server 2008 Transact-SQL Recipes"', 1033, 5, 0)
```

This returns return a list of each keyword, along with how they are treated (noise word/stop-word or exact match):

```
display_term    special_term
sql             Noise Word
server          Noise Word
2008            Exact Match
nn2008          Exact Match
transact        Exact Match
sql             Noise Word
transactsql     Exact Match
recipes         Exact Match
```

As you can see from the results, both SQL and Server are recognized as noise words (stop-words).

In this next query, I demonstrate removing a stopword from the stoplist (this is allowed even while the stoplist is actively bound to a full-text index):

```
ALTER FULLTEXT STOPLIST TSQLRecipes
DROP 'Server' LANGUAGE 'English';
```

To remove a stoplist, I use the DROP FULLTEXT STOPLIST command. Before I can drop it, it must be unbound from the full-text indexes using it. The last query of this recipe demonstrates removing the stoplist settings from the full-text index and then dropping the stoplist:

```
ALTER FULLTEXT INDEX ON dbo.SQLTopic
SET STOPLIST SYSTEM
GO

DROP FULLTEXT STOPLIST TSQLRecipes;
```

How It Works

This recipe demonstrated how to discard common strings from a full-text index by creating a user-defined stoplist that contained a list of stopwords. To create the stoplist, I used the CREATE FULLTEXT STOPLIST command. After creating the stoplist, I was then able to use ALTER FULLTEXT STOPLIST to add and remove stopword strings to the stoplist. I used the sys.fulltext_stoplists and sys.fulltext_stopwords system catalog views to confirm my settings. I then created a new table and full-text catalog, and then created a new full-text index that used the new stoplist by designating WITH STOPLIST = TSQLRecipes. I was able to test whether my stopwords in the stoplist would be properly ignored by using sys.dm_fts_parser. To remove the stoplist from the full-text index, I used ALTER FULLTEXT INDEX with SET STOPLIST, followed by the DROP FULLTEXT STOPLIST command.

Dropping a Full-Text Index

In this recipe, I'll demonstrate how to remove a full-text index from the full-text catalog using the DROP FULLTEXT INDEX command. The syntax is as follows:

```
DROP FULLTEXT INDEX ON table_name
```

This command only takes a single argument, the name of the table on which the full-text index should be dropped. For example:

```
DROP FULLTEXT INDEX ON Production.Document
```

How It Works

The DROP FULLTEXT INDEX ON command references the full-text indexed table. Since only one index is allowed on a single table, no other information is required to drop the full-text index.

Dropping a Full-Text Catalog

In this recipe, I demonstrate how to remove a full-text catalog from the database using the DROP FULLTEXT CATALOG command. The syntax is as follows:

```
DROP FULLTEXT CATALOG catalog_name
```

This command takes a single argument, the name of the catalog to drop. For example:

```
DROP FULLTEXT CATALOG cat_Production_Document
```

How It Works

The DROP FULLTEXT CATALOG references the catalog name and doesn't require any further information to remove it from the database. If the full-text catalog was set as the DEFAULT catalog, you'll see the following warning:

```
Warning: The fulltext catalog 'cat_Production_Document'
is being dropped and is currently set as default.
```

Basic Searching

Once you've created the full-text catalog and full-text indexes, you can get down to the business of querying the data with more sophisticated Transact-SQL predicates. Predicates are used in expressions in the WHERE or HAVING clauses, or join conditions of the FROM clause. Predicates return a TRUE, FALSE, or UNKNOWN response.

Beginning with the more simple commands, the FREETEXT command is used to search unstructured text data based on inflectional, literal, or synonymous matches. It is more intelligent than using LIKE because the text data is searched by meaning and not necessarily the exact wording.

The CONTAINS predicate is used to search unstructured textual data for precise or less-precise word and phrase matches. This command can also take into consideration the proximity of words to one another, allowing for weighted results.

These next two recipes will demonstrate basic searches using the FREETEXT and CONTAINS predicates. The examples depend on a full-text index on the Production.Document table's DocumentSummary column. I'll create that index here, before proceeding with the recipes:

```
USE AdventureWorks
GO
CREATE FULLTEXT CATALOG cat_Production_Document
```

```
CREATE FULLTEXT INDEX ON Production.Document
(DocumentSummary)
KEY INDEX PK_Document_DocumentNode
ON cat_Production_Document
WITH CHANGE_TRACKING AUTO,
     STOPLIST = SYSTEM
```

Using FREETEXT to Search Full-Text Indexed Columns

The FREETEXT predicate is used to search full-text columns based on inflectional, literal, or synonymous matches. The syntax is as follows:

```
FREETEXT ( { column_name | (column_list) | * }
         , 'freetext_string' [ , LANGUAGE language_term ] )
```

The arguments for this predicate are described in Table 6-8.

Table 6-8. *FREETEXT Arguments*

Argument	Description
column_name | column_list | *	Indicates the name of the column or columns that are full-text indexed and that you wish to be searched. Specifying * designates that all searchable columns are used.
freetext_string	Defines the text to search for.
language_term	Directs SQL Server to use a specific language for performing the search, accessing thesaurus information, and removing stopwords.

In this example, I'll use FREETEXT to search data based on the *meaning* of the search term. SQL Server looks at the individual words and searches for exact matches, inflectional forms, or extensions/replacements based on the specific language's thesaurus:

```
SELECT DocumentNode, DocumentSummary
FROM Production.Document
WHERE FREETEXT (DocumentSummary, 'change pedal' )
```

This returns

```
DocumentNode    DocumentSummary
0x7BC0          Detailed instructions for replacing pedals with Adventure Works Cycles
                replacement pedals. Instructions are applicable to all Adventure Works
                Cycles bicycle models and replacement pedals. Use only Adventure Works
                Cycles parts when replacing worn or broken components.
```

How It Works

In this recipe, FREETEXT was used to search the DocumentSummary column for the phrase "change pedal." Though neither the exact word "change" nor "pedal" exists in the data, a row was returned because of a match on the plural form of pedal ("pedals").

FREETEXT is, however, a less-precise way of searching full-text indexes compared to CONTAINS, which is demonstrated in the next few recipes.

Using CONTAINS for Word Searching

In this recipe, I demonstrate using the CONTAINS command to perform word searches. CONTAINS allows for more sophisticated full-text term searches than the FREETEXT predicate. The abridged syntax is as follows:

```
CONTAINS
  ( { column_name | (column_list) | * } ,
'< contains_search_condition >'    [ , LANGUAGE language_term ]  )
```

The arguments are identical to FREETEXT, only CONTAINS allows for a variety of search conditions (some demonstrated later on in the "Advanced Searching" section of this chapter).

This example demonstrates a simple search of rows, with a DocumentSummary searching for the words "replacing" or "pedals":

```
SELECT DocumentNode, DocumentSummary
FROM Production.Document
WHERE CONTAINS (DocumentSummary, '"replacing" OR "pedals"' )
```

This returns

DocumentNode	DocumentSummary
0x7BC0	Detailed instructions for replacing pedals with Adventure Works Cycles replacement pedals. Instructions are applicable to all Adventure Works Cycles bicycle models and replacement pedals. Use only Adventure Works Cycles parts when replacing worn or broken components.
0x7C20	Worn or damaged seats can be easily replaced following these simple instructions. Instructions are applicable to these Adventure Works Cycles models: Mountain 100 through Mountain 500. Use only Adventure Works Cycles parts when replacing worn or broken components.

How It Works

In this recipe, I performed a search against the DocumentSummary, finding any summary that contained either the words "replacing" OR "pedals." Unlike FREETEXT, the literal words are searched, and not the synonyms or inflectional form.

OR was used to search for rows with either of the words, but AND could also have been used to return rows only if both words existed for the DocumentSummary value.

■**Tip** For a term consisting of a single word, double quotes are not necessary, just the outer single quotes.

Advanced Searching

So far, this chapter has demonstrated examples of fairly straightforward word searches. However, using CONTAINS, you can perform more advanced searches against words or phrases. Some examples of this include the following:

- Using a wildcard search to find words or phrases that match a specific text prefix

- Searching for words or phrases based on inflections of a specific word

- Searching for words or phrases based on the proximity of words to one another

These next three recipes will demonstrate these more advanced searches using the CONTAINS predicate.

Using CONTAINS to Search with Wildcards

In this recipe, I demonstrate how to use wildcards within a CONTAINS search. A prefix term is designated, followed by the asterisk symbol:

```
SELECT DocumentNode, DocumentSummary
FROM Production.Document
WHERE CONTAINS (DocumentSummary, '"import*"' )
```

This returns

DocumentNode	DocumentSummary
0x5B40	It is important that you maintain your bicycle and keep it in good repair. Detailed repair and service guidelines are provided along with instructions for adjusting the tightness of the suspension fork.

How It Works

This recipe uses the asterisk symbol to represent a wildcard of one or more characters. This is similar to using LIKE, only you can benefit from the inherent performance of full-text indexing. Any match on a word that starts with "import" will be returned. In this case, one row that matches on the word "important" was returned.

When using a wildcard, the term must be embedded in double quotes; otherwise, SQL Server interprets the asterisk as a literal value to be searched for. For example, searching for 'import*' without the embedded quotes looks for the literal asterisk value as part of the search term.

Using CONTAINS to Search for Inflectional Matches

In this recipe, I'll demonstrate how to search for rows that match a search term based on inflectional variations. The syntax for searching for inflectional variations is as follows:

```
FORMSOF ( { INFLECTIONAL | THESAURUS } , < simple_term > [ ,...n ] )
```

In this example, the inflectional variation of "replace" is searched:

```
SELECT DocumentNode, DocumentSummary
FROM Production.Document
WHERE CONTAINS(DocumentSummary, ' FORMSOF  (INFLECTIONAL, replace) ')
```

This returns

DocumentNode	DocumentSummary
0x7B40	Reflectors are vital safety components of your bicycle. Always ensure your front and back reflectors are clean and in good repair. Detailed instructions and illustrations are included should you need to replace the front reflector or front reflector bracket of your Adventure Works Cycles bicycle.
0x7BC0	Detailed instructions for replacing pedals with Adventure Works Cycles replacement pedals. Instructions are applicable to all Adventure Works Cycles bicycle models and replacement pedals. Use only Adventure Works Cycles parts when replacing worn or broken components.

0x7C20   Worn or damaged seats can be easily replaced following these simple
                instructions. Instructions are applicable to these Adventure Works Cycles
                models: Mountain 100 through Mountain 500. Use only Adventure Works Cycles
                parts when replacing worn or broken components.

How It Works

This recipe searches for any rows with the inflectional version of "replace." Although the literal
value is not always found in that column, a row will also be returned that contains "replace*d*" or
"replac*ing*."

THESAURUS is the other option for the FORMSOF clause, allowing you to search based on synonymous terms (which are maintained in XML files in the $SQL_Server_Install_Path\Microsoft SQL
Server\<InstancePath>\MSSQL\FTDATA\ directory). For example, the French thesaurus XML file is
called tsFRA.xml. These XML files are updateable, so you can customize them according to your
own application requirements.

Using CONTAINS for Searching Results by Term Proximity

This recipe demonstrates how CONTAINS is used to find rows with specified words that are near one
another. The abridged syntax is as follows:

```
{ < simple_term > | < prefix_term > }
    { NEAR | ~ }
{ < simple_term > | < prefix_term > }
```

In this example, rows are returned where the word "oil" is near to "grease":

```
SELECT DocumentSummary
FROM Production.Document
WHERE CONTAINS(DocumentSummary, 'oil NEAR grease')
```

This returns

DocumentSummary
```
Guidelines and recommendations for lubricating the required components of your
Adventure Works Cycles bicycle. Component lubrication is vital to ensuring a smooth
and safe ride and should be part of your standard maintenance routine. Details
instructions are provided for each bicycle component requiring regular lubrication
including the frequency at which oil or grease should be applied.
```

How It Works

This recipe looked for any text that had the word "grease" near the word "oil." This example
searched for proximity between two words, although you can also test for proximity between multiple words, for example:

```
SELECT DocumentSummary
FROM Production.Document
WHERE CONTAINS(DocumentSummary, 'oil NEAR grease AND frequency')
```

In this case, all three words should be in near proximity to one another.

Ranked Searching

The previous examples demonstrated full-text index searches conducted in the WHERE clause of a SELECT query. SQL Server also has ranking functions available, which are referenced in the FROM clause of a query instead. Instead of just returning those rows that meet the search condition, the ranking functions CONTAINSTABLE and FREETEXTTABLE are used to return designated rows by relevance. The closer the match, the higher the system-generated rank, as these next two recipes will demonstrate.

Returning Ranked Search Results by Meaning

In this recipe, I demonstrate FREETEXTTABLE, which can be used to return search results ordered by rank, based on a search string.

The syntax and functionality between FREETEXT and FREETEXTTABLE is still very similar:

```
FREETEXTTABLE (table , { column_name | (column_list) | * }
        , 'freetext_string'
    [, LANGUAGE language_term ]
    [ ,top_n_by_rank ] )
```

The two additional arguments that differentiate FREETEXTTABLE from FREETEXT are the table and top_n_by_rank arguments. The table argument is the name of the table containing the full-text indexed column or columns. The top_n_by_rank argument, when designated, takes an integer value that represents the top matches in order of rank.

In this example, rows are returned from Production.Document in order of closest rank to the search term "bicycle seat":

```
SELECT   f.RANK, DocumentNode, DocumentSummary
FROM Production.Document d
INNER JOIN FREETEXTTABLE(Production.Document, DocumentSummary, 'bicycle seat') f
    ON d.DocumentNode = f.[KEY]
ORDER BY RANK DESC
```

This returns

RANK	DocumentNode	DocumentSummary
61	0x7C20	Worn or damaged seats can be easily replaced following these simple instructions. Instructions are applicable to these Adventure Works Cycles models: Mountain 100 through Mountain 500. Use only Adventure Works Cycles parts when replacing worn or broken c
37	0x6B40	Guidelines and recommendations for lubricating the required components of your Adventure Works Cycles bicycle. Component lubrication is vital to ensuring a smooth and safe ride and should be part of your standard maintenance routine. Details instructions a
37	0x7B40	Reflectors are vital safety components of your bicycle. Always ensure your front and back reflectors are clean and in good repair. Detailed instructions and illustrations are included should you need to replace the front reflector or front reflector bracke
21	0x7BC0	Detailed instructions for replacing pedals with Adventure Works Cycles replacement pedals. Instructions are applicable to all Adventure Works Cycles bicycle models and replacement pedals. Use only Adventure Works Cycles parts when replacing worn or broken
21	0x5B40	It is important that you maintain your bicycle and keep it in good repair. Detailed repair and service guidelines are provided along with instructions for adjusting the tightness of the suspension fork.

How It Works

FREETEXTTABLE is similar to FREETEXT in that it searches full-text indexed columns by meaning, and not literal value. FREETEXTTABLE is different from FREETEXT, however, in that it is referenced like a table in the FROM clause, allowing you to join data by its KEY. KEY and RANK are two columns that the FREETEXTTABLE returns in the result set. KEY is the unique/primary key defined for the full index, and RANK is the measure of how relevant a search result the row is estimated to be.

In this recipe, the FREETEXTTABLE result set searched the DocumentSummary column for "bicycle seat," joined by its KEY value to the Production.Document table's DocumentNode column:

```
INNER JOIN FREETEXTTABLE(Production.Document,
DocumentSummary,
'bicycle seat') f
   ON d.DocumentNode = f.[KEY]
```

RANK was returned sorted by descending order, based on the strength of the match:

```
ORDER BY RANK DESC
```

Returning Ranked Search Results by Weighted Value

In this recipe, I demonstrate returning search results based on a weighted pattern match value using the CONTAINSTABLE command. CONTAINSTABLE is equivalent to FREETEXTTABLE in that it acts as a table and can be referenced in the FROM clause. CONTAINSTABLE also has the same search capabilities and variations as CONTAINS.

Both CONTAINS and CONTAINSTABLE can be used to designate a row match's "weight," giving one term more importance than another, thus impacting result rank. This is achieved by using ISABOUT in the command, which assigns a weighted value to the search term.

The basic syntax for this is as follows:

```
ISABOUT { <search term> }   [ WEIGHT ( weight_value ) ]
```

This example demonstrates querying Production.Document by rank, giving the term "bicycle" a higher weighting than the term "seat":

```
SELECT f.RANK, d.DocumentNode, d.DocumentSummary
FROM Production.Document d
INNER JOIN CONTAINSTABLE(Production.Document, DocumentSummary,
'ISABOUT ( bicycle weight (.9), seat weight (.1))') f
   ON d.DocumentNode = f.[KEY]
ORDER BY RANK DESC
```

This returns

RANK	DocumentNode	DocumentSummary
23	0x6B40	Guidelines and recommendations for lubricating the required components of your Adventure Works Cycles bicycle. Component lubrication is vital to ensuring a smooth and safe ride and should be part of your standard maintenance routine. Details instructions a
23	0x7B40	Reflectors are vital safety components of your bicycle. Always ensure your front and back reflectors are clean and in good repair. Detailed instructions and illustrations are included should you need to replace the front reflector or front reflector bracke
11	0x7BC0	Detailed instructions for replacing pedals with Adventure Works Cycles replacement pedals. Instructions are applicable to all Adventure Works Cycles bicycle models and replacement pedals. Use only Adventure Works Cycles parts when replacing worn or broken

| 11 | 0x5B40 | It is important that you maintain your bicycle and keep it in good repair. Detailed repair and service guidelines are provided along with instructions for adjusting the tightness of the suspension fork. |

How It Works

The CONTAINSTABLE is a result set, joining to Production.Document by KEY and DocumentID. RANK was returned in the SELECT clause, and sorted in the ORDER BY clause. CONTAINSTABLE can perform the same kinds of searches as CONTAINS, including wildcard, proximity, inflectional, and thesaurus searches.

In this example, a weighted term search was performed, meaning that words are assigned values that impact their weight within the result ranking.

In this recipe, two words were searched, "bicycle" and "seat," with "bicycle" getting a higher rank than "seat":

```
'ISABOUT ( bicycle weight (.9), seat weight (.1))'
```

The weight value, which can be a number from 0.0 through 1.0, impacts how each row's matching will be ranked within CONTAINSTABLE. ISABOUT is put within the single quotes, and the column definition is within parentheses. Each term was followed by the word "weight" and the value 0.0 to 1.0 value in parentheses. Although the weight does not affect the rows returned from the query, it will impact the ranking value.

CHAPTER 7

■■■

Views

Views allow you to create a virtual representation of table data defined by a SELECT statement. The defining SELECT statement can join one or more tables and can include one or more columns. Once created, a view can be referenced in the FROM clause of a query.

Views can be used to simplify data access for query writers, obscuring the underlying complexity of the SELECT statement. Views are also useful for managing security and protecting sensitive data. If you wish to restrict direct table access by the end user, you can grant permissions exclusively to views, rather than to the underlying tables. You can also use views to expose only those columns that you wish the end user to see, including just the necessary columns in the view definition. Views can even allow direct data updates, under specific circumstances that I'll describe later in the chapter recipe "Modifying Data Through a View." Views also provide a standard interface to the back-end data, which shouldn't need to change unless there are significant changes to the underlying table structures.

In addition to regular views, you can also create indexed views, which are views that actually have index data persisted within the database (regular views do not actually store physical data). Also available are distributed-partitioned views, which allow you to represent one logical table made up of horizontally partitioned tables, each located across separate SQL Server instances. Table 7-1 shows the three types of views used in SQL Server.

Table 7-1. *SQL Server View Types*

View Type	Description
Regular view	This view is defined by a Transact-SQL query. No data is actually stored in the database, only the view definition.
Indexed view	This view is first defined by a Transact-SQL query, and then, after certain requirements are met, a clustered index is created on it in order to materialize the index data similar to table data. Once a clustered index is created, multiple nonclustered indexes can be created on the indexed view as needed.
Distributed partitioned view	This is a view that uses UNION ALL to combine multiple, smaller tables separated across two or more SQL Server instances into a single, virtual table for performance purposes and scalability (expansion of table size on each SQL Server instance, for example).

In this chapter, I'll present recipes that create each of these types of views, and I'll also provide methods for reporting view metadata.

Regular Views

Views are a great way to filter data and columns before presenting it to end users. Views can be used to obscure numerous table joins and column selections and can also be used to implement security by only allowing users authorization access to the view, and not to the actual underlying tables.

For all the usefulness of views, there are still some performance shortcomings to watch out for. When considering views for your database, consider the following best practices:

- Performance-tune your views as you would performance-tune a SELECT query, because a regular view is essentially just a "stored" query. Poorly performing views can have a significant impact on server performance.

- Don't nest your views more than one level deep. Specifically, do not define a view that calls another view, and so on. This can lead to confusion when you attempt to tune inefficient queries and can degrade performance with each level of view nesting.

- When possible, use stored procedures instead of views. Stored procedures can offer a performance boost, as the execution plan can reuse them. Stored procedures can also reduce network traffic, allow for more sophisticated business logic, and have fewer coding restrictions than a view (see Chapter 10 for more information).

When a view is created, its definition is stored in the database, but the actual data that the view returns is not stored separately from the underlying tables. The next few recipes will demonstrate how to create and manage views.

Creating a Basic View

A view is created using the CREATE VIEW command. The syntax is as follows:

```
CREATE VIEW [ schema_name . ] view_name [ (column [ ,...n ] ) ]
[ WITH [ ENCRYPTION ] [ SCHEMABINDING ] [ VIEW_METADATA ] [ ,...n ] ]
AS select_statement
[ WITH CHECK OPTION ]
```

The arguments of this command are described in Table 7-2. Some of these arguments will also be reviewed in more detail later on in the chapter.

Table 7-2. *CREATE VIEW Arguments*

Argument	Description
[schema_name .] view_name	This specifies the schema and name of the new view.
(column [,...n])	This is the optional list of column names to be used for the view. If not designated, the names used in the SELECT query will be used instead (unless there is no name specified for the column, and then there is an error).
ENCRYPTION	This encrypts the Transact-SQL view definition in the system tables so that it cannot be viewed without a saved copy of the original CREATE VIEW command.
SCHEMABINDING	SCHEMABINDING binds the view to the schema of the underlying tables, restricting any changes in the base table that would impact the view definition.

Argument	Description
VIEW_METADATA	When designated, APIs accessing information about the view will see view information instead of metadata from the underlying table or tables.
select_statement	This specifies the SELECT query used to return the rows and columns of the view.

The SELECT statement allows a view to have up to 1,024 defined columns. You cannot use certain SELECT elements in a view definition, including INTO, OPTION, COMPUTE, COMPUTE BY, or references to table variables or temporary tables. You also cannot use ORDER BY, unless used in conjunction with the TOP keyword.

This example demonstrates how to create a view that accesses data from both the Production.TransactionHistory and the Production.Product tables:

```
USE AdventureWorks
GO

CREATE VIEW dbo.v_Product_TransactionHistory
AS

SELECT   p.Name ProductName,
      p.ProductNumber,
      c.Name ProductCategory,
      s.Name ProductSubCategory,
      m.Name ProductModel,
      t.TransactionID,
      t.ReferenceOrderID,
      t.ReferenceOrderLineID,
      t.TransactionDate,
      t.TransactionType,
      t.Quantity,
      t.ActualCost
FROM Production.TransactionHistory t
INNER JOIN Production.Product p ON
   t.ProductID = p.ProductID
INNER JOIN Production.ProductModel m ON
   m.ProductModelID = p.ProductModelID
INNER JOIN Production.ProductSubcategory s ON
   s.ProductSubcategoryID = p.ProductSubcategoryID
INNER JOIN Production.ProductCategory c ON
   c.ProductCategoryID = s.ProductCategoryID
WHERE c.Name = 'Bikes'
GO
```

Next, I will query the new view to show transaction history for products by product name and model:

```
SELECT ProductName, ProductModel, ReferenceOrderID, ActualCost
FROM dbo.v_Product_TransactionHistory
ORDER BY ProductName
```

This returns the following abridged results:

ProductName	ProductModel	ReferenceOrderID	ActualCost
Mountain-200 Black, 38	Mountain-200	53457	1652.3928
Mountain-200 Black, 38	Mountain-200	53463	1652.3928
...			
Touring-3000 Yellow, 62	Touring-3000	71818	534.492
Touring-3000 Yellow, 62	Touring-3000	71822	534.492

```
(25262 row(s) affected)
```

How It Works

In this recipe, I define a view by using a SELECT query that referenced multiple tables in the FROM clause and qualified a specific product category of "Bikes." In this case, the view benefits anyone needing to write a query to access this data, as the user doesn't need to specify the many table joins each time she writes the query.

The view definition also used column aliases, using ProductName instead of just Name—making the column name unambiguous and reducing the possible confusion with other columns called Name. Qualifying what data is returned from the view in the WHERE clause also allows you to restrict the data that the query writer can see—in this case only letting the query writer reference products of a specific product category.

Querying the View Definition

You can view the Transact-SQL definition of a view by querying the sys.sql_modules system catalog view.

This example shows you how to query a view's SQL definition:

```
SELECT definition  FROM   sys.sql_modules
WHERE object_id = OBJECT_ID('v_Product_TransactionHistory')
```

This returns

```
definition
CREATE VIEW dbo.v_Product_TransactionHistory  AS
SELECT    p.Name ProductName,
          p.ProductNumber,
          c.Name ProductCategory,
          s.Name ProductSubCategory,
          m.Name
          ProductModel,
          t.TransactionID,
          t.ReferenceOrderID,
          t.ReferenceOrderLineID,
          t.TransactionDate,
          t.TransactionType,
          t.Quantity,
          t.ActualCost
FROM Production.TransactionHistory t
INNER JOIN Production.Product p ON
   t.ProductID = p.ProductID
INNER JOIN Production.ProductModel m ON
   m.ProductModelID = p.ProductModelID
INNER JOIN Production.ProductSubcategory s ON
```

```
    s.ProductSubcategoryID = p.ProductSubcategoryID
INNER JOIN Production.ProductCategory c ON
    c.ProductCategoryID = s.ProductCategoryID
WHERE c.Name = 'Bikes'
```

The T-SQL object definition can also be returned using the `OBJECT_DEFINITION` function, as the next query demonstrates:

```
SELECT OBJECT_DEFINITION ( OBJECT_ID('v_Product_TransactionHistory'))
```

This returns the same results as the previous query to `sys.sql_modules`.

How It Works

As you just saw, the `sys.sql_modules` system catalog view and `OBJECT_DEFINITION` function allow you to view the SQL text of a view. If the view has been encrypted (see the section "View Encryption" later in the chapter for a review of encryption), the `definition` column will return a `NULL` value. This `sys.sql_modules` system catalog view can also be used to view other procedural code object types described in later chapters, such as triggers, functions, and stored procedures.

Displaying Views and Their Structures

In this recipe, I use three different queries to return information about views in the current database.

The first query shows all views in the current database:

```
SELECT    s.name SchemaName,
        v.name ViewName
FROM sys.views v
INNER JOIN sys.schemas s ON
    v.schema_id = s.schema_id
ORDER BY s.name,
        v.name
```

This returns the following (abridged) results:

SchemaName	ViewName
dbo	v_Product_TransactionHistory
HumanResources	vEmployee
HumanResources	vEmployeeDepartment
...	
Sales	vStoreWithAddresses
Sales	vStoreWithContacts
Sales	vStoreWithDemographics

```
(21 row(s) affected)
```

This second query displays the columns exposed by each view in the current database:

```
SELECT  v.name ViewName,
        c.name ColumnName
FROM sys.columns c
INNER JOIN sys.views v ON
    c.object_id = v.object_id
ORDER BY v.name,
        c.name
```

This returns the following (abridged) results:

```
ViewName                              ColumnName
v_Product_TransactionHistory          ActualCost
v_Product_TransactionHistory          ProductCategory
v_Product_TransactionHistory          ProductModel
v_Product_TransactionHistory          ProductName
...
vVendorWithContacts                   PhoneNumberType
vVendorWithContacts                   Suffix
vVendorWithContacts                   Title

(270 row(s) affected)
```

How It Works

The first query in the recipe references the object catalog views `sys.views` and `sys.schemas` to return all views in the database:

```
FROM sys.views v
INNER JOIN sys.schemas s ON
    v.schema_id = s.schema_id
```

The second query reports on all columns returned by each view by querying the object catalog views `sys.columns` and `sys.views`:

```
FROM sys.columns c
INNER JOIN sys.views v ON
    c.object_id = v.object_id
```

■**Tip** Views can reference other views or tables within the view definition. These referenced objects are object dependencies (the view depends on them to return data). If you would like to query object dependencies for views, use the `sys.sql_expression_dependencies` catalog view. This catalog view is new in SQL Server 2008, and I cover it in Chapter 24.

Refreshing a View's Definition

When table objects referenced by the view are changed, the view's metadata can become outdated. For example, if you change the column width for a column referenced in a view definition, the new size may not be reflected until the metadata is refreshed. In this recipe, I'll show you how to refresh a view's metadata if the dependent objects referenced in the view definition have changed:

```
EXEC sp_refreshview 'dbo.v_Product_TransactionHistory'
```

You can also use the system stored procedure `sp_refreshsqlmodule`, which can be used not only for views, but also for stored procedures, triggers, and user-defined functions:

```
EXEC sys.sp_refreshsqlmodule  @name =  'dbo.v_Product_TransactionHistory'
```

How It Works

If the underlying object references for the view's SELECT query definition changes, you can use the sp_refreshview or sys.sp_refreshsqlmodule stored procedure to refresh the view's metadata. These system stored procedures take only one parameter, the view schema and name.

Modifying a View

The ALTER VIEW command is used to modify the definition of an existing view. The syntax is as follows:

```
ALTER VIEW [ schema_name . ] view_name [ ( column [ ,...n ] ) ]
[ WITH [ ENCRYPTION ] [ SCHEMABINDING ] [ VIEW_METADATA ] [ ,...n ] ]
AS select_statement
[ WITH CHECK OPTION ]
```

ALTER VIEW uses the same arguments as CREATE VIEW. This example demonstrates modifying an existing view:

```
-- Add a WHERE clause and remove
-- the ReferenceOrderID and ReferenceOrderLineID columns

ALTER VIEW dbo.v_Product_TransactionHistory
AS

SELECT    p.Name,
       p.ProductNumber,
       t.TransactionID,
       t.TransactionDate,
       t.TransactionType,
       t.Quantity,
       t.ActualCost
FROM Production.TransactionHistory t
INNER JOIN Production.Product p ON
   t.ProductID = p.ProductID
WHERE Quantity > 10

GO
```

How It Works

This recipe was used to remove two columns from the original view and add a WHERE clause—both by just redefining the SELECT statement after the AS keyword in the ALTER VIEW command. Note that if you alter an *indexed view* (reviewed later in the chapter), all indexes will be dropped and will need to be manually re-created.

Dropping a View

You can drop a view by using the DROP VIEW command. The syntax is as follows:

```
DROP VIEW [ schema_name . ] view_name [ ...,n ]
```

The command just takes one argument, containing the name or names of the views to drop from the database.

This example demonstrates dropping a view:

```
DROP VIEW dbo.v_Product_TransactionHistory
```

How It Works

Dropping a view will remove its definition from the system catalogs, as well as remove any indexes created for it if it were an *indexed* view.

Modifying Data Through a View

As I mentioned at the beginning of the chapter, you can perform inserts, updates, and deletes against a view, just like you would a regular table. In order to do this, any INSERT/UPDATE/DELETE operations can reference columns *only* from a single table. Also, the columns being referenced in the INSERT/UPDATE/DELETE cannot be derived—for example, they can't be calculated, based on an aggregate function, or be affected by a GROUP BY, DISTINCT, or HAVING clause.

As a real-world best practice, view updates may be appropriate for situations where the underlying data tables must be obscured from the query author. For example, if you are building a shrink-wrapped software application that allows users to directly update the data, providing views will allow you to filter the underlying columns that are viewed or provide more user-friendly column names than what you find used in the base tables.

In this example, a view is created that selects from the Production.Location table. A calculated column is also used in the query definition:

```
CREATE VIEW Production.vw_Location
AS
SELECT LocationID,
    Name LocationName,
    CostRate,
    Availability,
   CostRate/Availability CostToAvailabilityRatio
FROM Production.Location
GO
```

The following insert is attempted:

```
INSERT Production.vw_Location
(LocationName, CostRate, Availability, CostToAvailabilityRatio)
VALUES ('Finishing Cabinet', 1.22, 75.00, 0.01626 )
```

This returns the following error:

```
Msg 4406, Level 16, State 1, Line 1
Update or insert of view or function 'Production.vw_Location' failed
because it contains a derived or constant field.
```

This next insert is attempted, this time only referencing the columns that exist in the base table:

```
INSERT Production.vw_Location
(LocationName, CostRate, Availability)
VALUES ('Finishing Cabinet', 1.22, 75.00)
```

The results show that the insert succeeded:

```
(1 row(s) affected)
```

How It Works

In this recipe, I demonstrated performing an insert operation against a view. You can perform data modifications against views as long as your data modification and view meet the requirements. If your view can't meet these requirements, you can use an INSTEAD OF trigger to perform updates instead (an example of creating a view on a trigger is demonstrated in Chapter 12).

View Encryption

The ENCRYPTION OPTION in the CREATE VIEW and ALTER VIEW commands allows you to encrypt the Transact-SQL of a view. Once encrypted, you can no longer view the definition in the sys. sql_modules system catalog view. Software vendors who use SQL Server in the back end often encrypt their views or stored procedures in order to prevent tampering or reverse-engineering from clients or competitors. If you use encryption, be sure to save the original, unencrypted definition.

Encrypting a View

This example demonstrates encrypting the Transact-SQL definition of a new view:

```
CREATE VIEW dbo.v_Product_TopTenListPrice
WITH ENCRYPTION
AS

SELECT   TOP 10
        p.Name,
        p.ProductNumber,
        p.ListPrice
FROM Production.Product p
ORDER BY p.ListPrice DESC
GO
```

Next, the sys.sql_modules system catalog view is queried for the new view's Transact-SQL definition:

```
SELECT definition
FROM   sys.sql_modules
WHERE object_id = OBJECT_ID('v_Product_TopTenListPrice')
```

This returns

```
definition
NULL
```

How It Works

In this recipe, a new view was created using the WITH ENCRYPTION option. If you're using this option, be sure to retain your source code in a safe location, or use a version control program such as Visual SourceSafe. In general, if you must encrypt a view's definition, it should be performed just prior to deployment.

Indexed Views

A view is no more efficient than the underlying SELECT query that you use to define it. However, one way you can improve the performance of a frequently accessed view is to add an index to it. To do so, you must first create a unique, clustered index on the view. Once this index has been built, the data used to materialize the view is stored in much the same way as a table's clustered index. After creating the unique clustered index on the view, you can also create additional nonclustered indexes. The underlying (base) tables are not impacted physically by the creation of these view indexes, as they are separate underlying objects.

Indexed views can be created across all editions of SQL Server, although they require SQL Server Enterprise Edition in order for the Query Optimizer to automatically consider using an indexed view in a query execution plan. In SQL Server Enterprise Edition, an indexed view can automatically be used by the Query Optimizer when it is deemed useful, even if the SQL statement explicitly references the view's underlying base tables and not the view itself. In editions other than Enterprise Edition, you can manually force an indexed view to be used by the Query Optimizer by using the NOEXPAND table hint (reviewed later in the chapter in the "Forcing the Optimizer to Use an Index for an Indexed View" recipe).

Indexed views are particularly ideal for view definitions that aggregate data across many rows, as the aggregated values remain updated and materialized, and can be queried without continuous recalculation. Indexed views are ideal for queries referencing infrequently updated base tables, but creating them on highly volatile tables may result in degraded performance due to constant updating of the indexes. Base tables with frequent updates will trigger frequent index updates against the view, meaning that update speed will suffer at the expense of query performance.

Creating an Indexed View

In this recipe, I'll demonstrate how to create an indexed view. First, I will create a new view, and then create indexes (clustered and nonclustered) on it. In order to create an indexed view, you are required to use the WITH SCHEMABINDING option, which binds the view to the schema of the underlying tables. This prevents any changes in the base table that would impact the view definition. The WITH SCHEMABINDING option also adds additional requirements to the view's SELECT definition. Object references in a schema-bound view must include the two-part schema.object naming convention, and all referenced objects have to be located in the same database.

■Note There are also several other requirements that can determine whether or not an index can be created on top of a view. The exhaustive list won't be rehashed in this chapter, so be sure to check out the complete requirements in SQL Server Books Online.

The recipe begins by creating a new view with the SCHEMABINDING option:

```
CREATE VIEW dbo.v_Product_Sales_By_LineTotal
WITH SCHEMABINDING
AS

SELECT p.ProductID, p.Name ProductName,
       SUM(LineTotal) LineTotalByProduct,
       COUNT_BIG(*) LineItems
FROM Sales.SalesOrderDetail s
INNER JOIN Production.Product p ON
```

```
    s.ProductID = p.ProductID
GROUP BY p.ProductID, p.Name

GO
```

Before creating an index, we'll demonstrate querying the regular view, returning the query I/O cost statistics using the SET STATISTICS IO command (see Chapter 28 for more info on this command):

```
SET STATISTICS IO ON
GO

SELECT TOP 5 ProductName, LineTotalByProduct
FROM v_Product_Sales_By_LineTotal
ORDER BY LineTotalByProduct DESC
```

This returns the following results:

ProductName	LineTotalByProduct
Mountain-200 Black, 38	4400592.800400
Mountain-200 Black, 42	4009494.761841
Mountain-200 Silver, 38	3693678.025272
Mountain-200 Silver, 42	3438478.860423
Mountain-200 Silver, 46	3434256.941928

This also returns I/O information reporting the various scanning activities against the underlying base tables used in the view (if you are following along with this recipe, keep in mind that your actual stats may vary):

Table 'Product'. Scan count 0, logical reads 10, physical reads 0, read-ahead reads 0, lob logical reads 0, lob physical reads 0, lob read-ahead reads 0.

Table 'Worktable'. Scan count 0, logical reads 0, physical reads 0, read-ahead reads 0, lob logical reads 0, lob physical reads 0, lob read-ahead reads 0.

Table 'SalesOrderDetail'. Scan count 1, logical reads 1241, physical reads 7, read-ahead reads 1251, lob logical reads 0, lob physical reads 0, lob read-ahead reads 0.

Next, I'll add a clustered index that will be created on the regular view, based on the unique value of the ProductID view column:

```
CREATE UNIQUE CLUSTERED INDEX UCI_v_Product_Sales_By_LineTotal
  ON dbo.v_Product_Sales_By_LineTotal (ProductID)
GO
```

Once the clustered index is created, I can then start creating nonclustered indexes as needed:

```
CREATE NONCLUSTERED INDEX NI_v_Product_Sales_By_LineTotal
  ON dbo.v_Product_Sales_By_LineTotal (ProductName)
GO
```

Next, I'll execute the query I executed earlier against the regular view:

```
SELECT TOP 5 ProductName, LineTotalByProduct
FROM v_Product_Sales_By_LineTotal
ORDER BY LineTotalByProduct DESC
```

This returns the same results as before, but this time the I/O activity is different. Instead of two base tables being accessed, along with a worktable (tempdb used temporarily to process results), only a single object is accessed to retrieve results:

```
Table 'v_Product_Sales_By_LineTotal'. Scan count 1, logical reads 5, physical
reads 0, read-ahead reads 0, lob logical reads 0, lob physical reads 0, lob
read-ahead reads 0
```

How It Works

Indexed views allow you to materialize the results of the view as a physical object, similar to a regular table and associated indexes. This allows the SQL Server Query Optimizer to retrieve results from a single physical area instead of having to process the view definition query each time it is called.

In this example, a view was created using the SCHEMABINDING option:

```
CREATE VIEW dbo.v_Product_Sales_By_LineTotal
WITH SCHEMABINDING
AS
```

The remainder of the view was a regular SELECT query that aggregated the sum total of sales by product:

```
SELECT p.ProductID, p.Name ProductName,
       SUM(LineTotal) LineTotalByProduct,
       COUNT_BIG(*) LineItems
FROM Sales.SalesOrderDetail s
INNER JOIN Production.Product p ON
    s.ProductID = p.ProductID
GROUP BY p.ProductID, p.Name

GO
```

Notice that the query referenced the COUNT_BIG aggregate function. COUNT_BIG is required in order for SQL Server to maintain the number of rows in each group within the indexed view. Once the view was successfully created with SCHEMABINDING, a unique clustered index was then created on it:

```
CREATE UNIQUE CLUSTERED INDEX UCI_v_Product_Sales_By_LineTotal
  ON dbo.v_Product_Sales_By_LineTotal (ProductID)
GO
```

In order to index a view, you must first create a unique clustered index on it. Once this index has been built, the view data is stored in much the same way as a clustered index for a table is stored. After a clustered index is created, you can also create additional nonclustered indexes, as you would for a regular table. In the example, a nonclustered index was created on the ProductName column of the indexed view:

```
CREATE NONCLUSTERED INDEX NI_v_Product_Sales_By_LineTotal
  ON dbo.v_Product_Sales_By_LineTotal (ProductName)
GO
```

Once a view is indexed, view indexes can then be used by SQL Server Enterprise Edition whenever the view or underlying tables are referenced in a query. The SET STATISTICS IO command was used to demonstrate how SQL Server performs the data page retrieval both before and after the view was indexed.

Indexed views can provide performance benefits for relatively static data. Frequently updated base tables, on the other hand, are not an ideal choice for being referenced in an indexed view, as the updates will also cause frequent updates to the view's indexes, potentially reducing the benefit of any query performance gained. This is a trade-off between data modification speed and query speed.

Also, although indexed views can be created using any edition of SQL Server, they will be automatically considered during queries if you are using Enterprise Edition. To make sure SQL Server uses it in other editions, you need to use the view hint NOEXPAND, which is reviewed in the next recipe.

Forcing the Optimizer to Use an Index for an Indexed View

Once you've created an indexed view, if you're running on SQL Server Enterprise Edition, the Query Optimizer will automatically decide whether or not to use the indexed view in a query. For other editions, however, in order to make SQL Server use a specific indexed view, you must use the NOEXPAND keyword.

By adding the WITH (NOEXPAND) view hint after the FROM clause, SQL Server is directed only to use view indexes.

The view hint syntax is as follows:

```
{ NOEXPAND [ , INDEX ( index_val [ ,...n ] ) ] }
```

This recipe demonstrates how to force an indexed view's index to be used for a query:

```
SELECT ProductID
FROM dbo.v_Product_Sales_By_LineTotal
WITH (NOEXPAND)
WHERE ProductName = 'Short-Sleeve Classic Jersey, L'
```

NOEXPAND also allows you to specify one or more indexes to be used for the query, using the INDEX option. For example:

```
SELECT ProductID
FROM dbo.v_Product_Sales_By_LineTotal
WITH (NOEXPAND, INDEX(NI_v_Product_Sales_By_LineTotal))
WHERE ProductName = 'Short-Sleeve Classic Jersey, L'
```

How It Works

For those using non–Enterprise Edition versions of SQL Server, you can still take advantage of indexed views through the use of the NOEXPAND keyword. The drawback is that you must explicitly use hints whenever the indexed view must be utilized. Another drawback is that your hint usage could nullify a better SQL Server Query Optimizer choice that would have been made had the hint *not* been used.

Partitioned Views

Distributed partitioned views allow you to create a single logical representation (view) of two or more horizontally partitioned tables that are located across separate SQL Server instances.

In order to set up a distributed partitioned view, a large table is split into smaller tables based on a range of values defined in a CHECK constraint. This CHECK constraint ensures that each smaller table holds unique data that cannot be stored in the other tables. The distributed partitioned view is then created using a UNION ALL to join each smaller table into a single result set.

The performance benefit is realized when a query is executed against the distributed partitioned view. If the view is partitioned by a date range, for example, and a query is used to return rows that are only stored in a single table of the partition, SQL Server is smart enough to only search that one partition instead of all tables in the distributed-partitioned view.

Creating a Distributed-Partitioned View

In this recipe, I'll demonstrate how to create a distributed-partitioned view that spans two SQL Server instances. It's based on the following business scenario. There are two sibling corporations—MegaCorp and MiniCorp. Each has their own SQL Server instance to house website data, and each wants a table to track website hits. The numbers of hits are voluminous—and would require more storage than a single SQL Server instance could handle. The requirement is to create a unified view that references both tables in a single view. The business wants to be able to query either server and return either the same data or data just for its own company.

Since more than one SQL Server instance will be accessed in a distributed-partitioned view recipe, linked servers are added to both participating SQL Server instances (see Chapter 27 for more information on linked servers).

I'll begin this recipe by creating a linked server on the *first SQL Server* instance:

```
USE master
GO
EXEC sp_addlinkedserver
    'JOEPROD',
    N'SQL Server'
GO


-- skip schema checking of remote tables
EXEC sp_serveroption 'JOEPROD', 'lazy schema validation', 'true'
GO
```

On the second SQL Server instance, a linked server is created to the first SQL Server instance:

```
USE master
GO
EXEC sp_addlinkedserver
    'JOEPROD\SQL2008',
    N'SQL Server'
GO


-- skip schema checking of remote tables
EXEC sp_serveroption 'JOEPROD\SQL2008', 'lazy schema validation', 'true'
GO
```

Back on the first SQL Server instance, the following table is created to hold rows for MegaCorp website hits:

```
IF NOT EXISTS (SELECT name
               FROM sys.databases
               WHERE name = 'TSQLRecipeTest')
BEGIN
    CREATE DATABASE TSQLRecipeTest
END
GO


Use TSQLRecipeTest
GO
```

```
CREATE TABLE dbo.WebHits_MegaCorp
   (WebHitID uniqueidentifier NOT NULL,
    WebSite varchar(20) NOT NULL ,
    HitDT datetime NOT NULL,
    CHECK (WebSite = 'MegaCorp'),
    CONSTRAINT PK_WebHits PRIMARY KEY (WebHitID, WebSite))
```

On the second SQL Server instance, the following table is created to hold rows for MiniCorp website hits:

```
IF NOT EXISTS (SELECT name
                 FROM sys.databases
                 WHERE name = 'TSQLRecipeTest')
BEGIN
    CREATE DATABASE TSQLRecipeTest
END
GO

USE TSQLRecipeTest
GO

CREATE TABLE dbo.WebHits_MiniCorp
   (WebHitID uniqueidentifier NOT NULL ,
    WebSite varchar(20) NOT NULL ,
    HitDT datetime NOT NULL,
    CHECK (WebSite = 'MiniCorp') ,
    CONSTRAINT PK_WebHits PRIMARY KEY (WebHitID, WebSite))
```

Back on the first SQL Server instance, the following distributed partitioned view that references the local WebHits_MegaCorp table and the remote WebHits.MiniCorp table is created:

```
CREATE VIEW dbo.v_WebHits AS
   SELECT WebHitID,
          WebSite,
          HitDT
   FROM TSQLRecipeTest.dbo.WebHits_MegaCorp
UNION ALL
   SELECT WebHitID,
          WebSite,
          HitDT
   FROM JOEPROD.TSQLRecipeTest.dbo.WebHits_MiniCorp
GO
```

On the second SQL Server instance, the following distributed partitioned view is created—this time referencing the local WebHits_MiniCorp table and the remote WebHits_MegaCorp table:

```
CREATE VIEW dbo.v_WebHits AS
   SELECT WebHitID,
          WebSite,
          HitDT
   FROM TSQLRecipeTest.dbo.WebHits_MiniCorp
UNION ALL
   SELECT WebHitID,
          WebSite,
          HitDT
   FROM [JOEPROD\SQL2008].TSQLRecipeTest.dbo.WebHits_MegaCorp
GO
```

On the second SQL Server instance, the following batch of queries is executed to insert new rows:

```
-- For these inserts to work the setting XACT_ABORT must be ON and
-- the Distributed Transaction Coordinator service must be running

SET XACT_ABORT ON

INSERT dbo.v_WebHits
(WebHitID, WebSite, HitDT)
VALUES(NEWID(), 'MegaCorp', GETDATE())

INSERT dbo.v_WebHits
(WebHitID, WebSite, HitDT)
VALUES(NEWID(), 'MiniCorp', GETDATE())
```

This returns

```
(1 row(s) affected)

(1 row(s) affected)
```

Querying from the distributed-partitioned view returns the two newly inserted rows (from both underlying tables):

```
SET XACT_ABORT ON

SELECT WebHitID, WebSite, HitDT
FROM dbo.v_WebHits
```

This returns

WebHitID	WebSite	HitDT
E5994678-6066-45F4-8AE4-9F10CE412D1A	MegaCorp	2008-08-06 16:56:29.253
E1444A3F-7A2E-4A54-A156-C04FE742B453	MiniCorp	2008-08-06 16:56:29.353

Querying the MiniCorp table directly returns just the one MiniCorp row, as expected:

```
SELECT WebHitID, WebSite, HitDT
FROM JOEPROD.AdventureWorks.dbo.WebHits_MiniCorp
```

This returns

WebHitID	WebSite	HitDT
E1444A3F-7A2E-4A54-A156-C04FE742B453	MiniCorp	2005-08-06 16:56:29.353

Querying the MegaCorp table also returns the expected, single row:

```
SELECT WebHitID, WebSite, HitDT
FROM [JOEPROD\SQL2008].AdventureWorks.dbo.WebHits_MegaCorp
```

This returns

WebHitID	WebSite	HitDT
E5994678-6066-45F4-8AE4-9F10CE412D1A	MegaCorp	2005-08-06 16:56:29.253

How It Works

Distributed-partitioned views allow you to partition data across more than one SQL Server instance. This design option can be beneficial for very large databases and SQL Server instances with high volumes of transactions and read activity.

There's a lot going on in this recipe, so I'll walk through each step of the process. First, linked server references were created on each SQL Server instance so that both instances could use distributed queries to communicate with one another. Also, the linked server option lazy schema validation was enabled for performance reasons. This setting ensures that schema lookups are skipped prior to query execution.

Next, the table dbo.WebHits_MegaCorp was created on SQL Server Instance 1 (JOEPROD\SQL2008) and dbo.WebHits_MiniCorp on SQL Server Instance 2 (JOEPROD). Each was created with a CHECK constraint that restricted what values could be added to it. So that distributed-partitioned view updates are allowed, the CHECK constraints must be defined on the same column and cannot allow overlapping values in the member tables. In addition to this, only the operators <,>, =, >=, <=, AND, OR, and BETWEEN can be used in the CHECK constraint.

Other requirements you'll need to remember in order to allow view updates: the partitioning column, in this case WebSite, cannot allow null values; be a computed column; or be an identity, default, or timestamp column. The partition key, WebSite, also needed to be part of the primary key. Since WebSite wasn't unique by itself, it was added as a composite key with the uniqueidentifier data type WebHitID. Both partitioned tables were required to have primary keys on an identical number of columns:

```
CONSTRAINT PK_WebHits PRIMARY KEY (WebHitID, WebSite))
```

In the next step, the distributed partitioned views were created on each of the SQL Server instances. On the instance with the dbo.WebHits_MegaCorp table, the view referenced that table using the three-part database.schema.viewname format (because the table is local):

```
SELECT WebHitID,
       WebSite,
       HitDT
  FROM AdventureWorks.dbo.WebHits_MegaCorp
```

The table was then joined with UNION ALL (another requirement if you wish to perform data modifications against the distributed partitioned view):

```
UNION ALL
```

The columns defined in the SELECT list can't be referenced more than once in a single list, and should be in the same ordinal position for each SELECT that is UNIONed. Columns across each SELECT should also have the same data types and collations, as this recipe did.

In the FROM clause for the remote dbo.WebHits_MiniCorp table, the four-part name linked-servername.database.schema.viewname was used (since it is a remote table):

```
SELECT WebHitID,
       WebSite,
       HitDT
  FROM JOEPROD.AdventureWorks.dbo.WebHits_MiniCorp
GO
```

In the last batches in the recipe, SET XACT_ABORT was set ON in order to allow for the insert of rows into the distributed partitioned view. This option terminates and rolls back a transaction if a runtime error is encountered:

```
SET XACT_ABORT ON
```

As noted in the script comments, the Distributed Transaction Coordinator also needs to be running in order to invoke the distributed transaction of inserting a row across SQL Server instances. Two inserts were performed against the new distributed partitioned view—the first for a hit to MegaCorp, and the second for MiniCorp:

```
INSERT dbo.v_WebHits
(WebHitID, WebSite, HitDT)
VALUES(NEWID(), 'MegaCorp', GETDATE())

INSERT dbo.v_WebHits
(WebHitID, WebSite, HitDT)
VALUES(NEWID(), 'MiniCorp', GETDATE())
```

Querying the new distributed partitioned views, two rows are returned:

```
SELECT WebHitID, WebSite, HitDT
FROM dbo.v_WebHits
```

Querying the underlying horizontally partitioned tables, one row was automatically routed to the dbo.WebHits_MegaCorp table, and the other to the dbo.WebHits_MiniCorp table.

Based on which view is queried (for example, Instance 1 or Instance 2), SQL Server can determine whether a particular query request can be fulfilled from just querying the local partitioned table, or whether the remote table need also be queried. The end result is that SQL Server minimizes the amount of data needing to be transferred between the SQL Server instances.

■ ■ ■

SQL Server Functions

In this chapter, I'll demonstrate how to use SQL Server built-in functions in your Transact-SQL code. SQL Server built-in functions, not to be confused with the user-defined functions covered in Chapter 11, allow you to perform aggregations, mathematical operations, string manipulation, row ranking, and much more. SQL Server 2008 has added new functions as well, including GROUPING, SYSDATETIME, SYSDATETIMEOFFSET, SYSUTCDATETIME, SWITCHOFFSET, and TODATETIMEOFFSET—all of which I'll demonstrate. I'll also cover the new SQL Server 2008 improvement that allows you to return binary data in a string hexadecimal literal format.

Aggregate Functions

Aggregate functions are used to perform a calculation on one or more values, resulting in a single value. An example of a commonly used aggregate function is SUM, which is used to return the total value of a set of numeric values. Table 8-1 lists some of the more commonly used aggregate functions available in SQL Server.

Table 8-1. *Aggregate Functions*

Function Name	Description
AVG	The AVG aggregate function calculates the average of non-NULL values in a group.
CHECKSUM_AGG	The CHECKSUM_AGG function returns a checksum value based on a group of rows, allowing you to potentially track changes to a table. For example, adding a new row or changing the value of a column that is being aggregated will usually result in a new checksum integer value. The reason why I say "usually" is that there is a possibility that the checksum value does not change even if values are modified.
COUNT	The COUNT aggregate function returns an integer data type showing the count of rows in a group.
COUNT_BIG	The COUNT_BIG function works the same as COUNT, only it returns a bigint data type value.
GROUPING	The GROUPING function returns 1 (True) or 0 (False) depending on whether a NULL value is due to a CUBE, ROLLUP, or GROUPING SETS operation. If False, the column expression NULL value is from the natural data. See Chapter 1's recipe "Revealing Rows Generated by GROUPING."
MAX	The MAX aggregate function returns the highest value in a set of non-NULL values.
MIN	The MIN aggregate function returns the lowest value in a group of non-NULL values.

Continued

Table 8-1. *Continued*

Function Name	Description
SUM	The SUM aggregate function returns the summation of all non-NULL values in an expression.
STDEV	The STDEV function returns the standard deviation of all values provided in the expression based on a sample of the data population.
STDEVP	The STDEVP function also returns the standard deviation for all values in the provided expression, only it evaluates the entire data population.
VAR	The VAR function returns the statistical variance of values in an expression based on a sample of the provided population.
VARP	The VARP function also returns the variance of the provided values for the entire data population of the expression.

The next few recipes will demonstrate these aggregate functions.

Returning the Average of Values

The AVG aggregate function calculates the average of non-NULL values in a group. For example:

```
-- Average Product Review by Product
SELECT ProductID,
       AVG(Rating) AvgRating
FROM Production.ProductReview
GROUP BY ProductID
```

This returns

```
ProductID    AvgRating
709          5
798          5
937          3
```

This second example demonstrates averaging the DISTINCT values in the StandardCost column—meaning that only unique StandardCost values are averaged:

```
-- Average DISTINCT Standard Cost
SELECT AVG(DISTINCT StandardCost) AvgDistinctStandardCost
FROM Production.ProductCostHistory
```

This returns

```
AvgDistinctStandardCost
287.7111
```

How It Works

In this recipe, the first example returned the average product rating grouped by ProductID. The second example took an average of the DISTINCT StandardCost—meaning that only unique StandardCost values were averaged. Without the DISTINCT keyword, the default behavior of the AVG aggregate function is to average all values, duplicate values included.

Returning Row Counts

The COUNT aggregate function returns an integer showing the count of the rows in a group. For example, the following query groups rows by shelving assignment and returns the count of items on each shelf:

```
SELECT  Shelf,
        COUNT(ProductID) ProductCount
FROM   Production.ProductInventory
GROUP BY Shelf
ORDER BY Shelf
```

This returns the following (abridged) results:

Shelf	ProductCount
A	81
B	36
C	55
D	50
E	85
F	59
...	
S	17
T	28
U	38
V	7
W	14
Y	2

If you include the DISTINCT keyword within the COUNT function parentheses, you'll get the count of distinct values for that column. For example:

```
SELECT  COUNT(DISTINCT Shelf) ShelfCount
FROM   Production.ProductInventory
```

This returns

ShelfCount
21

How It Works

In the first example of this recipe, the number of products per shelf was counted. COUNT is the only aggregate function that does not ignore NULL values, so had ProductID been NULL, it would have still been included in the count. The second example demonstrated counting the number of DISTINCT shelf values from the Production.ProductInventory table. If you need to count a value larger than the integer data type can hold, use the COUNT_BIG aggregate function, which returns a bigint data type value.

Finding the Lowest and Highest Values from an Expression

The MAX aggregate function returns the highest value and the MIN aggregate function returns the lowest value in a group of non-NULL values. MIN and MAX can be used with numeric, character, and datetime columns. The minimum and maximum values for character data types are determined by using an ASCII alphabetical sort. `MIN` and `MAX` for `datetime` values are based on the earliest date to the most recent date.

In this example, I'll demonstrate how to use the `MIN` and `MAX` functions to find the lowest and highest value in the `Rating` numeric column from the `Production.ProductReview` table:

```
SELECT  MIN(Rating) MinRating,
        MAX(Rating) MaxRating
FROM  Production.ProductReview
```

This returns

MinRating	MaxRating
2	5

How It Works

This recipe demonstrated retrieving the minimum and maximum `Rating` values from the `Product.ProductReview` table. As with other aggregate functions, had there also been non-aggregated column references in the `SELECT` clause, they would have been included in a `GROUP BY` clause.

Returning the Sum of Values

The `SUM` aggregate function returns the summation of all non-`NULL` values in an expression. This example demonstrates how to use the `SUM` aggregate function to total the value of the `TotalDue` column for each `AccountNumber`:

```
SELECT  AccountNumber,
        SUM(TotalDue) TotalDueBySalesOrderID
FROM Sales.SalesOrderHeader
GROUP BY AccountNumber
ORDER BY AccountNumber
```

This returns the following abridged results:

AccountNumber	TotalDueBySalesOrderID
10-4020-000001	113098.7351
10-4020-000002	32733.9695
10-4020-000003	479506.3256
...	

How It Works

In this recipe, the sum of `TotalDue` by `AccountNumber` was calculated. Since `AccountNumber` wasn't aggregated itself, it was included in the `GROUP BY` clause. It was also included in the `ORDER BY` clause to order the grouped results.

Using Statistical Aggregate Functions

In this recipe, I'll demonstrate using the statistical functions `VAR`, `VARP`, `STDEV`, and `STDEVP`.

The `VAR` function returns the statistical variance of values in an expression based on a sample of the provided population (the `VARP` function also returns the variance of the provided values for the entire data population of the expression).

This first example returns the statistical variance of the TaxAmt value for all rows in the Sales.SalesOrderHeader table:

```
SELECT  VAR(TaxAmt) Variance_Sample,
        VARP(TaxAmt) Variance_EntirePopulation
FROM Sales.SalesOrderHeader
```

This returns

Variance_Sample	Variance_EntirePopulation
1177342.57277401	1177305.15524429

The STDEV function returns the standard deviation of all the values provided in the expression, based on a sample of the data population. The STDEVP function also returns the standard deviation for all values in the provided expression, only it evaluates the entire data population instead. This example returns the statistical standard deviation of the UnitPrice value for all rows in the Sales.SalesOrderDetail table:

```
SELECT  STDEV(UnitPrice) StandDevUnitPrice,
        STDEVP(UnitPrice)StandDevPopUnitPrice
FROM  Sales.SalesOrderDetail
```

This returns

StandDevUnitPrice	StandDevPopUnitPrice
751.885080772954	751.881981921885

How It Works

Although the use of each statistical function varies, the implementation is similar. Specifically, in this example, each function took a value expression, using a column name from the table. The function then acted on the set of data (zero or more rows) using the column specified in the SELECT clause, returning a single value.

Mathematical Functions

SQL Server offers several mathematical functions that can be used in your Transact-SQL code, as described in Table 8-2.

Table 8-2. *Mathematical Functions*

Function	Description
ABS	Calculates the absolute value
ACOS	Calculates the angle, the cosine of which is the specified argument, in radians
ASIN	Calculates the angle, the sine of which is the specified argument, in radians
ATAN	Calculates the angle, the tangent of which is the specified argument, in radians
ATN2	Calculates the angle, the tangent of which is between two float expressions, in radians
CEILING	Calculates the smallest integer greater than or equal to the provided argument
COS	Calculates the cosine

Continued

Table 8-2. *Continued*

Function	Description
COT	Calculates the cotangent
DEGREES	Converts radians to degrees
EXP	Calculates the exponential value of a provided argument
FLOOR	Calculates the largest integer less than or equal to the provided argument
LOG	Calculates the natural logarithm
LOG10	Calculates the Base-10 logarithm
PI	Returns the PI constant
POWER	Returns the value of the first argument to the power of the second argument
RADIANS	Converts degrees to radians
RAND	Produces a random float-type value ranging from 0 to 1
ROUND	Rounds a provided argument's value to a specified precision
SIGN	Returns -1 for negative values, 0 for zero values, and 1 if the provided argument is positive
SIN	Calculates the sine for a given angle in radians
SQUARE	Calculates the square of a provided expression
SQRT	Calculates the square root
TAN	Calculates the tangent

This next recipe will demonstrate mathematical functions in action.

Performing Mathematical Operations

This recipe will demonstrate four different mathematical functions, including POWER, SQRT, ROUND, and RAND.

This first example calculates 10 to the 2nd power:

```
SELECT POWER(10,2) Result
```

This returns

```
Result
100
```

This next example calculates the square root of 100:

```
SELECT SQRT(100) Result
```

This returns

```
Result
10
```

This example rounds a number to the third digit right of the decimal place:

```
SELECT ROUND(3.22245, 3) RoundedNumber
```

This returns

RoundedNumber
3.22200

This example returns a random float data type value between 0 and 1 (your result will vary from mine):

```
SELECT RAND() RandomNumber
```

This returns

RandomNumber
0.497749897248417

This last example in the recipe returns a fixed float data type value based on the provided integer value:

```
SELECT RAND(22) Result
```

This returns

Result
0.713983285609346

How It Works

In this recipe, I demonstrated four different mathematical functions, including POWER, SQRT, ROUND, and RAND. Each function takes different parameters based on the operation it performs. For some mathematical functions, such as RAND, an input value is optional.

String Functions

This next set of recipes demonstrates SQL Server's string functions. String functions provide a multitude of uses for your Transact-SQL programming, allowing for string cleanup, conversion between ASCII and regular characters, pattern searches, removal of trailing blanks, and much more.

Table 8-3 lists the different string functions available in SQL Server.

Table 8-3. *String Functions*

Function Name(s)	Description
ASCII and CHAR	The ASCII function takes the leftmost character of a character expression and returns the ASCII code. The CHAR function converts an integer value for an ASCII code to a character value instead.
CHARINDEX and PATINDEX	The CHARINDEX function is used to return the starting position of a string within another string. The PATINDEX function is similar to CHARINDEX, except that PATINDEX allows the use of wildcards when specifying the string for which to search.

Continued

Table 8-3. *Continued*

Function Name(s)	Description
DIFFERENCE and SOUNDEX	The two functions DIFFERENCE and SOUNDEX both work with character strings to evaluate those that sound similar. SOUNDEX assigns a string a four-digit code, and DIFFERENCE evaluates the level of similarity between the SOUNDEX outputs for two separate strings.
LEFT and RIGHT	The LEFT function returns a part of a character string, beginning at the specified number of characters from the left. The RIGHT function is like the LEFT function, only it returns a part of a character string beginning at the specified number of characters from the right.
LEN and DATALENGTH	The LEN function returns the number of characters in a string expression, excluding any blanks after the last character (trailing blanks). DATALENGTH, on the other hand, returns the number of bytes used for an expression.
LOWER and UPPER	The LOWER function returns a character expression in lowercase, and the UPPER function returns a character expression in uppercase.
LTRIM and RTRIM	The LTRIM function removes leading blanks, and the RTRIM function removes trailing blanks.
NCHAR and UNICODE	The UNICODE function returns the Unicode integer value for the first character of the character or input expression. The NCHAR function takes an integer value designating a Unicode character and converts it to its character equivalent.
QUOTENAME	The QUOTENAME function adds delimiters to a Unicode input string in order to make it a valid delimited identifier.
REPLACE	The REPLACE function replaces all instances of a provided string within a specified string with a new string.
REPLICATE	The REPLICATE function repeats a given character expression a designated number of times.
REVERSE	The REVERSE function takes a character expression and outputs the expression with each character position displayed in reverse order.
SPACE	The SPACE function returns a string of repeated blank spaces, based on the integer you designate for the input parameter.
STR	The STR function converts numeric data into character data.
STUFF	The STUFF function deletes a specified length of characters and inserts a designated string at the specified starting point.
SUBSTRING	The SUBSTRING function returns a defined chunk of a specified expression.

The next few recipes will demonstrate examples of how string functions are used.

Converting a Character Value to ASCII and Back to Character

The ASCII function takes the leftmost character of a character expression and returns the ASCII code, while the CHAR function converts an integer value for an ASCII code to a character value instead. Again, it should be stressed that ASCII only uses the first character of the string. If the string is empty or NULL, ASCII will return a NULL value (although a blank, single-space value is represented by a value of 32).

This first example demonstrates how to convert characters into the integer ASCII value:

```
SELECT ASCII('H'), ASCII('e'), ASCII('l'), ASCII('l'), ASCII('o')
```

This returns

72	101	108	108	111

Next, the CHAR function is used to convert the integer values back into characters again:

```
SELECT CHAR(72), CHAR(101), CHAR(108), CHAR(108), CHAR(111)
```

This returns

H	e	l	l	o

How It Works

In this recipe, the word "Hello" was deconstructed one character at a time and then converted into the numeric ASCII value, using the ASCII function. In the second T-SQL statement, the ASCII value was reversed back into character form using the CHAR function.

Returning Integer and Character Unicode Values

The UNICODE function returns the Unicode integer value for the first character of the character or input expression. The NCHAR function takes an integer value designating a Unicode character and converts it to its character equivalent. These functions are useful if you need to exchange data with external processes using the Unicode standard.

This first example converts single characters into an integer value representing the Unicode standard character code:

```
SELECT UNICODE('G'), UNICODE('o'), UNICODE('o'), UNICODE('d'), UNICODE('!')
```

This returns

71	111	111	100	33

Next, the Unicode integer values are converted back into characters:

```
SELECT NCHAR(71), NCHAR(111), NCHAR(111), NCHAR(100), NCHAR(33)
```

This returns

G	o	o	d	!

How It Works

In this recipe, the word "Good!" was deconstructed one character at a time and then converted into an integer value using the UNICODE function. In the second T-SQL statement, the integer value was reversed back into character form using the NCHAR function.

Finding the Start Position of a String Within Another String

The CHARINDEX function is used to return the starting position of a string within another string. The syntax is as follows:

```
CHARINDEX ( expression1 ,expression2 [ , start_location ] )
```

The expression1 argument is the string to be searched for. The expression2 argument is the string in which you are searching. The optional start_location value indicates the character position where you wish to begin looking.

This example demonstrates how to find the starting position of a string within another string:

```
SELECT CHARINDEX('String to Find',
    'This is the bigger string to find something in.')
```

This returns

```
20
```

How It Works

This function returned the starting character position, in this case the 20th character, where the first argument expression was found in the second expression. You can't use wildcards with this function. Also, note that search matches are based on the rules of your SQL Server instance's collation.

Finding the Start Position of a String Within Another String Using Wildcards

The PATINDEX function is similar to CHARINDEX, except that PATINDEX allows the use of wildcards in the string you are searching for. The syntax for PATINDEX is as follows:

```
PATINDEX ( '%pattern%' ,expression )
```

PATINDEX returns the start position of the first occurrence of the search pattern, but unlike CHARINDEX, it doesn't have a starting position option. In this example, rows are returned from Person.Address, where AddressLine1 contains the word fragment "olive" and has a street address beginning with the numbers 3 and 5:

```
SELECT  AddressID,
        AddressLine1
FROM  Person.Address
WHERE PATINDEX('[3][5]%olive%', AddressLine1) > 0
```

This returns the following results:

```
AddressID    AddressLine1
26857        3507 Olive Dr.
12416        3507 Olive Dr.
12023        3538 Olivewood Ct.
27157        3538 Olivewood Ct.

(4 row(s) affected)
```

How It Works

This example returned any row where the AddressLine1 column contained the word "Olive" that was also prefixed by a street number starting with 35 (using the wildcard pattern [3] and [5]). With the wildcard % on both the left and right of the word (without spaces between), the word "Olive" could also have been embedded within another word. The pattern can use different wildcard characters too.

Determining the Similarity of Strings

The two functions, DIFFERENCE and SOUNDEX, both work with character strings in order to evaluate those that sound similar, based on English phonetic rules. SOUNDEX assigns a string a four-digit code, and then DIFFERENCE evaluates the level of similarity between the SOUNDEX outputs for two separate strings. DIFFERENCE returns a value of 0 to 4, with 4 indicating the closest match in similarity.

This example demonstrates how to identify strings that sound similar—first by evaluating strings individually, and then comparing them in pairs:

```
SELECT  SOUNDEX('Fleas'),
        SOUNDEX('Fleece'),
        SOUNDEX('Peace'),
        SOUNDEX('Peas')
```

This returns

F420	F420	P200	P200

Next, string pairs are compared using DIFFERENCE:

```
SELECT  DIFFERENCE ( 'Fleas', 'Fleece')
```

This returns

```
4
```

Next, another string pair is compared:

```
SELECT  DIFFERENCE ( 'Fleece', 'Peace')
```

This returns

```
2
```

How It Works

In the first example, SOUNDEX was used to evaluate four similar-sounding words. The query results showed four codes, with "Fleas" and "Fleece" equal to F420, and "Peace" and "Peas" equal to P200. In the second example, DIFFERENCE was used to evaluate "Fleas" and "Fleece" and "Fleece" and "Peace." "Fleas" and "Fleece" were shown to be *more* similar, with a value of 4, than "Fleece" and "Peace," which have a comparison value of 2.

Taking the Leftmost or Rightmost Part of a String

The LEFT function returns a part of a character string, starting at the beginning and taking the specified number of characters from the leftmost side of the string. The RIGHT function is like the LEFT function, only it returns a part of a character string beginning at the specified number of characters from the right.

This recipe demonstrates how to return a subset of the leftmost and rightmost parts of a string. Also, a common string padding trick is demonstrated using these functions.

In the first example, the leftmost 10 characters are taken from a string:

```
SELECT LEFT('I only want the leftmost 10 characters.', 10)
```

This returns

```
I only wan
```

Next, the rightmost characters of a string:

```
SELECT RIGHT('I only want the rightmost 10 characters.', 10)
```

This returns

```
haracters.
```

This next example demonstrates zero-padding the ListPrice column's value:

```
-- Padding a number for business purposes
SELECT  TOP 3
        ProductID, RIGHT('0000000000' + CONVERT(varchar(10), ListPrice),10)
FROM  Production.Product
WHERE ListPrice > 0
```

This returns

ProductID	(No column name)
514	0000133.34
515	0000147.14
516	0000196.92

How It Works

This recipe demonstrated three examples of using LEFT and RIGHT. The first two examples demonstrated returning the leftmost or the rightmost characters of a string value. The third example demonstrated the padding of a string in order to conform to some expected business format. When presenting data to end users or exporting data to external systems, you may sometimes need to preserve or add leading values, such as leading zeros to fixed-length numbers or spaces to varchar fields. ListPrice was zero-padded by first concatenating ten zeros in a string to the converted varchar(10) value of the ListPrice. Then, outside of this concatenation, RIGHT was used to grab the last 10 characters of the concatenated string (thus taking leading zeros from the left side with it, when the ListPrice fell short of ten digits).

Determining the Number of Characters or Bytes in a String

The LEN function returns the number of characters in a string expression, excluding any blanks after the last character (trailing blanks). DATALENGTH, on the other hand, returns the number of bytes used for an expression. In this recipe, I'll demonstrate how to measure the number of characters and bytes in a string.

This first example returns the number of characters in the Unicode string (Unicode data takes two bytes for each character, whereas non-Unicode takes only one):

```
SELECT LEN(N'She sells sea shells by the sea shore.')
```

This returns

```
38
```

This next example returns the number of bytes in the Unicode string:

```
SELECT DATALENGTH(N'She sells sea shells by the sea shore.')
```

This returns

```
76
```

How It Works

This recipe used a Unicode string, which is defined by prefixing the string with an N as follows:

```
N'She sells sea shells by the sea shore.'
```

The number of characters for this string is 38 according to LEN, but since it is a Unicode string, DATALENGTH returns 76 bytes. SQL Server uses the Unicode UCS-2 encoding form, which consumes 2 bytes per character stored.

Replacing a Part of a String

The REPLACE function replaces all instances of a provided string within a specified string, and replaces it with a new string. One real strength of REPLACE is that, unlike PATINDEX and CHARINDEX, which return a specific location where a pattern is found, REPLACE can find multiple instances of a pattern within a specific character string.

The syntax for REPLACE is as follows:

```
REPLACE ( 'string_expression1' , 'string_expression2' , 'string_expression3' )
```

The first string expression argument is the string that will be modified. The second string expression is the string to be removed from the first string argument. The third string expression is the string to insert into the first argument.

This example demonstrates how to replace all instances of a provided string with a new string:

```
SELECT REPLACE('Zenon is our major profit center. Zenon leads the way.',
        'Zenon',
        'Xerxes')
```

This returns

```
Xerxes is our major profit center. Xerxes leads the way.
```

How It Works

In this recipe, the first string expression was the string to be searched, "Zenon is our major profit center. Zenon leads the way." The second expression was the expression to replace (Zenon), and the third expression was the value to substitute Zenon with, Xerxes. I used the REPLACE function to replace all occurrences of Zenon with Xerxes. Even though Zenon appeared twice in the original string, REPLACE substituted both occurrences of Xerxes with a single function call.

Stuffing a String into a String

The STUFF function deletes a specified length of characters and inserts a designated string at the specified starting point. The syntax is as follows:

```
STUFF ( character_expression, start, length, character_expression )
```

The first argument of this function is the character expression to be modified. The second argument is the starting position of the inserted string. The third argument is the number of characters to delete within the character expression. The fourth argument is the actual character expression that you want to insert. This example replaces a part of a string and inserts a new expression into the string body:

```
SELECT STUFF ( 'My cat''s name is X. Have you met him?',
        18,
        1,
        'Edgar' )
```

This returns

```
My cat's name is Edgar. Have you met him?
```

How It Works

The character expression in this recipe was "My cat's name is X. Have you met him?". The start value was 18, which means that the replacement will occur at the 18th position within the string (which is "X," in this case). The length value was 1, meaning only one character at position 18 would be deleted. The last character expression was Edgar, which is the value to stuff into the string.

Changing Between Lower- and Uppercase

The LOWER function returns a character expression in lowercase, and the UPPER function returns a character expression in uppercase.

■**Tip** There isn't a built-in proper case function, so in Chapter 11 I demonstrate creating a scalar user-defined function that allows you to do this.

Before showing the different functions in action, the following query I've presented will show the value of DocumentSummary for a specific row in the Production.Document table:

```
SELECT DocumentSummary
FROM Production.Document
WHERE FileName = 'Installing Replacement Pedals.doc'
```

This returns the following sentence-case value:

DocumentSummary
Detailed instructions for replacing pedals with Adventure Works Cycles replacement
pedals. Instructions are applicable to all Adventure Works Cycles bicycle models
and replacement pedals. Use only Adventure Works Cycles parts when replacing worn or
broken

This first example demonstrates setting values to lowercase:

```
SELECT LOWER(DocumentSummary)
FROM Production.Document
WHERE FileName = 'Installing Replacement Pedals.doc'
```

This returns

---

detailed instructions for replacing pedals with adventure works cycles replacement
pedals. instructions are applicable to all adventure works cycles bicycle models
and replacement pedals. use only adventure works cycles parts when replacing worn or
broken

Now for uppercase:

```
SELECT UPPER(DocumentSummary)
FROM Production.Document
WHERE FileName = 'Installing Replacement Pedals.doc'
```

This returns

DETAILED INSTRUCTIONS FOR REPLACING PEDALS WITH ADVENTURE WORKS CYCLES REPLACEMENT
PEDALS. INSTRUCTIONS ARE APPLICABLE TO ALL ADVENTURE WORKS CYCLES BICYCLE MODELS
AND REPLACEMENT PEDALS. USE ONLY ADVENTURE WORKS CYCLES PARTS WHEN REPLACING WORN OR
BROKEN

How It Works

The first example demonstrated the LOWER function, which returned a character expression in lower-case. The second example demonstrated the UPPER function, which returned a character expression in uppercase. In both cases, the function takes a single argument, the character expression containing the case to be converted to either upper- or lowercase.

Removing Leading and Trailing Blanks

The LTRIM function removes leading blanks, and the RTRIM function removes trailing blanks.

This first example demonstrates removing leading blanks from a string:

```
SELECT LTRIM('    String with leading blanks.')
```

This returns

```
String with leading blanks.
```

This second example demonstrates removing trailing blanks from a string:

```
SELECT RTRIM('"' + 'String with trailing blanks     ') + '"'
```

This returns

```
"String with trailing blanks"
```

How It Works

Both LTRIM and RTRIM take a single argument—a character expression that is to be trimmed. The function then trims the leading or trailing blanks. Note that there isn't a TRIM function (as seen in other programming languages) that can be used to remove both leading and trailing characters. To do this, you must use both LTRIM and RTRIM in the same expression.

Repeating an Expression *N* Number of Times

The REPLICATE function repeats a given character expression a designated number of times.
The syntax is as follows:

```
REPLICATE ( character_expression ,integer_expression )
```

The first argument is the character expression to be repeated. The second argument is the integer value of the number of times the character expression is to be repeated. This example demonstrates how to use the REPLICATE function to repeat a character expression a set number of times:

```
SELECT REPLICATE ('Z', 30)
```

This returns

```
ZZZZZZZZZZZZZZZZZZZZZZZZZZZZZZ
```

How It Works

In this recipe's example, the letter "Z" in the character expression was repeated 30 times. Use REPLICATE to repeat values rather than having to code the characters manually. The maximum return value is 8,000 bytes.

Repeating a Blank Space *N* Number of Times

The SPACE function returns a string of repeated blank spaces, based on the integer you designate for the input parameter. This is the same functionality as the REPLICATE function—only for a specific character constant.

This example demonstrates how to repeat a blank space a defined number of times:

```
SELECT  'Give me some' + SPACE(6) + 'space.'
```

This returns

```
Give me some    space.
```

How It Works

In this recipe, six blank spaces were concatenated into the middle of the string using the space function. The maximum return value for the SPACE function is 8,000 bytes.

Outputting an Expression in Reverse Order

The REVERSE function takes a character expression and outputs the expression with each character position displayed in reverse order.

This example demonstrates how to reverse a string expression:

```
SELECT  TOP 1
     GroupName,
     REVERSE(GroupName) GroupNameReversed
FROM HumanResources.Department
ORDER BY GroupName
```

This returns

```
GroupName                            GroupNameReversed
Executive General and Administration  noitartsinimdA dna lareneG evitucexE
```

How It Works

This recipe demonstrated using the REVERSE function to output a string's characters in reverse order.

Returning a Chunk of an Expression

The SUBSTRING function returns a defined chunk of a specified expression.

The syntax is as follows:

```
SUBSTRING ( expression, start, length )
```

The first argument of this function is the character expression that you should use to return a defined chunk. The second argument defines the character starting position of the chunk. The third argument is the length of the character chunk that you want to extract.

In this example, assume your application receives a bank account number from a customer. It is your company's policy to store only a masked representation of the bank number, retaining the middle four digits only:

```
DECLARE @BankAccountNumber char(14)
SET @BankAccountNumber = '1424-2342-3536'

SELECT 'XXXX-' + SUBSTRING(@BankAccountNumber, 6,4) + '-XXXX'
 Masked_BankAccountNumber
```

This returns

```
Masked_BankAccountNumber
XXXX-2342-XXXX
```

How It Works

In this recipe, the SUBSTRING function was used to get the middle four digits from a longer bank account number. The first parameter was the bank account number from which the middle four characters are to be taken. The second parameter was the starting position of the string, which was the sixth position (corresponding with the first 2), and the third parameter indicated how many characters to extract (in this case, four). The result was that the value 2342 was extracted from the bank account number and inserted into the masked string.

Working with NULLs

A NULL value can be tricky to code around because its value is unknown. SQL Server provides functions used to handle NULLs in your code, as described in Table 8-4.

Table 8-4. *NULL Functions*

Function	Description
ISNULL	ISNULL validates whether an expression is NULL, and if so, replaces the NULL value with an alternate value.
COALESCE	The COALESCE function returns the first non-NULL value from a provided list of expressions.
NULLIF	NULLIF returns a NULL value when the two provided expressions have the same value. Otherwise, the first expression is returned.

These next few recipes will demonstrate these functions in action.

Replacing a NULL Value with an Alternative Value

ISNULL validates whether an expression is NULL, and if so, replaces the NULL value with an alternate value.

In this example, any NULL value will be replaced with a different value:

```
SELECT JobCandidateID,
       BusinessEntityID,
       ISNULL(BusinessEntityID, 0) Cleaned_BusinessEntityID
FROM HumanResources.JobCandidate
```

This returns the following (abridged) results:

JobCandidateID	BusinessEntityID	Cleaned_BusinessEntityID
1	NULL	0
2	NULL	0
...		
13	NULL	0
8	212	212
4	274	274

How It Works

In this example, the BusinessEntityID column contained NULL values for some rows. I displayed the original row values in the second column of the query. In the third column of the query, I wrapped the BusinessEntityID in the ISNULL function. In the second argument of this function, I designated that NULL values be replaced with a 0 value.

Performing Flexible Searches Using ISNULL

In this recipe, I'll demonstrate how to perform flexible, dynamic searches in a query when the variables may or may not be populated. This recipe declares three local search variables for ProductID, StartDate, and StandardCost. By using this technique, your query can return results based on all, some, or none of the parameters being used. In this example, only a ProductID is supplied:

```
-- Local variables used for searches
DECLARE @ProductID int
DECLARE @StartDate datetime
DECLARE @StandardCost money

-- Only @ProductID is used
SET @ProductID = 711

SELECT ProductID, StartDate, StandardCost
FROM Production.ProductCostHistory
WHERE ProductID = ISNULL(@ProductID, ProductID) AND
    StartDate = ISNULL(@StartDate, StartDate) AND
    StandardCost = ISNULL(@StandardCost, StandardCost)
```

This returns

ProductID	StartDate	StandardCost
711	2001-07-01 00:00:00.000	12.0278
711	2002-07-01 00:00:00.000	13.8782
711	2003-07-01 00:00:00.000	13.0863

In this second example, a search is performed by a minimum and maximum StandardCost range:

```
-- Local variables used for searches
DECLARE @ProductID int
DECLARE @MinStandardCost money
DECLARE @MaxStandardCost money

SET @MinStandardCost = 3.3963
SET @MaxStandardCost = 10.0000

SELECT ProductID, StartDate, StandardCost
FROM Production.ProductCostHistory
WHERE ProductID = ISNULL(@ProductID, ProductID) AND
 StandardCost BETWEEN ISNULL(@MinStandardCost, StandardCost) AND
ISNULL(@MaxStandardCost, StandardCost)
ORDER BY StandardCost
```

This returns the following (abridged) results:

ProductID	StartDate	StandardCost
709	2001-07-01 00:00:00.000	3.3963
710	2001-07-01 00:00:00.000	3.3963
871	2003-07-01 00:00:00.000	3.7363
712	2002-07-01 00:00:00.000	5.2297
...		
932	2003-07-01 00:00:00.000	9.3463
860	2002-07-01 00:00:00.000	9.7136
859	2002-07-01 00:00:00.000	9.7136
858	2002-07-01 00:00:00.000	9.7136

How It Works

The benefit of the method demonstrated in this recipe is that your code will be more flexible, allowing for data to be searched in myriad ways, and keeping each search condition optional. The key to this recipe is in the WHERE clause. Each search condition uses ISNULL and the local variable name, followed by the column name itself:

```
WHERE ProductID = ISNULL(@ProductID, ProductID) AND
    StartDate = ISNULL(@StartDate, StartDate) AND
    StandardCost = ISNULL(@StandardCost, StandardCost)
```

If a parameter is not SET, it will remain NULL, and thus the search condition for each column will evaluate the column value against itself—always returning TRUE. Only the parameters that have been specified will be used to filter the results.

Returning the First Non-NULL Value in a List of Expressions

The COALESCE function returns the first non-NULL value from a provided list of expressions. The syntax is as follows:

```
COALESCE ( expression [ ,...n ] )
```

This recipe demonstrates how to use COALESCE to return the first occurrence of a non-NULL value:

```
DECLARE @Value1 int
DECLARE @Value2 int
DECLARE @Value3 int

SET @Value2 = 22
SET @Value3 = 955

SELECT COALESCE(@Value1, @Value2, @Value3)
```

This returns

22

How It Works

In this recipe, three local variables were created: @Value1, @Value2, and @Value3. Only @Value2 and @Value3 were SET to actual integer values. The variable not SET to a value, @Value1, is NULL. In COALESCE, the three values were checked, from @Value1 to @Value3. Since the @Value2 variable was the first variable with a non-NULL value, 22 was returned.

Returning a NULL Value When Two Expressions Are Equal: Otherwise Returning the First Expression

NULLIF returns a NULL value when the two provided expressions have the same value; otherwise, the first expression is returned.

This example demonstrates how to use NULLIF to evaluate two expressions. If the two expressions are equal, a NULL value will be returned; otherwise, the first evaluated expression is returned:

```
DECLARE @Value1 int
DECLARE @Value2 int

SET @Value1 = 55
SET @Value2 = 955

SELECT NULLIF(@Value1, @Value2)
```

This returns

```
55
```

The next example tests the values when both are equal:

```
DECLARE @Value1 int
DECLARE @Value2 int

SET @Value1 = 55
SET @Value2 = 55

SELECT NULLIF(@Value1, @Value2)
```

This returns

```
NULL
```

How It Works

In this recipe, the first batch had two differing values: 55 and 955. Since the values were different, the NULLIF condition is FALSE, and the first evaluated value is returned. In the second batch, both @Value1 and @Value2 were equal, so NULLIF returned a NULL value.

Date Functions

As I reviewed earlier in the book, SQL Server has several data types used to store date and time data: datetime, datetime2, date, time, datetimeoffset, and smalldatetime. SQL Server offers several functions used to manipulate and work with these data types, described in Table 8-5.

Table 8-5. *Date Functions*

Function(s)	Description
DATEADD	DATEADD returns a new date that is incremented or decremented based on the interval and number specified.
DATEDIFF	DATEDIFF subtracts the first date from the second date to produce a value in the format of the datepart code specified.
DATENAME	DATENAME returns a string value for the part of a date specified in the datepart code.
DATEPART	DATEPART returns an integer value for the part of a date specified in the datepart code.
DAY, MONTH, and YEAR	DAY returns an integer value for the day, MONTH returns the integer representing the month, and YEAR returns the integer representing the year of the evaluated date.
GETDATE, GETUTCDATE, and CURRENT_TIMESTAMP	GETDATE and CURRENT_TIMESTAMP both return the current date and time. GETUTCDATE returns the Coordinated Universal Time (UTC).
ISDATE	ISDATE returns a 1 (true) when an expression is a valid date or time and 0 (false) if not.
SYSDATETIME, SYSUTCDATETIME, and SYSDATETIMEOFFSET	SYSDATETIME returns the current date and time in datetime2 format, and SYSUTCDATETIME returns the UTC in datetime2 format. SYSDATETIMEOFFSET returns the current date and time along with the hour and minute offset between the current time zone and UTC in datetimeoffset format. These functions return timing accurate to 10 milliseconds.
SWITCHOFFSET	SWITCHOFFSET allows you to modify the existing time zone offset to a new offset in datetimeoffset data type format.
TODATETIMEOFFSET	TODATETIMEOFFSET allows you to modify a date and time value to a specific time zone offset, returning a value in datetimeoffset data type format.

The next few recipes will demonstrate these date functions.

Returning the Current Date and Time

GETDATE and CURRENT_TIMESTAMP both return the current date and time. GETUTCDATE returns the Coordinated Universal Time. The new SQL Server 2008 date functions SYSDATETIME and SYSUTCDATETIME provide date and time with accuracy to the nearest 10 milliseconds. SYSDATETIMEOFFSET also provides that level of accuracy, but also includes the hour and minute offset from UTC.

This example demonstrates how to return the current date and time, as well as the Coordinated Universal Time and associated offsets:

```
SET NOCOUNT ON

SELECT 'CurrDateAndTime_HighPrecision', SYSDATETIME()

SELECT 'UniversalTimeCoordinate_HighPrecision', SYSUTCDATETIME()

SELECT 'CurrDateAndTime_HighPrecision _UTC_Adjust', SYSDATETIMEOFFSET()
```

This returns

CurrDateAndTime_HighPrecision	2008-03-09 08:10:12.0861608
UniversalTimeCoordinate_HighPrecision	2008-03-09 14:10:12.0861608
CurrDateAndTime_HighPrecision _UTC_Adjust	2008-03-09 08:10:12.0861608 -06:00

How It Works

This recipe demonstrated methods for retrieving the current date and time. All functions can also be used as a DEFAULT value for date data types within a table column definition.

Converting Between Time Zones

The following recipe demonstrates using functions to adjust and convert datetimeoffset and datetime data type values to datetimeoffset data type values. In the first query, the SWITCHOFFSET function converts an existing datetimeoffset value from -05:00 to +03:00.

   Values in the datetimeoffset data type represent date and time values in specific time zones that are referenced to UTC time. For example, the U.S. Eastern Standard time zone is defined as UTC –5:00 (UTC minus five hours). You can convert datetimeoffset values between time zones by invoking the SWITCHOFFSET function. In the following example, an input value is converted from UTC –5:00 to UTC +3:00:

```
SELECT SWITCHOFFSET ( '2007-08-12 09:43:25.9783262 -05:00', '+03:00')
```

   The effect of the conversion is to change the datetime portion of the value such that the new, combined datetime and offset represent the exact same UTC time as before. In this case, the result is

```
2007-08-12 17:43:25.9783262 +03:00
```

   Both 2007-08-12 09:43:25.9783262 -05:00 (the input) and 2007-08-12 17:43:25.9783262 +03:00 (the output) represent the same moment in time. Both work out to 2007-08-12 14:43:25.9783262 in UTC time (offset 0:00).

   In this second query, TODATETIMEOFFSET takes a regular datatime data type value (no time zone associated with it) and converts it to a datetimeoffset data type value:

```
SELECT TODATETIMEOFFSET ( '2007-08-12 09:43:25' , '-05:00' )
```

   This returns

```
2007-08-12 09:43:25.0000000 -05:00
```

How It Works

This recipe used two new functions introduced in SQL Server 2008 to manipulate and convert values to the datetimeoffset data type. In the first example, the SWITCHOFFSET function took two input parameters: the datetimeoffset value to be adjusted, and the offset value to adjust the value to.

Whatever the original value's offset was, it gets converted to the offset value designated in the second argument.

In the second example, the TODATETIMEOFFSET function also took two input parameters: the datetime value to be converted and the offset value to use when converting the value to a datetimeoffset data type.

Incrementing or Decrementing a Date's Value

DATEADD returns a new date, which is the result of having incremented or decremented another date expression. The syntax is as follows:

```
DATEADD (datepart , number, date )
```

The datepart code, used to designate which unit of time the date will be modified by, is described in Table 8-6.

Table 8-6. *Datepart Codes*

Code	Description
yy or yyyy	Year
qq or q	Quarter
mm or m	Month
dy or y	Day of Year
dd or d	Day
wk or ww	Week
dw or w	Weekday
hh	Hour
mi or n	Minute
ss or s	Second
ms	Millisecond

The second argument of the DATEADD function is the numeric value to increment or decrement the date (negative or positive number). The third argument is the date to be modified.

This first example decreases the date by a year:

```
SELECT DATEADD(yy, -1, '4/2/2009')
```

This returns

```
2008-04-02 00:00:00.000
```

This next example increases the date by a quarter:

```
SELECT DATEADD(q, 1, '4/2/2009')
```

This returns

```
2009-07-02 00:00:00.000
```

This example decreases a date by six months:

```
SELECT DATEADD(mm, -6, '4/2/2009')
```

This returns

```
2008-10-02 00:00:00.000
```

This example increases a date by 50 days:

```
SELECT DATEADD(d, 50, '4/2/2009')
```

This returns

```
2009-05-22 00:00:00.000
```

This example decreases the date and time by 30 minutes:

```
SELECT DATEADD(mi, -30, '2009-09-01 23:30:00.000')
```

This returns

```
2009-09-01 23:00:00.000
```

How It Works

This recipe demonstrated using the DATEADD function to modify a date based on several granularities. The third argument of DATEADD for each of these examples was a literal date value. However, you can also reference a datetime data type table column or valid date expression. The first argument, datepart, is also used in different date functions, as you'll see in the next recipe.

Finding the Difference Between Two Dates

DATEDIFF subtracts one date from another to produce a value in the format of the datepart code specified. The syntax for DATEDIFF is as follows:

```
DATEDIFF ( datepart , startdate , enddate )
```

The first datepart code uses the same datepart codes as DATEADD. The second and third arguments are the date values that are part of the subtraction.

This example demonstrates how to use the DATEDIFF function to find the difference between two dates:

```
-- Find difference in months between now and EndDate
SELECT ProductID,
       GETDATE() Today,
       EndDate,
       DATEDIFF(m, EndDate, GETDATE()) MonthsFromNow
FROM Production.ProductCostHistory
WHERE EndDate IS NOT NULL
```

This returns the following (abridged) results:

ProductID	Today	EndDate	MonthsFromNow
707	2008-02-12 19:07:14.073	2002-06-30 00:00:00.000	68
707	2008-02-12 19:07:14.073	2003-06-30 00:00:00.000	56
708	2008-02-12 19:07:14.073	2002-06-30 00:00:00.000	68
708	2008-02-12 19:07:14.073	2003-06-30 00:00:00.000	56
...			

How It Works

In this recipe, the difference was calculated between the ProductCostHistory table's EndDate and today's current date, returning the difference by month. The next recipe demonstrates another function that also uses the datepart argument.

Displaying the String Value for Part of a Date

DATENAME returns a string value for the part of a date specified in the datepart code. The syntax is as follows:

```
DATENAME ( datepart , date )
```

The second parameter designates the date to base the string value on.

In this recipe, I'll demonstrate how to use DATENAME to return the day of the week for the date specified:

```
-- Show the EndDate's day of the week
SELECT ProductID,
       EndDate,
       DATENAME(dw, EndDate) WeekDay
FROM Production.ProductCostHistory
WHERE EndDate IS NOT NULL
```

This returns the following (abridged) results:

ProductID	EndDate	WeekDay
707	2002-06-30 00:00:00.000	Sunday
707	2003-06-30 00:00:00.000	Monday
708	2002-06-30 00:00:00.000	Sunday
708	2003-06-30 00:00:00.000	Monday
709	2002-06-30 00:00:00.000	Sunday

How It Works

In this recipe, the datepart argument was set to dw (weekday) and was based on the EndDate column date, resulting in the day of the week name to be returned.

Displaying the Integer Representation for Parts of a Date

This function returns an integer value for the part of a date specified in the date part selection. The syntax for DATEPART is as follows:

```
DATEPART ( datepart , date )
```

The second parameter, date, designates the date for which the integer value is calculated.

This example demonstrates how to return the integer value from a date based on the date part selected. The first example returns the year value:

```
SELECT DATEPART(yy, GETDATE())
```

This returns

2008

The next example shows the current month integer value:

```
SELECT DATEPART(m, GETDATE())
```

This returns

2

How It Works

In this recipe, the year, month, and day integer values were extracted from the current date and time using the DATEPART function. You can also show these values by using canned functions that don't require the datepart argument, as you'll see in the next recipe.

Displaying the Integer Value for Part of a Date Using YEAR, MONTH, and DAY

There are single parameter functions that you can also use to display the integer values for day, month, and year.

This example returns the current year:

```
SELECT YEAR(GETDATE())
```

This returns

2008

This example returns the current month:

```
SELECT MONTH(GETDATE())
```

This returns

9

This example returns the current day:

```
SELECT DAY(GETDATE())
```

This returns

30

How It Works

In this recipe, I demonstrated single argument date functions. DAY returns an integer value for the day, MONTH returns the integer representing the month, and YEAR returns the integer representing the year of the evaluated date.

Type Conversion

The CONVERT and CAST functions are both used to convert from one data type to another. The syntax for CAST is as follows:

```
CAST ( expression AS data_type [ (length ) ])
```

The first argument is the expression to convert (a table column or literal value, for example). The second argument is the data type to convert the expression to.

The syntax for CONVERT is as follows:

```
CONVERT ( data_type [ ( length ) ] ,expression [ ,style ] )
```

The first argument is the data type that you wish to convert the expression to. The second argument is the expression that you want to be converted. The third argument, style, allows you to configure specific date presentation formats. This third argument is not available using the CAST function.

Converting Between Data Types

In this recipe, I'll demonstrate how to convert the data type of an integer to a char(4) data type. In the first example, an integer value is concatenated to a character string:

```
SELECT 2000 + 'Cannot be concatenated'
GO
```

This returns the following error:

```
Msg 245, Level 16, State 1, Line 1

Conversion failed when converting a value of type varchar to type int. Ensure that
all values of the expression being converted can be converted to the target type, or
modify query to avoid this type conversion.
```

In the next example, CONVERT is used to change the integer value into the char data type:

```
SELECT CONVERT(char(4), 2008) + ' Can now be concatenated!'
```

This returns

```
2008 Can now be concatenated!
```

This example demonstrates performing the same type of conversion, this time using CAST:

```
SELECT BusinessEntityID, CAST(SickLeaveHours AS char(4)) +
       ' Sick Leave Hours Left' SickTime
FROM HumanResources.Employee
```

This returns the following (abridged) results:

```
BusinessEntityID    SickTime
1                   30   Sick Leave Hours Left
2                   41   Sick Leave Hours Left
3                   21   Sick Leave Hours Left
4                   80   Sick Leave Hours Left
5                   24   Sick Leave Hours Left
```

How It Works

The first query attempts to concatenate an integer and string value together. This results in an error, as the two data types must be compatible or of the same data type. The second attempt used CONVERT to change the data type of the expression to char(4) before concatenating it to the other string. CAST was also used to convert the data type of the smallint column so that it could be concatenated to a string.

Converting Dates to Their Textual Representation

As I mentioned earlier, CONVERT has an optional style parameter that allows you to convert datetime or smalldatetime to specialized character formats. Many people confuse how the date and time is stored with the actual presentation of the date in the query results. When using the style parameter, keep in mind that you are only affecting how the date is presented in its character-based form, and not how it is stored (unless, of course, you choose to store the presented data in a non-datetime data type column).

Some examples of available style formats using the CONVERT function are shown in Table 8-7.

Table 8-7. CONVERT Style Formats

Style Code	Format
101	mm/dd/yyyy
102	yy.mm.dd
103	dd/mm/yy
108	hh:mm:ss
110	mm-dd-yy
112	yymmdd

For example, the command

```
SELECT CONVERT(varchar(20), GETDATE(), 101)
```

returns today's date formatted as

```
02/12/2008
```

When a function like GETDATE() is executed and stored in a datetime column, both the specific date and time data are stored with it. If, however, you only wish to store data at the date level (storing no specific time of day), a common trick is to use CONVERT with a style designated to scrub all dates to the 00:00:00.000 time.

The following example converts a datetime value to a character value, and then reconverts it back to the datetime data type:

```
SELECT CONVERT(datetime, CONVERT( varchar(11), '2008-08-13 20:37:22.570', 101))
```

This returns

```
2008-08-13 00:00:00.000
```

Of course, now in SQL Server 2008, you can do the following datetime to date data type conversion instead if no time need be stored at all:

```
SELECT CONVERT(date,'2008-08-13 20:37:22.570')
```

This returns

```
2008-08-13 00:00:00.000
```

How It Works

In the first query of the recipe, I used the 101 value in the style option for CONVERT to return a date in an mm/dd/yyyy format. Query authors are usually concerned with the style option when presenting data back to the end user. This presentation is used when a datetime or smalldatetime is converted into a character data type. Keep in mind that if you convert the data type back to datetime and store the reconverted date, you can lose the precision of the original hour, minute, second, etc., depending on the style you chose for the character data!

In the second query, I demonstrated using CONVERT with the 101 style option to scrub the time out of a datetime value and setting it to a 00:00:00.000 value. In the last query of this recipe, I demonstrated another example of scrubbing out the time value by converting the datetime value to a date data type.

Representing Binary Data in String Literals

SQL Server 2008 introduces a new method for returning binary data in a string hexadecimal literal format. The CONVERT command allows for three binary styles: 0, 1, and 2. I'll demonstrate the usage of each value here.

Binary style 0 converts binary bytes to ASCII characters and ASCII characters to binary bytes. This is the behavior of previous versions of SQL Server. In this query, I'll demonstrate binary style 0:

```
SELECT CONVERT(char(29),
    0x53514C2053657276657220323030382054D53514C2052656369706573,
    0) ReturnValue
```

This returns

```
ReturnValue
SQL Server 2008 T-SQL Recipes
```

Next, I'll reverse the previous example by converting ASCII to varbinary:

```
SELECT CONVERT(varbinary, 'SQL Server 2008 T-SQL Recipes', 0) ReturnValue
```

This returns

```
ReturnValue
0x53514C20536572766572203230303820542D53514C2052656369706573
```

Using the new SQL Server 2008 functionality, binary style 1 and 2 are used to convert binary bytes to a character expression representing the hexadecimal value. Style 1 prefixes a value of 0x, and style 2 does not. The following query demonstrates style 1:

```
SELECT CONVERT(char(60),
       0x53514C20536572766572203230303820542D53514C2052656369706573,
       1) ReturnValue_Style_1
```

This returns

```
ReturnValue_Style_1
0x53514C20536572766572203230303820542D53514C2052656369706573
```

The next query demonstrates style 2:

```
SELECT CONVERT(char(60),
       0x53514C20536572766572203230303820542D53514C2052656369706573,
       2) ReturnValue_Style_2
```

This returns the following (notice that there is no 0x prefix):

```
ReturnValue_Style_2
53514C20536572766572203230303820542D53514C2052656369706573
```

You can also convert the character expression to binary; however, both style 1 and 2 will return the varbinary data type data with the 0x prefix (native to the data type).

How It Works

SQL Server 2008 introduces the ability to convert binary data into a string hexadecimal literal format. In previous versions, doing a CONVERT would translate the binary data into the ASCII format—and not an actual representation of the hexadecimal literal format. For maintaining this previous behavior, you use binary style 0. Otherwise, you can use style 1 or 2 to preserve the string hexadecimal literal format.

Evaluating the Data Type Returned by an Expression

When converting data types, it is sometimes useful to figure out what SQL Server thinks an expression's data type is. In this recipe, I'll demonstrate using ISDATE and ISNUMERIC functions to test the data type of an expression:

```
-- Returns 0
SELECT ISDATE('1/1/20000')

-- Returns 1
SELECT ISDATE('1/1/2008')
```

```
-- Returns 0
SELECT ISNUMERIC('123ABC')

-- Returns 1
SELECT ISNUMERIC('123')
```

This returns

```
0

(1 row(s) affected)


1

(1 row(s) affected)


0

(1 row(s) affected)


1

(1 row(s) affected)
```

How It Works

ISDATE determines whether an expression is a valid datetime value. ISNUMERIC determines whether or not an expression is a valid numeric data type value. Both ISNUMERIC and ISDATE return a 1 if the expression evaluates to TRUE and 0 if it is FALSE.

Ranking Functions

Ranking functions allow you to return ranking values associated to each row in a result set. Table 8-8 describes the four ranking functions.

Table 8-8. *Ranking Functions*

Function	Description
ROW_NUMBER	ROW_NUMBER returns an incrementing integer for each row in a set.
RANK	Similar to ROW_NUMBER, RANK increments its value for each row in the set. The key difference is if rows with tied values exist, they will receive the same rank value.
DENSE_RANK	DENSE_RANK is almost identical to RANK, only DENSE_RANK doesn't return gaps in the rank values when there are tied values.
NTILE	NTILE divides the result set into a specified number of groups, based on the ordering and optional partition clause.

The next four recipes will demonstrate the use of these four ranking functions.

Generating an Incrementing Row Number

The ROW_NUMBER function returns an incrementing integer for each row in a set. The syntax for ROW_NUMBER is as follows:

```
ROW_NUMBER ( )    OVER ( [ <partition_by_clause> ] <order_by_clause> )
```

The first optional argument, partition_by_clause, allows you to restart row numbering for each change in the partitioned column. The second argument, order_by_clause, determines the order in which the ROW_NUMBER is applied to the results.

This first example returns the six rows from the middle of the result set, ordered by name:

```
-- Select the rows 255 through 260 in the middle of the result set
SELECT  p.ProductID,
        p.Name,
        p.RowNumber
FROM
    (SELECT     ProductID,
            Name,
            ROW_NUMBER() OVER (ORDER BY Name) RowNumber
    FROM Production.Product) p
WHERE       p.RowNumber BETWEEN 255 AND 260
```

This returns

ProductID	Name	RowNumber
713	Long-Sleeve Logo Jersey, S	255
716	Long-Sleeve Logo Jersey, XL	256
462	Lower Head Race	257
857	Men's Bib-Shorts, L	258
856	Men's Bib-Shorts, M	259
855	Men's Bib-Shorts, S	260

The optional partition_by_clause allows you to restart row numbering for each change in the partitioned column. In this example, the results are partitioned by Shelf and ordered by ProductID:

```
SELECT  Shelf,
        ProductID,
        ROW_NUMBER() OVER
(PARTITION BY Shelf ORDER BY ProductID) RowNumber
FROM Production.ProductInventory
```

In the returned results, row numbering is incremented by ProductID, but with each change in Shelf, the row numbering is restarted at 1:

Shelf	ProductID	RowNumber
A	1	1
A	1	2
A	2	3
...		
Shelf	ProductID	RowNumber
B	1	1
B	2	2
B	3	3
...		

```
Shelf    ProductID    RowNumber
C        317          1
C        318          2
C        319          3
...
```

How It Works

In the first example, ROW_NUMBER was used to order the results by product name and then add an incrementing value for each row. ROW_NUMBER was referenced as the third column of the subquery (snipped out of main query):

```
...
  SELECT     ProductID,
        Name,
        ROW_NUMBER() OVER (ORDER BY Name) RowNumber
  FROM Production.Product
...
```

The ORDER BY clause in parentheses ordered the results by name, which impacted in which order the rows were returned, as well as each row's associated row number. Each row in the record set is given a number, incremented by 1 for each row. Since the query sorts the results by name, the first product will have a row number of 1. This query appeared as a subquery so that the ROW_NUMBER column could be referenced in the WHERE clause of the outer query, returning rows 255 through 260.

The second example demonstrated using the partition_by_clause argument. For each change in Shelf, the row numbering was restarted with 1. With the ROW_NUMBER ranking function, you can page through data (for example, "show me rows 25 through 50") without having to create excessive amounts of code that was necessary in pre-2005 versions of SQL Server.

Returning Rows by Rank

In this recipe, I'll demonstrate using the RANK function to apply rank values based on a SalesQuota value. RANK returns the rank of a row within a result set (or rank of row within a partition within a result set, if you designate the optional partition clause). The syntax for RANK is as follows:

```
RANK ( )    OVER ( [ < partition_by_clause > ] < order_by_clause > )
```

The key difference is if rows with tied values exist, they will receive the same rank value, as this example demonstrates:

```
SELECT  BusinessEntityID,
        QuotaDate,
        SalesQuota,
        RANK() OVER (ORDER BY SalesQuota DESC) as RANK
FROM Sales.SalesPersonQuotaHistory
WHERE SalesQuota BETWEEN 266000.00 AND  319000.00
```

This returns

BusinessEntityID	QuotaDate	SalesQuota	RANK
280	2003-07-01 00:00:00.000	319000.00	1
284	2003-04-01 00:00:00.000	304000.00	2
280	2002-04-01 00:00:00.000	301000.00	3
282	2003-01-01 00:00:00.000	288000.00	4
283	2003-04-01 00:00:00.000	284000.00	5

284	2003-01-01 00:00:00.000	281000.00	6
278	2004-01-01 00:00:00.000	280000.00	7
283	2002-01-01 00:00:00.000	280000.00	7
283	2002-04-01 00:00:00.000	267000.00	9
278	2002-01-01 00:00:00.000	266000.00	10

The OVER clause contains an optional partition_by_clause and a required order_by_clause, just like ROW_NUMBER. The order_by_clause determines the order that RANK values are applied to each row, and the optional partition_by_clause is used to further divide the ranking groups, as demonstrated in the next example:

```
SELECT  h.BusinessEntityID,
    s.TerritoryID,
    h.QuotaDate,
      h.SalesQuota,
RANK() OVER (PARTITION BY  s.TerritoryID ORDER BY h.SalesQuota DESC) as RANK
FROM Sales.SalesPersonQuotaHistory h
INNER JOIN Sales.SalesPerson s ON
    h.BusinessEntityID = s.BusinessEntityID
WHERE s.TerritoryID IN (5,6,7)
```

This returns ranking of SalesQuota partitioned by the salesperson's TerritoryID:

SalesPersonID	TerritoryID	QuotaDate	SalesQuota	RANK
279	5	2003-07-01 00:00:00.000	950000.00	1
279	5	2001-10-01 00:00:00.000	917000.00	2
...				
282	6	2003-07-01 00:00:00.000	1051000.00	1
282	6	2004-04-01 00:00:00.000	830000.00	2
282	6	2001-10-01 00:00:00.000	767000.00	3
282	6	2003-10-01 00:00:00.000	707000.00	4
282	6	2002-01-01 00:00:00.000	583000.00	5
282	6	2002-04-01 00:00:00.000	583000.00	5
282	6	2004-01-01 00:00:00.000	569000.00	7
...				

How It Works

RANK increments its values based on the ordered column, only unlike ROWNUMBER, which increments on each row, RANK will return the same value for matching ordered values.

For example, in this recipe, the query specified a RANK ordered by SalesQuota with a descending sort. Because two SalesQuota values were equal at 280000.00, they both received a rank of 7:

278	280000.00	7
283	280000.00	7

Also, you should notice that the next SalesQuota value had a rank of 9 (not 8). The RANK function didn't use the 8th position because there were two rows tied for 7th, meaning that the next rank value is 9. If the three rows had been tied, the next rank value would be 10, and so on.

In the second example, RANK was partitioned by TerritoryID, causing the RANK value to restart at 1 for each change in TerritoryID.

Returning Rows by Rank Without Gaps

In this recipe, I'll demonstrate DENSE_RANK, which is almost identical to RANK, only DENSE_RANK doesn't return gaps in the rank values:

```
SELECT  BusinessEntityID,
    SalesQuota,
DENSE_RANK() OVER (ORDER BY SalesQuota DESC) as DENSE_RANK
FROM Sales.SalesPersonQuotaHistory
WHERE SalesQuota BETWEEN 266000.00 AND  319000.00
```

This returns

BusinessEntityID	SalesQuota	DENSE_RANK
280	319000.00	1
287	304000.00	2
280	301000.00	3
282	288000.00	4
283	284000.00	5
287	281000.00	6
278	280000.00	7
283	280000.00	7
283	267000.00	8
278	266000.00	9

How It Works

The syntax and usage is identical to RANK, only DENSE_RANK doesn't create a gap in the rank value when there are tied records. In this recipe's example, two values were tied with a value of 7 due to the same SalesQuota of 280000.00:

278	280000.00	7
283	280000.00	7
283	267000.00	8

The next DENSE_RANK value after 7 was 8.

Using NTILE

NTILE divides the result set into a specified number of groups based on the ordering and optional partition. The syntax is very similar to the other ranking functions, only it also includes an integer_expression:

```
NTILE (integer_expression)  OVER ( [ < partition_by_clause > ] < order_by_clause > )
```

The integer_expression is used to determine the number of groups to divide the results into. This example demonstrates the NTILE ranking function against the Sales.SalePersonQuotaHistory table:

```
SELECT  BusinessEntityID,
        SalesQuota,
NTILE(4) OVER (ORDER BY SalesQuota DESC) as NTILE
FROM Sales.SalesPersonQuotaHistory
WHERE SalesQuota BETWEEN 266000.00 AND  319000.00
```

This returns

BusinessEntityID	SalesQuota	NTILE
280	319000.00	1
287	304000.00	1
280	301000.00	1
282	288000.00	2
283	284000.00	2
287	281000.00	2
278	280000.00	3
283	280000.00	3
283	267000.00	4
278	266000.00	4

How It Works

In this example, the result set was divided into four percentile groups. The results were ordered by SalesQuota (descending order) and determined the order of NTILE group assignment. Notice that the first two groups, 1 and 2, both had three rows each, whereas groups 3 and 4 had two rows each. If the number of rows isn't divisible by the number of groups, the first few groups will have more rows than the latter groups. Otherwise, if the rows are divisible by the number of groups, each group will have the same number of rows.

Probing Server, Database, and Connection-Level Settings Using System Functions

SQL Server includes several system configuration functions that can be used to determine system settings for the SQL Server instance. Some of these functions are prefixed with @@ and were called variables in previous versions of SQL Server. Other system functions don't have the @@ prefix, and these accept parameters that help gather information about the SQL Server instance or database.

The next few recipes will demonstrate these system functions in action.

Determining the First Day of the Week

The @@DATEFIRST function returns the value of the specified first day of the week for the SQL Server instance. This is important to note because this value defines the calculation for the weekday datepart used in other date functions such as DATEPART and DATEADD. In this example, I'll demonstrate returning the current first day of the week setting for the SQL Server instance:

```
SELECT @@DATEFIRST 'First Day of the Week'
```

This returns

```
First Day of the Week
7
```

How It Works

The @@DATEFIRST function shows the first day of the week setting. To change the first day value, you can use the SET DATEFIRST command. For example:

```
SET DATEFIRST 7
```

When changing this value, 7 is Sunday and 1 is Monday, and so on. This directly impacts the returned value for the dw (day of week) code for DATEPART and DATEADD functions.

Viewing the Language Used in the Current Session

The @@LANGID system function returns a smallint data type value representing the local language identifier for the current user session, and the @@LANGUAGE system function returns the language name.

This example returns the local language setting currently used in the current query session:

```
SELECT  @@LANGID LanguageID,
        @@LANGUAGE Language
```

This query returns

```
LanguageID    Language
0             us_english
```

In this next query, I'll use the SET LANGUAGE command to configure a new session default language in conjunction with a check of the language ID and name:

```
SET LANGUAGE 'Español'

SELECT  @@LANGID LanguageID,
        @@LANGUAGE Language
```

This returns

```
Se cambió la configuración de idioma a Español.

LanguageID    Language
5             Español
```

How It Works

This recipe demonstrated returning the language for the SQL Server instance. Your default will vary based on the locale and collation used to set up the SQL Server instance. I also executed SET LANGUAGE to change the default language for my session, which ends up impacting the language of system messages and also the format of datetime data type data.

Viewing and Setting Current Connection Lock Timeout Settings

The SET LOCK_TIMEOUT command configures the number of milliseconds a statement will wait in the current session for locks to be released by other connections. The @@LOCK_TIMEOUT function is used to display the current connection lock timeout setting in milliseconds.

This example demonstrates setting and viewing the current session's lock timeout value:

```
-- 1000 milliseconds, 1 second
SET LOCK_TIMEOUT 1000

SELECT @@LOCK_TIMEOUT

-- Unlimited
SET LOCK_TIMEOUT -1
```

This returns

```
1000
```

How It Works

In this example, I started off by setting the lock timeout to 1000 milliseconds. To view the change, I used @@LOCK_TIMEOUT. After that, I changed the lock timeout back again to -1, which specified an unlimited wait time. A lock timeout value tells us how long a statement will wait on a blocked resource, canceling the statement automatically if the threshold has been exceeded, and then returning an error message.

Displaying the Nesting Level for the Current Stored Procedure Context

@@NESTLEVEL returns the current nesting level for the stored procedure context. A stored procedure nesting level indicates how many times a stored procedure has called another stored procedure. SQL Server allows stored procedures to make up to a maximum of 32 nested (incomplete) calls.

This recipe demonstrates how to capture the current nesting level for the stored procedure context (see Chapter 10):

```
-- First procedure
CREATE PROCEDURE dbo.usp_QuickAndDirty
AS
SELECT @@NESTLEVEL
GO

-- Second procedure
CREATE PROCEDURE dbo.usp_Call_QuickAndDirty
AS
SELECT @@NESTLEVEL
EXEC dbo.usp_QuickAndDirty
GO
```

After creating the two stored procedures, I use the @@NESTLEVEL function prior to calling the usp_Call_QuickAndDirty stored procedure:

```
-- Returns 0 nest level
SELECT @@NESTLEVEL

-- Returns 1 and 2 nest level
EXEC dbo.usp_Call_QuickAndDirty
```

This returns three result sets:

```
0
1
2
```

How It Works

In this recipe, I created two stored procedures. The first stored procedure, in this case
usp_QuickAndDirty, executed @@NESTLEVEL. The second stored procedure also called @@NESTLEVEL,
and then executed the first stored procedure. Before calling the procedure, @@NESTLEVEL returned 0.
At each execution nesting, the value of @@NESTLEVEL is incremented.

Returning the Current SQL Server Instance Name and SQL Server Version

@@SERVERNAME displays the local server name, and @@VERSION returns the SQL Server instance version,
date, and processor information.

This example returns the current SQL Server instance's name and version information:

```
SELECT  @@SERVERNAME ServerName,
        @@VERSION VersionInformation
```

How It Works

In this recipe, I demonstrated returning the current SQL Server instance name and version information. Like the system configuration functions before it, no parameters were required.

Returning the Current Connection's Session ID (SPID)

@@SPID returns the current connection's session ID, which you can use to identify additional information in the sp_who system-stored procedure or via Dynamic Management Views such as
sys.dm_exec_sessions.

This recipe returns the current SQL connection's server process identifier:

```
SELECT  @@SPID  SPID
```

This returns

```
SPID
53
```

How It Works

In this recipe, I demonstrated returning the session ID of the current connection's query session.

Returning the Number of Open Transactions

The @@TRANCOUNT system function displays active transactions for the current connection. You can use this function to determine the number of open transactions within the current session, and based on that information, either COMMIT or ROLLBACK the transactions accordingly. This recipe demonstrates how to return the number of active transactions in the current connection:

```
BEGIN TRAN t1

SELECT @@TRANCOUNT -- Returns 1

    BEGIN TRAN t2

    SELECT @@TRANCOUNT -- Returns 2

        BEGIN TRAN t3

        SELECT @@TRANCOUNT -- Returns 3

        COMMIT TRAN

    SELECT @@TRANCOUNT -- Returns 2

    ROLLBACK TRAN

SELECT @@TRANCOUNT -- After ROLLBACK, always Returns 0!
```

This returns

```
1
2
3
2
0
```

How It Works

In this recipe, each time a BEGIN TRAN was issued, the value of @@TRANCOUNT was incremented. Each time a COMMIT TRAN occurred, @@TRANCOUNT was decremented. When ROLLBACK TRAN was executed, @@TRANCOUNT was set to 0. ROLLBACK TRAN rolls back all open transactions for the session, no matter how many levels deep the transactions are nested.

Retrieving the Number of Rows Affected by the Previous Statement

@@ROWCOUNT returns the integer value of the number of rows affected by the last Transact-SQL statement in the current scope. @@ROWCOUNT_BIG returns the bigint value.

In this example, I'll demonstrate how to return the rows affected by the previous Transact-SQL statement:

```
SELECT TOP 3 ScrapReasonID
FROM Production.ScrapReason

SELECT @@ROWCOUNT Int_RowCount, ROWCOUNT_BIG() BigInt_RowCount
```

This returns two result sets:

```
ScrapReasonID
1
2
4
```

```
Int_RowCount    BigInt_RowCount
3               3
```

How It Works

In this example, the first statement returned three rows from the Production.ScrapReason table—so @@ROWCOUNT is set to 3 in order to indicate that three rows were returned. The ROWCOUNT_BIG function is just like @@ROWCOUNT, only it is capable of returning bigint data type counts, instead of @@ROWCOUNT's integer data type. @@ROWCOUNT and @@ROWCOUNT_BIG are often used for error handling; for example, checking to make sure the expected number of rows were impacted by the previous statement (see Chapter 16).

Retrieving System Statistics

SQL Server has several built-in system statistical functions, which are described in Table 8-9.

Table 8-9. *System Statistical Functions*

Function	Description
@@CONNECTIONS	Returns the number of connections made to the SQL Server instance since it was last started.
@@CPU_BUSY	Shows the number of busy CPU milliseconds since the SQL Server instance was last started.
@@IDLE	Displays the total idle time of the SQL Server instance in milliseconds since the instance was last started.
@@IO_BUSY	Displays the number of milliseconds spent performing I/O operations since the SQL Server instance was last started.
@@PACKET_ERRORS	Displays the total network packet errors that have occurred since the SQL Server instance was last started.
@@PACK_RECEIVED	Returns the total input packets read from the network since the SQL Server instance was last started. You can monitor whether the number increments or stays the same, thus surmising whether there is a network availability issue.
@@PACK_SENT	Returns the total output packets sent to the network since the SQL Server instance was last started.
@@TIMETICKS	Displays the number of microseconds per tick. A *tick* is a unit of measurement designated by a specified number of milliseconds (31.25 milliseconds for the Windows OS).
@@TOTAL_ERRORS	Displays read/write errors encountered since the SQL Server instance was last started.
@@TOTAL_READ	Displays the number of non-cached disk reads by the SQL Server instance since it was last started.
@@TOTAL_WRITE	Displays the number of disk writes by the SQL Server instance since it was last started.

This example demonstrates using system statistical functions in a query:

```
SELECT  'Connections' FunctionNM, @@CONNECTIONS  Value
UNION
SELECT  'CPUBusy', @@CPU_BUSY
UNION
SELECT  'IDLE', @@IDLE
UNION
SELECT  'IOBusy', @@IO_BUSY
UNION
SELECT  'PacketErrors', @@PACKET_ERRORS
UNION
SELECT  'PackReceived', @@PACK_RECEIVED
UNION
SELECT  'PackSent', @@PACK_SENT
UNION
SELECT  'TimeTicks', @@TIMETICKS
UNION
SELECT  'TotalErrors', @@TOTAL_ERRORS
UNION
SELECT  'TotalRead', @@TOTAL_READ
UNION
SELECT  'TotalWrite', @@TOTAL_WRITE
```

This returns

FunctionNM	Value
Connections	369
CPUBusy	3333
IDLE	6374793
IOBusy	1916
PacketErrors	2
PackReceived	3606
PackSent	6592
TimeTicks	31250
TotalErrors	0
TotalRead	4688
TotalWrite	5542

How It Works

This recipe demonstrated a SELECT query referencing multiple system statistical functions. You can use them to track various statistics in your SQL Server instance.

Displaying Database and SQL Server Settings

The DATABASEPROPERTYEX system function allows you to retrieve information about database options. DATABASEPROPERTYEX uses the following syntax:

```
DATABASEPROPERTYEX ( database , property )
```

The first argument is the database name you want to probe. The second argument is the database property you want to look up.

This example demonstrates how to report the collation, status, and recovery mode for the AdventureWorks database:

```
SELECT DATABASEPROPERTYEX('AdventureWorks', 'Collation'),
       DATABASEPROPERTYEX('AdventureWorks', 'Recovery'),
       DATABASEPROPERTYEX('AdventureWorks', 'Status')
```

This returns

SQL_Latin1_General_CP1_CI_AS	SIMPLE	ONLINE

The SERVERPROPERTY system function allows you to retrieve information about your SQL Server instance. Its syntax, since not database specific, only requires the property name:

```
SERVERPROPERTY (propertyname )
```

This example demonstrates returning the instance's edition and default collation:

```
SELECT SERVERPROPERTY ('Collation'),
SERVERPROPERTY ('Edition')
```

This returns

SQL_Latin1_General_CP1_CI_AS	Enterprise Edition

How It Works

Both DATABASEPROPERTYEX and SERVERPROPERTY can be used to retrieve important system configuration settings. In both examples, the function was referenced in the SELECT clause of a query.

■**Note** I show how these functions are used in this book, but I don't rehash the list of available properties. For a complete list, see SERVERPROPERTY and DATABASEPROPERTYEX topics in SQL Server Books Online.

Returning the Current Database ID and Name

This DB_ID function returns the database integer ID, and DB_NAME returns the database name for the current database (unless there are parameters supplied).

This example demonstrates how to retrieve the current database system ID and name:

```
SELECT  DB_ID() DatabaseID, DB_NAME() DatabaseNM
```

This returns

DatabaseID	DatabaseNM
8	AdventureWorks

How It Works

In this example, the internal database ID (assigned by SQL Server when the database was created) is returned along with the database name. The functions will return information based on the current database context.

Both also accept parameters, for example:

```
SELECT  DB_ID('master') DatabaseID, DB_NAME(1) DatabaseNM
```

This returns

DatabaseID	DatabaseNM
1	master

Using parameters of these functions allow you to look up an explicit database ID or name value without switching the database context to the actual database.

Tip You can also just query `sys.databases` to retrieve `name` and `database_id`.

Returning a Database Object Name and ID

OBJECT_ID returns the database object identifier number, as assigned internally within the database. OBJECT_NAME returns the object's name based on its object identifier number.

In this example, I'll demonstrate how to return a database object's name and ID:

```
SELECT OBJECT_ID('AdventureWorks.HumanResources.Department'),
       OBJECT_NAME(773577794, DB_ID('AdventureWorks'))
```

This returns

757577737	DF_Department_ModifiedDate

How It Works

Both OBJECT_NAME and OBJECT_ID are often used in conjunction with system catalog views or system functions that reference a database object's identifier. The OBJECT_ID function is used to find the internal database identifier of a specific object (note that object IDs are only unique within a specified database). Its first argument is the name of the object. The second optional argument is the object type; for example, U for user-defined table, V for view, PK for primary key, and other values that you can reference in the type column of the sys.objects catalog view.

OBJECT_NAME is used to return the object name given the object identifier. The first argument is the object ID. The second optional argument is the database ID—which is useful when there are identical IDs across databases for different objects.

Returning the Application and Host for the Current User Session

In this recipe, I'll demonstrate the different functions used to return information about the current connection's context. APP_NAME returns the name of the application for the current SQL Server connection. HOST_ID returns the workstation identification number for the current connection, and HOST_NAME returns the workstation name for the current connection.

This example shows how to show the current application and host used to connect to the SQL Server instance:

```
SELECT APP_NAME() as 'Application',
       HOST_ID() as 'Host ID',
       HOST_NAME() as 'Host Name'
```

This returns

Application	Host ID	Host Name
Microsoft SQL Server Management Studio - Query	3388	CAESAR

How It Works

All three functions used in this example were used within a SELECT clause and didn't require any arguments. This information is useful for tracking information on a client and application connection, and thus helping you establish identity.

Reporting Current User and Login Context

The SYSTEM_USER function returns the Windows or SQL login name, and the USER function returns the current user's database user name.

In this first example, I'll demonstrate how to return the current user and login context:

```
SELECT  SYSTEM_USER, -- Login
        USER -- Database User
```

This returns

CAESAR\Administrator	dbo

These two functions can also be used as table DEFAULT values, as this next example demonstrates:

```
CREATE TABLE #TempExample
   (ExampleColumn varchar(10) NOT NULL,
    ModifiedByLogin varchar(55) NOT NULL DEFAULT SYSTEM_USER,
    ModifiedByUser varchar(55) NOT NULL DEFAULT USER)
GO

INSERT #TempExample
(ExampleColumn)
VALUES ('Value A')

SELECT ExampleColumn, ModifiedByLogin, ModifiedByUser
FROM #TempExample
```

This returns the following results:

ExampleColumn	ModifiedByLogin	ModifiedByUser
Value A	CAESAR\Administrator	dbo

How It Works

In this recipe, the SYSTEM_USER and USER functions were used within a regular query, and also as the DEFAULT value for a table. These functions are ideal for database change auditing—capturing the current user when a data modification occurs, for example.

Viewing User Connection Options

In this recipe, I'll demonstrate how to view the SET properties for the current user connection using the SESSIONPROPERTY function (for information on SET options, see Chapter 22):

```
SELECT  SESSIONPROPERTY  ('ANSI_NULLS') ANSI_NULLS,
    SESSIONPROPERTY ('ANSI_PADDING') ANSI_PADDING,
    SESSIONPROPERTY ('ANSI_WARNINGS') ANSI_WARNINGS,
    SESSIONPROPERTY ('ARITHABORT') ARITHABORT,
    SESSIONPROPERTY ('CONCAT_NULL_YIELDS_NULL')  CONCAT_NULL_YIELDS_NULL,
    SESSIONPROPERTY ('NUMERIC_ROUNDABORT') NUMERIC_ROUNDABORT,
    SESSIONPROPERTY ('QUOTED_IDENTIFIER') QUOTED_IDENTIFIER
```

This returns the following results (modified for readability):

ANSI_NULLS	ANSI_PADDING	ANSI_WARNINGS
1	1	1
ARITHABORT	CONCAT_NULL_YIELDS_NULL	
1	1	
NUMERIC_ROUNDABORT	QUOTED_IDENTIFIER	
0	1	

How It Works

SESSIONPROPERTY allows you to see the various database connection settings for the current user. It takes one argument, the name of the property to check. The function returned a 1 when the option was ON and 0 when it is OFF.

IDENTITY and uniqueidentifier Functions

With the last three recipes of this chapter, I'll review how to work with IDENTITY values for a table and how to generate new uniqueidentifier values.

As you may recall from Chapter 4, the IDENTITY column property is defined on a specific column of a table and allows you to define an automatically incrementing numeric value for a single column in a table.

Unlike the IDENTITY column, which guarantees uniqueness within the defined table, the ROWGUIDCOL property ensures a very high level of uniqueness. This unique ID is stored in a uniqueidentifier data type and is generated by the NEWID system function. You can also use the NEWSEQUENTIALID system function, which also produces a uniqueidentifier return type; however, it differs from NEWID because each newly generated GUID will be a greater value than any GUID previously generated on the scoped server. Because NEWSEQUENTIALID produces greater values on each execution, this behavior can reduce page splitting on the key, as well as random page lookups.

Returning the Last Identity Value

In this recipe, I'll demonstrate three methods for returning last generated identity values. In the first example, the IDENT_CURRENT function is used to return the last generated identity value for a specific table. This command takes a single argument: the name of the table to evaluate:

```
SELECT IDENT_CURRENT('Production.Product') LastIdentityValue
```

This returns

```
LastIdentityValue
999
```

Next, a new row is inserted into a table that has an IDENTITY column defined within it. Immediately after the INSERT, the last identity value generated is retrieved using the SCOPE_IDENTITY and @@IDENTITY functions (the difference is described after the example):

```
-- Example insert, generates IDENTITY value in the table
INSERT HumanResources.Department
(Name, GroupName)
VALUES ('TestDept', 'TestGroup')

-- Last identity value generated for any table
-- in the current session, for the current scope
SELECT SCOPE_IDENTITY()
```

This returns the last identity value generated from a table INSERT in the current session, for the current scope. Scope means that if this INSERT caused a trigger to fire that inserted another row into a different IDENTITY-based table, you would still only see the last IDENTITY value for the current session (not from the trigger sessions outside your scope):

```
17
```

Executing @@IDENTITY generates the last IDENTITY value generated for any table in the current session, but for any scope:

```
-- Last identity value generated for any table
-- in the current session, in any scope
SELECT @@IDENTITY
```

This returns

```
17
```

Although it is the same value for this example query, had a trigger fired off of the INSERT that in turn caused an INSERT into another IDENTITY-based table, you would see the latest identity value for the other table in the trigger's scope.

How It Works

This recipe demonstrated three methods of returning the last identity value generated. The first query used IDENT_CURRENT, which specified the last generated identity value for a specific table.

The next function demonstrated, SCOPE_IDENTITY, is specific to the current user session, and returns the last generated value for the current scope. The current scope, for example, refers to the current batch of SQL statements, current procedure, or current trigger.

In contrast, @@IDENTITY returns the last generated value for any table in the current session, *across any scope*. So if an INSERT in the current scope fires a trigger, which in turn inserts a record into a different table, @@IDENTITY will return the latest value from the inserted row impacted by the trigger, and not the original insert you may have intended to capture.

In short, use IDENT_CURRENT if you care about retrieving the latest IDENTITY value for a specific table, across any session or scope. Use SCOPE_IDENTITY if you wish to retrieve the latest IDENTITY value for any table in the current scope and session. Use @@IDENTITY if you want the last IDENTITY value for any table in the current session, regardless of scope.

Returning an Identity Column's Seed and Incrementing Value

The IDENT_INCR function displays the original increment value for the IDENTITY column of a specific table or referencing view. The IDENT_SEED function displays the originally defined seed value for the IDENTITY column of a specific table or referencing view. These functions are useful to determine at what increment and seed an IDENTITY column's value will progress as rows are inserted.

This example demonstrates returning the identity increment and seed for a specific table:

```
SELECT IDENT_INCR('Production.Product') IdentIncr,
    IDENT_SEED('Production.Product') IdentSeed
```

This returns

```
IdentIncr    IdentSeed
1            1
```

How It Works

In this recipe, the increment and seed for the Production.Product table was returned using IDENT_INCR and IDENT_SEED.

Creating a New uniqueidentifier Value

The NEWID function is used to create a uniqueidentifier data type value. The first example returns a new uniqueidentifier value in a SELECT statement:

```
SELECT NEWID()
```

This returns a value similar to the following (you'll see a different value from what I show here):

```
D04ED24F-671E-4559-A205-F6864B9C59A7
```

Next, a new temporary table is created that uses the NEWID function as a default:

```
CREATE TABLE #T4
    (MyValue uniqueidentifier NOT NULL DEFAULT NEWID())
```

Next, a new value is inserted into the table:

```
INSERT #T4 DEFAULT VALUES
```

Last, the value is retrieved from the table:

```
SELECT MyValue
FROM #T4
```

This returns

```
MyValue
2DD54CE0-5D26-42F9-A68D-7392DB89D0EF
```

The NEWSEQUENTIALID can also be used to generate new GUID values; only in this case, each new value generated on the computer will be greater than any value previously generated.

To demonstrate, first I'll create a new temporary table and populate it with five rows:

```
CREATE TABLE #T5
    (MyValue uniqueidentifier NOT NULL DEFAULT NEWSEQUENTIALID(),
     InsertDT datetime2 NOT NULL DEFAULT SYSDATETIME())
GO

INSERT #T5 DEFAULT VALUES
INSERT #T5 DEFAULT VALUES
INSERT #T5 DEFAULT VALUES
INSERT #T5 DEFAULT VALUES
INSERT #T5 DEFAULT VALUES
```

Next, I'll query the table ordering by the uniqueidentifier value:

```
SELECT MyValue, InsertDT
FROM #T5
ORDER BY MyValue
```

Notice that the ordering of the values also matches the order of date when they were inserted:

MyValue	InsertDT
EE78AB60-E548-DC11-A195-00188B28C9C5	2007-08-12 10:04:53.0833262
EF78AB60-E548-DC11-A195-00188B28C9C5	2007-08-12 10:04:53.8033262
F078AB60-E548-DC11-A195-00188B28C9C5	2007-08-12 10:04:54.3603262
F178AB60-E548-DC11-A195-00188B28C9C5	2007-08-12 10:04:54.9103262
F278AB60-E548-DC11-A195-00188B28C9C5	2007-08-12 10:04:55.3903262

How It Works

As this recipe shows, NEWID and NEWSEQUENTIALID can be used within a SELECT statement or as a DEFAULT column value in a CREATE or ALTER TABLE statement. Whereas NEWID provides random values, NEWSEQUENTIALID allows for incremental uniqueidentifier values. This behavior reduces page splitting on the key, as well as random page lookups.

■**Caution** Unlike with NEWID, the increment of values for NEWSEQUENTIALID can be derived based on existing values. For example, if a GUID is exposed on a URL, and a person wants to see someone else's data, she could potentially increment her own value to view consecutive records.

Also note, if your SQL Server instance doesn't have a network card (not a common configuration), unique values are generated within the contact of the server scope—meaning that duplicate values could be generated on other SQL instances.

CHAPTER 9

■■■

Conditional Processing, Control-of-Flow, and Cursors

In this chapter, I'll present recipes that demonstrate SQL Server Transact-SQL for

- *Conditional processing*: You'll learn how to use the CASE and IF...ELSE statements to evaluate conditions and return values accordingly. I'll review how to use the CASE function to evaluate a single input expression and return a value, and also how to evaluate one or more Boolean expressions. Finally, I'll demonstrate returning a value when the expressions are TRUE.

- *Control-of-flow functionality*: This recipe demonstrates how to control the execution of Transact-SQL statements or batches based on commands such as RETURN, WHILE, WAITFOR, and GOTO. RETURN is used to exit the current Transact-SQL batch immediately, and doesn't allow any code in the batch that executes after it. The WHILE command is used to repeat a specific operation or batch of operations while a condition remains TRUE. The WAITFOR command is used to delay the execution of Transact-SQL code for a specified length of time or until a specific time. GOTO is used to jump to a label in your Transact-SQL batch, passing over the code that follows it.

- *Creating and using cursors*: Here, I'll demonstrate Transact-SQL cursors, which allow you to work with one row at a time. Based on my experiences in the field, I'm not a big fan of cursors. Cursors can cause significant performance problems due to excessive singleton row calls, memory consumption, and code bloat issues when not implemented correctly. However, there still may be rare occasions when the use of a cursor is a better choice than a set-based solution.

An understanding of how and when (and when not) to use these techniques will allow you to create flexible and intelligent Transact-SQL code.

Conditional Processing

Conditional processing allows you to return a value, based on the value of an expression or group of expressions. The next few recipes will demonstrate SQL Server's conditional processing commands, including CASE and IF...ELSE.

The CASE function is used to return a value based on the value of an expression. It is most often used to translate codes into descriptive values or evaluate multiple conditions in order to return a value. (For example, "If the row is from the year 2008 and less than or equal to Current Quarter, return the Total Sales amount.")

The IF...ELSE construct evaluates a Boolean expression, and if TRUE, executes a Transact-SQL statement or batch. The uses for this command are many, allowing you to conditionally return result sets, update data, or execute stored procedures based on one or more search conditions.

The next three recipes will demonstrate conditional processing in action.

Using CASE to Evaluate a Single Input Expression

The CASE function is used to return a value based on the value of an expression. It can also be used to return a value based on the result of one or more Boolean expressions. The syntax for this usage of CASE is as follows:

```
CASE input_expression
    WHEN when_expression THEN result_expression
    [ ...n ]
    [
    ELSE else_result_expression
    ]
END
```

The arguments of this command are described in Table 9-1.

Table 9-1. *Input Expression CASE Arguments*

Argument	Description
input_expression	The input value to be evaluated in the CASE statement.
when_expression	The expression to compare to the input_expression. For example, if the input_expression is the Gender column, the when_expression could be 'F' or 'M'. If there is a match between the input_expression and the when_expression, the result_expression is returned.
result_expression	The value to be returned if the input_expression is equal to the when_expression.

This example demonstrates how to use CASE to evaluate one or more conditions, returning a result based on those conditions that evaluate to TRUE:

```
USE AdventureWorks
GO

-- Determine Conference Rooms Based on Department
SELECT DepartmentID,
    Name,
    GroupName,
    CASE GroupName
        WHEN 'Research and Development' THEN 'Room A'
        WHEN 'Sales and Marketing' THEN 'Room B'
        WHEN 'Manufacturing' THEN 'Room C'
        ELSE 'Room D'
    END ConferenceRoom
FROM HumanResources.Department
```

This returns the following (abridged) results:

```
DepartmentID    Name            GroupName                    ConferenceRoom
1               Engineering     Research and Development     Room A
2               Tool Design     Research and Development     Room A
```

3	Sales	Sales and Marketing	Room B
4	Marketing	Sales and Marketing	Room B
5	Purchasing	Inventory Management	Room D
...			

How It Works

In this recipe's example, CASE was used to assign a conference room based on the GroupName value. The CASE statement followed the Name column in the SELECT clause:

```
SELECT DepartmentID,
       Name,
       GroupName,
    CASE GroupName
```

The column to evaluate, GroupName, followed the CASE keyword. Next, a set of WHEN expressions were evaluated. Each department was assigned a different room, based on the value of GroupName:

```
WHEN 'Research and Development' THEN 'Room A'
WHEN 'Sales and Marketing' THEN 'Room B'
WHEN 'Manufacturing' THEN 'Room C'
```

The optional ELSE clause is used as a catch-all, assigning a default result expression if none of the WHEN expressions evaluated to TRUE:

```
ELSE 'Room D'
```

The END keyword is used to mark the end of the CASE statement, and in this recipe, it was followed by the aliased column name:

```
END ConferenceRoom
```

Using CASE to Evaluate Boolean Expressions

CASE offers an alternative syntax that doesn't use an initial input expression. Instead, one or more Boolean expressions are evaluated, returning a result expression when TRUE. The syntax is as follows:

```
CASE
    WHEN Boolean_expression THEN result_expression
    [ ...n ]
    [
    ELSE else_result_expression
    ]
END
```

The additional argument in this syntax, compared to the previous recipe, is the boolean_ expression, which is the expression being evaluated. Instead of an input expression, each WHEN evaluates a Boolean expression, and if TRUE, returns a result expression. This flavor of CASE allows for additional expressions above and beyond just evaluating the value of one input expression.

If none of the expressions evaluates to TRUE, the result_expression of the ELSE clause is returned, or a NULL value is returned if no ELSE clause was specified. If a row match is made against more than one Boolean expression, the first Boolean expression to evaluate to TRUE determines the result expression. In this example, the department name is evaluated in addition to other expressions, such as the department identifier and the room name starting with the letter "T":

```
SELECT DepartmentID,
       Name,
       CASE
          WHEN Name = 'Research and Development'
             THEN 'Room A'
          WHEN (Name = 'Sales and Marketing' OR
              DepartmentID = 10)
             THEN 'Room B'
          WHEN Name LIKE 'T%'
             THEN 'Room C'
          ELSE 'Room D'
       END ConferenceRoom
FROM HumanResources.Department
```

This returns the following (abridged) results:

DepartmentID	Name	ConferenceRoom
12	Document Control	Room D
1	Engineering	Room D
16	Executive	Room D
14	Facilities and Maintenance	Room D
10	Finance	Room B
9	Human Resources	Room D
...		
6	Research and Development	Room A
3	Sales	Room D
15	Shipping and Receiving	Room D
17	TestDept	Room C
2	Tool Design	Room C

How It Works

In this example, three Boolean expressions were used. If the department name was Research and Development, Room A would be returned:

```
WHEN Name = 'Research and Development'
             THEN 'Room A'
```

The second Boolean expression stated that if the department name was Sales and Marketing OR the DepartmentID was equal to 10, then Room B would be returned:

```
WHEN (Name = 'Sales and Marketing' OR
             DepartmentID = 10)
             THEN 'Room B'
```

The third Boolean expression looks for any department name that starts with the letter "T", causing Room C to be returned if there is a match:

```
WHEN Name LIKE 'T%'
       THEN 'Room C'
```

Using IF...ELSE

IF...ELSE evaluates a Boolean expression, and if TRUE, executes a Transact-SQL statement or batch. The syntax is as follows:

```
IF Boolean_expression
    { sql_statement | statement_block }
[ ELSE
    { sql_statement | statement_block } ]
```

The ELSE clause is invoked if the Boolean expression evaluates to FALSE, executing the Transact-SQL statement or batch that follows the ELSE.

This example recipe demonstrates executing a query conditionally based on the value of a local variable:

```
DECLARE @QuerySelector int
SET @QuerySelector = 3

IF @QuerySelector = 1
BEGIN
    SELECT TOP 3
        ProductID, Name, Color
    FROM Production.Product
    WHERE Color = 'Silver'
    ORDER BY Name
END
ELSE
BEGIN
    SELECT TOP 3
        ProductID, Name, Color
    FROM Production.Product
    WHERE Color = 'Black'
    ORDER BY Name
END
```

This returns

ProductID	Name	Color
322	Chainring	Black
863	Full-Finger Gloves, L	Black
862	Full-Finger Gloves, M	Black

How It Works

In this recipe, an integer local variable was created called @QuerySelector, which was set to the value of 3:

```
DECLARE @QuerySelector int
SET @QuerySelector = 3
```

The IF statement began by evaluating whether @QuerySelector was equal to 1:

```
IF @QuerySelector = 1
```

If the evaluation determined that @QuerySelector was indeed 1, the next block of code (starting with the BEGIN statement) would have been executed:

```
BEGIN
    SELECT TOP 3
        ProductID, Name, Color
    FROM Production.Product
    WHERE Color = 'Silver'
    ORDER BY Name
END
```

BEGIN is optional for single statements following IF, but for multiple statements that must be executed as a group, BEGIN and END must be used. As a best practice, it is easier to use BEGIN...END for single statements too, so that you don't forget to do so if/when the code is changed at a later time.

The optional ELSE clause is used as a catch-all, executing a search on black-colored products if the previous IF condition evaluated to FALSE:

```
ELSE
BEGIN
    SELECT TOP 3
        ProductID, Name, Color
    FROM Production.Product
    WHERE Color = 'Black'
    ORDER BY Name
END
```

Because the @QuerySelector variable was 3, the second block of T-SQL code was executed, returning products with Color = 'Black'.

Control-of-Flow

In the next few recipes, I'll demonstrate how to use the following SQL Server control-of-flow functions and commands.

- RETURN: This function is used to unconditionally exit the existing scope and return control to the calling scope. RETURN can also be used to communicate integer values back to the caller. This technique is often used to communicate business logic errors back to the calling procedure, or to confirm that everything in the batch/query/scope executed without error.

- WHILE: You can use this to repeatedly execute the same batch of Transact-SQL code while a Boolean condition evaluates to TRUE. WHILE is often used as an alternative to cursors (also reviewed in this chapter), as you can use it to loop through a result set one row at a time, performing actions for each row until the result set is empty. For example, you could populate a temporary table with a list of the names of indexes that have a fragmentation level greater than 50%. A WHILE statement can be invoked to keep looping for as long as there are rows in this table. For each iteration, you would grab the TOP 1 index row and perform an index rebuild on the first index name grabbed from the table. After that, you could delete that row from the table, and then keep looping through the indexes until the table is empty, ending the WHILE loop.

- GOTO: This function can be used to jump to a label in your Transact-SQL batch. It is often used to jump to a special error handler when an error occurs, or to skip over code if a certain business condition is or isn't met. GOTO has a reputation, which is duly earned, for being used in spaghetti code. This is because you have to jump between code blocks in order to fully understand what the batch or procedure is actually doing. Although use of GOTO should be minimal, it is still supported, and thus presented in a recipe here.

- WAITFOR: You can use this function to defer processing of consecutive Transact-SQL commands that follow it—for either a fixed period of time or *until* a specific time. This is useful in situations where activities are synchronous. For example, if your code cannot finish until an external task has completed in a set number of seconds/minutes/hours, or if you cannot perform an action until a specific time (non-business hours, for example).

Using RETURN

RETURN is used to exit the current Transact-SQL batch, query, or stored procedure immediately, and doesn't execute any code in the batch/query/procedure scope that follows after it. RETURN exits only the code executing in the current scope; if you have called stored procedure B from stored procedure A, and stored procedure B issues a RETURN, stored procedure B stops immediately, but stored procedure A continues as though B had completed successfully.

This example demonstrates how to use RETURN to unconditionally stop a query:

```
IF NOT EXISTS
(SELECT ProductID FROM Production.Product WHERE Color = 'Pink')
BEGIN
    RETURN
END

-- Won't execute
SELECT ProductID
FROM Production.Product
WHERE Color = 'Pink'
```

This returns

```
Command(s) completed successfully.
```

RETURN also allows for an optional integer expression:

```
RETURN [ integer_expression ]
```

This integer value can be used in a stored procedure to communicate issues to the calling application. For example:

```
-- Create a temporary Stored Procedure that raises a logical error
CREATE PROCEDURE #usp_TempProc
AS
SELECT 1/0
RETURN @@ERROR
GO
```

Next, the stored procedure is executing, capturing the RETURN code in a local variable:

```
DECLARE @ErrorCode int

EXEC @ErrorCode = #usp_TempProc
PRINT @ErrorCode
```

This returns the divide-by-zero error, followed by the error number that was printed:

```
Msg 8134, Level 16, State 1, Procedure #usp_TempProc_____00000B72,
Line 4
Divide by zero error encountered.
8134
```

How It Works

In this recipe, an `IF` condition checked for the existence of a pink-colored product:

```
IF NOT EXISTS
(SELECT ProductID FROM Production.Product WHERE Color = 'Pink')
```

If it evaluated to `TRUE` (no pink products exist), the `RETURN` statement is executed:

```
BEGIN
    RETURN
END

-- Won't execute
SELECT ProductID
FROM Production.Product
WHERE Color = 'Pink'
```

Since there are no pink products, `RETURN` is called, and the `SELECT` query following the `IF` statement is never executed.

The second example demonstrated creating a temporary stored procedure containing Transact-SQL that creates a divide-by-zero error. `RETURN` was used to capture the `@@ERRORCODE` value of 8134, which was passed back to the caller and printed in the `@ErrorCode` local variable. If an integer value isn't explicitly plugged into the `RETURN` call, a 0 value is sent by default.

Using WHILE

In this recipe, I demonstrate the `WHILE` command, which allows you to repeat a specific operation or batch of operations while a condition remains `TRUE`.

The syntax for `WHILE` is as follows:

```
WHILE Boolean_expression
    { sql_statement | statement_block }
    [ BREAK ]
    { sql_statement | statement_block }
    [ CONTINUE ]
    { sql_statement | statement_block }
```

`WHILE` will keep the Transact-SQL statement or batch processing while the Boolean expression remains `TRUE`. The `BREAK` keyword allows you to exit from the innermost `WHILE` loop, and the `CONTINUE` keyword causes the loop to restart.

In this example, the system stored procedure `sp_spaceused` is used to return the table space usage for each table in the `@AWTables` table variable:

```
-- Declare variables
DECLARE @AWTables TABLE (SchemaTable varchar(100))
DECLARE @TableName varchar(100)

-- Insert table names into the table variable
INSERT @AWTables
(SchemaTable)
SELECT TABLE_SCHEMA + '.' + TABLE_NAME
FROM INFORMATION_SCHEMA.tables
WHERE TABLE_TYPE = 'BASE TABLE'
ORDER BY  TABLE_SCHEMA + '.' + TABLE_NAME
```

```
-- Report on each table using sp_spaceused
WHILE (SELECT COUNT(*) FROM @AWTables)>0
BEGIN
    SELECT TOP 1 @TableName = SchemaTable
    FROM @AWTables
    ORDER BY SchemaTable

    EXEC sp_spaceused @TableName

    DELETE @AWTables
    WHERE SchemaTable = @TableName

END
```

This returns multiple result sets (one for each table). Three result sets are shown here:

name	rows	reserved	data	index_size	unused
Shift	3	48 KB	8 KB	40 KB	0 KB

name	rows	reserved	data	index_size	unused
Department	20	32 KB	8 KB	24 KB	0 KB

name	rows	reserved	data	index_size	unused
EmployeeAddress	290	48 KB	16 KB	32 KB	0 KB

As described earlier in the summary of the WHILE command, you can also use the keywords BREAK and CONTINUE in your code. BREAK is used to exit the WHILE loop, whereas CONTINUE is used to resume a WHILE loop. For example:

```
WHILE (1=1)
BEGIN
    PRINT 'Endless While, because 1 always equals 1'
    IF 1=1
    BEGIN
        PRINT 'But we didn''t let the endless loop happen'
        BREAK
    END
    ELSE
    BEGIN
        CONTINUE
    END
END
```

This returns

```
Endless While, because 1 always equals 1
But we didn't let the endless loop happen
```

How It Works

In this recipe, WHILE is used to loop through each table in the AdventureWorks database, reporting information using the sp_spaceused system stored procedure.

This recipe began by declaring two variables:

```
DECLARE @AWTables TABLE (SchemaTable varchar(100))
DECLARE @TableName varchar(100)
```

The table variable @AWTables was used to hold all the table names, and the @TableName variable to hold a single table name's value.

The table variable was populated with all the table names in the AdventureWorks database (populating a schema.table_name value):

```
INSERT @AWTables
(SchemaTable)
SELECT TABLE_SCHEMA + '.' + TABLE_NAME
FROM INFORMATION_SCHEMA.tables
WHERE TABLE_TYPE = 'BASE TABLE'
ORDER BY  TABLE_SCHEMA + '.' + TABLE_NAME
```

The WHILE loop was then started, looping as long as there were rows in the @AWTables table variable:

```
WHILE (SELECT COUNT(*) FROM @AWTables)>0
BEGIN
```

Within the WHILE, the @TableName local variable was populated with the TOP 1 table name from the @AWTables table variable:

```
    SELECT TOP 1 @TableName = SchemaTable
    FROM @AWTables
    ORDER BY SchemaTable
```

Using the @TableName variable, EXEC sp_spaceused was executed:

```
    EXEC sp_spaceused @TableName
```

Lastly, the row for the reported table was deleted from the table variable:

```
    DELETE @AWTables
    WHERE SchemaTable = @TableName
END
```

WHILE will continue to execute sp_spaceused until all rows are deleted from the @AWTables table variable.

In the second example of the recipe, BREAK was used to exit a loop if a certain condition is met (or threshold tripped). Use BREAK as an extra precaution against endless loops.

Using GOTO

This recipe demonstrates GOTO, which is used to jump to a label in your Transact-SQL batch, passing over the code that follows it. The syntax is

```
    GOTO label
label definition: code
```

In this example, I check to see whether a department name is already in use by an existing department. If so, the INSERT is bypassed using GOTO. If not, the INSERT is performed:

```
DECLARE @Name nvarchar(50) = 'Engineering'
DECLARE @GroupName nvarchar(50) = 'Research and Development'
DECLARE @Exists bit = 0

IF EXISTS (SELECT Name
          FROM HumanResources.Department
          WHERE Name = @Name)
BEGIN
   SET @Exists = 1
   GOTO SkipInsert
END

INSERT HumanResources.Department
(Name, GroupName)
VALUES(@Name , @GroupName)

SkipInsert:
IF @Exists = 1
BEGIN
     PRINT @Name + ' already exists in HumanResources.Department'
END
ELSE
BEGIN
     PRINT 'Row added'
END
```

This returns

```
Engineering already exists in HumanResources.Department
```

How It Works

In this recipe's example, two local variables were declared and set to values in preparation for being inserted into the HumanResources.Department table:

```
DECLARE @Name nvarchar(50) = 'Engineering'
DECLARE @GroupName nvarchar(50) = 'Research and Development'
```

Another variable was also defined to hold a bit value. This value acted as a flag to mark whether a row already existed in the table (used later on in the recipe):

```
DECLARE @Exists bit = 0
```

Next, an IF statement was used to check for the existence of any row with the same department name as the local variable. If such a row exists, the bit variable is set to 1 and the GOTO command is invoked. GOTO references the label name that you want to skip to, in this case called SkipInsert:

```
IF EXISTS (SELECT Name
          FROM HumanResources.Department
          WHERE Name = @Name)
BEGIN
   SET @Exists = 1
   GOTO SkipInsert
END
```

An INSERT follows the IF statement; however, in this example, it is skipped over because the department Engineering does already exist in the HumanResources.Department table:

```
INSERT HumanResources.Department
(Name, GroupName)
VALUES(@Name , @GroupName)
```

The label to be skipped to is then defined, suffixed with a colon:

```
SkipInsert:
```

Following the label is another IF statement. If the bit flag was enabled, a PRINT statement designates that the row already exists:

```
IF @Exists = 1
BEGIN
    PRINT @Name + ' already exists in HumanResources.Department'
END
```

Otherwise, a message is printed that the row was successfully added:

```
ELSE
BEGIN
    PRINT 'Row added'
END
```

As a best practice, when given a choice between using GOTO and other control-of-flow methods, you should choose something other than GOTO. GOTO can decrease the clarity of the code, as you'll have to jump around the batch or stored procedure code in order to understand the original intention of the query author.

Using WAITFOR

In this recipe, I demonstrate the WAITFOR command, which delays the execution of Transact-SQL code for a specified length of time.

The syntax for WAITFOR is as follows:

```
WAITFOR
{
    DELAY 'time_to_pass'
  | TIME 'time_to_execute'
  | ( receive_statement ) [ , TIMEOUT timeout ]
}
```

The time_to_pass parameter for WAITFOR DELAY is the number of seconds, minutes, and hours to wait before executing the command. The WAITFOR TIME time_to_execute parameter is used to designate an actual time (hour, minute, second) to execute the batch. The receive_statement and TIMEOUT options are used in conjunction with Service Broker (see Chapter 20).

In this first example, a 10-second delay is created by WAITFOR before a SELECT query is executed:

```
WAITFOR DELAY '00:00:10'
BEGIN
    SELECT TransactionID, Quantity
    FROM Production.TransactionHistory
END
```

In this second example, a query is not executed until a specific time, in this case 7:01 p.m.:

```
WAITFOR TIME '19:01:00'
BEGIN
    SELECT COUNT(*)
    FROM Production.TransactionHistory
END
```

How It Works

In this recipe, two different versions of WAITFOR were used to delay processing of a Transact-SQL batch.

The first query waited 10 seconds before executing the batch:

```
WAITFOR DELAY '00:00:10'
```

Waiting for a certain amount of time is useful when you know another operation must execute asynchronously while your current batch process must wait. For example, if you have kicked off an asynchronous SQL Server Agent job using the sp_start_job system stored procedure, control is returned immediately to the batch after the job starts to execute. If you know that the job you just kicked off takes at least 5 minutes to run, and your consecutive tasks are dependent on the completion of the job, WAITFOR can be used to delay processing until the job is complete.

The second query waited until the next instance of the specified time:

```
WAITFOR TIME '19:01:00'
```

WAITFOR TIME is useful for when certain operations must occur at specific time periods in the day. For example, say you have a stored procedure which performs data warehouse aggregations from transaction processing tables. The aggregations may take a couple of hours to complete, but you don't want to load the finished data from the staging to the production tables until after business hours. Using WAITFOR TIME in the procedure, you can stop the final load of the tables until non-business hours.

Cursors

Query authors with a programming background are often more comfortable using Transact-SQL cursors than the set-based alternatives for retrieving or updating rows. For example, a programmer may decide he wishes to loop through one row at a time, updating rows in a singleton fashion, instead of updating an entire set of rows in a single operation. Unfortunately, cursors can eat up a SQL Server instance's memory, reduce concurrency, decrease network bandwidth, lock resources, and can often require an excessive amount of code compared to a set-based alternative. Transact-SQL is a set-based language, meaning that it excels at manipulating and retrieving sets of rows, rather than performing single row-by-row processing.

Nevertheless, your application or business requirements may require the single, row-by-row processing that Transact-SQL cursors can provide. In general, you should only consider using cursors after exhausting other methods for doing row-level processing, such as WHILE loops, subqueries, temporary tables, or table variables, to name a few.

The general life cycle of a Transact-SQL cursor is as follows:

- A cursor is defined via a SQL statement that returns a valid result set.

- The cursor is then populated (opened).

- Once opened, rows can be fetched from the cursor, one at a time or in a block. The rows can also be fetched moving forward or backward, depending on the original cursor definition.

- Depending on the cursor type, the data can be modified while scrolling through the rows, or read and used with other operations.

- Finally, after the cursor has been used, it should then be explicitly closed and de-allocated from memory.

The DECLARE CURSOR command is used to create a cursor, and has many options that impact the flexibility and locking behavior of the cursor. The basic syntax is as follows:

```
DECLARE cursor_name CURSOR
[ LOCAL | GLOBAL ]
[ FORWARD_ONLY | SCROLL ]
[ STATIC | KEYSET | DYNAMIC | FAST_FORWARD ]
[ READ_ONLY | SCROLL_LOCKS | OPTIMISTIC ]
[ TYPE_WARNING ]
FOR select_statement[ FOR UPDATE [ OF column_name [ ,...n ] ] ]
```

There are several options that can impact whether or not the cursor data can be updated, and whether or not you can move backward and forward within the rows populated within the cursor. Table 9-2 briefly describes the available options.

Table 9-2. *Cursor Options*

Option	Description
LOCAL or GLOBAL	If LOCAL is selected, the cursor is only available within the scope of the SQL batch, trigger, or stored procedure. If GLOBAL is selected, the cursor is available to the connection itself (for example, a connection that executes a stored procedure that creates a cursor can use the cursor that was created in the stored procedure execution).
FORWARD_ONLY or SCROLL	The FORWARD_ONLY option only allows you to move forward from the first row of the cursor and onward. SCROLL, on the other hand, allows you to move backward and forward through the cursor result set using all fetch options (FIRST, LAST, NEXT, PRIOR, ABSOLUTE, and RELATIVE). If performance is a consideration, stick to using FORWARD_ONLY—as this cursor type incurs less overhead than the SCROLL.
STATIC or KEYSET or DYNAMIC or FAST_FORWARD	When STATIC is specified, a snapshot of the cursor data is held in the DYNAMIC or FAST_FORWARD tempdb database, and any changes made at the original data source aren't reflected in the cursor data. KEYSET allows you to see changes to rows made outside of the cursor, although you can't see inserts that would have met the cursor's SELECT query or deletes after the cursor has been opened. DYNAMIC allows you to see updates, inserts, and deletes in the underlying data source while the cursor is open. FAST_FORWARD defines two behaviors: setting the cursor to read-only and forward-only status (this is usually the best-performing cursor option, but the least flexible). When faced with a performance decision, and your desired functionality is not complicated, use this option.
READ_ONLY or SCROLL_LOCKS or OPTIMISTIC	The READ_ONLY option means that updates cannot be made through the cursor. If performance and concurrency are considerations, use this option. SCROLL_LOCKS places locks on rows so that updates or deletes are guaranteed to be made after the cursor is closed. The OPTIMISTIC option places no locks on updated or deleted rows, and will only maintain modifications if an update has not occurred outside of the cursor since the last data read.

Option	Description
TYPE_WARNINGS	When TYPE_WARNINGS is specified, a warning will be sent to the client if the cursor is implicitly converted from one type to a different type.

The select_statement argument is the query used to define the data within the cursor. Avoid using a query that has more columns and rows than will actually be used, because cursors, while open, are kept in memory. The UPDATE [OF column_name [,...n]] is used to specify those columns that are allowed to be updated by the cursor.

Once a cursor is declared using DECLARE CURSOR, the next step is to open it up and populate it using the OPEN command. The syntax is as follows:

```
OPEN  { [ GLOBAL ] cursor_name }
```

A cursor can be opened locally (the default) or globally. Once opened, you can begin using the FETCH command to navigate through rows in the cursor. The syntax for FETCH NEXT is as follows:

```
FETCH    [ [ NEXT | PRIOR | FIRST | LAST
                  | ABSOLUTE { n | @nvar }
                  | RELATIVE { n | @nvar } ]
           FROM   ]
{ [ GLOBAL ] cursor_name }
[ INTO @variable_name [ ,...n ] ]
```

FETCH provides several options for navigating through rows in the cursor, by populating the results into local variables for each column in the cursor definition (this is demonstrated in the next recipe).

The @@FETCH_STATUS function is used after a FETCH operation to determine the FETCH status, returning 0 if successful, -1 for unsuccessful, or -2 for missing.

Once you are finished with the opened cursor, execute the CLOSE command to release the result set from memory. The syntax is as follows:

```
CLOSE { [ GLOBAL ] cursor_name }
```

At this point, you can still reopen the cursor if you want to. If you are finished, however, you should remove internal system references to the cursor by using the DEALLOCATE command. This frees up any resources used by the cursor. For example, if scroll locks are held on the cursor referenced in the table, these locks are then released after a DEALLOCATE. The syntax is as follows:

```
DEALLOCATE { [ GLOBAL ] cursor_name }
```

This next recipe will demonstrate each of these commands in action.

Creating and Using Transact-SQL Cursors

Although I recommend avoiding cursors whenever possible, using cursors for ad hoc, periodic database administration information gathering, as I demonstrate in this next example, is usually perfectly justified.

This recipe demonstrates a cursor that loops through each session ID currently active on the SQL Server instance, and executes DBCC OUTPUTBUFFER to see the ASCII and hexadecimal output buffer of each session (if it is executing anything at that moment):

```
-- I won't show rowcounts in the results
SET NOCOUNT ON

DECLARE @session_id smallint

-- Declare the cursor
DECLARE session_cursor CURSOR
FORWARD_ONLY READ_ONLY
FOR SELECT session_id
    FROM sys.dm_exec_requests
    WHERE status IN ('runnable', 'sleeping', 'running')

-- Open the cursor
OPEN session_cursor

-- Retrieve one row at a time from the cursor
FETCH NEXT
FROM session_cursor
INTO @session_id

-- Keep retrieving rows while the cursor has them
WHILE @@FETCH_STATUS = 0
BEGIN

    PRINT 'Spid #: ' + STR(@session_id)
    EXEC ('DBCC OUTPUTBUFFER (' + @session_id + ')')

    -- Grab the next row
    FETCH NEXT
    FROM session_cursor
    INTO @session_id

END

-- Close the cursor
CLOSE session_cursor

-- Deallocate the cursor
DEALLOCATE session_cursor
```

This returns the output buffer for any active requests on the SQL Server instance.

How It Works

The recipe started off by setting SET NOCOUNT ON, which suppresses the SQL Server row count messages in order to provide cleaner output:

```
-- Don't show rowcounts in the results
SET NOCOUNT ON
```

Next, a local variable was defined to hold the individual value of the server process ID to be fetched from the cursor:

```
DECLARE @session_id smallint
```

The cursor was then defined using DECLARE CURSOR. The cursor contained the session_id column from the sys.dm_exec_requests Dynamic Management View:

```
-- Declare the cursor
DECLARE session_cursor CURSOR
FORWARD_ONLY READ_ONLY
FOR SELECT session_id
   FROM sys.dm_exec_requests
   WHERE status IN ('runnable', 'sleeping', 'running')
```

After the cursor was defined, it was then opened (populated):

```
OPEN session_cursor
```

Once opened, the first row value was retrieved into the @session_id local variable using
FETCH NEXT:

```
FETCH NEXT
FROM session_cursor
INTO @session_id
```

FETCH NEXT was used to retrieve the first row. After the first fetch, a WHILE condition was defined
that told SQL Server to continue the loop of statements until the cursor's fetch status was no longer
successful (meaning no more rows could be retrieved):

```
WHILE @@FETCH_STATUS = 0
BEGIN
```

@@FETCH_STATUS was used to return the status of the cursor FETCH statement last issued against
the open cursor, returning 0 if the last FETCH was successful, -1 for unsuccessful, or -2 for missing.

Within the WHILE statement, the @session_id variable is printed and used with EXEC command
to create a dynamic query:

```
PRINT 'Spid #: ' + STR(@session_id)
EXEC ('DBCC OUTPUTBUFFER (' + @session_id + ')')
```

The dynamic query executes DBCC OUTPUTBUFFER for each individual session_id. After this,
another FETCH NEXT was run to populate the next @SPID value:

```
-- Grab the next row
FETCH NEXT
FROM session_cursor
INTO @session_id

END
```

After all session_ids are retrieved, the WHILE loop exits (because @@FETCH_STATUS will return -1).
The cursor was then closed using the CLOSE command:

```
-- Close the cursor
CLOSE session_cursor
```

At this point, the cursor can still be opened with the OPEN command; however, to completely
remove the cursor from memory, DEALLOCATE was used:

```
-- Deallocate the cursor
DEALLOCATE session_cursor
```

Although useful, cursors should be handled with care, as they can consume excessive resources
and often don't perform as well as set-based equivalents. Be sure to explore all set-based alternatives before considering cursors in your Transact-SQL development.

■ ■ ■

Stored Procedures

A *stored procedure* groups one or more Transact-SQL statements into a logical unit, stored as an object in a SQL Server database. After the stored procedure is created, its T-SQL definition is accessible from the sys.sql_module catalog view.

When a stored procedure is executed for the first time, SQL Server creates an execution plan and stores it in the plan memory cache. SQL Server can then reuse the plan on subsequent executions of this stored procedure. Plan reuse allows stored procedures to provide fast and reliable performance compared to non-compiled and unprepared ad hoc query equivalents.

■Note It is also possible to create a stored procedure that utilizes a .NET Common Language Runtime (CLR) assembly. This is discussed in Chapter 13.

This chapter contains recipes for creating and manipulating stored procedures. I'll begin the chapter with a basic overview of when stored procedures can be used and what benefits they offer.

Stored Procedure Basics

Over the years, I have developed a strong bias toward the use of stored procedures whenever possible. There are many good reasons to use stored procedures, and in my experience, very few bad ones. Usually, reasons against using stored procedures come from application developers who are more comfortable using ad hoc SQL within the application tier, and may not be trained in the use of stored procedures. In companies with a separate application and database administration staff, stored procedures also imply a loss of control over the Transact-SQL code from the application developer to the database administration staff. Assuming your database administration team is competent and willing to assist with a move to stored procedures in a timely fashion, the benefits of using them should far outweigh any loss of control.

Some of the benefits of using stored procedures:

- Stored procedures help centralize your Transact-SQL code in the data tier. Web sites or applications that embed ad hoc SQL are notoriously difficult to modify in a production environment. When ad hoc SQL is embedded in an application, you may spend too much time trying to find and debug the embedded SQL. Once you've found the bug, chances are you'll need to recompile the program executable, causing unnecessary application outages or application distribution nightmares. If you centralize your Transact-SQL code in stored procedures, you'll have a centralized place to look for SQL code or SQL batches. If you document and standardize the code properly, your stored procedures will improve overall supportability of the application.

- Stored procedures can help reduce network traffic for larger ad hoc queries. Programming your application call to execute a stored procedure, rather than push across a 500-line SQL call, can have a positive impact on your network and application performance, particularly if the call is repeated thousands of times a minute.

- Stored procedures encourage code reusability. For example, if your web application uses a drop-down menu containing a list of cities, and this drop-down is used in multiple web pages, you can call the stored procedure from each web page rather than embed the same SQL in multiple places.

- Stored procedures allow you to obscure the method of data retrieval. If you change the underlying tables from which the source data is pulled, stored procedures (similar to views) can obscure this change from the application. This allows you to make changes without forcing a code change at the application tier. You can swap in new tables for the old, and so long as the same columns and data types are sent back to the application, the application is none the wiser.

- Unlike views, stored procedures can take advantage of control-of-flow techniques, temporary tables, table variables, and much more.

- Stored procedures have a stabilizing influence on query response time. If you've worked extensively with ad hoc queries, you may have noticed that sometimes the amount of time it takes to return results from a query can vary wildly. This may be due to external factors, such as concurrent activity against the table (locking) or resource issues (memory, CPU). On the other hand, an ad hoc query may be performing erratically because SQL Server periodically chooses less-efficient execution plans. With stored procedures, you gain more reliable query-plan caching, and hence reuse. Notice that I use the word "reliable" here, rather than "faster." Ad hoc queries can sometimes perform better than their stored procedure counterparts, but it all depends on the circumstances in which the execution plan was cached (which parameters were "sniffed") and how you have tested, tuned, and then implemented the code within.

If none of these previous reasons convinced you that stored procedures are largely beneficial, let's review the security benefits. Direct table access (or worse, sysadmin access) to the SQL Server instance and its database poses a security risk. Inline ad hoc code is more vulnerable to *SQL injection* attacks. A SQL injection occurs when harmful Transact-SQL is inserted into an existing application's Transact-SQL code prior to being sent to the SQL Server instance. Aside from SQL injection attacks, if someone gets ahold of the inline code, he'll be able to glean information about the underlying schema of your database and direct his hacking attempts accordingly. Keeping all SQL within stored procedures keeps only the stored procedure reference in the application—instead of each individual column and table name.

Another security benefit to stored procedures is that you can grant database users and/or database roles access to them specifically instead of having to grant direct access to tables. The stored procedure can act as a control layer, allowing you to choose which columns and rows can and cannot be modified by the stored procedure (and also by the caller).

Creating a Basic Stored Procedure

Stored procedures can be used for many different activities including simple SELECTs, INSERTs, UPDATEs, DELETEs, and much more. Many of the features or statements reviewed in the chapters of this book can be used within the body of a stored procedure. Transact-SQL activities can be mixed within a single procedure, or you can create stored procedures in a modular fashion, creating multiple stored procedures for each task or set of tasks.

The basic syntax for non-parameterized stored procedures is as follows:

```
CREATE PROCEDURE  [schema_name.] procedure_name
AS { <sql_statement> [ ...n ] }
```

The first arguments of the command are the schema and new procedure name. The sql_statement argument is the Transact-SQL body of your stored procedure. This argument contains one or more tasks that you wish to accomplish. In this example, I demonstrate how to create a basic stored procedure that queries data from the AdventureWorks database:

```
USE AdventureWorks
GO

CREATE PROCEDURE dbo.usp_SEL_ShoppingCartDisplay
AS

SELECT sc.ShoppingCartID,
       sc.ShoppingCartItemID,
       sc.Quantity,
       sc.ProductID,
       p.Name ProductName,
       p.ListPrice
FROM Sales.ShoppingCartItem sc
INNER JOIN Production.Product p ON
       sc.ProductID = p.ProductID

GO
```

Next, the new stored procedure is executed using the EXEC command:

```
EXEC dbo.usp_SEL_ShoppingCartDisplay
```

This returns the following results:

ShoppingCartID	ShoppingCartItemID	Quantity	ProductID	ProductName	ListPrice
14951	2	3	862	Full-Finger Gloves, M	37.99
20621	4	4	881	Short-Sleeve Classic Jersey, S	53.99
20621	5	7	874	Racing Socks, M	8.99

How It Works

In this recipe, I demonstrated creating a stored procedure that queried the contents of two tables, returning a result set. This stored procedure works like a view, only it will now have a cached query plan when executed for the first time, which will also make its runtime consistent in consecutive executions.

The example started off by creating a stored procedure called usp_SEL_ShoppingCartDisplay:

```
CREATE PROCEDURE dbo.usp_SEL_ShoppingCartDisplay
AS
```

The Transact-SQL query definition then followed the AS keyword:

```
SELECT sc.ShoppingCartID,
       sc.ShoppingCartItemID,
       sc.Quantity,
       sc.ProductID,
       p.Name ProductName,
       p.ListPrice
```

```
FROM Sales.ShoppingCartItem sc
INNER JOIN Production.Product p ON
        sc.ProductID = p.ProductID

GO
```

The GO keyword was used to mark the end of the stored procedure.

After the procedure in this recipe was created, it was then executed using the EXEC command:

```
EXEC dbo.usp_SEL_ShoppingCartDisplay
```

During the stored procedure creation process, SQL Server checks that the SQL syntax is correct, but it doesn't check for the existence of referenced tables. This means that you can reference a table name incorrectly, and the name will not cause an error until runtime. This is called *deferred name resolution*, and it allows you to create or reference the objects in the database that don't exist yet. This also means that you can drop, alter, or modify the objects referenced in the stored procedure without invalidating it.

Creating a Parameterized Stored Procedure

In the previous recipe, I demonstrated a non-parameterized stored procedure, meaning that no external parameters were passed to it. The ability to pass parameters to them is part of why stored procedures are one of the most important database objects in SQL Server. Using parameters, you can pass information into the body of the procedure in order to return customized search information, or use parameters to influence or execute INSERT, UPDATE, or DELETE statements against tables. A procedure can have up to 2,100 parameters (although it's unlikely you'll want to use nearly that many).

The syntax for creating a stored procedure is as follows:

```
CREATE { PROC | PROCEDURE } [schema_name.] procedure_name [ ; number ]
    [ { @parameter [ type_schema_name. ] data_type }
        [ VARYING ] [ = default ] [ OUT | OUTPUT ] [READONLY]
    ] [ ,...n ]
[ WITH <procedure_option> [ ,...n ] ]
[ FOR REPLICATION ]
AS { <sql_statement> [;][ ...n ] | <method_specifier> }
```

A parameter is prefixed by the @ sign, followed by the data type and optional default value. Parameters come in two flavors: input and output. Where input parameters are used to pass information into the stored procedure for processing, OUTPUT parameters are used to return information back to the stored procedure caller.

In this example, a new stored procedure is created that can accept three parameters. Based on the values of these parameters, either an existing row in a table will be updated or a new row will be inserted:

```
CREATE PROCEDURE dbo.usp_UPD_ShoppingCartItem
(@ShoppingCartID nvarchar(50),
@Quantity int = 1, -- defaulted to quantity of 1
@ProductID int)
AS
-- If the same ShoppingCartID and ProductID is sent
-- in the parameters, update the new quantity

IF EXISTS(SELECT *
FROM Sales.ShoppingCartItem
WHERE ShoppingCartID = @ShoppingCartID AND
```

```
  ProductID = @ProductID )
BEGIN
    UPDATE Sales.ShoppingCartItem
    SET Quantity = @Quantity
    WHERE ShoppingCartID = @ShoppingCartID AND
      ProductID = @ProductID

    PRINT 'UPDATE performed. '
END
ELSE
BEGIN
    -- Otherwise insert a new row
    INSERT Sales.ShoppingCartItem
    (ShoppingCartID, ProductID, Quantity)
    VALUES (@ShoppingCartID, @ProductID, @Quantity)

     PRINT 'INSERT performed. '
END

GO
```

Next, the new stored procedure is called, passing three values for each expected parameter:

```
EXEC usp_UPD_ShoppingCartItem '1255', 2, 316
```

This returns

```
(1 row(s) affected)
INSERT performed.
```

How It Works

This recipe demonstrated the creation of a stored procedure that could accept parameters. In the example, three parameters were defined for the procedure:

```
CREATE PROCEDURE usp_UPD_ShoppingCartItem
(@ShoppingCartID nvarchar(50),
@Quantity int = 1, -- defaulted to quantity of 1
@ProductID int)
AS
```

The first parameter and third parameter were required parameters, as neither designated a default value. The second parameter was optional, however, because it defined a default @Quantity value of 1.

The body of the stored procedure followed the AS keyword, starting with the first block of code, which checks for the existence of rows in an IF statement:

```
IF EXISTS(SELECT *
FROM Sales.ShoppingCartItem
WHERE ShoppingCartID = @ShoppingCartID AND
  ProductID = @ProductID )
BEGIN
```

If the row already existed for that specific ProductID and ShoppingCartID, its quantity would be updated based on the new @Quantity value:

```
    UPDATE Sales.ShoppingCartItem
    SET Quantity = @Quantity
    WHERE ShoppingCartID = @ShoppingCartID AND
      ProductID = @ProductID

    PRINT 'UPDATE performed. '
END
```

Otherwise, if a row didn't already exist, a new INSERT would be performed:

```
ELSE
BEGIN
    -- Otherwise insert a new row
    INSERT Sales.ShoppingCartItem
    (ShoppingCartID, ProductID, Quantity)
    VALUES (@ShoppingCartID, @ProductID, @Quantity)

    PRINT 'INSERT performed. '

END

GO
```

After the procedure was created, it was then executed along with the required parameter values:

```
EXEC usp_UPD_ShoppingCartItem '1255', 2, 316
```

In this case, since the specific ShoppingCartID and ProductID combination didn't exist in the table yet, a new row was inserted into Sales.ShoppingCartItem.

Using OUTPUT Parameters

In the previous recipe, you saw that there was syntax for including OUTPUT parameters in your stored procedure definition. OUTPUT parameters allow you to pass information back to the caller of the stored procedure, whether it's another stored procedure making the call or an ad hoc call made by an application.

In this example, I create a stored procedure that returns the list of departments for a specific group. In addition to returning the list of departments, an OUTPUT parameter is defined to store the number of departments returned for the specific group:

```
CREATE PROCEDURE dbo.usp_SEL_Department
    @GroupName nvarchar(50),
    @DeptCount int OUTPUT
AS

SELECT Name
FROM HumanResources.Department
WHERE GroupName = @GroupName
ORDER BY Name

SELECT @DeptCount = @@ROWCOUNT

GO
```

Next, the new stored procedure is called. A local variable is defined to hold the OUTPUT parameter value:

```
DECLARE @DeptCount int

EXEC dbo.usp_SEL_Department 'Executive General and Administration',
@DeptCount OUTPUT

PRINT @DeptCount
```

This returns the following result set:

```
Name
Executive
Facilities and Maintenance
Finance
Human Resources
Information Services
```

In addition to the results, the result row count is also returned via the PRINT command:

```
5
```

How It Works

I started off this recipe by creating a stored procedure with a defined parameter called @DeptCount, followed by the data type and OUTPUT keyword:

```
@DeptCount int OUTPUT
```

Within the definition of the stored procedure, the parameter was then assigned to the row count value, based on the previous SELECT statement that was executed before it.

```
SELECT @DeptCount = @@ROWCOUNT
```

To use the OUTPUT value in Transact-SQL code, a local variable was declared and used within the EXEC statement:

```
DECLARE @DeptCount int
```

Notice that the OUTPUT keyword followed the second parameter, in order to designate that it was receiving and not sending an actual value:

```
EXEC dbo.usp_SEL_Department 'Executive General and Administration',
                        @DeptCount OUTPUT
```

You can use OUTPUT parameters as an alternative or additional method for returning information back to the caller of the stored procedure. Capturing the OUTPUT results allows you to then pass the variable's value into another stored procedure or process. If you're using OUTPUT just to communicate information back to the calling application, it's usually just as easy to create a second result set containing the information you need. This is because .NET applications, for example, can easily consume the multiple result sets that are returned from a stored procedure. The technique of using OUTPUT parameters versus using an additional result set to return information is often just a matter of preference.

Modifying a Stored Procedure

The ALTER PROCEDURE command is used to modify the definition of a stored procedure, allowing you to change everything but the original stored procedure name. The syntax is almost identical to CREATE PROCEDURE.

In this recipe, I'll demonstrate modifying the existing stored procedure created in the previous recipe, in order to return the number of departments returned by the query as a separate result set, instead of using an OUTPUT parameter:

```
ALTER PROCEDURE dbo.usp_SEL_Department
    @GroupName nvarchar(50)
AS

SELECT Name
FROM HumanResources.Department
WHERE GroupName = @GroupName
ORDER BY Name

SELECT @@ROWCOUNT DepartmentCount
GO
```

Next, the modified stored procedure is executed:

```
EXEC dbo.usp_SEL_Department 'Research and Development'
```

This returns two result sets:

```
Name
Engineering
Research and Development
Tool Design
```

and

```
DepartmentCount
3
```

How It Works

In this recipe, ALTER PROCEDURE was used to modify the definition of an existing stored procedure—both removing a parameter and adding a second result set. Using this command, you can change everything but the procedure name itself. Using ALTER PROCEDURE also preserves any existing permissions on the stored procedure without having to explicitly redefine them after the change.

Dropping Stored Procedures

You can drop a stored procedure from the database using the DROP PROCEDURE command.

The syntax for dropping a stored procedure is

```
DROP PROCEDURE { [ schema_name. ] procedure } [ ,...n ]
```

This command takes one argument; the name of the procedure or procedures to drop. For example:

```
DROP PROCEDURE dbo.usp_SEL_Department
```

How It Works

Once a stored procedure is dropped, its definition information is removed from the database's system tables. Any cached query execution plans are also removed for that stored procedure. Code references to the stored procedure by other stored procedures or triggers will fail upon execution once the stored procedure has been dropped.

Executing Stored Procedures Automatically at SQL Server Startup

You can designate a stored procedure to be executed whenever the SQL Server service is started. You may wish to do this to perform any cleanup tasks your SQL Server instance requires (for example, documenting when the service started or clearing out work tables).

This automatic execution of a stored procedure is achieved using the sp_procoption system stored procedure. The command looks like it takes several different options, but in SQL Server, it really only performs a single task, which is setting a stored procedure to execute automatically when the SQL Server service restarts.

In this example, a stored procedure is set to execute automatically whenever SQL Server is started. First, the database context is set to the master database (which is the only place that auto-executable stored procedures can be placed):

```
USE master
GO
```

Next, for the example, a startup logging table is created:

```
CREATE TABLE dbo.SQLStartupLog
(SQLStartupLogID int IDENTITY(1,1) NOT NULL PRIMARY KEY,
 StartupDateTime datetime NOT NULL)
GO
```

Now, a new stored procedure is created to insert a value into the new table (so you can see whenever SQL Server was restarted using the table):

```
CREATE PROCEDURE dbo.usp_INS_TrackSQLStartups
AS

INSERT dbo.SQLStartupLog
(StartupDateTime)
VALUES (GETDATE())

GO
```

Next, the sp_procoption stored procedure is used to set this new procedure to execute when the SQL Server service restarts:

```
EXEC sp_procoption @ProcName = 'usp_INS_TrackSQLStartups',
  @OptionName = 'startup',
  @OptionValue = 'true'
```

Once the service restarts, a new row is inserted into the table. To disable the stored procedure again, the following command would need to be executed:

```
EXEC sp_procoption @ProcName = 'usp_INS_TrackSQLStartups',
  @OptionName = 'startup',
  @OptionValue = 'false'
```

How It Works

In this recipe, a new table was created in the master database that tracks SQL Server startups. A stored procedure was also created in the master database to insert a row into the table with the current date and time of execution.

■**Caution** I'm not espousing the creation of objects in the system databases, as it isn't generally a good idea. However, if you must use auto-execution functionality as discussed in this recipe, you have no choice but to do it (for example, if your IT department requires a log of SQL Server service start times for tracking purposes).

Next, sp_procoption was called to set the startup value of the stored procedure:

```
EXEC sp_procoption @ProcName = 'usp_INS_TrackSQLStartups',
  @OptionName = 'startup',
  @OptionValue = 'true'
```

After sp_procoption was used, whenever the SQL Server service is restarted, a new row will be inserted into the dbo.SQLStartupLog table. The stored procedure must be created in the master database; otherwise you'll see the following error message when trying to use sp_procoption:

```
Msg 15398, Level 11, State 1, Procedure sp_procoption, Line 73
Only objects in the master database owned by dbo
can have the startup setting changed.
```

Reporting Stored Procedure Metadata

You can use the sys.sql_modules catalog view to explore stored procedure metadata (useful for other object types as well), as I demonstrate in this recipe:

```
SELECT definition,
       execute_as_principal_id,
       is_recompiled,
       uses_ansi_nulls,
       uses_quoted_identifier
FROM  sys.sql_modules m
INNER JOIN sys.objects o ON
       m.object_id = o.object_id
WHERE o.type = 'P'
```

How It Works

The sys.sql_modules view is used to view the definition and settings of stored procedures, triggers, views, and other SQL-defined objects. In this recipe, sys.sql_modules was joined to sys.objects so that only sys.objects rows of type P (stored procedures) will be returned.

The query returns the stored procedure definition (if not encrypted), the EXECUTE AS security context ID, whether or not the stored procedure has WITH RECOMPILE set, and a 1 if the ANSI NULL or QUOTED IDENTIFIER options were ON when it was created.

■**Tip** Encryption, EXECUTE AS, and WITH RECOMPILE will all be discussed in this chapter.

Documenting Stored Procedures

This next recipe is more of a best practice, rather than a review of a command or function. It is important to comment your stored procedure code very well, so that future support staff, authors, and editors will understand the business rules and intents behind your Transact-SQL code. Although some code may seem "self-evident" at the time of authoring, the original logic may not seem so clear a few months after it was written. Business logic is often transient and difficult to understand over time, so including this in the body of the code can often save hours of troubleshooting and investigation.

For brevity, the stored procedure examples in this chapter have not included extensive comments or headers. However, in your production database, you should at the very least define headers for each stored procedure created in a production database.

The following is an example of a standard stored procedure header:

```
CREATE PROCEDURE dbo.usp_IMP_DWP_FactOrder
AS


-----------------------------------------------------------
-- Purpose: Populates the data warehouse, Called by Job
--
-- Maintenance Log
--
-- Update By      Update Date     Description
-- -----------    ---------       ---------------------------
-- Joe Sack       8/15/2008       Created
-- Joe Sack       8/16/2008       A new column was added to
--the base table, so it was added here as well.
... Transact-SQL code here
```

How It Works

This example demonstrated how to include header information within the body of a new stored procedure. It tracks the purpose, the application where it will be called, and a maintenance log.

■**Caution** One drawback of self-documenting is that other developers who edit your code may not include documentation of their own changes. You may end up being blamed for code you didn't write, just because you were the last person to log a change. This is where your company should strongly consider a source control system to track all check-in and check-out activities, as well as be able to compare changes between procedure versions.

No doubt you'll see other procedure headers out in the field with much more information. I'm a firm believer in not demanding too much documentation. Include enough to bring clarity, but not so much that you introduce redundancy. For example, if you include the stored procedure name in the header, in addition to the actual CREATE PROCEDURE, you'll soon start seeing code where the header name doesn't match the stored procedure name. Why not just document the information that isn't already included in the stored procedure definition?

Stored Procedure Security

I mentioned at the beginning of the chapter that stored procedures have inherent security benefits, and I'll go over that again now.

Inline ad hoc code is more susceptible to SQL injection attacks, allowing the hacker to see the embedded SQL calls and search for words like "Social Security Number" or "Credit Card," for example. Embedding your SQL code in a stored procedure allows you to obscure the schema from any external influences.

Also, using stored procedures instead of direct table access provides greater security for the base tables. You can control how modifications are made and the data that is retrieved (both at the column and row level). Instead of granting table access, you can grant EXECUTE permissions to the user in order to execute the stored procedure instead. This is also the only call that travels to the database server, so any snooping elements won't see your SELECT statement.

In addition to these inherent benefits (all you have to do is *use* stored procedures in order to benefit from them), there are also a couple of features you should be aware of. The next recipe shows you how to encrypt your stored procedure so that the query definition can't be viewed.

After that recipe, I'll demonstrate how to define a custom security context for your stored procedure.

Encrypting a Stored Procedure

Just like a view, stored procedure Transact-SQL definitions can have their contents encrypted in the database, removing the ability to read the procedure's definition. Software vendors who use SQL Server in their back end often encrypt stored procedures in order to prevent tampering or reverse-engineering from clients or competitors. If you use encryption, be sure to save the original T-SQL definition, as it can't easily be decoded later (legally and reliably, anyhow). It should also be encrypted only prior to a push to production.

In order to encrypt the stored procedure, WITH ENCRYPTION is designated after the name of the new stored procedure, as this next example demonstrates:

```
CREATE PROCEDURE dbo.usp_SEL_EmployeePayHistory
WITH ENCRYPTION
AS

SELECT EmployeeID, RateChangeDate, Rate, PayFrequency, ModifiedDate
FROM HumanResources.EmployeePayHistory

GO
```

Once you've created WITH ENCRYPTION, you'll be unable to view the procedure's text definition:

```
-- View the procedure's text
EXEC sp_helptext usp_SEL_EmployeePayHistory
```

This returns

```
The text for object 'usp_SEL_EmployeePayHistory' is encrypted.
```

How It Works

Encryption can be defined using either CREATE PROCEDURE or ALTER PROCEDURE, but be sure to save your source code, as the existing encrypted text cannot be decrypted easily.

Using EXECUTE AS to Specify the Procedure's Security Context

The WITH EXECUTE AS clause allows you to specify the security context that a stored procedure executes under, overriding the default security of the stored procedure caller. In this case, security context refers to the permissions of the user executing the stored procedure.

■Note This recipe discusses several security features and concepts that I also cover in Chapters 17 and 18.

You have the option to execute a stored procedure under

- The security context of the caller
- The person who authored or last altered the procedure
- A specific login (if you have IMPERSONATE permissions for that person's login)
- The owner of the stored procedure

First, let me present you with a quick aside about caller permissions and ownership chaining. An *ownership chain* occurs when an object, such a stored procedure or view, is created and used to perform an INSERT, UPDATE, DELETE, or SELECT against another database object. If the schema of the stored procedure object is the same as the schema of the object referenced within, SQL Server only checks that the stored procedure caller has EXECUTE permissions to the stored procedure. Again, this ownership chaining only applies to the INSERT, UPDATE, DELETE, or SELECT commands. This is why stored procedures are excellent for securing the database—as you can grant a user access to execute a stored procedure without giving her access to the underlying tables.

An issue arises, however, when you are looking to execute commands that are *not* INSERT, UPDATE, DELETE, or SELECT. In those situations, even if a caller has EXECUTE permissions to a stored procedure that, for example, truncates a table using the TRUNCATE TABLE command, he must still have permissions to use the TRUNCATE TABLE command in the first place. For example, the following stored procedure is created, which deletes all data from a table:

```
USE AdventureWorks
GO

CREATE PROCEDURE dbo.usp_DEL_ALLEmployeeSalary
AS

-- Deletes all rows prior to the data feed
DELETE dbo.EmployeeSalary

GO
```

To set up this scenario, I'll create and populate the dbo.EmployeeSalary table:

```
CREATE TABLE dbo.EmployeeSalary
(EmployeeID int NOT NULL PRIMARY KEY CLUSTERED,
 SalaryAMT money NOT NULL)
 GO

INSERT dbo.EmployeeSalary (EmployeeID, SalaryAMT)
VALUES (1,45000.00), (343, 100000.00),(93, 3234993.00)
```

Next, EXECUTE permission on this new stored procedure is granted to your employee BrianG:

```
USE master
GO

CREATE LOGIN BrianG WITH PASSWORD = '1301C636F9D'

USE AdventureWorks
GO

CREATE USER BrianG
GO
GRANT EXEC ON usp_DEL_ALLEmployeeSalary  to BrianG
```

Now, if BrianG attempts to execute this procedure, ownership chaining has got him covered:

```
EXECUTE  dbo.usp_DEL_ALLEmployeeSalary
```

BrianG has no other permissions in the database except to the new stored procedure, but it still works:

```
(3 row(s) affected)
```

But now the procedure is changed to use the TRUNCATE TABLE command instead of DELETE:

```
ALTER PROCEDURE dbo.usp_DEL_ALLEmployeeSalary
AS

-- Deletes all rows prior to the data feed
TRUNCATE TABLE dbo.EmployeeSalary

GO
```

Now, if BrianG attempts to execute this procedure again, SQL Server will check BrianG's ability to use the TRUNCATE TABLE command and will return the following error (since he only has permissions to execute the procedure):

```
Msg 1088, Level 16, State 7, Procedure usp_DEL_ALLEmployeeSalary, Line 5
Cannot find the object "EmployeeSalary" because it does not exist
or you do not have permissions.
```

Now consider the use of the EXECUTE AS option for stored procedures. Using EXECUTE AS, you can designate that any caller of the stored procedure run under your security context. For example, suppose the previous stored procedure was written as follows:

```
ALTER PROCEDURE dbo.usp_DEL_ALLEmployeeSalary
WITH EXECUTE AS OWNER
AS

-- Deletes all rows prior to the data feed
TRUNCATE TABLE dbo.EmployeeSalary

GO
```

With the added WITH EXECUTE AS OWNER, BrianG only needs EXECUTE permissions on the stored procedure and can execute the procedure under the stored procedure owner's security context.

Assuming the owner has permission to TRUNCATE a table, the stored procedure execution will be successful.

The same "gotcha" goes for dynamic SQL within a stored procedure. SQL Server will ensure that the caller has both EXECUTE *and* the appropriate permissions in order to perform the task the dynamic SQL is attempting to perform, even if that dynamic SQL is performing an INSERT, UPDATE, DELETE, or SELECT.

For example, the following procedure contains dynamic SQL, allowing you to select the row count from any table based on the schema and table name designated in the @SchemaAndTable input parameter:

```
CREATE PROCEDURE dbo.usp_SEL_CountRowsFromAnyTable
@SchemaAndTable nvarchar(255)
AS

EXEC ('SELECT COUNT(*) FROM ' + @SchemaAndTable)

GO
```

If you have the permissions to EXECUTE this procedure and have access to the designated table, SQL Server will allow you to return the row count:

```
EXEC dbo.usp_SEL_CountRowsFromAnyTable 'HumanResources.Department'
```

This returns

```
17
```

However, granting the EXECUTE permission isn't enough. Because this is dynamic SQL, if the user doesn't have SELECT permission to the underlying table, SQL Server will check both EXECUTE permissions on the procedure and SELECT permissions on the table. If the user BrianG didn't have SELECT permissions, he'd see the following error:

```
Msg 229, Level 14, State 5, Line 1
SELECT permission denied on object 'Department',
database 'AdventureWorks', schema 'HumanResources'.
```

Again, this is a situation that can be remedied using EXECUTE AS (if you are comfortable with BrianG having these permissions, of course). This time, an explicit user name will be designated as the security context for the procedure (I also create the user SteveP, who has permission to read from the HumanResources.Employee table):

```
USE master
GO

CREATE LOGIN SteveP WITH PASSWORD = '533B295A-D1F0'

USE AdventureWorks
GO

CREATE USER SteveP

GRANT SELECT ON OBJECT::HumanResources.Employee TO SteveP
GO
```

```
ALTER PROCEDURE dbo.usp_SEL_CountRowsFromAnyTable
    @SchemaAndTable nvarchar(255)
WITH EXECUTE AS 'SteveP'
AS

-- Will work for any tables that SteveP can SELECT from
EXEC ('SELECT COUNT(*) FROM ' + @SchemaAndTable)

GO
```

Assuming SteveP had the proper permissions to any tables passed as dynamic SQL in the procedure, now if BrianG has permission to the procedure and executes it, he will see results returned as though BrianG were SteveP. SQL Server will not check BrianG's permissions, but will use SteveP's security context instead.

How It Works

In this recipe, EXECUTE AS was demonstrated within a stored procedure, allowing you to define the security context under which a stored procedure is executed, regardless of the caller.

The options for EXECUTE AS in a stored procedure are as follows:

```
EXECUTE AS { CALLER | SELF | OWNER | 'user_name' }
```

The default behavior for EXECUTE AS is the CALLER option, which means that the permissions of the executing user are used (and if the user doesn't have proper access, that execution will fail). If the SELF option is used, the execution context of the stored procedure will be that of the user who created or last altered the stored procedure. When the OWNER option is designated, the owner of the stored procedure's schema is used. The user_name option is an explicit reference to a database user whose security context the stored procedure will be executed under.

Recompilation and Caching

Stored procedures can provide performance benefits due to the cached query execution plan, allowing SQL Server to reuse an existing plan instead of generating a new one. Stored procedures also have a stabilizing effect on query response time compared to the sometimes varying response times of ad hoc queries.

■**Note** For more information on assessing query performance and the procedure cache, see Chapter 28.

With that said, stored procedures are not the magic bullet for query performance. You still need to account for the performance of individual statements within the body of your stored procedure and to make sure that the tables are indexed properly and that the database is designed efficiently. Several of the features discussed in other chapters of this book can be utilized within the body of a stored procedure, but you must use them with the same consideration as you would had they been used outside of a stored procedure.

In the next two recipes, I'll discuss situations where you may *not* want a query execution plan to be cached, the first covering the RECOMPILE option and the second the DBCC FREEPROCCACHE command.

RECOMPILE(ing) a Stored Procedure Each Time It Is Executed

A recompilation occurs when a stored procedure's plan is re-created either automatically or explicitly. Recompilations occur automatically during stored procedure execution when underlying table or other object changes occur to objects that are referenced within a stored procedure. They can also occur with changes to indexes used by the plan or after a large number of updates to table keys referenced by the stored procedure. The goal of an automatic recompilation is to make sure the SQL Server execution plan is using the most current information and not using out-of-date assumptions about the schema and data.

SQL Server also uses statement-level recompiles within the stored procedure, instead of recompiling the entire stored procedure. Since recompiles cause extra overhead in generating new plans, statement-level recompiles help decrease this overhead by correcting only what needs to be corrected.

Although recompilations are costly and should be avoided most of the time, there may sometimes be reasons why you would want to force a recompilation. For example, your procedure may produce wildly different query results based on the application calling it due to varying selectivity of qualified columns—so much so that the retained execution plan causes performance issues when varying input parameters are used.

For example, if one parameter value for City returns a match of one million rows, while another value for City returns a single row, SQL Server may not necessarily cache the correct execution plan. SQL Server may end up caching a plan that is optimized for the single row instead of the million rows, causing a long query execution time. If you're looking to use stored procedures for benefits other than caching, you can use the WITH RECOMPILE command.

In this example, I demonstrate how to force a stored procedure to recompile each time it is executed:

```
CREATE PROCEDURE dbo.usp_SEL_BackupMBsPerSecond
(@BackupStartDate datetime,
 @BackupFinishDate datetime)
WITH RECOMPILE -- Plan will never be saved
AS

-- Procedure measure db backup throughput
SELECT  (SUM(backup_size)/1024)/1024 as 'MB',
        DATEDIFF ( ss , MIN(backup_start_date),
        MAX(backup_finish_date)) as 'seconds',
        ((SUM(backup_size)/1024)/1024 )/
            DATEDIFF ( ss , MIN(backup_start_date) ,
                MAX(backup_finish_date)) as 'MB per second'
FROM msdb.dbo.backupset
WHERE backup_start_date >= @BackupStartDate AND
backup_finish_date < @BackupFinishDate AND
type = 'd'
GO
```

Now whenever this procedure is called, a new execution plan will be created by SQL Server.

How It Works

This procedure used WITH RECOMPILE to ensure that a query plan is not cached for the procedure during creation or execution.

You will no doubt only have need to use WITH RECOMPILE under rare circumstances, as generally the cached plan chosen by SQL Server will suffice. Use this option if you still wish to take advantage of a stored procedure's other benefits (such as security and modularization), but don't want SQL Server to store an inefficient plan ("parameter sniff") based on wildly varying result sets.

> **■Note** See Chapter 28 for more information on query execution plans.

Flushing the Procedure Cache

In this recipe, I'll demonstrate how to remove all plans from the procedure cache. This technique is often used in order to test procedure performance in a "cold" cache, reproducing the cache as though SQL Server had just been restarted. This is an option for you on a development SQL Server instance, if you want to make sure existing cached query plans don't have an impact on your stored procedure performance testing.

> **■Caution** Don't use this command in a production environment, as you could be knocking out several cached query plans that are perfectly fine.

In this example, a count of cached query plans is executed prior to executing DBCC FREEPROCCACHE:

```
SELECT COUNT(*) 'CachedPlansBefore'
FROM sys.dm_exec_cached_plans
```

This returns

```
CachedPlansBefore
42
```

Next, the procedure cache for the entire SQL Server instance is cleared:

```
DBCC FREEPROCCACHE

SELECT COUNT(*) 'CachedPlansAfter'
FROM sys.dm_exec_cached_plans
```

This returns

```
DBCC execution completed. If DBCC printed error messages,
contact your system administrator.
CachedPlansAfter
0

(1 row(s) affected)
```

How It Works

DBCC FREEPROCCACHE was used in this recipe to clear out the procedure cache. If you try this yourself, the count of cached plans will vary based on the activity on your SQL Server instance. This includes any background processes or jobs that may be running before or after the clearing of the cache. The dynamic management view sys.dm_exec_cached_plans was used to demonstrate the impact of this DBCC command, showing an original count of 42 plans versus 0 afterward (although your results may vary depending on the ongoing activity of your SQL Server instance).

■■■

User-Defined Functions and Types

In this chapter, I'll present recipes for user-defined functions and types. User-defined *functions* (UDFs) allow you to encapsulate both logic and subroutines into a single function that can then be used within your Transact-SQL queries and programmatic objects. User-defined *types* (UDTs) allow you to create an alias type based on an underlying system data type, enforcing a specific data type, length, and nullability.

At the end of this chapter, I'll also cover the SQL Server 2008 user-defined table type, which can be used as a user-defined table parameter for passing table result sets within your T-SQL code.

Note This chapter covers how to create both user-defined functions and types using Transact-SQL. However, Chapter 13 briefly discusses how to create these objects using the new Common Language Runtime (CLR) functionality. As of SQL Server 2008, a CLR-based UDT is no longer limited to 8000 bytes.

UDF Basics

Transact-SQL user-defined functions fall into three categories; *scalar, inline table-valued*, and *multi-statement table-valued*.

A scalar user-defined function is used to return a single value based on zero or more parameters. For example, you could create a scalar UDF that accepts a CountryID as a parameter and returns the CountryNM.

Caution If you use a scalar user-defined function in the SELECT clause, the function will be executed for each row in the FROM clause, potentially resulting in poor performance, depending on the design of your function.

An inline table-valued UDF returns a table data type based on a single SELECT statement that is used to define the returned rows and columns. Unlike a stored procedure, an inline UDF can be referenced in the FROM clause of a query, as well as be joined to other tables. Unlike a view, an inline UDF can accept parameters.

A multi-statement table-valued UDF also returns a tabular result set and is referenced in the FROM clause. Unlike inline table-valued UDFs, they aren't constrained to use a single SELECT statement within the function definition and instead allow multiple Transact-SQL statements in the body of the UDF definition in order to define a single, final result set to be returned.

UDFs can also be used in places where a stored procedure can't, like in the FROM and SELECT clause of a query. UDFs also encourage code reusability. For example, if you create a scalar UDF that returns the CountryNM based on a CountryID, and the same function is needed across several different stored procedures, rather than repeat the 20 lines of code needed to perform the lookup, you can call the UDF function instead.

In the next few recipes, I'll demonstrate how to create, drop, modify, and view metadata for each of these UDF types.

Creating Scalar User-Defined Functions

A scalar user-defined function accepts zero or more parameters and returns a single value. Scalar UDFs are often used for converting or translating a current value to a new value, or performing other sophisticated lookups based on specific parameters. Scalar functions can be used within search, column, and join expressions.

The simplified syntax for a scalar UDF is as follows:

```
CREATE FUNCTION [ schema_name. ] function_name
( [ { @parameter_name [ AS ][ type_schema_name. ] parameter_data_type
    [ = default ] [ READONLY ] }
    [ ,...n ]
  ]
)
RETURNS return_data_type
    [ WITH <function_option> [ ,...n ] ]
    [ AS ]
    BEGIN
                function_body
        RETURN scalar_expression
    END
```

■**Note** The full syntax for CREATE FUNCTION can be found in SQL Server Books Online.

Table 11-1 gives a brief description of each argument's intended use.

Table 11-1. Scalar UDF Arguments

Argument	Description
[schema_name.] function_name	This argument defines the optional schema name and required function name of the new scalar UDF.
@parameter_name	This is the name of the parameter to pass to the UDF, and it must be prefixed with an @ sign.
[type_schema_name.] scalar_parameter_data_type	This is the optional schema of parameter data type and the associated parameter data type.
[,...n]	Although not an actual argument, this syntax element indicates that one or more parameters can be defined (up to 1024).
return_data_type	This specifies the data type the user-defined function will return.
function_body	This function body contains one or more of the Transact-SQL statements that are used to produce and evaluate a scalar value.
scalar_expression	This is the actual value that will be returned by the scalar function (notice that it is defined after the function body).

This example creates a scalar UDF that accepts a varchar(max) data type parameter. It returns a bit value (1 or 0) based on whether the passed parameter contains suspicious values (as defined by the function). So if the input parameter contains a call to a command such as DELETE or SHUTDOWN, the flag is set to 1:

```
-- Create a function to check for any suspicious behaviors
-- from the application
CREATE FUNCTION dbo.udf_CheckForSQLInjection
    (@TSQLString varchar(max))
RETURNS BIT
AS

BEGIN

DECLARE @IsSuspect bit

-- UDF assumes string will be left padded with a single space
SET @TSQLString = ' ' + @TSQLString

IF    (PATINDEX('% xp_%' , @TSQLString ) <> 0 OR
    PATINDEX('% sp_%' , @TSQLString ) <> 0  OR
    PATINDEX('% DROP %' , @TSQLString ) <> 0 OR
    PATINDEX('% GO %' , @TSQLString ) <> 0 OR
    PATINDEX('% INSERT %' , @TSQLString ) <> 0 OR
    PATINDEX('% UPDATE %' , @TSQLString ) <> 0 OR
    PATINDEX('% DBCC %' , @TSQLString ) <> 0 OR
    PATINDEX('% SHUTDOWN %' , @TSQLString )<> 0 OR
    PATINDEX('% ALTER %' , @TSQLString )<> 0 OR
    PATINDEX('% CREATE %' , @TSQLString ) <> 0OR
    PATINDEX('%;%' , @TSQLString )<> 0 OR
    PATINDEX('% EXECUTE %' , @TSQLString )<> 0 OR
    PATINDEX('% BREAK %' , @TSQLString )<> 0 OR
    PATINDEX('% BEGIN %' , @TSQLString )<> 0 OR
    PATINDEX('% CHECKPOINT %' , @TSQLString )<> 0 OR
    PATINDEX('% BREAK %' , @TSQLString )<> 0 OR
    PATINDEX('% COMMIT %' , @TSQLString )<> 0 OR
    PATINDEX('% TRANSACTION %' , @TSQLString )<> 0 OR
    PATINDEX('% CURSOR %' , @TSQLString )<> 0 OR
    PATINDEX('% GRANT %' , @TSQLString )<> 0 OR
    PATINDEX('% DENY %' , @TSQLString )<> 0 OR
    PATINDEX('% ESCAPE %' , @TSQLString )<> 0 OR
    PATINDEX('% WHILE %' , @TSQLString )<> 0 OR
    PATINDEX('% OPENDATASOURCE %' , @TSQLString )<> 0 OR
    PATINDEX('% OPENQUERY %' , @TSQLString )<> 0 OR
    PATINDEX('% OPENROWSET %' , @TSQLString )<> 0 OR
    PATINDEX('% EXEC %' , @TSQLString )<> 0)

BEGIN
    SELECT @IsSuspect = 1
END
ELSE
BEGIN
    SELECT @IsSuspect = 0
END
```

```
    RETURN (@IsSuspect)
END
```

```
GO
```

Next, you should test the function by evaluating three different string input values. The first contains a SELECT statement:

```
SELECT dbo.udf_CheckForSQLInjection
('SELECT * FROM HumanResources.Department')
```

This returns

0

The next string contains the SHUTDOWN command:

```
SELECT dbo.udf_CheckForSQLInjection
(';SHUTDOWN')
```

This returns

1

The last string tested contains the DROP command:

```
SELECT dbo.udf_CheckForSQLInjection
('DROP HumanResources.Department')
```

This returns

1

In this next example, I will create a user-defined function that can be used to set a string to proper case:

```
CREATE FUNCTION dbo.udf_ProperCase(@UnCased varchar(max))
RETURNS varchar(max)
AS
BEGIN

    SET @UnCased = LOWER(@UnCased)

    DECLARE @C int
    SET @C = ASCII('a')

    WHILE @C <= ASCII('z')
    BEGIN

  SET @UnCased = REPLACE( @UnCased, ' ' + CHAR(@C), ' ' +  CHAR(@C-32))
        SET @C = @C + 1
    END

    SET @UnCased = CHAR(ASCII(LEFT(@UnCased, 1))-32) + RIGHT(@UnCased,
LEN(@UnCased)-1)
```

```
    RETURN @UnCased
END

GO
```

Once the user-defined function is created, the string to modify to proper case can be used as the function parameter:

```
SELECT  dbo.udf_ProperCase(DocumentSummary)
FROM Production.Document
WHERE FileName = 'Installing Replacement Pedals.doc'
```

This returns

```
Detailed Instructions For Replacing Pedals With Adventure Works Cycles Replacement
Pedals.  Instructions Are Applicable To All Adventure Works Cycles Bicycle Models
And Replacement Pedals. Use Only Adventure Works Cycles Parts When Replacing Worn Or
Broken Components.
```

How It Works

This recipe demonstrated a scalar UDF, which in this case accepted one parameter and returned a single value. Some of the areas where you can use a scalar function in your Transact-SQL code include

- A column expression in a SELECT or GROUP BY clause
- A search condition for a JOIN in a FROM clause
- A search condition of a WHERE or HAVING clause

The recipe began by defining the UDF name and parameter:

```
CREATE FUNCTION dbo.udf_CheckForSQLInjection
    (@TSQLString varchar(max))
```

The @TSQLString parameter held the varchar(max) string to be evaluated.

In the next line of code, the scalar_return_data_type was defined as bit. This means that the single value returned by the function will be the bit data type:

```
RETURNS BIT
AS
```

The BEGIN marked the start of the function_body, where the logic to return the bit value was formulated:

```
BEGIN
```

A local variable was created to hold the bit value. Ultimately, this is the parameter that will be passed as the function's output:

```
DECLARE @IsSuspect bit
```

Next, the string passed to the UDF has a space concatenated to the front of it:

```
-- UDF assumes string will be left padded with a single space
SET @TSQLString = ' ' + @TSQLString
```

The @TSQLString was padded with an extra space in order to make the search of suspicious words or patterns easier to do. For example, if the suspicious word is at the beginning of the

@TSQLString, and you were searching for the word DROP, you would have to use PATINDEX to search for both '%DROP %' and '% DROP %'. Of course, searching '%DROP %' could give you false positives, such as the word "gumdrop," so you should prevent this confusion by padding the beginning of the string with a space.

In the IF statement, @TSQLString is evaluated using PATINDEX. For each evaluation, if a match is found, the condition will evaluate to TRUE:

```
IF    (PATINDEX('% xp_%' , @TSQLString ) <> 0 OR
    PATINDEX('% sp_%' , @TSQLString ) <> 0  OR
    PATINDEX('% DROP %' , @TSQLString ) <> 0 OR
    PATINDEX('% GO %' , @TSQLString ) <> 0 OR
    PATINDEX('% BREAK %' , @TSQLString )<> 0 OR
...
```

If any of the conditions evaluate to TRUE, the @IsSuspect bit flag will be set to 1:

```
BEGIN
    SELECT @IsSuspect = 1
END
ELSE
BEGIN
    SELECT @IsSuspect = 0
END
```

The RETURN keyword is used to pass the scalar value of the @IsSuspect variable back to the caller:

```
RETURN (@IsSuspect)
```

The END keyword is then used to close the UDF, and GO is used to end the batch:

```
END

GO
```

The new scalar UDF created in this recipe was then used to check three different string values. The first string, SELECT * FROM HumanResources.Department, comes up clean, but the second strings, ;SHUTDOWN and DROP HumanResources.Department, both return a bit value of 1 because they match the suspicious word searches in the function's IF clause.

SQL Server doesn't provide a built-in proper case function, so in my second example, I demonstrate creating a user-defined function that performs this action. The first line of the CREATE FUNCTION definition defines the name and parameter expected—in this case, a varchar(max) data type parameter:

```
CREATE FUNCTION dbo.udf_ProperCase(@UnCased varchar(max))
```

The RETURNS keyword defined what data type would be returned by the function after the logic has been applied:

```
RETURNS varchar(max)
AS
BEGIN
```

Next, the variable passed to the function was first modified to lowercase using the LOWER function:

```
    SET @UnCased = LOWER(@UnCased)
```

A new integer local variable, @C, was set to the ASCII value of the letter "a":

```
DECLARE @C int
SET @C = ASCII('a')
```

A WHILE loop was initiated to go through every letter in the alphabet, and for each, search for a space preceding that letter, and then replace each occurrence of a letter preceded by a space with the uppercase version of the character:

```
WHILE @C <= ASCII('z')
   BEGIN
   SET @UnCased = REPLACE( @UnCased, ' ' + CHAR(@C), ' ' + CHAR(@C-32))
      SET @C = @C + 1
   END
```

The conversion to uppercase is performed by subtracting 32 from the ASCII integer value of the lowercase character. For example, the ASCII value for a lowercase "a" is 97, while the uppercase "A" is 65.

```
SET @UnCased = CHAR(ASCII(LEFT(@UnCased, 1))-32) + RIGHT(@UnCased, LEN(@UnCased)-1)
```

The final proper case string value of @UnCased is then returned from the function:

```
   RETURN @UnCased
END
GO
```

Next, I used the new scalar UDF in the SELECT clause of a query to convert the DocumentSummary text to proper case:

```
SELECT  dbo.udf_ProperCase(DocumentSummary)
...
```

Creating Inline User-Defined Functions

An inline UDF returns a table data type. In the UDF definition, you do not explicitly define the returned table, but use a single SELECT statement for defining the returned rows and columns instead. An inline UDF uses one or more parameters and returns data using a single SELECT statement. Inline UDFs are very similar to views, in that they are referenced in the FROM clause. However, unlike views, UDFs can accept parameters that can then be used in the function's SELECT statement.

The basic syntax is as follows:

```
CREATE FUNCTION [ schema_name. ] function_name
        ( [ { @parameter_name [ AS ]
[ type_schema_name. ] scalar_parameter_data_type [ = default ]
        } [ ,...n ]
     ]
     )
RETURNS TABLE
[ AS ]
RETURN [ ( ] select_stmt [ ) ]
```

■Note The full syntax for CREATE FUNCTION can be found in SQL Server Books Online.

Table 11-2 details the arguments of this command.

Table 11-2. *Inline UDF Arguments*

Argument	Description
`[ schema_name. ] function_name`	This defines the optional schema name and required function name of the new inline UDF.
`@parameter_name`	This is the name of the parameter to pass to the UDF. It must be prefixed with an @ sign.
`[ type_schema_name. ] scalar_parameter_data_type`	This is the @parameter_name data type and the optional scalar_parameter_data_type owning schema (used if you are employing a user-defined type).
`[ ,...n ]`	Although not an actual argument, this syntax element indicates that one or more parameters can be defined (up to 1024).
`select_stmt`	This is the single SELECT statement that will be returned by the inline UDF.

This example demonstrates creating an inline table UDF that accepts an integer parameter and returns the associated addresses of a business entity:

```
CREATE FUNCTION  dbo.udf_ReturnAddress
   ( @BusinessEntityID int)
RETURNS TABLE
   AS
RETURN (
        SELECT t.Name AddressTypeNM,
               a.AddressLine1,
               a.City,
               a.StateProvinceID,
               a.PostalCode
        FROM Person.Address a
     INNER JOIN  Person.BusinessEntityAddress e ON
          a.AddressID = e.AddressID
     INNER JOIN Person.AddressType t ON
          e.AddressTypeID = t.AddressTypeID
     WHERE e.BusinessEntityID  = @BusinessEntityID  )

GO
```

Next, the new function is tested in a query, referenced in the FROM clause for business entity 332:

```
SELECT AddressTypeNM, AddressLine1, City, PostalCode
FROM dbo.udf_ReturnAddress(332)
```

This returns

```
AddressTypeNM    AddressLine1          City       PostalCode
Shipping         26910 Indela Road     Montreal   H1Y 2H5
Main Office      25981 College Street  Montreal   H1Y 2H5
```

How It Works

In this recipe, I created an inline table UDF to retrieve the addresses of a business entity based on the @BusinessEntityID value passed. The UDF started off just like a scalar UDF, only the RETURNS command used a TABLE data type (which is what distinguishes it from a scalar UDF):

```
CREATE FUNCTION  dbo.udf_ReturnAddress
  ( @BusinessEntityID int)
RETURNS TABLE
   AS
```

After the AS keyword, the RETURN statement was issued with a single SELECT statement in parentheses:

```
RETURN (
       SELECT t.Name AddressTypeNM,
              a.AddressLine1,
              a.City,
              a.StateProvinceID,
              a.PostalCode
      FROM Person.Address a
    INNER JOIN  Person.BusinessEntityAddress e ON
         a.AddressID = e.AddressID
    INNER JOIN Person.AddressType t ON
         e.AddressTypeID = t.AddressTypeID
    WHERE e.BusinessEntityID  = @BusinessEntityID  )
```

```
GO
```

After it was created, the new inline UDF was then used in the FROM clause of a SELECT query. The @BusinessEntityID value of 332 was passed into the function in parentheses:

```
SELECT AddressTypeNM, AddressLine1, City, PostalCode
FROM dbo.udf_ReturnAddress(332)
```

This function then returns a result set, just like when you are querying a view or a table. Also, just like a view or stored procedure, the query you create to define this function must be tuned as you would a regular SELECT statement. Using an inline UDF offers no inherent performance benefits over using a view or stored procedure.

Creating Multi-Statement User-Defined Functions

Multi-statement table UDFs are referenced in the FROM clause just like inline UDFs, but unlike inline UDFs, they are not constrained to use a single SELECT statement within the function definition. Instead, multi-statement UDFs can use multiple Transact-SQL statements in the body of the UDF definition in order to define that a single, final result set be returned.

The basic syntax of a multi-statement table UDF is as follows:

```
CREATE FUNCTION [ schema_name. ] function_name
( [ { @parameter_name [ AS ] [ type_schema_name. ] parameter_data_type
    [ = default ] [READONLY] }
    [ ,...n ]
  ]
)
RETURNS @return_variable TABLE <table_type_definition>
    [ WITH <function_option> [ ,...n ] ]
    [ AS ]
    BEGIN
                function_body
        RETURN
    END
```

Table 11-3 describes the arguments of this command.

Table 11-3. *Multi-Statement UDF Arguments*

Argument	Description
`[ schema_name. ] function_name`	This specifies the optional schema name and required function name of the new inline UDF.
`@parameter_name`	This is the name of the parameter to pass to the UDF. It must be prefixed with an @ sign.
`[ type_schema_name. ] scalar_parameter_data_type`	This is the data type of the `@parameter_name` and the `scalar_parameter_data_type` optional owning schema (used if you are using a user-defined type).
`[ ,...n ]`	Although not an actual argument, this syntax element indicates that one or more parameters can be defined (up to 1024).
`@return_variable`	This is the user-defined name of the table variable that will hold the results to be returned by the UDF.
`< table_type_definition >`	This argument contains one or more column definitions for the table variable. Each column definition contains the name and data type, and can optionally define a PRIMARY KEY, UNIQUE, NULL, or CHECK constraint.
`function_body`	The function body contains one or more Transact-SQL statements that are used to populate and modify the table variable that will be returned by the UDF.

Notice the RETURNS keyword, which defines a *table variable* definition. Also notice the RETURN keyword at the end of the function, which doesn't have any parameter or query after it, as it is assumed that the defined table variable will be returned.

In this example, a multi-statement UDF will be created that accepts two parameters: one to hold a string, and the other to define how that string will be delimited. The string is then broken apart into a result set based on the defined delimiter:

```
-- Creates a UDF that returns a string array as a table result set
CREATE FUNCTION dbo.udf_ParseArray
    ( @StringArray varchar(max),
      @Delimiter char(1) )
RETURNS @StringArrayTable  TABLE (Val varchar(50))
AS
BEGIN
   DECLARE @Delimiter_position int

   IF RIGHT(@StringArray,1) != @Delimiter
   SET @StringArray = @StringArray + @Delimiter

   WHILE CHARINDEX(@Delimiter, @StringArray) <> 0
     BEGIN
       SELECT @Delimiter_position =
          CHARINDEX(@Delimiter, @StringArray)

       INSERT @StringArrayTable
       VALUES (left(@StringArray, @Delimiter_position - 1))

       SELECT @StringArray = STUFF(@StringArray, 1,
@Delimiter_position, '')
     END
```

```
RETURN
END

GO
```

Now it will be used to break apart a comma-delimited array of values:

```
SELECT Val
FROM dbo.udf_ParseArray('A,B,C,D,E,F,G', ',')
```

This returns the following results:

```
Val
A
B
C
D
E
F
G
```

How It Works

The multi-statement table UDF in this recipe was created using two parameters, the first to hold a string and the second to define the character that delimits the string:

```
CREATE FUNCTION dbo.udf_ParseArray
   ( @StringArray varchar(max),
     @Delimiter char(1) )
```

Next, a table variable was defined after the RETURNS token. The @StringArrayTable was used to hold the values of the string array after being shredded into the individual values:

```
RETURNS @StringArrayTable  TABLE (Val varchar(50))
```

The function body started after AS and BEGIN:

```
AS
BEGIN
```

A local variable was created to hold the delimiter position in the string:

```
DECLARE @Delimiter_position int
```

If the last character of the string array wasn't the delimiter value, then the delimiter value was concatenated to the end of the string array:

```
IF RIGHT(@StringArray,1) != @Delimiter
SET @StringArray = @StringArray + @Delimiter
```

A WHILE loop was created, looping until there were no remaining delimiters in the string array:

```
WHILE CHARINDEX(@Delimiter, @StringArray) <> 0
   BEGIN
```

Within the loop, the position of the delimiter was identified using CHARINDEX:

```
SELECT @Delimiter_position =
   CHARINDEX(@Delimiter, @StringArray)
```

The LEFT function was used with the delimiter position to extract the individual-delimited string part into the table variable:

```
INSERT @StringArrayTable
VALUES (left(@StringArray, @Delimiter_position - 1))
```

The inserted chunk was then removed from the string array using the STUFF function:

```
SELECT @StringArray = STUFF(@StringArray, 1, @Delimiter_position, '')
```

STUFF is used to delete a chunk of characters and insert another character string in its place. This first parameter of the STUFF function is the character expression, which in this example is the string array. The second parameter is the starting position of the deleted and inserted text, and in this case I am removing text from the string starting at the first position and stopping at the first delimiter. The third parameter is the length of the characters to be deleted, which for this example is the delimiter-position variable value. The last argument is the string to be inserted, which in this case was a blank string represented by two single quotes. The net effect is that the first comma-separated entry was replaced by an empty string—the same result as if the first entry had been deleted.

This process of inserting values continued until there were no longer delimiters in the string array. After this, the WHILE loop ended, and RETURN was called to return the table variable result set.

```
      END
RETURN
END
GO
```

The new UDF was then referenced in the FROM clause. The first parameter of the UDF was a comma-delimited list of letters. The second parameter was the delimiting parameter (a comma):

```
-- Now use it to break apart a comma-delimited array
SELECT Val
FROM dbo.udf_ParseArray('A,B,C,D,E,F,G', ',')
```

The list was then broken into a result set, with each individual letter as its own row. As you can see, multi-statement table UDFs allow for much more sophisticated programmability than an inline table value, which can only use a single SELECT statement.

Modifying User-Defined Functions

A function can be modified by using the ALTER FUNCTION command, as I demonstrate in this next recipe:

```
ALTER FUNCTION dbo.udf_ParseArray
   ( @StringArray varchar(max),
 @Delimiter char(1) ,
 @MinRowSelect int,
 @MaxRowSelect int)
RETURNS @StringArrayTable  TABLE (RowNum int IDENTITY(1,1), Val
varchar(50))
AS
BEGIN
   DECLARE @Delimiter_position int

   IF RIGHT(@StringArray,1) != @Delimiter
   SET @StringArray = @StringArray + @Delimiter

   WHILE CHARINDEX(@Delimiter, @StringArray) <> 0
      BEGIN
```

```
        SELECT @Delimiter_position =
            CHARINDEX(@Delimiter, @StringArray)

        INSERT @StringArrayTable
        VALUES (left(@StringArray, @Delimiter_position - 1))

        SELECT @StringArray = stuff(@StringArray, 1,
@Delimiter_position, '')
        END

DELETE @StringArrayTable
WHERE RowNum < @MinRowSelect OR
    RowNum > @MaxRowSelect

RETURN
END

GO

-- Now use it to break apart a comma delimited array
SELECT RowNum, Val
FROM dbo.udf_ParseArray('A,B,C,D,E,F,G', ',', 3, 5)
```

This returns

RowNum	Val
3	C
4	D
5	E

How It Works

ALTER FUNCTION allows you to modify an existing UDF by using syntax that is almost identical to that of CREATE FUNCTION, with some limitations:

- You can't change the name of the function using ALTER FUNCTION. What you're doing is replacing the code of an *existing* function—therefore the function needs to exist first.

- You can't convert a scalar UDF to a table UDF (either inline or multi-statement), nor can you convert a table UDF to a scalar UDF.

In this recipe, the udf_ParseArray from the previous recipe was modified to add two new parameters, @MinRowSelect and @MaxRowSelect:

```
ALTER FUNCTION dbo.udf_ParseArray
    ( @StringArray varchar(max),
      @Delimiter char(1) ,
      @MinRowSelect int,
      @MaxRowSelect int)
```

The @StringArrayTable table variable also had a new column added to it called RowNum, which was given the IDENTITY property (meaning that it will increment an integer value for each row in the result set):

```
RETURNS @StringArrayTable  TABLE (RowNum int IDENTITY(1,1), Val varchar(50))
```

The other modification came after the WHILE loop was finished. Any RowNum values below the minimum or maximum values were deleted from the @StringArrayTable table array:

```
DELETE @StringArrayTable
WHERE RowNum < @MinRowSelect OR
    RowNum > @MaxRowSelect
```

After altering the function, the function was called using the two new parameters to define the row range to view (in this case rows 3 through 5):

```
SELECT RowNum, Val
FROM udf_ParseArray('A,B,C,D,E,F,G', ',', 3, 5)
```

This returned the third, fourth, and fifth characters from the string array passed to the UDF.

Viewing UDF Metadata

In this recipe, I demonstrate how to view a list of UDFs in the current database (I don't show the results because this query includes the actual UDF T-SQL definition):

```
SELECT name, type_desc, definition
FROM sys.sql_modules s
INNER JOIN sys.objects o
    ON s.object_id = o.object_id
WHERE TYPE IN ('IF', -- Inline Table UDF
    'TF', -- Multistatement Table UDF
    'FN') -- Scalar UDF
```

How It Works

The sys.sql_modules and sys.objects system views are used to return the UDF name, type description, and SQL definition in a query result set:

```
FROM sys.sql_modules s
INNER JOIN sys.objects o
    ON s.object_id = o.object_id
```

Because sys.sql_modules contains rows for other object types, sys.objects must also be qualified to only return UDF rows:

```
WHERE TYPE IN ('IF', -- Inline Table UDF
    'TF', -- Multistatement Table UDF
    'FN') -- Scalar UDF
```

Dropping User-Defined Functions

In this recipe, I demonstrate how to drop a user-defined function. The syntax, like other DROP commands, is very straightforward:

```
DROP FUNCTION { [ schema_name. ] function_name } [ ,...n ]
```

Table 11-4 details the arguments of this command.

Table 11-4. *DROP FUNCTION Arguments*

Argument	Description
[schema_name.] function_name	This defines the optional schema name and required function name of the user-defined function.
[,...n]	Although not an actual argument, this syntax element indicates that one or more user-defined functions can be dropped in a single statement.

This recipe demonstrates how to drop the dbo.udf_ParseArray function created in earlier recipes:

```
DROP FUNCTION dbo.udf_ParseArray
```

How It Works

Although there are three different types of user-defined functions (scalar, inline, and multi-statement), you need only drop them using the single DROP FUNCTION command.

You can also drop more than one UDF in a single statement, for example:

```
DROP FUNCTION dbo.udf_ParseArray, dbo.udf_ReturnEmployeeAddress,
dbo.udf_CheckForSQLInjection
```

Benefitting from UDFs

User-defined functions are useful for both the performance enhancements they provide because of their cached execution plans and their ability to encapsulate reusable code. In this next section, I'll discuss some of the benefits of UDFs. For example, scalar functions in particular can be used to help make code more readable and allow you to apply lookup rules consistently across an application rather than repeating the same code multiple times throughout different stored procedures or views.

Table-valued functions are also useful for allowing you to apply parameters to results, for example, using a parameter to define row-level security for a data set (demonstrated later on).

■Caution When designing user-defined functions, consider the multiplier effect. For example, if you create a scalar user-defined function that performs a lookup against a million-row table in order to return a single value, and a single lookup with proper indexing takes 30 seconds, chances are you are going to see a significant performance hit if you use this UDF to return values based on each row of another large table. If scalar user-defined functions reference other tables, make sure that the query you use to access the table information performs well, and doesn't return a result set that is too large.

The next few recipes will demonstrate some of the more common and beneficial ways in which user-defined functions are used in the field.

Maintaining Reusable Code

Scalar UDFs allow you to reduce code bloat by encapsulating logic within a single function, rather than repeating the logic multiple times wherever it happens to be needed.

For example, the following scalar, user-defined function is used to determine the kind of personal computer that an employee will receive. There are several lines of code that evaluate different input parameters, including the title of the employee, the employee's hire date, and salaried status. Rather than include this logic in multiple areas across your database application, you can encapsulate the logic in a single function:

```
CREATE FUNCTION dbo.udf_GET_AssignedEquipment
 (@Title nvarchar(50), @HireDate datetime, @SalariedFlag bit)
RETURNS nvarchar(50)
AS
BEGIN

DECLARE @EquipmentType nvarchar(50)

IF @Title LIKE 'Chief%' OR
   @Title LIKE 'Vice%' OR
   @Title = 'Database Administrator'
BEGIN
  SET @EquipmentType = 'PC Build A'
END

IF @EquipmentType IS NULL AND @SalariedFlag = 1
BEGIN
  SET @EquipmentType = 'PC Build B'
END

IF @EquipmentType IS NULL AND @HireDate < '1/1/2002'
BEGIN
  SET @EquipmentType = 'PC Build C'
END

IF @EquipmentType IS NULL
BEGIN
  SET @EquipmentType = 'PC Build D'
END

RETURN @EquipmentType
END

GO
```

Once you've created it, you can use this scalar function in many areas of your Transact-SQL code without having to recode the logic within. For example, the new scalar function is used in the SELECT, GROUP BY, and ORDER BY clauses of a query:

```
SELECT dbo.udf_GET_AssignedEquipment
           (JobTitle, HireDate, SalariedFlag) PC_Build,
       COUNT(*) Employee_Count
FROM HumanResources.Employee
GROUP BY dbo.udf_GET_AssignedEquipment
           (JobTitle, HireDate, SalariedFlag)
ORDER BY dbo.udf_GET_AssignedEquipment
           (JobTitle, HireDate, SalariedFlag)
```

This returns

PC_Build	Employee_Count
PC Build A	7
PC Build B	45
PC Build C	238

This second query uses the scalar function in both the SELECT and WHERE clauses, too:

```
SELECT JobTitle,
       BusinessEntityID,
       dbo.udf_GET_AssignedEquipment
           (JobTitle, HireDate, SalariedFlag) PC_Build
FROM HumanResources.Employee
WHERE dbo.udf_GET_AssignedEquipment
           (JobTitle, HireDate, SalariedFlag) IN
                 ('PC Build A', 'PC Build B')
```

This returns the following (abridged) results:

JobTitle	BusinessEntityID	PC_Build
Chief Executive Officer	1	PC Build A
Vice President of Engineering	2	PC Build A
Engineering Manager	3	PC Build B
Design Engineer	5	PC Build B
Design Engineer	6	PC Build B
...		

How It Works

Scalar, user-defined functions can help you encapsulate business logic so that it isn't repeated across your code, providing a centralized location for you to make a single modification to a single function when necessary. This also provides consistency, so that you and other database developers are consistently using and writing the same logic in the same way. One other benefit is code readability, particularly with large queries that perform multiple lookups or evaluations.

Cross-Referencing Natural Key Values

Recall from Chapter 1 that a *surrogate key* is an artificial primary key, as opposed to a *natural key*, which represents a unique descriptor of data (for example, a Social Security Number is an example of a natural key, but an IDENTITY property column is a surrogate key). IDENTITY values are often used as surrogate primary keys but are also referenced as foreign keys.

In my own OLTP and star schema database designs, I assign each table a surrogate key by default, unless there is a significant reason not to do so. Doing this helps you abstract your own unique key from any external legacy natural keys. If you are using, for example, an EmployeeNumber that comes from the HR system as your primary key instead, you could run into trouble later on if that HR system decides to change its data type (forcing you to change the primary key, any foreign key references, and composite primary keys). Surrogate keys help protect you from changes like this because they are under your control, and so they make good primary keys. You can keep your natural keys' unique constraints without worrying about external changes impacting your primary or foreign keys.

When importing data from legacy systems into production tables, you'll often still need to reference the natural key in order to determine which rows get inserted, updated, or deleted. This isn't very tricky if you're just dealing with a single column (for example, `EmployeeID`, `CreditCardNumber`, `SSN`, `UPC`). However, if the natural key is made up of multiple columns, the cross-referencing to the production tables may not be quite so easy.

The following demonstrates a scalar, user-defined function that can be used to simplify natural key lookups, by checking for their existence prior to performing an action. To set up the example, I'll execute a few objects and commands.

First, I'll create a new table that uses its own surrogate keys, along with three columns that make up the composite natural key (these three columns form the unique value that received from the legacy system):

```
CREATE TABLE dbo.DimProductSalesperson
(DimProductSalespersonID int IDENTITY(1,1) NOT NULL PRIMARY KEY,
 ProductCD char(10) NOT NULL,
 CompanyNBR int NOT NULL,
 SalespersonNBR int NOT NULL
)
GO
```

■**Caution** This recipe doesn't add indexes to the tables; however, in a real-life scenario, you'll want to add indexes for key columns used for join operations or qualified in the WHERE clause of a query.

Next, I'll create a staging table that holds rows from the external legacy data file. For example, this table could be populated from an external text file that is dumped out of the legacy system. This table doesn't have a primary key, as it is just used to hold data prior to being moved to the `dbo.DimProductSalesperson` table:

```
CREATE TABLE dbo.Staging_PRODSLSP
( ProductCD char(10) NOT NULL,
 CompanyNBR int NOT NULL,
 SalespersonNBR int NOT NULL
)
GO
```

Next, I'll insert two rows into the staging table:

```
INSERT dbo.Staging_PRODSLSP
(ProductCD, CompanyNBR, SalespersonNBR)
VALUES ('2391A23904', 1, 24)

INSERT dbo.Staging_PRODSLSP
(ProductCD, CompanyNBR, SalespersonNBR)
VALUES ('X129483203', 1, 34)
```

Now, these two rows can be inserted into the `DimProductSalesperson` table using the following query, which *doesn't* use a scalar UDF:

```
INSERT dbo.DimProductSalesperson
(ProductCD, CompanyNBR, SalespersonNBR)
SELECT s.ProductCD, s.CompanyNBR, s.SalespersonNBR
FROM dbo.Staging_PRODSLSP s
LEFT OUTER JOIN dbo.DimProductSalesperson d ON
   s.ProductCD = d.ProductCD AND
```

```
   s.CompanyNBR = d.CompanyNBR AND
   s.SalespersonNBR = d.SalespersonNBR
WHERE d.DimProductSalespersonID IS NULL
```

Because each column forms the natural key, I must LEFT join each column from the inserted table against the staging table, and then check to see whether the row does not already exist in the destination table using IS NULL.

An alternative to this, allowing you to reduce the code in each INSERT/UPDATE/DELETE, is to create a scalar UDF like the following:

```
CREATE FUNCTION dbo.udf_GET_Check_NK_DimProductSalesperson
 (@ProductCD char(10),  @CompanyNBR int,  @SalespersonNBR int )
RETURNS bit
AS
BEGIN

DECLARE @Exists bit

IF EXISTS (SELECT DimProductSalespersonID
           FROM dbo.DimProductSalesperson
           WHERE @ProductCD = @ProductCD   AND
                 @CompanyNBR = @CompanyNBR   AND
                 @SalespersonNBR = @SalespersonNBR)
BEGIN
   SET @Exists = 1
END
ELSE
BEGIN
   SET @Exists = 0
END

RETURN @Exists
END

GO
```

The UDF certainly looks like more code up front, but you'll obtain the benefit later during the data import process. For example, now you can rewrite the INSERT operation demonstrated earlier, as follows:

```
INSERT dbo.DimProductSalesperson
(ProductCD, CompanyNBR, SalespersonNBR)
SELECT ProductCD, CompanyNBR, SalespersonNBR
FROM dbo.Staging_PRODSLSP
WHERE dbo.udf_GET_Check_NK_DimProductSalesperson
(ProductCD, CompanyNBR, SalespersonNBR) = 0
```

How It Works

In this recipe, I demonstrated how to create a scalar UDF that returned a bit value based on three parameters. If the three values already existed for a row in the production table, a 1 was returned; otherwise a 0 was returned. Using this function simplifies the INSERT/UPDATE/DELETE code that you must write in situations where a natural key spans multiple columns.

Walking through the UDF code, the first lines defined the UDF name and parameters. Each of these parameters is for the composite natural key in the staging and production table:

```
CREATE FUNCTION dbo.udf_GET_Check_NK_DimProductSalesperson
 (@ProductCD char(10),  @CompanyNBR int,  @SalespersonNBR int )
```

Next, a bit data type was defined to be returned by the function:

```
RETURNS bit
AS
BEGIN
```

A local variable was created to hold the bit value:

```
DECLARE @Exists bit
```

An IF was used to check for the existence of a row matching all three parameters for the natural composite key. If there is a match, the local variable is set to 1. If not, it is set to 0:

```
IF EXISTS (SELECT DimProductSalespersonID
           FROM dbo.DimProductSalesperson
           WHERE @ProductCD = @ProductCD   AND
                 @CompanyNBR = @CompanyNBR   AND
                 @SalespersonNBR = @SalespersonNBR)
BEGIN
   SET @Exists = 1
END
ELSE
BEGIN
   SET @Exists = 0
END
```

The local variable was then passed back to the caller:

```
RETURN @Exists
END

GO
```

The function was then used in the WHERE clause, extracting from the staging table those rows that returned a 0 from the scalar UDF, and therefore do not exist in the DimProductSalesperson table:

```
WHERE dbo.udf_GET_Check_NK_DimProductSalesperson
(ProductCD, CompanyNBR, SalespersonNBR) = 0
```

Replacing Views with Multi-Statement UDFs

Multi-statement UDFs allow you to return data in the same way you would from a view, only with the ability to manipulate data like a stored procedure.

In this example, a multi-statement UDF is created to apply row-based security based on the caller of the function. Only rows for the specified salesperson will be returned. In addition to this, the second parameter is a bit flag that controls whether rows from the SalesPersonQuotaHistory table will be returned in the results:

```
CREATE FUNCTION dbo.udf_SEL_SalesQuota
   ( @BusinessEntityID int,
     @ShowHistory bit )
RETURNS @SalesQuota TABLE
    (BusinessEntityID int,
     QuotaDate datetime,
     SalesQuota money)
```

```
AS
BEGIN
    INSERT @SalesQuota
    (BusinessEntityID, QuotaDate, SalesQuota)
    SELECT BusinessEntityID, ModifiedDate, SalesQuota
    FROM Sales.SalesPerson
    WHERE BusinessEntityID = @BusinessEntityID

    IF @ShowHistory = 1
    BEGIN

      INSERT @SalesQuota
      (BusinessEntityID, QuotaDate, SalesQuota)
      SELECT BusinessEntityID, QuotaDate, SalesQuota
      FROM Sales.SalesPersonQuotaHistory
      WHERE BusinessEntityID = @BusinessEntityID

    END

    RETURN
END

GO
```

After the UDF is created, the following query is executed to show sales quota data for a specific salesperson from the SalesPerson table:

```
SELECT  BusinessEntityID, QuotaDate, SalesQuota
FROM dbo.udf_SEL_SalesQuota (275,0)
```

This returns

BusinessEntityID	QuotaDate	SalesQuota
275	2001-06-24 00:00:00.000	300000.00

Next, the second parameter is switched from a 0 to a 1, in order to display additional rows for SalespersonID 275 from the SalesPersonQuotaHistory table:

```
SELECT  BusinessEntityID, QuotaDate, SalesQuota
FROM dbo.udf_SEL_SalesQuota (275,1)
```

This returns the following (abridged) results:

BusinessEntityID	QuotaDate	SalesQuota
275	2001-06-24 00:00:00.000	300000.00
275	2001-07-01 00:00:00.000	367000.00
275	2001-10-01 00:00:00.000	556000.00
275	2002-01-01 00:00:00.000	502000.00
275	2002-04-01 00:00:00.000	550000.00
275	2002-07-01 00:00:00.000	1429000.00
275	2002-10-01 00:00:00.000	1324000.00
...		

How It Works

This recipe demonstrated a multi-statement table-valued UDF to return sales quota data based on the BusinessEntityID value that was passed. It also included a second bit flag that controlled whether or not history was also returned.

Walking through the function, you'll notice that the first few lines defined the input parameters (something that a view doesn't allow):

```
CREATE FUNCTION dbo.udf_SEL_SalesQuota
    ( @BusinessEntityID int,
      @ShowHistory bit )
```

After this, the table columns that are to be returned by the function were defined:

```
RETURNS @SalesQuota TABLE
    (BusinessEntityID int,
     QuotaDate datetime,
     SalesQuota money)
```

The function body included two separate batch statements, the first being an INSERT into the table variable of rows for the specific salesperson:

```
AS
BEGIN
    INSERT @SalesQuota
    (BusinessEntityID, QuotaDate, SalesQuota)
    SELECT BusinessEntityID, ModifiedDate, SalesQuota
    FROM Sales.SalesPerson
    WHERE BusinessEntityID = @BusinessEntityID
```

Next, an IF statement (another construct not allowed in views) evaluated the bit parameter. If equal to 1, quota history will also be inserted into the table variable:

```
IF @ShowHistory = 1
    BEGIN

        INSERT @SalesQuota
        (BusinessEntityID, QuotaDate, SalesQuota)
        SELECT BusinessEntityID, QuotaDate, SalesQuota
        FROM Sales.SalesPersonQuotaHistory
        WHERE BusinessEntityID = @BusinessEntityID

    END
```

Lastly, the RETURN keyword signaled the end of the function (and, unlike a scalar function, no local variable is designated after it):

```
    RETURN
END

GO
```

Although the UDF contained Transact-SQL not allowed in a view, it was still able to be referenced in the FROM clause:

```
SELECT  BusinessEntityID, QuotaDate, SalesQuota
FROM dbo.udf_SEL_SalesQuota (275,0)
```

The results could be returned in a view using a UNION statement, but with that you wouldn't be able to have the control logic to either show or not show history in a single view.

In this recipe, I demonstrated a method to create your own parameter-based result sets. This can be used to implement row-based security. Row-level security is not built natively into the SQL Server security model. You can use functions to return only the rows that are allowed to be viewed by designating input parameters that are used to filter the data.

UDT Basics

User-defined types are useful for defining a consistent data type that is named after a known business or application-centric attribute, such as PIN, PhoneNBR, or EmailAddress. Once a user-defined type is created in the database, it can be used within columns, parameters, and variable definitions, providing a consistent underlying data type. The next two recipes will show you how to create and drop user-defined types. Note that unlike some other database objects, there isn't a way to modify an existing type using an ALTER command.

Creating and Using User-Defined Types

This recipe demonstrates how to create a user-defined type (also called an *alias data type*), which is a specific configuration of a data type that is given a user-specified name, data type, length, and nullability. You can use all base data types except the new xml data type.

■**Caution** One drawback when using user-defined data types is their inability to be changed without cascading effects, as you'll see in the last recipe of this chapter.

The basic syntax for creating a user-defined type is as follows:

```
CREATE TYPE [ schema_name. ] type_name
{
    FROM base_type
  [ (precision [ ,scale ] ) ]
  [ NULL | NOT NULL ] }
```

Table 11-5 details the arguments of these commands.

Table 11-5. *CREATE TYPE Arguments*

Argument	Description
[schema_name.] type_name	This specifies the optional schema name and required type name of the new user-defined type.
base_type	This is the base data type used to define the new user-defined type. You are allowed to use all base system data types except the xml data type.
(precision [,scale])	If using a numeric base type, precision is the maximum number of digits that can be stored both left and right of the decimal point. scale is the maximum number of digits to be stored right of the decimal point.
NULL	NOT NULL	This defines whether or not your new user-defined type allows NULL values.

In this recipe, I'll create a new type based on a 14-character string:

```
-- In this example, we assume the company's Account number will
-- be used in multiple tables, and that it will always have a fixed
-- 14 character length and will never allow NULL values

CREATE TYPE dbo.AccountNBR
FROM char(14) NOT NULL
GO
```

Next, I'll use the new type in the column definition of two tables:

```
-- The new data type is now used in two different tables

CREATE TABLE dbo.InventoryAccount
   (InventoryAccountID int NOT NULL,
   InventoryID int NOT NULL,
   InventoryAccountNBR AccountNBR)
GO

CREATE TABLE dbo.CustomerAccount
   (CustomerAccountID int NOT NULL,
   CustomerID int NOT NULL,
   CustomerAccountNBR AccountNBR)
GO
```

This type can also be used in the definition of a local variable or input parameter. For example, the following stored procedure uses the new data type to define the input parameter for a stored procedure:

```
CREATE PROCEDURE dbo.usp_SEL_CustomerAccount
   @CustomerAccountNBR AccountNBR
AS

SELECT CustomerAccountID, CustomerID, CustomerAccountNBR
FROM dbo.CustomerAccount
WHERE CustomerAccountNBR = CustomerAccountNBR
GO
```

Next, a local variable is created using the new data type and is passed to the stored procedure:

```
DECLARE @CustomerAccountNBR AccountNBR
SET @CustomerAccountNBR = '1294839482'

EXEC dbo.usp_SEL_CustomerAccount @CustomerAccountNBR
```

To view the underlying base type of the user-defined type, you can use the sp_help system stored procedure:

```
EXEC sp_help 'dbo.AccountNBR'
```

This returns the following results (only a few columns are displayed for presentation purposes):

Type_name	Storage_type	Length	Nullable
AccountNbr	char	14	no

How It Works

In this recipe, a new user-defined type called dbo.AccountNBR was created with a char(14) data type and NOT NULL. Once the user-defined type was created, it was then used in the column definition of two different tables:

```
CREATE TABLE dbo.InventoryAccount
   (InventoryAccountID int NOT NULL,
   InventoryID int NOT NULL,
   InventoryAccountNBR AccountNBR)
```

Because NOT NULL was already inherent in the data type, it wasn't necessary to explicitly define it in the column definition.

After creating the tables, a stored procedure was created that used the new data type in the input parameter definition. The procedure was then called using a local variable that also used the new type.

Although Transact-SQL types may be an excellent convenience for some developers, creating your application's data dictionary and abiding by the data types may suit the same purpose. For example, if an AccountNBR is always 14 characters, as a DBA/developer, you can communicate and check to make sure that new objects are using a consistent name and data type.

Identifying Columns and Parameters with Dependencies on User-Defined Types

Before showing you how to remove a user-defined data type, you'll need to know how to identify all database objects that depend on that type. As you'll see later on, removing a UDT doesn't automatically cascade changes to the dependent table.

This example shows you how to identify which database objects are using the specified user-defined type. This first query in the recipe displays all columns that use the AccountNBR user-defined type:

```
SELECT OBJECT_NAME(c.object_id) Table_Name, c.name Column_Name
FROM sys.columns c
INNER JOIN sys.types t ON
   c.user_type_id = t.user_type_id
WHERE t.name = 'AccountNBR'
```

This returns

Table_Name	Column_Name
InventoryAccount	InventoryAccountNBR
CustomerAccount	CustomerAccountNBR

This next query shows any procedures or functions that have parameters defined using the AccountNBR user-defined type:

```
-- Now see what parameters reference the AccountNBR data type
SELECT OBJECT_NAME(p.object_id) Table_Name, p.name Parameter_Name
FROM sys.parameters p
INNER JOIN sys.types t ON
```

```
      p.user_type_id = t.user_type_id
WHERE t.name = 'AccountNBR'
```

This returns

Table_Name	Parameter_Name
usp_SEL_CustomerAccount	@CustomerAccountNBR

How It Works

In order to report which table columns use the user-defined type, the system catalog views `sys.columns` and `sys.types` are used:

```
FROM sys.columns c
INNER JOIN sys.types t ON
   c.user_type_id = t.user_type_id
```

The `sys.columns` view contains a row for each column defined for a table-valued function, table, and view in the database. The `sys.types` view contains a row for each user and system data type.

To identify which function or procedure parameters reference the user-defined type, the system catalog views `sys.parameters` and `sys.types` are used:

```
FROM sys.parameters p
INNER JOIN sys.types t ON
   p.user_type_id = t.user_type_id
```

The `sys.parameters` view contains a row for each database object that can accept a parameter, including stored procedures, for example.

Identifying which objects reference a user-defined type is necessary if you plan on dropping the user-defined type, as the next recipe demonstrates.

Dropping User-Defined Types

In this recipe, I demonstrate how to remove a user-defined type (also called an alias data type) from the database. As with most `DROP` commands, the syntax for removing a user-defined type is very straightforward:

```
DROP TYPE [ schema_name. ] type_name
```

The `DROP TYPE` command uses the schema and type name, as this recipe will demonstrate. First, however, any references to the user-defined type need to be removed beforehand. In this example, the `AccountNBR` type is changed to the base equivalent for two tables and a stored procedure:

```
ALTER TABLE dbo.InventoryAccount
ALTER COLUMN InventoryAccountNBR char(14)
GO

ALTER TABLE dbo.CustomerAccount
ALTER COLUMN CustomerAccountNBR char(14)
GO

ALTER PROCEDURE dbo.usp_SEL_CustomerAccount
   @CustomerAccountNBR char(14)
AS
```

```
SELECT CustomerAccountID, CustomerID, CustomerAccountNBR
FROM dbo.CustomerAccount
WHERE CustomerAccountNBR = CustomerAccountNBR
GO
```

With the referencing objects now converted, it is okay to go ahead and drop the type:

```
DROP TYPE dbo.AccountNBR
```

How It Works

In order to remove a type, you must first change or remove any references to the type in a database table. If you are going to change the definition of a UDT, you need to remove *all* references to that UDT everywhere in *all* database objects that use that UDT. That means changing tables, views, stored procedures, etc., first before dropping the type. This can be very cumbersome if your database objects depend very heavily on them. Also, if any schema-bound stored procedures, functions, or triggers use the data type as parameters or variables, these references must be changed or removed. In this recipe, ALTER TABLE... ALTER COLUMN was used to change the data type to the system data type:

```
ALTER TABLE dbo.InventoryAccount
ALTER COLUMN InventoryAccountNBR char(14)
```

A stored procedure parameter was also modified using ALTER PROCEDURE:

```
ALTER PROCEDURE usp_SEL_CustomerAccount
(@CustomerAccountNBR char(14))
...
```

Passing Table-Valued Parameters

SQL Server 2008 introduces *table-valued parameters* that can be used to pass rowsets to stored procedures and user-defined functions. This functionality allows you to encapsulate multi-rowset capabilities within stored procedures and functions without having to make multiple row-by-row calls to data modification procedures or create multiple input parameters that inelegantly translate to multiple rows.

For example, the following stored procedure has several input parameters that are used to insert rows into the Department table:

```
CREATE PROCEDURE dbo.usp_INS_Department_Oldstyle
    @Name_1 nvarchar(50),
    @GroupName_1 nvarchar(50),
    @Name_2 nvarchar(50),
    @GroupName_2 nvarchar(50),
    @Name_3 nvarchar(50),
    @GroupName_3 nvarchar(50),
    @Name_4 nvarchar(50),
    @GroupName_4 nvarchar(50),
    @Name_5 nvarchar(50),
    @GroupName_5 nvarchar(50)
AS

INSERT HumanResources.Department
(Name, GroupName)
VALUES (@Name_1, @GroupName_1)
```

```
INSERT HumanResources.Department
(Name, GroupName)
VALUES (@Name_2, @GroupName_2)

INSERT HumanResources.Department
(Name, GroupName)
VALUES (@Name_3, @GroupName_3)

INSERT HumanResources.Department
(Name, GroupName)
VALUES (@Name_4, @GroupName_4)

INSERT HumanResources.Department
(Name, GroupName)
VALUES (@Name_5, @GroupName_5)

GO
```

This previous example procedure has several limitations. First of all, it assumes that each call will contain five rows. If you have ten rows, you must call the procedure twice. If you have three rows, you need to modify the procedure to test for NULL values in the parameters and skip inserts accordingly. If NULL values are allowed in the underlying table, you would also need a method to indicate when a NULL should be stored, and when a NULL represents a value not to be stored.

A more common technique is to create a singleton insert procedure:

```
CREATE PROCEDURE dbo.usp_INS_Department_Oldstyle_V2
    @Name nvarchar(50),
    @GroupName nvarchar(50)
AS

INSERT HumanResources.Department
(Name, GroupName)
VALUES (@Name, @GroupName)

GO
```

If you have five rows to be inserted, you would call this procedure five times. This may be acceptable in many circumstances—however, if you will always be inserting multiple rows in a single batch, SQL Server 2008 provides a better alternative. Instead of performing singleton calls, you can pass the values to be inserted into a single parameter that represents a table of values. Such a parameter is called a *table-valued parameter*.

In order to use a table-valued parameter, the first step is to define a user-defined table data type as I demonstrate here:

```
CREATE TYPE Department_TT AS TABLE
(Name nvarchar(50),
 GroupName nvarchar(50))
GO
```

Once the new table type is created in the database, I can now reference it in module definitions and within the code:

```
CREATE PROCEDURE dbo.usp_INS_Department_NewStyle
    @DepartmentTable as Department_TT READONLY
AS

INSERT HumanResources.Department
(Name, GroupName)
```

```
SELECT Name, GroupName
FROM @DepartmentTable

GO
```

Let's assume that an external process is used to populate a list of values, which I will then pass to the procedure. In your own applications, the data source that you pass in can be generated from a populated staging table, directly from an application rowset, or from a constructed rowset, as demonstrate next:

```
-- I can declare our new type for use within a T-SQL batch
DECLARE @StagingDepartmentTable as Department_TT

-- Insert multiple rows into this table-type variable
INSERT @StagingDepartmentTable
(Name, GroupName)
VALUES ('Archivists', 'Accounting')

INSERT @StagingDepartmentTable
(Name, GroupName)
VALUES ('Public Media', 'Legal')

INSERT @StagingDepartmentTable
(Name, GroupName)
VALUES ('Internal Admin', 'Office Administration')

-- Pass this table-type variable to the procedure in a single call
EXEC dbo.usp_INS_Department_NewStyle @StagingDepartmentTable
```

How It Works

In order to pass result sets to modules, I must first define a user-defined table type within the database. I used the CREATE TYPE command and defined it AS TABLE:

```
CREATE TYPE Department_TT AS TABLE
```

Next, I defined the two columns that made up the table, just as one would for a regular table:

```
(Name nvarchar(50),
 GroupName nvarchar(50))
GO
```

I could have also defined the table type with PRIMARY KEY, UNIQUE, and CHECK constraints. I can also designate nullability, as well as define whether or not the column was computed.

Next, I created a new procedure that uses the newly created table type. In the input parameter argument list, I created an input parameter with a type of Department_TT:

```
CREATE PROCEDURE dbo.usp_INS_Department_NewStyle
    @DepartmentTable as Department_TT READONLY
AS
```

Notice the READONLY keyword after the data type designation. This is a requirement for stored procedure and user-defined function input parameters, as you are not allowed to modify the table-valued result set in this version of SQL Server.

The next block of code handled the INSERT to the table, using the input parameter as the data source of the multiple rows:

```
INSERT HumanResources.Department
(Name, GroupName)
SELECT Name, GroupName
FROM @DepartmentTable

GO
```

After that, I demonstrated declaring a local variable that would contain multiple rows that will be passed to the procedure. The DECLARE statement defines the variable name, followed by the name of the table user-defined type defined earlier in the recipe:

```
DECLARE @StagingDepartmentTable as Department_TT
```

Once declared, I inserted multiple rows into this table, and then passed it as a parameter to the stored procedure call:

```
INSERT @StagingDepartmentTable
(Name, GroupName)
VALUES ('Archivists', 'Accounting')
...

EXEC dbo.usp_INS_Department_NewStyle @StagingDepartmentTable
```

The benefits of this new functionality come into play when you consider procedures that handle business processes. For example, if you have a web site that handles product orders, you can now pass result sets to a single procedure that includes the general header information, along with multiple rows representing the products that were ordered. This application process can be constructed as a single call versus having to issue several calls for each unique product line item ordered. For extremely busy systems, using table-valued parameters allows you to reduce the chatter between the application and the database server, resulting in increased network bandwidth and more efficient batching of transactions on the SQL Server side.

CHAPTER 12

■■■■

Triggers

In this chapter, I'll present recipes for creating and using Data Manipulation Language (DML) and Data Definition Language (DDL) triggers. *DML triggers* contain Transact-SQL code that is used to respond to an INSERT, UPDATE, or DELETE operation against a table or view. *DDL triggers* respond to server or database events instead of data modifications. For example, you can create a DDL trigger that writes to an audit table whenever a database user issues the CREATE TABLE or DROP TABLE command.

■Tip In SQL Server 2008, system stored procedures that perform DDL operations will now fire DDL triggers.

Triggers, when used properly, can provide a convenient automatic response to specific actions. They are appropriate for situations where you must create a business-level response to an action. Triggers should not be used in place of constraints (for example, primary key or unique constraints) because constraints will perform better and are better suited to these operations. You should also be cognizant of the Transact-SQL used to define the trigger, being careful to ensure that the code is properly optimized. If a trigger takes several seconds to execute for each UPDATE, overall performance can suffer.

In my experience, triggers always seem to be the forgotten database object when it comes to troubleshooting performance issues. I'll hear complaints about a poorly performing data modification and spend time trying to optimize it, only to find out that it was a poorly tuned trigger that caused the performance issue. It's one of the major reasons that I use DML triggers sparingly—and when I do use them, I take extra care to make sure they are fast and bug-free. Nonetheless, application requirements may dictate that a DML trigger be used. Not to mention that SQL Server DDL triggers open up a whole new range of functionality not available in previous versions, providing features that can't easily be replaced by other database object types.

In this chapter, I'll review the following topics:

- How to create an AFTER DML trigger
- How to create an INSTEAD OF DML trigger
- How to create a DDL trigger
- How to modify or drop an existing trigger
- How to enable or disable triggers
- How to limit trigger nesting, set the firing order, and control recursion
- How to view trigger metadata
- How to use triggers to respond to logon events

First, however, I'll start off with a background discussion of DML triggers.

Note This chapter covers how to create triggers using Transact-SQL. However, Chapter 13 covers how to create triggers using the new Common Language Runtime (CLR) functionality.

DML Triggers

DML triggers respond to user INSERT, UPDATE, or DELETE operations against a table or a view. When a data modification event occurs, the trigger performs a set of actions defined within the trigger. Similar to stored procedures, triggers are defined in Transact-SQL and allow a full range of activities to be performed.

A DML trigger can be defined specifically as FOR UPDATE, FOR INSERT, FOR DELETE, or any combination of the three. UPDATE triggers respond to modifications against one or more columns within the table, INSERT triggers respond to new data being added to the database, and DELETE triggers respond to data being deleted from the database. There are two types of DML triggers: AFTER and INSTEAD OF.

AFTER triggers are only allowed for tables, and they execute *after* the data modification has been completed against the table. INSTEAD OF triggers execute *instead of* the original data modification and can be created for both tables and views.

DML triggers allow you to perform actions in response to data modifications in a table. For example, you can create a trigger that populates an audit table based on the operation performed, or perhaps use the trigger to decrement the value of a quantity. Although this ability to trigger actions automatically is a powerful feature, there are a few things to keep in mind before your use of triggers proliferates:

- Triggers can often become a hidden and hence forgotten problem. When troubleshooting performance or logical issues, DBAs can forget that triggers are executing in the background. Make sure that your use of triggers is "visible" in your data documentation.

- If you can ensure that all your data modifications flow through a stored procedure, I would strongly recommend you perform all activities within the stored procedure, rather than use a trigger. For example, if you need to update a quantity in a related table, after inserting a sales record, why not put this logic in the stored procedure instead? The advantages are manageability (one place to look) and supportability (one place to troubleshoot), when the procedure needs modifications or performs unexpected actions.

- Always keep performance in mind, and this means writing triggers that execute quickly. Long-running triggers can significantly slow down data modification operations. Take particular care in putting triggers into databases with frequent data modifications.

- Non-logged updates do not cause a DML trigger to fire (for example WRITETEXT, TRUNCATE TABLE, and bulk insert operations).

- Constraints usually run faster than a DML trigger, so if your business requirements can be fulfilled by a constraint, use constraints instead. AFTER triggers run *after* the data modification has already occurred, so they cannot be used to prevent a constraint violation.

- Don't allow result sets from a SELECT statement to be returned within your trigger. Most applications can't consume these in an elegant fashion, and embedded queries can hurt the trigger's performance.

As long as you keep these general guidelines in mind and use them properly, triggers are an excellent means of enforcing business rules in your database.

■**Caution** Some of the triggers demonstrated in the chapter may interfere with existing triggers on the SQL instance and database. If you are following along with the code, be sure to test this functionality only on a development SQL Server environment.

Creating an AFTER DML Trigger

An AFTER DML trigger executes after an INSERT, UPDATE, and/or DELETE modification has been completed successfully against a table. The specific syntax for an AFTER DML trigger is as follows:

```
CREATE TRIGGER [ schema_name . ]trigger_name
ON  table
[ WITH <dml_trigger_option> [ ...,n ] ]
AFTER
{ [ INSERT ] [ , ] [ UPDATE ] [ , ] [ DELETE ] }
[ NOT FOR REPLICATION ]
AS { sql_statement [ ...n ]}
```

Table 12-1 details the arguments of this command.

Table 12-1. *CREATE TRIGGER Arguments*

Argument	Description
[schema_name .]trigger_name	Defines the optional schema owner and required user-defined name of the new trigger.
table	Defines the table name that the trigger applies to.
<dml_trigger_option> [...,n]	Allows you to specify the ENCRYPTION and/or EXECUTE AS clause. ENCRYPTION will encrypt the Transact-SQL definition of the trigger, making it unviewable within the system tables. EXECUTE AS allows you to define the security context that the trigger will be executed under.
[INSERT] [,] [UPDATE] [,] [DELETE]	Defines which DML event or events the trigger will react to, including INSERT, UPDATE, and DELETE. A single trigger can react to one or more of these actions against the table.
NOT FOR REPLICATION	Designates that the trigger should not be executed when a replication modification is performed against the table.
sql_statement [...n]	Allows one or more Transact-SQL statements, which can be used to carry out actions such as performing validations against the DML changes or performing other table DML actions.

Before proceeding to the recipe, it is important to note that SQL Server creates two "virtual" tables that are available specifically for triggers, called the deleted and inserted tables. These two tables capture the before and after pictures of the modified rows. Table 12-2 shows the tables that each DML operation impacts.

Table 12-2. *Inserted and Deleted Virtual Tables*

DML Operation	Inserted Table Holds . . .	Deleted Table Holds . . .
INSERT	Inserted rows	
UPDATE	New rows (rows with updates)	Old rows (pre-update)
DELETE		Deleted rows

The inserted and deleted tables can be used within your trigger to access the data both before and after the data modifications that caused the trigger to fire. These tables will store data for both single and multi-row updates. Be sure to program your triggers with both types of updates (single and multi-row) in mind. For example, a DELETE operation can impact either a single row or 50 rows—so make sure that the trigger is programmed to handle this accordingly.

In this recipe, I demonstrate using a trigger to track row inserts or deletes from the Production. ProductInventory table:

```
USE AdventureWorks
GO

-- Track all Inserts, Updates, and Deletes
CREATE TABLE Production.ProductInventoryAudit
   (ProductID int NOT NULL  ,
    LocationID smallint NOT NULL  ,
    Shelf nvarchar(10) NOT NULL  ,
    Bin tinyint NOT NULL  ,
    Quantity smallint NOT NULL  ,
    rowguid uniqueidentifier NOT NULL  ,
    ModifiedDate datetime NOT NULL  ,
    InsOrUPD char(1) NOT NULL  )
GO

-- Create trigger to populate Production.ProductInventoryAudit table
CREATE TRIGGER Production.trg_uid_ProductInventoryAudit
ON  Production.ProductInventory
AFTER  INSERT, DELETE
AS

SET NOCOUNT ON

-- Inserted rows
INSERT Production.ProductInventoryAudit
(ProductID, LocationID, Shelf, Bin, Quantity,
rowguid, ModifiedDate, InsOrUPD)
SELECT DISTINCT i.ProductID, i.LocationID, i.Shelf, i.Bin, i.Quantity,
i.rowguid, GETDATE(),  'I'
FROM inserted i

-- Deleted rows

INSERT Production.ProductInventoryAudit
(ProductID, LocationID, Shelf, Bin, Quantity,
rowguid, ModifiedDate, InsOrUPD)
SELECT d.ProductID, d.LocationID, d.Shelf, d.Bin, d.Quantity,
d.rowguid, GETDATE(), 'D'
FROM deleted d
```

```
GO

-- Insert a new row
INSERT Production.ProductInventory
(ProductID, LocationID, Shelf, Bin, Quantity)
VALUES (316, 6, 'A', 4, 22)

-- Delete a row

DELETE Production.ProductInventory
WHERE ProductID = 316 AND
    LocationID = 6

-- Check the audit table
SELECT ProductID, LocationID, InsOrUpd
FROM Production.ProductInventoryAudit
```

This returns

ProductID	LocationID	InsOrUpd
316	6	I
316	6	D

How It Works

This recipe started off by having you create a new table for holding inserted or deleted rows from the Production.ProductInventory table. The new table's schema matches the original table, only this time a new column was added called InsOrUPD to indicate whether the row was an INSERT or UPDATE operation:

```
CREATE TABLE Production.ProductInventoryAudit
    (ProductID int NOT NULL   ,
      LocationID smallint NOT NULL   ,
      Shelf nvarchar(10) NOT NULL   ,
      Bin tinyint NOT NULL   ,
      Quantity smallint NOT NULL   ,
      rowguid uniqueidentifier NOT NULL   ,
      ModifiedDate datetime NOT NULL   ,
      InsOrUPD char(1) NOT NULL   )
GO
```

Next, an AFTER DML trigger is created using CREATE TRIGGER. The owning schema and new trigger name is designated in the first line of the statement:

```
CREATE TRIGGER Production.trg_uid_ProductInventoryAudit
```

The table (which when updated will cause the trigger to fire) is designated in the ON clause:

```
ON  Production.ProductInventory
```

Two types of DML activity will be monitored, inserts and deletes:

```
AFTER  INSERT, DELETE
```

The body of the trigger begins after the AS keyword:

```
AS
```

The SET NOCOUNT is set ON in order to suppress the "rows affected" messages from being returned back to the calling application whenever the trigger is fired:

```
SET NOCOUNT ON
```

The first statement inserts a new row into the new audit table for rows that exist in the virtual inserted table:

```
INSERT Production.ProductInventoryAudit
(ProductID, LocationID, Shelf, Bin, Quantity,
rowguid, ModifiedDate, InsOrUPD)
SELECT DISTINCT i.ProductID, i.LocationID, i.Shelf, i.Bin, i.Quantity,
i.rowguid, GETDATE(), 'I'
FROM inserted i
```

The second statement inserts a new row into the new audit table for rows that exist in the virtual deleted table, but not the inserted table:

```
INSERT Production.ProductInventoryAudit
(ProductID, LocationID, Shelf, Bin, Quantity,
rowguid, ModifiedDate, InsOrUPD)
SELECT d.ProductID, d.LocationID, d.Shelf, d.Bin, d.Quantity,
d.rowguid, GETDATE(), 'D'
FROM deleted d

GO
```

After creating the trigger, in order to test it, a new row was inserted into the Production.ProductInventory table and then deleted right afterwards:

```
-- Insert a new row
INSERT Production.ProductInventory
(ProductID, LocationID, Shelf, Bin, Quantity)
VALUES (316, 6, 'A', 4, 22)

-- Delete a row

DELETE Production.ProductInventory
WHERE ProductID = 316 AND
    LocationID = 6
```

As you can see, a query was executed against the audit table, and there were two rows tracking the insert and delete activities against the Production.ProductInventory table:

```
SELECT ProductID, LocationID, InsOrUpd
FROM Production.ProductInventoryAudit
```

Creating an INSTEAD OF DML Trigger

INSTEAD OF DML triggers execute *instead of* the original data modification that fired the trigger and are allowed for both tables and views. INSTEAD OF triggers are often used to handle data modifications to views that do not allow for data modifications (see Chapter 7 for a review of what rules a view must follow in order to be updateable).

DML triggers use the following syntax:

```
CREATE TRIGGER [ schema_name . ]trigger_name
ON { table | view }
[ WITH <dml_trigger_option> [ ...,n ] ]
INSTEAD OF
```

```
{ [ INSERT ] [ , ] [ UPDATE ] [ , ] [ DELETE ] }
[ NOT FOR REPLICATION ]
AS { sql_statement [ ...n ] }
```

Table 12-3 details the arguments of this command.

Table 12-3. *INSTEAD OF Trigger Arguments*

Argument	Description
[schema_name .]trigger_name	Defines the optional schema owner and required user-defined name of the new trigger.
table | view	Defines the name of the table or view that the trigger applies to.
<dml_trigger_option> [...,n]	Allows you to specify the ENCRYPTION and/or EXECUTE AS clause. ENCRYPTION will encrypt the Transact-SQL definition of the trigger. EXECUTE AS allows you to define the security context under which the trigger will be executed.
[INSERT] [,] [UPDATE] [,] [DELETE]	Defines which DML event or events the trigger will react to, including INSERT, UPDATE, and DELETE. A single trigger can react to one or more of these actions against the table.
NOT FOR REPLICATION	Designates that the trigger should not be executed when a replication modification is performed against the table.
sql_statement [...n]	Allows one or more Transact-SQL statements, which can be used to carry out actions such as performing validations against the DML changes or performing other table DML actions. These statements perform actions instead of the specified DML operation that fired the trigger code.

In this recipe, I'll create a new table that will hold "pending approval" rows for the HumanResources.Department table. These are new departments that require manager approval before being added to the actual table. A view will be created to display all "approved" and "pending approval" departments from the two tables, and an INSTEAD OF trigger will be created on the view for inserts, causing inserts to be routed to the new approval table, instead of the actual HumanResources.Department table:

```
USE AdventureWorks
GO

-- Create Department "Approval" table
CREATE TABLE HumanResources.DepartmentApproval
   (Name nvarchar(50) NOT NULL UNIQUE,
     GroupName nvarchar(50) NOT NULL,
     ModifiedDate datetime NOT NULL DEFAULT GETDATE())
GO


-- Create view to see both approved and pending approval departments
CREATE VIEW HumanResources.vw_Department
AS
```

```
SELECT Name, GroupName, ModifiedDate, 'Approved' Status
FROM HumanResources.Department
UNION
SELECT Name, GroupName, ModifiedDate, 'Pending Approval' Status
FROM HumanResources.DepartmentApproval

GO

-- Create an INSTEAD OF trigger on the new view
CREATE TRIGGER HumanResources.trg_vw_Department
ON HumanResources.vw_Department
INSTEAD OF
INSERT
AS

SET NOCOUNT ON
INSERT HumanResources.DepartmentApproval
(Name, GroupName)
SELECT i.Name, i.GroupName
FROM inserted i
WHERE i.Name NOT IN (SELECT Name FROM HumanResources.DepartmentApproval)

GO


-- Insert into the new view, even though view is a UNION
-- of two different tables
INSERT HumanResources.vw_Department
(Name, GroupName)
VALUES ('Print Production', 'Manufacturing')


-- Check the view's contents
SELECT Status, Name
FROM  HumanResources.vw_Department
WHERE GroupName = 'Manufacturing'
```

This returns the following result set:

Status	Name
Approved	Production
Approved	Production Control
Pending Approval	Print Production

How It Works

The recipe began by creating a separate table to hold "pending approval" department rows:

```
CREATE TABLE HumanResources.DepartmentApproval
   (Name nvarchar(50) NOT NULL UNIQUE,
    GroupName nvarchar(50) NOT NULL,
    ModifiedDate datetime NOT NULL DEFAULT GETDATE())
```

Next, a view was created to display both "approved" and "pending approval" departments:

```
CREATE VIEW HumanResources.vw_Department
AS

SELECT Name, GroupName, ModifiedDate, 'Approved' Status
FROM HumanResources.Department
UNION
SELECT Name, GroupName, ModifiedDate, 'Pending Approval' Status
FROM HumanResources.DepartmentApproval

GO
```

The UNION in the CREATE VIEW prevents this view from being updateable, as any inserts against it will be ambiguous. INSTEAD OF triggers allow you to enable data modifications against non-updateable views.

A trigger was created to react to INSERTs, routing them to the approval table so long as the department name was unique:

```
CREATE TRIGGER HumanResources.trg_vw_Department
ON HumanResources.vw_Department
INSTEAD OF
INSERT
AS

SET NOCOUNT ON
INSERT HumanResources.DepartmentApproval
(Name, GroupName)
SELECT i.Name, i.GroupName
FROM inserted i
WHERE i.Name NOT IN (SELECT Name FROM HumanResources.DepartmentApproval)
```

A new INSERT was tested against the view to see if it would be inserted in the approval table:

```
INSERT HumanResources.vw_Department
(Name, GroupName)
VALUES ('Print Production', 'Manufacturing')
```

The view was then queried, showing that the row was inserted, and displayed a "pending approval status."

Handling Transactions Within DML Triggers

In this recipe, I'll demonstrate the use of DML triggers and their interactions with transactions—both within the trigger and within the initiating event that caused the trigger to fire. For these examples, we'll be working with the objects created in the "Creating an AFTER DML Trigger" recipe.

When a trigger is fired, SQL Server always creates a transaction around it, allowing any changes made by the firing trigger, or the caller, to roll back to the previous state. For example, the trg_uid_ProductInventoryAudit trigger has been rewritten to fail if certain Shelf or Quantity values are encountered. If they are, ROLLBACK is used to cancel the trigger and undo any changes:

```
USE AdventureWorks
GO

-- Remove trigger if one already exists with same name
IF  EXISTS
(SELECT 1
 FROM sys.triggers
 WHERE object_id =
   OBJECT_ID(N'[Production].[trg_uid_ProductInventoryAudit]'))
```

```
DROP TRIGGER [Production].[trg_uid_ProductInventoryAudit]
GO

CREATE TRIGGER Production.trg_uid_ProductInventoryAudit
ON  Production.ProductInventory
AFTER  INSERT, DELETE
AS

SET NOCOUNT ON

IF EXISTS
(SELECT Shelf
FROM inserted
WHERE Shelf = 'A')
BEGIN
    PRINT 'Shelf ''A'' is closed for new inventory.'
    ROLLBACK
END

-- Inserted rows
INSERT Production.ProductInventoryAudit
(ProductID, LocationID, Shelf, Bin, Quantity,
rowguid, ModifiedDate, InsOrUPD)
SELECT DISTINCT i.ProductID, i.LocationID, i.Shelf, i.Bin, i.Quantity,
i.rowguid, GETDATE(), 'I'
FROM inserted i

-- Deleted rows

INSERT Production.ProductInventoryAudit
(ProductID, LocationID, Shelf, Bin, Quantity,
rowguid, ModifiedDate, InsOrUPD)
SELECT d.ProductID, d.LocationID, d.Shelf, d.Bin, d.Quantity,
d.rowguid, GETDATE(), 'D'
FROM deleted d

IF EXISTS
(SELECT Quantity
FROM deleted
WHERE Quantity > 0)
BEGIN
    PRINT 'You cannot remove positive quantity rows!'
    ROLLBACK
END

GO
```

Now I'll attempt an insert of a row using Shelf "A":

```
INSERT Production.ProductInventory
(ProductID, LocationID, Shelf, Bin, Quantity)
VALUES (316, 6, 'A', 4, 22)
```

Because this is not allowed based on the trigger logic, the trigger neither inserts a row into the audit table nor allows the calling INSERT:

```
Shelf 'A' is closed for new inventory.
Msg 3609, Level 16, State 1, Line 2
The transaction ended in the trigger. The batch has been aborted.
```

In the previous example, the INSERT that caused the trigger to fire didn't use an explicit transaction; however, the operation was still rolled back. This next example demonstrates two deletions, one that is allowed (according to the rules of the trigger) and another that is not allowed. Both inserts are embedded within an explicit transaction:

```
BEGIN TRANSACTION

-- Deleting a row with a zero quantity
DELETE Production.ProductInventory
WHERE ProductID = 853 AND
   LocationID = 7

-- Deleting a row with a non-zero quantity
DELETE Production.ProductInventory
WHERE ProductID = 999 AND
   LocationID = 60

COMMIT TRANSACTION
```

This returns the following output:

```
(1 row(s) affected)
You cannot remove positive quantity rows!
Msg 3609, Level 16, State 1, Line 9
The transaction ended in the trigger. The batch has been aborted.
```

Because the trigger issued a rollback, the outer transaction is also invalidated (meaning that it doesn't remain open). Also, even though the first row was a valid deletion, because they were in the same calling transaction, neither row was deleted:

```
SELECT ProductID, LocationID
FROM Production.ProductInventory
WHERE (ProductID = 853 AND
   LocationID = 7) OR
(ProductID = 999 AND
   LocationID = 60)
```

This returns

```
ProductID    LocationID
853          7
999          60
```

How It Works

This recipe demonstrated the interaction between triggers and transactions. In a nutshell, if your trigger issues a ROLLBACK command, any data modifications performed by the trigger or the rest of the statements in the transaction are undone. The Transact-SQL query or batch that invoked the trigger in the first place will also be cancelled and rolled back. If the invoking caller was embedded in an explicit transaction, the entire calling transaction is cancelled and rolled back. If you use explicit transactions within a trigger, SQL Server will treat it like a nested transaction. As I mentioned in Chapter 3, a ROLLBACK rolls back all transactions, no matter how many levels deep they may be nested.

Controlling DML Triggers Based on Modified Columns

When a trigger is fired, you can determine which columns have been modified by using the UPDATE function.

UPDATE, not to be confused with the DML command, returns a TRUE value if an INSERT or DML UPDATE has occurred against a column. For example, the following DML UPDATE trigger checks to see whether a specific column has been modified, and if so, returns an error and rolls back the modification:

```
USE AdventureWorks
GO

CREATE TRIGGER HumanResources.trg_U_Department
ON   HumanResources.Department
AFTER   UPDATE
AS

IF UPDATE(GroupName)
BEGIN
    PRINT 'Updates to GroupName require DBA involvement.'
    ROLLBACK
END
GO
```

An attempt is made to update a GroupName value in this next query:

```
UPDATE HumanResources.Department
SET GroupName = 'Research and Development'
WHERE DepartmentID = 10
```

This returns the warning message and error telling us that the batch has been aborted (no updates made):

```
Updates to GroupName require DBA involvement.
Msg 3609, Level 16, State 1, Line 1
The transaction ended in the trigger. The batch has been aborted.
```

How It Works

When your trigger logic is aimed at more granular, column-based changes, use the UPDATE function and conditional processing to ensure that code is only executed against specific columns. Embedding the logic in conditional processing can help reduce the overhead each time the trigger fires—at least for columns that may be unrelated to the purpose of the trigger.

Viewing DML Trigger Metadata

This next recipe demonstrates how to view information about the triggers in the current database.

The first example queries the `sys.triggers` catalog view, returning the name of the view or table, the associated trigger name, whether the trigger is `INSTEAD OF`, and whether the trigger is disabled:

```
-- Show the DML triggers in the current database
SELECT OBJECT_NAME(parent_id) Table_or_ViewNM,
       name TriggerNM,
       is_instead_of_trigger,
       is_disabled
FROM sys.triggers
WHERE parent_class_desc = 'OBJECT_OR_COLUMN'
ORDER BY OBJECT_NAME(parent_id), name
```

This returns the following (abridged) results:

Table_or_ViewNM	TriggerNM	is_instead_of_trigger	is_disabled
Department	trg_U_Department	0	0
Employee	dEmployee	1	0
Person	iuPerson	0	0
…			
Vendor	dVendor	1	0
vw_Department	trg_vw_Department	1	0
WorkOrder	iWorkOrder	0	0
WorkOrder	uWorkOrder	0	0

To display a specific trigger's Transact-SQL definition, you can query the `sys.sql_modules` system catalog view:

```
-- Displays the trigger SQL definition
--(if the trigger is not encrypted)
SELECT o.name, m.definition
FROM sys.sql_modules m
INNER JOIN sys.objects o ON
    m.object_id = o.object_id
WHERE o.type = 'TR'
```

How It Works

The first query in this recipe queried the `sys.triggers` catalog view to show all the DML triggers in the current database. There are DDL triggers in the `sys.triggers` catalog view too, so to prevent them from being displayed in the results, the `parent_class_desc` was qualified to `OBJECT_OR_COLUMN`. This is because DDL triggers, as you'll see in the next section, are scoped at the database or SQL Server instance level—and not at the schema scope.

The second query showed the actual Transact-SQL trigger name and definition of each trigger in the database. If the trigger was encrypted (similar to an encrypted view or stored procedure, for example), the trigger definition will display a `NULL` value in this query.

DDL Triggers

DDL triggers respond to server or database events, rather than table data modifications. For example, you can create a DDL trigger that writes to an audit table whenever a database user issues the CREATE TABLE or DROP TABLE command. Or, at the server level, you can create a DDL trigger that responds to the creation of a new login (for example, preventing a certain login from being created).

■**Tip** In SQL Server 2008, system stored procedures that perform DDL operations will now fire DDL triggers. For example, sp_create_plan_guide and sp_control_plan_guide will fire the CREATE_PLAN_GUIDE event.

Database DDL triggers are stored as objects within the database they were created in, whereas Server DDL triggers, which track changes at the server level, are stored in the master database.

The syntax for a DDL trigger is as follows:

```
CREATE TRIGGER trigger_name
ON { ALL SERVER | DATABASE }
[ WITH <ddl_trigger_option> [ ...,n ] ]
FOR { event_type | event_group } [ ,...n ]
AS { sql_statement [ ...n ]}
```

Table 12-4 details the arguments of this command.

Table 12-4. *CREATE TRIGGER (DDL) Arguments*

Argument	Description
trigger_name	This argument is the user-defined name of the new DDL trigger (notice that a DDL trigger does not have an owning schema, since it isn't related to an actual database table or view).
ALL SERVER | DATABASE	This argument designates whether the DDL trigger will respond to server-scoped (ALL SERVER) or DATABASE-scoped events.
<ddl_trigger_option> [...,n]	This argument allows you to specify the ENCRYPTION and/or EXECUTE AS clause. ENCRYPTION will encrypt the Transact-SQL definition of the trigger. EXECUTE AS allows you to define the security context under which the trigger will be executed.
{ event_type | event_group } [,...n]	An event_type indicates a single DDL server or database event that can be reacted to by the trigger: for example, CREATE_TABLE, ALTER_TABLE, DROP_INDEX, and more. An event_group is a logical grouping of event_type events. A single DDL trigger can be created to react against one or more event types or groups. For example, the DDL_PARTITION_FUNCTION_EVENTS group reacts to the following individual events: CREATE_PARTITION_FUNCTION, ALTER_PARTITION_FUNCTION, and DROP_PARTITION_FUNCTION. You can find a complete list of trigger event types in the SQL Server Books Online topic "DDL Events for Use with DDL Triggers" and a complete list of trigger event groups in the SQL Server Books Online topic "Event Groups for Use with DDL Triggers."
sql_statement [...n]	This argument defines one or more Transact-SQL statements that can be used to carry out actions in response to the DDL database or server event.

Creating a DDL Trigger That Audits Database-Level Events

This recipe demonstrates creating an audit table that can contain information on any attempts at the creation, alteration, or dropping of indexes in the AdventureWorks database.

First, I'll create the audit table:

```
USE master
GO

CREATE TABLE dbo.ChangeAttempt
    (EventData xml NOT NULL,
      AttemptDate datetime NOT NULL DEFAULT GETDATE(),
      DBUser char(50) NOT NULL)
GO
```

Next, I'll create a database DDL trigger to track index operations, inserting the event data to the newly created table:

```
CREATE TRIGGER db_trg_RestrictINDEXChanges
ON DATABASE
FOR CREATE_INDEX, ALTER_INDEX, DROP_INDEX
AS

SET NOCOUNT ON

INSERT dbo.ChangeAttempt
(EventData, DBUser)
VALUES (EVENTDATA(), USER)

GO
```

Now I'll attempt an actual index creation in the database:

```
CREATE NONCLUSTERED INDEX ni_ChangeAttempt_DBUser ON
    dbo.ChangeAttempt(DBUser)
GO
```

Next, I'll query the ChangeAttempt audit table to see whether the new index creation event was captured by the trigger:

```
SELECT EventData
FROM dbo.ChangeAttempt
```

This returns the actual event information, stored in XML format (see Chapter 14 for more information on XML in SQL Server):

```
<EVENT_INSTANCE>
  <EventType>CREATE_INDEX</EventType>
  <PostTime>2008-02-26T11:29:38.480</PostTime>
  <SPID>53</SPID>
  <ServerName>CAESAR\AUGUSTUS</ServerName>
  <LoginName>CAESAR\Administrator</LoginName>
  <UserName>dbo</UserName>
  <DatabaseName>AdventureWorks</DatabaseName>
  <SchemaName>dbo</SchemaName>
  <ObjectName>ni_ChangeAttempt_DBUser</ObjectName>
  <ObjectType>INDEX</ObjectType>
  <TargetObjectName>ChangeAttempt</TargetObjectName>
  <TargetObjectType>TABLE</TargetObjectType>
  <TSQLCommand>
```

```
      <SetOptions ANSI_NULLS="ON" ANSI_NULL_DEFAULT="ON"
       ANSI_PADDING="ON" QUOTED_IDENTIFIER="ON" ENCRYPTED="FALSE" />
      <CommandText>CREATE NONCLUSTERED INDEX ni_ChangeAttempt_DBUser ON
       dbo.ChangeAttempt(DBUser)
</CommandText>
    </TSQLCommand>
  </EVENT_INSTANCE>
```

How It Works

The recipe began with creating a table that could contain audit information on index modification and login creation attempts. The EventData column uses SQL Server's xml data type, which was populated by the new EVENTDATA function (described later on in this recipe):

```
CREATE TABLE dbo.ChangeAttempt
    (EventData xml NOT NULL,
    AttemptDate datetime NOT NULL DEFAULT GETDATE(),
    DBUser char(50) NOT NULL)
GO
```

The first trigger created in the recipe applied to the current database. The new DDL trigger responded to CREATE INDEX, ALTER INDEX, or DROP INDEX commands:

```
CREATE TRIGGER db_trg_RestrictINDEXChanges
ON DATABASE
FOR CREATE_INDEX, ALTER_INDEX, DROP_INDEX
AS
```

The SET NOCOUNT command was used in the trigger to suppress the number of row-affected messages from SQL Server (otherwise every time you make an index modification, you'll see a "1 row affected" message):

```
SET NOCOUNT ON
```

An INSERT was then made to the new audit table, populating it with the event data and user:

```
INSERT dbo.ChangeAttempt
(EventData, DBUser)
VALUES (EVENTDATA(), USER)
```

```
GO
```

The EVENTDATA function returns server and data event information in an XML format, and is also used for SQL Server's SQL Service Broker functionality.

■**Note** See Chapter 20 for more information on event notifications.

The XML data captured by the EVENTDATA function included useful information such as the event, the login name that attempted the CREATE INDEX, the target object name, and the time that it occurred.

Creating a DDL Trigger That Audits Server-Level Events

In this recipe, I demonstrate using a server-level DDL trigger to restrict users from creating new logins on the SQL Server instance.

I'll start by creating the DDL trigger:

```
USE master
GO

-- Disallow new Logins on the SQL instance
CREATE TRIGGER srv_trg_RestrictNewLogins
ON ALL SERVER
FOR CREATE_LOGIN
AS
PRINT 'No login creations without DBA involvement.'

    ROLLBACK
GO
```

Next, an attempt is made to add a new SQL login:

```
CREATE LOGIN JoeS WITH PASSWORD = 'A235921'
GO
```

This returns

```
No login creations without DBA involvement.
Msg 3609, Level 16, State 2, Line 1
The transaction ended in the trigger. The batch has been aborted.
```

I discuss the DROP TRIGGER command in the "Dropping a Trigger" recipe later in the chapter; however, following is the cleanup code to remove this trigger:

```
DROP TRIGGER srv_trg_RestrictNewLogins
ON ALL SERVER
```

How It Works

This recipe demonstrated using a server-level DDL trigger to restrict a SQL login from being created. The FOR statement of the trigger was set to the CREATE LOGIN event:

```
CREATE TRIGGER srv_trg_RestrictNewLogins
ON ALL SERVER
FOR CREATE_LOGIN
AS
```

The body of the trigger used a PRINT statement to warn end users that their attempt was not allowed:

```
PRINT 'No login creations without DBA involvement.'
```

This was followed by a ROLLBACK, which cancels the CREATE LOGIN attempt from the trigger:

```
    ROLLBACK
GO
```

Using a Logon Trigger

Logon triggers fire synchronously in response to a logon event to the SQL Server instance. You can use logon triggers to create reactions to specific logon events or simply to track information about a logon event.

■**Caution** Be very careful about how you design your logon trigger. Test it out in a development environment first before deploying to production. If you are using a logon trigger to restrict entry to the SQL Server instance, be careful that you do not restrict all access.

In this recipe, I'll demonstrate creating a logon trigger that restricts a login from accessing SQL Server during certain time periods. I'll also log the logon attempt in a separate table.

First, I'll create the new login:

```
CREATE LOGIN nightworker WITH PASSWORD = 'E74A53C6'
GO
```

Next, I'll create an audit database and a table to track the logon attempts:

```
CREATE DATABASE ExampleAuditDB
GO

USE ExampleAuditDB
GO

CREATE TABLE dbo.RestrictedLogonAttempt
   (LoginNM sysname NOT NULL,
    AttemptDT datetime NOT NULL)
GO
```

I'll now create the logon trigger to restrict the new login from logon from 7:00 a.m. to 5:00 p.m:

```
USE master
GO

CREATE TRIGGER trg_logon_attempt
ON ALL SERVER
WITH EXECUTE AS 'sa'
FOR LOGON
AS
BEGIN

IF ORIGINAL_LOGIN()='nightworker' AND
   DATEPART(hh,GETDATE()) BETWEEN 7 AND 17
   BEGIN
      ROLLBACK
      INSERT ExampleAuditDB.dbo.RestrictedLogonAttempt
      (LoginNM, AttemptDT)
      VALUES (ORIGINAL_LOGIN(), GETDATE())
   END
END
GO
```

Now attempt to log on as the nightworker login during the specified time range, and you will see the following error message:

```
Logon failed for login 'nightworker' due to trigger execution.
```

After the attempt, I'll query the audit table to see if the logon was tracked:

```
SELECT LoginNM, AttemptDT
FROM ExampleAuditDB.dbo.RestrictedLogonAttempt
```

This returns the following (results will vary based on when you execute this recipe yourself):

```
LoginNM         AttemptDT
nightworker     2008-2-26 11:37:15.127
```

How It Works

Logon triggers allow you to restrict and track logon activity after authentication to the SQL Server instance but before an actual session is generated. If you wish to apply custom business rules to logons above and beyond what is offered within the SQL Server feature set, you can implement them using the logon trigger.

In this recipe, I created a test login, a new auditing database, and an auditing table to track attempts. In the master database, I created a logon trigger. Stepping through the code, note that ALL SERVER is used to set the scope of the trigger execution:

```
CREATE TRIGGER trg_logon_attempt
ON ALL SERVER
```

The EXECUTE AS clause is used to define the permissions under which the trigger will execute. I could have used a lesser login—for example, a login that had permissions to write to the audit table:

```
WITH EXECUTE AS 'sa'
```

The FOR LOGON keywords designated the type of trigger I am creating:

```
FOR LOGON
AS
```

The body of the trigger logic then started at the BEGIN keyword:

```
BEGIN
```

The original security context of the logon attempt was then evaluated. In this case, I am only interested in enforcing logic if the login is for nightworker:

```
IF ORIGINAL_LOGIN()='nightworker' AND
```

Included in this logic is an evaluation of the hour of the day. If the current time is between 7 a.m. and 5 p.m., two actions will be performed:

```
DATEPART(hh,GETDATE()) BETWEEN 7 AND 17
BEGIN
```

The first action is to roll back the logon attempt:

```
    ROLLBACK
```

The second action is to track the attempt to the audit table:

```
    INSERT  ExampleAuditDB.dbo.RestrictedLogonAttempt
    (LoginNM, AttemptDT)
    VALUES (ORIGINAL_LOGIN(), GETDATE())
```

```
        END
END
GO
```

Again, it is worthwhile to remind you that how you code the logic of a logon trigger is very important. Improper logging can cause unexpected results. Also, if your logon trigger isn't performing the actions you expect, be sure to check out your latest SQL log for clues. Logon trigger attempts that are rolled back also get written to the SQL log. If something was miscoded in the trigger, for example, if I hadn't designated the proper fully qualified table name for `RestrictedLogonAttempt`, the SQL log would have shown the error message "Invalid object name 'dbo.RestrictedLogon-Attempt'."

Note Don't forget about removing this recipe's trigger when you are finished testing it out. To drop it, execute `DROP TRIGGER trg_logon_attempt ON ALL SERVER` in the master database.

Viewing DDL Trigger Metadata

In this recipe, I demonstrate the retrieval of DDL trigger metadata.

The first example queries the `sys.triggers` catalog view, returning the associated *database-scoped* trigger name and trigger enabled/disabled status:

```
USE AdventureWorks
GO

-- Show the DML triggers in the current database
SELECT name TriggerNM, is_disabled
FROM sys.triggers
WHERE parent_class_desc = 'DATABASE'
ORDER BY OBJECT_NAME(parent_id), name
```

This returns the following (abridged) results:

TriggerNM	is_disabled
ddlDatabaseTriggerLog	1

This next example queries the `sys.server_triggers` and `sys.server_trigger_events` system catalog views to retrieve a list of server-scoped DDL triggers. This returns the name of the DDL trigger, the type of trigger (Transact-SQL or CLR), the disabled state of the trigger, and the events the trigger is fired off of (you'll see one row for each event a trigger is based on):

```
SELECT name, s.type_desc SQL_or_CLR,
is_disabled, e.type_desc FiringEvents
FROM sys.server_triggers s
INNER JOIN sys.server_trigger_events  e ON
   s.object_id = e.object_id
```

This returns data based on the previous server-level trigger created earlier:

name	SQL_or_CLR	is_disabled	FiringEvents
trg_logon_attempt	SQL_TRIGGER	0	LOGON

To display *database-scoped* DDL trigger Transact-SQL definitions, you can query the `sys.sql_modules` system catalog view:

```
SELECT t.name, m.Definition
FROM sys.triggers AS t
INNER JOIN sys.sql_modules m ON
t.object_id = m.object_id
WHERE t.parent_class_desc = 'DATABASE'
```

To display *server-scoped* DDL triggers, you can query the sys.server_sql_modules and
sys.server_triggers system catalog views:

```
SELECT t.name, m.definition
FROM sys.server_sql_modules m
INNER JOIN sys.server_triggers t ON
   m.object_id = t.object_id
```

How It Works

The first query in this recipe returns a list of database-scoped triggers using the sys.triggers
system catalog view. In order to only display DDL database-scoped triggers, I had to qualify the
parent_class_desc value to DATABASE. The second query was written to return a list of server-scoped
triggers and their associated triggering events. In that situation, the sys.server_triggers and
sys.server_trigger_events system catalogs were queried.

The third query was used to return the Transact-SQL definitions of database-scoped triggers by
qualifying sys.triggers to sys.sql_modules. To return server-scoped trigger Transact-SQL definitions, the sys.server_sql_modules and sys.server_triggers system catalog views were queried.

Managing Triggers

The next set of recipes demonstrate how to modify, drop, enable, disable, and control trigger
options. Some of the commands I'll be demonstrating include ALTER TRIGGER to modify a trigger's
definition, DROP TRIGGER to remove it from the database, ALTER DATABASE to set trigger recursion
options, sp_configure to control trigger nesting, and sp_settriggerorder to set the firing order of a
trigger.

Modifying a Trigger

You can modify an existing DDL or DML trigger by using the ALTER TRIGGER command. ALTER
TRIGGER takes the same arguments as the associated DML or DDL CREATE TRIGGER syntax does.

In this example, I modify a trigger created in the previous recipe (that trigger was dropped earlier in the chapter for cleanup purposes, so you can re-create it for demonstration purposes here).
Instead of restricting users from creating new logins, the login event will be allowed, followed by a
warning and an INSERT into an auditing table:

```
USE master
GO

ALTER TRIGGER srv_trg_RestrictNewLogins
ON ALL SERVER
FOR CREATE_LOGIN
AS

SET NOCOUNT ON

PRINT 'Your login creation is being monitored.'
```

```
INSERT AdventureWorks.dbo.ChangeAttempt
(EventData, DBUser)
VALUES (EVENTDATA(), USER)

GO
```

How It Works

ALTER TRIGGER allows you to modify existing DDL or DML triggers. The arguments for ALTER TRIGGER are the same as for CREATE TRIGGER. You can't use it to change the actual trigger name, however, so in this example, the trigger name is no longer applicable to the actual actions the DDL trigger will take (in this case just monitoring, no longer restricting new logins).

Enabling and Disabling Table Triggers

Sometimes triggers must be disabled if they are causing problems that you need to troubleshoot, or if you need to import or recover data that shouldn't fire the trigger. In this recipe, I demonstrate how to disable a trigger from firing using the DISABLE TRIGGER command, as well as how to re-enable a trigger using ENABLE TRIGGER.

The syntax for DISABLE TRIGGER is as follows:

```
DISABLE TRIGGER [ schema . ] trigger_name
ON { object_name | DATABASE | SERVER }
```

The syntax for enabling a trigger is as follows:

```
ENABLE TRIGGER [ schema_name . ] trigger_name
ON { object_name | DATABASE | SERVER }
```

Table 12-5 details the arguments of this command.

Table 12-5. *ENABLE and DISABLE Trigger Arguments*

Argument	Description
[schema_name .]trigger_name	The optional schema owner and required user-defined name of the trigger you want to disable.
object_name	DATABASE	SERVER	object_name is the table or view that the trigger was bound to (if it's a DML trigger). Use DATABASE if the trigger was a DDL database-scoped trigger and SERVER if the trigger was a DDL server-scoped trigger.

This example starts off by creating a trigger (which is enabled by default) that prints a message back to a connection that is performing an INSERT against the HumanResources.Department table:

```
USE AdventureWorks
GO

CREATE TRIGGER HumanResources.trg_Department
ON  HumanResources.Department
AFTER  INSERT
AS

PRINT 'The trg_Department trigger was fired'

GO
```

The trigger is then disabled using the `DISABLE TRIGGER` command:

```
DISABLE TRIGGER HumanResources.trg_Department
ON HumanResources.Department
```

Because the trigger was disabled, no printed message will be returned when the following `INSERT` is executed:

```
INSERT HumanResources.Department
(Name, GroupName)
VALUES ('Construction', 'Building Services')
```

This returns

```
(1 row(s) affected)
```

Next, the trigger is enabled using the `ENABLE TRIGGER` command:

```
ENABLE TRIGGER HumanResources.trg_Department
ON HumanResources.Department
```

Now when another `INSERT` is attempted, the trigger will fire, returning a message back to the connection:

```
INSERT HumanResources.Department
(Name, GroupName)
VALUES ('Cleaning', 'Building Services')
```

This returns

```
The trg_Department trigger was fired

(1 row(s) affected)
```

How It Works

This recipe started by creating a new trigger that printed a statement whenever a new row was inserted into the `HumanResources.Department` table.

After creating the trigger, the `DISABLE TRIGGER` command was used to keep it from firing (although the trigger's definition still stays in the database):

```
DISABLE TRIGGER HumanResources.trg_Department
ON HumanResources.Department
```

An insert was then performed that did not fire the trigger. The `ENABLE TRIGGER` command was then executed, and then another insert was attempted, this time firing off the trigger.

Limiting Trigger Nesting

Trigger nesting occurs when a trigger is fired, which performs an action (for example, inserting into a different table), which in turn fires another trigger, which then initiates the firing of other triggers. An infinite loop firing of triggers is prevented by SQL Server's maximum level of nesting, which is 32 levels deep.

You can also modify the SQL Server instance to not allow trigger nesting at all. Disabling the `nested triggers` option prevents any `AFTER` trigger from causing the firing of another trigger.

This example demonstrates how to disable or enable this behavior:

```
USE master
GO

-- Disable nesting
EXEC sp_configure 'nested triggers', 0
RECONFIGURE WITH OVERRIDE
GO

-- Enable nesting
EXEC sp_configure 'nested triggers', 1
RECONFIGURE WITH OVERRIDE
GO
```

This returns

```
Configuration option 'nested triggers' changed from 1 to 0.
Run the RECONFIGURE statement to install.
Configuration option 'nested triggers' changed from 0 to 1.
Run the RECONFIGURE statement to install.
```

How It Works

This recipe used the sp_configure system stored procedure to change the nested trigger behavior at the server level. To disable nesting altogether, sp_configure was executed for the "nested trigger" server option, followed by the parameter 0, which disables nesting:

```
EXEC sp_configure 'nested triggers', 0
RECONFIGURE WITH OVERRIDE
GO
```

Because server options contain both a current configuration versus an actual runtime configuration value, the RECONFIGURE WITH OVERRIDE command was used to update the runtime value so that it takes effect right away.

In order to enable nesting again, this server option is set back to 1 in the second batch of the recipe.

■**Note** For more information on configuring server options, see Chapter 21.

Controlling Trigger Recursion

Trigger nesting is considered to be recursive if the action performed when a trigger fires causes the *same* trigger to fire again. Recursion can also occur when a trigger's fire impacts a different table, which also has a trigger that impacts the original table, thus causing the trigger to fire again.

You can control whether recursion is allowed by configuring the RECURSIVE_TRIGGERS database option. If you allow recursion, your AFTER triggers will still be impacted by the 32-level nesting limit, preventing an infinite looping situation.

This example demonstrates enabling and disabling this option:

```
-- Allows recursion
ALTER DATABASE AdventureWorks
SET RECURSIVE_TRIGGERS ON
```

```
-- View the db setting
SELECT is_recursive_triggers_on
FROM sys.databases
WHERE name = 'AdventureWorks'

-- Prevents recursion
ALTER DATABASE AdventureWorks
SET RECURSIVE_TRIGGERS OFF

-- View the db setting
SELECT is_recursive_triggers_on
FROM sys.databases
WHERE name = 'AdventureWorks'
```

This returns

```
is_recursive_triggers_on
1

is_recursive_triggers_on
0
```

How It Works

ALTER DATABASE was used to configure database-level options, including whether or not triggers were allowed to fire recursively within the database. The option was enabled by setting RECURSIVE_TRIGGERS ON:

```
ALTER DATABASE AdventureWorks
SET RECURSIVE_TRIGGERS ON
```

The option was then queried by using the sys.databases system catalog view, which showed the current database option in the is_recursive_triggers_on field (1 for on, 0 for off):

```
SELECT is_recursive_triggers_on
FROM sys.databases
WHERE name = 'AdventureWorks'
```

The recipe then disabled trigger recursion by setting the option OFF, and then confirming it again in a sys.databases query.

■**Note** For more information on ALTER DATABASE and database options, see Chapter 22.

Setting Trigger Firing Order

In general, you should try to consolidate triggers that react to the same event (or events) by placing all their business logic into just one trigger. This improves manageability and supportability of the triggers, because you'll have an easier time finding the code you are looking for, and be able to troubleshoot accordingly. You'll also avoid the issue of trying to figure out which trigger ran first. Instead, you can define multiple triggers on the same table, referencing the same DML types (for example multiple INSERT triggers). DDL triggers can also be set on the same database or server scope events or event groups.

If you find that you must have separate triggers referencing the same database objects (perhaps you've added triggers so as not to overlap a third party's code), and if the order in which they are fired is important to you, you should configure it using the sp_settriggerorder system stored procedure.

The syntax for sp_settriggerorder is as follows:

```
sp_settriggerorder [ @triggername = ] '[ triggerschema. ] triggername'
      , [ @order = ] 'value'
      , [ @stmttype = ] 'statement_type'
      [ , [ @namespace = ] { 'DATABASE' | 'SERVER' | NULL } ]
```

Table 12-6 details the arguments of this command.

Table 12-6. *sp_settriggerorder Arguments*

Argument	Description
'[triggerschema.] triggername'	This defines the optional schema owner and required user-defined name of the trigger to be ordered.
[@order =] 'value'	This can be either First, None, or Last. Any triggers in between these will be fired in a random order after the first and last firings.
[@stmttype =] 'statement_type'	This designates the type of trigger to be ordered, for example, INSERT, UPDATE, DELETE, CREATE_INDEX, ALTER_INDEX, and so forth.
[@namespace =] { 'DATABASE'	'SERVER'	NULL}	This designates whether this is a DDL trigger, and if so, whether it is database- or server-scoped.

This recipe will create a test table and add three DML INSERT triggers to it. The sp_settriggerorder will then be used to define the firing order:

```
CREATE TABLE dbo.TestTriggerOrder
   (TestID int  NOT NULL)
GO

CREATE TRIGGER dbo.trg_i_TestTriggerOrder
ON dbo.TestTriggerOrder
AFTER INSERT
AS
PRINT 'I will be fired first.'
GO

CREATE TRIGGER dbo.trg_i_TestTriggerOrder2
ON dbo.TestTriggerOrder
AFTER INSERT
AS
PRINT 'I will be fired last.'
GO
```

```
CREATE TRIGGER dbo.trg_i_TestTriggerOrder3
ON dbo.TestTriggerOrder
AFTER INSERT
AS
PRINT 'I won''t be first or last.'
GO

EXEC sp_settriggerorder 'trg_i_TestTriggerOrder', 'First', 'INSERT'
EXEC sp_settriggerorder 'trg_i_TestTriggerOrder2', 'Last', 'INSERT'

INSERT dbo.TestTriggerOrder
(TestID)
VALUES (1)
```

This returns

```
I will be fired first.
I won't be first or last.
I will be fired last.
```

How It Works

This recipe started off by creating a single column test table. Three DML INSERT triggers were then added to it. Using sp_settriggerorder, the first and last triggers to fire were defined:

```
EXEC sp_settriggerorder 'trg_i_TestTriggerOrder', 'First', 'INSERT'
EXEC sp_settriggerorder 'trg_i_TestTriggerOrder2', 'Last', 'INSERT'
```

An INSERT was then performed against the table, and the trigger messages were returned in the expected order.

To reiterate this point, if you can, use a single trigger on a table when you can. If you must create multiple triggers of the same type, and your trigger contains ROLLBACK functionality if an error occurs, be sure to set the trigger that has the most likely chance of failing as the first trigger to execute. This way only the first-fired trigger need execute, preventing the other triggers from having to fire and roll back transactions unnecessarily.

Dropping a Trigger

The syntax for dropping a trigger differs by trigger type (DML or DDL).

The syntax for dropping a DML trigger is as follows:

```
DROP TRIGGER schema_name.trigger_name [ ,...n ]
```

Table 12-7 details the argument of this command.

Table 12-7. *DROP TRIGGER Argument (DML)*

Argument	Description
schema_name.trigger_name	The owning schema name of the trigger and the DML trigger name to be removed from the database.

The syntax for dropping a DDL trigger is as follows:

```
DROP TRIGGER trigger_name [ ,...n ]
ON { DATABASE | ALL SERVER }
```

Table 12-8 details the arguments of this command.

Table 12-8. *DROP TRIGGER Arguments (DDL)*

Argument	Description
trigger_name	Defines the DDL trigger name to be removed from the database (for a database-level DDL trigger) or SQL Server instance (for a server-scoped trigger)
DATABASE	ALL SERVER	Defines whether you are removing a DATABASE-scoped DDL trigger or a server-scoped trigger (ALL SERVER)

In the case of both DDL and DML syntax statements, the [,...n] syntax block indicates that more than one trigger can be dropped at the same time.

This example demonstrates dropping a DML and a DDL trigger:

```
-- Drop a DML trigger
DROP TRIGGER dbo.trg_i_TestTriggerOrder

-- Drop multiple DML triggers
DROP TRIGGER dbo.trg_i_TestTriggerOrder2, dbo.trg_i_TestTriggerOrder3

-- Drop a DDL trigger
DROP TRIGGER db_trg_RestrictINDEXChanges
ON DATABASE
```

How It Works

In this recipe, DML and DDL triggers were explicitly dropped using the DROP TRIGGER command. You will also drop all DML triggers when you drop the table or view that they are bound to. You can also remove multiple triggers in the same DROP command if each of the triggers were created using the same ON clause.

CHAPTER 13

■ ■ ■

CLR Integration

Although this book focuses on the Transact-SQL language, there are significant areas of overlap between Common Language Runtime (CLR) and Transact-SQL, which I'll discuss in this chapter, along with a few recipes to get you started.

In some people's eyes, the inclusion of the CLR within the database is the major advancement in SQL Server. As a result of the inclusion, developers don't always have to use Transact-SQL to create procedural database objects such as stored procedures, functions, and triggers. They can now create these objects using any of the .NET languages (VB .NET, C#, C++ and so on) and compile them into .NET *assemblies*. These assemblies are deployed inside the database and run by the CLR, which in turn is hosted inside the SQL Server memory space.

T-SQL, the traditional programming language for the SQL Server database, is a powerful language for data-intensive operations, but is limited in its computational complexity. For these complex operations in the database, the developer traditionally had to resort to the notoriously difficult extended procedures written in C++, or create hideously long and awkward stored procedure code.

In theory, CLR integration offers the "best of both worlds." Your code can be hosted in the secure environment of the database, delegating memory management, garbage collection, and thread support to the robust database engine, while exploiting .NET's computational power, advanced data type support, and rich array of built-in classes.

Although this book is focused on Transact-SQL functionality, I'll still be introducing the basic methods for creating assemblies, importing them into the database, and then associating them to database objects. I'll start off by describing the basic end-to-end steps, and then going into the variations that exist for the different CLR database object types. Discussions and recipes in this chapter include the following:

- A discussion of both when and when not to use assemblies in SQL Server
- Available SQL Server CLR database objects, and how to create them
- A recipe-by-recipe walk-through of creating a CLR stored procedure
- Creating a CLR scalar user-defined function
- Creating a CLR trigger
- Viewing, modifying, and removing assemblies from the database

First, however, I'll begin the chapter with a brief overview of the Common Language Runtime (CLR).

CLR Overview

Before getting too far into the discussion of SQL Server integration, I need to cover some of the basics for those of you who are new to the *.NET Framework*. First of all, the .NET Framework is a programmatic platform that is used to build Microsoft Windows applications and services. This framework can be used to create Windows forms, web services, and ASP.NET applications (to name a few). The major parts of the framework include the CLR, the framework classes and libraries (containing reusable functionality and programming models for your applications to use), and ASP.NET (which allows the creation of web-based applications).

■**Note** Programming in .NET requires the actual Microsoft .NET Framework. This is why Microsoft Windows .NET Framework is a software prerequisite to installing SQL Server.

The *Common Language Runtime* is the environment where .NET programs are actually executed and managed. The CLR is used to execute .NET programs, manage memory, and maintain program metadata. As of SQL Server 2005 and continuing into SQL Server 2008, the CLR is hosted *within* the SQL Server process. This means that reserved space within the SQL Server process handles memory management, security, and execution context.

When you write managed .NET code (code that is executed and managed within the CLR), *assemblies* are the packaged DLL or executable file that is used to deploy the functionality. You can then associate this assembly with various database objects, such as triggers, types, procedures, user-defined functions (UDFs), and so on. Using CLR-based database objects opens up a wide range of functionality, allowing you to perform complex calculations, access data from external sources, integrate with other business applications, and solve problems that cannot be addressed using Transact-SQL.

You can write your assemblies in the .NET language with which you are most comfortable—the two most common being Visual Basic .NET and C# ("c-sharp"). One reason why you can choose your preferred .NET language is because the code is compiled into an *intermediate language* (IL) form first. It's the IL form that is read and executed by the CLR. Code written in C# or VB .NET (short for Visual Basic .NET) that performs the same tasks usually ends up with intermediate language instructions that look almost identical to one another.

Aside from the programming language, you also have your choice in how you actually develop your code. One obvious choice is Visual Studio, which includes templates that can ease the creation of SQL Server database CLR objects. You don't have to use Visual Studio, however, as there are other free open source .NET development environments that you can download off the Web. You can also hand-code your .NET applications in Windows Notepad. Although not ideal for development projects, this method requires no additional software, and it is the method I'll use in this chapter. I'm using this low-tech method in order to keep the focus on CLR integration with Transact-SQL and not get too deeply into the many features and considerations of Visual Studio.

When (and When Not) to Use Assemblies

The announcement of the CLR and .NET Framework integration with SQL Server caused a great deal of conflicting emotions among seasoned SQL Server professionals and developers. At one extreme, people had the vision of an all .NET database environment usurping Transact-SQL entirely. At the other end were the anxious, hardcore database administrators and developers, some without any .NET programming background, many of whom vowed early on to keep this feature locked away indefinitely.

The first and most obvious thing to note is that .NET-based database objects are *not* a replacement for T-SQL-created database objects. Transact-SQL is still very much alive. There are major units of functionality that would be impossible to implement without Transact-SQL, and several .NET constructs and programming models that end up using Transact-SQL under the covers anyway.

There are two main reasons to consider using CLR database objects:

- You have "data-specific" logic that was previously impossible to implement in the database, using existing functionality and T-SQL. Therefore you have created extended stored procedures or modules in the middle tier or client layers.

- You have forced T-SQL to perform a highly complex or calculation intensive task, resulting in complex and inelegant/inefficient Transact-SQL code.

In some ways, the replacement of extended stored procedures with .NET CLR counterparts is the most clear-cut case for using assemblies. In previous versions of SQL Server, if you needed to add functionality to SQL Server that didn't already exist, or needed to access external resources, a common option was to use *extended stored procedures*. Database users called extended stored procedures and optionally passed parameters to them, just as with regular stored procedures. Extended stored procedures could be written in the programming language (such as C++), resulting in a DLL file. The sp_addextendedproc system stored procedure was used to create a new procedure and bind it to the DLL file (which had to exist on the SQL Server instance). The DLL file was not imported into the SQL Server database, so it needed to exist on the SQL Server instance machine. Because a DLL was loaded and used within SQL Server without any special management or protection, there was an increased risk of memory leaks or performance issues, depending on how the DLL code was written. If the DLL misbehaved, SQL Server could crash.

CLR integration addresses several of the inherent issues of extended stored procedures. When using managed code, memory leaks are not possible, and security is fully integrated with the SQL Server environment. In short, assemblies are generally safer to use than extended stored procedures. So if you have

- A database application that must perform very complex calculations that cannot be performed (or are very difficult to perform) using Transact-SQL

- A database application that needs access to functionality that exists in the .NET Framework, but not in Transact-SQL

- A database application that needs access to external data sources (web services, files, system settings), that you cannot access using Transact-SQL

then you may well want to consider assemblies as a potential solution. If you have already deployed such functionality using extended stored procedures in your system, then these should be the first candidates for conversion to CLR.

If you have complex business logic that exists in other tiers of the system (whether client or middle tier), then you need to assess and test on a case-by-case basis whether it would be wise to move that functionality into an assembly in the database. Database applications, integration with other applications, and ad hoc reporting against the same database are all common components of today's applications. If there are business rules central to the data itself, then it may well make sense to encapsulate this logic within the database so that each different data consumer does not have to duplicate these rules.

One thing is for sure, though: CLR database objects should *not* be used to replace functionality that already exists in Transact-SQL. Set-based processing using SELECT/INSERT/UPDATE/DELETE will always be the preferred and best-performing method for data-intensive retrieval and modification. If an action can be performed efficiently within the database using Transact-SQL, you should use Transact-SQL over CLR methods.

CLR Objects Overview

In order to use CLR within SQL Server, you must create and compile an assembly into a DLL, and then import the new assembly (using CREATE ASSEMBLY) into a SQL Server database. Once integrated in the database, it is backed up along with your tables, data, and other database objects—since it is a database object just like any other. Once an assembly is added, you can then associate it to different database objects, including user-defined functions, stored procedures, triggers, user-defined types, and aggregate functions:

- *User-defined functions*: These create scalar or table-valued functions that can access .NET Framework calculation classes and access external resources. Later on in the chapter, you'll see an example of using regular expressions functionality within a scalar function (something you could not do using Transact-SQL).

- *Stored procedures*: This is probably the SQL Server database object with the most creative potential. You can use CLR-stored procedures to replace extended stored procedures, utilize .NET Framework classes, and perform calculation-heavy or external resource activities that aren't possible using Transact-SQL.

- *Triggers*: These allow you to create .NET programmatic responses to data manipulation language (INSERT/UPDATE/DELETE) or data definition language (CREATE, ALTER, DROP).

- *User-defined types*: These allow you to create new complex data types (unlike Transact-SQL user-defined types, which are based on predefined data types). CLR user-defined types include methods and properties along the lines of a .NET object/class. This may be one of the more controversial additions to SQL Server, because the multiple properties for a single type can fly in the face of basic relational database design principles. CLR user-defined types do allow you to implement data verification and string formatting, which *isn't* possible for Transact-SQL user-defined types.

- *User-defined aggregate functions*: You cannot create aggregate functions using Transaction-SQL. To create new aggregate functions in SQL Server, you can create a CLR-based user-defined aggregate function. User-defined aggregate functions can be used to create your own complex statistical analysis aggregates not available natively in SQL Server, or to collect multiple string values into a single business-defined result.

The rest of this chapter will focus on creating CLR stored procedures, user-defined functions, and triggers, as these are the most directly analogous to their T-SQL counterparts (in terms of the way that they are accessed and executed) and therefore are the most relevant for this book.

Creating CLR Database Objects

The recipes in this section walk through the creation of three CLR-based objects, namely a CLR stored procedure, a CLR UDF, and a CLR trigger. In the case of the *CLR stored procedure*, I'll actually present a series of four subrecipes that describe each of the following steps:

1. Use the system stored procedure sp_configure to enable CLR functionality for the SQL Server instance. Set the database where you will be using CLR database objects to TRUSTWORTHY if you plan on using CLR database objects with EXTERNAL_ACCESS or UNSAFE permissions.

2. Create the assembly code using your .NET language of choice, and your tool of choice. For example, you can use C# or VB .NET to create the assembly. Using Visual Studio makes the process of creating CLR assemblies easier; however, you can use something as simple as Notepad and the vsc.exe compiler.

3. Compile the code into a DLL file.

4. Use the CREATE ASSEMBLY Transact-SQL command to load the new assembly into the database. Choose the safety level based on the functionality of the assembly. Try to build code that is covered by either SAFE or EXTERNAL_ACCESS safety levels. These levels offer more stability for the SQL Server instance and help avoid the potential issues that unsafe code may incur.

After that, I'll demonstrate how to create a *CLR scalar user-defined function*, following the similar steps (in a single recipe), but with a new assembly and a few twists on the code. Finally, I'll take a look at a CLR trigger.

Enabling CLR Support in SQL Server

When SQL Server is installed, CLR functionality is disabled by default. To enable the use of CLR database objects, the system stored procedure sp_configure must be used to configure the 'clr enabled' option (see Chapter 21 for a full review of this system stored procedure):

```
EXEC sp_configure 'clr enabled', 1
RECONFIGURE WITH OVERRIDE
GO
```

This returns

```
Configuration option 'clr enabled' changed from 0 to 1.
Run the RECONFIGURE statement to install.
```

If you plan on using CLR database objects that require EXTERNAL_ACCESS or UNSAFE security permissions, you must enable the TRUSTWORTHY database option to ON. For example:

```
IF NOT EXISTS (SELECT 1 FROM sys.databases WHERE name = 'BookStore')
BEGIN
    CREATE DATABASE BookStore
END
GO

ALTER DATABASE BookStore
SET TRUSTWORTHY ON
```

How It Works

This example demonstrated enabling CLR functionality for the SQL Server instance. After executing the command, CLR functionality is enabled immediately without having to restart the SQL Server instance. I then enabled the TRUSTWORTHY option for the BookStore database, in order to allow EXTERNAL_ACCESS and UNSAFE security permissions later on (although I'll only be demonstrating a CLR database object that requires external access, and not demoing anything that is unsafe!).

In the next recipe, I'll demonstrate creating an assembly using VB .NET.

Writing an Assembly for a CLR Stored Procedure

In this recipe, I'll demonstrate creating the code for an assembly. Specifically, VB .NET code is used to read data from an external text file and then output the text file data in a result set.

Before getting to the actual code, I first need to discuss a few new concepts regarding assemblies themselves.

So far I've discussed CLR assemblies as though they are used on a one-for-one basis with database objects. Assemblies, however, can contain code for use by one or more CLR database objects. For example, the code I'll be using in this recipe is intended for a single stored procedure. You can, however, put several subroutines or types within a single assembly, for use in different CLR database objects. As a best practice, try to group related functionality within a single assembly. This is important (if not necessary) if your various functions or methods have dependencies on one another. Take a situation where you have a set of functionalities that will all cross-reference with an external mapping application. For example, your assembly could contain code that can be used by a CLR stored procedure to return driving directions, a CLR user-defined function to return mapping coordinates based on address input information, and a new user-defined CLR type that contains the varying address details.

Another important concept to understand is assembly security. When you use managed code, you must consider how much access to specific resources that your code requires. In the "Loading the Assembly into SQL Server" recipe, you'll see that when an assembly is added to SQL Server, you'll need to indicate the level of permissions that the assembly requires. You'll have three choices, SAFE, EXTERNAL_ACCESS, and UNSAFE, which I'll describe in more detail later on in the chapter.

This assembly example demonstrates creating a class and function using VB .NET, which then takes a file and path name as an input value, opens the file for reading, and, finally, returns the results back to the SQL Server connection context that made the call. I'll discuss the elements of this script in the "How It Works" section:

```
Imports System.Data
Imports System.Data.Sql
Imports System.Data.SqlTypes
Imports Microsoft.SqlServer.Server
Imports System.IO

Public Class ReadFiles

Public Shared Sub Main(ByVal sFile As SqlString)

    Dim sReader As StreamReader = New StreamReader(sFile)
    Dim sLine As String
    Dim sPipe As SqlPipe = SqlContext.Pipe

    Do
    sLine = sReader.ReadLine()
 If Not sLine Is Nothing Then
   sPipe.Send(sLine)
End If
    Loop Until sLine Is Nothing

    sReader.Close()

    End Sub
End Class
```

How It Works

This current recipe's example contains a class and function that will be associated specifically to a CLR stored procedure. CLR database objects require specific namespaces to exist within the assembly so that SQL Server can reference built-in CLR assemblies in your assembly code. For example, the code included the following namespaces:

```
Imports System.Data
Imports System.Data.Sql
Imports System.Data.SqlTypes
Imports Microsoft.SqlServer.Server
```

You can also include other namespaces, depending on the required functionality of the assembly. For example, the System.IO namespace contains the functions needed to read and write from file system files:

```
Imports System.IO
```

The example continued declaring a public class called ReadFiles:

```
Public Class ReadFiles
```

Next, a public, shared subroutine included a single parameter string value (in this case expecting the name and path of the file to be read):

```
Public Shared Sub Main(ByVal sFile As SqlString)
```

Notice that the sFile input parameter was defined as the SqlString type. As you work with CLR assemblies, you'll need to understand the SQL Server data types that associate to specific SQL CLR .NET data types. Table 13-1 lists some of the available data types and their CLR versus SQL Server translations (notice that with some types you can pick and choose, due to overlap).

Table 13-1. *Converting SQL Server to CLR Data Types*

CLR Data Type(s)	SQL Server Data Type(s)
SqlBytes	varbinary, binary
SqlBinary	varbinary, binary
SqlChars (ideal for data access and retrieval)	nvarchar, nchar
SqlString (ideal for string operation)	nvarchar, nchar
SqlGuid	uniqueidentifier
SqlBoolean	bit
SqlByte	tinyint
SqlInt16	smallint
SqlInt32	int
SqlInt64	bigint
SqlMoney	smallmoney, money
SqlDecimal	decimal, numeric
SqlSingle	real
SqlDouble	float
SqlDateTime	smalldatetime, datetime, date, datetime2
TimeSpan	time
SqlXml	xml

Continuing the walk-through of the example, you'll note that a StreamReader object was declared and set to the passed file name and path. The StreamReader class is used to read text data from a file. Because it is not a Transact-SQL function, you would not normally be able to reference this function in your code. CLR assemblies allow you to use these .NET commands from your SQL Server database:

```
Dim sReader As StreamReader = New StreamReader(sFile)
```

A string variable is created to hold a single line of data from the file:

```
Dim sLine As String
```

Next, I use two classes, SqlPipe and SqlContext:

```
Dim sPipe As SqlPipe = SqlContext.Pipe
```

The SqlPipe object is used to send zero or more rows back to the connected caller's connection. So, if I execute a CLR stored procedure that I expect will return a list of results (similar to a SELECT query), the Send method of the SqlPipe object is used. This SqlContext class maintains and accesses the SQL Server caller's context, meaning if I execute a stored procedure, SqlContext knows that it is my action and that the results belong to my client. A SqlPipe is spawned based on the SqlContext of a user's connection using the Pipe method of SqlContext.

Next, a Do loop (similar to a Transact-SQL WHILE) is created to read through each line of the file until there are no longer any rows:

```
Do
```

The sLine variable is set to the first line of the file using the ReadLine method of the StreamReader object:

```
sLine = sReader.ReadLine()
```

If something exists in the line from the file, the values of that line are sent back to the SQL Server connection using the Send method of the SqlPipe object:

```
 If Not sLine Is Nothing Then
   sPipe.Send(sLine)
End If
```

Once the file is complete, however, the Do loop is finished and the connection to the file is closed:

```
Loop Until sLine Is Nothing

sReader.Close()
```

Finishing off the assembly, I ended the sub, and then the class definition.

```
   End Sub
End Class
```

Now that you have seen how to write the assembly in VB .NET, you can move to the next step, which is compiling the assembly code into a DLL file, which can then be imported into SQL Server. In preparation for this exercise, I'll create a file directory called C:\Apress\Recipes\CLR\ and then save this file as ReadFiles.vb.

Compiling an Assembly into a DLL File

Use vbc.exe to compile the assembly file without the use of Visual Studio. The vbc.exe compiler can be found on the SQL Server instance machine under the latest version of C:\WINDOWS\MICROSOFT. NET\framework\ directory.

In this example, I'll execute the following command to create the DLL assembly file based on the ReadFiles.vb code using the vbc executable at the command prompt (notice that the reference to `sqlaccess.dll` will vary based on your SQL instance directory path):

```
vbc /t:library /out:C:\Apress\Recipes\CLR\ReadFiles.DLL /r:"C:\Program
 Files\Microsoft SQL Server\MSSQL10.AUGUSTUS\MSSQL\Binn\sqlaccess.dll"
"C:\Apress\Recipes\CLR\ReadFiles.vb"
```

How It Works

Executing the `vbc.exe` executable in this recipe creates a DLL file under the `C:\Apress\Recipes\CLR` directory, which can then be used to create an assembly in SQL Server. I'll review how to do that next.

Loading the Assembly into SQL Server

To load the new assembly into a SQL Server 2008 database, use the `CREATE ASSEMBLY` command. The basic syntax, as used in this example, is as follows:

```
CREATE ASSEMBLY assembly_name
[ AUTHORIZATION owner_name ]
FROM { '[\\computer_name\]share_name\[path\]manifest_file_name'
  | '[local_path\]manifest_file_name'|
{ varbinary_literal | varbinary_expression }}
[ WITH PERMISSION_SET = { SAFE | EXTERNAL_ACCESS | UNSAFE } ]
```

Table 13-2 describes this command's arguments.

Table 13-2. *CREATE ASSEMBLY Arguments*

Argument	Description
`assembly_name`	This defines the name of the new database assembly.
`owner_name`	This defines the user or role owner of the assembly.
`'[\\computer_name\]share_name\[path\]manifest_file_name'` | `'[local_path\]manifest_file_name'|`	This defines the path and file name of the assembly to be loaded.
`varbinary_literal	varbinary_expression`	Instead of an actual file, the binary values that make up the assembly can be passed to the command.
`SAFE	EXTERNAL_ACCESS	UNSAFE`	This references the safety permission level for the assembly, per the discussion earlier in this section.

The safety permission levels for the assembly require special consideration. `SAFE` permissions allow you to run code that only requires access to the local SQL Server instance. Using this default mode, your assembly won't be able to access the network, external files (even files on the same machine as the SQL Server instance), the registry, or environment variables. `EXTERNAL_ACCESS` permissions permit access to the network, external files, the registry, environment variables, and web services. Both the `SAFE` and `EXTERNAL_ACCESS` modes have a specific level of internal safety. These internal measures include the protection of the memory space of other applications, as well as a restriction from any action that could hurt the SQL Server instance.

UNSAFE permissions are most similar to the extended stored procedures discussed earlier in the chapter. This level of permission doesn't put any restrictions on how the assembly accesses resources, allowing for the potential of memory space violations or performing actions that could hurt the stability of the SQL Server instance. As you may suspect, this is the permission level you should avoid unless necessary, and only under conditions where you can ensure the assembly is thoroughly tested and free of negative side effects.

Continuing with this section's example of creating a CLR stored procedure, a new assembly is created based on the ReadFiles.DLL, using the EXTERNAL_ACCESS option, since the assembly needs to read from the file system:

```
USE BookStore
GO

CREATE ASSEMBLY ReadFiles FROM 'C:\Apress\Recipes\CLR\ReadFiles.DLL'
WITH PERMISSION_SET = EXTERNAL_ACCESS
GO
```

How It Works

When creating a new assembly, the actual assembly contents are loaded into the database. This means that database backups will also back up the assemblies contained within. In our example, a new assembly called ReadFiles was created based on the assembly DLL file. The permission was set to EXTERNAL_ACCESS because the assembly is used to read data from a file and return it back as a result set to the SQL Server caller.

Importing an assembly into SQL Server isn't enough to start using its functionality. You must then associate that assembly to a CLR database object. The next recipe demonstrates how to do this.

Creating the CLR Stored Procedure

CLR database objects are created similarly to their regular Transact-SQL equivalents, only the procedural definition references an assembly instead. The following commands each have the CLR option of EXTERNAL NAME:

- CREATE PROCEDURE
- CREATE FUNCTION
- CREATE TRIGGER
- CREATE TYPE

As a side note, the CREATE AGGREGATE command, which creates a user-defined SQL Server aggregate function, can't be written in Transact-SQL and is only used in conjunction with a .NET assembly.

■**Tip** In SQL Server 2008, CLR user-defined types are no longer restricted to 8,000 bytes in size.

The specific extension syntax for creating a CLR-based stored procedure, user-defined function, or trigger is as follows:

```
EXTERNAL NAME assembly_name.class_name.method_name
```

For creating a new CLR data type or aggregate, only the assembly and class name are referenced:

```
EXTERNAL NAME assembly_name [ .class_name ]
```

This example demonstrates creating a new CLR stored procedure using the EXTERNAL NAME extension of the CREATE PROCEDURE command to map to your new assembly, created in the previous recipe:

```
CREATE PROCEDURE dbo.usp_FileReader
(@FileName nvarchar(1024))
AS EXTERNAL NAME ReadFiles.ReadFiles.Main
GO
```

ReadFiles appears twice because it is the CLR assembly name and the class within the VB .NET code block.

Once created, the CLR stored procedure is executed like a normal Transact-SQL defined stored procedure. Continuing this example, the contents of a SQL Server error log file are returned in the results of the stored procedure (looking at an error log that is not currently being used by the SQL Server instance):

```
EXEC dbo.usp_FileReader
N'C:\Program Files\Microsoft SQL Server\MSSQL10.AUGUSTUS\MSSQL\LOG\ERRORLOG.1'
```

This returns the contents of the ERRORLOG file as a result set (abridged here):

```
...
2007-10-14 08:09:18.91 Server      Using locked pages for buffer pool.
2007-10-14 08:09:18.92 Server      Using dynamic lock allocation.
Initial allocation of 2500 Lock blocks and 5000 Lock Owner blocks per node.
This is an informational message only.  No user action is required.
2007-10-14 08:09:19.16 Server      Node configuration: node 0: CPU mask:
0x0000000000000003 Active CPU mask: 0x0000000000000003.
This message provides a description of the NUMA configuration for this computer.
This is an informational message only. No user action is required.
2007-10-14 08:09:19.27 Server      FILESTREAM: effective level = 0, configured level
= 0, file system access share name = 'CAESAR'.
2007-10-14 08:09:19.27 Server      Attempting to initialize
Microsoft Distributed Transaction Coordinator (MS DTC).
This is an informational message only. No user action is required.
2007-10-14 08:09:20.65 Server      Attempting to recover in-doubt distributed
transactions involving Microsoft Distributed Transaction Coordinator (MS DTC).
This is an informational message only. No user action is required.
2007-10-14 08:09:20.65 Server      Database mirroring has been enabled on this
instance of SQL Server.
2007-10-14 08:09:20.67 spid7s      Starting up database 'master'
....
```

Once created, database CLR objects can be altered or dropped using the normal ALTER or DROP commands for the database object type.

How It Works

This recipe demonstrated how to create a CLR stored procedure. The parameters required for the stored procedure depend on the parameters expected by the .NET assembly methods. In this case, the Main method of the ReadFiles assembly expected a string parameter for the file and path name to be read, so a @FileName nvarchar data type parameter is used in the stored procedure reference. In the EXTERNAL NAME clause, the ReadFiles assembly was referenced, followed by the ReadFiles class, and Main method.

Using the .NET Framework, the procedure was able to access external resources and iterate through the contents of a file. With CLR integration, the functional scope of SQL Server now extends out to the capabilities of the .NET Framework.

Creating a CLR Scalar User-Defined Function

As explained in the introduction at the beginning of the chapter, you'll benefit most from CLR when using it to execute high-complexity computational operations. Using CLR for scalar UDF functions that don't focus on data retrieval from SQL Server may often perform quite well over a Transact-SQL equivalent. CLR scalar UDFs are also useful for operations that simply aren't possible using Transact-SQL (for example, accessing external data or using .NET library functionality that doesn't exist in Transact-SQL).

In this example, an assembly is created that contains a class and method intended for use with a CLR user-defined scalar function. I'm going to take advantage of the System.Text. RegularExpressions .NET Framework namespace. This contains a class called Regex, which will allow us to break apart a single string into an array of values based on a specific delimiter. Regular expression functionality, which is often used for pattern matching, isn't built into SQL Server 2008, but now, with CLR integration, you can safely and efficiently use the regular expression libraries written for VB .NET.

The goal of this example is to create a scalar UDF that takes three parameters. The first parameter is a delimited string of values. The second parameter is the delimiter character used to separate the string. The third parameter is the value from the array that I would like to select. I'll walk through the code in more detail in the "How It Works" section, but in the meantime, this example compiles the following code using vbc.exe:

```
Imports System.Data
Imports System.Data.Sql
Imports System.Data.SqlTypes
Imports Microsoft.SqlServer.Server
Imports System.Text.RegularExpressions

Public Class SQLArrayBuilder

Public Shared Function ChooseValueFromArray(ArrayString as String,
ArrayDelimiter as String, ArrayItemSelection as SqlInt16) as SqlString

Dim NewArrayString as String() = Regex.Split(ArrayString, ArrayDelimiter)

Dim NewArrayItemSelection as SqlInt16=ArrayItemSelection-1

Dim ReturnString as SQLString = NewArrayString(NewArrayItemSelection)


Return ReturnString

End Function

End Class
```

After saving the VB file SQLArrayBuilder.vb and compiling this assembly using vbc, it can then be imported into the database. Because nothing in the assembly accesses external resources, I can use a SAFE permission level:

```
CREATE ASSEMBLY SQLArrayBuilder FROM 'C:\Apress\Recipes\CLR\SQLArrayBuilder.DLL'
WITH PERMISSION_SET = SAFE
GO
```

Next, I'll associate the new assembly to a scalar user-defined function. Notice that the syntax is the same as if it were a Transact-SQL command, except that after AS, the EXTERNAL NAME keywords are used to designate the assembly, class, and function:

```
CREATE FUNCTION dbo.CountSalesOrderHeader
(@ArrayString nvarchar(4000), @ArrayDelimiter nchar(1),
@ArrayItemSelection smallint)
RETURNS nvarchar(4000)
AS
EXTERNAL NAME SQLArrayBuilder.SQLArrayBuilder.ChooseValueFromArray
GO
```

Now to test the function, the first parameter will include three comma-separated values. The second parameter designates a comma as the delimiter, and the third value indicates the value you would like to choose from the array:

```
SELECT dbo.CountSalesOrderHeader
('Brian,Steve,Boris,Tony,Russ', ',', 3) Choice
```

This returns

```
Choice
Boris
```

This time the second value is selected from the array:

```
SELECT dbo.CountSalesOrderHeader
('Brian,Steve,Boris,Tony,Russ', ',', 2) Choice
```

This returns

```
Choice
Steve
```

How It Works

This recipe shares the same general setup steps as the CLR stored procedure example. Once again, an assembly was created and then compiled. Next, the assembly was added to the database using CREATE ASSEMBLY. A new user-defined function was then created, using the expected three input parameters and the appropriate output parameter data type. The UDF also included a reference to the assembly, class, and function name.

Walking through the code, you'll see that I included the core namespaces also seen in the stored procedure example:

```
Imports System.Data
Imports System.Data.Sql
Imports System.Data.SqlTypes
Imports Microsoft.SqlServer.Server
```

The reference to the regular expressions namespace was also included, so that you could use the functionality of the Regex object, which is a collection of library classes created and shipped with .NET:

```
Imports System.Text.RegularExpressions
```

Our class name was then declared, which will be the reference that is used during the creation of the CLR function:

```
Public Class SQLArrayBuilder
```

The function was declared, including the three input parameters in parentheses, followed by the expected return data type (SqlString) of the function:

```
Public Shared Function ChooseValueFromArray(ArrayString as String,
ArrayDelimiter as String, ArrayItemSelection as SqlInt16) as SqlString
```

Next, a new string array variable was declared and populated with the array generated from the Regex.Split method, which is used to split an array of strings at the positions defined by a regular expression match (in this case, our delimiter):

```
Dim NewArrayString as String() =
Regex.Split(ArrayString, ArrayDelimiter)
```

VB .NET arrays are zero-based—meaning the first value in the array is indexed at 0, followed by 1, 2, and so on. Because the SQL Server caller of the scalar UDF will want to pass an array selection value based on a one-based value, I take the input array item selection and subtract "1" from it, so as to select the appropriate value from the array:

```
Dim NewArrayItemSelection as SqlInt16=ArrayItemSelection-1
```

After the array is populated, a new string variable is created to hold the selected value:

```
Dim ReturnString as SQLString = NewArrayString(NewArrayItemSelection)
```

This value is the passed back using the Return command, followed by the end of the function and class definition:

```
Return ReturnString

End Function

End Class
```

After that, the assembly was compiled, and then imported into the database using CREATE ASSEMBLY. The function was then created using CREATE FUNCTION referencing the assembly, class, and function:

```
SQLArrayBuilder.SQLArrayBuilder.ChooseValueFromArray
```

The function was then tested, parsing out a comma-delimited string and returning the desired scalar value.

■**Caution** The examples in this chapter are written in order to introduce the core concepts and functionality of CLR integration with SQL Server 2008. Although this function works properly when the appropriate values are passed to the function, it does not contain error trapping code to handle unexpected values. Using SAFE and EXTERNAL_ACCESS limits the damage surface area, although bad input values may cause rather unfriendly error messages returned to the end user. In your production .NET code, be sure to add error handling.

Creating a CLR Trigger

In this next recipe, I'll demonstrate creating a CLR trigger, which is used to generate an external "control file" that can in turn be used to notify an outside hypothetical application that a process is finished.

In this example scenario, I have a table called dbo.DataWarehouseLoadHistory. This table contains a row inserted whenever the daily data warehouse load finishes. When a row is inserted, the trigger will output a control file to an external directory, notifying the legacy system (and I'm assuming this is a system that cannot access SQL Server 2008 programmatically).

First, I'll create the new demonstration table in a user-defined database:

```
USE BookStore
GO

CREATE TABLE dbo.DataWarehouseLoadHistory
(DataWarehouseLoadHistoryID int
   NOT NULL IDENTITY(1,1) PRIMARY KEY ,
LoadDT datetime NOT NULL)
GO
```

Next, the following assembly code is compiled using vbc.exe:

```
Imports System
Imports System.Data
Imports System.Data.Sql
Imports System.Data.SqlTypes
Imports System.Data.SqlClient
Imports Microsoft.SqlServer.Server
Imports System.IO


Public Class DW_Trigger

  Public Shared Sub ExportFile()

   Dim DWTrigger As SqlTriggerContext
   DWTrigger = SqlContext.TriggerContext

    If (DWTrigger.TriggerAction = _
     TriggerAction.Insert) Then

    Dim DWsw As StreamWriter = New _
     StreamWriter("C:\DataWarehouseLoadTrigger.txt")

    DWsw.WriteLine(Now())
    DWsw.Close()

    End If

   End Sub

End Class
```

After compiling the assembly into a DLL, it is then imported into SQL Server using CREATE ASSEMBLY:

```
CREATE ASSEMBLY DataWarehouseLoadNotification
FROM 'C:\Apress\Recipes\CLR\DataWarehouseLoadNotification.dll'
WITH PERMISSION_SET = EXTERNAL_ACCESS
GO
```

Next, I'll create a trigger that is mapped to the assembly subroutine:

```
CREATE TRIGGER dbo.trg_i_DWNotify
ON dbo.DataWarehouseLoadHistory  AFTER INSERT
AS
EXTERNAL NAME DataWarehouseLoadNotification.DW_Trigger.ExportFile
```

To demonstrate the new trigger, I'll insert a new row into the DataWarehouseLoadHistory table:

```
INSERT dbo.DataWarehouseLoadHistory
(LoadDT)
VALUES(GETDATE())
```

This INSERT causes the CLR trigger to fire and then create a notification file under the C:\ drive of the SQL Server instance machine (of course in a production scenario, I'd be putting this file someplace else for the legacy system to pick up). The file contains the current date and time that the trigger was fired:

```
2/17/2008 2:43:47 PM
```

How It Works

This recipe demonstrated creating a CLR trigger that created a text file in response to an INSERT into a table. Of course, this CLR database object would *not* have been a good idea to create for a table that receives numerous new rows each day (continually overlaying a file non-stop)! But in this scenario, I'm assuming that the data is only updated periodically, and that the external legacy application is monitoring any changes in the file.

The steps to creating this CLR trigger were similar to creating a user-defined function and stored procedure: a new assembly was compiled, added to SQL Server, and then associated to a database object using CREATE TRIGGER.

Something to point out, however, is the SqlTriggerContext class, which was used to define the context information for the trigger within SQL Server:

```
Dim DWTrigger As SqlTriggerContext
DWTrigger = SqlContext.TriggerContext
```

Once the object was created, it was then used to find out the actions that cause the trigger to fire or determine which columns were modified. In this example, the SqlTriggerContext object was used to determine whether the trigger firing event was an INSERT, and if so, the external file would be written:

```
If (DWTrigger.TriggerAction = _
  TriggerAction.Insert) Then
...
```

After compiling the DLL, an assembly was created and then bound to a trigger on the DataWarehouseLoadHistory table. An INSERT was tested, causing a notification file under the C:\ drive to be created.

Administering Assemblies

The next three recipes will demonstrate how to administer database assemblies. I'll demonstrate how to view assembly metadata, modify an assembly's permissions, and remove an assembly from the database.

Viewing Assembly Metadata

To view all assemblies in the current database, you can query the sys.assemblies system catalog view. For example:

```
SELECT name, permission_set_desc
FROM sys.assemblies
```

This returns

name	permission_set_desc
Microsoft.SqlServer.Types	UNSAFE_ACCESS
ReadFiles	EXTERNAL_ACCESS
SQLArrayBuilder	SAFE_ACCESS
DataWarehouseLoadNotification	EXTERNAL_ACCESS

How It Works

The system catalog view sys.assemblies can be used to view the name of the assemblies and the security profile assigned to it.

Modifying an Assembly's Permissions

You can use the ALTER ASSEMBLY command (which uses many of the same options as CREATE ASSEMBLY) to modify specific configurations of an existing assembly permissions.

In this example, the permissions of an assembly are set from EXTERNAL_ACCESS to SAFE:

```
ALTER ASSEMBLY ReadFiles
WITH PERMISSION_SET = SAFE
```

After executing this command, an attempt is made to execute the stored procedure associated to this assembly:

```
EXEC dbo.usp_FileReader
N'C:\Program Files\Microsoft SQL Server\MSSQL10.AUGUSTUS\MSSQL\LOG\ERRORLOG.1'
```

This returns the following (abridged) error:

```
Msg 6522, Level 16, State 1, Procedure usp_FileReader, Line 0
A .NET Framework error occurred during execution of
user defined routine or aggregate 'usp_FileReader':
System.Security.SecurityException: Request for the permission of type
'System.Security.Permissions.FileIOPermission, mscorlib,
Version=2.0.0.0, Culture=neutral, PublicKeyToken=b77a5c561934e089' failed.
```

How It Works

Although SQL Server allowed me to change the permission level of the assembly, external operations (reading from a file) attempted by the assembly were now no longer allowed. This means that
when you write your assembly, you must think about what level of permissions it will need. If you
think your assembly only needs SAFE access, but it actually needs access to external resources, you
can use ALTER ASSEMBLY to change the permissions.

Removing an Assembly from the Database

To remove an assembly from the database, use the DROP ASSEMBLY command. The abridged syntax is
as follows:

```
DROP ASSEMBLY assembly_name [ ,...n ]
```

The first argument is the name or comma-delimited list of assembly names to be dropped
from the database. For example:

```
DROP ASSEMBLY ReadFiles
```

How It Works

This example demonstrated dropping an assembly. Any existing CLR object references (stored procedure, for example) must be dropped prior to removing the assembly from the database. If you
don't drop referencing objects first, you'll see an error message like the following:

```
Msg 6590, Level 16, State 1, Line 1
DROP ASSEMBLY failed because 'ReadFiles' is referenced by object 'usp_FileReader'.
```

XML, Hierarchies, and Spatial Data

In this chapter, I'll present recipes discussing and demonstrating the various integration points between XML and SQL Server. I'll also introduce the new hierarchyid, geometry, and geography data types, which are now native to SQL Server 2008.

Working with Native XML

In SQL Server 2000, if you wanted to store XML data within the database, you had to store it in a character or binary format. This wasn't too troublesome if you just used SQL Server for XML document storage, but attempts to query or modify the stored document within SQL Server were not so straightforward. Introduced in SQL Server 2005, the SQL Server native xml data type helps address this issue.

Relational database designers may be concerned about this data type, and rightly so. The normalized database provides performance and data integrity benefits that put into question why we would need to store XML documents in the first place. Having an xml data type allows you to have your relational data stored alongside your unstructured data. By providing this data type, Microsoft isn't suggesting that you run your high-speed applications based on XML documents. Rather, you may find XML document storage is useful when data must be "somewhat" structured. For example, let's say your company's web site offers an online contract. This contract is available over the Web for your customer to fill out and then submit. The submitted data is stored in an xml data type. You might choose to store the submitted data in an XML document because your legal department is always changing the document's fields. Also, since this document is only submitted a few times a day, throughput is not an issue. Another good reason to use native xml data type is for "state" storage. For example, if your .NET applications use XML configuration files, you can store them in a SQL Server database in order to maintain a history of changes and as a backup/recovery option.

These next few recipes will demonstrate xml data type columns in action.

Creating XML Data Type Columns

Native xml data types can be used as a data type for columns in a table, local variables, or parameters. Data stored in the xml data type can contain an XML document or XML fragments. An *XML fragment* is an XML instance without a single top-level element for the contents to nest in. Creating an XML data type column is as easy as just using it in the table definition. For example, the ChapterDESC column uses an XML data type in the following table:

```
IF NOT EXISTS (SELECT name FROM sys.databases
                WHERE name = 'TestDB')
BEGIN
     CREATE DATABASE TestDB
END
GO

USE TestDB
GO

CREATE TABLE dbo.Book
(BookID int IDENTITY(1,1) PRIMARY KEY,
 ISBNNBR char(10) NOT NULL,
 BookNM varchar(250) NOT NULL,
 AuthorID int NOT NULL,
 ChapterDESC XML NULL)
GO
```

In this second example, a local variable called @Book is given an xml data type and is set to an xml value (in the next recipe, I'll demonstrate how that value can be used):

```
DECLARE @Book XML

SET @Book =
CAST('<Book name="SQL Server 2000 Fast Answers">
<Chapters>
<Chapter id="1"> Installation, Upgrades... </Chapter>
<Chapter id="2"> Configuring SQL Server </Chapter>
<Chapter id="3"> Creating and Configuring Databases </Chapter>
<Chapter id="4"> SQL Server Agent and SQL Logs </Chapter>
</Chapters>
</Book>' as XML)
```

In the third example, an xml data type input parameter is used for a stored procedure:

```
CREATE PROCEDURE dbo.usp_INS_Book
    @ISBNNBR char(10),
    @BookNM varchar(250),
    @AuthorID int,
    @ChapterDESC xml
AS

INSERT dbo.Book
(ISBNNBR, BookNM, AuthorID, ChapterDESC)
VALUES (@ISBNNBR, @BookNM, @AuthorID, @ChapterDESC)

GO
```

How It Works

This recipe demonstrated how to use the xml data type in the column definition of a table, a local variable, and the input parameter for a stored procedure. The syntax is not different from what you'd use with other SQL Server data types. The next recipe demonstrates how to INSERT XML data into a table using Transact-SQL.

Inserting XML Data into a Column

In this recipe, I'll demonstrate inserting an XML document into the table created in the previous recipe. The INSERT command is used, and the XML document is embedded in single quotes (as a string would be) but is also CAST explicitly into the xml data type:

```
INSERT dbo.Book
(ISBNNBR, BookNM, AuthorID, ChapterDESC)
VALUES ('570X000000',
      'SQL Server 2008 T-SQL Recipes',
      55,
CAST('<Book name="SQL Server 2008 T-SQL Recipes">
<Chapters>
<Chapter id="1"> SELECT </Chapter>
<Chapter id="2"> INSERT,UPDATE,DELETE </Chapter>
<Chapter id="3"> Transactions, Locking, Blocking, and Deadlocking </Chapter>
<Chapter id="4"> Tables </Chapter>
<Chapter id="5"> Indexes </Chapter>
<Chapter id="6"> Full-text search </Chapter>
</Chapters>
</Book>' as XML))
```

This returns

```
(1 row(s) affected)
```

In this second example, a local variable called @Book is given an xml data type and is set to an xml value. That value is then used in a table INSERT:

```
DECLARE @Book XML

SET @Book =
CAST('<Book name="SQL Server 2000 Fast Answers">
<Chapters>
<Chapter id="1"> Installation, Upgrades... </Chapter>
<Chapter id="2"> Configuring SQL Server </Chapter>
<Chapter id="3"> Creating and Configuring Databases </Chapter>
<Chapter id="4"> SQL Server Agent and SQL Logs </Chapter>
</Chapters>
</Book>' as XML)

INSERT dbo.Book
(ISBNNBR, BookNM, AuthorID, ChapterDESC)
VALUES ('1590591615',
      'SQL Server 2000 Fast Answers',
      55,
      @Book)
```

This returns

```
(1 row(s) affected)
```

How It Works

In both the INSERT examples, the XML data for the ChapterDESC column was converted explicitly to xml using the CAST function and was checked by SQL Server to ensure that it was well formed (*well formed*, in this case, means that it follows the general rules of an XML document). For example, if the document fragment had been missing the closing </Book> element, the following error would have been raised:

```
Msg 9400, Level 16, State 1, Line 1
XML parsing: line 9, character 12, unexpected end of input
```

The xml column defined in the example, however, was untyped. When an xml column is *untyped*, it means that the contents inserted into the column are not validated against an XML schema. An XML schema is used to define the allowed elements and attributes for an XML document, and is discussed in the next recipe.

Validating XML Data Using Schemas

An XML Schema (also referred to as XML Schema Definition, or XSD) defines the elements, attributes, data types, and allowed values for an XML document. Using CREATE XML SCHEMA COLLECTION, you can add XML Schema definitions to SQL Server and use them in constraining XML data type columns, local variables, or parameters.

■**Tip** For a review of XML Schema fundamentals, visit the World Wide Web Consortium (W3C) standards site at http://www.w3.org/TR/XMLschema-0/.

The CREATE XML SCHEMA COLLECTION command is used to add new XML schemas and uses the following syntax:

```
CREATE XML SCHEMA COLLECTION [ <relational_schema>. ]sql_identifier
AS Expression
```

The command takes two arguments, the first being the unique name of the new XML Schema, while the second is the body of the XML Schema or Schemas.

To add additional XML Schemas to an existing collection, you can use the ALTER XML SCHEMA COLLECTION. The syntax is as follows:

```
ALTER XML SCHEMA COLLECTION [ relational_schema. ]sql_identifier
ADD 'Schema Component'
```

To remove the entire XML Schema collection from the database, use the DROP XML SCHEMA command. The syntax is as follows:

```
DROP XML SCHEMA COLLECTION [ relational_schema. ]sql_identifier
```

The only argument for dropping an existing XML Schema collection is the name of the collection.

In this example, a new XML Schema collection is created called BookStoreCollection, which contains a single XML Schema defined within:

```
CREATE XML SCHEMA COLLECTION BookStoreCollection
AS
N'<xsd:schema targetNamespace="http://JOEPROD/BookStore"
xmlns:xsd="http://www.w3.org/2001/XMLSchema"
xmlns:sqltypes="http://schemas.microsoft.com/sqlserver/2004/sqltypes"
elementFormDefault="qualified">
<xsd:import namespace=
"http://schemas.microsoft.com/sqlserver/2004/sqltypes" />
<xsd:element name="Book">
    <xsd:complexType>
      <xsd:sequence>
        <xsd:element name="BookName" minOccurs="0">
          <xsd:simpleType>
            <xsd:restriction base="sqltypes:varchar">
              <xsd:maxLength value="50" />
            </xsd:restriction>
          </xsd:simpleType>
        </xsd:element>
<xsd:element name="ChapterID" type="sqltypes:int"
minOccurs="0" />
        <xsd:element name="ChapterNM" minOccurs="0">
          <xsd:simpleType>
            <xsd:restriction base="sqltypes:varchar">
              <xsd:maxLength value="50" />
            </xsd:restriction>
          </xsd:simpleType>
        </xsd:element>
      </xsd:sequence>
    </xsd:complexType>
  </xsd:element>
</xsd:schema>'
```

This returns

```
Command(s) completed successfully.
```

Once created, you can verify an XML Schema's existence using the system catalog views sys.XML_schema_collections and sys.XML_schema_namespaces. This first query shows all schema collections defined in the database:

```
SELECT name
FROM sys.XML_schema_collections
ORDER BY create_date
```

This returns

```
name
sys
BookStoreCollection
```

This second query shows namespaces found in a specific XML Schema collection (namespaces uniquely identify the scope of elements and attributes, helping uniquely identify these components):

```
SELECT n.name
FROM sys.XML_schema_namespaces n
INNER JOIN sys.XML_schema_collections  c ON
   c.XML_collection_id = n.XML_collection_id
WHERE c.name = 'BookStoreCollection'
```

This returns

```
name
http://JOEPROD/BookStore
```

Once a schema collection is available, you can bind it to an xml column in a table by referencing it in parentheses after the data type definition. For example, the ChapterDESC column is bound to the BookStoreCollection XML Schema collection:

```
CREATE TABLE dbo.BookInfoExport
(BookID int IDENTITY(1,1) PRIMARY KEY,
 ISBNNBR char(10) NOT NULL,
 BookNM varchar(250) NOT NULL,
 AuthorID int NOT NULL,
 ChapterDESC xml (BookStoreCollection) NULL)
```

This xml column will now only allow typed xml values (XML documents that conform to the defined XML Schema collection). Attempting to assign XML values that do not conform to the XSD specified for the column will raise an error (for example, if expected elements or attributes are missing). Using the keyword DOCUMENT or CONTENT with the schema collection reference lets you determine whether the allowed XML will allow only a full XML document (DOCUMENT) or XML fragments (CONTENT) instead.

For example, the following local variable requires a full XML document that conforms to the XML Schema collection:

```
DECLARE @Book XML (DOCUMENT BookStoreCollection)
```

How It Works

This recipe provided a quick tour through the XML Schema functionality built into SQL Server. Using an XML Schema collection, you can validate and constrain the content of XML data within the xml data type. Untyped XML data will still be validated for general XML structure, but by using XML Schema collections, you can apply more sophisticated validation and constraints.

■**Tip** SQL Server 2008 now allows lax validation for wildcard content. SQL Server 2005 supported strict and skip. The strict value meant that all contents were fully validated; otherwise, skip designated that contents would not be validated. The new lax value directs SQL Server to validate attributes and elements defined in the schema but skip validation of undefined attributes and elements.

Retrieving XML Data

The xml data type column can be queried using XQuery methods. *XQuery* is a query language that is used to search XML documents. These XQuery methods described in Table 14-1 are integrated into SQL Server and can be used in regular Transact-SQL queries.

Table 14-1. *XQuery Methods*

Method	Description
exist	Returns 1 for an XQuery expression when it evaluates to TRUE; otherwise, it returns 0 for FALSE.
modify	Performs updates against XML data (demonstrated after this recipe).
nodes	Shreds XML data to relational data, identifying nodes-to-row mapping.
query	Returns XML results based on an XQuery expression.
value	Returns a scalar SQL data type value based on an XQuery expression.

■**Tip** For an in-depth review of XQuery fundamentals, visit the World Wide Web Consortium (W3C) standards site at http://www.w3.org/TR/xquery/. XQuery supports iteration syntax using the for, let, where, order by, and return clauses (acronym FLWOR). In SQL Server 2005, let was not supported. SQL Server 2008 now supports let.

To demonstrate each of these methods, I'll create a new table with an xml data type column and insert three rows:

```
CREATE TABLE dbo.BookInvoice
(BookInvoiceID int IDENTITY(1,1) PRIMARY KEY,
 BookInvoiceXML XML NOT NULL)
GO

INSERT dbo.BookInvoice
(BookInvoiceXML)
VALUES ('<BookInvoice invoicenumber="1" customerid="22" orderdate="7/1/2008">
<OrderItems>
<Item id="22" qty="1" name="SQL Fun in the Sun"/>
<Item id="24" qty="1" name="T-SQL Crossword Puzzles"/>
</OrderItems>
</BookInvoice>')

INSERT dbo.BookInvoice
(BookInvoiceXML)
VALUES ('<BookInvoice invoicenumber="1" customerid="40" orderdate="7/11/2008">
<OrderItems>
<Item id="11" qty="1" name="MCDBA Cliff Notes"/>
</OrderItems>
</BookInvoice>')

INSERT dbo.BookInvoice
(BookInvoiceXML)
VALUES ('<BookInvoice invoicenumber="1" customerid="9" orderdate="7/22/2008">
<OrderItems>
<Item id="11" qty="1" name="MCDBA Cliff Notes"/>
<Item id="24" qty="1" name="T-SQL Crossword Puzzles"/>
</OrderItems>
</BookInvoice>')
```

In the first example, the exists method is used to find all rows from the table for purchases of the item with an ID of 11:

```
SELECT BookInvoiceID
FROM dbo.BookInvoice
WHERE BookInvoiceXML.exist
('/BookInvoice/OrderItems/Item[@id=11]') = 1
```

This returns

```
BookInvoiceID
2
3
```

This next example demonstrates the nodes method, which shreds a document into a relational rowset. A local variable is used to populate a single XML document from the BookInvoice table, which is then referenced using the nodes method. This query retrieves a document and lists out the ID element of each BookInvoice/OrderItems/Item node:

```
DECLARE @BookInvoiceXML xml

SELECT @BookInvoiceXML = BookInvoiceXML
FROM dbo.BookInvoice
WHERE BookInvoiceID = 2

SELECT BookID.value('@id','integer') BookID
FROM   @BookInvoiceXML.nodes('/BookInvoice/OrderItems/Item')
AS BookTable(BookID)
```

The last query returns the item ID values in the virtual BookTable table:

```
BookID
11
```

The next example demonstrates the query method, which is used to return the two item elements from a specific XML document:

```
DECLARE @BookInvoiceXML XML

SELECT @BookInvoiceXML = BookInvoiceXML
FROM dbo.BookInvoice
WHERE BookInvoiceID = 3

SELECT @BookInvoiceXML.query('/BookInvoice/OrderItems')
```

This returns

```
<OrderItems>
  <Item id="11" qty="1" name="MCDBA Cliff Notes" />
  <Item id="24" qty="1" name="T-SQL Crossword Puzzles" />
</OrderItems>
```

The last example of this recipe demonstrates the value method, which is used to find the distinct book names from the first and second items within the BookInvoiceXML xml column:

```
SELECT DISTINCT
BookInvoiceXML.value
('(/BookInvoice/OrderItems/Item/@name)[1]', 'varchar(30)') as BookTitles
FROM dbo.BookInvoice
```

```
UNION
SELECT DISTINCT
BookInvoiceXML.value
('(/BookInvoice/OrderItems/Item/@name)[2]', 'varchar(30)')
FROM dbo.BookInvoice
```

Two result sets were combined together using UNION, as two levels of the /BookInvoice/ OrderItems/Item node were explored in two separate queries (the NULL value is from the stored XML fragment that only had a single item):

```
BookTitles
NULL
MCDBA Cliff Notes
SQL Fun in the Sun
T-SQL Crossword Puzzles
```

How It Works

XQuery methods enable you to query and modify data (modifications demonstrated later in this chapter) within an xml data type. Most of the examples in this recipe used a similar format of XMLColumn.MethodName.

For example, the exist method was used on the BookInvoiceXML xml column to show items with an ID of 11. The XQuery expression followed the method name in parentheses:

```
BookInvoiceXML.exist ('/BookInvoice/OrderItems/Item[@id=11]') = 1
```

The nodes function example included an XQuery expression to define the results to return in a shredded format, followed by the name of the new result table and column name in parentheses:

```
@BookInvoiceXML.nodes('/BookInvoice/OrderItems/Item')
AS BookTable(BookID)
```

The query method example used a simple XQuery expression in order to return item elements in the results:

```
@BookInvoiceXML.query('/BookInvoice/OrderItems/Item')
```

The value method included the XQuery expression that returns a scalar value for each row, defined by the data type in the second parameter:

```
BookInvoiceXML.value
('(/BookInvoice/OrderItems/Item/@name)[2]', 'varchar(30)')
```

Modifying XML Data

The xml data type column can be modified using the modify method in conjunction with UPDATE, allowing you to insert, update, or delete an XML node in the xml data type column.

This example demonstrates the modify method by inserting a new item into an existing XML document (specifically, a new item into the /BookInvoice/OrderItems node):

```
UPDATE dbo.BookInvoice
SET BookInvoiceXML.modify
('insert <Item id="920" qty="1" name="SQL Server 2008 Transact-SQL Recipes"/>
into (/BookInvoice/OrderItems)[1]')
WHERE BookInvoiceID = 2
```

Checking the BookInvoice XML document for this row confirms that the new item was added:

```
SELECT BookInvoiceXML
FROM dbo.BookInvoice
WHERE BookInvoiceID = 2
```

This returns

```
<BookInvoice invoicenumber="1" customerid="40" orderdate="7/11/2008">
  <OrderItems>
    <Item id="11" qty="1" name="MCDBA Cliff Notes" />
    <Item id="920" qty="1" name="SQL Server 2008 Transact-SQL Recipes" />
  </OrderItems>
</BookInvoice>
```

How It Works

The modify function also used the XMLColumn.MethodName format and an XQuery insert expression in parentheses to insert a new item element into an existing document:

```
BookInvoiceXML.modify
('insert <Item id="920" qty="1" name="SQL Server 2008 T-SQL Recipes"/>
into (/BookInvoice/OrderItems)[1]')
```

The insert command used to add a new item element is an extension to the XQuery language and is called *XML DML*. Other XML DML commands include the replace statement, which updates XML data, and the delete statement, which removes a node from an XML document or fragment.

Indexing XML Data

You can improve performance of queries against XML data type columns by using XML indexes. To create an XML index, the table must first already have a clustered index defined on the primary key of the table.

XML columns can only have *one* primary XML index defined, and then up to *three* secondary indexes (of different types described in a bit). The CREATE INDEX command is used to define XML indexes. The abridged syntax is as follows:

```
CREATE [ PRIMARY ] XML INDEX index_name
    ON <object> ( xml_column_name )
    [ USING XML INDEX xml_index_name
        [ FOR { VALUE | PATH | PROPERTY } ] ]
    [ WITH ( <xml_index_option> [ ,...n ] ) ][ ; ]
```

Creating an index for an XML column uses several of the same arguments as a regular table index (see Chapter 5 for more information). The XML-specific arguments of this command are described in Table 14-2.

Table 14-2. *CREATE XML INDEX Arguments*

Argument	Description
Object	This specifies the name of the table the index is being added to.
XML_column_name	This defines the name of the XML data type column.
XML_index_name	This is the unique name of the XML index.

Argument	Description
VALUE | PATH | PROPERTY	These are arguments for secondary indexes only and relate to XQuery optimization. A VALUE secondary index is used for indexing based on imprecise paths. A PATH secondary index is used for indexing via a path and value. A PROPERTY secondary index is used for indexing based on a querying node values based on a path.

In this first example, a primary XML index is created on an xml data type column:

```
CREATE PRIMARY XML INDEX idx_XML_Primary_Book_ChapterDESC
    ON dbo.Book(ChapterDESC)
GO
```

Next, a secondary VALUE index is created on the same xml column, but with a different name. The USING clause is added for secondary indexes, specifying in the FOR clause that the xml data type column be given a VALUE index in addition to the existing primary index:

```
CREATE XML INDEX idx_XML_Value_Book_ChapterDESC
    ON dbo.Book(ChapterDESC)
  USING XML INDEX idx_XML_Primary_Book_ChapterDESC
FOR VALUE
GO
```

You can use the sys.XML_indexes system catalog view to view the XML indexes used in a database. In this query, all XML indexes are listed for a specific table:

```
SELECT  name, secondary_type_desc
FROM    sys.XML_indexes
WHERE object_id = OBJECT_ID('dbo.Book')
```

This query returns the name of the XML indexes, and if the index is a secondary index, the type:

name	secondary_type_desc
idx_XML_Primary_Book_ChapterDESC	NULL
idx_XML_Value_Book_ChapterDESC	VALUE

Once created, XML indexes can be modified or removed just like regular indexes using the ALTER INDEX and DROP INDEX commands.

How It Works

Because XML documents can store up to 2GB for a single column and row, query performance can suffer when you are trying to query the data stored in the XML column. Make use of XML indexes if you plan on frequently querying XML data type data. Indexing xml data types internally persists the tabular form of the XML data, allowing for more efficient querying of hierarchical data.

XML indexes may look a little odd at first because you are adding secondary indexes to the same xml data type column. Adding the different types of secondary indexes helps benefit performance, based on the different types of XQuery queries you plan to execute. All in all, you can have up to four indexes on a single xml data type column: one primary and three secondary. A primary XML index must be created prior to being able to create secondary indexes. A secondary PATH index is used to enhance performance for queries that specify a path and value from the xml column using XQuery. A secondary PROPERTY index is used to enhance performance of queries that retrieve specific node values by specifying a path using XQuery. The secondary VALUE index is used to enhance performance of queries that retrieve data using an imprecise path (for example, for an XPath expression that employs //, which can be used to find nodes in a document no matter where they exist).

Converting Between XML Documents and Relational Data

In the next recipe, I'll demonstrate how to convert relational data sets into a hierarchical XML format using FOR XML. After that, I'll demonstrate how to use OPENXML to convert an XML format into a relational data set.

Formatting Relational Data As XML

Introduced in SQL Server 2000, FOR XML extends a SELECT statement by returning the relational query results in an XML format. FOR XML operates in four different modes: RAW, AUTO, EXPLICIT, and PATH.

In RAW mode, a single row element is generated for each row in the result set, with each column in the result converted to an attribute within the element.

In this example, FOR XML RAW is used to return the results of the HumanResources.Shift table in an XML format. The TYPE option is used to return the results in the XML data type, and ROOT is used to define a top-level element where the results will be nested:

```
USE AdventureWorks
GO

SELECT ShiftID, Name
FROM HumanResources.Shift
FOR XML RAW('Shift'), ROOT('Shifts'), TYPE
```

This returns

```
<Shifts>
    <Shift ShiftID="1" Name="Day" />
    <Shift ShiftID="2" Name="Evening" />
    <Shift ShiftID="3" Name="Night" />
</Shifts>
```

The FOR XML AUTO mode creates XML elements in the results of a SELECT statement, and also automatically nests the data, based on the columns in the SELECT clause. AUTO shares the same options as RAW.

In this example, Employee, Shift, and Department information is queried from AdventureWorks—with XML AUTO automatically arranging the hierarchy of the results:

```
SELECT  TOP 3 BusinessEntityID,
        Shift.Name,
        Department.Name
FROM   HumanResources.EmployeeDepartmentHistory Employee
INNER JOIN HumanResources.Shift Shift ON
    Employee.ShiftID = Shift.ShiftID
INNER JOIN HumanResources.Department Department ON
    Employee.DepartmentID = Department.DepartmentID
ORDER BY BusinessEntityID
FOR XML AUTO, TYPE
```

This returns

```xml
<Employee BusinessEntityID="1">
  <Shift Name="Day">
    <Department Name="Executive" />
  </Shift>
</Employee>
<Employee BusinessEntityID="2">
  <Shift Name="Day">
    <Department Name="Engineering" />
  </Shift>
</Employee>
<Employee BusinessEntityID="3">
  <Shift Name="Day">
    <Department Name="Engineering" />
  </Shift>
</Employee>
```

Notice that the third INNER JOIN caused the values from the Department table to be children of the Shift table's values. The Shift element was then included as a child of the Employee element. Rearranging the order of the columns in the SELECT clause, however, impacts how the hierarchy is returned. For example:

```sql
SELECT  TOP 3
      Shift.Name,
      Department.Name,
      BusinessEntityID
FROM   HumanResources.EmployeeDepartmentHistory Employee
INNER JOIN HumanResources.Shift Shift ON
   Employee.ShiftID = Shift.ShiftID
INNER JOIN HumanResources.Department Department ON
   Employee.DepartmentID = Department.DepartmentID
ORDER BY Shift.Name, Department.Name, BusinessEntityID
FOR XML AUTO, TYPE
```

This time the top of the hierarchy is the Shift, with the child element of Department, and Employees children of the Department elements:

```xml
<Shift Name="Day">
  <Department Name="Document Control">
    <Employee BusinessEntityID="217" />
    <Employee BusinessEntityID="219" />
    <Employee BusinessEntityID="220" />
  </Department>
</Shift>
```

The FOR XML EXPLICIT mode allows you more control over the XML results, letting you define whether columns are assigned to elements or attributes. The EXPLICIT parameters have the same use and meaning as for RAW and AUTO; however, EXPLICIT also makes use of *directives*, which are used to define the resulting elements and attributes. For example, the following query displays the VendorID and CreditRating columns as attributes, and the VendorName column as an element. The column is defined after the column alias using an element name, tag number, attribute, and directive:

```
SELECT TOP 3
    1 AS Tag,
    NULL AS Parent,
    BusinessEntityID AS [Vendor!1!VendorID],
    Name AS [Vendor!1!VendorName!ELEMENT],
    CreditRating AS [Vendor!1!CreditRating]
FROM Purchasing.Vendor
ORDER BY CreditRating
FOR XML EXPLICIT, TYPE
```

This returns

```
<Vendor VendorID="1496" CreditRating="1">
  <VendorName>Advanced Bicycles</VendorName>
</Vendor>
<Vendor VendorID="1492" CreditRating="1">
  <VendorName>Australia Bike Retailer</VendorName>
</Vendor>
<Vendor VendorID="1500" CreditRating="1">
  <VendorName>Morgan Bike Accessories</VendorName>
</Vendor>
```

The Tag column in the SELECT clause is required in EXPLICIT mode in order to produce the XML document output. Each tag number represents a constructed element. The Parent column alias is also required, providing the hierarchical information about any parent elements. The Parent column references the tag of the parent element. If the Parent column is NULL, this indicates that the element has no parent and is top-level.

The TYPE directive in the FOR XML clause of the previous query was used to return the results as a true SQL Server native xml data type, allowing you to store the results in XML or query it using XQuery.

Next, the FOR XML PATH option defines column names and aliases as XPath expressions. XPath is a language used for searching data within an XML document.

■**Tip** For information on XPath, visit the World Wide Web Consortium (W3C) standards site at http://www.w3.org/TR/xpath.

FOR XML PATH uses some of the same arguments and keywords as other FOR XML variations. Where it differs, however, is in the SELECT clause, where XPath syntax is used to define elements, subelements, attributes, and data values.

For example:

```
SELECT Name as "@Territory",
       CountryRegionCode as "@Region",
       SalesYTD
FROM Sales.SalesTerritory
WHERE SalesYTD > 6000000
ORDER BY SalesYTD DESC
FOR XML PATH('TerritorySales'), ROOT('CompanySales'), TYPE
```

This returns

```
<CompanySales>
   <TerritorySales Territory="Southwest" Region="US">
      <SalesYTD>8351296.7411</SalesYTD>
   </TerritorySales>
   <TerritorySales Territory="Canada" Region="CA">
      <SalesYTD>6917270.8842</SalesYTD>
   </TerritorySales>
</CompanySales>
```

This query returned results with a root element of CompanySales and a subelement of TerritorySales. The TerritorySales element was then attributed based on the territory and region code (both prefaced with ampersands [@] in the SELECT clause). The SalesYTD, which was unmarked with XPath directives, became a subelement to TerritorySales.

How It Works

The FOR XML command is included at the end of a SELECT query in order to return data in an XML format. The AUTO and RAW modes allow for a quick and semi-automated formatting of the results, whereas EXPLICIT and PATH provide more control over the hierarchy of data and the assignment of elements versus attributes. FOR XML PATH, on the other hand, is an easier alternative to EXPLICIT mode for those developers who are more familiar with the XPath language.

The FOR XML options I demonstrated in this recipe were the most common variations you will see when trying to create XML from a result set. Generating XML document fragments using FOR XML eases the process of having to create the hierarchy using other manual methods in Transact-SQL. Keep in mind that you always have the option of programmatic XML document creation too (using .NET, for example).

Converting XML to a Relational Form

Whereas FOR XML converts relational query results to an XML format, OPENXML converts XML format to a relational form. To perform this conversion, the sp_XML_preparedocument system stored procedure is used to create an internal pointer to the XML document, which is then used with OPENXML in order to return the rowset data.

The syntax for the OPENXML command is as follows:

```
OPENXML(idoc ,rowpattern, flags)
[WITH (SchemaDeclaration | TableName)]
```

The arguments for this command are described in Table 14-3.

Table 14-3. *OPENXML Arguments*

Argument	Description
idoc	This is the internal representation of the XML document as represented by the sp_XML_preparedocument system stored procedure.
rowpattern	This defines the XPath pattern used to return nodes from the XML document.

Continued

Table 14-3. *Continued*

Argument	Description
flags	When the flag 0 is used, results default to attribute-centric mappings. When flag 1 is used, attribute-centric mapping is applied first, and then element-centric mapping for columns that are not processed. Flag 2 uses element-centric mapping. Flag 8 specifies that consumed data should not be copied to the overflow property.
SchemaDeclaration | TableName	SchemaDeclaration defines the output of the column name (rowset name), column type (valid data type), column pattern (optional XPath pattern), and optional metadata properties (about the XML nodes). If Tablename is used instead, a table must already exist for holding the rowset data.

In this example, an XML document is stored in a local variable and is then passed to a stored procedure that uses OPENXML in order to convert it into a relational rowset. First, I'll create the stored procedure:

```
CREATE PROCEDURE dbo.usp_SEL_BookXML_Convert_To_Relational
    @XMLDoc xml
AS

DECLARE @docpointer int

EXEC sp_XML_preparedocument @docpointer OUTPUT, @XMLdoc

SELECT    Chapter, ChapterNM
FROM      OPENXML (@docpointer, '/Book/Chapters/Chapter',0)
            WITH (Chapter int '@id',
              ChapterNM varchar(50) '@name' )
GO
```

Next, I'll populate a local xml data type variable and send it to the new stored procedure:

```
DECLARE @XMLdoc XML
SET @XMLdoc =
'<Book name="SQL Server 2000 Fast Answers">
   <Chapters>
      <Chapter id="1" name="Installation, Upgrades"/>
      <Chapter id="2" name="Configuring SQL Server"/>
      <Chapter id="3" name="Creating and Configuring Databases"/>
      <Chapter id="4" name="SQL Server Agent and SQL Logs"/>
   </Chapters>
   </Book>'

EXEC dbo.usp_SEL_BookXML_Convert_To_Relational @XMLdoc
```

This returns

```
Chapter    ChapterNM
1          Installation, Upgrades
2          Configuring SQL Server
3          Creating and Configuring Databases
4          SQL Server Agent and SQL Logs
```

How It Works

The example started off by creating a stored procedure that would be used to convert an XML document fragment into a relational data set. The procedure had a single input parameter defined of an xml data type:

```
CREATE PROCEDURE dbo.usp_SEL_BookXML_Convert_To_Relational
    @XMLDoc xml
AS
```

A local variable was declared for use as an output parameter in the sp_XML_preparedocument system stored procedure to hold the value of the internal document pointer:

```
DECLARE @docpointer int
```

Next, the system stored procedure is called with the OUTPUT parameter, the second argument being the input xml data type parameter:

```
EXEC sp_XML_preparedocument @docpointer OUTPUT, @XMLdoc
```

Next, a SELECT statement referenced the OPENXML function in the FROM clause, with the name of the two columns to be returned in the results:

```
SELECT    Chapter, ChapterNM
FROM      OPENXML
```

The first argument in the OPENXML command was the internal pointer variable. The second argument was the XPath expression of the node to be used in the XML document. The third argument was the flag, which designated an attribute-centric mapping:

```
(@docpointer, '/Book/Chapters/Chapter',0)
```

The WITH clause defined the actual result output. Two columns were defined, one for the Chapter and the other for the ChapterNM. The @id designated the ID attribute to be mapped to the Chapter column and the @name attribute designated the name mapped to the ChapterNM column:

```
        WITH (Chapter int '@id',
          ChapterNM varchar(50) '@name' )
```

After creating the stored procedure, a local variable was then populated with an XML fragment, and then passed to the stored procedure, returning two columns and four rows.

Working with Native Hierarchical Data

SQL Server 2008 introduces the new hierarchyid data type, which can be used to natively store and manage a position within a tree hierarchy. This new data type allows you to *compactly* represent a position of a node within a hierarchy, and similar to the xml data type, hierarchyid includes several built-in methods that you can use to manipulate or traverse hierarchies. This new improvement helps facilitate simplified storage and querying of hierarchical data without having to produce your own methods.

The next few recipes will demonstrate how to store, manipulate, and query hierarchical data using the hierarchyid data type.

Storing Hierarchical Data

This recipe demonstrates storing a web page layout hierarchy. In this example, I want to represent a root web page followed by two levels of pages and associated siblings.

I'll start by creating a table that will store the web page hierarchy. The first column in the table definition, WebpageLayoutID, will contain the hierarchyid data type data. The second column, PositionDESC, is a calculated column that uses the GetLevel method of a hierarchyid data type column to show the position of the specific row in the tree. The final column, PageURL, will just contain the actual web page URL.

■**Note** The hierarchyid data type includes several methods that can be used to manipulate and traverse node values. These will be explained and demonstrated in more detail in the next recipe.

```
USE TestDB
GO

CREATE TABLE dbo.WebpageLayout
   (WebpageLayoutID hierarchyid NOT NULL,
    PositionDESC as WebpageLayoutID.GetLevel(),
    PageURL nvarchar(50) NOT NULL)
GO
```

Continuing with the recipe, I'll insert a new row representing the root of the web site hierarchical structure:

```
INSERT dbo.WebpageLayout
(WebpageLayoutID, PageURL)
VALUES
('/', 'http://joesack.com')
```

Notice that the string version representing the root of the hierarchy is /. This is automatically converted upon insert into the native hierarchyid format (binary format). Next, I'll query the data to see how it is stored:

```
SELECT WebpageLayoutID, PositionDESC, PageURL
FROM dbo.WebpageLayout
```

This returns

WebpageLayoutID	PositionDESC	PageURL
0x	0	http://joesack.com

Notice that the original / value was redefined as the hex value of 0x. Hierarchy paths are represented using the slash character. A single slash is used to represent the root of a tree. Consecutive levels are formed using integer values separated by slashes.

Next, I'll insert two new rows representing children of the root web page. These two web pages are on the same level (so they are siblings):

```
INSERT dbo.WebpageLayout
(WebpageLayoutID, PageURL)
VALUES
('/1/', 'http://joesack.com/WordPress/')

INSERT dbo.WebpageLayout
(WebpageLayoutID, PageURL)
VALUES
('/2/', 'http://joesack.com/SQLFastTOC.htm')
```

Again, I'll query the results so far:

```
SELECT WebpageLayoutID, PositionDESC, PageURL
FROM dbo.WebpageLayout
```

This returns

WebpageLayoutID	PositionDESC	PageURL
0x	0	http://joesack.com
0x58	1	http://joesack.com/WordPress/
0x68	1	http://joesack.com/SQLFastTOC.htm

Notice that the PositionDESC shows the root web page as a position of 0 and the two children as a position of 1.

Next, I'll demonstrate adding two new web pages that are children for the http://joesack.com/WordPress/ page. Unlike with previous examples, I'll use the GetDescendant method of the hierarchyid data type to populate the WebpageLayoutID:

```
DECLARE @ParentWebpageLayoutID hierarchyid
SELECT @ParentWebpageLayoutID = CONVERT(hierarchyid, '/1/')

INSERT dbo.WebpageLayout
(WebpageLayoutID, PageURL)
VALUES
(@ParentWebpageLayoutID.GetDescendant(NULL,NULL),
'http://joesack.com/WordPress/?page_id=2')

INSERT dbo.WebpageLayout
(WebpageLayoutID, PageURL)
VALUES
(@ParentWebpageLayoutID.GetDescendant(NULL,NULL),
'http://joesack.com/WordPress/?page_id=9')
```

This returns

```
(1 row(s) affected)

(1 row(s) affected)
```

Instead of showing the native format of WebpageLayoutID, this next query shows the string representation of the hierarchyid data type using the ToString method:

```
SELECT WebpageLayoutID.ToString() as WebpageLayoutID, PositionDESC, PageURL
FROM dbo.WebpageLayout
```

Notice that the newly inserted row was placed beneath the proper parent by using the GetDescendant method rather than having to hard-code the value into the INSERT:

WebpageLayoutID	PositionDESC	PageURL
/	0	http://joesack.com
/1/	1	http://joesack.com/WordPress/
/1/1/	2	http://joesack.com/WordPress/?page_id=2
/1/1/	2	http://joesack.com/WordPress/?page_id=9
/2/	1	http://joesack.com/SQLFastTOC.htm

How It Works

This recipe introduced the SQL Server 2008 hierarchyid data type and started off by demonstrating how to create a table with the hierarchyid data type. After that, I inserted a new row for the root web page. Hierarchy paths are represented using the slash character. A single slash is used to represent the root of a tree. Consecutive levels are formed using integer values separated by slashes:

```
/
/1/
/1/1/
/2/
/2/1/
/2/2/
```

Tip Node ordering on the same level can also be designated by using dots—for example, /1/1.5/.

After inserting the root node, I queried the table to show that the slash had been converted to a hex value. I then inserted two new pages that were children of the root node. For one of the child nodes, I then created two new children, but instead of manually designating the node path, I used the GetDescendant function to define the path for me. Querying the table after the INSERT revealed that the proper position and path had been used.

Returning a Specific Ancestor

The previous recipe introduced how to get started with using the native hierarchyid data type. The hierarchyid data type includes a set of methods that you can use to retrieve and traverse data values. I'll walk you through examples of how each is used over the next few recipes.

The GetAncestor method allows you return a position in the hierarchy by moving up a certain number of levels from a specific position. The input parameter defines the number of levels to move up. In this example, I create two local variables to hold the original node value and then the value of the ancestor one level above:

```
DECLARE @WebpageLayoutID hierarchyid
DECLARE @New_WebpageLayoutID hierarchyid
SELECT @WebpageLayoutID = CONVERT(hierarchyid, '/1/1/')

SELECT @New_WebpageLayoutID = @WebpageLayoutID.GetAncestor( 1 )
SELECT @New_WebpageLayoutID.ToString()
```

This returns the parent of the 1/1 node, which is /1/:

```
/1/
```

How It Works

This recipe demonstrated how to work with the various methods available with the hierarchyid data type. These methods are referenced using the dot notation off of the data value contained in the local variable, which is similar to methods used with the xml data type demonstrated earlier in the chapter (for example, the modify method).

The technique used to prep the value prior to using the method was to declare the hierarchyid variable first:

```
DECLARE @WebpageLayoutID hierarchyid
```

A second variable was defined to hold the new hierarchyid value:

```
DECLARE @New_WebpageLayoutID hierarchyid
```

After that, the variable value was assigned using a SELECT:

```
SELECT @WebpageLayoutID = CONVERT(hierarchyid, '/1/1/')
```

This could also have been configured using a SET command, or from retrieving a single hierarchyid value from a table.

Next, the GetAncestor method is used to populate the second declared hierarchyid variable:

```
SELECT @New_WebpageLayoutID = @WebpageLayoutID.GetAncestor( 1 )
```

In order to print the populated value of the variable, I used the ToString method:

```
SELECT @New_WebpageLayoutID.ToString()
```

ToString converts the native hierarchyid node value into the string representation.

If you wanted to reverse the string back into the actual hierarchyid node value, you could use the Parse method. For example:

```
SELECT hierarchyid::Parse ('/1/1/')
```

This returns

```
0x5AC0
```

Notice that Parse is bound to the general class of hierarchyid and not an actual local variable itself.

Returning Child Nodes

The GetDescendant returns the child of a specific hierarchical position. It takes two inputs, which can be NULL, or specifies children of the specific node in order to define the boundaries of which child is returned of that parent. In this case, I am looking for the descendant node of the path /1/:

```
DECLARE @WebpageLayoutID hierarchyid
DECLARE @New_WebpageLayoutID hierarchyid
SELECT @WebpageLayoutID = CONVERT(hierarchyid, '/1/')

SELECT @New_WebpageLayoutID = @WebpageLayoutID.GetDescendant(NULL,NULL)
SELECT @New_WebpageLayoutID.ToString()
```

This returns

```
/1/1/
```

How It Works

Similar to the last recipe, the GetDescendant method was used in conjunction with the hierarchyid local variable using a variable.method format:

```
SELECT @New_WebpageLayoutID = @WebpageLayoutID.GetDescendant(NULL,NULL)
```

This function returned the child node of the local variable's parent, /1/1/.

Returning a Node's Depth

The GetLevel method returns the depth of the specified node in the tree. The following example returns the level integer value for /1/1/1/1/:

```
DECLARE @WebpageLayoutID hierarchyid
SELECT @WebpageLayoutID = CONVERT(hierarchyid, '/1/1/1/1/')

SELECT @WebpageLayoutID.GetLevel()
```

This returns

```
4
```

How It Works

The GetLevel method is used in conjunction with the hierarchyid local variable using a variable.method format:

```
SELECT @WebpageLayoutID.GetLevel()
```

This function returned the integer-valued depth of the local variable's node.

Returning the Root Node

The GetRoot method returns the hierarchyid root value of the tree. This function is not used in conjunction with a user-defined hierarchyid local variable. To demonstrate, I'll use GetRoot to help me get the root row from the table I created in the previous recipe:

```
SELECT PageURL
FROM dbo.WebpageLayout
WHERE WebpageLayoutID = hierarchyid::GetRoot()
```

This returns

```
PageURL
http://joesack.com
```

How It Works

In this recipe, the query returned the root web page by using the GetRoot method:

```
WHERE WebpageLayoutID = hierarchyid::GetRoot()
```

Notice that GetRoot was bound to the general class of hierarchyid and not an actual local variable itself.

Determining Whether a Node Is a Child of the Current Node

The IsDescendantOf method returns a Boolean value with true (1) or false (0) designating whether or not a node is a child of the current node. This method takes one input parameter that defines the child node to be evaluated, as the next query demonstrates:

```
DECLARE @WebpageLayoutID hierarchyid
SELECT @WebpageLayoutID = CONVERT(hierarchyid, '/1/')

SELECT @WebpageLayoutID.IsDescendantOf('/')
SELECT @WebpageLayoutID.IsDescendantOf('/1/1/')
```

This returns

```
1

(1 row(s) affected)

0

(1 row(s) affected)
```

How It Works

This recipe demonstrated using the IsDescendantOf method to evaluate whether a node is a child of the current node. The first evaluation by IsDescendantOf checked to see whether the root node was a descendant of /1/. Since it was, a 1 was returned. The second use of IsDescendantOf checked to see whether 1/1 is a descendant of /1/. Since it is not, a 0 was returned.

Changing Node Locations

The GetReparentedValue method returns the node value of the new path given two input parameters, the old root and the new root, as the following query demonstrates:

```
DECLARE @WebpageLayoutID hierarchyid
DECLARE @New_WebpageLayoutID hierarchyid
SELECT @WebpageLayoutID = CONVERT(hierarchyid, '/1/1/')

SELECT @New_WebpageLayoutID = @WebpageLayoutID.GetReparentedValue('/1/', '/2/')
SELECT @New_WebpageLayoutID.ToString()
```

This returns

```
/2/1/
```

How It Works

This recipe demonstrated changing the node parent of an existing node using the GetReparentedValue method. The hierarchyid value of 1/1 contained in the @WebpageLayoutID local variable was reparented from /1/ to /2 to become /2/1/.

Native Spatial Data

Prior to SQL Server 2008, database storage of spatial data required use of non-native methods including the creation of custom CLR assemblies. SQL Server 2008 introduces native storage of spatial data, providing two new data types, geography and geometry. Fundamentally, these data types provide built-in capabilities for location and mapping applications (such as Microsoft Virtual Earth) and representation of geometric shapes.

The geometry data type represents flat-earth (Euclidean) coordinate spatial data, and also allows for storage of points, polygons, curves, and collections.

■**Tip** Polygons within geography or geometry data type context can be used to define regions and areas referencing locations on the earth. Note that the data that is of the geography data type is still two-dimensional in SQL Server 2008.

The geography data type is used for round-earth spatial storage, allowing for latitude and longitude coordinates and storage of points, polygons, curves, and collections. This will likely be a more commonly used data type for mapping/location-aware applications.

SQL Server 2008 supports the Well-Known Text (WKT), Well-Known Binary (WKB), and Geography Markup Language (GML) XML transport formats for representing vector geometry mapping objects. These formats are regulated by the Open Geospatial Consortium (OGC), and I'll be using the WKT format in this recipe in conjunction with the geography data type.

■**Tip** For more on OGC and the WKT/WKB/GML XML transport formats, visit http://www.opengeospatial.org/standards/sfa and http://www.opengeospatial.org/standards/sfs for standards documentation.

The next two recipes will demonstrate how to store and query native spatial data type data.

Storing Spatial Data

In this recipe, I'll demonstrate how to store spatial data within the geography data type. Specifically, I will create a table that will be used to contain the location and shapes of lakes found in Minneapolis. Once stored, I'll demonstrate how to use various functions to work with the geography data. SQL Server 2008 provides several built-in functions for performing geometric and geographic calculations. Examples of computational capabilities include the ability to define intersections between points, distances, and areas.

I'll begin by creating a new table that will contain the geography data type data that represents the polygon shape and location of lakes in Minneapolis:

```
USE TestDB
GO

CREATE TABLE dbo.MinneapolisLake
    (MinneapolisLakeID int NOT NULL IDENTITY(1,1) PRIMARY KEY,
    LakeNM varchar(50) NOT NULL,
    LakeLocationGEOG Geography NOT NULL,
    LakeLocationWKT AS LakeLocationGEOG.STAsText())
GO
```

Notice that the LakeLocationWKT column is actually a calculated column based on the LakeLocationGEOG Geography column. The STAsText method of the geography data type returns the WKT representation of the geometry column (I'll demonstrate the difference later on in this recipe).

Now that the table is created, I'll insert three rows representing three lakes. I'll use the Parse method of the geography instance in order to input the WKT value for the polygons representing each lake.

■**Caution** Community Technical Preview (CTP) versions of SQL Server 2008 used a coordinate order of latitude-longitude for WKT and WKB formats employed against the geography data type. As of RTM, the order has been reversed, using longitude-latitude ordering. Using the incorrect ordering will raise an error upon INSERT or UPDATE.

Lake Calhoun and Lake Harriet both are relatively round/oval shapes, so the polygon is defined with four longitude and latitude pairs—as well as a repeat of the first longitude and latitude pair in order to complete the polygon ring:

```
-- Lake Calhoun
INSERT dbo.MinneapolisLake
(LakeNM, LakeLocationGEOG)
VALUES ('Lake Calhoun',
geography::Parse('POLYGON((-93.31593 44.94821 , -93.31924 44.93603 ,
-93.30666 44.93577 , -93.30386 44.94321 , -93.31593 44.94821 ))'))

-- Lake Harriet
INSERT dbo.MinneapolisLake
(LakeNM, LakeLocationGEOG)
VALUES ('Lake Harriet',
geography::Parse('POLYGON((-93.30776 44.92774 , -93.31379 44.91889 ,
-93.30122 44.91702 , -93.29739 44.92624 ,-93.30776 44.92774 ))'))
```

If I had not repeated the start and end points of the polygon ring, I would have gotten this error message:

```
The Polygon input is not valid because the start and end points of the exterior
ring are not the same. Each ring of a polygon must have the same start and end
points.
```

Next, I'll insert the polygon representing Lake of the Isles, which has a more unusual shape than the previous two lakes and is therefore represented with seven distinct polygon longitude and latitude pairs (and an eighth pair to close the polygon ring):

```
-- Lake of the Isles (notice several points, as this lake has an odd shape)
INSERT dbo.MinneapolisLake
(LakeNM, LakeLocationGEOG)
VALUES ('Lake of the Isles',
geography::Parse(
  'POLYGON(( -93.30924 44.95847,
            -93.31291 44.95360,
            -93.30607 44.95178,
            -93.30158  44.95543,
            -93.30349 44.95689,
            -93.30372  44.96261,
            -93.3068  44.95720 8,
            -93.30924  44.95847))'))
```

I'll now query the table to demonstrate what the stored data looks like:

```
SELECT LakeNM, LakeLocationGEOG, LakeLocationWKT
FROM dbo.MinneapolisLake
```

This returns

LakeNM	LakeLocationGEOG	LakeLocationWKT
Lake Calhoun	0xE6100000010405000000BEDEFDF15E794640 D1747632385457C09609BFD4CF774640CDE49B 6D6E5457C0F949B54FC777464072BF4351A053 57C04DA1F31ABB78464001A43671725357C0BE DEFDF15E794640D1747632385457C001000000 020000000001000000FFFFFFFF0000000003	POLYGON ((44.94821 -93.31593, 44.93603 -93.31924, 44.93577 -93.30666, 44.94321 -93.30386, 44.94821 -93.31593))
Lake Harriet	0xE6100000010405000000074982F2FC0764640 16C1FF56B25357C08B4F01309E754640F5F3A6 22155457C093E34EE960754640AC3940304753 57C09F1F46088F764640130A1170085357C074 982F2FC076464016C1FF56B25357C001000000 020000000001000000FFFFFFFF0000000003	POLYGON ((44.92774 -93.30776, 44.91889 -93.31379, 44.91702 -93.30122, 44.92624 -93.29739, 44.92774 -93.30776))
Lake of the Isles	0xE6100000010408000003B191C25AF7A4640 5DA79196CA5357C099BB96900F7A4640D925AA B7065457C0527E52EDD37946405A12A0A69653 57C003CFBD874B7A46402C4833164D5357C04A EF1B5F7B7A46406F2A52616C5357C0BA66F2CD 367B464008C90226705357C098DD9387857A46 40FAF202ECA35357C03B191C25AF7A46405DA7 9196CA5357C001000000020000000001000000 FFFFFFFF0000000003	POLYGON ((44.95847 -93.30924, 44.9536 -93.31291, 44.95178 -93.30607, 44.95543 -93.30158, 44.95689 -93.30349, 44.96261 -93.30372, 44.9572 -93.30688, 44.95847 -93.30924))

Notice that the native geography data in `LakeLocationGEOG` was not human readable—which is why I defined the `LakeLocationWKT` calculated column using the `STAsText` method to show the WKT human-readable text instead.

How It Works

This recipe demonstrated how to store native spatial data in the geography data type. I started off by creating a table that would hold one row for each lake. The `LakeLocationGEOG` column was defined with the geography data type:

```
LakeLocationGEOG Geography NOT NULL,
```

I also defined a calculated column that referenced my geography column and the method call to `STAsText`—in order to show the human-readable WKT format of the geography instance:

```
LakeLocationWKT AS LakeLocationGEOG.STAsText())
```

Next, I started inserting rows for three different lakes. In the `VALUES` argument of the `INSERT`, I used the `Parse` command (prefixed by `geography::`, and then followed by the WKT definition of the polygon and associated longitude and latitude points that defined the boundaries of the lake):

```
VALUES ('Lake Calhoun',
geography::Parse('POLYGON((-93.31593 44.94821, -93.31924 44.93603, -93.30666
44.93577, -93.30386 44.94321, -93.31593 44.94821))'))
```

The `POLYGON` keyword represented the type of object (other types can be instantiated in SQL Server 2008, including line strings, multi-line strings, multi-polygons, points, and multi-points.).

Also notice that the each longitude and latitude pair in the previous code snippet was separated with a comma for the POLYGON instantiated type.

Note Geography data types can also be used to store elevation and measure values; however, these values are not used in any computations and are just stored as metadata. Stored data is treated as two-dimensional.

The Parse method is functionally equivalent to the STGeomFromText method, only it makes some assumptions about the spatial reference ID (SRID). A SRID defines the reference system used for the geometry and geography data types. In this case, Parse maps to a SRID of 4326 for the geography data type, which translates to WGS 84 (World Geodetic System 1984) as a reference for geographic mapping. If I had used the STGeomFromText method instead of Parse, I could have designated a second SRID parameter to be a different spatial reference type. The sys.spatial_reference_systems catalog view contains all SRIDs recognized by SQL Server 2008.

Querying Spatial Data

Now that I have the geography values stored in the table, I can take advantage of SQL Server 2008's native computational functionality to reveal a variety of data points.

Tip SQL Server 2008 provides several methods for working with geography and geometry data types. This chapter demonstrates some of them, but for a complete list, reference SQL Server Books Online.

For example, I can determine the internal areas in square meters of each lake using the STArea method and total length in meters using the STLength method:

```
SELECT LakeNM,
       LakeLocationGEOG.STLength() Length,
       LakeLocationGEOG.STArea() Area
FROM dbo.MinneapolisLake
```

This returns

LakeNM	Length	Area
Lake Calhoun	4330.60504437253	1131010.52091503
Lake Harriet	4010.50193580554	982158.281167269
Lake of the Isles	3473.37155877733	448936.179574728

Now, let's say that the Twin Cities marathon plans on running from downtown Minneapolis all the way to one of the lakes in my table. If I have the longitude and latitude of my starting position (represented by a point), I can use the STDistance method to determine the shortest distance between downtown Minneapolis and each lake, as I demonstrate next (I'll walk through each line in the "How It Works" section):

```
DECLARE @DowntownStartingPoint geography
SET @DowntownStartingPoint = geography::Parse('POINT(-93.26319 44.97846)')

SELECT LakeNM,
       LakeLocationGEOG.STDistance(@DowntownStartingPoint) Distance
FROM dbo.MinneapolisLake
ORDER BY LakeLocationGEOG.STDistance(@DowntownStartingPoint)
```

This returns the distance in meters from downtown to each lake:

```
LakeNM              Distance
Lake of the Isles   3650.39170324889
Lake Calhoun        5063.86366294861
Lake Harriet        6400.09741657171
```

Continuing the example of the marathon, let's assume that a small plane will be flying overhead with a banner cheering on the runners as they head from downtown to the lakes.

So far, I have demonstrated the point and polygon geography types; however, the flight path in this case will be represented by a Linestring. In this next query, I will use the STIntersects method of the geography data type to determine whether or not the flight path will intersect any of the lakes (fly over any of the lakes):

```
DECLARE @FlightPath geography
SET @FlightPath = geography::Parse('LINESTRING(-93.26319 44.97846, -93.30862
44.91695  )')

SELECT LakeNM,
       LakeLocationGEOG.STIntersects(@FlightPath) IntersectsWithFlightPath
FROM dbo.MinneapolisLake
```

The results show that the flight path from Minneapolis downtown will intersect only with Lake Harriet:

```
LakeNM              IntersectsWithFlightPath
Lake Calhoun        0
Lake Harriet        1
Lake of the Isles   0
```

So far, I have not used any of the geography data type methods within the context of a WHERE clause. Assuming a much larger result set than what I'm demonstrating here, there can be a significant computational performance overhead with using some of the spatial methods within the context of a search condition. To address this, SQL Server 2008 provides spatial index support of your geometry and geography data types.

Methods such as STDistance and STIntersects are supported by spatial indexes when used within the WHERE clause of a query. Spatial indexes improve the performance of spatial data type searches by filtering the underlying grid representation of the area. Creating a spatial index involves decomposing the spatial plain into a four-level grid hierarchy, which allows for faster data filtering by the SQL Server.

A spatial index is created with the command CREATE SPATIAL INDEX. The syntax for CREATE SPATIAL INDEX has overlap with that of a regular clustered or nonclustered index (there are several index options in common such as PAD_INDEX, FILLFACTOR, DROP_EXISTING, and more). If you plan on indexing a geometry data type, you have different indexing considerations regarding the boundaries of the index (geography boundaries are already predefined) as defined by a BOUNDING_BOX option. You can also use the GRIDS option to define the density of each level of grid (four-level grid) and associated cells per defined spatial object using the CELLS_PER_OBJECT option.

Continuing with the recipe, I'll now create a spatial index for the geography column in the MinneapolisLake table created earlier:

```
CREATE SPATIAL INDEX Spatial_Index_MinneapolisLake_LakeLocationGEOG
  ON dbo.MinneapolisLake(LakeLocationGEOG)
```

Currently the number of rows in the table hardly justifies the index; however, as the table scales up, having an index can help the internal filtering process significantly, improving the performance of queries such as the following.

Note The final query in this recipe will likely produce a clustered index scan against the table because there are very few rows populated in it. If you add 1000 additional rows (representing lakes) to the table, it will switch to a clustered index seek on the spatial index.

In this last example of this recipe, I would like to determine which lake my boat is floating in by providing the latitude and longitude:

```
DECLARE @LocationOfMyBoat geography
SET @LocationOfMyBoat= geography::Parse('POINT(-93.31329 44.94088)')

SELECT LakeNM
FROM dbo.MinneapolisLake
WHERE LakeLocationGEOG.STIntersects(@LocationOfMyBoat) = 1
```

This returns

```
LakeNM
Lake Calhoun
```

How It Works

This recipe demonstrated how to use built-in methods to evaluate and perform calculations against the data. The first demonstration was of calculating the length of each polygon (in meters) and associated polygon area in square meters. The syntax in the SELECT clause just required a reference to the geography data type column, followed by a dot, and then the method name (notice that neither of the functions took input parameters, so they were suffixed with empty parentheses):

```
LakeLocationGEOG.STLength() Length,
LakeLocationGEOG.STArea() Area
```

Next, I demonstrated how to calculate the distance of each lake from a designated point. I started off by declaring a variable to hold the geography data type point:

```
DECLARE @DowntownStartingPoint geography
```

Next, I set the variable using the geography::Parse method, defining a point with a single latitude and longitude pair:

```
SET @DowntownStartingPoint = geography::Parse('POINT(-93.26319 44.97846)')
```

Once the variable was populated, I used it as an input parameter to the STDistance method to calculate the shortest distance between the lake and the input parameter point:

```
LakeLocationGEOG.STDistance(@DowntownStartingPoint) Distance
```

Next, I demonstrated how to calculate the intersection of a line representing a flight path over the three lakes. I started off by first declaring a geography type variable to contain the line string type:

```
DECLARE @FlightPath geography
```

Like the previous example, I used the Parse method to define the line string using two longitude and latitude pairs to represent the two endpoints of the line:

```
SET @FlightPath = geography::Parse('LINESTRING
(-93.26319 44.97846, -93.30862 44.91695  )')
```

Once the variable was populated, I then used it as an input parameter to the STIntersects method, which returned a 1 if the lake intersected with the line string or 0 if it did not:

```
    LakeLocationGEOG.STIntersects(@FlightPath) IntersectsWithFlightPath
```

Next, I discussed the use of spatial indexes to improve the performance of searches when using spatial methods in the WHERE clause. The CREATE SPATIAL INDEX command was used, followed by the user-defined name of the index:

```
CREATE SPATIAL INDEX Spatial_Index_MinneapolisLake_LakeLocationGEOG
```

The second line of the index defined the name of the table, and the name of the spatial data type column in parentheses:

```
    ON dbo.MinneapolisLake(LakeLocationGEOG)
```

I didn't use the GRIDS option with this statement. This option allows you to define the density of each level of the internal index grid structure that is used to filter the data. The options are LOW (4×4 grid), MEDIUM (8×8 grid), and HIGH (16×16 grid). The default is MEDIUM, so by default my index uses an 8×8 grid on all four levels of the internal index grid structure.

Once an index is mapped to a four-level grid hierarchy, SQL Server reads the spatial column data and performs a process called tessellation. The *tessellation* process defines how many grid cells the spatial object touches—which allows the index to locate objects more efficiently within the defined space. CREATE SPATIAL INDEX has a CELLS_PER_OBJECT option, which defines the limit on the number of internal cells per spatial object (allowed between 1 and 8192). The default is 16, which is what my index uses. The more cells you allow per object, the more space required by the spatial index.

After creating the index, I demonstrated using the STIntersects method in the WHERE clause of a SELECT query. I started off by defining a spatial point type that represented the location of my boat in a lake:

```
DECLARE @LocationOfMyBoat geography
SET @LocationOfMyBoat= geography::Parse('POINT(-93.31329 44.94088)')
```

Once the variable was populated, I provided it as the input of the STIntersects method—requesting any rows where my boat intersected with a lake:

```
WHERE LakeLocationGEOG.STIntersects(@LocationOfMyBoat) = 1
```

This query returned the name of the lake where my boat intersected, Lake Calhoun. Had my table been populated with 10,000 lakes, the existence of a spatial index would have proven beneficial for performance.

■ ■ ■

Hints

SQL Server's query optimization process is responsible for producing a query execution plan when a SELECT query is executed. Typically SQL Server will choose an efficient plan over an inefficient one. When this doesn't happen, you will want to examine the query execution plan, table statistics, supporting indexes, and other factors that are discussed in more detail in Chapter 28.

Ultimately, after researching the query performance, you may decide to override the decision-making process of the SQL Server query optimizer by using *hints*.

Caution You should almost always let SQL Server's Query Optimization process formulate the query execution plan without the aid of hints. Even if your hint works for the short term, keep in mind that in the future there may be more efficient query plans that could be used as the contents of the database change, but won't be, because you have overridden the optimizer with the specified hint. Also, the validity of or effectiveness of a hint may change when new service packs or editions of SQL Server are released.

I will review examples of the different kinds of hints available in SQL Server, including the new SQL Server 2008 hint, FORCESEEK, which you can use to replace index scans with index seeks. In most cases, this new hint will not be necessary; however, under some conditions you may encounter scenarios where the Query Optimizer simply doesn't choose to use an index seek on an index when you would otherwise expect it to.

Using Join Hints

A join "hint" is a misnomer in this case, as a join hint will *force* the query optimizer to join the tables in the way you command. Join hints force the internal JOIN operation used to join two tables in a query. Available join hints are described in Table 15-1.

Table 15-1. *Join Hints*

Hint Name	Description
LOOP	LOOP joins operate best when one table is small and the other is large, with indexes on the joined columns.
HASH	HASH joins are optimal for large unsorted tables.
MERGE	MERGE joins are optimal for medium or large tables that are sorted on the joined column.
REMOTE	REMOTE forces the join operation to occur at the site of the table referenced on the right (the second table referenced in a JOIN clause). For performance benefits, the left table should be the local table and should have fewer rows than the remote right table.

Forcing a HASH Join

Before showing how the join hint works, the example starts off with the original, non-hinted query:

```
-- (More on SHOWPLAN_XML in Chapter 28)
SET SHOWPLAN_XML ON
GO

SELECT   p.Name,
      r.ReviewerName,
      r.Rating
FROM   Production.Product p
INNER JOIN Production.ProductReview r ON
   r.ProductID = p.ProductID
GO

SET SHOWPLAN_XML OFF
GO
```

This returns the following excerpt (SHOWPLAN_XML returns information about how the query *may be* processed, but it doesn't actually execute the query):

```
  <RelOp NodeId="0" PhysicalOp="Nested Loops" LogicalOp="Inner Join"
EstimateRows="4" EstimateIO="0" EstimateCPU="1.672e-005" AvgRowSize="82"
EstimatedTotalSubtreeCost="0.0115181" Parallel="0" EstimateRebinds="0"
EstimateRewinds="0">
```

The next example submits the same query, only this time using a join hint:

```
SET SHOWPLAN_XML ON
GO

SELECT   p.Name,
      r.ReviewerName,
      r.Rating
FROM   Production.Product p
INNER HASH JOIN Production.ProductReview r ON
   r.ProductID = p.ProductID
GO

SET SHOWPLAN_XML OFF
GO
```

This returns the following excerpt:

```
<RelOp NodeId="0" PhysicalOp="Hash Match" LogicalOp="Inner Join" EstimateRows="4"
EstimateIO="0" EstimateCPU="0.0350031" AvgRowSize="82"
EstimatedTotalSubtreeCost="0.0443511" Parallel="0" EstimateRebinds="0"
EstimateRewinds="0">
```

How It Works

In the first, non-hinted, query, SET SHOWPLAN_XML was used to view how the query may be executed by SQL Server.

SET SHOWPLAN_XML returned an XML rendering of the query execution plan. The excerpt for the RelOp fragment for logical join (INNER JOIN) operation showed a nested loop physical join operation.

In the second query, a hint was added to force the nested loop join to perform a hash join operation instead. To do this, HASH was added between the INNER and JOIN keywords:

```
INNER HASH JOIN Production.ProductReview r ON
    r.ProductID = p.ProductID
```

Now in the second SHOWPLAN_XML result set, the query execution switched to using a hash join to join the two tables.

Using Query Hints

Some query hints, like the join hints discussed in the previous recipe, are instructions sent with the query to override SQL Server's query optimizer decision making. Using query hints may provide a short-term result that satisfies your current situation, but may not always be the most efficient result over time. Nonetheless, there are times when you may decide to use them, if only to further understand the choices that the query optimizer automatically makes.

Query hints can be used in SELECT, INSERT, UPDATE, and DELETE statements, described in Table 15-2.

Table 15-2. *Query Hints*

Hint Name	Description
{HASH | ORDER} GROUP	When used in conjunction with the GROUP BY clause, specifies whether hashing or ordering is used for GROUP BY and COMPUTE aggregations.
{CONCAT | HASH | MERGE} UNION	Designates the strategy used to join all result sets for UNION operations.
{LOOP | MERGE | HASH} JOIN	Forces *all* join operations to perform the loop, merge, or hash join in the entire query.
FAST integer	Speeds up the retrieval of rows for the top *integer* value designated.
FORCE ORDER	When designated, performs table joins in the order in which the tables appear.
MAXDOP number_of_processors	Overrides the "max degree of parallelism" server configuration option for the query.

Continued

Table 15-2. *Continued*

Hint Name	Description
OPTIMIZE FOR (@variable_name = literal_constant) [,...n]	Directs SQL Server to use a particular variable value or values for a variable when the query is compiled and optimized. You could, for example, plug in a literal constant that returns the best performance across the range of expected parameters.
ROBUST PLAN	Creates a query plan with the assumption that the row size of a table will be at maximum width.
KEEP PLAN	"Relaxes" the recompile threshold for the query.
KEEPFIXED PLAN	Forces the query optimizer NOT to recompile due to statistics or indexed column changes. Only schema changes or sp_recompile will cause the query plan to be recompiled.
EXPAND VIEWS	Keeps the query optimizer from using indexed views when the base table is referenced.
MAXRECURSION number	Designates the maximum number of recursions (1 to 32757) allowed for the query. If 0 is chosen, no limit is applied. The default recursion limit is 100. This option is used in conjunction with Common Table Expressions (CTEs).
USE PLAN 'xml_plan'	USE PLAN directs SQL SERVER to use a potentially better performing query plan (provided in the xml_plan literal value) that you know can cause the query to perform better. See Chapter 28 for more details.
PARAMETERIZATION { SIMPLE | FORCED }	Relates to the new PARAMETERIZATION database setting, which controls whether or not all queries are parameterized (literal values contained in a query get substituted with parameters in the cached query plan). When PARAMETERIZATION SIMPLE is chosen, SQL Server decides which queries are parameterized or not. When PARAMETERIZATION FORCED is used, all queries in the database will be parameterized. For more information on this database setting, see Chapter 28.
RECOMPILE	Forces SQL Server to throw out the query execution plan after it is executed, meaning that the next time the query executes, it will be forced to recompile a new query plan. Although usually SQL Server reuses effective query plans, sometimes a less efficient query plan is reused. Recompiling forces SQL Server to come up with a fresh plan (but with the overhead of a recompile).

Forcing a Statement Recompile

This example uses the RECOMPILE query hint to recompile the query, forcing SQL Server to discard the plan generated for the query after it executes. With the RECOMPILE query hint, a new plan will be generated the next time the same or similar query is executed. You may decide you wish to do this for volatile query plans, where differing search condition values for the same plan cause extreme fluctuations in the number of rows returned. In that scenario, using a compiled query plan may hurt, not help, the query performance. The benefit of a cached and reusable query execution plan (the avoided cost of compilation) may occasionally be outweighed by the actual performance of the query.

■**Note** SQL Server uses statement-level recompilation. Instead of an entire batch recompiling when indexes are added or data is changed to the referenced tables, only individual statements within the batch impacted by the change are recompiled.

Typically, you will want to use this RECOMPILE query hint within a stored procedure—so that you can control which statements automatically recompile—instead of having to recompile the entire stored procedure.

To begin this recipe, I will execute the following query without a query hint:

```
DECLARE @CarrierTrackingNumber nvarchar(25) = '5CE9-4D75-8F'

SELECT   SalesOrderID,
    ProductID,
    UnitPrice,
    OrderQty
FROM Sales.SalesOrderDetail
WHERE CarrierTrackingNumber = @CarrierTrackingNumber
ORDER BY   SalesOrderID,
        ProductID
```

This returns

SalesOrderID	ProductID	UnitPrice	OrderQty
47964	760	469.794	1
47964	789	1466.01	1
47964	819	149.031	4
47964	843	15.00	1
47964	844	11.994	6

(5 row(s) affected)

Now I can query the Dynamic Management View sys.dm_exec_cached_plans (see Chapter 22 for a review of this DMV) to see whether this query produced a compiled plan in memory that can potentially be reused:

```
SELECT cacheobjtype, objtype, usecounts
FROM sys.dm_exec_cached_plans
CROSS APPLY sys.dm_exec_sql_text(plan_handle)
WHERE text LIKE 'DECLARE @CarrierTrackingNumber%'
```

This returns the cache object type and number of times the object has been used for query execution:

cacheobjtype	objtype	usecounts
Compiled Plan	Adhoc	1

(1 row(s) affected)

Next, I will execute the original query again to test whether the cached plan is reused. After executing the original query and then querying `sys.dm_exec_cached_plans`, I will see the following incremented count, meaning that the compiled ad hoc plan was reused:

cacheobjtype	objtype	usecounts
Compiled Plan	Adhoc	2

Now I'll demonstrate the `RECOMPILE` hint. Before doing this, I'll clear the procedure cache (don't try this in a production SQL Server instance—only use this in a test environment):

```
DBCC FREEPROCCACHE
```

This clears out the cache, and now I will direct SQL Server *not* to create or reuse an existing plan:

```
DECLARE @CarrierTrackingNumber nvarchar(25) = '5CE9-4D75-8F'

SELECT    SalesOrderID,
    ProductID,
    UnitPrice,
    OrderQty
FROM Sales.SalesOrderDetail
WHERE CarrierTrackingNumber = @CarrierTrackingNumber
ORDER BY    SalesOrderID,
          ProductID
OPTION (RECOMPILE)
```

Querying `sys.dm_exec_cached_plans` again, I don't see a plan generated for reuse:

cacheobjtype	objtype	usecounts

```
(0 row(s) affected)
```

How It Works

This query demonstrated using a query hint, which was referenced in the `OPTION` clause at the end of the query:

```
OPTION (RECOMPILE)
```

Without the hint, the original query generated a cached query plan that could then be reused for consecutive executions. By adding this hint, I have overridden the behavior by forcing the query to compile a new plan each time it is executed.

It bears repeating that SQL Server should be relied upon most of the time to make the correct decisions when processing a query. Query hints *can* provide you with more control for those exceptions when you need to override SQL Server's choices.

Using Table Hints

Table hints, like query hints, can be used to override `SELECT`, `INSERT`, `UPDATE`, and `DELETE` default processing behavior. You can use multiple table hints for one query, separated by commas, so long as they do not belong to the same category grouping. Be sure to test the performance of your queries with and without the query hints (see Chapter 28 for more details on examining query performance).

Table 15-3 lists available table hints. Some hints cannot be used together, so they have been grouped in the table accordingly. You can't, for example, use both NOLOCK and HOLDLOCK for the same query.

Table 15-3. *Table Hints*

Hint Name	Description
FASTFIRSTROW	This hint is deprecated and will be removed in future versions of SQL Server.
FORCESEEK	New in SQL Server 2008, this hint allows you to force a query to only consider clustered or nonclustered index *seek* access paths for a specified table or view instead of a *scan*. You can leave it to the optimizer to select the index to seek, or optionally you can also couple FORCESEEK with an INDEX hint (described next).
INDEX (index_val [,... n])	This hint overrides SQL Server's index choice and forces a specific index for the table to be used.
NOEXPAND	When an indexed view is referenced, the query optimizer will not access the data structures of the data objects used to define the view. Only indexes on the indexed view are used for the purposes of the query.
HOLDLOCK, SERIALIZABLE, REPEATABLEREAD, READCOMMITTED, READCOMMITTEDLOCK, READUNCOMMITTED, NOLOCK	Selecting one of these hints determines the isolation level for the table. For example, designating NOLOCK means that the operation (SELECT for example) will place no locking on the table.
ROWLOCK, PAGLOCK, TABLOCK, TABLOCKX	This hint designates the granularity of locking for the table, for example, selecting ROWLOCK to force only row locks for a query.
READPAST	This hint skips locked rows and does not read them.
UPDLOCK	This hint will force update locks instead of shared locks to be generated (not compatible with NOLOCK or XLOCK).
XLOCK	This hint forces exclusive locks on the resources being referenced (not compatible with NOLOCK or UPDLOCK).
KEEPIDENTITY	This option applies to the OPENROWSET function's BULK insert functionality (see Chapter 27) and impacts how rows are inserted into a table with an IDENTITY column. If you use this hint, SQL Server will use the identity values from the data file, instead of generating its own. For more on the IDENTITY column, see Chapter 4.
KEEPDEFAULTS	Like KEEPIDENTITY, this table hint applies to the OPENROWSET function. Using this hint specifies that columns not included in the bulk-load operation will be assigned to the column default. For more on default columns, see Chapter 4.
IGNORE_CONSTRAINTS	Another OPENROWSET hint, IGNORE_CONSTRAINTS directs SQL Server to ignore CHECK constraints when importing data. See Chapter 4 for more on CHECK constraints.
IGNORE_TRIGGERS	This query hint directs INSERT triggers *not* to fire when importing using the BULK option of OPENROWSET.

Executing a Query Without Locking

This example returns the DocumentID and Title from the Production.Document table where the Status column is equal to 1. It uses the NOLOCK table hint, which means the query will not place shared locks on the Production.Document table:

```
SELECT DocumentID,
       Title
FROM Production.Document
WITH (NOLOCK)
WHERE Status = 1
```

How It Works

The crux of this example is the WITH keyword, which uses the NOLOCK table hint in parentheses:

```
WITH (NOLOCK)
```

NOLOCK causes the query not to place shared locks on the impacted rows/data pages—allowing you to read without being blocked or blocking others (although you are now subject to "dirty reads").

Forcing a SEEK over a SCAN

SQL Server 2008 introduces the new FORCESEEK table hint, which you can use to replace index scans with index seeks. In most cases, this hint will not be necessary; however, under some conditions, you may encounter scenarios where the Query Optimizer simply doesn't choose to use an index seek on an index when you would otherwise expect it to.

Bad query plans can happen for several reasons. For example, if your table data is highly volatile and your statistics are no longer accurate, a bad plan could be produced. Another example would be a query with a poorly constructed WHERE clause that doesn't provide sufficient or useful information to the query optimization process.

If the intent of your query is to perform a singleton lookup against a specific value, and instead you see that the query scans the entire index before retrieving your single row, the I/O costs of the scan can be significant (particularly for very large tables). In situations where you have done due diligence (updated statistics, optimized the query), you may then consider using the new FORCESEEK table hint.

The following example uses SET SHOWPLAN XML to return the estimated query execution plan. I cover SET SHOWPLAN XML in more detail in Chapter 28. In this recipe, I start by setting SHOWPLAN XML on, and then execute the query that will perform a clustered index scan against the Production. TransactionHistory table:

```
SET SHOWPLAN_XML ON
GO

SELECT DISTINCT TransactionID, TransactionDate
FROM Production.TransactionHistory
WHERE ReferenceOrderID BETWEEN 1000 AND 100000
GO

SET SHOWPLAN_XML OFF
```

This returns the estimated execution plan of the query. You can see from the following fragment embedded in the XML results that a clustered index scan operation will be used:

```
<RelOp NodeId="0" PhysicalOp="Clustered Index Scan" LogicalOp="Clustered Index Scan"
 EstimateRows="112121" EstimateIO="0.586088" EstimateCPU="0.124945" AvgRowSize="23"
EstimatedTotalSubtreeCost="0.711033" Parallel="0" EstimateRebinds="0"
EstimateRewinds="0">
```

The referenced table, Production.TransactionHistory, has one clustered index on the TransactionID column, a nonclustered index on ProductID, and then a composite index on ReferenceOrderID and ReferenceOrderLineID. In this situation, the range of ReferenceOrderID values probably justifies a scan, but let's say for the purposes of the example you would like to have it use a seek operation instead. For example, if the actual table values between the range of 1000 and 100000 should return only a few rows, but for some reason the statistics of the indexes indicate something different, you can use the FORCESEEK to help push a different data access method.

■**Caution** This example is for illustrative purposes only. The forced seek in this next query is non-optimal.

```
SET SHOWPLAN_XML ON
GO

SELECT DISTINCT TransactionID, TransactionDate
FROM Production.TransactionHistory WITH (FORCESEEK)
WHERE ReferenceOrderID BETWEEN 1000 AND 100000
GO

SET SHOWPLAN_XML OFF
```

This time you see from the estimated query plan XML output that an index seek operation will be used:

```
<RelOp NodeId="3" PhysicalOp="Index Seek" LogicalOp="Index Seek"
EstimateRows="112121" EstimateIO="0.15794" EstimateCPU="0.0617452" AvgRowSize="11"
 EstimatedTotalSubtreeCost="0.219685" Parallel="1" EstimateRebinds="0"
EstimateRewinds="0">
```

You also see within the XML output that the specific indexed used was the nonclustered index made up of the ReferenceOrderID and ReferenceOrderLineID columns:

```
<Object Database="[AdventureWorks]" Schema="[Production]"
Table="[TransactionHistory]"
Index="[IX_TransactionHistory_ReferenceOrderID_ReferenceOrderLineID]" />
```

In the previous query, I allowed SQL Server to choose which index to seek; however, I also have the option to force a seek operation and also designate which index should be used. For example:

```
SELECT DISTINCT TransactionID, TransactionDate
FROM Production.TransactionHistory WITH (FORCESEEK, INDEX
(IX_TransactionHistory_ReferenceOrderID_ReferenceOrderLineID))
WHERE ReferenceOrderID BETWEEN 1000 AND 100000
```

How It Works

The FORCESEEK command is a query hint that should be infrequently used, but can be extremely useful in situations where you are sure a non-optimal access path is being chosen by SQL Server. FORCESEEK can be used in the FROM clause of a SELECT, UPDATE, or DELETE.

In this recipe, I referenced the table hint by placing the WITH keyword followed by the hint name in parentheses:

```
FROM Production.TransactionHistory WITH (FORCESEEK)
```

This overrides the query's original clustered index scan access path. If you have multiple indexes on a table, using this hint alone will tell SQL Server to choose the best seek across the choice of indexes. However, you can further narrow down the instructions by designating the INDEX hint as well, which I included as follows:

```
FROM Production.TransactionHistory WITH (FORCESEEK, INDEX
(IX_TransactionHistory_ReferenceOrderID_ReferenceOrderLineID))
```

The INDEX hint was followed by the name of the index within parentheses. You could have also used the index number. As with FORCESEEK, in general you should not designate the INDEX hint if you don't have to—as SQL Server will choose the most optimal seek path available at that moment.

CHAPTER 16

■ ■ ■

Error Handling

In this chapter, I'll present recipes for creating, raising, and handling SQL Server errors using Transact-SQL.

System-Defined and User-Defined Error Messages

This first batch of recipes is concerned with the viewing and raising of system and user-defined error messages. The sys.messages table contains one row for each user-defined and built-in error message on the SQL Server instance. *Built-in error messages* are those that are raised in response to standard SQL Server errors. *User-defined error messages* are often used in third-party applications that define a set of error messages for use within an application. User-defined error messages allow for *parameterization*, meaning that you can create custom messages that allow for customizable messages based on parameters (as you'll see demonstrated later on in the chapter when I discuss RAISERROR).

Viewing System Error Information

You can use the sys.messages system catalog view to see all system and user-defined error messages in the SQL Server instance, as this example demonstrates:

```
SELECT message_id, severity, is_event_logged, text
FROM sys.messages
ORDER BY severity DESC, text
```

This returns the following abridged results (the output has been truncated and formatted for clarity):

message_id	severity	is_event_logged	text
832	24	1	A page that should have been constant has changed (expected checksum: %08x, actual checksum: %08x, database %d, file '%ls', page %S_PGID). This usually indicates a memory failure or other hardware or OS corruption.
1459	24	1	An error occurred while accessing the database mirroring metadata. Drop mirroring (ALTER DATABASE database_name SET PARTNER OFF) and reconfigure it.
17405	24	1	An image corruption/hotpatch detected while reporting exceptional situation. This may be a sign of a hardware problem. Check SQLDUMPER_ERRORLOG.log for details.

How It Works

In this recipe, a simple SELECT query returned the following information about both SQL Server built-in error messages and the custom error messages defined for this particular instance of SQL Server:

- message_id: This is the error message identifier.
- severity: This is the severity level.
- is_event_logged: This is used if the error writes to the Windows event log.
- text: This is the text of the message.

The severity level ranges from 1 to 25, with the following implied categorizations:

- Severity levels 0 through 10 denote informational messages.
- Severity levels 11 through 16 are database engine errors that can be corrected by the user (database objects that are missing when the query is executed, incompatible locking hints, transaction deadlocks, denied permissions, and syntax errors). For example, a PRIMARY KEY violation will return a level 14 severity-level error. A divide-by-zero error returns a level 16 severity-level error.
- Severity levels 17 through 19 are for errors needing sysadmin attention (for instance, if SQL Server has run out of memory resources, or if database engine limits have been reached).
- Severity levels 20 through 25 are fatal errors and system issues (hardware or software damage that impacts the database, integrity problems, and media failures).

The text column in sys.messages contains the actual error message to be presented to the user from the database engine. Notice that the first message in the recipe's results had percentage signs and other symbols combined within it:

```
A page that should have been constant has changed (expected checksum: %08x, actual
checksum: %08x, database %d, file '%ls', page %S_PGID). This usually indicates a
memory failure or other hardware or OS corruption.
```

The % sign is a substitution parameter that allows the database engine to customize error message output based on the current database context and error event. The values concatenated to the % sign indicate the data type and length of the substitution parameter.

Creating a User-Defined Error Message

In this recipe, I demonstrate how to create a new user-defined error message using the sp_addmessage system stored procedure. You may wish to create user-defined, custom messages for your application to use, ensuring consistency across your application-specific error handling routines. Creating a new error message adds it to the sys.messages system catalog view and allows you to invoke it with the RAISERROR command (reviewed in the next recipe).

The syntax for this system stored procedure is as follows:

```
sp_addmessage [ @msgnum = ] msg_id ,
    [ @severity = ] severity ,
    [ @msgtext = ] 'msg'
    [ , [ @lang = ] 'language' ]
    [ , [ @with_log = ] 'with_log' ]
    [ , [ @replace = ] 'replace' ]
```

The parameters are briefly described in Table 16-1.

Table 16-1. *sp_addmessage Arguments*

Parameter	Description
msg_id	This is the user-supplied error ID, which can be between 50,001 and 2,147,483,647. The message ID is not the unique key or primary key of this table; rather, the unique composite key is the combination of the message ID and the language ID.
severity	This defines the severity level of your message (1 through 25).
msg	This represents the actual error message, which uses a data type of nvarchar(255).
language	This specifies the language in which the error message is written.
with_log	This defines whether or not the message will be written to the Windows Application error log when the error is invoked.
Replace	When specified, the existing user-defined error (based on message ID and language) is overwritten with the new parameters passed to the system stored procedure.

In this recipe, a new error message will be created to warn the user that his group can't update a specific table (which you might use if you were building your own application-based security system in a database, for example):

```
-- Creating the new message
USE master
GO

EXEC sp_addmessage
     100001,
     14,
   N'The current table %s is not updateable by your group!'
GO

-- Using the new message (RAISERROR reviewed in the next recipe)
RAISERROR (100001, 14, 1, N'HumanResources.Employee')
```

This returns

```
Msg 100001, Level 14, State 1, Line 3
The current table HumanResources.Employee is not updateable by your group!
```

How It Works

In this recipe, a new message was created using sp_addmessage:

```
EXEC sp_addmessage
     100001,
     14,
   N'The current table %s is not updateable by your group!'
```

The first parameter, 100001, was the new message ID. You can use an integer value between 50,001 and 2,147,483,647. The second parameter value of 14 indicated the severity level, and the third parameter was the actual error message.

A substitution parameter value was included within the body of the message, %s, where the s tells you that the parameter is a string value. You can also designate a parameter as a signed integer (d or i), unsigned octal (o), unsigned integer (u), or unsigned hexadecimal (x or X).

The other optional parameters such as language, with_log, and replace were not used. The last command in this recipe, RAISERROR, was used to raise an instance of the newly created error:

```
RAISERROR (100001, 14, 1, N'HumanResources.Employee')
```

RAISERROR is often used to return errors related to application or business logic—for example, errors based on conditions that are syntactically correct, yet violate some condition or requirement of the application or business.

In this example, the first parameter was the new error message ID, the second parameter was the severity level, the third parameter was the state (a number you can use to identify which part of your code throws the error), and the fourth was the Unicode substitution parameter that passes to the error message. The argument can take substitution parameters for the int, tinyint, smallint, varchar, char, nchar, nvarchar, varbinary, and binary data types. The new error message was then returned to the SQL user with the value HumanResources.Employee plugged into the substitution parameter value.

Dropping a User-Defined Error Message

In this recipe, I demonstrate how to remove a user-defined error message from the sys.messages table. The syntax is as follows:

```
sp_dropmessage [ @msgnum = ] message_number
[ , [ @lang = ] 'language' ]
```

The parameters are briefly described in Table 16-2.

Table 16-2. *sp_dropmessage Arguments*

Parameter	Description
message_number	This is the message number of the user-defined error message.
language	This is the language of the message to drop. If you designate ALL and a message exists with the same message number but in different languages, all messages for that number will be dropped.

This recipe drops the user-defined error message created in the previous recipe:

```
EXEC sp_dropmessage 100001
```

How It Works

This recipe dropped the user-defined error message created in the previous recipe by using the system stored procedure sp_dropmessage. This system stored procedure can only be used to drop user-added messages, which have message IDs greater than 49,999.

Manually Raising an Error

The RAISERROR command allows you to invoke either a user-defined error message from the sys.messages system catalog view or an error message produced from a string or string variable. The syntax of RAISERROR is as follows:

```
RAISERROR ( { msg_id | msg_str | @local_variable }
    { ,severity ,state }
    [ ,argument [ ,...n ] ] )
    [ WITH option [ ,...n ] ]
```

The parameters are briefly described in Table 16-3.

Table 16-3. *RAISERROR Arguments*

Parameter	Description
msg_id | msg_str | @local_variable	When using RAISERROR, you can choose one of three options for this parameter. The msg_id option is a user-defined error message number from the sys.messages table. The msg_str option is a user-defined message with up to 2,047 characters. The @local_variable option is a string variable used to pass this message string.
severity	This defines the severity level of your message (1 through 25).
state	This specifies a user-defined number between 1 and 127 that can be used for identifying the location of the failing code (if your code is divided into multiple sections, for example).
argument [,...n]	This defines one or more substitution parameters to be used within the error message.
WITH option [,...n]	Three options are allowed in the WITH clause: LOG, NOWAIT, and SETERROR. LOG writes to the SQL Server error log and Windows Application error log. NOWAIT sends the messages immediately to the client. SETERROR sets the @@ERROR and ERROR_NUMBER values to the error message ID (or 50,000 if not using an error from sys.messages).

Invoking an Error Message

In this recipe, I create a stored procedure to INSERT a new row into the HumanResources.Department table. When an attempt is made to insert a new department into the HumanResources.Department table, the group name will be evaluated first to see whether it is Research and Development. If it isn't, the insert will not occur, and an error using RAISERROR will be invoked:

```
USE AdventureWorks
GO

CREATE PROCEDURE dbo.usp_INS_Department
   @DepartmentName nvarchar(50),
    @GroupName nvarchar(50)
AS
IF  @GroupName = 'Research and Development'
BEGIN
   INSERT HumanResources.Department
   (Name, GroupName)
   VALUES (@DepartmentName, @GroupName)
END
ELSE
BEGIN
RAISERROR('%s group is being audited
for the next %i days.
No new departments for this group can be added
during this time.',
        16,
```

```
        1,
        @GroupName,
        23)
END

GO
```

Next, the new procedure is executed:

```
EXEC dbo.usp_INS_Department 'Mainframe Accountant', 'Accounting'
```

This returns

```
Msg 50000, Level 16, State 1, Procedure usp_INS_Department, Line 13
Accounting group is being audited
for the next 23 days.
No new departments for this group can be added during this time.
```

An alternative to creating the error message within the stored procedure is to create it as a user-defined message (as discussed earlier in the chapter). For example:

```
EXEC sp_addmessage
        100002,
        14,
   N'%s group is being audited for the next %i
days. No new departments for this group can be added
during this time.'
GO
```

Then, by rewriting the previous RAISERROR example, you can reference the user-defined error message number instead:

```
...
ELSE
BEGIN
    RAISERROR(100002,
            16,
            1,
            @GroupName,
            23)
END
```

How It Works

This recipe used RAISERROR to return an error if a specific IF condition was not met. RAISERROR is often used to send errors to the calling application from Transact-SQL batches, stored procedures, and triggers—especially for data or logical conditions that wouldn't normally cause a syntactic error to be raised.

Within the body of the stored procedure, the value of the group name was evaluated. If it had been equal to Research and Development, the insert would have happened:

```
IF  @GroupName = 'Research and Development'
BEGIN
    INSERT HumanResources.Department
    (Name, GroupName)
    VALUES (@DepartmentName, @GroupName)
END
```

Because the group was *not* equal to `Research and Development`, the `ELSE` clause initiates the `RAISERROR` command instead:

```
ELSE
BEGIN
   RAISERROR('%s group is being audited for the next %i
days. No new departments for this group can be added
during this time.',
         16,
         1,
         @GroupName,
         23)
END
```

The first parameter of the `RAISERROR` command was the error message text, which used two substitution parameters: one for the group name, and the second for the number of days the group will be audited. The second parameter, 16, was the severity level. The third parameter, 1, was the state. The last two parameters, `@GroupName` and 23, were the substitution parameters to be plugged into the error message when it was invoked.

This recipe also demonstrated adding a user-defined message and then invoking it with `RAISERROR`, instead of creating the text on the fly. This technique is useful for error messages that must be used in multiple areas of your database, and it prevents you from having to retype the message in each referencing procedure or script. It also ensures the consistency of the error message.

Trapping and Handling Application Errors

The `TRY...CATCH` command can be used to capture execution errors within your Transact-SQL code. `TRY...CATCH` can catch any execution error with a severity level greater than 10 (so long as the raised error doesn't forcefully terminate the Transact-SQL user session). `TRY...CATCH` can also handle severity-level errors (greater than 10) invoked using `RAISERROR`.

The syntax for `TRY...CATCH` is as follows:

```
BEGIN TRY
     { sql_statement | statement_block }
END TRY
BEGIN CATCH
     { sql_statement | statement_block }
END CATCH
```

The arguments used in both the `TRY` and `CATCH` sections are `sql_statement` and `statement_block`. In a nutshell, statements within the `TRY` block are those you wish to execute. If errors are raised within the `TRY` block, then the `CATCH` block of code is executed. The `CATCH` block is then used to handle the error. Handling just means that you wish to take some action in response to the error, whether it's to report the error's information, log information in an error table, or roll back an open transaction.

The benefit of `TRY...CATCH` is in the ability to nest error handling inside code blocks, allowing you to handle errors more gracefully and with less code than non-`TRY...CATCH` methods. `TRY...CATCH` also allows you to use SQL Server error logging and transaction state functions that capture granular error information about an error event. Table 16-4 details the use of each.

Table 16-4. *Error and Transaction State Functions*

Function	Description
ERROR_LINE	This defines the error line number in the SQL statement or block where the error was raised.
ERROR_MESSAGE	This is the error message raised in the SQL statement or block.
ERROR_NUMBER	This is the error number raised in the SQL statement or block.
ERROR_PROCEDURE	This defines the name of the trigger or stored procedure where the error was raised (assuming TRY...CATCH was used in a procedure or trigger).
ERROR_SEVERITY	This indicates the severity level of the error raised in the SQL statement or block.
ERROR_STATE	This specifies the state of the error raised in the SQL statement or block.
XACT_STATE	In the CATCH block, XACT_STATE reports on the state of open transactions from the TRY block. If 0 is returned, there are no open transactions from the TRY block. If 1 is returned, an active user transaction is currently open. If -1 is returned, an error occurred in the TRY block, and the transaction must be rolled back. XACT_STATE can also be used outside of a TRY...CATCH command.

If an error is encountered in a TRY batch, SQL Server will exit at the point of the error and move to the CATCH block, without processing any of the other statements in the TRY batch (the exception to the rule is if you're using nested TRY...CATCH blocks, which I'll demonstrate later on in the chapter).

TRY...CATCH can be used within a trigger or stored procedure or used to encapsulate the actual execution of a stored procedure (capturing any errors that "bubble up" from the procedure execution and then handling them accordingly).

Warnings and most informational attention messages (severity level of 10 or less) are *not* caught by TRY...CATCH, and neither are syntax and object name resolution errors. Nonetheless, this new construct is now an ideal choice for capturing many other common error messages that in previous versions required bloated and inelegant Transact-SQL code.

In general, you'll want to make sure that every block of non-anonymous Transact-SQL code that modifies data in some way or participates in a transaction has an error handler. I'm not part of the group that believes in going overboard with error handling, however. I've seen some coders put error handling around each and every SELECT statement they write. I personally think this is overkill, as any issues that would cause a SELECT statement to "break" will require manual intervention of some sort. Also, with .NET error handling capabilities, wrappers around your SELECT queries often redundantly handle errors that may already be handled in the application tier.

In the next two recipes, I demonstrate two different scripts: one that uses an outdated method of trapping error messages, and one that demonstrates the TRY...CATCH syntax method for doing the same thing. After those recipes, I'll demonstrate how to apply TRY...CATCH to a stored procedure and then how to use nested TRY...CATCH calls.

Old-Style Error Handling

Prior to SQL Server 2005, error handling generally involved checking the T-SQL @@ERROR function after every statement was executed. You would then use GOTO statements to point to a centralized error handling block where, if an error had occurred, the process would be terminated and the transaction rolled back.

This is demonstrated by the following code:

```
DECLARE @ErrorNBR int

BEGIN TRAN

    INSERT Production.Location
    (Name, CostRate, Availability)
    VALUES
    ('Tool Verification', 0.00, 0.00)

    SELECT @ErrorNBR = @@ERROR
    IF @ErrorNBR <> 0
    GOTO UndoTran

    INSERT Production.Location
    (Name, CostRate, Availability)
    VALUES
    ('Frame Forming', 0.00, 0.00)

    SELECT @ErrorNBR = @@ERROR
    IF @ErrorNBR <> 0
    GOTO UndoTran

COMMIT TRAN

UndoTran:
IF @ErrorNBR <> 0
BEGIN
PRINT CAST(@ErrorNBR as varchar(6)) +
' occurred after an attempt to insert into Production.Location'
ROLLBACK TRAN
END
```

This returns

```
(1 row(s) affected)
Msg 2601, Level 14, State 1, Line 17
Cannot insert duplicate key row in object 'Production.Location'
with unique index 'AK_Location_Name'.
The statement has been terminated.
2601 occurred after an attempt to insert into Production.Location
```

How It Works

The first example in this recipe demonstrated an error trapping method used prior to SQL Server 2005. The first line of code created an integer variable to hold the value of @@ERRORNBR after each statement was executed. @@ERRORNBR's value changes after each statement's execution, so a local variable will allow you to retain the original value of the error number:

```
DECLARE @ErrorNBR int
```

Next, a transaction was begun:

```
BEGIN TRAN
```

Two inserts were attempted against the Production.Location table. The first inserted a value that doesn't already exist in the table, and therefore succeeds:

```
INSERT Production.Location
(Name, CostRate, Availability)
VALUES
('Tool Verification', 0.00, 0.00)
```

Immediately after this insert, the value of @@ERROR was captured and stored in @ErrorNBR:

```
SELECT @ErrorNBR = @@ERROR
```

Since the insert succeeded, the value is 0. Had the insert failed, the value would have been equal to the appropriate error message ID as found in sys.messages.

Next, an IF statement evaluated the local variable value, and since it was 0, it didn't invoke the IF condition:

```
IF @ErrorNBR <> 0
GOTO UndoTran
```

Another insert was then attempted, this time using a location name that already exists in the table. This insert failed this time due to a unique constraint on the location name:

```
INSERT Production.Location
(Name, CostRate, Availability)
VALUES
('Frame Forming', 0.00, 0.00)
```

The error trapping logic from the first insert was repeated for the second insert, and when executed, the GOTO section was invoked, since the value of @ErrorNBR is no longer equal to 0:

```
SELECT @ErrorNBR = @@ERROR
IF @ErrorNBR <> 0
GOTO UndoTran
```

Because the GOTO command was invoked, the COMMIT TRAN was skipped:

```
COMMIT TRAN
```

The UndoTran label code printed the error number and a message and rolled back the transaction:

```
UndoTran:
IF @ErrorNBR <> 0
BEGIN
PRINT CAST(@ErrorNBR as varchar(6)) + ' occurred after an
attempt to insert into Production.Location'
ROLLBACK TRAN
END
```

It's clear from this example that this method requires repetitive code to trap possible errors for each and every statement. For larger procedures or batch scripts, this can significantly increase the amount of Transact-SQL code required in order to achieve statement-level error trapping.

Error Handling with TRY...CATCH

In this recipe, I'll demonstrate the same error handling functionality, this time using TRY...CATCH:

```
BEGIN TRY

    BEGIN TRAN

    INSERT Production.Location
    (Name, CostRate, Availability)
    VALUES
    ('Tool Verification', 0.00, 0.00)

    INSERT Production.Location
    (Name, CostRate, Availability)
    VALUES
    ('Frame Forming', 0.00, 0.00)

    COMMIT TRANSACTION

END TRY
BEGIN CATCH
    SELECT   ERROR_NUMBER() ErrorNBR, ERROR_SEVERITY() Severity,
             ERROR_LINE () ErrorLine, ERROR_MESSAGE() Msg

        ROLLBACK TRANSACTION

END CATCH
```

This returns the following results:

ErrorNBR	Severity	ErrorLine	Msg
2601	14	5	Cannot insert duplicate key row in object 'Production.Location' with unique index 'AK_Location_Name'.

How It Works

This recipe duplicates the previous recipe's results, only this time using TRY...CATCH. The batch started with the BEGIN TRY command, and the starting of a new transaction:

```
BEGIN TRY

    BEGIN TRAN
```

Next, the two inserts used in the previous example were attempted again, this time *without* individual error trapping blocks following each statement:

```
INSERT Production.Location
(Name, CostRate, Availability)
VALUES
('Tool Verification', 0.00, 0.00)

INSERT Production.Location
(Name, CostRate, Availability)
VALUES
('Frame Forming', 0.00, 0.00)
```

The TRY batch, which included the statements I wished to error-check, was completed with the END TRY keywords:

```
END TRY
```

The BEGIN CATCH marked the beginning of the error handling code block:

```
BEGIN CATCH
```

Using some of the error functions described at the beginning of this recipe, information on the *first* error that occurred within the TRY block was reported:

```
SELECT   ERROR_NUMBER() ErrorNBR, ERROR_SEVERITY() Severity,
      ERROR_LINE () ErrorLine, ERROR_MESSAGE() Msg
```

Next, the open transaction declared earlier in the batch was then rolled back:

```
    ROLLBACK TRANSACTION
```

The END CATCH command was used to mark the ending of the error handling CATCH block.

Applying Error Handling Without Recoding a Stored Procedure

You don't have to recode each of your database's stored procedures in order to start benefiting from the new TRY...CATCH construct. Instead, you can use TRY...CATCH to capture and handle errors from outside a procedure's code.

To demonstrate, I'll create a stored procedure that by design will return an error when executed:

```
CREATE PROCEDURE usp_SEL_DivideByZero
AS

SELECT 1/0

GO
```

The stored procedure included no error handling whatsoever, but this doesn't pose a problem if I use TRY...CATCH as follows:

```
BEGIN TRY
   EXEC dbo.usp_SEL_DivideByZero
END TRY
BEGIN CATCH
   SELECT   ERROR_NUMBER() ErrorNBR, ERROR_SEVERITY() Severity,
         ERROR_LINE () ErrorLine, ERROR_MESSAGE() Msg
   PRINT 'This stored procedure did not execute properly.'
END CATCH
```

This returns

ErrorNBR	Severity	ErrorLine	Msg
8134	16	4	Divide by zero error encountered.

How It Works

Although the stored procedure created in this exercise didn't include error handling, I was still able to add a programmatic response to errors by using TRY...CATCH to execute the stored procedure.

The procedure was called from within the TRY block, and the error information and message caught and handled by the CATCH block.

```
BEGIN TRY
    EXEC dbo.usp_SEL_DivideByZero
END TRY
BEGIN CATCH
    SELECT  ERROR_NUMBER() ErrorNBR, ERROR_SEVERITY() Severity,
         ERROR_LINE () ErrorLine, ERROR_MESSAGE() Msg
    PRINT 'This stored procedure did not execute properly.'
END CATCH
```

Nesting Error Handling

TRY...CATCH statements can be nested, which means you can use the TRY...CATCH statements within other TRY...CATCH blocks. This allows you to handle errors that may happen, even in your error handling.

In this example, I'll create a new stored procedure to handle INSERTs into the HumanResources. Department table. This procedure includes two levels of error handling. If an error occurs when attempting the first INSERT, a second attempt is made with a different department name:

```
CREATE PROCEDURE dbo.usp_INS_Department
    @Name nvarchar(50),
    @GroupName nvarchar(50)
AS


BEGIN TRY

    INSERT HumanResources.Department (Name, GroupName)
    VALUES (@Name, @GroupName)

END TRY
BEGIN CATCH

    BEGIN TRY

    PRINT 'The first department attempt failed.'

    INSERT HumanResources.Department (Name, GroupName)
    VALUES ('Misc', @GroupName)

    END TRY
    BEGIN CATCH
        PRINT 'A Misc department for that group already exists.'
    END CATCH

END CATCH

GO
```

Executing the code for the existing department Engineering causes the first INSERT to fail, but the second INSERT of the Misc department for the Research and Development department succeeds:

```
EXEC dbo.usp_INS_Department 'Engineering', 'Research and Development'
```

This returns

```
(0 row(s) affected)
The first department attempt failed.
(1 row(s) affected)
```

If this same exact department and group INSERT is attempted again, both INSERTs will fail, causing the second nested CATCH to return a printed error too:

```
EXEC dbo.usp_INS_Department 'Engineering', 'Research and Development'
```

This returns

```
(0 row(s) affected)
The first department attempt failed.

(0 row(s) affected)
A Misc department for that group already exists.
```

How It Works

This recipe demonstrated nesting a TRY...CATCH within another TRY...CATCH. This allows you to add error handling around your error handling, in cases where you anticipate that this is necessary. Walking through the code, the first few lines of the stored procedure defined the input parameters for use with inserting into the HumanResources.Department table:

```
CREATE PROCEDURE dbo.usp_INS_Department
    @Name nvarchar(50),
    @GroupName nvarchar(50)
AS
```

Next, the first level TRY block was begun with an attempt to INSERT the new row into the table:

```
BEGIN TRY

    INSERT HumanResources.Department (Name, GroupName)
    VALUES (@Name, @GroupName)

END TRY
```

In case this fails, the CATCH block contained another TRY block:

```
BEGIN CATCH

    BEGIN TRY
```

A statement was printed, and then another attempt was made to INSERT into the table, this time using a generic name of Misc instead of the original department name sent by the input parameter:

```
    PRINT 'The first department attempt failed.'

    INSERT HumanResources.Department (Name, GroupName)
    VALUES ('Misc', @GroupName)

    END TRY
```

If this were to fail, the nested CATCH would print a second message telling the user that the Misc department for the specified group already exists:

```
BEGIN CATCH
    PRINT 'A Misc department for that group already exists.'
END CATCH

END CATCH

GO
```

The stored procedure was then tested, using a department that already existed in the table. Because there is a UNIQUE constraint on the department name, the first INSERT failed, and control was passed to the CATCH block. The TRY block within the CATCH then successfully inserted the Misc department name into the table

On a second execution of the stored procedure, both INSERTs failed, but were handled by returning a PRINT statement warning you about it.

CHAPTER 17

■■■

Principals

$\mathbf{M}$icrosoft uses a set of terminology to describe SQL Server security functionality, which separates the security architecture into

- *Principals*: These are objects (for example a user login, a role, or an application) that may be granted permission to access particular database objects.

- *Securables*: These are objects (a table or view, for example) to which access can be controlled.

- *Permissions*: These are individual rights, granted (or denied) to a principal, to access a securable object.

Principals are the topic of this chapter, and securables and permissions are discussed in the next chapter.

Principals fall into three different scopes:

- *Windows principals* are principals based on Windows domain user accounts, domain groups, local user accounts, and local groups. Once added to SQL Server and given permissions to access objects, these types of principals gain access to SQL Server based on Windows Authentication.

- *SQL Server principals* are SQL Server–level logins and fixed server roles. SQL logins are created within SQL Server and have a login name and password independent of any Windows entity. Server roles are groupings of SQL Server instance-level permissions that other principals can become members of, inheriting that server role's permissions.

- *Database principals* are database users, database roles (fixed and user-defined), and application roles—all of which I'll cover in this chapter.

I'll start this chapter off with a discussion of Windows principals.

Windows Principals

Windows principals allow access to a SQL Server instance using Windows Authentication. SQL Server allows us to create Windows logins based on Windows user accounts or groups, which can belong either to the local machine or to a domain. A Windows login can be associated with a domain user, local user, or Windows group. When adding a Windows login to SQL Server, the name of the user or group is bound to the Windows account. Windows logins added to SQL Server don't require separate password logins; in that case, Windows handles the login authentication process.

When users log on to SQL Server using Windows Authentication, their current user account must be identified as a login to the SQL Server instance, or they must belong to a Windows user group that exists as a login.

Windows logins apply only at the server operating system level: you can't grant Windows principals access to specific database objects. To grant permissions based on Windows logins, you need to create a database user and associate it with the login. You'll see how to do this when I discuss database principals.

When installing SQL Server, you are asked to decide between Windows-only and mixed authentication modes. Whichever authentication method you choose, you can always change your mind later. Microsoft Windows Authentication allows for tighter security than SQL Server logins, because security is integrated with the Windows operating system, local machine, and domain, and because no passwords are ever transmitted over the network. When using mixed authentication mode, you can create your own database logins and passwords within SQL Server.

Use the CREATE LOGIN command to add a Windows group or login to the SQL Server instance. The abridged syntax for creating a login from a Windows group or user login is as follows:

```
CREATE LOGIN login_name
FROM   WINDOWS
[ WITH DEFAULT_DATABASE = database
    | DEFAULT_LANGUAGE = language
]
    | CERTIFICATE certname
    | ASYMMETRIC KEY asym_key_name
```

The arguments of this command are described in Table 17-1.

Table 17-1. *CREATE LOGIN Arguments*

Argument	Description
login_name	This option defines the name of the Windows user or group.
DEFAULT_DATABASE = database	This option specifies the default database context of the Windows login, with the master system database being the default.
DEFAULT_LANGUAGE = language	This option specifies the default language of the Windows login, with the server default language being the login default if this option isn't specified.
CERTIFICATE certname	This option allows you to bind a certificate to a Windows login. See Chapter 19 for more information on certificates, and Chapter 20 for an example of doing so.
ASYMMETRIC KEY asym_key_name	This option binds a key to a Windows login. See Chapter 19 for more information on keys.

Creating a Windows Login

In this recipe, I assume that you already have certain Windows accounts and groups on the local machine or in your domain. This example creates a Windows *login* on the SQL Server instance, which is internally mapped to a Windows user:

```
CREATE LOGIN [CAESAR\Livia]
FROM WINDOWS
WITH DEFAULT_DATABASE = AdventureWorks,
DEFAULT_LANGUAGE = English
```

In the second example, a new Windows login is created, based on a Windows group. This is identical to the previous example, except that you are mapping to a Windows group instead of a Windows user:

```
CREATE LOGIN [CAESAR\Senators]
FROM WINDOWS
WITH DEFAULT_DATABASE= AdventureWorks
```

How It Works

This recipe demonstrated adding access for a Windows user and Windows group to the SQL Server instance. In the first example, the CREATE LOGIN designated the Windows user in square brackets:

```
CREATE LOGIN [CAESAR\Livia]
```

On the next line, the WINDOWS keyword was used to designate that this is a new login associated to a Windows account:

```
FROM WINDOWS
```

Next, the default database and languages were designated in the WITH clause:

```
WITH DEFAULT_DATABASE = AdventureWorks,
DEFAULT_LANGUAGE = English
```

In the second example, I demonstrated how to add a Windows group to SQL Server, which again requires square brackets in the CREATE LOGIN command:

```
CREATE LOGIN [CAESAR\Senators]
```

The FROM WINDOWS clause designated that this was a Windows group, followed by the default database:

```
FROM WINDOWS
WITH DEFAULT_DATABASE= AdventureWorks
```

When a Windows group is associated to a SQL Server login, it enables any member of the Windows group to inherit the access and permissions of the Windows login. Therefore, any members of this group will also have access to the SQL Server instance without explicitly having to add each Windows account to the SQL Server instance separately.

Viewing Windows Logins

You can view Windows logins and groups by querying the sys.server_principals system catalog view. This example shows the name of each Windows login and group with access to SQL Server, along with the security identifier (sid). Each principal in the system catalog view has a sid, which helps uniquely identify it on the SQL Server instance:

```
SELECT name, sid
FROM sys.server_principals
WHERE type_desc IN ('WINDOWS_LOGIN', 'WINDOWS_GROUP')
ORDER BY type_desc
```

This returns the following results (your own results will vary):

name	sid
BUILTIN\Administrators	0x01020000000000052000000020020000
CAESAR\SQLServerMSSQLUser$caesar$AUGUSTUS	0x0105000000000005150000019B2983B6D2CB3A E17D79646EE030000
CAESAR\SQLServerMSFTEUser$CAESAR$AUGUSTUS	0x0105000000000005150000019B2983B6D2CB3A E17D79646EB030000

CAESAR\SQLServerSQLAgentUser$CAESAR$AUGUSTUS	0x0105000000000000051500000019B2983B6D2CB3A E17D79646EF030000
CAESAR\Senators	0x0105000000000000051500000019B2983B6D2CB3A E17D79646F1030000
NT AUTHORITY\SYSTEM	0x010100000000000512000000
CAESAR\Administrator	0x0105000000000000051500000019B2983B6D2CB3A E17D79646F4010000
CAESAR\Livia	0x0105000000000000051500000019B2983B6D2CB3A E17D79646F0030000

How It Works

In this recipe, I demonstrated how to query Windows logins on the SQL Server instance using the sys.server_principals system catalog view. This view actually allows you to see other principal types too, which will be reviewed later in the chapter.

Altering a Windows Login

Once a Windows login is added to SQL Server, it can be modified using the ALTER LOGIN command (this command has several more options that are applicable to SQL logins, as you'll see reviewed later in the chapter). Using this command, you can perform tasks such as

- Changing the default database of the login
- Changing the default language of the login
- Enabling or disabling a login from being used

The abridged syntax is as follows (arguments similar to CREATE LOGIN):

```
ALTER LOGIN login_name
    {
    ENABLE | DISABLE
    |
WITH
    | DEFAULT_DATABASE = database
    | DEFAULT_LANGUAGE = language    }
```

In the first example, a Windows login (associated with a Windows user) is disabled from use in SQL Server. This prevents the login from accessing SQL Server, and if connected, ceases any further activity on the SQL Server instance:

```
ALTER LOGIN [CAESAR\Livia]
DISABLE
```

This next example demonstrates enabling this account again:

```
ALTER LOGIN [CAESAR\Livia]
ENABLE
```

In this example, the default database is changed for a Windows group:

```
ALTER LOGIN [CAESAR\Senators]
WITH DEFAULT_DATABASE = master
```

How It Works

In the first example, a Windows login was disabled using ALTER LOGIN and the login name:

```
ALTER LOGIN [CAESAR\Livia]
```

Following this was the DISABLE keyword, which removes this account's access to the SQL Server instance (it removes the account's access, but still keeps the login in the SQL Server instance for the later option of reenabling access):

```
DISABLE
```

The second example demonstrated reenabling access to the login by using the ENABLE keyword.

The third example changed the default database for a Windows group. The syntax for referencing Windows logins and groups is the same—both principal types are designated within square brackets:

```
ALTER LOGIN [CAESAR\Senators]
```

The second line then designated the new default database context for the Windows group:

```
WITH DEFAULT_DATABASE = master
```

Dropping a Windows Login

In this recipe, I'll demonstrate dropping a login from the SQL Server instance entirely by using the DROP LOGIN command. This removes the login's permission to access the SQL Server instance. If the login is currently connected to the SQL Server instance when the login is dropped, any actions attempted by the connected login will no longer be allowed.

The syntax is as follows:

```
DROP LOGIN login_name
```

The only parameter is the login name—which can be a Windows or SQL login (demonstrated later in the chapter), as this recipe demonstrates:

```
-- Windows Group login
DROP LOGIN [CAESAR\Senators]

-- Windows user login
DROP LOGIN [CAESAR\Livia]
```

How It Works

This recipe demonstrated the simple DROP LOGIN command, which removes a login from SQL Server. If a login owns any securables (see the next chapter for more information on securables), the DROP attempt will fail. For example, if the CAESAR\Livia login had been a database owner, an error like the following would have been raised:

```
Msg 15174, Level 16, State 1, Line 3
Login 'CAESAR\Livia' owns one or more database(s).
Change the owner of the database(s) before
dropping the login.
```

Denying SQL Server Access to a Windows User or Group

Use the DENY CONNECT SQL command to deny a Windows user or group access to SQL server. For example:

```
USE [master]
GO
DENY CONNECT SQL TO [CAESAR\Helen]
GO
```

To allow access again, you can use GRANT:

```
USE [master]
GO
GRANT CONNECT SQL TO [CAESAR\Helen]
GO
```

How It Works

This section is a sneak preview of Chapter 18, where GRANT and DENY will be explained in more detail. In a nutshell, the GRANT command grants permissions to securables, and DENY denies permissions to them. Use DENY CONNECT to restrict the Windows User or Group login from accessing a SQL Server instance the next time a login attempt is made. In both GRANT CONNECT and DENY CONNECT, it is assumed that the Windows user or group already has a login in SQL Server. Keep in mind that there are limitations to which logins you can deny permissions to. For example, if you try to DENY CONNECT to your own login with the following code:

```
DENY CONNECT SQL TO [CAESAR\Administrator]
```

it returns the following warning:

```
Cannot grant, deny, or revoke permissions to sa, dbo, information_schema,
sys, or yourself.
```

SQL Server Principals

Windows Authentication relies on the underlying operating system to perform authentication (determining who a particular user is), which means that SQL Server performs the necessary authorization (determining what actions an authenticated user is entitled to perform). When working with SQL Server principals and SQL Server authentication, SQL Server itself performs both authentication and authorization.

As noted earlier, when using mixed authentication mode, you can create your own login and passwords within SQL Server. These SQL logins only exist in SQL Server and do not have an outside Windows user/group mapping. With SQL logins, the passwords are stored within SQL Server. These user credentials are stored in SQL Server and are used to authenticate the user in question and to determine her appropriate access rights.

Because the security method involves explicit passwords, it is inherently less secure than using Windows Authentication alone. However, SQL Server logins are still commonly used with third-party and non-Windows operating system applications. SQL Server *has* improved the password protection capabilities by enabling Windows-like password functionality, such as forced password changes, expiration dates, and other password policies (e.g., password complexity), with Windows 2003 Server and higher.

As with Windows logins, SQL Server logins apply only at the server level; you can't grant permissions on these to specific database objects. Unless you are granted membership to a fixed server role such as sysadmin, you must create database users associated to the login before you can begin working with database objects.

As in previous versions of SQL Server, SQL Server supports principals based on both individual logins and server roles, which multiple individual users can be assigned to.

To create a new SQL Server login, use the CREATE LOGIN command:

```
CREATE LOGIN login_name
[WITH PASSWORD = ' password ' [ HASHED ] [ MUST_CHANGE ],
    SID = sid],
    DEFAULT_DATABASE = database,
    DEFAULT_LANGUAGE = language,
    CHECK_EXPIRATION = { ON | OFF},
    CHECK_POLICY = { ON | OFF},
    CREDENTIAL = credential_name ]
```

The arguments of this command are described in Table 17-2.

Table 17-2. *CREATE LOGIN Arguments*

Argument	Description
login_name	This is the login name.
' password ' [HASHED] [MUST_CHANGE]	This is the login's password. Specifying the HASHED option means that the provided password is already hashed (made into an unreadable and secured format). If MUST_CHANGE is specified, the user is prompted to change the password the first time the user logs in.
SID = sid	This explicitly specifies the sid that will be used in the system tables of the SQL Server instance. This can be based on a login from a different SQL Server instance (if you're migrating logins). If this isn't specified, SQL Server generates its own sid in the system tables.
DEFAULT_DATABASE = database	This option specifies the default database context of the SQL login, with the master system database being the default.
DEFAULT_LANGUAGE = language	This option specifies the default language of the login, with the server default language being the login default if this option isn't specified.
CHECK_EXPIRATION = { ON	OFF},	When set to ON (the default), the SQL login will be subject to a password expiration policy. A password expiration policy affects how long a password will remain valid before it must be changed. This functionality requires Windows 2003 Server or higher versions.
CHECK_POLICY = { ON	OFF},	When set to ON (the default), Windows password policies are applied to the SQL login (for example, policies regarding the password's length, complexity, and inclusion of non-alphanumeric characters). This functionality requires Windows 2003 Server or higher versions.
CREDENTIAL = credential_name	This option allows a server credential to be mapped to the SQL login. See Chapter 18 for more information on credentials.

Creating a SQL Server Login

This example first demonstrates how to create a SQL Server login with a password and a default database designated:

```
CREATE LOGIN Veronica
WITH PASSWORD = 'InfernoII',
DEFAULT_DATABASE = AdventureWorks
```

Assuming you are using Windows 2003 Server or higher, as well as mixed authentication, the recipe goes on to create a SQL login with a password that must be changed the first time the user logs in. This login also is created with the CHECK_POLICY option ON, requiring it to comply with Windows password policies:

```
CREATE LOGIN Trishelle
WITH PASSWORD = 'ChangeMe' MUST_CHANGE ,
    CHECK_EXPIRATION = ON,
        CHECK_POLICY = ON
```

How It Works

The first example in this recipe demonstrated creating a SQL login named Veronica. The login name was designated after CREATE LOGIN:

```
CREATE LOGIN Veronica
```

The second line designated the login's password:

```
WITH PASSWORD = 'InfernoII',
```

The last line of code designated the default database that the login's context would first enter after logging into SQL Server:

```
DEFAULT_DATABASE = AdventureWorks
```

The second SQL login example demonstrated how to force a password to be changed on the first login by designating the MUST CHANGE token after the password:

```
CREATE LOGIN Trishelle
WITH PASSWORD = 'ChangeMe' MUST_CHANGE ,
```

This password policy integration requires Windows 2003 Server, as did the password expiration and password policy options also designated for this login:

```
    CHECK_EXPIRATION = ON,
        CHECK_POLICY = ON
```

Viewing SQL Server Logins

Again, you can view SQL Server logins (and other principals) by querying the sys.server_principals system catalog view:

```
SELECT name, sid
FROM sys.server_principals
WHERE type_desc IN ('SQL_LOGIN')
ORDER BY name
```

This returns the following results:

name	sid
Boris	0xC2692B07894DFD45913C5595C87936B9
BrianG	0x4EC3966D4E33844F89680AFD87D2D5BD
JoeSa	0xB64D3C39533CC648B581884EC143F2D4
Prageeta	0x00CACEF1F0E0CE429B7C808B11A624E7
sa	0x01
SteveP	0xAAA2CD258750C641BBE9584627CAA11F
Veronica	0xE08E462A75D8C047A4561D4E9292296D

How It Works

This recipe's query returned the name and sid of each SQL login on the SQL Server instance by querying the sys.server_principals catalog view.

Altering a SQL Server Login

Once a login is added to SQL Server, it can be modified using the ALTER LOGIN command. Using this command, you can perform several tasks:

- Change the login's password.
- Change the default database or language.
- Change the name of the existing login without disrupting the login's currently assigned permissions.
- Change the password policy settings (enabling or disabling them).
- Map or remove mapping from a SQL login credential.
- Enable or disable a login from being used.
- Unlock a locked login.

The syntax arguments are similar to CREATE LOGIN (I'll demonstrate usage in this recipe):

```
ALTER LOGIN login_name
    {
    ENABLE | DISABLE
    |
WITH  PASSWORD = ' password '
    [ OLD_PASSWORD = ' oldpassword '
      | [ MUST_CHANGE | UNLOCK ] ]
    | DEFAULT_DATABASE = database
    | DEFAULT_LANGUAGE = language
    | NAME = login_name
    | CHECK_POLICY = { ON | OFF }
    | CHECK_EXPIRATION = { ON | OFF }
    | CREDENTIAL = credential_name
    | NO CREDENTIAL
    }
```

In the first example of this recipe, a SQL login's password is changed from InfernoII to InfernoIII:

```
ALTER LOGIN Veronica
WITH  PASSWORD = 'InfernoIII'
OLD_PASSWORD = 'InfernoII'
```

The OLD_PASSWORD is the current password that is being changed; however, sysadmin fixed server role members don't have to know the old password in order to change it.

This second example demonstrates changing the default database of the Veronica SQL login:

```
ALTER LOGIN Veronica
WITH DEFAULT_DATABASE = [AdventureWorks]
```

This third example in this recipe demonstrates changing both the name and password of a SQL login:

```
ALTER LOGIN Veronica
WITH NAME = Angela,
PASSWORD = 'B0S2004'
```

Changing the login name instead of just dropping and creating a new one offers one major benefit—the permissions associated to the original login are not disrupted when the login is renamed. In this case, the Veronica login is renamed to Angela, but the permissions remain the same.

How It Works

In the first example of this recipe, ALTER LOGIN was used to change a password designating the old password and the new password. If you have sysadmin fixed server role permissions, you only need to designate the new password. The second example demonstrated how to change the default database of a SQL login. The last example demonstrated how to change a login's name from Veronica to Angela, as well as change the login's password.

Managing a Login's Password

SQL Server provides the LOGINPROPERTY function to return information about login and password policy settings and state. Using this function, you can determine the following qualities of a SQL login:

- Whether the login is locked or expired

- Whether the login has a password that must be changed

- Bad password counts and the last time an incorrect password was given

- Login lockout time

- The last time a password was set and the length of time the login has been tracked using password-policies

- The password hash for use in migration (to another SQL instance, for example)

This function takes two parameters; the name of the SQL login and the property to be checked. In this example, I will list all available properties of a specific login:

```
SELECT LOGINPROPERTY('Angela', 'IsLocked') IsLocked,
       LOGINPROPERTY('Angela', 'IsExpired') IsExpired,
       LOGINPROPERTY('Angela', 'IsMustChange') IsMustChange,
       LOGINPROPERTY('Angela', 'BadPasswordCount') BadPasswordCount,
       LOGINPROPERTY('Angela', 'BadPasswordTime') BadPasswordTime,
       LOGINPROPERTY('Angela', 'HistoryLength') HistoryLength,
       LOGINPROPERTY('Angela', 'LockoutTime') LockoutTime,
       LOGINPROPERTY('Angela', 'PasswordLastSetTime') PasswordLastSetTime,
       LOGINPROPERTY('Angela', 'PasswordHash') PasswordHash
```

This returns

IsLocked	IsExpired	IsMustChange	BadPassword Count	BadPassword Time	HistoryLength	LockoutTime	PasswordLast SetTime	PasswordHash
0	0	0	0	1900-01-01 00:00:00.000	0	1900-01-01 00:00:00.000	2007-12-22 07:07:33.590	0x01000D175F71 610D24501843F3 F3E08E518B8DF7 73E9006C4DFA

How It Works

LOGINPROPERTY allows you to validate the properties of a SQL login. You can use it to manage password rotation, for example, checking the last time a password was set and then modifying any logins that haven't changed within a certain period of time.

You can also use the password hash property in conjunction with CREATE LOGIN and the hashed_password HASHED argument to re-create a SQL login with the preserved password on a new SQL Server instance.

Dropping a SQL Login

This recipe demonstrates dropping a SQL login from a SQL Server instance by using the DROP LOGIN command.

The syntax is as follows:

```
DROP LOGIN login_name
```

The only parameter is the login name—which can be a Windows or SQL login, as this recipe demonstrates:

```
DROP LOGIN Angela
```

How It Works

This recipe demonstrated the simple DROP LOGIN command, which removes a login from SQL Server. The process is simple; however, if a login owns any securables (see the next chapter for information on securables), the DROP attempt will fail. For example, if the Angela login had been a database owner, an error like the following would have been raised:

```
Msg 15174, Level 16, State 1, Line 3
Login 'Angela' owns one or more database(s).
Change the owner of the database(s) before dropping the
 login.
```

Managing Server Role Members

Fixed server roles are predefined SQL groups that have specific SQL Server–scoped (as opposed to database- or schema-scoped) permissions assigned to them. You cannot create new fixed server roles; you can only add or remove membership to such a role from other SQL or Windows logins.

The sysadmin fixed server role is the role with the highest level of permissions in a SQL Server instance. Although server roles are permissions based, they have members (SQL or Windows logins/groups) and are categorized by Microsoft as principals.

To add a login to a fixed server role, use the sp_addsrvrolemember system stored procedure.

The syntax is as follows:

```
sp_addsrvrolemember [ @loginame= ] 'login',
[ @rolename = ] 'role'
```

The first parameter of the system stored procedure is the login name to add to the fixed server role. The second parameter is the fixed server role you are adding the login to.

In this example, the login Veronica is created and then added to the sysadmin fixed server role:

```
CREATE LOGIN Veronica
WITH PASSWORD = 'PalmTree1'
GO

EXEC master..sp_addsrvrolemember
'Veronica',
'sysadmin'
GO
```

To remove a login from a fixed server role, the system stored procedure sp_dropsrvrolemember is used. The syntax is almost identical to sp_addsrvrolemember:

```
sp_dropsrvrolemember [ @loginame= ] 'login' ,
[ @rolename= ] 'role'
```

This example *removes* the Veronica login from the sysadmin fixed role membership:

```
EXEC master..sp_dropsrvrolemember
'Veronica',
'sysadmin'
GO
```

How It Works

Once a login is added to a fixed server role, that login receives the permissions associated with the fixed server role. The sp_addsrvrolemember system stored procedure was used to add a new login to a fixed role membership, and sp_dropsrvrolemember was used to remove a login from a fixed role membership.

Adding SQL or Windows logins to a fixed server role should never be done lightly. Fixed server roles contain far-reaching permissions—so as a rule of thumb, seek to grant only those permissions that are absolutely necessary for the job at hand. For example, don't give sysadmin membership to someone who just needs SELECT permission on a table.

Reporting Fixed Server Role Information

Fixed server roles define a grouping of SQL Server-scoped permissions (such as backing up a database or creating new logins). Like SQL or Windows logins, fixed server roles have a security identifier and can be viewed in the sys.server_principals system catalog view. Unlike SQL or Windows logins, fixed server roles can have members (SQL and Windows logins) defined within them that inherit the permissions of the fixed server role.

To view fixed server roles, query the sys.server_principals system catalog view:

```
SELECT name
FROM sys.server_principals
WHERE type_desc = 'SERVER_ROLE'
```

This returns

```
name
public
sysadmin
securityadmin
serveradmin
setupadmin
processadmin
diskadmin
dbcreator
bulkadmin
```

You can also view a list of fixed server roles by executing the sp_helpserverrole system stored procedure:

```
EXEC sp_helpsrvrole
```

This returns

```
ServerRole                Description
sysadmin                  System Administrators
securityadmin             Security Administrators
serveradmin               Server Administrators
setupadmin                Setup Administrators
processadmin              Process Administrators
diskadmin                 Disk Administrators
dbcreator                 Database Creators
bulkadmin                 Bulk Insert Administrators

(8 row(s) affected)
```

Table 17-3 details the permissions granted to each fixed server role.

Table 17-3. *Server Role Permissions*

Server Role	Granted Permissions
sysadmin	GRANT option (can GRANT permissions to others), CONTROL SERVER
setupadmin	ALTER ANY LINKED SERVER
serveradmin	ALTER SETTINGS, SHUTDOWN, CREATE ENDPOINT, ALTER SERVER STATE, ALTER ANY ENDPOINT, ALTER RESOURCES
securityadmin	ALTER ANY LOGIN
processadmin	ALTER SERVER STATE, ALTER ANY CONNECTION
diskadmin	ALTER RESOURCES
dbcreator	CREATE DATABASE
bulkadmin	ADMINISTER BULK OPERATIONS

To see the members of a fixed server role, you can execute the sp_helpsrvrolemember system stored procedure:

```
EXEC sp_helpsrvrolemember 'sysadmin'
```

This returns the following results:

ServerRole	MemberName	MemberSID
sysadmin	sa	0x01
sysadmin	NT AUTHORITY\SYSTEM	0x010100000000000512000000
sysadmin	BUILTIN\Administrators	0x01020000000000052000000020 020000
sysadmin	CAESAR\SQLServerMSSQLUser$caesar$AUGUSTUS	0x010500000000000051500000019 B2983B6D2CB3AE17D79646EE0300 00
sysadmin	CAESAR\SQLServerMSFTEUser$CAESAR$AUGUSTUS	0x010500000000000051500000019 B2983B6D2CB3AE17D79646EB0300 00
sysadmin	CAESAR\Administrator	0x010500000000000051500000019 B2983B6D2CB3AE17D79646F40100 00
sysadmin	CAESAR\SQLServerSQLAgentUser$CAESAR$AUGUSTUS	0x010500000000000051500000019 B2983B6D2CB3AE17D79646EF0300 00

How It Works

You can query the system catalog view `sys.server_principals` in order to view fixed server roles, or you can use the `sp_helpsrvrole` system stored procedure to view descriptions for each of the roles. To view members of a role (other principals), use the `sp_helpsrvrolemember` system stored procedure.

The next recipe will show you how to *add* or *remove* other principals to a fixed server role.

Database Principals

Database principals are the objects that represent users to which you can assign permissions to access databases or particular objects within a database. Whereas logins operate at the server level and allow you to perform actions such as connecting to a SQL Server, database principals operate at the database level, and allow you to select or manipulate data, to perform DDL statements on objects within the database, or to manage users' permissions at the database level.

SQL Server recognizes four different types of database principals:

- *Database users*: Database user principals are the database-level security context under which requests within the database are executed, and are associated with either SQL Server or Windows logins.

- *Database roles*: Database roles come in two flavors, fixed and user-defined. Fixed database roles are found in each database of a SQL Server instance, and have database-scoped permissions assigned to them (such as SELECT permission on all tables or the ability to CREATE tables). User-defined database roles are those that you can create yourself, allowing you to manage permissions to securables more easily than if you had to individually grant similar permissions to multiple database users.

- *Application roles*: Application roles are groupings of permissions that don't allow members. Instead, you can "log in" as the application role. When you use an application role, it overrides all of the other permissions your login would otherwise have, giving you only those permissions granted to the application role.

In this section, I'll review how to create, modify, report on, and drop database users. I'll also cover how to work with database roles (fixed and user-defined) and application roles.

Creating Database Users

Once a login is created, it can then be mapped to a database user. A login can be mapped to multiple databases on a single SQL Server instance—but only one user for each database it has access to. Users are granted access with the CREATE USER command.

The syntax is as follows:

```
CREATE USER user_name
    [ FOR
        { LOGIN login_name
        | CERTIFICATE cert_name
        | ASYMMETRIC KEY asym_key_name
        }
    ]
    [ WITH DEFAULT_SCHEMA = schema_name ]
```

The arguments of this command are described in Table 17-4.

Table 17-4. *CREATE USER Arguments*

Argument	Description
user_name	This defines the name of the user in the database.
login_name	This defines the name of the SQL or Windows login that is mapping to the database user.
cert_name	When designated, this specifies a certificate that is bound to the database user. See Chapter 19 for more information on certificates.
asym_key_name	When designated, this specifies an asymmetric key that is bound to the database user. See Chapter 19 for more information on keys.
schema_name	This indicates the default schema that the user will belong to, which will determine what schema is checked first when the user references database objects. If this option is unspecified, the dbo schema will be used. This schema name can also be designated for a schema not yet created in the database.

In this first example of the recipe, a new user called Veronica is created in the TestDB database:

```
IF NOT EXISTS (SELECT name
                FROM sys.databases
                WHERE name = 'TestDB')
BEGIN
    CREATE DATABASE TestDB
END
GO

USE TestDB
GO
CREATE USER Veronica
```

In the second example, a Windows login is mapped to a database user called Joe with a default schema specified:

```
USE TestDB
GO

CREATE USER Helen
FOR LOGIN [CAESAR\Helen]
WITH DEFAULT_SCHEMA = HumanResources
```

How It Works

In the first example of the recipe, a user named Veronica was created in the TestDB database. If you don't designate the FOR LOGIN clause of CREATE USER, it is assumed that the user maps to a login with the same name (in this case, a login named Veronica). Notice that the default schema was not designated, which means Veronica's default schema will be dbo.

In the second example, a new user named Helen was created in the AdventureWorks database, mapped to a Windows login named [CAESAR\Helen] (notice the square brackets). The default schema was also set for the Helen login to HumanResources. For any unqualified object references in queries performed by Helen, SQL Server will first search for objects in the HumanResources schema.

Reporting Database User Information

You can report database user (and role) information for the current database connection by using the sp_helpuser system stored procedure.

The syntax is as follows:

```
sp_helpuser [ [ @name_in_db= ] ' security_account ' ]
```

The single, optional parameter is the name of the database user for which you wish to return information. For example:

```
EXEC sp_helpuser 'Veronica'
```

This returns the following results:

UserName	RoleName	LoginName	DefDBName	DefSchemaName	UserID	SID
Veronica	public	Veronica	master	dbo	5	0x3057F4EEC4F07A46B F126AB2434F104D

How It Works

The sp_helpuser system stored procedure returns the database users defined in the current database. From the results, you can determine important information such as the user name, login name, default database and schema, and the user's security identifier. If a specific user isn't designated, sp_helpuser returns information on all users in the current database you are connected to.

Modifying a Database User

You can rename a database user or change the user's default schema by using the ALTER USER command.

The syntax is as follows (argument usages are demonstrated in this recipe):

```
ALTER USER user_name
    WITH  NAME = new_user_name
    | DEFAULT_SCHEMA = schema_name
```

In this first example of this recipe, the default schema of the Joe database user is changed:

```
USE TestDB
GO

ALTER USER Helen
WITH DEFAULT_SCHEMA = Production
```

In the second example of this recipe, a database user name is changed:

```
USE TestDB
GO

ALTER USER Veronica
WITH NAME = VSanders
```

How It Works

The ALTER USER command allows you to perform one of two changes: renaming a database user or changing a database user's default schema. The first example changed the default schema of the Helen login to the Production schema. The second example renamed the database user Veronica to VSanders.

Removing a Database User from the Database

Use the DROP USER command to remove a user from the database.

The syntax is as follows:

```
DROP USER user_name
```

The user_name is the name of the database user, as this example demonstrates:

```
USE TestDB
GO

DROP USER VSanders
```

How It Works

The DROP USER command removes a user from the database, but does not impact the Windows or SQL login that is associated to it. Like DROP LOGIN, you can't drop a user that is the owner of database objects. For example, if the database user Helen is the schema owner for a schema called Test, you'll get an error like the following:

```
Msg 15138, Level 16, State 1, Line 2
The database principal owns a schema in the database, and cannot be dropped.
```

Fixing Orphaned Database Users

When you migrate a database to a new server (by using BACKUP/RESTORE, for example) the relationship between logins and database users can break. A login has a security identifier, which uniquely identifies it on the SQL Server instance. This sid is stored for the login's associated database user in each database that the login has access to. Creating another SQL login on a different SQL Server instance with the same name will not re-create the same sid unless you specifically designated it with the sid argument of the CREATE LOGIN statement.

The following query demonstrates this link by joining the sys.database_principals system catalog view to the sys.server_principals catalog view on the sid column in order to look for orphaned database users in the database:

```
SELECT dp.name OrphanUser, dp.sid OrphanSid
FROM sys.database_principals dp
LEFT OUTER JOIN sys.server_principals sp ON
    dp.sid = sp.sid
WHERE sp.sid IS NULL AND
      dp.type_desc = 'SQL_USER' AND
      dp.principal_id > 4
```

This returns

OrphanUser	OrphanSid
Sonja	0x40C455005F34E44FB95622488AF48F75

If you RESTORE a database from a different SQL Server instance onto a new SQL Server instance—and the database users don't have associated logins on the new SQL Server instance—the database users can become "orphaned." If there are logins with the same name on the new SQL Server instance that match the name of the database users, the database users still may be orphaned in the database if the login sid doesn't match the restored database user sid.

Beginning in the previous version of SQL Server, SQL Server 2005, Service Pack 2, you can use the ALTER USER WITH LOGIN command to remap login/user associations. This applies to both SQL and Windows accounts, which is very useful if the underlying Windows user or group has been re-created in Active Directory and now has an identifier that no longer maps to the generated sid on the SQL Server instance.

The following query demonstrates remapping the orphaned database user Sonja to the associated server login:

```
ALTER USER Sonja
WITH LOGIN = Sonja
```

The next example demonstrates mapping a database user, [Helen], to the login [CAESAR\Helen] (assuming that the user became orphaned from the Windows account or the sid of the domain account was changed due to a drop/re-create outside of SQL Server):

```
ALTER USER [Helen]
WITH LOGIN = [CAESAR\Helen]
```

This command also works with remapping a user to a new login—whether or not that user is orphaned.

How It Works

In this recipe, I demonstrated querying the sys.database_principals and sys.server_principals catalog views to view any database users with a sid that does not exist at the server scope (no associated login sid). I then demonstrated using ALTER USER to map the database user to a login with the same name (but different sid). I also demonstrated how to remap a Windows account in the event that it is orphaned using ALTER USER.

■**Tip** In previous versions of SQL Server, you could use the `sp_change_users_login` to perform and report on `sid` remapping. This stored procedure has been deprecated in favor of `ALTER USER WITH LOGIN`.

Reporting Fixed Database Roles Information

Fixed database roles are found in each database of a SQL Server instance and have database-scoped permissions assigned to them (such as `SELECT` permission on all tables or the ability to `CREATE` tables). Like fixed server roles, fixed database roles have members (database users) that inherit the permissions of the role.

A list of fixed database roles can be viewed by executing the `sp_helpdbfixedrole` system stored procedure:

```
EXEC sp_helpdbfixedrole
```

This returns the following results:

DBFixedRole	Description
db_owner	DB Owners
db_accessadmin	DB Access Administrators
db_securityadmin	DB Security Administrators
db_ddladmin	DB DDL Administrators
db_backupoperator	DB Backup Operator
db_datareader	DB Data Reader
db_datawriter	DB Data Writer
db_denydatareader	DB Deny Data Reader
db_denydatawriter	DB Deny Data Writer

To see the database members of a fixed database role (or any user-defined or application role), you can execute the `sp_helprolemember` system stored procedure:

```
EXEC sp_helprolemember
```

This returns the following results (the member `sid` refers to the `sid` of the login mapped to the database user):

DbRole	MemberName	MemberSid
db_backupoperator	Joe	0x0105000000000000515000000527A777BF094B3850F
db_datawriter	Joe	0x0105000000000000515000000527A777BF094B3850FF83D0
db_owner	dbo	0x01

How It Works

Fixed database roles are found in each database on a SQL Server instance. A fixed database role groups important database permissions together. These permissions can't be modified or removed.

In this recipe, I used `sp_helpdbfixedrole` to list the available fixed database roles:

```
EXEC sp_helpdbfixedrole
```

After that, the sp_helprolemember system stored procedure was used to list the members of each fixed database role (database users), showing the role name, database user name, and login sid:

```
EXEC sp_helprolemember
```

As with fixed server roles, it's best not to grant membership to them without assurance that all permissions are absolutely necessary for the database user. Do not, for example, grant a user db_owner membership when only SELECT permissions on a table are needed.

The next recipe shows you how to add or remove database users to a fixed database role.

Managing Fixed Database Role Membership

To associate a database user or role with a database role (user-defined or application role), use the sp_addrolemember system stored procedure.

The syntax is as follows:

```
sp_addrolemember [ @rolename = ] 'role',
    [ @membername = ] 'security_account'
```

The first parameter of the system stored procedure takes the role name, and the second parameter the name of the database user.

To remove the association between a database user and role, use the sp_droprolemember system stored procedure:

```
sp_droprolemember [ @rolename= ] 'role' ,
        [ @membername= ] 'security_account'
```

Like sp_addrolemember, the first parameter of the system stored procedure takes the role name, and the second parameter takes the name of the database user.

This first example demonstrates adding the database user Helen to the fixed db_datawriter and db_datareader roles:

```
USE TestDB
GO
EXEC sp_addrolemember 'db_datawriter', 'Helen'
EXEC sp_addrolemember 'db_datareader', 'Helen'
```

This second example demonstrates how to *remove* the database user Helen from the db_datawriter role:

```
USE TestDB
GO
EXEC sp_droprolemember 'db_datawriter', 'Helen'
```

How It Works

This recipe began by discussing sp_addrolemember, which allows you to add a database user to an existing database role. The database user Helen was added to db_datawriter and db_datareader, which gives her cumulative permissions to SELECT, INSERT, UPDATE, or DELETE from any table or view in the AdventureWorks database:

```
EXEC sp_addrolemember 'db_datawriter', 'Helen'
EXEC sp_addrolemember 'db_datareader', 'Helen'
```

The first parameter of the stored procedure was the database role, and the second parameter was the name of the database user (or role) that the database role is associated to.

After that, the `sp_droprolemember` was used to remove Helen's membership from the `db_datawriter` role:

```
EXEC sp_droprolemember 'db_datawriter', 'Helen'
```

Managing User-Defined Database Roles

User-defined database roles allow you to manage permissions to securables more easily than if you had to individually grant the same permissions to multiple database users over and over again. Instead, you can create a database role, grant it permissions to securables, and then add one or more database users as members to that database role. When permission changes are needed, you only have to modify the permissions of the single database role, and the members of the role will then automatically inherit those permission changes.

Use the `CREATE ROLE` command to create a user-defined role in a database.

The syntax is as follows:

```
CREATE ROLE role_name [ AUTHORIZATION owner_name ]
```

The command takes the name of the new role and an optional role owner name. The owner name is the name of the user or database role that owns the new database role (and thus can manage it).

You can list all database roles (fixed, user-defined, and application) by executing the `sp_helprole` system stored procedure:

```
EXEC sp_helprole
```

This returns the following abridged results (the `IsAppRole` column shows as a 1 if the role is an application role and 0 if not):

RoleName	RoleId	IsAppRole
public	0	0
db_owner	16384	0
...	...	...

Once a database role is created in a database, you can grant or deny it permissions as you would a regular database user (see the next chapter for more on permissions). I'll also demonstrate granting permissions to a database role in a moment.

If you wish to change the name of the database role, *without* also disrupting the role's current permissions and membership, you can use the `ALTER ROLE` command, which has the following syntax:

```
ALTER ROLE role_name WITH NAME = new_name
```

The command takes the name of the original role as the first argument and the new role name in the second argument.

To drop a role, use the `DROP ROLE` command. The syntax is as follows:

```
DROP ROLE role_name
```

If a role owns any securables, you'll need to transfer ownership to a new owner before you can drop the role.

In this example, I'll create a new role in the `AdventureWorks` database:

```
USE AdventureWorks
GO
CREATE ROLE HR_ReportSpecialist AUTHORIZATION db_owner
```

After being created, this new role doesn't have any database permissions yet. In this next query, I'll grant the HR_ReportSpecialist database role permission to SELECT from the HumanResources. Employee table:

```
GRANT SELECT ON HumanResources.Employee TO HR_ReportSpecialist
```

To add Veronica as a member of this new role, I execute the following:

```
EXEC sp_addrolemember 'HR_ReportSpecialist',
        'Veronica'
GO
```

If, later on, I decide that the name of the role doesn't match its purpose, I can change its name using ALTER ROLE:

```
ALTER ROLE HR_ReportSpecialist WITH NAME = HumanResources_RS
```

Even though the role name was changed, Veronica remains a member of the role.

This last example demonstrates dropping a database role:

```
DROP ROLE HumanResources_RS
```

This returns an error message, because the role must be emptied of members before it can be dropped:

```
Msg 15144, Level 16, State 1, Line 1
The role has members. It must be empty before it can be dropped.
```

So, the single member of this role is then dropped, prior to dropping the role:

```
EXEC sp_droprolemember 'HumanResources_RS',
        'Veronica'
GO

DROP ROLE HumanResources_RS
```

How It Works

The CREATE ROLE command creates a new database role in a database. Once created, you can apply permissions to the role as you would a regular database user. Roles allow you to administer permissions at a group level—allowing individual role members to inherit permissions in a consistent manner instead of applying permissions to individual users, which may or may not be identical.

This recipe demonstrated several commands related to managing user-defined database roles. The sp_helprole system stored procedure was used to list all database roles in the current database. CREATE ROLE was used to create a new user-defined role owned by the db_owner fixed database role:

```
CREATE ROLE HR_ReportSpecialist AUTHORIZATION db_owner
```

I then granted permissions to the new role to SELECT from a table:

```
GRANT SELECT ON HumanResources.Employee TO HR_ReportSpecialist
```

The Veronica user was then added as a member of the new role:

```
EXEC sp_addrolemember 'HR_ReportSpecialist',
        'Veronica'
```

The name of the role was changed using ALTER ROLE (still leaving membership and permissions intact):

```
ALTER ROLE HR_ReportSpecialist WITH NAME = HumanResources_RS
```

The Veronica user was then dropped from the role (so that I could drop the user-defined role):

```
EXEC sp_droprolemember 'HumanResources_RS',
        'Veronica'
```

Once emptied of members, the user-defined database role was then dropped:

```
DROP ROLE HumanResources_RS
```

Managing Application Roles

An application role is a hybrid between a login and a database role. You can assign permissions to application roles in the same way that you can assign permissions to user-defined roles. Application roles differ from database and server roles, however, in that application roles *do not allow members.* Instead, an application role is *activated* using a password-enabled system stored procedure. When you use an application role, it overrides all of the other permissions your login would otherwise have.

Because an application role has no members, it requires a password for the permissions to be enabled. In addition to this, once a session's context is set to use an application role, any existing user or login permissions are nullified. Only the application role's permissions apply.

To create an application role, use the CREATE APPLICATION ROLE, which has the following syntax:

```
CREATE APPLICATION ROLE application_role_name
    WITH PASSWORD = ' password ' [ , DEFAULT_SCHEMA = schema_name ]
```

The arguments of this command are described in Table 17-5.

Table 17-5. *CREATE APPLICATON ROLE Arguments*

Argument	Description
application_role_name	The name of the application role
password	The password to enable access to the application role's permissions
schema_name	The default database schema of the application role that defines which schema is checked for unqualified object names in a query

In this example, a new application role name, DataWareHouseApp, is created and granted permissions to a view in the AdventureWorks database:

```
USE AdventureWorks
GO
CREATE APPLICATION ROLE DataWareHouseApp
WITH PASSWORD =  'mywarehouse123!',
 DEFAULT_SCHEMA = dbo
```

An application role by itself is useless without first granting it permissions to do something. So, in this example, the application role is given SELECT permissions on a specific database view:

```
-- Now grant this application role permissions
GRANT SELECT ON  Sales.vSalesPersonSalesByFiscalYears
TO DataWareHouseApp
```

The system stored procedure sp_setapprole is used to enable the permissions of the application role for the current user session. In this next example, I activate an application role and query two tables:

```
EXEC sp_setapprole 'DataWareHouseApp', -- App role name
    'mywarehouse123!' -- Password

-- Works
SELECT COUNT(*)
FROM Sales.vSalesPersonSalesByFiscalYears

-- Doesn't work
SELECT COUNT(*)
FROM HumanResources.vJobCandidate
```

This returns

```
-----------
14

(1 row(s) affected)

Msg 229, Level 14, State 5, Line 7
SELECT permission denied on object 'vJobCandidate',
database 'AdventureWorks', schema
'HumanResources'.
```

Even though the original connection login was for a login with sysadmin permissions, using sp_setapprole to enter the application permissions means that only that role's permissions apply. So, in this case, the application role had SELECT permission for the Sales.vSalesPersonSalesByFis-calYears view, but not the HumanResources.vJobCandidate view queried in the example.

To revert back to the original login's permissions, you must close out the connection and open a new connection.

You can modify the name, password, or default database of an application role using the ALTER APPLICATION ROLE command.

The syntax is as follows:

```
ALTER APPLICATION ROLE application_role_name
WITH  NAME = new_application_role_name
    | PASSWORD = ' password '
    | DEFAULT_SCHEMA = schema_name
```

The arguments of the command are described in Table 17-6.

Table 17-6. *ALTER APPLICATION ROLE Arguments*

Parameter	Description
new_application_role_name	The new application role name
password	The new application role password
schema_name	The new default schema

In this example, the application role name and password are changed:

```
ALTER APPLICATION ROLE DataWareHouseApp
WITH  NAME = DW_App, PASSWORD = 'newsecret!123'
```

To remove an application role from the database, use DROP APPLICATION ROLE, which has the following syntax:

```
DROP APPLICATION ROLE rolename
```

This command takes only one argument, the name of the application role to be dropped. For example:

```
DROP APPLICATION ROLE DW_App
```

How It Works

This recipe demonstrated how to

- Create a new application role using CREATE APPLICATION ROLE.
- Activate the role permissions using sp_setapprole.
- Modify an application role using ALTER APPLICATION ROLE.
- Remove an application role from a database using DROP APPLICATION ROLE.

Application roles are a convenient solution for application developers who wish to grant users access *only through an application*. Savvy end users may figure out that their SQL login can also be used to connect to SQL Server with other applications such as Microsoft Access or SQL Server Management Studio. To prevent this, you can change the login account to have minimal permissions for the databases, and then use an application role for the required permissions. This way, the user can only access the data through the application, which is then programmed to use the application role.

CHAPTER 18

■■■

Securables, Permissions, and Auditing

In the previous chapter, I discussed principals, which are security accounts that can access SQL Server. In this chapter, I'll discuss and demonstrate securables and permissions. *Securables* are resources that SQL Server controls access to through permissions. Securables in SQL Server fall into three nested hierarchical scopes. The top level of the hierarchy is the *server scope*, which contains logins, databases, and endpoints. The *database scope*, which is contained within the server scope, controls securables such as database users, roles, certificates, and schemas. The third and inner-most scope is the *schema scope*, which controls securables such as the schema itself, and objects within the schema such as tables, views, functions, and procedures.

Permissions enable a principal to perform actions on securables. Across all securable scopes, the primary commands used to control a principal's access to a securable are GRANT, DENY, and REVOKE. These commands are applied in similar ways, depending on the scope of the securable that you are targeting. GRANT is used to enable access to securables. DENY explicitly restricts access, trumping other permissions that would normally allow a principal access to a securable. REVOKE removes a specific permission on a securable altogether, whether it was a GRANT or DENY permission.

Once permissions are granted, you may still have additional business and compliance auditing requirements that mandate tracking of changes or knowing which logins are accessing which tables. To address this need, SQL Server 2008 introduces the SQL Server Audit object, which can be used to collect SQL instance– and database-scoped actions that you are interested in monitoring. This audit information can be set to a file, the Windows Application event log, or the Windows Security event log.

In this chapter, I'll discuss how permissions are granted to principals at all three securable scopes. In addition to permissions, this chapter also presents the following related securable and permissions recipes:

- How to manage schemas using CREATE, ALTER, and DROP SCHEMA
- How to report allocated permissions for a specific principal by using the fn_my_permissions function
- How to determine a connection's permissions to a securable using the system function Has_perms_by_name, as well as using EXECUTE AS to define your connection's security context to a different login or user to see their permissions, too
- How to query all granted, denied, and revoked permissions using sys.database_permissions and sys.server_permissions
- How to change a securable's ownership using ALTER AUTHORIZATION

- How to provide Windows external resource permissions to a SQL login using `CREATE CREDENTIAL` and `ALTER LOGIN`

- How to audit SQL instance– and database-level actions using SQL Server 2008's new SQL Server Audit functionality

This chapter starts off with a general discussion of SQL Server permissions.

Permissions Overview

Permissions apply to SQL Server objects within the three securable scopes (server, database, and schema). SQL Server uses a set of common permission names that are applied to different securables (and at different scopes) and imply different levels of authorization against a securable. Table 18-1 shows those permissions that are used for multiple securables (however, this isn't the exhaustive list).

Table 18-1. *Major Permissions*

Permission	Description
ALTER	Enables the grantee the use of `ALTER`, `CREATE`, or `DROP` commands for the securable. For example, using `ALTER TABLE` requires `ALTER` permissions on that specific table.
AUTHENTICATE	Enables the grantee to be trusted across database or SQL Server scopes.
CONNECT	Enables a grantee the permission to connect to a SQL Server resources (such as an endpoint or the SQL Server instance).
CONTROL	Enables all available permissions on the specific securable to the grantee, as well as any nested or implied permissions within (so if you `CONTROL` a schema, for example, you also control any tables, views, or other database objects within that schema).
CREATE	Enables the grantee to create a securable (which can be at the server, database, or schema scope).
IMPERSONATE	Enables the grantee to impersonate another principal (login or user). For example, using the `EXECUTE AS` command for a login requires `IMPERSONATE` permissions. I demonstrated using `EXECUTE AS` in Chapter 10's recipe, "Using `EXECUTE AS` to Specify the Procedure's Security Context." In this chapter, I'll also go over how to use `EXECUTE AS` to set your security context outside of a module.
TAKE OWNERSHIP	Enables the grantee to take ownership of a granted securable.
VIEW	Enables the grantee to see system metadata regarding a specific securable.

To report available permissions in SQL Server, as well as view that specific permission's place in the permission hierarchy, use the `sys.fn_builtin_permissions` system catalog table function.

The syntax is as follows:

```
sys.fn_builtin_permissions
( [ DEFAULT | NULL ] | empty_string |
APPLICATION ROLE | ASSEMBLY | ASYMMETRIC KEY |
CERTIFICATE | CONTRACT | DATABASE |
ENDPOINT | FULLTEXT CATALOG| LOGIN |
MESSAGE TYPE | OBJECT | REMOTE SERVICE BINDING |
ROLE | ROUTE | SCHEMA | SERVER | SERVICE |
SYMMETRIC KEY | TYPE   | USER | XML SCHEMA COLLECTION )
```

The arguments of this command are described in Table 18-2.

Table 18-2. *fn_builtin_permissions Arguments*

Argument	Description
DEFAULT | NULL | empty_string	Designating any of these first three arguments results in all permissions being listed in the result set.
APPLICATION ROLE | ASSEMBLY | ASYMMETRIC KEY | CERTIFICATE | CONTRACT | DATABASE | ENDPOINT | FULLTEXT CATALOG| LOGIN | MESSAGE TYPE | OBJECT | REMOTE SERVICE BINDING |ROLE | ROUTE | SCHEMA | SERVER | SERVICE | SYMMETRIC KEY | TYPE | USER | XML SCHEMA COLLECTION	Specify any one of these securable types in order to return permissions for that type.

In addition to the permission name, you can determine the nested hierarchy of permissions by looking at the covering_permission_name (a permission within the same class that is the superset of the more granular permission), parent_class_desc (the parent class of the permission—if any), and parent_covering_permission_name (the parent covering permission—if any) columns in the result set, which you'll see demonstrated in the next recipe.

Reporting SQL Server Assignable Permissions

In this recipe, I show you how to view the available permissions within SQL Server and explain their place within the permissions hierarchy. In the first example, I'll return all permissions, regardless of securable scope:

```
SELECT class_desc, permission_name, covering_permission_name,
parent_class_desc, parent_covering_permission_name
FROM sys.fn_builtin_permissions(DEFAULT)
ORDER BY class_desc, permission_name
```

This returns the following (abridged) result set:

class_desc	permission_name	covering_permission_name	parent_class_desc	parent_covering_permission_name
APPLICATION ROLE	ALTER	CONTROL	DATABASE	ALTER ANY APPLICATION ROLE
APPLICATION ROLE	CONTROL		DATABASE	CONTROL
APPLICATION ROLE	VIEW DEFINITION	CONTROL	DATABASE	VIEW DEFINITION
...				
SERVER	ALTER ANY DATABASE	CONTROL SERVER	...	...
...				
XML SCHEMA COLLECTION	REFERENCES	CONTROL	SCHEMA	REFERENCES
XML SCHEMA COLLECTION	TAKE OWNERSHIP	CONTROL	SCHEMA	CONTROL
XML SCHEMA COLLECTION	VIEW DEFINITION	CONTROL	SCHEMA	VIEW DEFINITION

This next example only shows permissions for the schema securable scope:

```
SELECT permission_name, covering_permission_name, parent_class_desc
FROM sys.fn_builtin_permissions('schema')
ORDER BY permission_name
```

This returns the following result set:

permission_name	covering_permission_name	parent_class_desc
ALTER	CONTROL	DATABASE
CONTROL		DATABASE
DELETE	CONTROL	DATABASE
EXECUTE	CONTROL	DATABASE
INSERT	CONTROL	DATABASE
REFERENCES	CONTROL	DATABASE
SELECT	CONTROL	DATABASE
TAKE OWNERSHIP	CONTROL	DATABASE
UPDATE	CONTROL	DATABASE
VIEW CHANGE TRACKING	CONTROL	DATABASE
VIEW DEFINITION	CONTROL	DATABASE

How It Works

The sys.fn_builtin_permissions system catalog function allows you to view available permissions in SQL Server.

The first example in this recipe, sys.fn_builtin_permissions, was used to display all permissions by using the DEFAULT option. The first line of code referenced the column names to be returned from the function:

```
SELECT class_desc, permission_name, covering_permission_name,
parent_class_desc, parent_covering_permission_name
```

The second line referenced the function in the FROM clause, using the DEFAULT option to display all permissions:

```
FROM sys.fn_builtin_permissions(DEFAULT)
```

The last line of code allowed me to order by the permission's class and name:

```
ORDER BY class_desc, permission_name
```

The results displayed the securable class description, permission name, and covering permission name (the *covering permission name* is the name of a permission class that is higher in the nested permission hierarchy). For example, for the APPLICATION ROLE class, you saw that the CONTROL permission was a child of the DATABASE class and ALTER ANY APPLICATION permission, but was not subject to any covering permission in the APPLICATION ROLE class (because CONTROL enables all available permissions on the specific securable to the grantee, as well as any nested or implied permissions within):

class_desc	permission_name	covering_permission_name	parent_class_desc	parent_covering_permission_name
...				
APPLICATION ROLE	CONTROL	DATABASE	CONTROL	
...				

For the OBJECT class, you saw that the ALTER permission was a child of the SCHEMA parent class and ALTER permission. Within the OBJECT class, the ALTER permissions was also a child of the covering CONTROL permission (as seen in the covering_permission_name column):

class_desc ...	permission_name	covering_permission_name	parent_class_desc	parent_covering_permission_name
OBJECT ...	ALTER	CONTROL	SCHEMA	ALTER

For the SERVER class and ALTER ANY DATABASE permission, the covering permission for the SERVER class was CONTROL SERVER. Notice that the SERVER class does *not* have a parent class and permission:

class_desc ...	permission_name	covering_permission_name	parent_class_desc	parent_covering_permission_name
SERVER ...	ALTER ANY DATABASE		CONTROL SERVER	... ...

The second example in this recipe returned permissions for just the schema-securable class. The first line of code included just three of the columns this time:

```
SELECT permission_name, covering_permission_name, parent_class_desc
```

The second line included the word "schema" in order to show permissions for the schema-securable class:

```
FROM sys.fn_builtin_permissions('schema')
```

The results were then ordered by the permission name:

```
ORDER BY permission_name
```

Permissions that control database objects contained within a schema (such as views, tables, etc.) were returned. For example, you saw that the DELETE permission is found within the schema scope and is covered by the CONTROL permission. Its parent class is the DATABASE securable:

permission_name ...	covering_permission_name	parent_class_desc
DELETE ...	CONTROL	DATABASE

Server-Scoped Securables and Permissions

Server-scoped securables are objects that are unique within a SQL Server instance, including end-points, logins, and databases. Permissions on server-scoped securables can be granted only to server-level principals (SQL Server logins or Windows logins), and not to database-level principals such as users or database roles.

At the top of the permissions hierarchy, server permissions allow a grantee to perform activities such as creating databases, logins, or linked servers. Server permissions also give you the ability to shut down the SQL Server instance (using SHUTDOWN) or use SQL Profiler (using the ALTER TRACE permission). When allocating permissions on a securable to a principal, the person doing the allocating is the *grantor*, and the principal receiving the permission is the *grantee*.

The abridged syntax for granting server permissions is as follows:

```
GRANT Permission  [ ,...n ]
TO  grantee_principal [ ,...n ]
[ WITH GRANT OPTION ]
[ AS grantor_principal ]
```

The arguments of this command are described in Table 18-3.

Table 18-3. *GRANT Arguments*

Argument	Description
Permission [,...n]	You can grant one or more server permissions in a single GRANT statement.
TO grantee_principal [,...n]	This is the grantee, also known as the principal (SQL Server login or logins), who you are granting permissions to.
WITH GRANT OPTION	When designating this option, the grantee will then have permission to grant the permission(s) to other grantees.
AS grantor_principal	This optional clause specifies where the grantor derives its right to grant the permission to the grantee.

To explicitly *deny* permissions on a securable to a server-level principal, use the DENY command.

The syntax is as follows:

```
DENY  permission  [ ,...n ]
TO grantee_principal [ ,...n ]
[ CASCADE ]
[ AS grantor_principal ]
```

The arguments of this command are described in Table 18-4.

Table 18-4. *DENY Arguments*

Argument	Description
permission [,...n]	This specifies one or more server-scoped permissions to deny.
grantee_principal [,...n]	This defines one or more logins (Windows or SQL) that you can deny permissions to.
CASCADE	When this option is designated, if the grantee principal granted any of these permissions to others, those grantees will also have their permissions denied.
AS grantor_principal	This optional clause specifies where the grantor derives his right to deny the permission to the grantee.

To *revoke* permissions on a securable to a principal, use the REVOKE command. Revoking a permission means you'll neither be granting nor denying that permission—revoke *removes* the specified permission(s) that had previously been either granted or denied.

The syntax is as follows:

```
REVOKE [ GRANT OPTION FOR ]  permission   [ ,...n ]
FROM < grantee_principal > [ ,...n ]
 [ CASCADE ]
 [ AS grantor_principal ]
```

The arguments of this command are described in Table 18-5.

Table 18-5. *REVOKE Arguments*

Argument	Description
GRANT OPTION FOR	When specified, the right for the grantee to grant the permission to other grantees is revoked.
permission [,...n]	This specifies one or more server-scoped permissions to revoke.
grantee_principal [,...n]	This defines one or more logins (Windows or SQL) to revoke permissions from.
CASCADE	When this option is designated, if the grantee principal granted any of these permissions to others, those grantees will also have their permissions revoked.
AS grantor_principal	This optional clause specifies where the grantor derives its right to revoke the permission to the grantee.

Managing Server Permissions

In this first example of this recipe, the SQL login Veronica is granted the ability to use the SQL Profiler tool to monitor SQL Server activity. This permission is given with the WITH GRANT OPTION, so Veronica can also GRANT the permission to others. Keep in mind that permissions at the server scope can only be granted when the current database is master, so I start off the batch by switching database context:

```
USE master
GO

-- Create recipe login if it doesn't exist
IF NOT EXISTS
    (SELECT name
     FROM sys.server_principals
     WHERE name = 'Veronica')
BEGIN
    CREATE LOGIN [Veronica]
    WITH PASSWORD=N'test!#1',
    DEFAULT_DATABASE=[master],
    CHECK_EXPIRATION=OFF,
    CHECK_POLICY=OFF
END

GRANT ALTER TRACE TO Veronica
WITH GRANT OPTION
```

In this second example, the Windows login [JOEPROD\TestUser] is granted the permissions to create and view databases on the SQL Server instance:

```
USE master
GO

GRANT CREATE ANY DATABASE, VIEW ANY DATABASE TO [JOEPROD\TestUser]
```

In this next example, the right to execute the SHUTDOWN command is denied the Windows login [JOEPROD\TestUser]:

```
DENY SHUTDOWN TO [JOEPROD\TestUser]
```

In the last example, the permission to use SQL Profiler is revoked from Veronica, including any other grantees she may have given this permission to as well:

```
USE master
GO
REVOKE ALTER TRACE FROM Veronica CASCADE
```

How It Works

Permissions on server-scoped securables are granted using GRANT, denied with DENY, and removed with REVOKE. Using these commands, one or more permissions can be assigned in the same command, as well as allocated to one or more logins (Windows or SQL).

This recipe dealt with assigning permissions at the server scope, although you'll see in future recipes that the syntax for assigning database and schema permissions are very similar.

Querying Server-Level Permissions

You can use the sys.server_permissions catalog view to identify permissions at the SQL instance level. In this recipe, I will query all permissions associated with a login named TestUser2. To start, I'll create the new login:

```
USE master
GO
CREATE LOGIN TestUser2
WITH PASSWORD = 'abcde1111111!'
```

Next, I'll grant another server-scoped permission and deny a server-scoped permission:

```
DENY SHUTDOWN TO TestUser2

GRANT CREATE ANY DATABASE TO TestUser2
```

Querying sys.server_permissions and sys.server_principals returns all server-scoped permissions for the new login created earlier:

```
SELECT p.class_desc,
       p.permission_name,
       p.state_desc
FROM sys.server_permissions p
INNER JOIN sys.server_principals s ON
    p.grantee_principal_id = s.principal_id
WHERE s.name = 'TestUser2'
```

This returns

class_desc	permission_name	state_desc
SERVER	CONNECT SQL	GRANT
SERVER	CREATE ANY DATABASE	GRANT
SERVER	SHUTDOWN	DENY

Even though I only explicitly executed one GRANT and one DENY, just by virtue of creating the login, I have implicitly granted the new login CONNECT permissions to the SERVER scope.

How It Works

In this recipe, I queried `sys.server_permissions` and `sys.server_principals` in order to return the server-scoped permissions associated with the new login I created. In the `SELECT` clause, I returned the class of the permission, the permission name, and the associated state of the permission:

```
SELECT p.class_desc,
       p.permission_name,
       p.state_desc
```

In the `FROM` clause, I joined the two catalog views by the grantee's principal ID. The grantee is the target recipient of granted or denied permissions:

```
FROM sys.server_permissions p
INNER JOIN sys.server_principals s ON
    p.grantee_principal_id = s.principal_id
```

In the `WHERE` clause, I designated the name of the login I wished to see permissions for:

```
WHERE s.name = 'TestUser2'
```

Database-Scoped Securables and Permissions

Database-level securables are unique to a specific database, and include several SQL Server objects such as roles, assemblies, cryptography objects (keys and certificates), Service Broker objects, full-text catalogs, database users, schemas, and more.

You can grant permissions on these securables to database principals (database users, roles). The abridged syntax for granting database permissions is as follows:

```
GRANT permission [ ,...n ]
TO database_principal [ ,...n ]
[ WITH GRANT OPTION ]
[ AS database_principal ]
```

The arguments of this command are described in Table 18-6.

Table 18-6. *GRANT Arguments*

Argument	Description
permission [,...n]	This specifies one or more database permissions to be granted to the principal(s).
database_principal [,...n]	This defines grantees of the new permissions.
WITH GRANT OPTION	When designating this option, the grantee has permissions to grant the permission(s) to other grantees.
AS database_principal	This optional clause specifies where the grantor derives its right to grant the permission to the grantee. For example, if your current database user context does not have permission to GRANT a specific permission, but you have an IMPERSONATE permission on a database user that does, you can designate that user in the AS clause.

To *deny* database-scoped permissions to a grantee, the DENY command is used. The abridged syntax is as follows:

```
DENY permission [ ,...n ]
TO database_principal [ ,...n ] [ CASCADE ]
[ AS database_principal ]
```

The arguments of this command are described in Table 18-7.

Table 18-7. *DENY Arguments*

Argument	Description
permission [,...n]	This specifies one or more database-scoped permissions to deny.
< database_principal > [,...n]	This defines one or more database principals to deny permissions for.
CASCADE	When this option is designated, if the grantee principal granted any of these permissions to others, those grantees will also have their permissions denied.
AS database_principal	This optional clause specifies where the grantor derives its right to deny the permission to the grantee.

To *revoke* database-scoped permissions to the grantee, the REVOKE command is used. The abridged syntax is as follows:

```
REVOKE permission [ ,...n ]
FROM  < database_principal > [ ,...n ]
[ CASCADE ]
[ AS database_principal]
```

The arguments of this command are described in this Table 18-8.

Table 18-8. *REVOKE Arguments*

Argument	Description
database_permission [,...n]	This specifies one or more database-scoped permissions to revoke.
< database_principal > [,...n]	This defines one or more database principals to revoke permissions from.
CASCADE	When this option is designated, if the grantee principal granted any of these permissions to others, those grantees will also have their permissions revoked.
AS database_principal	This optional clause specifies where the grantor derives its right to revoke the permission to the grantee.

Managing Database Permissions

Starting off this recipe, I'll set up the logins and users if they don't already exist or haven't already been created earlier in the chapter:

```
-- Create recipe login if it doesn't exist
IF NOT EXISTS (SELECT name FROM sys.server_principals WHERE name = 'Danny')
BEGIN
```

```
      CREATE LOGIN [Danny] WITH PASSWORD=N'test!#23',
      DEFAULT_DATABASE=[master], CHECK_EXPIRATION=OFF, CHECK_POLICY=OFF
END

-- Create DB for recipe if it doesn't exist
IF NOT EXISTS (SELECT name FROM sys.databases WHERE name = 'TestDB')
BEGIN
    CREATE DATABASE TestDB
END
GO

USE TestDB
GO

-- Create db users if they don't already exist
IF NOT EXISTS (SELECT name FROM sys.database_principals WHERE name = 'Veronica')
BEGIN
   CREATE USER Veronica FROM LOGIN Veronica
END

IF NOT EXISTS (SELECT name FROM sys.database_principals WHERE name = 'Danny')
BEGIN
   CREATE USER Danny FROM LOGIN Danny
END
```

This first example demonstrates granting database permissions to the Veronica database user in the TestDB database:

```
USE TestDB
GO

GRANT ALTER ANY ASSEMBLY, ALTER ANY CERTIFICATE
TO VERONICA
```

This second example demonstrates denying permissions to the Danny database user:

```
DENY ALTER ANY DATABASE DDL TRIGGER TO Danny
```

The last example demonstrates revoking database permissions to connect to the TestDB database from the Danny user:

```
REVOKE CONNECT FROM Danny
```

How It Works

This recipe demonstrated how to grant, revoke, or deny database-scoped permissions to database principals. As you may have noticed, the syntax for granting database-scoped permissions is almost identical to server-scoped permissions. Schema-scoped permissions are also managed with the same commands, but with slight variations.

Before reviewing how to manage schema permissions, in this next recipe I'll demonstrate how to manage schemas in general.

Querying Database Permissions

You can use the sys.database_permissions catalog view to identify permissions in a database. In this recipe, I will query all permissions associated with a user named TestUser in the AdventureWorks database. To start, I'll create the new login and user:

```
USE master
GO
CREATE LOGIN TestUser WITH PASSWORD = 'abcde1111111!'

USE AdventureWorks
GO
CREATE USER TestUser FROM LOGIN TestUser
```

Next, I'll grant and deny various permissions:

```
GRANT SELECT ON HumanResources.Department TO TestUser
DENY SELECT ON Production.ProductPhoto TO TestUser
GRANT EXEC ON HumanResources.uspUpdateEmployeeHireInfo TO TestUser
GRANT CREATE ASSEMBLY TO TestUser
GRANT SELECT ON Schema::Person TO TestUser
DENY IMPERSONATE ON USER::dbo TO TestUser
DENY SELECT ON HumanResources.Employee(Birthdate) TO TestUser
```

I'll now query the sys.database_principals to determine the identifier of the principal:

```
SELECT principal_id
FROM sys.database_principals
WHERE name = 'TestUser'
```

This returns the following results (if you are following along with this recipe, keep in mind that your principal identifier may be different):

```
principal_id
5
```

Now I can use the principal ID of 5 with the grantee principal ID in the sys.database_ permissions table (I could have integrated the prior query into this next query, but I've separated them in order to give a clearer picture of what each catalog view does):

```
SELECT
    p.class_desc,
    p.permission_name,
    p.state_desc,
    ISNULL(o.type_desc,'') type_desc,
    CASE p.class_desc
      WHEN 'SCHEMA'
        THEN schema_name(major_id)
      WHEN 'OBJECT_OR_COLUMN'
        THEN CASE
                WHEN minor_id = 0
                   THEN object_name(major_id)
                ELSE (SELECT
                         object_name(object_id) +
                         '.'+
                         name
                      FROM sys.columns
                      WHERE object_id = p.major_id AND
                            column_id = p.minor_id) END
                ELSE '' END AS object_name
FROM sys.database_permissions p
LEFT OUTER JOIN sys.objects o ON
    o.object_id = p.major_id
WHERE grantee_principal_id = 5
```

This returns

class_desc	permission_name	state_desc	type_desc	object_name
DATABASE	CONNECT	GRANT		
DATABASE	CREATE ASSEMBLY	GRANT		
OBJECT_OR_COLUMN	SELECT	GRANT	USER_TABLE	Department
OBJECT_OR_COLUMN	SELECT	DENY	USER_TABLE	Employee.BirthDate
OBJECT_OR_COLUMN	EXECUTE	GRANT	SQL_STORED_PROCEDURE	uspUpdateEmployee HireInfo
OBJECT_OR_COLUMN	SELECT	DENY	USER_TABLE	ProductPhoto
SCHEMA	SELECT	GRANT		Person
DATABASE_PRINCIPAL	IMPERSONATE	DENY		

```
(8 row(s) affected)
```

How It Works

This recipe demonstrated querying system catalog views to determine the permissions of a specific database user. I created the login and user, and then granted and denied various permissions for it.

After that, I queried sys.database_principals to determine the ID of this new user.

Walking through the last and more complicated query in the recipe, the first few columns of the query displayed the class description, permission name, and state (for example, GRANT or DENY):

```
SELECT
    p.class_desc,
    p.permission_name,
    p.state_desc,
```

The type description was actually taken from the sys.objects view, which I used to pull information regarding the object targeted for the permission. If it is NULL, I return no characters in the result set:

```
ISNULL(o.type_desc,'') type_desc,
```

The next expression was the CASE statement evaluating the class description. When the class is a schema, I return the schema's name:

```
CASE p.class_desc
    WHEN 'SCHEMA'
        THEN schema_name(major_id)
```

When the class is an object or column, I nest another CASE statement:

```
    WHEN 'OBJECT_OR_COLUMN'
        THEN CASE
```

If the minor ID is zero, I know that this is an object and not a column, and so I return the object name:

```
                WHEN minor_id = 0
                    THEN object_name(major_id)
```

Otherwise, I am dealing with a column name, so I perform a subquery to concatenate the object name with the name of the column:

```
                ELSE (SELECT
                        object_name(object_id) +
                        '.'+
```

```
                        name
                  FROM sys.columns
                  WHERE object_id = p.major_id AND
                        column_id = p.minor_id) END
            ELSE '' END AS object_name
```

I queried the permissions with a `LEFT OUTER JOIN` on `sys.objects`. I didn't use an `INNER` join because not all permissions are associated with objects—for example, the `GRANT` on the `CREATE ASSEMBLY` permission:

```
FROM sys.database_permissions p
LEFT OUTER JOIN sys.objects o ON
    o.object_id = p.major_id
```

Lastly, I qualified that the grantee is the ID of the user I created. The grantee is the recipient of the permissions. The `sys.database_permissions` also has the `grantor_principal_id`, which is the grantor of permissions for the specific row. I didn't want to designate this—rather I just wanted the rows of permissions granted to the specified user:

```
WHERE grantee_principal_id = 5
```

Schema-Scoped Securables and Permissions

Schema-scoped securables are contained within the database securable scope and include user-defined data types, XML schema collections, and objects. The object securable also has other securable object types within it, but I'll review this later in the chapter.

As of SQL Server 2005 and 2008, users are separated from direct ownership of a database object (such as tables, views, and stored procedures). This separation is achieved by the use of schemas, which are basically containers for database objects. Instead of having a direct object owner, the object is contained within a schema, and that schema is then owned by a user.

One or more users can own a schema or use it as their default schema for creating objects. What's more, you can apply security at the schema level. This means any objects within the schema can be managed as a unit, instead of at the individual object level.

Every database comes with a `dbo` schema, which is where your objects go if you don't specify a default schema. But if you wish to create your own schemas, you can use the `CREATE SCHEMA` command.

The abridged syntax is as follows:

```
CREATE SCHEMA schema_name [AUTHORIZATION owner_name ]
```

The arguments of this command are described in Table 18-9.

Table 18-9. *CREATE SCHEMA Arguments*

Argument	Description
schema_name	This is the name of the schema and the schema owner.
owner_name	The owner is a database principal that can own one or more schemas in the database.

To remove an existing schema, use the `DROP SCHEMA` command.

The syntax is as follows:

```
DROP SCHEMA schema_name
```

The command only takes a single argument: the name of the schema to drop from the database. Also, you can't drop a schema that contains objects, so the objects must either be dropped or transferred to a new schema.

Note See the topic "Changing an Object's Schema" in Chapter 24 for a review of using ALTER SCHEMA to transfer schema ownership of an object.

Like with server- and database-scoped permissions, permissions for schemas are managed using the GRANT, DENY, and REVOKE commands.

The abridged syntax for granting permissions on a schema is as follows:

```
GRANT permission [ ,...n ] ON SCHEMA :: schema_name
TO  database_principal [ ,...n]
[ WITH GRANT OPTION ][ AS granting_principal ]
```

The arguments of this command are described in Table 18-10.

Table 18-10. *GRANT Arguments*

Argument	Description
permission [,...n]	This specifies one or more schema permissions to be granted to the grantee.
schema_name	This defines the name of the schema the grantee is receiving permissions to.
database_principal	This specifies the database principal permissions recipient.
WITH GRANT OPTION	When designating this option, the grantee has permissions to grant the schema permission(s) to other grantees.
AS granting_principal	This optional clause specifies where the grantor derives its right to grant the schema-scoped permission to the grantee.

To deny schema-scoped permissions to a grantee, the DENY command is used. The abridged syntax is as follows:

```
DENY permission [ ,...n ]  ON SCHEMA :: schema_name
TO  database_principal [ ,...n ]
 [ CASCADE ]
 [ AS denying_principal ]
```

The arguments of this command are described in Table 18-11.

Table 18-11. *DENY Arguments*

Argument	Description
permission [,...n]	This specifies one or more schema-scoped permissions to deny.
schema_name	This defines the name of the schema where permissions will be denied.
database_principal [,...n]	This specifies one or more database principals to deny permissions for.

Continued

Table 18-11. *Continued*

Argument	Description
CASCADE	When this option is designated, if the grantee principal granted any of these permissions to others, those grantees will also have their permissions denied.
AS denying_principal	This optional clause specifies where the grantor derives its right to deny the permission to the grantee.

To revoke schema-scoped permissions to the grantee, the REVOKE command is used. The abridged syntax is as follows:

```
REVOKE [ GRANT OPTION FOR ]
permission [ ,...n ]
 ON SCHEMA :: schema_name
{ TO | FROM } database_principal [ ,...n ]
 [ CASCADE ] [ AS principal ]
```

The arguments of this command are described in Table 18-12.

Table 18-12. *REVOKE Arguments*

Argument	Description
permission [,...n]	This specifies one or more schema-scoped permissions to revoke.
schema_name	This defines the name of the schema of which the permissions will be revoked.
database_principal [,...n]	This specifies one or more database principals to revoke permissions for.
CASCADE	When this option is designated, if the grantee principal granted any of these permissions to others, those grantees will also have their permissions revoked.
AS principal	This optional clause specifies where the grantor derives its right to revoke the permission to the grantee.

Managing Schemas

In this recipe, I'll create a new schema in the TestDB database called Publishers:

```
USE TestDB
GO
CREATE SCHEMA Publishers AUTHORIZATION db_owner
```

I now have a schema called Publishers, which can be used to contain other database objects. It can be used to hold all objects related to publication functionality, for example, or used to hold objects for database users associated to publication activities.

To start using the new schema, use the schema.object_name two-part naming format:

```
CREATE TABLE Publishers.ISBN
(ISBN char(13) NOT NULL PRIMARY KEY,
 CreateDT datetime NOT NULL DEFAULT GETDATE())
GO
```

This next example demonstrates making the Publishers schema a database user's default schema. For this example, I'll create a new SQL login in the master database:

```
USE master
GO
CREATE LOGIN Nancy
WITH PASSWORD=N'test123',
    DEFAULT_DATABASE=TestDB,
    CHECK_EXPIRATION=OFF,
    CHECK_POLICY=OFF
GO
```

Next, I'll create a new database user in the TestDB database:

```
USE TestDB
GO
CREATE USER Nancy FOR LOGIN Nancy
GO
```

Now I'll change the default schema of the existing database user to the Publishers schema. Any objects this database user creates by default will belong to this schema (unless the database user explicitly uses a different schema in the object creation statement):

```
USE TestDB
GO
ALTER USER Nancy WITH DEFAULT_SCHEMA=Publishers
GO
```

Chapter 24 reviews how to transfer the ownership of an object from one schema to another using ALTER SCHEMA. You'll need to use this in situations where you wish to drop a schema. For example, if I tried to drop the Publishers schema right now, with the Publishers.ISBN table still in it, I would get an error warning me that there are objects referencing that schema. This example demonstrates using ALTER SCHEMA to transfer the table to the dbo schema prior to dropping the Publishers schema from the database:

```
ALTER SCHEMA dbo TRANSFER Publishers.ISBN
GO

DROP SCHEMA Publishers
```

How It Works

Schemas act as a container for database objects. Unlike when a database user owns objects directly, a database user now can own a schema (or, in other words, have permissions to use the objects within it).

In this recipe, CREATE SCHEMA was used to create a new schema called Publishers. A new table was created in the new schema called Publishers.ISBN. After that, a new login and database user was created for the TestDB database. ALTER USER was used to make that new schema the default schema for the new user.

Since a schema cannot be dropped until all objects are dropped or transferred from it, ALTER SCHEMA was used to transfer Publishers.ISBN into the dbo schema. DROP SCHEMA was used to remove the Publishers schema from the database.

Managing Schema Permissions

In this next set of examples, I'll show you how to manage schema permissions. Before showing you this though, I would like to quickly point out how you can identify which schemas exist for a particular database. To view the schemas for a database, you can query the sys.schemas system catalog view. This example demonstrates listing the schemas that exist within the AdventureWorks database:

```
USE AdventureWorks
GO

SELECT s.name SchemaName, d.name SchemaOwnerName
FROM sys.schemas s
INNER JOIN sys.database_principals d ON
    s.principal_id= d.principal_id
ORDER BY s.name
```

This returns a list of built-in database schemas (the fixed database roles, dbo, guest, sys, and INFORMATION_SCHEMA) along with user-defined schemas (Person, Production, Purchasing, Sales, HumanResources):

SchemaName	SchemaOwnerName
db_accessadmin	db_accessadmin
db_backupoperator	db_backupoperator
db_datareader	db_datareader
db_datawriter	db_datawriter
db_ddladmin	db_ddladmin
db_denydatareader	db_denydatareader
db_denydatawriter	db_denydatawriter
db_owner	db_owner
db_securityadmin	db_securityadmin
dbo	dbo
guest	guest
HumanResources	dbo
INFORMATION_SCHEMA	INFORMATION_SCHEMA
Person	dbo
Production	dbo
Purchasing	dbo
Sales	dbo
sys	sys

Within the AdventureWorks database, I'll now demonstrate assigning permissions on schemas to database principals. In this example, the database user TestUser is granted TAKE OWNERSHIP permissions to the Person schema, which enables the grantee to take ownership of a granted securable:

```
GRANT TAKE OWNERSHIP
ON SCHEMA ::Person
TO TestUser
```

In the next example, I'll grant the database user TestUser multiple permissions in the same statement, including the ability to ALTER a schema, EXECUTE stored procedures within the schema, or SELECT from tables or views in the schema. Using the WITH GRANT OPTION, TestUser can also grant other database principals these permissions too:

```
GRANT ALTER, EXECUTE, SELECT
ON SCHEMA  ::Production
TO TestUser
WITH GRANT OPTION
```

In this next example, the database user TestUser is denied the ability to INSERT, UPDATE, or DELETE data from any tables within the Production schema:

```
DENY INSERT, UPDATE, DELETE
ON SCHEMA ::Production
TO TestUser
```

In the last example of this recipe, TestUser's right to ALTER the Production schema or SELECT from objects within the Production schema is revoked, along with the permissions she may have granted to others (using CASCADE):

```
REVOKE ALTER, SELECT
ON SCHEMA ::Production
TO TestUser
CASCADE
```

How It Works

Granting, denying, or revoking permissions occurs with the same commands that are used with database- and server-level-scoped permissions. One difference, however, is the reference to ON SCHEMA, where a specific schema name is the target of granted, denied, or revoked permissions. Notice, also, that the name of the schema was prefixed with two colons (called a scope qualifier). A scope *qualifier* is used to scope permissions to a specific object type.

Object Permissions

Objects are nested within the schema scope, and they can include tables, views, stored procedures, functions, and aggregates. Defining permissions at the schema scope (such as SELECT or EXECUTE) can allow you to define permissions for a grantee on all objects within a schema. You can also define permissions at the object level. Object permissions are nested within schema permissions, schema permissions within database-scoped permissions, and database-scoped permissions within server-level permissions.

Like server-level, database-scoped, and schema-scoped permissions, you can use GRANT, DENY, and REVOKE to define permissions on specific database objects.

The abridged syntax for granting object permissions is as follows:

```
GRANT permission ON
[ OBJECT :: ][ schema_name ]. object_name [ ( column [ ,...n ] ) ]
TO <database_principal> [ ,...n ]
[ WITH GRANT OPTION ] [ AS database_principal ]
```

The arguments of this command are described in Table 18-13.

Table 18-13. *GRANT Arguments*

Argument	Description
permission [,...n]	This specifies one or more object permissions to be granted to the grantee.
[OBJECT ::][schema_name]. object_name [(column [,...n])]	This defines the target object (and if applicable, columns) for which the permission is being granted.
database_principal	This specifies the database principal permissions recipient.

Continued

Table 18-13. *Continued*

Argument	Description
WITH GRANT OPTION	When designating this option, the grantee has permissions to grant the permission(s) to other grantees.
AS database_principal	This optional clause specifies where the grantor derives its right to grant the permission to the grantee.

To deny object permissions to a grantee, the DENY command is used. The abridged syntax is as follows:

```
DENY permission  [ ,...n ] ON
  [ OBJECT :: ][ schema_name ]. object_name [ ( column [ ,...n ] ) ]
TO <database_principal> [ ,...n ]
[ CASCADE ] [ AS <database_principal> ]
```

The arguments of this command are described in Table 18-14.

Table 18-14. *DENY Arguments*

Argument	Description
[OBJECT ::][schema_name]. object_name [(column [,...n])]	This specifies the target object (and if applicable, columns) for which the permission is being denied.
< database_principal > [,...n]	This specifies one or more database principals to deny permissions for.
CASCADE	When this option is designated, if the grantee principal granted any of these permissions to others, those grantees will also have their permissions denied.
AS database_principal	This optional clause specifies where the grantor derives its right to deny the permission to the grantee.

To revoke object permissions to the grantee, the REVOKE command is used. The abridged syntax is as follows:

```
REVOKE [ GRANT OPTION FOR ]
permission  [ ,...n ]
ON  [ OBJECT :: ][ schema_name ]. object_name [ ( column [ ,...n ] ) ]
FROM <database_principal> [ ,...n ]
 [ CASCADE ] [ AS <database_principal> ]
```

The arguments of this command are described in Table 18-15.

Table 18-15. *REVOKE Arguments*

Argument	Description
GRANT OPTION FOR	When this option is used, the right to grant the permission to other database principals is revoked.
permission [,...n]	This specifies one or more object permissions to be revoked from the grantee.
[OBJECT ::][schema_name]. object_name [(column [,...n])]	This defines the target object (and if applicable, columns) for which the permission is being revoked.
< database_principal > [,...n]	This specifies one or more database principals to revoke permissions from.
CASCADE	When this option is designated, if the grantee principal granted any of these permissions to others, those grantees will also have their permissions revoked.
AS database_principal	This optional clause specifies where the grantor derives its right to revoke the permission to the grantee.

Managing Object Permissions

In this recipe, I grant the database user TestUser the permission to SELECT, INSERT, DELETE, and UPDATE data in the HumanResources.Department table:

```
USE AdventureWorks
GO

GRANT DELETE, INSERT, SELECT, UPDATE
ON HumanResources.Department
TO TestUser
```

Here, the database role called ReportViewers is granted the ability to execute a procedure, as well as view metadata regarding that specific object in the system catalog views:

```
CREATE ROLE ReportViewers

GRANT EXECUTE, VIEW DEFINITION
ON dbo.uspGetManagerEmployees
TO ReportViewers
```

In this next example, ALTER permission is denied to the database user TestUser for the HumanResources.Department table:

```
DENY ALTER ON HumanResources.Department TO TestUser
```

In this last example, INSERT, UPDATE, and DELETE permissions are revoked from TestUser on the HumanResources.Department table:

```
REVOKE INSERT, UPDATE, DELETE
ON HumanResources.Department
TO TestUser
```

How It Works

This recipe demonstrated granting object permissions to specific database securables. Object permissions are granted by designating the specific object name and the permissions that are applicable to the object. For example, EXECUTE permissions can be granted to a stored procedure, but not SELECT.

Permissions can be superseded by other types of permissions. For example, if the database user TestUser has been granted SELECT permissions on the HumanResources.Department table, but has been denied permissions on the HumanResources schema itself, TestUser will receive the following error message when attempting to SELECT from that table, as the DENY overrides any GRANT SELECT permissions:

```
Msg 229, Level 14, State 5, Line 2
SELECT permission denied on object 'Department', database 'AdventureWorks', schema
'HumanResources'.
```

Managing Permissions Across Securable Scopes

Now that I've reviewed the various securable scopes and the methods by which permissions can be granted to principals, in the next set of recipes I'll show you how to report and manage the permissions a principal has on securables across the different scopes.

Determining a Current Connection's Permissions to a Securable

With SQL Server's nested hierarchy of securable permissions (server, database, and schema), permissions can be inherited by higher-level scopes. Figuring out what permissions your current login/database connection has to a securable can become tricky, especially when you add server or database roles to the equation.

Understanding what permissions your database connection has added to a securable can be determined by using the Has_perms_by_name function. This system scalar function returns a 1 if the current user has granted permissions to the securable and 0 if not.

The syntax for this function is as follows:

```
Has_perms_by_name ( securable , securable_class , permission
      [ , sub-securable ] [ , sub-securable_class ] )
```

The arguments for this function are described in Table 18-16.

Table 18-16. *Has_perms_by_name Arguments*

Parameter	Description
securable	The name of the securable that you want to verify permissions for.
securable_class	The name of the securable class that you want to check. Class names (for example, DATABASE or SCHEMA) can be retrieved from the class_desc column in the sys.fn_builtin_permissions function.
permission	The name of the permission to check.
sub-securable	The name of the securable subentity.
sub-securable_class	The name of the securable subentity class.

This example demonstrates how to check whether the current connected user has permissions to `ALTER` the `AdventureWorks` database:

```
USE AdventureWorks
GO

SELECT Has_perms_by_name ('AdventureWorks', 'DATABASE', 'ALTER')
```

This returns 0, which means the current connection *does not* have permission to `ALTER` the `AdventureWorks` database:

```
0
```

This next query tests the current connection to see whether the `Person.Address` table can be updated or selected from by the current connection:

```
SELECT  CASE Has_perms_by_name ('Person.Address', 'OBJECT', 'UPDATE')
         WHEN 1 THEN 'Yes'
         ELSE 'No'
       END UpdateTable,
        CASE Has_perms_by_name ('Person.Address', 'OBJECT', 'SELECT')
         WHEN 1 THEN 'Yes'
         ELSE 'No'
       END SelectFromTable
```

This returns

```
UpdateTable    SelectFromTable
Yes            No
```

How It Works

The `Has_perms_by_name` system function evaluates whether or not the current connection has granted permissions to access a specific securable (granted permissions either explicitly or inherently through a higher-scoped securable). In both examples in this recipe, the first parameter used was the securable name (the database name or table name). The second parameter was the securable class, for example, `OBJECT` or `DATABASE`. The third parameter used was the actual permission to be validated, for example, `ALTER`, `UPDATE`, or `SELECT` (depending on which permissions are applicable to the securable being checked).

Reporting the Permissions for a Principal by Securable Scope

In this recipe, I'll demonstrate using the `fn_my_permissions` function to return the assigned permissions for the currently connected principal. The syntax for this function is as follows:

```
fn_my_permissions ( securable , 'securable_class')
```

The arguments for this command are described in Table 18-17.

Table 18-17. *fn_my_permissions Arguments*

Argument	Description
securable	The name of the securable to verify. Use NULL if you are checking permissions at the server or database scope.
securable_class	The securable class that you are listing permissions for.

In this first example, I demonstrate how to check the server-scoped permissions for the current connection:

```
SELECT permission_name
FROM fn_my_permissions(NULL, N'SERVER')
ORDER BY permission_name
```

This returns the following results (this query example was executed under the context of sysadmin, so in this case, all available server-scoped permissions are returned):

```
ADMINISTER BULK OPERATIONS
ALTER ANY CONNECTION
ALTER ANY CREDENTIAL
ALTER ANY DATABASE
ALTER ANY ENDPOINT
ALTER ANY EVENT NOTIFICATION
ALTER ANY LINKED SERVER
ALTER ANY LOGIN
ALTER RESOURCES
ALTER SERVER STATE
ALTER SETTINGS
ALTER TRACE
AUTHENTICATE SERVER
CONNECT SQL
CONTROL SERVER
CREATE ANY DATABASE
CREATE DDL EVENT NOTIFICATION
CREATE ENDPOINT
CREATE TRACE EVENT NOTIFICATION
EXTERNAL ACCESS ASSEMBLY
SHUTDOWN
UNSAFE ASSEMBLY
VIEW ANY DATABASE
VIEW ANY DEFINITION
VIEW SERVER STATE
```

If you have IMPERSONATE permissions on the login or database user, you can also check the permissions of another principal other than your own by using the EXECUTE AS command. In Chapter 10, I demonstrated how to use EXECUTE AS to specify a stored procedure's security context. You can also use EXECUTE AS in a stand-alone fashion, using it to switch the security context of the current database session. You can then switch back to your original security context by issuing the REVERT command.

The simplified syntax for EXECUTE AS is as follows:

```
EXECUTE AS { LOGIN | USER } = 'name'
[ WITH { NO REVERT } ]
```

The arguments of this command are described in Table 18-18.

Table 18-18. *EXECUTE AS Abridged Syntax Arguments*

Argument	Description
{ LOGIN | USER } = 'name'	Select LOGIN to impersonate a SQL or Windows login or USER to impersonate a database user. The name value is the actual login or user name.
NO REVERT	If NO REVERT is designated, you cannot use the REVERT command to switch back to your original security context.

To demonstrate EXECUTE AS's power, the previous query is reexecuted, this time by using the security context of the Veronica login:

```
USE master
GO

EXECUTE AS LOGIN = N'Veronica'
GO

SELECT permission_name
FROM fn_my_permissions(NULL, N'SERVER')
ORDER BY permission_name
GO

REVERT
GO
```

This returns a much smaller list of server permissions, as you are no longer executing the call under a login with sysadmin permissions:

```
CONNECT SQL
VIEW ANY DATABASE
```

This next example demonstrates returning database-scoped permissions for the Veronica database user:

```
USE TestDB
GO

EXECUTE AS USER = N'Veronica'
GO

SELECT permission_name
FROM fn_my_permissions(N'TestDB', N'DATABASE')
ORDER BY permission_name
GO

REVERT
GO
```

This returns

```
ALTER ANY ASSEMBLY
ALTER ANY CERTIFICATE
CONNECT
CREATE ASSEMBLY
CREATE CERTIFICATE
```

In this next example, permissions are checked for the current connection on the Production.
Culture table, this time showing any subentities of the table (meaning any explicit permissions on
table columns):

```
USE AdventureWorks
GO

SELECT subentity_name, permission_name
FROM fn_my_permissions(N'Production.Culture', N'OBJECT')
ORDER BY permission_name, subentity_name
```

This returns the following results (when the subentity_name is populated, this is a column
reference):

subentity_name	permission_name
	ALTER
	CONTROL
	DELETE
	EXECUTE
	INSERT
	RECEIVE
	REFERENCES
CultureID	REFERENCES
ModifiedDate	REFERENCES
Name	REFERENCES
	SELECT
CultureID	SELECT
ModifiedDate	SELECT
Name	SELECT
	TAKE OWNERSHIP
	UPDATE
CultureID	UPDATE
ModifiedDate	UPDATE
Name	UPDATE
	VIEW CHANGE TRACKING
	VIEW DEFINITION

How It Works

This recipe demonstrated how to return permissions for the current connection using the
fn_my_permissions function. The first example used a NULL in the first parameter and SERVER in the
second parameter in order to return the server-scoped permissions of the current connection:

```
...
FROM fn_my_permissions(NULL, N'SERVER')
```

I then used EXECUTE AS to execute the same query, this time under the Veronica login's context,
which returned server-scoped permissions for her login:

```
EXECUTE AS LOGIN = N'Veronica'
GO
...

REVERT
GO
```

The next example showed database-scoped permissions by designating the database name in the first parameter and DATABASE in the second parameter:

```
FROM fn_my_permissions(N'TestDB', N'DATABASE')
```

The last example checked the current connection's permissions to a specific table:

```
...
FROM fn_my_permissions(N'Production.Culture', N'OBJECT')
```

This returned information at the table level *and* column level. For example, the ALTER and CONTROL permissions applied to the table level, while those rows with a populated entity_name (for example, CultureID and ModifiedDate) refer to permissions at the table's column level.

Changing Securable Ownership

As described earlier in the chapter, objects are contained within schemas, and schemas are then owned by a database user or role. Changing a schema's owner does not require the objects to be renamed. Aside from schemas, however, other securables on a SQL Server instance still do have direct ownership by either a server- or database-level principal.

For example, schemas have database principal owners (such as database user) and endpoints have server-level owners, such as a SQL login.

Assuming that the login performing the operation has the appropriate TAKE OWNERSHIP permission, you can use the ALTER AUTHORIZATION command to change the owner of a securable.

The abridged syntax for ALTER AUTHORIZATION is as follows:

```
ALTER AUTHORIZATION
ON [ <entity_type> :: ] entity_name
TO { SCHEMA OWNER | principal_name }
```

The arguments for this command are described in Table 18-19.

Table 18-19. *ALTER AUTHORIZATION Arguments*

Argument	Description
entity_type	This designates the class of securable being given a new owner.
entity_name	This specifies the name of the securable.
SCHEMA OWNER	principal_name	This indicates the name of the new schema owner, or the name of the database or server principal taking ownership of the securable.

In this example, the owner of the HumanResources schema is changed to the database user TestUser:

```
USE AdventureWorks
GO

ALTER AUTHORIZATION ON Schema::HumanResources
TO TestUser
```

In this second example, the owner of an endpoint is changed to a SQL login. Before doing so, the existing owner of the endpoint is verified using the sys.endpoints and sys.server_principals system catalog views:

```
SELECT p.name OwnerName
FROM sys.endpoints e
INNER JOIN sys.server_principals p ON
    e.principal_id = p.principal_id
WHERE e.name = 'ProductWebsite'
```

This returns

```
OwnerName
JOEPROD\Owner
```

Next, the owner is changed to a different SQL login:

```
ALTER AUTHORIZATION ON Endpoint::ProductWebSite TO TestUser
```

Reexecuting the query against sys.server_principals and sys.endpoints, the new owner is displayed:

```
OwnerName
TestUser
```

How It Works

This recipe demonstrated how to change object ownership. You may wish to change ownership when a login or database user needs to be removed. If that login or database user owns securables, you can use ALTER AUTHORIZATION to change that securables owner prior to dropping the SQL login or database user.

In this recipe, ALTER AUTHORIZATION was used to change the owner of a schema to a different database user, and the owner of an endpoint to a different SQL login (associated to a Windows account). In both cases, the securable name was prefixed by the :: scope qualifier, which designates the type of object you are changing ownership of.

Allowing SQL Logins to Access Non-SQL Server Resources

In this chapter, I've discussed permissions and securables within a SQL Server instance; however, sometimes a SQL login (not associated to a Windows user or group) may need permissions outside of the SQL Server instance. A Windows principal (a Windows user or group) has implied permissions outside of the SQL Server instance, but a SQL login does not, because a SQL login and password is created inside SQL Server. To address this, you can bind a SQL login to a Windows credential, giving the SQL login the implied Windows permissions of that credential. This SQL login can then use more advanced SQL Server functionality, where outside resource access may be required. This credential can be bound to more than one SQL login (although one SQL login can only be bound to a single credential).

To create a credential, use the CREATE CREDENTIAL command.

The syntax is as follows:

```
CREATE CREDENTIAL credential_name WITH IDENTITY = ' identity_name '
    [ , SECRET = ' secret ' ]
[ FOR CRYPTOGRAPHIC_PROVIDER cryptographic_provider_name ]
```

The arguments for this command are described in Table 18-20.

Table 18-20. *CREATE CREDENTIAL Arguments*

Argument	Description
credential_name	The name of the new credential
identity_name	The external account name (a Windows user, for example)
secret	The credential's password
cryptographic_provider_name	The name of the Enterprise Key Management (EKM) provider (used when associating an EKM provider with a credential)

In this example, a new credential is created that is mapped to the JOEPROD\Owner Windows user account:

```
USE master
GO

CREATE CREDENTIAL AccountingGroup
WITH IDENTITY = N'JOEPROD\AccountUser1',
SECRET = N'mypassword!'
```

Once created, the credential can be bound to existing or new SQL logins using the CREDENTIAL keyword in CREATE LOGIN and ALTER LOGIN:

```
USE master
GO
ALTER LOGIN Veronica
WITH CREDENTIAL = AccountingGroup
GO
```

How It Works

A credential allows SQL authentication logins to be bound to Windows external permissions. In this recipe, a new credential was created called AccountingGroup. It was mapped to the Windows user JOEPROD\AccountUser1 and given a password in the SECRET argument of the command. After creating the credential, it was then bound to the SQL login Veronica by using ALTER LOGIN and WITH CREDENTIAL. Now the Veronica login, using credentials, has outside–SQL Server permissions equivalent to the JOEPROD\AccountUser1 Windows account.

Auditing SQL Instance and Database-Level Activity of Principals Against Securables

SQL Server 2008 Enterprise Edition introduces the native capability to audit SQL Server instance– and database-scoped activity. This activity is captured to a target data destination using a *Server Audit* object, which defines whether the audit data is captured to a file, to the Windows Application event log, or to the Windows Security event log. A Server Audit object also allows you to designate whether or not the SQL Server instance should be shut down if it is unable to write to the target.

Once a Server Audit object is created, you can bind a Server Audit Specification or Database Audit Specification object to it. A *Server Audit Specification* is used to define which events you wish to capture at the SQL Server instance scope. A *Database Audit Specification* object allows you to define which events you wish to capture at the database scope. Only one Server Audit Specification can be bound to a Server Audit object, whereas one or more Database Audit Specifications can be bound to a Server Audit object. A single Server Audit object can be collocated with a Server Audit Specification and one or more Database Audit Specifications.

In the next few recipes, I will demonstrate how to create a Server Audit object that writes event-captured data to a target file. I will then demonstrate how to associate SQL instance-level and database-scoped events to the audit file, and I'll demonstrate how to read the audit data contained in the binary file.

Defining Audit Data Sources

The first step in configuring auditing for SQL Server 2008 Enterprise Edition is to create a Server Audit object. This is done by using the CREATE SERVER AUDIT command. The syntax for this command is as follows:

```
CREATE SERVER AUDIT audit_name
    TO { [ FILE (<file_options> [, ...n]) ] | APPLICATION_LOG | SECURITY_LOG }
    [ WITH ( <audit_options> [, ...n] ) ]
}
[ ; ]
<file_options>::=
{
      FILEPATH = 'os_file_path'
    [, MAXSIZE = { max_size { MB | GB | TB } | UNLIMITED } ]
    [, MAX_ROLLOVER_FILES = integer]
    [, RESERVE_DISK_SPACE = { ON | OFF } ]
}

<audit_options>::=
{
    [  QUEUE_DELAY = integer ]
    [, ON_FAILURE = CONTINUE | SHUTDOWN ]
    [, AUDIT_GUID = uniqueidentifier ]
}
```

The arguments for this command are described in Table 18-21.

Table 18-21. *CREATE SERVER AUDIT Arguments*

Argument	Description
audit_name	This specifies the user-defined name of the Server Audit object.
FILE (<file_options> [, ...n])] |	This designates that the Server Audit object will write events to a file.
APPLICATION_LOG	This designates that the Server Audit object will write events to the Windows Application event log.
SECURITY_LOG	This designates that the Server Audit object will write events to the Windows Security event log.
FILEPATH	If FILE was chosen, this designates the OS file path of the audit log.
MAXSIZE	If FILE was chosen, this argument defines the maximum size in MB, GB, or TB. UNLIMITED can also be designated.
MAX_ROLLOVER_FILES	If FILE was chosen, this designates the maximum number of files to be retained on the file system. When 0 is designated, no limit is enforced.

Argument	Description
RESERVE_DISK_SPACE	This argument takes a value of either ON or OFF. When enabled, this option reserves the disk space designated in MAXSIZE.
QUEUE_DELAY	This value designates the milliseconds that can elapse before audit actions are processed. The minimum and default value is 1000 milliseconds.
ON_FAILURE	This argument takes a value of either CONTINUE or SHUTDOWN. If SHUTDOWN is designated, the SQL instance will be shut down if the target can't be written to.
AUDIT_GUID	This option takes the unique identifier of a Server Audit object. If you restore a database that contains a Database Audit Specification, this object will be orphaned on the new SQL instance unless the original Server Audit object is re-created with the matching GUID.

In this recipe, I will create a new Server Audit object that will be configured to write to a local file directory. The maximum size I'll designate per log will be 500 megabytes, with a maximum number of 10 rollover files. I won't reserve disk space, and the queue delay will be 1 second (1000 milliseconds). If there is a failure for the audit to write, I will not shut down the SQL Server instance:

```
USE master
GO

CREATE SERVER AUDIT Caesar_Augustus_Server_Audit
TO FILE
    ( FILEPATH = 'C:\Apress\',
      MAXSIZE = 500 MB,
      MAX_ROLLOVER_FILES = 10,
      RESERVE_DISK_SPACE = OFF)
WITH ( QUEUE_DELAY = 1000,
      ON_FAILURE = CONTINUE)
```

To validate the configurations of the new Server Audit object, I can check the sys.server_audits catalog view:

```
SELECT audit_id,
       type_desc,
       on_failure_desc,
       queue_delay,
       is_state_enabled
FROM sys.server_audits
```

This returns

audit_id	type_desc	on_failure_desc	queue_delay	is_state_enabled
65536	FILE	CONTINUE	1000	0

As you can see from the is_state_enabled column of sys.server_audits, the Server Audit object is created in a disabled state. Later on, I'll demonstrate how to enable it in the "Querying Captured Audit Data" recipe, but in the meantime, I will leave it disabled until I define Server and Database Audit Specifications associated with it.

In order to see more details around the file configuration of the Server Audit object I just created, I can query the sys.server_file_audits catalog view:

```
SELECT    name,
          log_file_path,
          log_file_name,
          max_rollover_files,
          max_file_size
FROM sys.server_file_audits
```

This returns the following result set (reformatted for presentation purposes):

Column	Result
name	Caesar_Augustus_Server_Audit
log_file_path	C:\Apress\
log_file_name	Caesar_Augustus_Server_Audit_1F55EE1E-1BD3-4112-B108-F453330AF279. sqlaudit
max_rollover_files	10
max_file_size	500

How It Works

This recipe demonstrated how to create a Server Audit object that defines the target destination of collected audit events. This is the first step in the process of setting up an audit. Walking through the code, in the first line I designated the name of the Server Audit object:

```
CREATE SERVER AUDIT Caesar_Augustus_Server_Audit
```

Since the target of the collected audit events will be forwarded to a file, I designated TO FILE:

```
TO FILE
```

Next, I designated the file path where the audit files would be written (since there are rollover files, each file is dynamically named—so I just used the path and not an actual file name):

```
( FILEPATH = 'C:\Apress\',
```

I then designated the maximum size of each audit file and the maximum number of rollover files:

```
MAXSIZE = 500 MB,
MAX_ROLLOVER_FILES = 10,
```

I also chose not to prereserve disk space (as a best practice, you should write your audit files to a dedicated volume or LUN where sufficient disk space can be ensured):

```
RESERVE_DISK_SPACE = OFF)
```

Lastly, I designated that the queue delay remain at the default level of 1000 milliseconds (1 second) and that if there was a failure to write to the target, the SQL Server instance will continue to run (for mission-critical auditing, where events *must* be captured, you may then consider shutting down the SQL instance if there are issues writing to the target file):

```
WITH ( QUEUE_DELAY = 1000,
       ON_FAILURE = CONTINUE)
```

After creating the new Server Audit object, I used sys.server_audits to validate the primary Server Audit object settings and sys.server_file_audits to validate the file options.

In the next recipe, I'll demonstrate how to capture SQL instance–scoped events to the Server Audit object created in this recipe.

Capturing SQL Instance–Scoped Events

A Server Audit Specification is used to define what SQL instance–scoped events will be captured to the Server Audit object. The command to perform this action is CREATE SERVER AUDIT SPECIFICATION, and the syntax is as follows:

```
CREATE SERVER AUDIT SPECIFICATION audit_specification_name
FOR SERVER AUDIT audit_name
{
    { ADD ( { audit_action_group_name } )
        } [, ...n]
    [ WITH ( STATE = { ON | OFF } ) ]
}
```

The arguments for this command are described in Table 18-22.

Table 18-22. *CREATE SERVER AUDIT SPECIFICATION Arguments*

Argument	Description
audit_specification_name	This specifies the user-defined name of the Server Audit Specification object.
audit_name	This defines the name of the preexisting Server Audit object (target file or event log).
audit_action_group_name	This indicates the name of the SQL instance–scoped action groups. For a list of auditable action groups, you can query the sys.dm_audit_actions catalog view.
STATE	This argument takes a value of either ON or OFF. When ON, collection of records begins.

In this recipe, I will create a new Server Audit Specification that will capture three different audit action groups. To determine what audit action groups can be used, I can query the sys.dm_audit_actions system catalog view:

```
SELECT name
FROM sys.dm_audit_actions
WHERE class_desc = 'SERVER' AND
      configuration_level = 'Group'
ORDER BY name
```

This returns the following abridged results:

```
name
APPLICATION_ROLE_CHANGE_PASSWORD_GROUP
AUDIT_CHANGE_GROUP
BACKUP_RESTORE_GROUP
BROKER_LOGIN_GROUP
DATABASE_CHANGE_GROUP
DATABASE_MIRRORING_LOGIN_GROUP
DATABASE_OBJECT_ACCESS_GROUP
...
DBCC_GROUP
FAILED_LOGIN_GROUP
LOGIN_CHANGE_PASSWORD_GROUP
LOGOUT_GROUP
...
```

```
SERVER_OBJECT_PERMISSION_CHANGE_GROUP
SERVER_OPERATION_GROUP
SERVER_PERMISSION_CHANGE_GROUP
SERVER_PRINCIPAL_CHANGE_GROUP
SERVER_PRINCIPAL_IMPERSONATION_GROUP
SERVER_ROLE_MEMBER_CHANGE_GROUP
SERVER_STATE_CHANGE_GROUP
SUCCESSFUL_LOGIN_GROUP
TRACE_CHANGE_GROUP
```

In this recipe scenario, I would like to track any time a DBCC command was executed, BACKUP operation was taken, or server role membership was performed:

```
CREATE SERVER AUDIT SPECIFICATION Caesar_Augustus_Server_Audit_Spec
FOR SERVER AUDIT Caesar_Augustus_Server_Audit
    ADD (SERVER_ROLE_MEMBER_CHANGE_GROUP),
    ADD (DBCC_GROUP),
    ADD (BACKUP_RESTORE_GROUP)
WITH (STATE = ON)
```

Once the Server Audit Specification is created, I can validate the settings by querying the sys.server_audit_specifications catalog view:

```
SELECT server_specification_id,
       name,
       is_state_enabled
FROM sys.server_audit_specifications
```

This returns

server_specification_id	name	is_state_enabled
65538	Caesar_Augustus_Server_Audit_Spec	1

I can also query the details of this specification by querying the sys.server_audit_specification_details catalog view (I use the server specification ID returned from the previous query to qualify the following result set):

```
SELECT server_specification_id,
       audit_action_name
FROM sys.server_audit_specification_details
WHERE server_specification_id = 65538
```

This returns

server_specification_id	audit_action_name
65538	SERVER_ROLE_MEMBER_CHANGE_GROUP
65538	BACKUP_RESTORE_GROUP
65538	DBCC_GROUP

The entire auditing picture is not yet complete since I have not yet enabled the Server Audit object (Caesar_Augustus_Server_Audit). Before I turn the Server Audit object on, I will also add a Database Audit Specification object, and then I'll demonstrate actual audit event captures and how to query the audit log.

How It Works

In this recipe, I demonstrated how to create a Server Audit Specification that defines which SQL instance-scoped events will be captured and forwarded to a specific Server Audit object target (in this case, a file under C:\Apress).

I started off the recipe first by querying sys.dm_audit_actions to get a list of action groups that I could choose to audit for the SQL Server instance. The sys.dm_audit_actions catalog view actually contains a row for all audit actions—at both the SQL instance and database scopes. So in the WHERE clause of my query, I designated that the class of audit action should be for the SERVER and that the configuration level should be for a group (I'll demonstrate the non-group action-level configuration level in the next recipe):

```
...
WHERE class_desc = 'SERVER' AND
      configuration_level = 'Group'
...
```

Next, I used the CREATE SERVER AUDIT SPECIFICATION command to define which action groups I wished to track. The first line of code designated the name of the new Server Audit Specification:

```
CREATE SERVER AUDIT SPECIFICATION Caesar_Augustus_Server_Audit_Spec
```

The next line of code designated the target of the event collection, the name of the Server Audit object:

```
FOR SERVER AUDIT Caesar_Augustus_Server_Audit
```

After that, I designated each action group I wished to capture:

```
ADD (SERVER_ROLE_MEMBER_CHANGE_GROUP),
ADD (DBCC_GROUP),
ADD (BACKUP_RESTORE_GROUP)
```

Lastly, I designated that the state of the Server Audit Specification should be enabled upon creation:

```
WITH (STATE = ON)
```

In the next recipe, I'll demonstrate how to create a Database Audit Specification to capture database-scoped events. Once all of the specifications are created, I'll then demonstrate actual captures of actions and show you how to read the Server Audit log.

Capturing Database-Scoped Events

A Database Audit Specification is used to define what database-scoped events will be captured to the Server Audit object. The command to perform this action is CREATE DATABASE AUDIT SPECIFICATION, and the abridged syntax is as follows (it does not show action specification syntax—however, I'll demonstrate this within the recipe):

```
CREATE DATABASE AUDIT SPECIFICATION audit_specification_name
{
    [ FOR SERVER AUDIT audit_name ]
    [ { ADD (
            { <audit_action_specification> | audit_action_group_name }
              )
      } [, ...n] ]
    [ WITH ( STATE = { ON | OFF } ) ]
}
```

The arguments for this command are described in Table 18-23.

Table 18-23. *CREATE DATABASE AUDIT SPECIFICATION Arguments*

Argument	Description
audit_specification_name	This specifies the user-defined name of the Database Audit Specification object.
audit_name	This defines the name of the preexisting Server Audit object (target file or event log).
audit_action_specification	This indicates the name of a auditable database-scoped action. For a list of auditable database-scoped actions, you can query the sys.dm_audit_actions catalog view.
audit_action_group_name	This defines the name of the database-scoped action group. For a list of auditable action groups, you can query the sys.dm_audit_actions catalog view.
STATE	This argument takes a value of either ON or OFF. When ON, collection of records begins.

In this recipe, I will create a new Database Audit Specification that will capture both audit action groups and audit events. *Audit action groups* are related groups of actions at the database scope, and *audit events* are singular events. For example, I can query the sys.dm_audit_actions system catalog view to view specific audit events against the object securable scope (for example, tables, views, stored procedures, and functions) by executing the following query:

```
SELECT name
FROM sys.dm_audit_actions
WHERE configuration_level = 'Action' AND
      class_desc = 'OBJECT'
ORDER BY name
```

This returns a result set of atomic events that can be audited against an object securable scope:

```
name
DELETE
EXECUTE
INSERT
RECEIVE
REFERENCES
SELECT
UPDATE
```

I can also query the sys.dm_audit_actions system catalog view to see audit action groups at the database scope:

```
SELECT  name
FROM sys.dm_audit_actions
WHERE configuration_level = 'Group' AND
      class_desc = 'DATABASE'
ORDER BY name
```

This returns the following abridged results:

```
name
APPLICATION_ROLE_CHANGE_PASSWORD_GROUP
```

```
AUDIT_CHANGE_GROUP
BACKUP_RESTORE_GROUP
CONNECT
DATABASE_CHANGE_GROUP
DATABASE_OBJECT_ACCESS_GROUP

...
DBCC_GROUP
SCHEMA_OBJECT_ACCESS_GROUP
SCHEMA_OBJECT_CHANGE_GROUP
SCHEMA_OBJECT_OWNERSHIP_CHANGE_GROUP
SCHEMA_OBJECT_PERMISSION_CHANGE_GROUP
```

In this recipe scenario, I would like to track any time a INSERT, UPDATE, or DELETE is performed against the HumanResources.Department table by *any* database user. I would also like to track whenever impersonation is used within the AdventureWorks database (for example, using the EXECUTE AS command):

```
USE AdventureWorks
GO

CREATE DATABASE AUDIT SPECIFICATION AdventureWorks_DB_Spec
FOR SERVER AUDIT Caesar_Augustus_Server_Audit
    ADD (DATABASE_PRINCIPAL_IMPERSONATION_GROUP),
    ADD (INSERT, UPDATE, DELETE
        ON HumanResources.Department
        BY public)
WITH (STATE = ON)
GO
```

I can validate the settings of my Database Audit Specification by querying the sys.database_audit_specifications system catalog view:

```
SELECT database_specification_id,name,is_state_enabled
FROM sys.database_audit_specifications
```

This returns

database_specification_id	name	is_state_enabled
65538	AdventureWorks_DB_Spec	1

For a detailed look at what I'm auditing for the new Database Audit Specification, I can query the sys.database_audit_specification_details system catalog view (I'll walk through the logic in the "How It Works" section):

```
SELECT audit_action_name,
       class_desc,
       is_group,
       CASE
           WHEN major_id > 0 THEN OBJECT_NAME(major_id, DB_ID())
           ELSE 'N/A'
       END ObjectNM
FROM sys.database_audit_specification_details
WHERE database_specification_id = 65538
```

This returns

audit_action_name	class_desc	is_group	ObjectNM
DATABASE_PRINCIPAL_IMPERSONATION_GROUP	DATABASE	1	N/A
DELETE	OBJECT_OR_COLUMN	0	Department
INSERT	OBJECT_OR_COLUMN	0	Department
UPDATE	OBJECT_OR_COLUMN	0	Department

Although the Database Audit Specification is enabled, I have still not enabled the overall Server Audit object. I'll be demonstrating that in the next recipe, where you'll also learn how to query the captured audit data from a binary file.

How It Works

In this recipe, I demonstrated how to create a Database Audit Specification that designated which database-scoped events would be captured to the Server Audit object. To perform this action, I used the CREATE DATABASE AUDIT SPECIFICATION command. I started off by changing the context to the database I wished to audit (since this is a database-scoped object):

```
USE AdventureWorks
GO
```

The first line of the CREATE DATABASE AUDIT SPECIFICATION command designated the user-defined name, followed by a reference to the Server Audit object I would be forwarding the database-scoped events to:

```
CREATE DATABASE AUDIT SPECIFICATION AdventureWorks_DB_Spec
FOR SERVER AUDIT Caesar_Augustus_Server_Audit
```

After that, I used the ADD keyword followed by an open parenthesis, defined the audit action group I wished to monitor, and then entered a closing parenthesis and a comma (since I planned on defining more than one action to monitor):

```
ADD (DATABASE_PRINCIPAL_IMPERSONATION_GROUP),
```

Next, I designated the ADD keyword again, followed by the three actions I wished to monitor for the HumanResources.Department table:

```
ADD (INSERT, UPDATE, DELETE
    ON HumanResources.Department
```

The object-scoped actions required a reference to the database principal that I wished to audit actions for. In this example, I wished to view actions by all database principals. Since all database principals are by default a member of public, this was what I designated:

```
    BY public)
```

After that, I used the WITH keyword followed by the STATE argument, which I set to enabled:

```
WITH (STATE = ON)
GO
```

I then used the sys.database_audit_specifications to view the basic information of the new Database Audit Specification. I queried the sys.database_audit_specification_details catalog view to list the events that the Database Audit Specification captures. In the first three lines of code, I looked at the audit action name, class description, and is_group field, which designates whether or not the audit action is an audit action group or individual event:

```
SELECT audit_action_name,
       class_desc,
       is_group,
```

I used a CASE statement to evaluate the major_id column. If the major_id is a non-zero value, this indicates that the audit action row is for a database object, and therefore I used the OBJECT_NAME function to provide that object's name:

```
CASE
    WHEN major_id > 0 THEN OBJECT_NAME(major_id, DB_ID())
    ELSE 'N/A'
END ObjectNM
```

In the last two lines of the SELECT, I designated the catalog view name, and specified the database specification ID (important if you have more than one Database Audit Specification defined for a database—which is allowed):

```
FROM sys.database_audit_specification_details
WHERE database_specification_id = 65538
```

Now that I have defined the Server Audit object, Server Audit Specification, and Database Audit Specification, in the next recipe, I'll demonstrate enabling the Server Audit object and creating some auditable activity, and then show how to query the captured audit data.

Querying Captured Audit Data

The previous recipes have now built up to the actual demonstration of SQL Server 2008's auditing capabilities. To begin the recipe, I will enable the Server Audit object created a few recipes ago. Recall that I had defined this Server Audit object to write to a binary file under the C:\Apress folder.

To enable the audit, I use the ALTER SERVER AUDIT command and configure the STATE option:

```
USE master
GO

ALTER SERVER AUDIT [Caesar_Augustus_Server_Audit] WITH (STATE = ON)
```

Now I will perform a few actions at both the SQL Server scope and within the AdventureWorks database in order to demonstrate the audit collection process. I've added comments before each group of statements so that you can follow what actions I'm trying to demonstrate:

```
USE master
GO

-- Create new login (not auditing this, but using it for recipe)
CREATE LOGIN TestAudit WITH PASSWORD = 'C83D7F50-9B9E'

-- Add to server role bulkadmin
EXEC sp_addsrvrolemember 'TestAudit', 'bulkadmin'
GO

-- Back up AdventureWorks database
BACKUP DATABASE AdventureWorks
TO DISK = 'C:\Apress\Example_AW.BAK'
GO

-- Perform a DBCC on AdventureWorks
DBCC CHECKDB('AdventureWorks')
GO
```

```
-- Perform some AdventureWorks actions
USE AdventureWorks
GO

-- Create a new user and then execute under that
-- user's context
CREATE USER TestAudit FROM LOGIN TestAudit

EXECUTE AS USER = 'TestAudit'

-- Revert back to me (in this case a login with sysadmin perms)
REVERT

-- Perform an INSERT, UPDATE, and DELETE
-- from HumanResources.Department

INSERT HumanResources.Department
(Name, GroupName)
VALUES('Traffic', 'Advertising')

UPDATE HumanResources.Department
SET Name = 'Media Planning'
WHERE Name = 'Traffic'

DELETE HumanResources.Department
WHERE Name = 'Media Planning'
```

Now that I have performed several events that are covered by the Server Audit Specification and Database Audit Specification created earlier, I can use the fn_get_audit_file table-valued function to view the contents of my Server Audit binary file. The syntax for this function is as follows:

```
fn_get_audit_file
( file_pattern,
 {default | initial_file_name | NULL },
 {default | audit_file_offset | NULL } )
```

The arguments for this command are described in Table 18-24.

Table 18-24. *fn_get_audit_file Arguments*

Argument	Description
file_pattern	Designates the location of the audit file or files to be read. You can use a drive letter or network share for the path and use the single asterisk (*) wildcard to designate multiple files.
{default | initial_file_name | NULL }	Designates the name and path for a specific file you would like to begin reading from. Default and NULL are synonymous and indicate no selection for the initial file name.
{default | audit_file_offset | NULL }	Designates the buffer offset from the initial file (when initial file is selected). Default and NULL are synonymous and indicate no selection for the audit file offset.

In this first call to the fn_get_audit_file function, I'll look for any changes to server role memberships. Notice that I am using the sys.dm_audit_actions catalog view in order to translate the action ID into the actual action event name (you can use this view to find which event names you need to filter by):

```
SELECT af.event_time,
       af.succeeded,
       af.target_server_principal_name,
       object_name
FROM fn_get_audit_file
     ('C:\Apress\Caesar_Augustus_Server_Audit_*',
      default, default) af
INNER JOIN sys.dm_audit_actions aa ON
       af.action_id = aa.action_id
WHERE aa.name = 'ADD MEMBER' AND
      aa.class_desc = 'SERVER ROLE'
```

This returns the event time, success flag, server principal name, and server role name:

event_time	succeeded	target_server_principal_name	object_name
2008-09-02 15:06:54.702	1	TestAudit	bulkadmin

In this next example, I'll take a look at deletion events against the HumanResources.Department table:

```
SELECT af.event_time,
       af.database_principal_name
FROM fn_get_audit_file
     ('C:\Apress\Caesar_Augustus_Server_Audit_*',
      default, default) af
INNER JOIN sys.dm_audit_actions aa ON
       af.action_id = aa.action_id
WHERE aa.name = 'DELETE' AND
      aa.class_desc = 'OBJECT' AND
      af.schema_name = 'HumanResources' AND
      af.object_name = 'Department'
```

This returns

event_time	database_principal_name
2008-09-02 15:13:24.542	dbo

The fn_get_audit_file function also exposes the SQL statement when applicable to the instantiating event. The following query demonstrates capturing the actual BACKUP DATABASE text used for the audited event:

```
SELECT event_time, statement
FROM fn_get_audit_file
     ('C:\Apress\Caesar_Augustus_Server_Audit_*',
      default, default) af
INNER JOIN sys.dm_audit_actions aa ON
       af.action_id = aa.action_id
WHERE aa.name = 'BACKUP' AND
      aa.class_desc = 'DATABASE'
```

This returns the event time and associated BACKUP statement text:

```
event_time              statement
2008-02-02 15:07:29.482 BACKUP DATABASE AdventureWorks TO DISK =
                        'C:\Apress\Example_AW.BAK'
```

The last query of this recipe demonstrates querying each distinct event and the associated database principal that performed it, along with the target server principal name (when applicable) or target object name:

```
SELECT DISTINCT
       aa.name,
       database_principal_name,
       target_server_principal_name,
       object_name
FROM fn_get_audit_file
       ('C:\Apress\Caesar_Augustus_Server_Audit_*',
        default, default) af
INNER JOIN sys.dm_audit_actions aa ON
       af.action_id = aa.action_id
```

This returns the various events I performed earlier that were defined in the Server and Database Audit Specifications. It also includes audit events by default—for example, AUDIT SESSION CHANGED:

name	database_principal_name	target_server_principal_name	object_name
ADD MEMBER	dbo	TestAudit	bulkadmin
AUDIT SESSION CHANGED			
BACKUP	dbo		AdventureWorks
DBCC	dbo		
DELETE	dbo		EmployeePayHistory
IMPERSONATE	dbo		TestAudit
INSERT	dbo		EmployeePayHistory
UPDATE	dbo		EmployeePayHistory

How It Works

I started off this recipe by enabling the overall Server Audit object using the ALTER SERVER AUDIT command. After that, I performed several SQL instance– and database-scoped activities—focusing on events that I had defined for capture in the Server and Database Audit Specifications bound to the Caesar_Augustus_Server_Audit audit. After that, I demonstrated how to use the fn_get_audit_file function to retrieve the event data from the binary file created under the C:\Apress directory.

■Note I could have also defined the Server Audit object to write events to the Windows Application or Windows Security event log instead, in which case I would not have used fn_get_audit_file to retrieve the data, as this function only applies to the binary file format.

Each query to fn_get_audit_file I also joined to the sys.dm_audit_actions object in order to designate the audit action name and, depending on the action, the class description as well. For example:

```
...
FROM fn_get_audit_file
      ('C:\Apress\Caesar_Augustus_Server_Audit_*',
        default, default) af
INNER JOIN sys.dm_audit_actions aa ON
      af.action_id = aa.action_id
WHERE aa.name = 'ADD MEMBER' AND
      aa.class_desc = 'SERVER ROLE'
...
```

In the next and last recipe of this chapter, I'll demonstrate how to manage, modify, and remove audit objects.

Managing, Modifying, and Removing Audit Objects

This recipe will demonstrate how to add and remove actions from existing Server and Database Audit Specifications, disable Server and Database Audit Specifications, modify the Server Audit object, and remove audit objects from the SQL instance and associated databases.

To modify an existing Server Audit Specification, I use the ALTER SERVER AUDIT SPECIFICATION command. In this first query demonstration, I'll remove one audit action type from the Server Audit Specification I created in an earlier recipe and also add a new audit action.

Before I can modify the specification, however, I must first disable it:

```
USE master
GO

ALTER SERVER AUDIT SPECIFICATION [Caesar_Augustus_Server_Audit_Spec]
WITH (STATE = OFF)
```

Next, I will drop one of the audit actions:

```
ALTER SERVER AUDIT SPECIFICATION [Caesar_Augustus_Server_Audit_Spec]
DROP (BACKUP_RESTORE_GROUP)
```

Now I'll demonstrate adding a new audit action group to an existing Server Audit Specification:

```
ALTER SERVER AUDIT SPECIFICATION [Caesar_Augustus_Server_Audit_Spec]
ADD (LOGIN_CHANGE_PASSWORD_GROUP)
```

To have these changes take effect and resume auditing, I must reenable the Server Audit Specification:

```
ALTER SERVER AUDIT SPECIFICATION [Caesar_Augustus_Server_Audit_Spec]
WITH (STATE = ON)
```

To modify the audit actions of a Database Audit Specification, I must use the ALTER DATABASE AUDIT SPECIFICATION command. Similar to Server Audit Specifications, a Database Audit Specification must have a disabled state prior to making any changes to it:

```
USE AdventureWorks
GO

ALTER DATABASE AUDIT SPECIFICATION [AdventureWorks_DB_Spec]
WITH (STATE = OFF)
```

This next query demonstrates removing an existing audit event from the Database Audit Specification I created earlier:

```
ALTER DATABASE AUDIT SPECIFICATION [AdventureWorks_DB_Spec]
DROP (INSERT ON [HumanResources].[Department] BY public)
```

Next, I demonstrate how to add a new audit event to the existing Database Audit Specification:

```
ALTER DATABASE AUDIT SPECIFICATION [AdventureWorks_DB_Spec]
ADD (DATABASE_ROLE_MEMBER_CHANGE_GROUP)
```

To have these changes go into effect, I need to reenable the Database Audit Specification:

```
ALTER DATABASE AUDIT SPECIFICATION [AdventureWorks_DB_Spec]
WITH (STATE = ON)
```

To modify the Server Audit object itself, I use the `ALTER SERVER AUDIT` command. Similar to the Server and Database Audit Specification objects, the Server Audit object needs to be disabled before changes can be made to it. In this next example, I demonstrate disabling the Server Audit, making a change to the logging target so that it writes to the Windows Application event log instead, and then reenabling it:

```
USE master
GO

ALTER SERVER AUDIT [Caesar_Augustus_Server_Audit]
WITH (STATE = OFF)

ALTER SERVER AUDIT [Caesar_Augustus_Server_Audit]
TO APPLICATION_LOG

ALTER SERVER AUDIT [Caesar_Augustus_Server_Audit]
WITH (STATE = ON)
```

Once the target is changed, audit events are now forwarded to the Windows Application event log. For example, if I execute a `DBCC CHECKDB` command again, I would see this reflected in the Windows Application event log with an event ID of 33205. The following is an example of a Windows Application event log entry:

```
Audit event: event_time:2008-09-02 18:17:49.4704464
sequence_number:1
action_id:DBCC
succeeded:true
permission_bitmask:0
is_column_permission:false
session_id:57
server_principal_id:263
database_principal_id:1
target_server_principal_id:0
target_database_principal_id:0
object_id:0
class_type:DB
session_server_principal_name:CAESAR\Administrator
server_principal_name:CAESAR\Administrator
server_principal_sid:010500000000000515000000 6bb13b36a981eb9a2b3859a8f4010000
database_principal_name:dbo
target_server_principal_name:
target_server_principal_sid:
target_database_principal_name:
server_instance_name:CAESAR\AUGUSTUS
database_name:AdventureWorks
schema_name:
object_name:
```

```
statement:DBCC CHECKDB('AdventureWorks')
additional_information:
```

To remove a Database Audit Specification, I need to disable it and then use the DROP DATABASE
AUDIT SPECIFICATION—as demonstrated next:

```
USE AdventureWorks
GO

ALTER DATABASE AUDIT SPECIFICATION [AdventureWorks_DB_Spec]
WITH (STATE = OFF)

DROP DATABASE AUDIT SPECIFICATION [AdventureWorks_DB_Spec]
```

To remove a Server Audit Specification, I need to disable it and then use the DROP SERVER AUDIT
SPECIFICATION command:

```
USE master
GO

ALTER SERVER AUDIT SPECIFICATION [Caesar_Augustus_Server_Audit_Spec]
WITH (STATE = OFF)

DROP SERVER AUDIT SPECIFICATION [Caesar_Augustus_Server_Audit_Spec]
```

Finally, to drop a Server Audit object, I need to first disable it and then use the DROP SERVER
AUDIT command, as demonstrated next:

```
ALTER SERVER AUDIT [Caesar_Augustus_Server_Audit] WITH (STATE = OFF)

DROP SERVER AUDIT [Caesar_Augustus_Server_Audit]
```

Any binary log files created from the auditing will still remain after removing the Server Audit
object.

How It Works

This recipe demonstrated several commands used to manage audit objects. For each of these exist-
ing audit objects, I was required to disable the state prior to making changes. I used ALTER SERVER
AUDIT SPECIFICATION to add and remove audit events from the Server Audit Specification and DROP
SERVER AUDIT SPECIFICATION to remove the definition from the SQL Server instance.

I used ALTER DATABASE AUDIT SPECIFICATION to add and remove audit events from the Database Audit Specification and DROP DATABASE AUDIT SPECIFICATION to remove the definition from the
user database. I used ALTER SERVER AUDIT to modify an existing Server Audit object—changing the
target logging method from a binary file to the Windows Application event log instead. Lastly, I used
DROP SERVER AUDIT to remove the Server Audit object from the SQL Server instance.

■ ■ ■

Encryption

Prior to SQL Server 2005 and 2008, if you wanted to encrypt sensitive data such as financial information, salary, or personal identification numbers, you were forced to rely on outside application programs and algorithms. SQL Server 2005 introduced built-in data encryption capabilities using a combination of certificates, keys, and system functions.

Similar to a digital certificate that is issued by a certificate authority, a SQL Server certificate contains a pair of keys: a public key as well as a private key, which is used to encrypt and decrypt data. SQL Server also has the ability to create asymmetric and symmetric keys. An *asymmetric key* is similar to a certificate, in that a public key is used to encrypt data, and the private key is used to decrypt data. Both asymmetric keys and certificates provide powerful encryption strength, but with more performance overhead due to the complexity of the encryption/decryption process. A lower-overhead solution, which is more appropriate for the encryption of large amounts of data, is a *symmetric key*, which is a single key that is used to both encrypt and decrypt the same data.

SQL Server allows you to layer these encryption capabilities into an encryption hierarchy. When SQL Server is installed, a server-level certificate called the *Service Master Key* is created in the master database and is bound to the SQL Server service account login by default. The Service Master Key is used to encrypt all other database certificates and keys created within the SQL Server instance. Additionally, you can also create a *Database Master Key* in a user database, which you can use to encrypt database certificates and keys.

In SQL Server 2008, Microsoft introduces *transparent data encryption (TDE)*, which enables the entire database to be encrypted without requiring modification of any applications that access it. The data, log files, and associated database backups are encrypted. If the database is stolen, the data cannot be accessed without the Database Encryption Key (DEK). I'll demonstrate in this chapter how to enable this new feature.

■**Tip** SQL Server 2008 also introduces support for Extensible Key Management (EKM), meaning that SQL Server can use Hardware Security Modules (HSM) for storing and managing encryption keys. HSM allows a decoupling of the data from the actual encryption keys.

I'll start the chapter by first discussing and then demonstrating how to encrypt data without the use of certificates and keys.

Encryption by Passphrase

For a quick-and-dirty encryption of data that doesn't involve certificates or keys, you can simply encrypt/decrypt data based on a password supplied by the user. A passphrase is simply a password that allows spaces in it. This passphrase is not stored in the database, which can be advantageous because it means that internal passwords cannot be "cracked" using stored system data. Because the password can include spaces, you can create a long, easy-to-remember sentence that can be used to encrypt and decrypt sensitive data.

In the next recipe, I'll demonstrate how to encrypt and decrypt data using passphrase functions.

Using a Function to Encrypt by Passphrase

To encrypt data with a user-supplied passphrase, you can call the EncryptByPassPhrase function.

The syntax is as follows:

```
EncryptByPassPhrase(
 { ' passphrase ' | @passphrase }
, { ' cleartext ' | @cleartext }
[ , { add_authenticator | @add_authenticator }
, { authenticator | @authenticator } ]    )
```

The arguments of this command are described in Table 19-1.

Table 19-1. *EncryptByPassPhrase Arguments*

Argument	Description
' passphrase ' | @passphrase	The passphrase that is used to encrypt the data
' cleartext ' | @cleartext	The text to be encrypted
add_authenticator | @add_authenticator	A Boolean value (1 or 0) determining whether an authenticator will be used with the encrypted value
authenticator | @authenticator	The data used for the authenticator

To decrypt the encrypted value, the DecryptByPassPhrase function is used, which includes the same arguments as EncryptByPassPhrase except that it takes encrypted text instead of clear text:

```
DecryptByPassPhrase(
{ ' passphrase ' | @passphrase }
, { ' ciphertext ' | @ciphertext }
[ , { add_authenticator | @add_authenticator }
, { authenticator | @authenticator } ] )
```

In this recipe, the "my secure secret text" string is encrypted using a passphrase:

```
-- Table used to store the encrypted data
-- for the purposes of this recipe
CREATE TABLE #SecretInfo
(Secret varbinary(8000) NOT NULL)
GO

INSERT #SecretInfo
(Secret)
SELECT    EncryptByPassPhrase(
          'My Password Used To Encrypt This String in 2008.',
          'This is the text I need to secure.')

SELECT Secret
FROM #SecretInfo
```

This returns the following (your results may vary):

```
0x0100000031AF7E0656FB1C3253AE708B4DB5F3F1EDEA48C832E5BE493E01655D8E7783D6C21E
2B94817636EAD39328D940B8BD4F9718081E6EB837BE
```

Taking the returned varbinary value from the #SecretInfo table, I can decrypt the text using the same passphrase (using an incorrect passphrase will return a NULL value):

```
SELECT CAST(DecryptByPassPhrase(
'My Password Used To Encrypt This String in 2008.',
Secret) as varchar(50))
FROM #SecretInfo
```

This returns

```
This is the text I need to secure.
```

How It Works

In this recipe, a temporary table was used to hold the encrypted output of the EncryptByPassPhrase function. I defined the column with a varbinary(8000) data type (8000 is the maximum size allowed to be encrypted by this function):

```
CREATE TABLE #SecretInfo
(Secret varbinary(8000) NOT NULL)
GO
```

Next, I inserted a new row into the temporary table, using INSERT...SELECT:

```
INSERT #SecretInfo
(Secret)
```

The SELECT references the EncryptByPassPhrase function. The first parameter was the actual password (in this case an entire sentence) that was used to encrypt the string. The second parameter was the string to be encrypted:

```
SELECT  EncryptByPassPhrase('My Password Used To Encrypt This String in 2008.',
        'This is the text I need to secure.')
```

The next step queried the varbinary(8000) value that was inserted, returning an unintelligible value:

```
SELECT Secret
FROM #SecretInfo
```

The data was then decrypted using the DecryptByPassPhrase function, which took the password as the first parameter (the one originally used to encrypt the data in the first place), and a reference to the encrypted data in the Secret column of the #SecretInfo temporary table:

```
SELECT CAST(DecryptByPassPhrase(
'My Password Used To Encrypt This String in 2008.',
Secret) as varchar(50))
FROM #SecretInfo
```

Passphrase encryption functions allow you to encrypt data without fear of even sysadmin server role members reading the data (sysadmin server role members, as you'll see in this chapter, have inherent permissions to read other forms of encrypted data).

The encrypted data will be protected from database backup theft or even the infiltration of the database while on the SQL Server instance, assuming that you haven't stored the password in a table or used the password in any of your modules (stored procedures, triggers, and so on). If the passphrase is improperly shared, the data can be decrypted.

Master Keys

Encryption in SQL Server is handled in a hierarchical manner in order to provide multi-level security. SQL Server includes two key types that are used to encrypt data. The *Service Master Key* is at the top of the hierarchy and is automatically created when SQL Server is installed. The Service Master Key is also used to encrypt Database Master Keys below it. *Database Master Keys* are then used to encrypt certificates and both asymmetric and symmetric keys. This layering of keys and certificates provides stronger encryption. In this section, I'll discuss these two different types of keys: the Service Master Key and Database Master Key.

As stated before, the Service Master Key is at the top of the encryption hierarchy in SQL Server and is responsible for encrypting system data, linked server logins, and Database Master Keys. The Service Master Key is automatically generated the first time it is used by SQL Server to encrypt a credential, Database Master Key, or linked server password, and it is generated using the Windows credentials of the SQL Server service account. If you have to change the SQL Server service account, Microsoft recommends that you use SQL Server Configuration Manager, because this tool will perform the appropriate decryptions and encryptions required to generate a new Service Master Key, while keeping the encryption hierarchy intact.

The Database Master Key is an additional layer of SQL Server security in the encryption hierarchy that allows you to encrypt database certificates and asymmetric keys. Each database can contain only a single Database Master Key, which, when created, is encrypted by the Service Master Key.

When you're creating an asymmetric key (reviewed later in the chapter in the "Asymmetric Key Encryption" section), you can decide whether or not to include a password for encrypting the private key of the asymmetric key pair. If a password is not included, the Database Master Key is then used to encrypt the private key instead. This is a good example of using the Database Master Key to encrypt other objects.

In this next group of recipes, I'll demonstrate how to manage these two different key types.

Backing Up and Restoring a Service Master Key

Because of the Service Master Key's critical role in SQL Server, it is very important for you to back up this key to a safe location in the event that it is damaged or modified. This is performed by using the `BACKUP SERVICE MASTER KEY` command.

The syntax is as follows:

```
BACKUP SERVICE MASTER KEY TO FILE = 'path_to_file'
    ENCRYPTION BY PASSWORD = 'Password'
```

This command takes two arguments; the first argument is the name of the path and file name where the key backup will be exported. The second argument is the password used to encrypt the file containing the key backup. After backing up a Service Master Key, the backup file should then be backed up to tape or copied off the server to a safe location.

In the event that a Service Master Key must be recovered from backup on the SQL Server instance, the `RESTORE SERVICE MASTER KEY` command is used.

The syntax is as follows:

```
RESTORE SERVICE MASTER KEY FROM FILE = 'path_to_file'
    DECRYPTION BY PASSWORD = 'password' [FORCE]
```

This command takes the name of the backup file and the encryption password. The FORCE argument is used to force a replacement of the existing Service Master Key even in the event of data loss (so it should only be used under dire circumstances and if you can afford to lose the encrypted data that cannot be decrypted).

This recipe demonstrates backing up and then restoring the Service Master Key.

In the first example, BACKUP SERVICE MASTER KEY is used to back up to a file on the C:\Apress\ Recipes directory:

```
BACKUP SERVICE MASTER KEY
TO FILE = 'C:\Apress\Recipes\SMK.bak'
ENCRYPTION BY PASSWORD = 'MakeItAGoodOne!1AB'
```

The following code demonstrates recovering the Service Master Key from a backup file:

```
RESTORE SERVICE MASTER KEY
FROM FILE = 'C:\Apress\Recipes\SMK.bak'
DECRYPTION BY PASSWORD = 'MakeItAGoodOne!1AB'
```

How It Works

In the first example, the Service Master Key was backed up to a file. The second line of code designated the file name to back up the file to:

```
BACKUP SERVICE MASTER KEY
TO FILE = 'C:\Apress\Recipes\SMK.bak'
```

The third line of code designated the password used to protect the file (and is required in order to initiate a restore):

```
ENCRYPTION BY PASSWORD = 'MakeItAGoodOne!1AB'
```

In the second example, a Service Master Key restore was initiated. The second line of code designated the file name to restore the Service Master Key from:

```
RESTORE SERVICE MASTER KEY
FROM FILE = 'C:\Apress\Recipes\SMK.bak'
```

The third line of code designated the password that was used to protect and generate the Service Master Key backup:

```
DECRYPTION BY PASSWORD = 'MakeItAGoodOne!1AB'
```

If you are testing this example out yourself, you'll see that if you perform a backup and restore without any actual change in the Service Master Key, you'll see the following message during a RESTORE operation:

```
The old and new master keys are identical. No data re-encryption is required.
```

Creating, Regenerating, and Dropping a Database Master Key

The Database Master Key, when explicitly created, adds an extra layer of security by automatically encrypting new certificates or asymmetric keys in the database, serving to further protect encrypted data.

To create a Database Master Key, the CREATE MASTER KEY command is used. The syntax is as follows:

```
CREATE MASTER KEY ENCRYPTION BY PASSWORD = 'password'
```

Like the Service Master Key, the Database Master Key doesn't have an explicit name, and uses a single argument, the Database Master Key's password. The Database Master Key can be regenerated by using the ALTER MASTER KEY command. The syntax for regenerating the Database Master Key is as follows:

```
ALTER MASTER KEY
[FORCE] REGENERATE WITH ENCRYPTION BY PASSWORD = 'password'
```

This command only takes a single argument, the password of the regenerated key. Regenerating the key decrypts all objects encrypted by the key and reencrypts them using the newly regenerated key. If there is an error during the decryption (for data that cannot be decrypted for various reasons), the FORCE option forces the regeneration process, but, and this is important, *with the danger of rendering some encrypted data inaccessible.*

To remove the Database Master Key entirely, the DROP MASTER KEY command is used (no additional arguments needed).

For example:

```
USE BookStore
GO
DROP MASTER KEY
```

You won't be able to drop the Database Master Key, however, if it is still being used to encrypt other database objects.

In this first example, I'll create a Database Master Key for the BookStore database:

```
IF NOT EXISTS (SELECT name
            FROM sys.databases
            WHERE name = 'BookStore')
BEGIN
    CREATE DATABASE BookStore
END
GO

USE BookStore
GO
CREATE MASTER KEY ENCRYPTION BY PASSWORD = '99a555ac-cf60-472b-9c1e-ed735ffbb089'
```

Next, I'll demonstrate regenerating the Database Master Key with a new password:

```
Use BookStore
GO
ALTER MASTER KEY
REGENERATE WITH ENCRYPTION BY PASSWORD = 'uglypassword1C3ED8CF'
```

Lastly, I will drop the Database Master Key (it isn't being used to encrypt other keys, so I am allowed to do this):

```
DROP MASTER KEY
```

How It Works

This example demonstrated creating a Database Master Key for the BookStore database. The only user-provided information was the password used to encrypt the Database Master Key:

```
CREATE MASTER KEY ENCRYPTION BY PASSWORD = '99a555ac-cf60-472b-9c1e-ed735ffbb089'
```

The second example also only required a single user-provided argument; the password used to regenerate the new Database Master Key:

```
ALTER MASTER KEY
REGENERATE WITH ENCRYPTION BY PASSWORD = 'uglypassword1C3ED8CF'
```

The Database Master Key was then dropped using the following command:

```
DROP MASTER KEY
```

Backing Up and Restoring a Database Master Key

Like a Service Master Key, the Database Master Key can also be backed up to disk using the
BACKUresP MASTER KEY command. The syntax is as follows:

```
BACKUP MASTER KEY TO FILE = 'path_to_file'
    ENCRYPTION BY PASSWORD = 'Password'
```

The command takes two arguments, the first being the path and file name (that the Database
Master Key will be backed up to), and the second being the password used to protect the backup
file.

To restore a Database Master Key from the file backup, the RESTORE MASTER KEY command is
used. The syntax is as follows:

```
RESTORE MASTER KEY FROM FILE = 'path_to_file'
    DECRYPTION BY PASSWORD = 'password'
    ENCRYPTION BY PASSWORD = 'password'
    [FORCE]
```

This command takes the file name and path, the password used to decrypt the backup file, and
the new password to encrypt the new Database Master Key. The FORCE option forces the Database
Master Key restore, even if all dependent encrypted data in the database cannot be reencrypted
using the new key. This means dependent encrypted data would be unavailable because it cannot
be decrypted—so use this option with caution and as a last resort!

In this first example, I create a master key in the BookStore database and then back up the
Database Master Key to a file:

```
USE BookStore
GO

CREATE MASTER KEY ENCRYPTION BY PASSWORD = 'MagneticFields!'
GO

BACKUP MASTER KEY TO FILE = 'C:\Apress\Recipes\BookStore_Master_Key.BAK'
    ENCRYPTION BY PASSWORD = '4D280837!!!'
```

Next, I demonstrate restoring the Database Master Key from file:

```
RESTORE MASTER KEY FROM FILE = 'C:\Apress\Recipes\BookStore_Master_Key.BAK'
DECRYPTION BY PASSWORD = '4D280837!!!'
ENCRYPTION BY PASSWORD = 'MagneticFields!'
```

How It Works

As you'll see in upcoming recipes, the Database Master Key is used to encrypt other subordinate
encryption objects. Therefore, it's a good idea for you to back up the Database Master Key immediately after it is first created.

In this recipe, I created a Database Master Key for the user database, and then I backed up the
Database Master Key to file, which was designated in the first argument of the BACKUP MASTER KEY
command:

```
BACKUP MASTER KEY TO FILE = 'C:\Apress\Recipes\BookStore_Master_Key.BAK'
```

The second line of code designated the password used to encrypt the backup file:

```
 ENCRYPTION BY PASSWORD = '4D280837!!!'
```

The second example demonstrated restoring the Database Master Key from file. The first line of code designated the name of the backup file:

```
RESTORE MASTER KEY FROM FILE = 'C:\Apress\Recipes\BookStore_Master_Key.BAK'
```

The second line designated the password used to originally encrypt the backup file:

```
DECRYPTION BY PASSWORD = '4D280837!!!'
```

The third line of code designated the password used to encrypt the Database Master Key once it is restored:

```
ENCRYPTION BY PASSWORD = 'MagneticFields!'
```

If you tested this example out on your own SQL Server instance, and your Database Master Key hadn't changed between the backup and restore, you would see the following message:

```
The old and new master keys are identical. No data re-encryption is required.
```

Removing Service Master Key Encryption from the Database Master Key

When a Database Master Key is created, it is encrypted using two methods by default: the Service Master Key and the password used in the CREATE MASTER KEY command. If you don't wish to have the Database Master Key encrypted by the Service Master Key (so that SQL Server logins with sysadmin permissions can't access the encrypted data without knowing the Database Master Key password), you can drop it using a variation of the ALTER MASTER KEY command.

The abridged syntax is as follows:

```
ALTER MASTER KEY
ADD ENCRYPTION BY SERVICE MASTER KEY |
DROP ENCRYPTION BY SERVICE MASTER KEY
```

Since the Service Master Key allows for automatic decryption of the Database Master Key by users with appropriate permissions (sysadmin, for example), once you drop encryption by the Service Master Key, you must use a new command to access the Database Master Key if you wish to modify it. This command is OPEN MASTER KEY, which has the following syntax:

```
OPEN MASTER KEY DECRYPTION BY PASSWORD = 'password'
```

The CLOSE MASTER KEY command is used once the example is finished using the Database Master Key (with no additional arguments).

In this example, encryption by the Service Master Key is dropped for the BookStore database:

```
USE BookStore
GO

ALTER MASTER KEY DROP ENCRYPTION BY SERVICE MASTER KEY
```

To reenable encryption by the Service Master Key, I must first open access to the Database Master Key, Service Master Key encryption is re-added to the Database Master Key, and then the Database Master Key is closed again:

```
OPEN MASTER KEY DECRYPTION BY PASSWORD = 'MagneticFields!'

ALTER MASTER KEY ADD ENCRYPTION BY SERVICE MASTER KEY

CLOSE MASTER KEY
```

Once the Service Master Key is used to encrypt the Database Master Key, the Database Master Key no longer needs to be explicitly opened or closed.

How It Works

This recipe demonstrated removing encryption of the Database Master Key by the Service Master Key using the ALTER MASTER KEY command:

```
ALTER MASTER KEY DROP ENCRYPTION BY SERVICE MASTER KEY
```

Once this is done, any modification of the Database Master Key requires password access using OPEN MASTER KEY. This was used in order to reapply encryption by the Service Master Key:

```
OPEN MASTER KEY DECRYPTION BY PASSWORD = 'MagneticFieldS!'
```

The ALTER MASTER KEY was used then to add Service Master Key encryption back again:

```
ALTER MASTER KEY ADD ENCRYPTION BY SERVICE MASTER KEY
```

After finishing the ALTER MASTER KEY operation, the Database Master Key was closed:

```
CLOSE MASTER KEY
```

Asymmetric Key Encryption

An asymmetric key contains a database-side internal public and private key, which can be used to encrypt and decrypt data in the SQL Server database. Asymmetric keys can be imported from an external file or assembly, and can also be generated within the SQL Server database.

Unlike a certificate (which is discussed later in the chapter), asymmetric keys cannot be backed up to a file. This means that if an asymmetric key is created within SQL Server, there isn't an easy mechanism for reusing that same key in other user databases.

Asymmetric keys are a highly secure option for data encryption, but they also require more SQL Server resources when in use. In the next set of recipes, I'll demonstrate how to create, manage, and use asymmetric key encryption.

Creating an Asymmetric Key

In this recipe, I'll demonstrate creating an asymmetric key, which will then be used for encrypting and decrypting data. The abridged and simplified syntax for creating an asymmetric key is as follows:

```
CREATE ASYMMETRIC KEY Asym_Key_Name
[ FROM PROVIDER Provider_Name ]
   [ AUTHORIZATION database_principal_name ]
   {FROM <Asym_Key_Source>|
      WITH ALGORITHM = <key_option>
   [ ENCRYPTION BY PASSWORD = 'password' ]
```

The arguments of this command are described in Table 19-2.

Table 19-2. *CREATE ASYMMETRIC KEY Arguments*

Argument	Description
Asym_Key_Name	The name of the asymmetric key.
Provider_Name	The Extensible Key Management provider name.
database_principal_name	The owner of the asymmetric key.
Asym_Key_Source	Options that allow you to define external key sources (file, assembly, EKM provider).
key_option	Algorithm options used when generating a new key, allowing you to select the security type (RSA_512, RSA_1024, RSA_2048). key_option also allows you to designate the key name from an EKM provider and either create or open a key on the EKM device.
Password	The password used to encrypt the private key. When not used, the private key is automatically encrypted by the Database Master Key.

In this example, I create a new asymmetric key in the BookStore database:

```
USE BookStore
GO

CREATE ASYMMETRIC KEY asymBookSellerKey
WITH ALGORITHM = RSA_512
ENCRYPTION BY PASSWORD = 'EEB0B4DD!!!'
```

How It Works

This example demonstrated creating an asymmetric key in the BookStore database. The first line of code designated the name of the new key:

```
CREATE ASYMMETRIC KEY asymBookSellerKey
```

The second line of code designated the encryption security type:

```
WITH ALGORITHM = RSA_512
```

The third line of code designated the password used to encrypt the asymmetric key:

```
ENCRYPTION BY PASSWORD = 'EEB0B4DD!!!'
```

Viewing Asymmetric Keys in the Current Database

You can view all asymmetric keys in the current database by querying the sys.asymmetric_keys system catalog view. For example:

```
SELECT name, algorithm_desc, pvt_key_encryption_type_desc
FROM sys.asymmetric_keys
```

This returns

```
name                    algorithm_desc    pvt_key_encryption_type_desc
asymBookSellerKey       RSA_512           ENCRYPTED_BY_PASSWORD
```

How It Works

The sys.asymmetric_keys system catalog view was used to see asymmetric keys in the current database. The first line of code designated the name, security type, and method by which the private key was encrypted:

```
SELECT name, algorithm_desc, pvt_key_encryption_type_desc
```

The second line designated the system catalog view in the FROM clause:

```
FROM sys.asymmetric_keys
```

Modifying the Asymmetric Key's Private Key Password

You can also modify the password of the private key by using the ALTER ASYMMETRIC KEY command with the ENCRYPTION BY PASSWORD and DECRYPTION BY PASSWORD options.

This recipe's example demonstrates giving the asymmetric key a new password:

```
ALTER ASYMMETRIC KEY asymBookSellerKey
WITH PRIVATE KEY
(ENCRYPTION BY PASSWORD = 'newpasswordE4D352F280E0',
DECRYPTION BY PASSWORD = 'EEB0B4DD!!!')
```

How It Works

In this recipe, I used ALTER ASYMMETRIC KEY to change the private key password. The first line of code designated the asymmetric key name:

```
ALTER ASYMMETRIC KEY asymBookSellerKey
```

I designated the new password in the ENCRYPTION BY PASSWORD argument:

```
WITH PRIVATE KEY
(ENCRYPTION BY PASSWORD = 'newpasswordE4D352F280E0',
```

The old private key password was designated in the DECRYPTION BY PASSWORD argument:

```
DECRYPTION BY PASSWORD = 'EEB0B4DD!!!')
```

Encrypting and Decrypting Data Using an Asymmetric Key

Using an asymmetric key to encrypt data is a very secure method of maintaining the secrecy of the data, because a public and private key pair are used.

■**Caution** Encryption by asymmetric key is a more costly operation when used in conjunction with large data sets compared to the faster option of encrypting symmetric keys, which use a single key to both encrypt and decrypt data.

Granted that encrypting data by an asymmetric key is not recommended, you do still have this as an option. Once an asymmetric key is added to the database, it can be used to encrypt and decrypt data. To encrypt data, the EncryptByAsmKey function is used.

The syntax is as follows:

```
EncryptByAsymKey ( Asym_Key_ID , { 'plaintext' | @plaintext } )
```

The arguments of this command are described in Table 19-3.

Table 19-3. *EncryptByAsymKey Arguments*

Argument	Description
Asym_Key_ID	The ID of the asymmetric key to be used to encrypt the data. The AsymKey_ID function can be used to return the ID of the asymmetric key.
'plaintext ' | @plaintext	The unencrypted text to be encrypted (from a string or a local variable).

As with encrypting data via a certificate, the EncryptByAsymKey function returns varbinary encrypted data.

To decrypt data encrypted by a specific asymmetric key, the DecryptByAsymKey function is used. The syntax is as follows:

```
DecryptByAsymKey ( Asym_Key_ID ,
                 { ' ciphertext ' | @ciphertext }
                 [ , ' Asym_Key_Password ' ] )
```

The arguments of this command are described in Table 19-4.

Table 19-4. *DecryptByAsymKey Arguments*

Argument	Description
Asym_Key_ID	The ID of the asymmetric key to be used to decrypt the data. The Asym_Key_ID system function can be used to return the ID of the asymmetric key.
'ciphertext' | @ciphertext	The encrypted text to be decrypted.
'Asym_Key_Password '	The password of the asymmetric key's private key (password used when the asymmetric key was created).

In this example, I'll create a table containing bank routing information for specific booksellers:

```
Use BookStore
GO

CREATE TABLE dbo.BookSellerBankRouting
(BookSellerID int NOT NULL PRIMARY KEY,
 BankRoutingNBR varbinary(300) NOT NULL)
```

Next, a new row is inserted into the table using the EncryptByAsymKey on the yet-to-be-encrypted bank routing number:

```
INSERT dbo.BookSellerBankRouting
(BookSellerID, BankRoutingNBR)
VALUES (22,
EncryptByAsymKey(AsymKey_ID('asymBookSellerKey'),
            '137492837583249ABR'))
```

Querying the value of BankRoutingNBR for the newly inserted row returns cipher text:

```
SELECT CAST(BankRoutingNBR as varchar(100)) BankRoutingNBR
FROM dbo.BookSellerBankRouting
WHERE BookSellerID = 22
```

This returns

```
BankRoutingNBR
m(Ì_'dc`Ó«·"ÆöÖï2ö]Œ¡ìåßo'a8___.§6øovPgîÎwñ@lÈ__µq-@'cda_?Lÿ<_3p'85íàj_{
```

Next, I'll use the `DecryptByAsymKey` function to decrypt the `BankRoutingNBR` column value. I'll also use `CAST` to convert the varbinary data into varchar data type:

```
SELECT CAST(DecryptByAsymKey
        ( AsymKey_ID('asymBookSellerKey'),
                BankRoutingNBR,
            N'newpasswordE4D352F280E0') as varchar(100)) BankRoutingNBR
FROM dbo.BookSellerBankRouting
WHERE BookSellerID = 22
```

This returns

```
BankRoutingNBR
137492837583249ABR
```

How It Works

I started this recipe off by creating a table to store encrypted bank routing numbers. The `BankRoutingNBR` column was given a varbinary data type in order to stored the encrypted data. I then performed an `INSERT` of a row into the table. The two columns to be inserted into were designated:

```
INSERT dbo.BookSellerBankRouting
(BookSellerID, BankRoutingNBR)
```

The `BookSellerID` was set to a value of 22:

```
VALUES (22,
```

The `BankRoutingNBR` was populated using the `EncryptByAsymKey` function:

```
EncryptByAsymKey(
```

This function took a first parameter of the asymmetric key's system ID, using the `AsymKey_ID` function to convert the key name to the key ID integer value:

```
AsymKey_ID('asymBookSellerKey'),
```

The second parameter contained the bank routing number to be encrypted:

```
'137492837583249ABR'))
```

The data was then stored in the table in encrypted cipher text. To decrypt the data, the `DecryptByAsymKey` function was used. The `CAST` function was wrapped around it in order to convert the varbinary value into varchar:

```
SELECT CAST(
```

The first parameter of the `DecryptByAsymKey` function was the asymmetric key's system ID, again using the `AsymKey_ID` to convert the asymmetric key name into the ID:

```
DecryptByAsymKey
        ( AsymKey_ID('asymBookSellerKey'),
```

The second parameter was the `BankRoutingNBR` column from the `dbo.BookSellerBankRouting` table:

```
        BankRoutingNBR,
```

The third parameter was the password of the asymmetric key's private key:

```
        N'newpasswordE4D352F280E0')
```

The data type was then converted to `varchar(100)`:

```
as varchar(100)) BankRoutingNBR
FROM dbo.BookSellerBankRouting
WHERE BookSellerID = 22
```

This returned the bank routing number in clear, decrypted text.

Dropping an Asymmetric Key

To drop an asymmetric key, use the `DROP ASYMMETRIC KEY` command. This command takes just one argument—the name of the asymmetric key.

In this recipe, I drop the asymmetric key created in the previous recipe:

```
DROP ASYMMETRIC KEY asymBookSellerKey
```

How It Works

This example demonstrated the simple method of dropping an asymmetric key. Keep in mind that an asymmetric key can't be dropped if it was used to encrypt other keys or is mapped to a login. If you used it to directly encrypt data (not recommended), you will be removing the decryption method.

Symmetric Key Encryption

Certificates (reviewed later in the chapter) and asymmetric keys encrypt data using a database-side internal public key and decrypt data using a database-side internal private key. Symmetric keys are simpler. They contain a key that is used for *both* encryption and decryption. Consequently, symmetric keys encrypt data faster and are more suitable for use against large data sets. Although a trade-off in terms of encryption complexity, symmetric keys are still considered to be a good option for encrypting secret data within the database.

In the next set of recipes, I'll demonstrate how to create, manage, and use symmetric key encryption.

Creating a Symmetric Key

A symmetric key is a less resource-intensive method of encrypting large amounts of data. Unlike certificates or asymmetric keys, a symmetric key both encrypts and decrypts the data with a single internal key. The distinguishing feature of symmetric keys is that the key must be opened for use within a database session, prior to the encrypting or decrypting of data.

To create a symmetric key, the `CREATE SYMMETRIC KEY` command is used. The abridged and simplified syntax is as follows:

```
CREATE SYMMETRIC KEY key_name [ AUTHORIZATION owner_name ]
   [ FROM PROVIDER Provider_Name ]
   WITH <key_options> [ , ... n ] |
   ENCRYPTION BY <encrypting_mechanism> [ , ... n ]
```

The arguments of this command are described in Table 19-5.

Table 19-5. *CREATE SYMMETRIC KEY Arguments*

Argument	Description
key_name	Defines the name of the new symmetric key. If prefixed with a # sign, a temporary key can be created for the current session and user.
owner_name	Specifies the database user that owns the key.
Provider_Name	Defines the Extensible Key Management provider name.
key_options	Specifies options used to define the key source, algorithm (DES | TRIPLE_DES | TRIPLE_DES_3KEY | RC2 | RC4 | DESX | AES_128 | AES_192 | AES_256), and optional identity phrase (character-based phrase is used to generate a GUID that tags data with a temporary key).
Encrypting_mechanism	Defines how the symmetric key is protected (certificate, password, asymmetric key, or another symmetric key).

In this recipe, a new symmetric key is created that is encrypted by an existing database asymmetric key:

```
USE BookStore
GO

-- Create asymmetric key used to encrypt symmetric key
CREATE ASYMMETRIC KEY asymBookSellerKey
WITH ALGORITHM = RSA_512
ENCRYPTION BY PASSWORD = 'EEBOB4DD!!!'

-- Create symmetric key
CREATE SYMMETRIC KEY sym_BookStore
WITH ALGORITHM = TRIPLE_DES
ENCRYPTION BY ASYMMETRIC KEY asymBookSellerKey
```

How It Works

In this recipe, I demonstrated the creation of a symmetric key, which will then be used to encrypt data. It must be encrypted using a certificate, password, asymmetric key, or another symmetric key. In this case, I used an asymmetric key to encrypt it.

After creating the asymmetric key, I used CREATE SYMMETRIC KEY. The first line of code for this command designated the symmetric key name:

```
CREATE SYMMETRIC KEY sym_BookStore
```

The second line of code designated the encryption algorithm used to create the encrypting key:

```
WITH ALGORITHM = TRIPLE_DES
```

The last line of code defined the asymmetric key in the current database that would be used to encrypt the symmetric key:

```
ENCRYPTION BY ASYMMETRIC KEY asymBookSellerKey
```

Viewing Symmetric Keys in the Current Database

You can see the symmetric keys in the current database by querying the sys.symmetric_keys system catalog view:

```
SELECT name, algorithm_desc
FROM sys.symmetric_keys
```

This returns

name	algorithm_desc
##MS_DatabaseMasterKey##	TRIPLE_DES
sym_BookStore	TRIPLE_DES

How It Works

The sys.symmetric_keys system catalog view was used to return the name and encryption algorithm of symmetric keys in the current database. Notice that this query against sys.symmetric_keys also returned a row for the Database Master Key.

Changing How a Symmetric Key Is Encrypted

In this recipe, I'll demonstrate how to change the way a symmetric key is encrypted using ALTER SYMMETRIC KEY. Before doing this, however, I must first open it using the OPEN SYMMETRIC KEY command.

The syntax for OPEN SYMMETRIC KEY is as follows:

```
OPEN SYMMETRIC KEY Key_name DECRYPTION BY < decryption_mechanism >
```

The decryption mechanism for opening the key depends on how the key was originally encrypted. For example, the following symmetric key is opened using the private key password of an encryption key:

```
OPEN SYMMETRIC KEY sym_BookStore
DECRYPTION BY ASYMMETRIC KEY asymBookSellerKey
WITH PASSWORD = 'EEB0B4DD!!!'
```

Once opened for use, the key can be changed to use encryption by a password instead (adding the password encryption first, and *then* removing the asymmetric key encryption):

```
ALTER SYMMETRIC KEY sym_BookStore
ADD ENCRYPTION BY PASSWORD = 'hushhush!123'

ALTER SYMMETRIC KEY sym_BookStore
DROP ENCRYPTION BY ASYMMETRIC KEY asymBookSellerKey
```

Once finished with the operations, the CLOSE SYMMETRIC KEY command closes the key for use in the database session:

```
CLOSE SYMMETRIC KEY sym_BookStore
```

How It Works

This example demonstrated ways to change how a symmetric key is encrypted, in this case from using an asymmetric key to using a password instead.

First, OPEN SYMMETRIC KEY was used to open the key up for modification. The first line of code designated the symmetric key name:

```
OPEN SYMMETRIC KEY sym_BookStore
```

The second line of code designated the name of the asymmetric key used to encrypt the symmetric key:

```
DECRYPTION BY ASYMMETRIC KEY asymBookSellerKey
```

The third line of code designated the private key password of the asymmetric key:

```
WITH PASSWORD = 'EEB0B4DD!!!'
```

Once opened for use, the key was changed to use encryption by a password. The first line of code designated the symmetric key to modify:

```
ALTER SYMMETRIC KEY sym_BookStore
```

The second line of code designated that the symmetric key would be encrypted by a password:

```
ADD ENCRYPTION BY PASSWORD = 'hushhush!123'
```

After that, ALTER SYMMETRIC KEY was called again to drop the asymmetric key encryption. The first line of code designated the symmetric key to be modified:

```
ALTER SYMMETRIC KEY sym_BookStore
```

The second line of code designated the asymmetric key encryption to be dropped:

```
DROP ENCRYPTION BY ASYMMETRIC KEY asymBookSellerKey
```

Once I finished, the CLOSE SYMMETRIC KEY command was used to close the key for use in the database session:

```
CLOSE SYMMETRIC KEY sym_BookStore
```

Using Symmetric Key Encryption and Decryption

To encrypt data using a symmetric key, the symmetric key must first be opened, and then the EncryptByKey function used.

The syntax for this function is as follows:

```
EncryptByKey( key_GUID , { ' cleartext ' | @cleartext }
[ , { add_authenticator | @add_authenticator }
, { authenticator | @authenticator } ])
```

The arguments of this command are described in Table 19-6.

Table 19-6. *EncryptByKey Arguments*

Argument	Description
key_GUID	The symmetric key global unique identifier (GUID), which can be derived by using the Key_GUID system function.
'cleartext' | @cleartext	The text to be encrypted.

Continued

Table 19-6. *Continued*

Argument	Description
add_authenticator | @add_authenticator	A Boolean value (1 or 0) determining whether an authenticator will be used with the encrypted value. The data being encrypted can be further encrypted by using an additional binding value—for example, the table's primary key. If the authenticator is modified (or tampered with), the encrypted data will not be able to be decrypted.
authenticator | @authenticator	The data column used for the authenticator. For example, you can bind the encrypted data along with the primary key of the table.

In this example, I will create a new table to hold password hints for customers. The answer to the password hint is to be encrypted in the table:

```
USE BookStore
GO

CREATE TABLE dbo.PasswordHint
(CustomerID int NOT NULL PRIMARY KEY,
 PasswordHintQuestion varchar(300) NOT NULL,
 PasswordHintAnswer varbinary(200) NOT NULL)
GO
```

Next, I'll insert a new row into the dbo.PasswordHint table that encrypts the PasswordHintAnswer column using a symmetric key:

```
OPEN SYMMETRIC KEY sym_BookStore
DECRYPTION BY PASSWORD = 'hushhush!123'

INSERT dbo.PasswordHint
(CustomerID, PasswordHintQuestion, PasswordHintAnswer)
VALUES
(23, 'What is the name of the hospital you were born in?',
EncryptByKey(Key_GUID('sym_BookStore '), 'Mount Marie'))

CLOSE SYMMETRIC KEY sym_BookStore
```

To decrypt data that was encrypted by a symmetric key, I'll use the DecryptByKey command. Notice that unlike the EncryptByKey command, DecryptByKey doesn't use the symmetric key GUID, so the correct symmetric key session must be opened in order to decrypt the data:

```
OPEN SYMMETRIC KEY sym_BookStore
DECRYPTION BY PASSWORD = 'hushhush!123'

SELECT CAST(DecryptByKey(PasswordHintAnswer) as varchar(200)) PasswordHintAnswer
FROM dbo.PasswordHint
WHERE CustomerID = 23

CLOSE SYMMETRIC KEY sym_BookStore
```

This returns

```
PasswordHintAnswer
Mount Marie
```

If you attempted to query the value with the previous query without first opening the symmetric key that was used to encrypt the data, a NULL value would have been returned instead:

```
PasswordHintAnswer
NULL
```

As was shown in the EncryptByKey syntax earlier, you can also include an extra authenticator column value to be used in the encryption of the text data. This additional information helps further obscure the cipher text from any meaningful value that could potentially be derived from the cipher text and other non-encrypted columns in the table.

In this next example, I'll use the primary key column from the dbo.PasswordHint table. To demonstrate, I'll create a new table and add an unencrypted row to it:

```
CREATE TABLE dbo.BookSellerLogins
(LoginID int NOT NULL PRIMARY KEY,
 Password varbinary(256) NOT NULL)
GO

INSERT dbo.BookSellerLogins
(LoginID, Password)
VALUES(22, CAST('myeasypassword' as varbinary))
```

Next, I'll open the symmetric key and encrypt the values of the password column in an UPDATE statement using the symmetric key and the LoginID of the row:

```
OPEN SYMMETRIC KEY sym_BookStore
DECRYPTION BY PASSWORD = 'hushhush!123'

UPDATE dbo.BookSellerLogins
SET Password =
   EncryptByKey(Key_GUID('sym_BookStore'),
           Password,
           1,
           CAST(LoginID as varbinary))

CLOSE SYMMETRIC KEY sym_BookStore
```

Now, to decrypt the value of this updated row, the DecryptByKey must also include the authenticator column in the function call:

```
OPEN SYMMETRIC KEY sym_BookStore
DECRYPTION BY PASSWORD = 'hushhush!123'

SELECT LoginID,
CAST(DecryptByKey(Password, 1,
CAST(LoginID as varbinary)) as varchar(30)) Password
FROM dbo.BookSellerLogins

CLOSE SYMMETRIC KEY sym_BookStore
```

This returns

```
LoginID    Password
22         myeasypassword
```

How It Works

In this recipe, I demonstrated how to encrypt data using EncryptByKey and decrypt it using DecryptByKey. Before using the function, the symmetric key first had to be opened. The first line of OPEN SYMMETRIC KEY referenced the symmetric key name:

```
OPEN SYMMETRIC KEY sym_BookStore
```

The second line included the password used to access the symmetric key for use:

```
DECRYPTION BY PASSWORD = 'hushhush!123'
```

A new row was then inserted, with an encrypted value using EncryptByKey. The first argument used the Key_GUID function to return the system ID of the symmetric key to be used. The second argument was the text to be encrypted by the symmetric key:

```
...
EncryptByKey(Key_GUID('sym_BookStore '), 'Mount Marie'))
```

The key was then closed after finishing the encryption, referencing the symmetric key for the argument:

```
CLOSE SYMMETRIC KEY sym_BookStore
```

To decrypt the data, the symmetric key was reopened:

```
OPEN SYMMETRIC KEY sym_BookStore
DECRYPTION BY PASSWORD = 'hushhush!123'
```

The DecryptByKey function was used, taking just the table column where the encrypted data was stored as an argument:

```
SELECT CAST(DecryptByKey(PasswordHintAnswer) as varchar(200)) PasswordHintAnswer
FROM dbo.PasswordHint
WHERE CustomerID = 23
```

After returning the decrypted data, the symmetric key was then closed:

```
CLOSE SYMMETRIC KEY sym_BookStore
```

Encrypting data using an authenticator was also demonstrated. In the example, the third parameter was a flag indicating that an authenticator value would be used (1 for True), followed by the column authenticator (LoginID):

```
EncryptByKey(Key_GUID('sym_BookStore'),
        Password,
        1,
        CAST(LoginID as varbinary))
```

The LoginID was converted to varbinary prior to being included in the encrypted data. Using an authenticator further secures the encrypted data. However, if the accompanying authenticator LoginID value was changed for the specific row, the encrypted data can no longer be decrypted with the modified LoginID value.

In the example, the symmetric key was opened, and the DecryptByKey function was used, including the encrypted column in the first argument, the authenticator flag in the second argument, and the authenticator column in the third argument (CAST as a varbinary data type):

```
SELECT LoginID,
CAST(DecryptByKey(Password, 1,
CAST(LoginID as varbinary)) as varchar(30)) Password
FROM dbo.BookSellerLogins
```

After returning the decrypted data, the symmetric key was then closed.

Dropping a Symmetric Key

You can remove a symmetric key from the database by using the DROP SYMMETRIC KEY command, which takes the name of the symmetric key as its single argument.

For example:

```
DROP SYMMETRIC KEY sym_BookStore
```

How It Works

In this recipe, I demonstrated dropping a symmetric key from the database. It took a single argument—the name of the symmetric key. Keep in mind that if the key were open, the DROP command would fail with an error.

Certificate Encryption

Certificates can be used to encrypt and decrypt data within the database. A certificate contains a key pair, information about the owner of the certificate, and the valid start and end expiration dates for the certificate in question. A certificate contains both a public and a private key. As you'll see in later recipes, the public key of the certificate is used to *encrypt* data, and the private key is used to *decrypt* data. SQL Server can generate its own certificates, or, if you like, you can load one from an external file or assembly. Certificates are more portable than asymmetric keys, because they can be backed up and then loaded from files, whereas asymmetric keys cannot. This means that the same certificate can easily be reused in multiple user databases. Once a certificate is created, certificate encryption and decryption functions can then be used against database data.

■**Tip** Both certificates *and* asymmetric key database objects provide a very secure method for encrypting data. This strong method of encryption comes with a performance cost, however. Encrypting very large data sets with a certificate or asymmetric key may incur too much overhead for your environment. A lower overhead option (but a less secure one as well) is using a symmetric key, which was reviewed earlier.

In the next set of recipes I'll demonstrate how to create, manage, and use certificate-based encryption.

Creating a Database Certificate

To create a new database certificate, the CREATE CERTIFICATE command is used. The simplified and abridged syntax for creating a new certificate in the database is as follows:

```
CREATE CERTIFICATE certificate_name [ AUTHORIZATION user_name ]
    { FROM <existing_keys> | <generate_new_keys> }
```

The arguments of this command are described in Table 19-7.

Table 19-7. *CREATE CERTIFICATE Arguments*

Argument	Description
certificate_name	The name of the new database certificate
user_name	The database user who owns the certificate
existing_keys	The arguments for creating certificates from an existing assembly or certificate file (and private key file)
generate_new_keys	The arguments used for creating a new certificate, including the password, certificate subject, start date, expiration date, and private key encryption options

In this example, a new certificate is created in the BookStore database:

```
USE BookStore
GO

CREATE CERTIFICATE cert_BookStore
ENCRYPTION BY PASSWORD = 'AA5FA6AC!!!'
WITH SUBJECT = 'BookStore Database Encryption Certificate',
START_DATE = '2/20/2008', EXPIRY_DATE = '10/20/2009'
```

How It Works

In this recipe, I created a new certificate that will be used to encrypt and decrypt data. The first line of code included the name of the new certificate:

```
CREATE CERTIFICATE cert_BookStore
```

The second line included the password used to encrypt the certificate:

```
ENCRYPTION BY PASSWORD = 'AA5FA6AC!!!'
```

The third line designated the subject of the certificate, followed by the start and expiration date for the certificate:

```
WITH SUBJECT = 'BookStore Database Encryption Certificate',
START_DATE = '2/20/2008', EXPIRY_DATE = '10/20/2009'
```

Viewing Certificates in the Database

Once the certificate is created in the database, you can view it by querying the sys.certificates system catalog view:

```
SELECT name, pvt_key_encryption_type_desc, issuer_name
FROM sys.certificates
```

This returns

```
name                  pvt_key_encryption_type_desc    issuer_name
cert_BookStore        ENCRYPTED_BY_PASSWORD           BookStore ...
```

How It Works

I queried the sys.certificates system catalog view to see certificates in the current database. The name column returned the name of the certificate. The pvt_key_encryption_type_desc column in the result set described how the private key of the certificate was encrypted. The issuer_name returned the certificate subject.

Backing Up and Restoring a Certificate

Once a certificate is created, it can also be backed up to file for safekeeping or for use in restoring in other databases using the BACKUP CERTIFICATE command.

The syntax is as follows:

```
BACKUP CERTIFICATE certname TO FILE = 'path_to_file'
    [ WITH PRIVATE KEY
        ( FILE = 'path_to_private_key_file' ,
            ENCRYPTION BY PASSWORD = 'encryption_password'
[ , DECRYPTION BY PASSWORD = 'decryption_password' ]   ) ]
```

The arguments of this command are described in Table 19-8.

Table 19-8. *BACKUP CERTIFICATE Arguments*

Argument	Description
path_to_file	The file name and path that the certificate backup is written to
path_to_private_key_file	The path and file name to the private key file
encryption_password	The private key password used when the certificate was created
decryption_password	The private key password used to decrypt the key prior to backup

This example demonstrates backing up the certificate (it assumes I have a matching path of C:\Apress\Recipes\Certificates on the SQL Server instance):

```
BACKUP CERTIFICATE cert_BookStore
TO FILE = 'C:\Apress\Recipes\Certificates\certBookStore.BAK'
WITH PRIVATE KEY ( FILE = 'C:\Apress\Recipes\Certificates\certBookStorePK.BAK' ,
ENCRYPTION BY PASSWORD = '3439F6A!!!',
DECRYPTION BY PASSWORD = 'AA5FA6AC!!!' )
```

This backup creates two files, one for the certificate containing the public key (used to encrypt data), and another containing the password-protected private key (used to decrypt data).

Once backed up, you can use the certificate in other databases, or drop the existing certificate using the DROP CERTIFICATE command (which uses the certificate name as its argument) and restore it from backup, as this example demonstrates:

```
DROP CERTIFICATE cert_BookStore
GO

CREATE CERTIFICATE cert_BookStore
FROM FILE = 'C:\Apress\Recipes\Certificates\certBookStore.BAK'
WITH PRIVATE KEY (FILE = 'C:\Apress\Recipes\Certificates\certBookStorePK.BAK',
            DECRYPTION BY PASSWORD = '3439F6A!!!',
            ENCRYPTION BY PASSWORD = 'AA5FA6AC!!!')
```

How It Works

This recipe demonstrated backing up a certificate to external files using BACKUP CERTIFICATE, dropping it using DROP CERTIFICATE, and then re-creating it from file using CREATE CERTIFICATE.

Walking through the code, the first line of the backup referenced the certificate name:

```
BACKUP CERTIFICATE cert_BookStore
```

The TO FILE clause included the file name where the public key of the certificate would be backed up to:

```
TO FILE = 'C:\Apress\Recipes\Certificates\certBookStore.BAK'
```

The WITH PRIVATE KEY clause designated the file where the private key backup would be output to, along with the encryption (the private key password used when the certificate was created) and decryption (the private key password used to decrypt the key prior to back up) passwords:

```
WITH PRIVATE KEY ( FILE = 'C:\Apress\Recipes\Certificates\certBookStorePK.BAK' ,
ENCRYPTION BY PASSWORD = '3439F6A!!!',
DECRYPTION BY PASSWORD = 'AA5FA6AC!!!' )
```

After removing the existing certificate using DROP CERTIFICATE, the certificate was then re-created from the backup files. The first line of CREATE CERTIFICATE referenced the certificate name:

```
CREATE CERTIFICATE cert_BookStore
```

The FROM FILE clause designated the location of the public key backup file:

```
FROM FILE =
'C:\Apress\Recipes\Certificates\certBookStore.BAK'
```

The WITH PRIVATE KEY clause designated the location of the private key file, followed by the decryption and encryption passwords:

```
WITH PRIVATE KEY (FILE = 'C:\Apress\Recipes\Certificates\certBookStorePK.BAK',
          DECRYPTION BY PASSWORD = '3439F6A!!!',
          ENCRYPTION BY PASSWORD = 'AA5FA6AC!!!')
```

Managing a Certificate's Private Key

You can add or remove the private key of a certificate by using the ALTER CERTIFICATE command. This command allows you to remove the private key (defaulting to encryption by the Database Master Key), add the private key, or change the private key password.

The following example drops the private key from the certificate:

```
ALTER CERTIFICATE cert_BookStore
REMOVE PRIVATE KEY
```

As with CREATE CERTIFICATE, you can also re-add a private key from a backup file to an existing certificate using ALTER CERTIFICATE:

```
ALTER CERTIFICATE cert_BookStore
WITH PRIVATE KEY
(FILE = 'C:\Apress\Recipes\Certificates\certBookStorePK.BAK',
        DECRYPTION BY PASSWORD = '3439F6A!!!',
            ENCRYPTION BY PASSWORD = 'AA5FA6AC!!!')
```

ALTER CERTIFICATE can also be used to change the password of an existing private key:

```
ALTER CERTIFICATE cert_BookStore
WITH PRIVATE KEY (DECRYPTION BY PASSWORD = 'AA5FA6AC!!!',
ENCRYPTION BY PASSWORD = 'mynewpassword!!!Efsj')
```

The `DECRYPTION BY PASSWORD` was the old private key password, and the `ENCRYPTION BY PASSWORD` the new private key password.

How It Works

This recipe demonstrated how to modify the way that a certificate is encrypted. The private key was removed from the certificate using `ALTER CERTIFICATE` and `REMOVE PRIVATE KEY`:

```
ALTER CERTIFICATE cert_BookStore
REMOVE PRIVATE KEY
```

To add it back again, I also used `ALTER CERTIFICATE`. The first line referenced the certificate name:

```
ALTER CERTIFICATE cert_BookStore
```

The `WITH PRIVATE KEY` clause designated the location of the private key file, along with the decryption and encryption passwords:

```
WITH PRIVATE KEY
(FILE = 'C:\Apress\Recipes\Certificates\certBookStorePK.BAK',
        DECRYPTION BY PASSWORD = '3439F6A!!!',
            ENCRYPTION BY PASSWORD = 'AA5FA6AC!!!')
```

Finally, I modified the certificate's private key password. The first line referenced the certificate name:

```
ALTER CERTIFICATE cert_BookStore
```

The `WITH PRIVATE KEY` clause designated the decryption password and the new encryption password:

```
WITH PRIVATE KEY (DECRYPTION BY PASSWORD = 'AA5FA6AC!!!',
ENCRYPTION BY PASSWORD = 'mynewpassword!!!Efsj')
```

Using Certificate Encryption and Decryption

Once you have a certificate in the database, you can use the `EncryptByCert` system function to encrypt data using the certificate's public key. Encryption allows you to protect sensitive table data. Without the associated private key, the data will be unreadable.

The syntax for `EncryptByCert` is as follows:

```
EncryptByCert ( certificate_ID , { ' cleartext ' | @cleartext } )
```

The arguments of this command are described in Table 19-9.

Table 19-9. *EncryptByCert Arguments*

Argument	Description
certificate_ID	The certificate ID of the certificate used to encrypt the data
' cleartext '	@cleartext	The unencrypted text to be encrypted

In order to retrieve the certificate ID of a specific database certificate, you can use the `Cert_ID` function, which takes the certificate name as its single argument:

```
Cert_ID ( ' cert_name ' )
```

To decrypt data that has been encrypted by a certificate, use the `DecryptByCert` function. This function uses the internal private key of the certificate to decrypt the data (the private key requires the private key password defined when the certificate was created):

```
DecryptByCert ( certificate_ID ,
              { ' ciphertext ' | @ciphertext }
              [ , { ' cert_password ' | @cert_password } ] )
```

The arguments of this command are described in Table 19-10.

Table 19-10. *DecryptByCert Arguments*

Argument	Description
certificate_ID	The certificate ID of the certificate used to decrypt the data
' ciphertext ' | @ciphertext	The encrypted text to be decrypted
' cert_password ' | @cert_password	The private key password of the certificate used to decrypt the data

In this example, I'll perform an `INSERT` into the `PasswordHintAnswer` table with data that is encrypted by the public key of the certificate:

```
USE BookStore
GO

INSERT dbo.PasswordHint
(CustomerID, PasswordHintQuestion, PasswordHintAnswer)
VALUES
(1, 'What is the name of the hospital you were born in?',
   EncryptByCert(Cert_ID('cert_BookStore'), 'Hickman Hospital'))
```

The next query shows the newly inserted row:

```
SELECT CAST(PasswordHintAnswer as varchar(200)) PasswordHintAnswer
FROM dbo.PasswordHint
WHERE CustomerID = 1
```

This returns unintelligible cipher text instead of the original text value:

```
PasswordHintAnswer
o‹_*_1/2bYy-X-_Î`´5BuÄ*n«ßR_.´jõÑ†£sÙ_"ùüÔ_ÄÆ7(c)±w__Àa_3U_'c9_›¨
```

This next example demonstrates querying the `PasswordHintAnswer` column, this time using the private key of the certificate to view the decrypted results:

```
SELECT CAST(DecryptByCert(
              Cert_ID('cert_BookStore'),
              PasswordHintAnswer,
              N'mynewpassword!!!Efsj')
                  as varchar(200)) PasswordHintAnswer
FROM dbo.PasswordHint
WHERE CustomerID = 1
```

This returns

```
PasswordHintAnswer
Hickman Hospital
```

How It Works

In this recipe's example, a table was created with a varbinary data type column that was used to hold encrypted information. This data type was chosen because the EncryptByCert function returns varbinary encrypted data. The first parameter of the EncryptByCert function took the certificate ID, followed by the text to be encrypted:

```
EncryptByCert(Cert_ID('cert_BookStore'), 'Hickman Hospital')
```

This text to be encrypted can be of the nvarchar, varchar, char, or nchar data types. The data is actually stored, however, in varbinary. If you attempt to convert the varbinary data to the original text data type, without the DecryptByCert function and the appropriate certificate and password, only encrypted garble is returned.

The encrypted string was then decrypted using the private key of the same certificate. The function's first parameter was the certificate ID, followed by the encrypted text in the second parameter. The third parameter was the private key password used when the certificate was created:

```
DecryptByCert(Cert_ID('cert_BookStore'), PasswordHintAnswer,
 N'mynewpassword!!!Efsj') PasswordHintAnswer
```

The results of the function were also CAST back into the varchar data type, in order to display the original text.

Automatically Opening and Decrypting via a Symmetric Key

Earlier in the chapter, you saw a demonstration of opening a symmetric key that was encrypted by an asymmetric key. This operation involved two steps, the first being an OPEN SYMMETRIC KEY command, followed by the actual DecryptByKey function call. SQL Server also provides two additional decryption functions that allow you to combine the two aforementioned steps into a single operation: DecryptByKeyAutoAsymKey for symmetric keys encrypted by asymmetric keys and DecryptByKeyAutoCert for symmetric keys encrypted by certificates.

DecryptByKeyAutoAsymKey and DecryptByKeyAutoCert both use similar syntax to their counterparts, only they also include an argument containing the asymmetric key or certificate password.

I'll begin this recipe by creating a new asymmetric key, and then a symmetric key that will be encrypted by the new asymmetric key (the asymmetric key in this scenario will be encrypted by the Database Master Key, so no password is used). Here's the code involved:

```
USE BookStore
GO
CREATE ASYMMETRIC KEY asymBookSell_V2
WITH ALGORITHM = RSA_512

CREATE SYMMETRIC KEY sym_BookStore_V2
WITH ALGORITHM = TRIPLE_DES
ENCRYPTION BY ASYMMETRIC KEY asymBookSell_V2
```

Next, I will insert a new row into the dbo.PasswordHint table:

```
OPEN SYMMETRIC KEY sym_BookStore_V2
DECRYPTION BY ASYMMETRIC KEY asymBookSell_V2

INSERT dbo.PasswordHint
(CustomerID, PasswordHintQuestion, PasswordHintAnswer)
VALUES
(45, 'What is the name of the hospital you were born in?',
EncryptByKey(Key_GUID('sym_BookStore_V2'), 'Sister Helen'))

CLOSE SYMMETRIC KEY sym_BookStore_V2
```

Now I will demonstrate the DecryptByKeyAutoAsymKey function, which allows me to avoid having to use two separate operations to decrypt the table value:

```
SELECT CAST(
    DecryptByKeyAutoAsymKey
    (ASYMKEY_ID('asymBookSell_V2'),
     NULL,
     PasswordHintAnswer) as varchar)
FROM dbo.PasswordHint
WHERE CustomerID = 45
```

This returns

```
Sister Helen
```

How It Works

In this recipe, I created a new asymmetric key and then a symmetric key encrypted by the newly created asymmetric key. After that, I opened up the key and inserted a new row, encrypting the value of the PasswordHintAnswer column. To view the decrypted data, I did not have to reopen the symmetric key. Instead, I called the DecryptByKeyAutoAsymKey function. The first argument of the function call was the asymmetric key ID of the asymmetric key:

```
SELECT CAST(
    DecryptByKeyAutoAsymKey
    (ASYMKEY_ID('asymBookSell_V2'),
```

The second parameter was for the asymmetric key password. Since the asymmetric key I created was by encrypted implicitly by the Database Master Key, I used a NULL value for the argument:

```
    NULL,
```

The third parameter was the encrypted column to be decrypted:

```
    PasswordHintAnswer) as varchar)
FROM dbo.PasswordHint
WHERE CustomerID = 45
```

The entire function call was wrapped in a CAST function in order to display the results in the varchar data type.

Transparent Data Encryption

SQL Server 2008 introduces Transparent Data Encryption, or TDE, which allows you to fully encrypt the database files without modifying application code. When a user database is available and has TDE enabled, encryption occurs at the page level when written to disk. Decryption takes place when the data page is read into memory. If the database files or database backup are stolen, they will not be accessible without the certificate originally used to encrypt it.

The following two recipes will demonstrate how to enable and maintain Transparent Data Encryption.

Enabling Transparent Data Encryption

In this recipe, I'll demonstrate how to enable Transparent Data Encryption for a user-defined database. The first step in preparing a database for TDE is to create a master key and certificate in the master system database:

```
USE master
GO

CREATE MASTER KEY ENCRYPTION
BY PASSWORD = '834BACDA-10E6-4BBC-A698-952533E54337'
GO

CREATE CERTIFICATE TDE_Server_Certificate
WITH SUBJECT = 'Server-level cert for TDE'
GO
```

Now that I have a server-level certificate, I will use it to encrypt the Database Encryption Key of the database where I want to enable TDE. The DEK is the encryption key that will actually be used to encrypt the entire database. The syntax is relatively straightforward, so I'll continue with the recipe and explain some of the options in more detail in the "How It Works" section. I execute the following command in the context of the user database that I wish to encrypt:

```
USE BookStore
GO

CREATE DATABASE ENCRYPTION KEY
WITH ALGORITHM = TRIPLE_DES_3KEY
ENCRYPTION BY SERVER CERTIFICATE TDE_Server_Certificate
GO
```

Now that I have defined the DEK, the last step in this recipe is to actually encrypt the database. This is set using the ALTER DATABASE command and the ENCRYPTION option:

```
ALTER DATABASE BookStore
SET ENCRYPTION ON
GO
```

To validate that the database is actually encrypted, I will execute the following query against sys.databases:

```
SELECT is_encrypted
FROM sys.databases
WHERE name = 'BookStore'
```

This returns 1 for true:

```
is_encrypted
1
```

How It Works

This recipe demonstrated each of the steps required to enable TDE for a database. In the first step of this recipe, I am assuming that the master key hasn't already been created for the master system database. Assuming not, I created it, along with a certificate that I would then use to encrypt the DEK.

I then switched the database context to the user-defined database and created the DEK. The first line of code is standard—I didn't need to define a specific name for the key:

```
CREATE DATABASE ENCRYPTION KEY
```

In the second line of the command, I define the algorithm strength. My choices were AES_128, AES_192, AES_256, and TRIPLE_DES_3KEY:

```
WITH ALGORITHM = TRIPLE_DES_3KEY
```

The last line of the command defined which server-level certificate (existing in the master database) I would use to encrypt the DEK:

```
ENCRYPTION BY SERVER CERTIFICATE TDE_Server_Certificate
GO
```

After the DEK was created for the BookStore database, I was then able to enable TDE using the ALTER DATABASE command. The first line defined the target database:

```
 ALTER DATABASE BookStore
```

The second line defined that encryption should be set to ON:

```
SET ENCRYPTION ON
GO
```

Once enabled, your data files "at rest" are encrypted. Without the server certificate used to encrypt the DEK, a stolen database cannot be restored or properly attached to another SQL Server instance, nor can the files themselves be hacked.

If a DBA wishes to legitimately move the database from one SQL Server instance to another, she can back up the server-level certificate and create it on the second server. This will allow the TDE backup to be restored or data/log files to be attached.

Managing and Removing TDE

This next recipe will demonstrate common tasks for managing and also removing TDE from a database.

In this first query, I will demonstrate regenerating the algorithm strength of the existing DEK. Originally, the DEK was defined as TRIPLE_DES_3KEY, but in this next query I will change this to use AES_128:

```
ALTER DATABASE ENCRYPTION KEY
REGENERATE WITH ALGORITHM = AES_128
```

To validate my change, I can query the new catalog view sys.dm_database_encryption_keys:

```
SELECT DB_NAME(database_id) databasenm,
       CASE encryption_state
           WHEN 0 THEN 'No encryption'
           WHEN 1 THEN 'Unencrypted'
           WHEN 2 THEN 'Encryption in progress'
           WHEN 3 THEN 'Encrypted'
           WHEN 4 THEN 'Key change in progress'
           WHEN 5 THEN 'Decryption in progress'
       END encryption_state,
       key_algorithm,
       key_length
FROM sys.dm_database_encryption_keys
```

This returns information on all databases and associated DEK status. Notice that there are two rows in the result set. The tempdb database is included in this, as it too must now encrypt data—since the encryption processing for any user databases can involve tempdb processing as well:

Databasenm	encryption_state	key_algorithm	key_length
Tempdb	Encrypted	AES	256
BookStore	Encrypted	AES	128

In addition to changing the algorithm of the DEK, I can also change the server-level certificate that I can use to encrypt the DEK (in case you feel that the server certificate was compromised or you must rotate it periodically):

```
USE master
GO

CREATE CERTIFICATE TDE_Server_Certificate_V2
WITH SUBJECT = 'Server-level cert for TDE V2'
GO

USE BookStore
GO

ALTER DATABASE ENCRYPTION KEY
ENCRYPTION BY SERVER CERTIFICATE TDE_Server_Certificate_V2
```

To remove TDE for the database, I execute the following command:

```
ALTER DATABASE BookStore
SET ENCRYPTION OFF
GO
```

At this point, I can clean up my work and drop the DEK (you may need to give SQL Server time to decrypt the data before removing the key—particularly for larger databases):

```
USE BookStore
GO

DROP DATABASE ENCRYPTION KEY
```

How It Works

This recipe demonstrated how to manage a database that is configured with TDE, along with its associated DEK. The DEK algorithm can be modified using the `ALTER DATABASE ENCRYPTION KEY` command. This command is also used if you wish to modify which server-level certificate (in the master database) is used to encrypt the DEK. To remove encryption, I used `ALTER DATABASE` and `SET ENCRYPTION OFF`. At that point, I was then able to drop the database DEK. If this was the last user-defined database using TDE on the SQL Server instance, the system database `tempdb` will revert to unencrypted after the SQL Server instance is restarted.

CHAPTER 20

■■■

Service Broker

Service Broker allows you to build asynchronous, database-driven messaging applications. Using Service Broker, application tasks can keep moving forward while messages are handled in their own required timeframe. Service Broker allows one database to send a message to another without waiting for a response, so the sending database will continue to function, even if the remote database cannot process the message immediately. Service Broker is reviewed in this book because it can be managed entirely by using SQL Server Transact-SQL objects and commands.

Service Broker provides message queuing for SQL Server. It provides a means for you to send an asynchronous, transactional message from within a database to a queue, where it will be picked up and processed by another service, possibly running on another database or server. Again, with asynchronous programs, a message is sent, and the application can proceed with other related tasks without waiting for confirmation that the original message was received or processed. Once the specific task is finished, the conversation between the two Service Broker services is explicitly ended by both sides.

Service Broker includes several out-of-the-box features that address complex factors you may often encounter when trying to build your own asynchronous messaging system. For example, Service Broker messages are guaranteed to be received in the *proper order*, or in the order in which they were initially sent. These messages are also only received *once* (the broker guarantees that there will be no duplicate reads) and can be sent as part of the same conversation, correlated to the same instance of a task. Another benefit of Service Broker is the guaranteed *delivery* of messages. If the target database (the recipient of the first message) isn't available when the first message transmission is attempted, the message will be queued on the initiator database (the sender of the first message), and an attempt will be made to send the message when the receiving database becomes available. These messages are also recoverable in the event of a database failure, as Service Broker is built within a SQL Server database and can be backed up along with the rest of the database.

This chapter will provide a high-level overview of Service Broker objects and commands by setting up the BookStore/BookDistribution Service Broker application, using a stored procedure to automatically process messages in a Service Broker queue, and enabling Service Broker applications to communicate remotely across SQL Server instances. For very active Service Broker applications, SQL Server 2008 introduces the ability to prioritize conversations using the CREATE BROKER PRIORITY command, which I will also demonstrate in this chapter. Using this functionality, you can designate the priority of less or more important conversations in order to make sure messages flow appropriately.

I'll finish the chapter with a review and demonstration of event notification functionality. Event notifications work with Service Broker to allow you to track database and SQL Server instance events, similar to SQL Trace—only unlike SQL Trace, the event notifications are asynchronous and have a minimal impact on overall SQL Server instance performance.

Example Scenario: Online Bookstore

In a hypothetical online bookstore, an order is placed by a customer for a book. The purchase is made and recorded to the BookStore database, which uses built-in Service Broker functionality to send a message to the BookDistribution database. The BookDistribution database is used by a separate application that handles warehouse stocking and distribution delivery. These two separate databases can exist on the same or different SQL Server instances.

Continuing with the hypothetical example, the BookStore database starts a *conversation* with the other database by submitting a book order message. This book order is sent to a *queue* on the BookDistribution database, where the receiving service program can either pick up the message right away or defer processing for a later time. The original transaction on the BookStore database is not held up because the communication is being conducted asynchronously. For example, the application can proceed with other tasks, such as sending an order confirmation to the customer or updating other dependent tables used within the hypothetical application. When the BookDistribution database is ready to process the order, Service Broker allows it to pluck the message from the queue, extract the message information, and process it accordingly. The BookDistribution program can then send a message back to the BookStore database confirming that the order was received, and then take its own actions to get the book sent to the customer.

Creating a Basic Service Broker Application

In this next set of recipes, I'll demonstrate setting up an application that places a book order in the BookStore database. This book order is sent asynchronously to the BookDistribution database on the same SQL Server instance. Once the BookDistribution database gets a chance to process it, BookDistribution will send an order confirmation response. The task is then finished, and the conversation between Service Broker services is ended.

The following is a general list of steps used to put together a Service Broker application when both databases reside on the same SQL Server instance:

1. Define the asynchronous tasks that you want your application to perform. Service Broker is ideal for applications that perform loosely coupled actions, such as triggering messages and responses that can span over several minutes, hours, or days, while still letting other application tasks move ahead with other actions.

2. Determine whether the Service Broker initiator and target services will be created on the same SQL Server instance or span two SQL Server instances. Multi-instance communication requires extra steps to establish authentication via certificates or NT security and to create endpoints, routes, and dialog security.

3. If not already enabled, set the ENABLE_BROKER and TRUSTWORTHY database options for the participating databases using ALTER DATABASE.

4. Create a Database Master Key for each participating database (see Chapter 19 for more on the Database Master Key).

5. Create the message types that you wish to be sent between services. *Message types* define the type of data contained within a message that is sent from a Service Broker endpoint (initiator service or target service). These should be added on *both* databases participating in the Service Broker application.

6. Create a contract to define the kinds of message types that can be sent by the initiator and the message types that can be sent by the target. Contracts define which message types can be sent or received at a task level. This contract should be added to *both* participating databases.

7. Create a queue on both participating databases to hold messages. A queue stores messages. You can query a queue with the SELECT statement or use the RECEIVE command to retrieve one or more messages from the queue. Each queue can also be defined with an activation stored procedure or application, which will automatically handle messages when they are received in the queue.

8. Create a service on both participating databases that binds the specific contract to a specific queue. A service defines the endpoint, which is used to bind a message queue to one or more contracts.

Once these steps are followed, you are ready to create new dialog conversations (a *dialog conversation* is the act of exchanging messages between services) and send/receive messages between the Service Broker services. The first recipe in this section will demonstrate how to enable SQL Server databases for Service Broker activity.

■**Tip** As you'll see in this chapter, several Service Broker commands require that if the statement isn't the first statement in the batch, the preceding statement must be terminated with a semicolon statement terminator.

Enabling Databases for Service Broker Activity

The demonstration starts in the master database, where ALTER DATABASE is used to ensure that both the ENABLE_BROKER and TRUSTWORTHY database setting are enabled for both participating databases:

```
USE master
GO

IF NOT EXISTS (SELECT name
                FROM sys.databases
                WHERE name = 'BookStore')

CREATE DATABASE BookStore
GO

IF NOT EXISTS (SELECT name
                FROM sys.databases
                WHERE name = 'BookDistribution')

CREATE DATABASE BookDistribution
GO

ALTER DATABASE BookStore SET ENABLE_BROKER
GO
ALTER DATABASE BookStore SET TRUSTWORTHY ON
GO


ALTER DATABASE BookDistribution SET ENABLE_BROKER
GO
ALTER DATABASE BookDistribution SET TRUSTWORTHY ON
GO
```

How It Works

This recipe used `ALTER DATABASE` to enable Service Broker activity for the database. To disable Service Broker, you can use the `DISABLE_BROKER` database option.

Creating the Database Master Key for Encryption

Service Broker uses dialog security when conversations span multiple databases. In order for this security to take effect, each participating database must have a Database Master Key.

In the `BookStore` database, a Database Master Key is created, in order to allow for encrypted messages between the two local databases:

```
USE BookStore
GO

CREATE MASTER KEY
ENCRYPTION BY PASSWORD = 'D4C86597'
GO
```

Now the same is done for the `BookDistribution` database:

```
USE BookDistribution
GO

CREATE MASTER KEY
ENCRYPTION BY PASSWORD = '50255686DDC5'
GO
```

How It Works

See Chapter 19 for details on how to create Database Master Keys for a database. In this case, I created one for each database participating in the Service Broker application.

Managing Message Types

Message types define the type of data contained within a message sent from a Service Broker endpoint (initiator or target). Think of a message type as the message template (but not the actual message), defining the name, owner, and type of message content.

The `CREATE MESSAGE TYPE` command is used to create a new message type. Its syntax is as follows:

```
CREATE MESSAGE TYPE message_type_name
[ AUTHORIZATION owner_name ]
[ VALIDATION =
{ NONE | EMPTY    |
WELL_FORMED_XML   |
VALID_XML WITH SCHEMA COLLECTION  schema_collection_name } ]
```

The arguments of this command are described in Table 20-1.

Table 20-1. *CREATE MESSAGE TYPE Arguments*

Argument	Description
message_type_name	This option defines the name of the message type.
owner_name	This argument specifies the database owner of the message type.

Argument	Description
NONE |EMPTY |WELL FORMED XML | VALID XML WITH SCHEMA COLLECTION schema_collection_name	These settings define the message validation. When NONE, no validation is performed. When EMPTY, the message body has to be NULL. When WELL FORMED XML is chosen, the body has to contain well-formed XML. When VALID XML WITH SCHEMA COLLECTION is chosen, the message body must conform to a specific XML schema.

Continuing with the online bookstore example, the first Service Broker objects created are the two message types that will be exchanged between the databases. The first is a message type that is used to send the book order:

```
Use BookStore
GO

CREATE MESSAGE TYPE [//SackConsulting/SendBookOrder]
VALIDATION = WELL_FORMED_XML
GO
```

The second message type will be sent by the target database to confirm that it has received the book order. Both message types will use a well-formed XML message body, which means that valid XML must be supplied as message content, but no schema-based validation will be performed on the message content:

```
CREATE MESSAGE TYPE [//SackConsulting/BookOrderReceived]
VALIDATION = WELL_FORMED_XML
GO
```

Now I'll change the database context to the BookDistribution database, and the same message types and contract that were created in the BookStore database are also created in the BookDistribution database. Without creating the same message types, the receiving database would not be able to accept the incoming message. Communication structures are a two-way street, with each side having to understand the messages to be exchanged in the dialog conversation:

```
USE BookDistribution
GO

CREATE MESSAGE TYPE [//SackConsulting/SendBookOrder]
VALIDATION = WELL_FORMED_XML
GO

CREATE MESSAGE TYPE [//SackConsulting/BookOrderReceived]
VALIDATION = WELL_FORMED_XML
GO
```

How It Works

In this recipe, two different recipe types were created in both databases that will participate in the online bookstore example. In the first line of code in the CREATE MESSAGE TYPE, the name was designated in square brackets. This is the name of the message type that will be used to send a book order message:

```
CREATE MESSAGE TYPE [//SackConsulting/SendBookOrder]
```

The message validation type was designated as well-formed XML:

```
VALIDATION = WELL_FORMED_XML
GO
```

Another message was created using the same validation type, this time with a different message type name. This is the message type that will be used to respond to book order messages:

```
CREATE MESSAGE TYPE [//SackConsulting/BookOrderReceived]
VALIDATION = WELL_FORMED_XML
GO
```

Notice that I don't actually define the contents of the message. The actual message is an instance of the message type and will be demonstrated in the "Initiating a Dialog" recipe.

Creating Contracts

Contracts define which message types can be sent or received at a task level. An example of a task could be "place a book order to the distribution center." Each task in your application should define a separate contract, based on the type of messages exchanged between the initiator of the conversation and the target. Contracts also define the intended direction of the message types (initiator to target, target to initiator).

To create a new contract, use the CREATE CONTRACT command. The abridged syntax is as follows:

```
CREATE CONTRACT contract_name
   [ AUTHORIZATION owner_name ]
( {    message_type_name }
SENT BY
{ INITIATOR | TARGET | ANY }
} [ ,...n] )
```

The arguments of this command are described in Table 20-2.

Table 20-2. *CREATE CONTRACT Arguments*

Argument	Description
contract_name	This defines the name of the new contract.
owner_name	This specifies the database owner of the contract.
message_type_name	This defines the name of the message type included in the contract.
INITIATOR | TARGET | ANY	The SENT BY options define which directions a message type can be sent. When INITIATOR, only the service that starts the conversation can send the specific message type. When TARGET, only the target of the conversation can send the specific message type. ANY allows the message to be sent by both the initiator and target.
[,...n]	More than one message type can be defined within the contract definition.

Continuing with the online bookstore example, a contract is created on the BookStore database that defines which messages can be sent by the initiator (BookStore database) or the target (BookDistribution database):

```
Use BookStore
GO
CREATE CONTRACT
    [//SackConsulting/BookOrderContract]
    ( [//SackConsulting/SendBookOrder]
```

```
            SENT BY INITIATOR,
        [//SackConsulting/BookOrderReceived]
            SENT BY TARGET
    )
GO
```

Now I'll switch context to the BookDistribution database and create the same contract:

```
USE BookDistribution
GO

CREATE CONTRACT
    [//SackConsulting/BookOrderContract]
    ( [//SackConsulting/SendBookOrder]
            SENT BY INITIATOR,
        [//SackConsulting/BookOrderReceived]
            SENT BY TARGET
    )
GO
```

How It Works

This recipe demonstrated creating a new contract in both the BookStore and BookDistribution databases. In order for the conversation to be successful, the contract definition must be identical for both the initiator and the target. The first argument of the CREATE CONTRACT command included the contract name:

```
CREATE CONTRACT
    [//SackConsulting/BookOrderContract]
```

In parentheses, the allowed message types created in the previous recipe are designated, along with a definition of which role can use a message type:

```
    ( [//SackConsulting/SendBookOrder]
            SENT BY INITIATOR,
        [//SackConsulting/BookOrderReceived]
            SENT BY TARGET
    )
GO
```

The BookStore database is where the [//SackConsulting/SendBookOrder] message will be sent from (the INITIATOR), and the BookDistribution database is from where the [//SackConsulting/BookOrderReceived] message will be sent (the TARGET).

Creating Queues

A queue stores messages. You can query a queue with a SELECT statement or use the RECEIVE command to retrieve one or more messages from the queue.

Upon creation, a queue can be bound to a stored procedure that will handle messages when they arrive (see the "Creating a Stored Procedure to Process Messages" section found later in the chapter). Retrieval programs can also be external to SQL Server (such as .NET-based programs); however, stored procedures provide an easy-to-implement solution.

To create a new queue, the CREATE QUEUE command is used. The syntax is as follows:

```
CREATE QUEUE <object>
    [ WITH
        [ STATUS = { ON | OFF }  [ , ] ]
```

```
[ RETENTION = { ON | OFF } [ , ] ]
[ ACTIVATION (
    [ STATUS = { ON | OFF } , ]
     PROCEDURE_NAME = <procedure> ,
     MAX_QUEUE_READERS = max_readers ,
     EXECUTE AS { SELF | 'user_name' | OWNER }
       ) ]
]
  [ ON { filegroup | [ DEFAULT ] } ] ]
```

The arguments of this command are described in Table 20-3.

Table 20-3. *CREATE QUEUE Arguments*

Argument	Description
object	This defines the database, schema, and associated name of the new queue.
STATUS = { ON	OFF }	When STATUS is ON, the queue is available for use. When OFF, messages can't be added or removed from the queue.
RETENTION = { ON	OFF }	When RETENTION is ON, received or sent messages for the queue are kept until the conversation is done (allowing a prolonged view of in-progress messages in the conversation). When OFF (which is the default), messages are not retained after being either sent or received (and retrieved). Retained messages are available for reporting within the queue, but without risk of duplicate sending or receiving.
STATUS	When ON, the designated stored procedure will be activated to receive messages (up to the number designated in the max_readers argument). When OFF, the stored procedure isn't activated for the queue.
PROCEDURE_NAME	This indicates the name of the stored procedure that will process [schema_name messages for the queue. This can be fully qualified, using the database name, schema, and stored procedure name.
MAX_QUEUE_READERS = max_readers	Multiple instances of the queue reader stored procedure can be activated at the same time, from 0 to 32767 instances.
EXECUTE AS	EXECUTE AS defines what database user account the stored procedure runs under. When SELF, it runs under the context of the current user. Otherwise, a specific user name can be designated.
ON { filegroup [DEFAULT] }	Like a table, a queue can be placed on a specific filegroup. If not explicitly designated, the queue is placed on the DEFAULT filegroup.

Continuing with the online bookstore application example, a queue is created in the BookStore database to hold incoming messages from the BookDistribution database. It is created with a status of enabled:

```
Use BookStore
GO

CREATE QUEUE BookStoreQueue
WITH STATUS=ON
GO
```

The CREATE QUEUE command also has activation options that allow you to bind a program to it for automatically processing messages. This will be demonstrated later on in the "Creating a Stored Procedure to Process Messages" section. But in the meantime, message exchanges from queues will be handled manually in this example.

Next, I'll create a new queue to the BookDistribution database for messages that will be received from the BookStore database:

```
USE BookDistribution
GO

CREATE QUEUE BookDistributionQueue
WITH STATUS=ON
GO
```

How It Works

In this example, a queue was created in both databases. The first queue created in BookStore was called BookStoreQueue:

```
CREATE QUEUE BookStoreQueue
```

The second line of code designated that the queue is created in an enabled state:

```
WITH STATUS=ON
```

The second queue was created in the BookDistribution database and used a different name, BookDistributionQueue. It too was created in an enabled state.

Creating Services

A service defines the endpoint, which is then used to bind a message queue to one or more contracts. Services make use of queues and contracts to define a task or set of tasks.

A service is both the initiator and the receiver of messages, enforcing the rules of the contract and routing the messages to the proper queue.

To create a new service, the CREATE SERVICE command is used. The abridged syntax is as follows:

```
CREATE SERVICE service_name
    [ AUTHORIZATION owner_name ]
    ON QUEUE [ schema_name. ]queue_name
    [ ( contract_name [ ,...n ] ) ]
```

The arguments of this command are described in Table 20-4.

Table 20-4. *CREATE SERVICE Arguments*

Argument	Description
service_name	The name of the new service.
owner_name	The owning database user or role of the service.
[schema_name.]queue_name	The name of the queue that receives messages.
contract_name [,...n]	The name of the contract(s) that can send messages to the new service. If none is designated, the new service can only initiate (and not receive) messages. If only an initiator, any contract can be used to send messages.

Continuing with the online bookstore example, a service is created in the BookStore database to bind the queue to a specific contract:

```
Use BookStore
GO

CREATE SERVICE [//SackConsulting/BookOrderService]
    ON QUEUE dbo.BookStoreQueue
    ([//SackConsulting/BookOrderContract])
GO
```

Now context is switched to the BookDistribution database, and a service is created to bind the queue to the contract:

```
USE BookDistribution
GO

CREATE SERVICE [//SackConsulting/BookDistributionService]
    ON QUEUE dbo.BookDistributionQueue
    ([//SackConsulting/BookOrderContract])
GO
```

How It Works

In this recipe, I created a service in both the BookStore and BookDistribution databases. The CREATE SERVICE command was used to bind a specific queue to a contract.

The first argument used in CREATE SERVICE for the BookStore service was the service name:

```
CREATE SERVICE [//SackConsulting/BookOrderService]
```

The second line of code designated the queue for which the contract will be bound (will accept messages from):

```
ON QUEUE dbo.BookStoreQueue
```

The third argument was the name of the contract bound to the queue and exposed by the service:

```
([//SackConsulting/BookOrderContract])
```

In the BookDistribution database, a service was created with a different service name and queue name, but was bound to the same contract as the service in the BookStore database:

```
CREATE SERVICE [//SackConsulting/BookDistributionService]
    ON QUEUE dbo.BookDistributionQueue
    ([//SackConsulting/BookOrderContract])
GO
```

Now that the messages, queues, contracts, and services have been created, you are ready to start communication between the two databases using Service Broker commands.

Initiating a Dialog

A *dialog conversation* is the act of exchanging messages between services. A new conversation is created using the BEGIN DIALOG CONVERSATION. Each new conversation generates a unique conversation handle of the uniqueidentifier data type.

The syntax is as follows:

```
BEGIN DIALOG [ CONVERSATION ] @dialog_handle
    FROM SERVICE initiator_service_name
    TO SERVICE 'target_service_name'
        [ , { 'service_broker_guid' | 'CURRENT DATABASE' } ]
    [ ON CONTRACT contract_name ]
    [ WITH
    [ { RELATED_CONVERSATION = related_conversation_handle
      | RELATED_CONVERSATION_GROUP = related_conversation_group_id } ]
    [ [ , ] LIFETIME = dialog_lifetime ]
    [ [ , ] ENCRYPTION = { ON | OFF } ] ]
```

The arguments of this command are described in Table 20-5.

Table 20-5. *BEGIN DIALOG Arguments*

Argument	Description
@dialog_handle	This specifies the uniqueidentifier data type local variable that is used to hold the new dialog handle.
initiator_service_name	This defines the service that initiates the conversation.
'target_service_name'	This indicates the target service that the initiating service will exchange messages with.
'service_broker_guid' | 'CURRENT DATABASE'	This specifies the service_broker_guid retrieved for the target service database from sys.databases. If CURRENT DATABASE is designated, the service_broker_guid is used from the current database.
contract_name	This defines the name of the contract that the conversation is based on.
related_conversation_handle	This indicates the uniqueidentifier value of the existing conversation group that the dialog belongs to.
related_conversation_group_id	This specifies the uniqueidentifier value of the existing conversation group that the new dialog is added to.
dialog_lifetime	This defines the number of seconds that the dialog is kept open.
ENCRYPTION = { ON | OFF }	When this is set to ON, encryption is used for messages sent outside of the initiator SQL Server instance.

The END CONVERSATION command finishes one side of the conversation. Messages can no longer be sent or received for the service that ends the conversation. Both services (initiator and target) must end the conversation in order for it to be completed.

The SEND command is used to send a message on a specific open conversation. In this command, the message type and message contents are also defined.

Continuing with the online bookstore example, and with the required objects established, I am now ready to initiate a dialog between the two Service Broker services.

On the BookStore database, I execute the following commands in a batch:

```
Use BookStore
GO

DECLARE @Conv_Handler uniqueidentifier
DECLARE @OrderMsg xml;

BEGIN DIALOG CONVERSATION @Conv_Handler
FROM SERVICE [//SackConsulting/BookOrderService]
TO SERVICE '//SackConsulting/BookDistributionService'
ON CONTRACT [//SackConsulting/BookOrderContract];

SET @OrderMsg =
'<order id="3439" customer="22" orderdate="7/15/2008">
<LineItem ItemNumber="1" ISBN="1-59059-592-0" Quantity="1" />
</order>';

SEND ON CONVERSATION @Conv_Handler
MESSAGE TYPE [//SackConsulting/SendBookOrder]
(@OrderMsg);
```

How It Works

In the previous batch of statements, two local variables were used to hold the dialog conversation handle and the order message XML document:

```
DECLARE @Conv_Handler uniqueidentifier
DECLARE @OrderMsg xml;
```

The BEGIN DIALOG CONVERSATION command was used to create a conversation between the two services, based on the established contract. The first argument passed was the @Conv_Handler local variable:

```
BEGIN DIALOG CONVERSATION @conv_handler
```

The initiator used to begin the dialog was designated in the second line and the target service in the third:

```
FROM SERVICE [//SackConsulting/BookOrderService]
TO SERVICE '//SackConsulting/BookDistributionService'
```

The contract name was then designated:

```
ON CONTRACT [//SackConsulting/BookOrderContract];
```

The @OrderMsg local variable was set to an XML document containing order and line item information:

```
SET @OrderMsg =
'<order id="3439" customer="22" orderdate="7/15/2008">
<LineItem ItemNumber="1" ISBN="1-59059-592-0" Quantity="1" />
</order>';
```

The SEND ON CONVERSATION command used the conversation handler local variable to send a message using the specified (and allowed) message type and the actual XML message content. The first argument in the command was the @Conv_Handler value populated from the BEGIN DIALOG CONVERSATION command:

```
SEND ON CONVERSATION @Conv_Handler
```

The second argument was the message type to be used, followed by the XML message in the local variable:

```
MESSAGE TYPE [//SackConsulting/SendBookOrder]
(@OrderMsg);
```

This message was then sent to the queue in the BookDistribution database.

Querying the Queue for Incoming Messages

Continuing with the online bookstore example, on the BookDistribution database, the queue is queried to view incoming messages using SELECT:

```
USE BookDistribution
GO

SELECT message_type_name, CAST(message_body as xml) message,
queuing_order, conversation_handle, conversation_group_id
FROM dbo.BookDistributionQueue
```

This returns the following result set (formatted for presentation):

Column	Value
Message_type_name	//SackConsulting/SendBookOrder
Message	<order id="3439" customer="22" orderdate="7/15/2008">
	<LineItem ItemNumber="1" ISBN="1-59059-592-0" Quantity="1" />
	</order>
Queuing_order	0
Conversation_handle	63558054-02EE-DC11-B4A4-0003FF25C9C5
Conversation_group_id	62558054-02EE-DC11-B4A4-0003FF25C9C5

How It Works

In this recipe, I demonstrated that you can SELECT from a queue the same way you would from a table. The data returned showed the message type, message contents, queuing order, and the uniqueidentifier values that designate the conversation's handle and group.

Receiving and Responding to a Message

The RECEIVE statement is used to read rows (messages) from the queue. Unlike a SELECT statement, RECEIVE can be used to remove the rows that have been read. The results of the RECEIVE can be populated into regular tables or used in local variables to perform other actions or send other Service Broker messages.

If the message is an xml data type message, Transact-SQL XQuery methods can be used to query the message contents by acting on the data according to your application needs (for example, by extracting the order ID or quantity of the product ordered).

Continuing with the online bookstore example in the BookDistribution database, I will create a new table to hold information about received book orders:

```
USE BookDistribution
GO

CREATE TABLE dbo.BookOrderReceived
    (BookOrderReceivedID int IDENTITY (1,1) NOT NULL,
    conversation_handle uniqueidentifier NOT NULL,
    conversation_group_id uniqueidentifier NOT NULL,
    message_body xml NOT NULL)
GO
```

To process the received message in the BookDistribution database, the RECEIVE command is used. This batch of statements (which are executed together) performs several actions:

```
-- Declare the local variables needed to hold the incoming message data
DECLARE @Conv_Handler uniqueidentifier
DECLARE @Conv_Group uniqueidentifier
DECLARE @OrderMsg xml
DECLARE @TextResponseMsg varchar(8000)
DECLARE @ResponseMsg xml
DECLARE @OrderID int;

-- Take the message from the queue, retrieving its values into the local variables
RECEIVE TOP(1)   @OrderMsg = message_body,
            @Conv_Handler = conversation_handle,
            @Conv_Group = conversation_group_id
FROM dbo.BookDistributionQueue;

-- Insert the local variable values into the new table
INSERT dbo.BookOrderReceived
(conversation_handle, conversation_group_id, message_body)
VALUES
(@Conv_Handler,@Conv_Group, @OrderMsg  )

-- Use XQuery against the received message to extract
-- the order ID, for use in the response message

SELECT @OrderID = @OrderMsg.value('(/order/@id)[1]', 'int' )

SELECT @TextResponseMsg =
    '<orderreceived id= "' +
    CAST(@OrderID as varchar(10)) +
    '"/>';

SELECT @ResponseMsg = CAST(@TextResponseMsg as xml);

-- Send the response message back to the initiator, using
-- the existing conversation handle
SEND ON CONVERSATION @Conv_Handler
MESSAGE TYPE [//SackConsulting/BookOrderReceived]
(@ResponseMsg );
```

How It Works

This recipe started off by creating a table to store the contents of the incoming Service Broker message. After that, six local variables were created to hold the incoming message data:

```
DECLARE @Conv_Handler uniqueidentifier
DECLARE @Conv_Group uniqueidentifier
DECLARE @OrderMsg xml
DECLARE @TextResponseMsg varchar(8000)
DECLARE @ResponseMsg xml
DECLARE @OrderID int;
```

The RECEIVE command was then used to return the message from the queue. The TOP clause in the first line designated the maximum number of messages to be returned, which in this case was 1:

```
RECEIVE TOP(1)
```

The next few lines populated the local variables with data from the message, similar to the way that you would perform a variable population using SELECT:

```
      @OrderMsg = message_body,
@Conv_Handler = conversation_handle,
    @Conv_Group = conversation_group_id
```

The last line of the RECEIVE command was the FROM clause referencing the queue where the message is found:

```
FROM dbo.BookDistributionQueue;
```

After that, an INSERT was performed, inserting a row containing values from the message body into a new table:

```
INSERT dbo.BookOrderReceived
(conversation_handle, conversation_group_id, message_body)
VALUES
(@Conv_Handler,@Conv_Group, @OrderMsg  )
```

An XQuery value method was used to retrieve the order ID from the stored xml data type data:

```
SELECT @OrderID = @OrderMsg.value
('(/order/@id)[1]', 'int' )
```

The value taken from the XQuery was then used to populate a local variable, embedding the value in an <orderreceived> XML element:

```
SELECT @TextResponseMsg =
    '<orderreceived id= "' +
    CAST(@OrderID as varchar(10)) +
    '"/>';
```

This variable was then converted to an xml data type in preparation for sending a response to the BookStore database:

```
SELECT @ResponseMsg = CAST(@TextResponseMsg as xml);
```

Using the existing conversation uniqueidentifier handle in the first line, a message is sent using SEND ON CONVERSATION. The second line includes the message type to send, and the local variable in parentheses the actual payload of the message:

```
SEND ON CONVERSATION @Conv_Handler
MESSAGE TYPE [//SackConsulting/BookOrderReceived]
(@ResponseMsg );
```

Ending a Conversation

A conversation involves both the sending and receiving of messages. This communication can continue for however many iterations are required by your application. Once a side is finished (initiator or target), you can notify the other side that you are done with the conversation by using the END CONVERSATION command.

In the previous recipe, an order confirmation was sent to BookStore based on an order message BookStore had sent. Continuing with the online bookstore example, I'll create a new table to store order confirmation information from the target service:

```
USE BookStore
GO

-- Create an order confirmation table
CREATE TABLE dbo.BookOrderConfirmation
    (BookOrderConfirmationID int IDENTITY (1,1) NOT NULL,
     conversation_handle uniqueidentifier NOT NULL,
     DateReceived datetime NOT NULL DEFAULT GETDATE(),
     message_body xml NOT NULL)
```

In the BookStore database, RECEIVE TOP is used to receive the response message and store it in the new table. Since the conversation for this particular BookOrder is complete once a response is received (when a dialog conversation should end depends on your own real-world task requirements), the END CONVERSATION command is used to notify the target database that it is done with its side of the conversation:

```
DECLARE @Conv_Handler uniqueidentifier
DECLARE @Conv_Group uniqueidentifier
DECLARE @OrderMsg xml
DECLARE @TextResponseMsg varchar(8000);

RECEIVE TOP(1)   @Conv_Handler = conversation_handle,
            @OrderMsg = message_body
FROM dbo.BookStoreQueue

INSERT dbo.BookOrderConfirmation
(conversation_handle, message_body)
VALUES (@Conv_Handler,@OrderMsg );

END CONVERSATION @Conv_Handler;
GO
```

On the BookDistribution database, the queue is checked again for new messages. When a conversation dialog is ended, an empty message with a message type name of http://schemas. microsoft.com/SQL/ServiceBroker/EndDialog is sent. This next batch of statements receives this message, and ends the conversation on its side if the message type is a dialog-ending message type:

```
USE BookDistribution
GO

DECLARE @Conv_Handler uniqueidentifier
DECLARE @Conv_Group uniqueidentifier
DECLARE @OrderMsg xml
DECLARE @message_type_name nvarchar(256);

RECEIVE TOP(1)   @Conv_Handler = conversation_handle,
        @OrderMsg = message_body,
```

```
            @message_type_name = message_type_name
FROM dbo.BookDistributionQueue

-- Both sides (initiator and target) must end the conversation

IF
@message_type_name = 'http://schemas.microsoft.com/SQL/ServiceBroker/EndDialog'
BEGIN
    END CONVERSATION @Conv_Handler;
END
```

I can check the status of conversations by querying the sys.conversation_endpoints view:

```
SELECT state_desc, conversation_handle
FROM sys.conversation_endpoints
```

This returns

state_desc	conversation_handle
CLOSED	237A7DD6-86FB-D911-AAF4-000FB522BF5A

How It Works

In this recipe, I demonstrated how to end an open conversation dialog. I began by creating a table to hold order confirmations in the BookStore database received by the BookDistribution database. After that, RECEIVE TOP(1) was used to grab the latest message from BookDistribution from the BookStoreQueue. The contents of the message were then inserted into the BookOrderConfirmation table. The conversation was then ended using END CONVERSATION and the uniqueidentifier value for the specific conversation:

```
END CONVERSATION @Conv_Handler;
```

Ending a conversation automatically sends a message type of http://schemas.microsoft.com/ SQL/ServiceBroker/EndDialog to the target database. Back on the BookDistribution database, the queue was checked again for new messages. RECEIVE TOP(1) was used to retrieve the latest response from the BookStore database. An IF statement was used to verify whether the message received was an END DIALOG request:

```
IF
@message_type_name =
'http://schemas.microsoft.com/SQL/ServiceBroker/EndDialog'
```

If it was, the conversation was also ended on the target database (BookDistribution):

```
BEGIN
    END CONVERSATION @Conv_Handler;
END
```

The status of conversations was then checked by querying the sys.conversation_endpoints view, which confirmed that the conversation was indeed CLOSED.

This entire section of recipes demonstrated a simple message exchange application used to send a book order message to a book distribution handling database. A book order was sent from the initiator, a response was sent back, and the conversation was ended using END CONVERSATION on both databases. Of course, a real-world scenario will involve more tasks, which may in turn translate to additional message types, contracts, services, and queues. Ideal tasks for Service Broker are those that can benefit from the asynchronous capabilities that prevent application holdups and bottlenecks.

Prioritizing Service Broker Conversations

For very active Service Broker applications, SQL Server 2008 introduces the ability to prioritize conversations using the CREATE BROKER PRIORITY command. Using this functionality, you can designate the priority of less or more important conversations in order to make sure messages flow appropriately.

In order to take advantage of this functionality, the Service Broker databases involved in the conversation must first have the new HONOR_BROKER_PRIORITY option enabled. In the first query of this recipe, I'll demonstrate enabling this option for both databases in my Service Broker application:

```
ALTER DATABASE BookStore
SET HONOR_BROKER_PRIORITY ON

ALTER DATABASE BOOKDistribution
SET HONOR_BROKER_PRIORITY ON
```

I can confirm that the database changes were made by querying sys.databases:

```
SELECT name, is_honor_broker_priority_on
FROM sys.databases
WHERE name IN ('BookStore', 'BookDistribution')
```

This returns

name	is_honor_broker_priority_on
BookStore	1
BookDistribution	1

Now I can use the CREATE BROKER PRIORITY command to define priorities for specified conversations based on the local service name, remote service name (more on remote services later), and the contract name. The priority level itself is a number between 1 and 10, where 1 is the lowest priority and 10 the highest. The default value for conversation priority is 5.

In this recipe, I'll demonstrate setting the priority level of a conversation to 10 based on a specified contract and local service:

```
USE BookStore
GO

CREATE BROKER PRIORITY Conv_Priority_BookOrderContract_BookOrderService
FOR CONVERSATION
SET (CONTRACT_NAME = [//SackConsulting/BookOrderContract],
    LOCAL_SERVICE_NAME = [//SackConsulting/BookOrderService],
    REMOTE_SERVICE_NAME = ANY,
    PRIORITY_LEVEL = 10)
```

Notice that I used the value of ANY for the REMOTE_SERVICE_NAME. ANY can be used as a value for the contract, local service, or remote service, and in this case indicates that the priority should be associated with any service or contract that is associated with the Service Broker endpoint.

Next, I can confirm the broker priority I just created by querying the sys.conversation_priorities catalog view:

```
SELECT name, priority, service_contract_id,
       local_service_id,remote_service_name
FROM sys.conversation_priorities cp
```

This returns

name	priority	service_contract_id	local_service_id	remote_service_name
Conv_Priority_BookOrderContract_ BookOrderService	10	65536	65536	NULL

You can associate the service and contract IDs returned from sys.conversation_priorities to the sys.service_contracts and sys.services catalog views, if you wish to also include the service and contract names.

Next, I'll also create a broker priority definition in the BookDistribution database in order to cover the priority of bidirectional communication:

```
USE BookDistribution
GO

CREATE BROKER PRIORITY Conv_Priority_BookOrderContract_BookDistributionService
FOR CONVERSATION
SET (CONTRACT_NAME = [//SackConsulting/BookOrderContract],
    LOCAL_SERVICE_NAME = [//SackConsulting/BookDistributionService],
    REMOTE_SERVICE_NAME = ANY,
    PRIORITY_LEVEL = 10)
```

I can modify an existing broker priority using the ALTER BROKER PRIORITY command. In this next query, I will change the remote service setting from ANY to that of a specific remote service:

```
USE BookStore
GO

ALTER BROKER PRIORITY Conv_Priority_BookOrderContract_BookOrderService
FOR CONVERSATION
SET (REMOTE_SERVICE_NAME = '//SackConsulting/BookDistributionService')
```

I can also use the ALTER BROKER PRIORITY command to change the broker priority:

```
ALTER BROKER PRIORITY Conv_Priority_BookOrderContract_BookOrderService
FOR CONVERSATION
SET (PRIORITY_LEVEL = 9)
```

To remove a broker priority definition, I use the DROP BROKER PRIORITY command as demonstrated here:

```
DROP BROKER PRIORITY Conv_Priority_BookOrderContract_BookOrderService
```

How It Works

In this recipe, I demonstrated how to define Service Broker conversation priorities. Before doing this, I had to enable the HONOR_BROKER_PRIORITY database option in the participating databases. When enabled, this option allows messages in Service Broker dialogs to be sent based on any broker priority rules defined.

After enabling the database option, I used the CREATE BROKER PRIORITY command to define a higher prioritization based on specific conversation qualities. Walking through the code I executed, the first line defined the name of the broker priority object:

```
CREATE BROKER PRIORITY Conv_Priority_BookOrderContract_BookOrderService
FOR CONVERSATION
```

Next, the SET statement has open parenthesis followed by the contract, local service, remote service, and priority arguments:

```
SET (CONTRACT_NAME = [//SackConsulting/BookOrderContract],
    LOCAL_SERVICE_NAME = [//SackConsulting/BookOrderService],
    REMOTE_SERVICE_NAME = ANY,
    PRIORITY_LEVEL = 10)
```

Once created, any message sent within a conversation dialog in the BookOrderContract contract and BookOrderService local service would be given a priority level of 10 (higher than the default value of 5).

I then created a second broker priority for the target service to handle conversation dialog traffic back to the initiating service. Lastly, I demonstrated how to modify the existing broker priority definition using ALTER BROKER PRIORITY and also demonstrated how to remove it using DROP BROKER PRIORITY.

For very active Service Broker applications, conversation prioritization allows you to control the importance of various conversations across contracts and services.

Creating a Stored Procedure to Process Messages

In the previous block of recipes, ad hoc Transact-SQL batches were used to process incoming messages from the queue. You can, however, create service programs using stored procedures or external applications to *automatically* activate and process messages in the queue. Using the CREATE QUEUE and ALTER QUEUE options, you can also designate the number of simultaneous and identical service programs that can be activated to process incoming messages on the same queue.

Creating the Bookstore Stored Procedure

Using the previous recipe's existing objects for setting up the stored procedure application, this example creates a stored procedure used to process incoming messages on the dbo. BookDistributionQueue. This procedure uses several of the RECEIVE and SEND commands employed in the previous recipe, only tailored to a stored procedure implementation:

```
USE BookDistribution
GO

CREATE PROCEDURE dbo.usp_SB_ReceiveOrders
AS

DECLARE @Conv_Handler uniqueidentifier
DECLARE @Conv_Group uniqueidentifier
DECLARE @OrderMsg xml
DECLARE @TextResponseMsg varchar(8000)
DECLARE @ResponseMsg xml
DECLARE @Message_Type_Name nvarchar(256);
DECLARE @OrderID int;

-- XACT_ABORT automatically rolls back the transaction when a runtime error occurs
SET XACT_ABORT ON

BEGIN TRAN;

    RECEIVE TOP(1)    @OrderMsg = message_body,
                @Conv_Handler = conversation_handle,
                @Conv_Group = conversation_group_id,
                @Message_Type_Name = message_type_name
    FROM dbo.BookDistributionQueue;
```

```
IF @Message_Type_Name = '//SackConsulting/SendBookOrder'
BEGIN
    INSERT dbo.BookOrderReceived
    (conversation_handle, conversation_group_id, message_body)
    VALUES
    (@Conv_Handler,@Conv_Group, @OrderMsg  )

    SELECT @OrderID = @OrderMsg.value('(/order/@id)[1]', 'int' )

    SELECT @TextResponseMsg =
        '<orderreceived id= "' +
        CAST(@OrderID as varchar(10)) +
        '"/>';

    SELECT @ResponseMsg = CAST(@TextResponseMsg as xml);

    SEND ON CONVERSATION @Conv_Handler
    MESSAGE TYPE [//SackConsulting/BookOrderReceived]
    (@ResponseMsg );
END

IF @Message_Type_Name = 'http://schemas.microsoft.com/SQL/ServiceBroker/EndDialog'
BEGIN
    END CONVERSATION @Conv_Handler;
END

COMMIT TRAN

GO
```

The procedure contains logic for processing the //SackConsulting/SendBookOrder and http://schemas.microsoft.com/SQL/ServiceBroker/EndDialog message types. If the latter is sent, the specific conversation for the specific conversation handle is ended. If a book order message type is received, its information is inserted into a table, and an order confirmation is returned.

You can modify an existing queue by using the ALTER QUEUE command. This command uses the same options as CREATE QUEUE, which allows you to change the status and retention of the queue, the stored procedure to be activated, the maximum number of queue reader stored procedure instances, and the security contact of the procedure.

ALTER QUEUE includes one additional parameter, DROP, which is used to drop all stored procedure activation settings for the queue.

To bind our stored procedure to an existing queue, the ALTER QUEUE command is used:

```
ALTER QUEUE dbo.BookDistributionQueue
WITH ACTIVATION (STATUS = ON,
            PROCEDURE_NAME = dbo.usp_SB_ReceiveOrders,
            MAX_QUEUE_READERS = 2,
            EXECUTE AS SELF)
```

I designated the procedure name, followed by the maximum number of simultaneous implementations of the same stored procedure that can independently process distinct messages from the queue.

To test the new service program on the BookStore database, a new conversation is started and a new order placed:

```
Use BookStore
GO

DECLARE @Conv_Handler uniqueidentifier
DECLARE @OrderMsg xml;

BEGIN DIALOG CONVERSATION @conv_handler
FROM SERVICE [//SackConsulting/BookOrderService]
TO SERVICE '//SackConsulting/BookDistributionService'
ON CONTRACT [//SackConsulting/BookOrderContract];

SET @OrderMsg =
'<order id="3490" customer="29" orderdate="7/22/2008">
<LineItem ItemNumber="1" ISBN="1-59059-592-0" Quantity="2" />
</order>';

SEND ON CONVERSATION @Conv_Handler
MESSAGE TYPE [//SackConsulting/SendBookOrder]
(@OrderMsg);
```

If the stored procedure on the target queue did its job and activated upon receipt of the new message, there should already be an order confirmation returned back into the dbo.BookStoreQueue:

```
SELECT conversation_handle, CAST(message_body as xml) message
FROM dbo.BookStoreQueue
```

This returns the following results:

conversation_handle	message
20E768EB-8EFB-D911-AAF4-000FB522BF5A	<orderreceived id="3490" />

How It Works

In this recipe, a stored procedure was created to handle messages in the queue. That stored procedure was bound to the queue using ALTER QUEUE. The first argument of this command was the name of the queue to be modified:

```
ALTER QUEUE dbo.BookDistributionQueue
```

The WITH ACTIVATION clause first designated that the status of the new application (the stored procedure) program is available to receive new messages:

```
WITH ACTIVATION (STATUS = ON,
```

Next, the name of the stored procedure bound to the queue is designated:

```
        PROCEDURE_NAME = dbo.usp_SB_ReceiveOrders,
```

The MAX QUEUE READERS option is used to designate a maximum of two stored procedure applications executing simultaneously:

```
        MAX_QUEUE_READERS = 2,
```

The EXECUTE AS argument was designated as SELF, meaning that the stored procedure will execute with the same permissions as the principal who executed the ALTER QUEUE command:

```
        EXECUTE AS SELF)
```

When the queue STATUS = ON and a new message arrives in the queue, the stored procedure is executed to handle the incoming message(s). You can use internal stored procedures or external applications to handle incoming messages to a queue. The benefit of using stored procedures, however, is that they provide a simple, encapsulated component for handling messages and automatically performing any required responses and associated business tasks.

Remote-Server Service Broker Implementations

To demonstrate the basics of setting up a Service Broker program, the examples in this chapter have involved two databases on the same SQL Server instance. In most cases, however, you'll be setting up Service Broker to work with multiple databases that exist on two or more SQL Server instances. The core components from this chapter remain the same, but to achieve cross-server communication, a few extra steps are required. Cross-server communication can be achieved through using either Windows authentication or certificate-based authentication (which is what you'll see demonstrated here in this chapter). These steps will be demonstrated in this next batch of recipes.

The following is a general list of tasks that I'll go through in this section to enable Service Broker communication across SQL Server instances:

1. *Enable transport security*: Transport security in Service Broker refers to the network connections between two SQL Server instances, enabling or restricting encrypted communication between them. This is set up in the master system databases of both SQL Server instances and, as you'll see, involves creating endpoints, certificates, logins, and users.

2. *Enable dialog security*: Dialog security for Service Broker provides authentication, authorization, and encryption for dialog conversations. On the actual databases used for the Service Broker implementation, certificates are created and their public keys exchanged between SQL Server instances. Users are created that are not associated to a login, but are instead given authorization to the certificate created from the public key of the other SQL Server instance.

3. *Create routes*: A route is used by Service Broker to determine where a service is located, be it local or remote.

4. *Create remote service bindings*: A remote service binding is used to map the security credentials used to open a conversation with a remote Service Broker service.

In this cross-server scenario, the online bookstore Service Broker program will use the BookStore database on the JOEPROD SQL Server instance, and the BookDistribution database on the JOEPROD\NODE2 SQL Server instance. Objects from the previous set of recipes will be used to demonstrate this functionality. Starting from scratch (if you happen to be following along), the example database is dropped and re-created with the BookStore database on JOEPROD and BookDistribution on JOEPROD\NODE2. The following objects and settings are then created and configured on the BookStore database of the JOEPROD instance:

```
USE master
GO

-- Enable Service Broker for the database

ALTER DATABASE BookStore SET ENABLE_BROKER
GO

ALTER DATABASE BookStore SET TRUSTWORTHY ON
GO
```

```
USE BookStore
GO

-- Create the messages

CREATE MESSAGE TYPE [//SackConsulting/SendBookOrder]
VALIDATION = WELL_FORMED_XML
GO

CREATE MESSAGE TYPE [//SackConsulting/BookOrderReceived]
VALIDATION = WELL_FORMED_XML
GO

-- Create the contract

CREATE CONTRACT
    [//SackConsulting/BookOrderContract]
    ( [//SackConsulting/SendBookOrder]
        SENT BY INITIATOR,
      [//SackConsulting/BookOrderReceived]
        SENT BY TARGET
    )
GO

-- Create the queue

CREATE QUEUE BookStoreQueue
WITH STATUS=ON
GO

-- Create the service

CREATE SERVICE [//SackConsulting/BookOrderService]
    ON QUEUE dbo.BookStoreQueue
    ([//SackConsulting/BookOrderContract])
GO
```

On the BookDistribution database of the JOEPROD\NODE2 instance, the following objects are set up:

```
USE master
GO

IF NOT EXISTS (SELECT name
                FROM sys.databases
                WHERE name = 'BookDistribution')

CREATE DATABASE BookDistribution
GO

-- Enable Service Broker for the database

ALTER DATABASE BookDistribution SET ENABLE_BROKER
GO

ALTER DATABASE BookDistribution SET TRUSTWORTHY ON
GO
```

```
USE BookDistribution
GO

-- Create the messages

CREATE MESSAGE TYPE [//SackConsulting/SendBookOrder]
VALIDATION = WELL_FORMED_XML
GO

CREATE MESSAGE TYPE [//SackConsulting/BookOrderReceived]
VALIDATION = WELL_FORMED_XML
GO

-- Create the contract

CREATE CONTRACT
    [//SackConsulting/BookOrderContract]
    ( [//SackConsulting/SendBookOrder]
        SENT BY INITIATOR,
     [//SackConsulting/BookOrderReceived]
        SENT BY TARGET
    )
GO

-- Create the queue

CREATE QUEUE BookDistributionQueue
WITH STATUS=ON
GO

-- Create the service

CREATE SERVICE [//SackConsulting/BookDistributionService]
    ON QUEUE dbo.BookDistributionQueue
    ([//SackConsulting/BookOrderContract])
GO
```

Enabling Transport Security

Transport security in Service Broker refers to the network connections between two SQL Server instances, and the enabling or restricting of encrypted communication between them. Transport security is at the SQL Server instance level, and therefore this recipe demonstrates creating objects in the master database of both SQL Server instances. You can choose from two forms of transport security: Windows authentication or certificate-based security.

This recipe includes several steps that involve working with objects that should be familiar to you from the previous chapters. Each of these steps requires activities on both SQL Server instances (this example includes JOEPROD and JOEPROD\NODE2). For this recipe, I'll only use the master system database, not the actual user databases, because transport security applies to the SQL Server instance itself.

I begin this recipe by creating a Database Master Key in the master system database of each of the SQL Server instances. This is created in order to encrypt the certificate used for certificate-based transport security:

```
-- Executed on JOEPROD
USE master
GO

CREATE MASTER KEY ENCRYPTION BY PASSWORD = '1294934A!'

-- Executed on JOEPROD\NODE2
USE master
GO

CREATE MASTER KEY ENCRYPTION BY PASSWORD = '1294934B!'
```

Next, I will create a new certificate in the master system database of each of the SQL Server instances:

```
-- Executed on JOEPROD
CREATE CERTIFICATE JOEPRODMasterCert
   WITH SUBJECT = 'JOEPROD Transport Security SB',
   EXPIRY_DATE = '10/1/2010'
GO

-- Executed on JOEPROD\NODE2
CREATE CERTIFICATE Node2MasterCert
   WITH SUBJECT = 'Node 2 Transport Security SB',
   EXPIRY_DATE = '10/1/2010'
GO
```

Next, I will back up each of these certificates to a file. The public key backup files will then be copied over for use in creating a certificate in the master database of the other SQL Server instance (this happens later in the recipe):

```
-- Executed on JOEPROD
BACKUP CERTIFICATE JOEPRODMasterCert
TO FILE = 'C:\Apress\JOEPRODMasterCert.cer'
GO

-- Executed on JOEPROD\NODE2
BACKUP CERTIFICATE Node2MasterCert
TO FILE = 'C:\Apress\Node2MasterCert.cer'
GO
```

On each SQL Server instance, I'll create a Service Broker endpoint. Both endpoints will use certificate-based authentication and will require encrypted communication.

```
-- Executed on JOEPROD

CREATE ENDPOINT SB_JOEPROD_Endpoint
STATE = STARTED
AS TCP
(LISTENER_PORT = 4020)
FOR SERVICE_BROKER
(AUTHENTICATION = CERTIFICATE JOEPRODMasterCert,
  ENCRYPTION = REQUIRED)
GO

-- Executed on JOEPROD\NODE2
```

```
CREATE ENDPOINT SB_NODE2_Endpoint
STATE = STARTED
AS TCP
(LISTENER_PORT = 4021)
FOR SERVICE_BROKER
(AUTHENTICATION = CERTIFICATE Node2MasterCert,
  ENCRYPTION = REQUIRED)
GO
```

On each SQL Server instance, I'll create a new login and user in the master system database that will be used for remote connections from the other SQL Server instance:

```
-- Executed on JOEPROD
CREATE LOGIN SBLogin
    WITH PASSWORD = 'Used4TransSec'
GO

CREATE USER SBUser
    FOR LOGIN SBLogin
GO

-- Executed on JOEPROD\NODE2

CREATE LOGIN SBLogin
    WITH PASSWORD = 'Used4TransSec'
GO

CREATE USER SBUser
    FOR LOGIN SBLogin
GO
```

Next, I will grant CONNECT permissions to the associated endpoint for each SQL Server instance's login:

```
-- Executed on JOEPROD

GRANT CONNECT ON Endpoint::SB_JOEPROD_Endpoint TO SBLogin
GO

-- Executed on JOEPROD\NODE2

GRANT CONNECT ON Endpoint::SB_NODE2_Endpoint TO SBLogin
GO
```

On each SQL Server instance, a new certificate is created based on the certificate backup created in the other SQL Server instance. The newly created login and user created in the previous step is given authorization permissions over this certificate:

```
-- Executed on JOEPROD

CREATE CERTIFICATE Node2MasterCert
AUTHORIZATION SBUser
FROM FILE = 'C:\Apress\Node2MasterCert.cer'
GO

-- Executed on JOEPROD\NODE2
```

```
CREATE CERTIFICATE JOEPRODMasterCert
AUTHORIZATION SBUser
FROM FILE = 'C:\Apress\JOEPRODMasterCert.cer'
GO
```

How It Works

In this recipe, I walked through the various steps required to establish transport security through certificates. The recipe started off by creating a Database Master Key that would be used to encrypt the certificates (as a requirement for Service Broker endpoints—if using certificate-based security, the certificate can't be password encrypted).

A certificate was created on each SQL Server instance and was then backed up and copied to the other SQL Server instance. This exchange of public keys will be used later on in this section. In the meantime, Service Broker endpoints were created on each SQL Server instance, and were configured to allow access from other servers based on certificate security.

After that, a login and user were created on both SQL Server instances. The login was granted CONNECT permissions to the endpoint. This is not enough to enable connectivity though, because that user must also have access to the public key of the certificate used on the other SQL Server instance. This permission was granted in order to exchange the keys with the other server. The new certificates were then bound to the newly created user on each instance. Because the user has permissions to the certificate of the other SQL Server instance, and because the endpoint is based on that certificate, the SQL Server instances will have encrypted transport security access to one another.

This is only half the requirement for allowing cross-server communication with Service Broker. The next step is dialog security at the user database level, which I demonstrate in the next recipe.

Enabling Dialog Security

Whereas transport security handles communication at the SQL Server instance level, dialog security for Service Broker provides authentication, authorization, and encryption for dialog conversations. Like the previous recipe, setting up dialog security involves several small steps, many of which involve commands that have been covered in previous chapters of this book.

These recipes will take place in the BookStore database on the JOEPROD SQL Server instance and in the BookDistribution database on the NODE2 SQL Server instance. A certificate is created on each SQL Server instance (which requires a Database Master Key in each database, which you created at the beginning of this section). Later on, the certificates will be exchanged across SQL Server instances similarly to the previous transport security recipe:

```
-- Executed on JOEPROD
USE BookStore
GO

CREATE MASTER KEY ENCRYPTION BY PASSWORD = '1294934A!'
GO

CREATE CERTIFICATE BookStoreCert
    WITH SUBJECT = 'BookStore SB cert',
    EXPIRY_DATE = '10/1/2010'
GO

-- Executed on NODE2
USE BookDistribution
GO
```

```
CREATE MASTER KEY ENCRYPTION BY PASSWORD = '1294934B!'
GO

CREATE CERTIFICATE BookDistributionCert
    WITH SUBJECT = 'BookDistributionCert SB cert',
    EXPIRY_DATE = '10/1/2010'
GO
```

Next, the certificates from each of the databases are backed up to file:

```
-- Executed on JOEPROD
USE BookStore
GO

BACKUP CERTIFICATE BookStoreCert
TO FILE = 'C:\Apress\BookStoreCert.cer'
GO

-- Executed on NODE2
USE BookDistribution
GO

BACKUP CERTIFICATE BookDistributionCert
TO FILE = 'C:\Apress\BookDistributionCert.cer'
GO
```

After that, I will create a user in each database. Neither user will be associated to a login. Instead, later on, I'll map each user to the public certificate of the other SQL Server instance:

```
-- Executed on JOEPROD
USE BookStore
GO

CREATE USER BookDistributionUser
WITHOUT LOGIN
GO

-- Executed on NODE2
USE BookDistribution
GO

CREATE USER BookStoreUser
WITHOUT LOGIN
GO
```

Next, I'll create a new certificate in each database based on the other database's certificate public key. The newly created user in each database is given authorization to this certificate:

```
-- Executed on JOEPROD
USE BookStore
GO

CREATE CERTIFICATE BookDistributionCert
AUTHORIZATION BookDistributionUser
FROM FILE = 'C:\Apress\BookDistributionCert.cer'
GO
```

```
-- Executed on NODE2
USE BookDistribution
GO

CREATE CERTIFICATE BookStoreCert
AUTHORIZATION BookStoreUser
FROM FILE = 'C:\Apress\BookStoreCert.cer'
GO
```

Lastly, the users for both databases need permissions to SEND rights on the associated Service Broker services:

```
-- Executed on JOEPROD
USE BookStore
GO

GRANT SEND ON
SERVICE::[//SackConsulting/BookOrderService] TO BookDistributionUser
GO

-- Executed on NODE2
USE BookDistribution
GO

GRANT SEND ON
SERVICE::[//SackConsulting/BookDistributionService]
TO BookStoreUser
```

How It Works

In this recipe, I demonstrated setting up dialog security, which handles authentication, authorization, and encryption between the two user-defined databases in a Service Broker application.

The first step included creating a Database Master Key in each database, which was then used to implicitly encrypt the certificates created in the BookStore and BookDistribution databases. After creating the certificates, a backup was made of each one, and the associated file was then copied to the other server.

After that, a new user was created in each database without an associated login. A new certificate was then created in each database based on the other database's certificate. The certificate creation included an AUTHORIZATION clause, which designated the new user in each database.

Lastly, the two users were each granted permissions to SEND messages to their associated Service Broker services.

This leaves only a couple more steps before the Service Broker application can begin communicating across SQL Server instances.

Creating Routes and Remote Service Bindings

Once the transport and dialog security objects are taken care of, the next step in this distributed online bookstore example is to set up routes and remote service bindings.

A route is used by Service Broker to determine where a service is located, be it local or remote. A route is created using the CREATE ROUTE command. The syntax is as follows:

```
CREATE ROUTE route_name
[ AUTHORIZATION owner_name ]
WITH
   [ SERVICE_NAME = 'service_name', ]
```

```
[ BROKER_INSTANCE = 'broker_instance_identifier' , ]
[ LIFETIME = route_lifetime , ]
ADDRESS =  'next_hop_address'
[ , MIRROR_ADDRESS = 'next_hop_mirror_address' ]
```

The arguments for this command are described in Table 20-6.

Table 20-6. *CREATE ROUTE Arguments*

Argument	Description
route_name	This option defines the new route name.
AUTHORIZATION owner_name	This option specifies the database principal owner of the route.
SERVICE_NAME = 'service_name'	This option defines the name of the remote service to be routed to.
BROKER_INSTANCE = 'broker_instance_identifier'	This option specifies the service_broker_ guid (from sys.databases) of the database hosting the target service.
LIFETIME = route_lifetime	This option allows you to designate for how many seconds a route is considered by SQL Server before it expires.
ADDRESS = 'next_hop_address'	This option defines the DNS, NetBios, or TCP/IP address of SQL Server instance housing the service. It also includes the port number of the Service Broker endpoint using a syntax of TCP://{ dns_name | netbios_name | ip_address } : port_number.
MIRROR_ADDRESS = 'next_hop_mirror_address'	If using database mirroring, this option allows you to specify the address for the mirrored database using the syntax of TCP://{ dns_name | netbios_name | ip_address } : port_number.

In this recipe's example, a route is created on JOEPROD that points to the NODE2 Service Broker endpoint (listening on port 4021) and references the BookDistribution database's //SackConsulting/BookDistributionService service:

```
-- Executed on JOEPROD
USE BookStore
GO

CREATE ROUTE Route_BookDistribution
WITH SERVICE_NAME = '//SackConsulting/BookDistributionService',
ADDRESS = 'TCP://192.168.0.105:4021'
GO
```

On NODE2, a route is created that points to the JOEPROD Service Broker endpoint (listening on port 4020), and referencing the BookStore database's //SackConsulting/BookStoreService service:

```
-- Executed on NODE2
USE BookDistribution
GO
```

```
CREATE ROUTE Route_BookStore
WITH SERVICE_NAME = '//SackConsulting/BookOrderService',
ADDRESS = 'TCP://192.168.0.105:4020'
GO
```

A remote service binding is used to map the security credentials used to open a conversation with a remote Service Broker service. Specifically, you use a remote service binding with the user that you created in the previous recipe (the one mapped to a certificate). A remote service binding is created using the CREATE REMOTE SERVICE BINDING command. The syntax is as follows:

```
CREATE REMOTE SERVICE BINDING binding_name
    [ AUTHORIZATION owner_name ]
    TO SERVICE 'service_name'
    WITH  USER = user_name [ , ANONYMOUS = { ON | OFF } ]
```

The arguments for this command are described in Table 20-7.

Table 20-7. *CREATE REMOTE SERVICE BINDING Arguments*

Argument	Description
binding_name	This option specifies the name of the new remote service binding.
AUTHORIZATION owner_name	This option defines the database principal owner of the binding.
service_name	This option indicates the name of the remote service to bind to.
USER = user_name	This option designates the database user that is mapped to the remote service's certificate.
ANONYMOUS = { ON	OFF }	When this option is ON, anonymous authentication under the context of the public fixed database role is used to connect to the remote database.

In this example on JOEPROD, a binding is made on BookStore to the //SackConsulting/BookDistributionService service, using the BookStore user that was mapped to the BookDistribution database's public certificate:

```
USE BookStore
GO

CREATE REMOTE SERVICE BINDING BookDistributionBinding
    TO SERVICE '//SackConsulting/BookDistributionService'
    WITH USER =  BookDistributionUser
GO
```

On NODE2, a similar binding is made in the BookDistribution database, only this time pointing to the //SackConsulting/BookOrderService service:

```
USE BookDistribution
GO

CREATE REMOTE SERVICE BINDING BookStoreBinding
    TO SERVICE '//SackConsulting/BookOrderService'
    WITH USER =  BookStoreUser
GO
```

With the routes and bindings set up, I am now ready to test sending a remote message from the JOEPROD server's BookStore database to the NODE2 server's BookDistribution database:

```
Use BookStore
GO

DECLARE @Conv_Handler uniqueidentifier
DECLARE @OrderMsg xml;

BEGIN DIALOG CONVERSATION @Conv_Handler
FROM SERVICE [//SackConsulting/BookOrderService]
TO SERVICE '//SackConsulting/BookDistributionService'
ON CONTRACT [//SackConsulting/BookOrderContract];

SET @OrderMsg =
'<order id="3439" customer="22" orderdate="9/25/2008">
<LineItem ItemNumber="22" ISBN="1-59059-592-0" Quantity="10" />
</order>';

SEND ON CONVERSATION @Conv_Handler
MESSAGE TYPE [//SackConsulting/SendBookOrder]
(@OrderMsg);
```

Moving over to the NODE2 server and the BookDistribution database, the queue is checked for the incoming message:

```
USE BookDistribution
GO

SELECT message_type_name, CAST(message_body as xml) message,
queuing_order, conversation_handle, conversation_group_id
FROM dbo.BookDistributionQueue
```

This returns the following result set (abridged for readability):

Column	Value
Message_type_name	//SackConsulting/SendBookOrder
Message	<order id="3439" customer="22" orderdate="9/25/2008"> <LineItem ItemNumber="22" ISBN="1-59059-592-0" Quantity="10" /> </order>
Queuing_order	0
Conversation_handle	8150EB31-07EE-DC11-B4A4-0003FF25C9C5
Conversation_group_id	8050EB31-07EE-DC11-B4A4-0003FF25C9C5

How It Works

This recipe started off by creating routes on both SQL Server instances. Each route included the service name of the other SQL Server instance, the address for which to connect to it, and the port number of the Service Broker endpoint.

After that, a remote service binding was created on both SQL Server instances that was used to map the local database user (the one associated to the public key certificate of the other SQL Server instance) to the remote service.

Once this was completed, a message was sent from the BookStore database that then arrived at the remote NODE2 server's BookDistribution database.

Event Notifications

Event notification is a tie-in to Service Broker functionality, allowing you to asynchronously capture SQL events on a SQL Server instance, routing the event information into a specified queue. With a minimal of system overhead, you can track events that occur on the SQL Server instance such as user logins, stored procedure recompiles, permission changes, object manipulation (for example, CREATE/ALTER/DROP events on databases, assemblies, roles, or tables).

Unlike creating your own Service Broker applications, with event notification you need only create the queue and Service Broker components, because the initiator components are handled for you. The initiator components (message type and contract) that are used to capture and send the event notifications are already built into SQL Server.

The next recipe will demonstrate this functionality in action.

Capturing Login Commands

In this recipe, I demonstrate how to capture any CREATE LOGIN, ALTER LOGIN, or DROP LOGIN commands that are executed on the SQL Server instance using event notifications. The command for creating an event notification is as follows:

```
CREATE EVENT NOTIFICATION event_notification_name
ON { SERVER | DATABASE | QUEUE queue_name }
[ WITH FAN_IN ]
FOR { event_type | event_group } [ ,...n ]
TO SERVICE 'broker_service' , { 'broker_instance_specifier' |
  'current database'}
```

The arguments of this command are described in Table 20-8.

Table 20-8. *CREATE EVENT NOTIFICATION Arguments*

Argument	Description
event_notification_name	This argument defines the name of the new event notification.
SERVER | DATABASE | QUEUE queue_name	These three arguments define the event notification scope, causing notifications to fire when an event occurs for the specific SQL Server instance (SERVER), current database (DATABASE), or specific queue (QUEUE queue_name).
WITH FAN_IN	This argument configures SQL Server to send only one message per event for event notifications that are created on the same event with the same principal and the same service and broker_instance_specifier.
{ event_type | event_group } [,...n]	The event_type is a Transact-SQL DDL, Service Broker, or SQL Trace event type to be monitored. The event_group is a predefined group of event types—and when designated, any member of the group will cause an event notification to be fired. An example of an event group is DDL_LOGIN_EVENTS, which contains the CREATE LOGIN, ALTER LOGIN, and DROP LOGIN events.

Argument	Description
`'broker_service'` , { `'broker_instance_specifier'` | `'current database'` }	The broker_service argument is the name of the broker service receiving event notification data. The broker_instance_specifier is the service_broker_guid (from sys.databases) of the destination database, with 'current database' used to specify the current database guid.

The example starts off in a database called EventTracking, where I'll create a new queue to hold the event information:

```
IF NOT EXISTS (SELECT name
               FROM sys.databases
               WHERE name = 'EventTracking')

CREATE DATABASE EventTracking
GO

USE EventTracking
GO

CREATE QUEUE SQLEventQueue
WITH STATUS=ON;
GO
```

Next, I'll create a new service on the queue, associated to the built-in event notification contract:

```
CREATE SERVICE [//JOEPROD/TrackLoginModificationService]
ON QUEUE SQLEventQueue
([http://schemas.microsoft.com/SQL/Notifications/PostEventNotification]);
GO
```

Next, I'll execute a query against the sys.databases system catalog view in order to retrieve the EventTracking database service_broker_guid (which will be used in the CREATE EVENT NOTIFICATION command):

```
select service_broker_guid
from sys.databases
WHERE name = 'EventTracking'
```

This returns the following (your GUID will vary):

```
service_broker_guid
C72069CD-ACBA-4EA8-80BB-5CC6FF3A40AA
```

Next, I'll create an event notification using the SERVER scope to track any login creation, modification, or drop from the SQL Server instance (your GUID will vary):

```
CREATE EVENT NOTIFICATION EN_LoginEvents
ON SERVER
FOR CREATE_LOGIN, ALTER_LOGIN, DROP_LOGIN
TO SERVICE '//JOEPROD/TrackLoginModificationService',
'C72069CD-ACBA-4EA8-80BB-5CC6FF3A40AA';
```

I'll test the new event notification by creating a new login:

```
CREATE LOGIN TrishelleN WITH PASSWORD = 'AR!3i2ou4'
GO
```

Next, I'll query the queue using `SELECT` or `RECEIVE` (`RECEIVE`, unlike `SELECT`, will also remove the event message from the queue):

```
SELECT CAST(message_body as xml) EventInfo
FROM dbo.SQLEventQueue
```

This returns XML-based information about the login event, including the added login name and the login that added it:

```
<EVENT_INSTANCE>
  <EventType>CREATE_LOGIN</EventType>
  <PostTime>2008-03-09T12:39:09.493</PostTime>
  <SPID>53</SPID>
  <ServerName>CAESAR\AUGUSTUS</ServerName>
  <LoginName>CAESAR\Administrator</LoginName>
  <ObjectName>TrishelleN</ObjectName>
  <ObjectType>LOGIN</ObjectType>
  <DefaultLanguage>us_english</DefaultLanguage>
  <DefaultDatabase>master</DefaultDatabase>
  <LoginType>SQL Login</LoginType>
  <SID>McTRGu1DYE2R8FTJYClN1w==</SID>
  <TSQLCommand>
    <SetOptions ANSI_NULLS="ON" ANSI_NULL_DEFAULT="ON" ANSI_PADDING="ON"
                QUOTED_IDENTIFIER="ON" ENCRYPTED="FALSE" />
    <CommandText>CREATE LOGIN TrishelleN WITH PASSWORD = '******'
</CommandText>
  </TSQLCommand>
</EVENT_INSTANCE>
```

How It Works

In this recipe, I demonstrated creating an event notification by performing the following steps:

1. Create a new queue in an existing database.

2. Create a new service that is bound to the new queue and the built-in event notification contract.

3. Use `CREATE EVENT NOTIFICATION` to track one or more events or event groups.

Event notification functionality provides a low-overhead method of tracking activities at the SQL Server instance, database, or Service Broker application level. As you saw in the example, very little coding was necessary in order to begin tracking events. This new functionality will be particularly useful for IT security or business-level auditing requirements. For example, when capturing the login creation event, the user that created it was also captured, along with the type of login (SQL login), default database, language, and security identifier of the new login.

CHAPTER 21

■ ■ ■ ■

Configuring and Viewing SQL Server Options

Although SQL Server automatically maintains and adjusts many settings and configurations behind the scenes, there are still several options that the database administrator can configure. In this brief chapter, I'll show you recipes for viewing and configuring SQL Server settings using Transact-SQL.

■**Note** For a review of the `SERVERPROPERTY`, `@@SERVERNAME`, and other SQL Server instance-level functions, see Chapter 8.

Viewing SQL Server Configurations

SQL Server configuration settings control a variety of behaviors, from the way memory is managed to the default fill factor of your indexes. Although the valid configuration values vary, based on the option you are modifying, you can use the `sp_configure` system stored procedure to view or make changes:

The syntax for `sp_configure` is as follows:

```
sp_configure [ [ @configname = ] 'option_name'
    [ , [ @configvalue = ] 'value' ] ]
```

The parameters are briefly described in Table 21-1.

Table 21-1. *sp_configure Parameters*

Parameter	Description
[@configname =] 'option_name'	The name of the SQL Server option to be configured
[@configvalue =] 'value'	The desired new value to be set for the SQL Server option

The sp_configure stored procedure is used to both modify and query the SQL Server instance configuration settings. You can also query configuration settings using the `sys.configurations` system catalog view. The `sys.configurations` view can be queried like any normal view, and it returns each configuration name, the value in use by the SQL Server instance, the configuration setting's description, whether the configuration requires a SQL Server instance restart, and whether the configuration is an advanced option.

This recipe demonstrates three methods for viewing SQL Server configurations. The first method, which follows immediately, shows basic options. The second method displays "advanced" options, or those that require extra consideration by an experienced database administrator before modification. The third and last example shows how to query the sys.configurations system catalog view.

```
-- Display basic options
EXEC sp_configure
GO
```

This returns basic configurations and their current values:

name	minimum	maximum	config_value	run_value
allow updates	0	1	0	0
backup compression default	0	1	0	0
clr enabled	0	1	0	0
cross db ownership chaining	0	1	0	0
default language	0	9999	0	0
filestream access level	0	2	2	2
max text repl size (B)	-1	2147483647	65536	65536
nested triggers	0	1	1	1
remote access	0	1	1	1
remote admin connections	0	1	0	0
remote login timeout (s)	0	2147483647	20	20
remote proc trans	0	1	0	0
remote query timeout (s)	0	2147483647	600	600
server trigger recursion	0	1	1	1
show advanced options	0	1	0	0
user options	0	32767	0	0

The next query shows advanced options (in addition to the basic options):

```
-- Display advanced options
EXEC sp_configure 'show advanced option', 1
RECONFIGURE
GO

EXEC sp_configure
GO
```

This returns both basic and advanced options (not all rows displayed):

name	minimum	maximum	config_value	run_value
Ad Hoc Distributed Queries	0	1	0	0
affinity I/O mask	-2147483648	2147483647	0	0
affinity mask	-2147483648	2147483647	0	0
Agent XPs	0	1	1	1
allow updates	0	1	0	0
...				
user options	0	32767	0	0
Web Assistant Procedures	0	1	0	0
xp_cmdshell	0	1	0	0

Finally, the sys.configurations view is queried to show SQL Server configurations, ordered by configuration name:

```
SELECT name, value, minimum, maximum, value_in_use, is_dynamic, is_advanced
FROM sys.configurations
ORDER BY name
```

This returns all options, in addition to other useful information such as whether the option is advanced and whether it's dynamic. If the option has an is_dynamic value of 1, the configuration change will take effect after the RECONFIGURE command is executed:

name	value	minimum	maximum	value_in_use	is_dynamic	is_advanced
Ad Hoc Distributed Queries	0	0	1	0	1	1
affinity I/O mask	0	-2147483648	2147483647	0	0	1
affinity mask	0	-2147483648	2147483647	0	1	1
affinity64 I/O mask	0	-2147483648	2147483647	0	0	1
affinity64 mask	0	-2147483648	2147483647	0	1	1
...						
Web Assistant Procedures	0	0	1	0	1	1
xp_cmdshell	0	0	1	0	1	1

How It Works

In the first part of the recipe, basic options were returned using the system stored procedure sp_configure. Examples of basic options included the clr enabled and nested triggers configurations. The clr enabled option shows you whether or not CLR-based objects are allowed in the SQL Server instance. The nested triggers configuration determines whether or not triggers can be fired that fire other triggers. These are basic settings that all SQL Server users can see by default.

The second part of the recipe demonstrated how to view *all* server options, including advanced options. To do this, an actual SQL Server configuration change was necessary. The "show advanced option" setting was configured from 0 (false) to 1 (true):

```
EXEC sp_configure 'show advanced option', 1
RECONFIGURE
GO
```

After executing sp_configure, the RECONFIGURE command was used. For those SQL Server options that don't require reboots, the RECONFIGURE command forces an update to the currently configured value. If an invalid or not recommended value is used, RECONFIGURE will reject it. Using RECONFIGURE WITH OVERRIDE will override this validation, in most cases. For example, take the recovery interval option, which designates the maximum database recovery time (in minutes). Setting the value of this option *above* 60 minutes using RECONFIGURE would raise a warning indicating that the value is not recommended. The warning, however, doesn't stop you from making the change. Using RECONFIGURE WITH OVERRIDE would force this option's value to be changed.

After changing the show advanced option value to 1, all options were returned by sp_configure:

```
EXEC sp_configure
GO
```

Last in the recipe, the sys.configurations system catalog view was queried to return all SQL Server options. It returned additional information for each setting, including whether the setting was dynamic and if it was an advanced option.

Changing SQL Server Configurations

SQL Server does a remarkable job of maintaining itself out of the box, and in most cases, the default settings will suffice. When you must change a default configuration value, you need to do so with care, making sure that you understand exactly what it is you are changing. For example, the locks configuration, which determines the maximum number of available locks SQL Server can issue, should be left to SQL Server to manage, allowing SQL Server to allocate, de-allocate, and escalate lock types as it sees fit.

In this recipe, I'll demonstrate using `sp_configure` to disable query parallelism, as well as to set a cap on the maximum amount of memory (in MBs) that the SQL Server instance is permitted to use. The `max degree of parallelism` option sets the limit on the number of processors used in a parallel plan execution. The default value for this option is to use all available processors (with the option equal to 0):

```
SELECT name, value_in_use
FROM sys.configurations
WHERE name IN ('max degree of parallelism')
```

This returns

name	value_in_use
max degree of parallelism	0

In this example, the `maximum degree of parallelism` is set to a single CPU:

```
EXEC sp_configure 'max degree of parallelism', 1
RECONFIGURE
GO
```

This returns

```
Configuration option 'max degree of parallelism' changed from 0 to 1.
Run the RECONFIGURE statement to install.
```

Now the value is checked again:

```
SELECT name, value_in_use
FROM sys.configurations
WHERE name IN ('max degree of parallelism')
```

This returns

name	value_in_use
max degree of parallelism	1

The `max server memory` option designates the maximum amount of memory SQL Server is allowed to use, measured in megabytes. The default value for this setting is no set maximum, as this query will show:

```
SELECT name, value_in_use
FROM sys.configurations
WHERE name IN ('max server memory (MB)')
```

This returns the default memory value (which is very large):

name	value_in_use
max server memory (MB)	2147483647

In this example, a cap of 2500MB is put on the SQL Server instance:

```
EXEC sp_configure 'max server memory', 2500
RECONFIGURE
GO
```

This returns

```
Configuration option 'max server memory (MB)' changed from 2147483647 to 2500.
Run the RECONFIGURE statement to install.
```

The new value is then verified:

```
SELECT name, value_in_use
FROM sys.configurations
WHERE name IN ('max server memory (MB)')
```

This returns

```
name                      value_in_use
max server memory (MB)    2500
```

How It Works

In this recipe, I demonstrated setting the max degree of parallelism to 1, which means that only a single processor will be used on a single query (disabling SQL Server's ability to use multiple CPUs for executing a single query). This recipe also demonstrated limiting the maximum server memory to 2500MB. As long as other options have not been configured to constrain SQL Server any further, SQL Server will still dynamically manage memory, but only up to the limit specified using sp_configure. Neither change in setting required a restart of the SQL Server instance, so the RECONFIGURE command was enough to set the value during execution time.

■ ■ ■

Creating and Configuring Databases

In this chapter, you'll see an assortment of recipes that revolve around creating and configuring a SQL Server database. Some of the things you'll learn to do with Transact-SQL include the following:

- Creating a new database
- Adding or removing files or filegroups from a database
- Viewing and modifying database settings
- Increasing or decreasing a database or database file size
- Removing a database from the SQL Server instance
- Detaching and reattaching a database from a SQL Server instance

I'll also review the various "state" settings, such as configuring the database to be read-only, or putting the database into single-user mode.

Creating, Altering, and Dropping Databases

In this first set of recipes, I cover how to create, modify, and drop databases in a SQL Server instance. Specifically, I'll be showing you how to

- Create a database based on the default configuration of the model system database.
- View information about a database's configuration.
- Create a database using explicit file options (instead of depending on the model system database).
- Create a database that uses a user-defined filegroup.
- Change the name of an existing database.
- Drop a database from the SQL Server instance.
- Detach a database from the SQL Server instance so that only the underlying data and log files remain. Reattach the database using those same files.

The primary commands you'll be using to create and modify databases are CREATE DATABASE and ALTER DATABASE. Similar to my discussion in Chapter 1 about the SELECT statement, in this chapter, each recipe will slice off the relevant components used to perform the specified task, instead of presenting the syntax in one large block.

Creating a Database with a Default Configuration

This recipe demonstrates how to create a database in its simplest form, by using the default configuration based on the model system database. The model database is a system database installed with SQL Server that defines the template for all other databases created on the SQL Server instance. If you create a database without specifying any options other than the database name, the options will be based on the model system database.

The syntax for creating a database based on model is as follows:

```
CREATE DATABASE database_name
```

The CREATE DATABASE command, in its simplest form, can take just a single argument: the new database name.

This recipe creates a new database called BookStore:

```
USE master
GO

IF NOT EXISTS (SELECT name
               FROM sys.databases
               WHERE name = 'BookStore')

CREATE DATABASE BookStore

GO
```

How It Works

In this recipe, a new database called BookStore was created, without any other options but the database name. By omitting details such as file locations, size, and file growth options, the new database is created based on the model system database. The database will include any user-defined objects that you've placed in the model database and will use a file-naming convention based on the new database name.

Although this is a quick way to create a new database, it doesn't give you much control over several of the options that I'll describe throughout this chapter.

Viewing Database Information

This recipe demonstrates how to view database properties and file information using the system stored procedure sp_helpdb:

```
EXEC sp_helpdb 'BookStore'
GO
```

This returns the following two result sets (albeit a bit packed due to the constraints of the printed page):

name	db_size	owner	dbid	created	status	compatibility_level
BookStore	1.62 MB	CAESAR\Administrator	6	Dec 23 2007	Status=ONLINE, Updateability=READ_WRITE, UserAccess=MULTI_USER, Recovery=FULL, Version=639, Collation=SQL_Latin1_ General_CP1_CI_AS, SQLSortOrder=52, IsAutoCreateStatistics, IsAutoUpdateStatistics, IsFullTextEnabled	100

name	fileid	filename	filegroup	size	maxsize	growth	usage
BookStore	1	C:\Program Files\ Microsoft SQL Server\ MSSQL10.AUGUSTUS\ MSSQL\DATA\ BookStore.mdf	PRIMARY	1152 KB	Unlimited	1024 KB	data only
BookStore_log	2	C:\Program Files\ Microsoft SQL Server\ MSSQL10.AUGUSTUS\ MSSQL\DATA\ BookStore_log.LDF	NULL	504 KB	2147483648 KB	10%	log only

How It Works

The system stored procedure sp_helpdb was used to view the properties of a database. This system stored procedure takes a single optional parameter, which in this case is the database name:

```
EXEC sp_helpdb 'BookStore'
```

Had the database name been omitted from this stored procedure, information for all the databases on the SQL Server instance would have been returned instead.

This system stored procedure returns information such as

- The database name and owner
- The date that the database was created
- The various database settings and options, such as the database's default collation or whether or not the database is configured to automatically update statistics (database options are described later in the chapter).
- A list of individual files that make up the database, along with their size, filegroup, and growth options

The output also includes the database's compatibility level. For example, a SQL Server 2008 database by default will have a compatibility level of 100. SQL Server 2005 would be level 90, and SQL Server 2000 level 80. Compatibility level allows you to keep databases in SQL Server 2008 that remain compatible with prior versions of SQL Server. This also means that you cannot use Transact-SQL extensions introduced in SQL Server 2008 with a SQL Server 2005–compatible database. In previous versions, you set this level using the sp_dbcmptlevel system stored procedure. In SQL Server 2008, you set the database compatibility using ALTER DATABASE. For example:

```
ALTER DATABASE AdventureWorks
SET COMPATIBILITY_LEVEL = 100
GO
```

Creating a Database Using File Options

Using the default options from the model system database to create a new database is fine if you're simply looking to create a quick-and-dirty test database, but in a production environment, you'll usually want to put more thought into the location, size, and growth options of the database data and log files. This recipe will demonstrate the use of specifying explicit file options when creating a new database.

The abridged syntax for CREATE DATABASE, as presented in this recipe, is as follows:

```
CREATE DATABASE database_name
   [ ON
      [ <filespec> [ ,...n ] ] ]
[ [ LOG ON { <filespec> [ ,...n ] } ] ]
```

The arguments of this syntax are briefly described in Table 22-1.

Table 22-1. *CREATE DATABASE File Arguments*

Argument	Description
database_name	Defines the name of the database
[ON [<filespec> [,...n]]]	Designates one or more explicitly defined data files for the database
[LOG ON { <filespec> [,...n] }]	Designates one or more explicitly defined transaction log files for the database

The syntax for the filespec argument, used both in creating a data file and a log file, is as follows:

```
[ PRIMARY ]
(
   [ NAME = logical_file_name , ]
   FILENAME = 'os_file_name'
      [ , SIZE = size [ KB | MB | GB | TB ] ]
      [ , MAXSIZE = { max_size [ KB | MB | GB | TB ] | UNLIMITED } ]
      [ , FILEGROWTH = growth_increment [ KB | MB | % ] ]
) [ ,...n ]
```

The filespec arguments are described in Table 22-2.

Table 22-2. *Filespec Arguments*

Argument	Description
PRIMARY	This optional keyword designates the data file in the filespec as the primary data file (entry point of the database that contains pointers to other files and is typically named with an .mdf file extension). Only one primary file can exist for a database, and if it is not explicitly designated, the first data file listed in CREATE DATABASE is used as the primary file.
logical_file_name	This defines the logical name of the database file.

Argument	Description
os_file_name	This specifies the physical path and file name of the database file.
size [KB | MB | GB | TB]	This defines the initial size of the file, based on the sizing attribute of choice (kilobytes, megabytes, gigabytes, terabytes).
MAXSIZE = { max_size [KB | MB | GB | TB] | UNLIMITED }	This specifies the maximum allowable size of the file. If UNLIMITED is chosen, the file can grow to the available space of the physical drive.
FILEGROWTH = growth_increment [KB | MB | %]	This dictates the amount that the file size increases when space is required. You can either designate the number of kilobytes or megabytes, or the percentage of existing file size to grow. If you select 0, file growth will not occur.
[,...n]	This indicates that you can have one or more files defined (up to 32,767 files per database).

In this recipe, I'll create a new database called BookStoreArchive using all the aforementioned CREATE DATABASE options:

```
USE master
GO

CREATE DATABASE BookStoreArchive
ON  PRIMARY
(   NAME = 'BookStoreArchive',
    FILENAME = 'F:\Apress\BookStoreArchive.mdf' ,
    SIZE = 3MB ,
    MAXSIZE = UNLIMITED,
    FILEGROWTH = 10MB ),
(   NAME = 'BookStoreArchive2',
    FILENAME = 'G:\Apress\BookStoreArchive2.ndf' ,
    SIZE = 1MB ,
    MAXSIZE = 30,
    FILEGROWTH = 5% )
 LOG ON
(   NAME = 'BookStoreArchive_log',
    FILENAME = 'H:\Apress\BookStoreArchive_log.LDF' ,
    SIZE = 504KB ,
    MAXSIZE = 100MB ,
    FILEGROWTH = 10%)
GO
```

How It Works

In this recipe, a new database called BookStoreArchive was created. The PRIMARY keyword was used to designate the first file as the primary data file:

```
CREATE DATABASE BookStoreArchive
ON  PRIMARY
```

The first file definition followed in parentheses. The logical file name was called BookStoreArchive:

```
(   NAME = 'BookStoreArchive',
```

The physical file name was designated on the F:\ drive. In production scenarios, you'll likely be putting your data files on different drive letters (which could support a RAID 5 or RAID 10 array):

```
FILENAME = 'F:\Apress\BookStoreArchive.mdf' ,
```

Next, the initial data file size was set to 3 megabytes:

```
SIZE = 3MB ,
```

The maximum size of the file was set to unlimited, meaning that it can keep growing as long as there is free space on the C:\ drive:

```
MAXSIZE = UNLIMITED,
```

The growth increment was set to 10-megabyte chunks. Whenever more space is needed on the file, the file size will expand in 10-megabyte increments:

```
FILEGROWTH = 10MB ),
```

The previous file definition ended with a comma, followed by a second data file definition:

```
(   NAME = 'BookStoreArchive2',
    FILENAME = 'G:\Apress\BookStoreArchive2.ndf' ,
```

The second data file was given a different logical name and physical file name. The physical file name ended in an .ndf file extension. Although that specific file extension isn't required, it does make it easier to identify the file type if you use .mdf for the primary file and .ndf for all secondary data files. Adding multiple files that are spread out over different drive letters, assuming each drive letter is RAID enabled and on a separate channel or controller, can allow you to spread out I/O activity and potentially improve performance for larger, high-traffic databases.

The size of the second file was set to 1 megabyte, with a cap on the maximum size of 30 megabytes. File growth was set to increment in 5% chunks, instead of in megabytes as the first data file was defined:

```
SIZE = 1MB ,
MAXSIZE = 30,
FILEGROWTH = 5% )
```

After the two data files were defined, the LOG ON keywords marked the beginning of the transaction log file definition:

```
LOG ON
(   NAME = 'BookStoreArchive_log',
```

The physical file name used an .ldf file extension, which is the standard for transaction log files:

```
FILENAME = 'H:\Apress\BookStoreArchive_log.LDF' ,
```

The initial size was set to 504 kilobytes, with a maximum transaction log size of 100 megabytes and a 10% file growth rate.

```
SIZE = 504KB ,
MAXSIZE = 100MB ,
FILEGROWTH = 10%)
```

Once the CREATE DATABASE command is executed, the associated files are automatically created on the server, and the database is then available for use.

Later on in the chapter, there will be recipes showing you how to modify existing file properties, as well as how to add new data or transaction files to the database.

Creating a Database with a User-Defined Filegroup

A database must have, at a minimum, one data file and one transaction log file. These files belong to a single database and therefore are not shared with other databases. By default, when a database is created, the data files belong to the primary filegroup. A *filegroup* is a named grouping of files for administrative and placement reasons. The primary filegroup contains the primary data file, as well as other data files that have not been explicitly assigned to a different filegroup. Data files (but *not* transaction log files) belong to filegroups.

In addition to the primary filegroup (which all SQL Server databases have), you can create secondary user-defined filegroups for placing your files. User-defined filegroups are often used in very large databases (VLDB), allowing you to partition the database across several arrays and manage backups at the filegroup level instead of the entire database.

■**Note** You can place tables or indexes on specific filegroups. See Chapter 4 for a review of filegroups and tables and Chapter 5 for a review of filegroups and indexes.

In this recipe, I demonstrate how to create a database with files on a user-defined filegroup. The syntax for doing so is as follows:

```
CREATE DATABASE database_name
[ ON
FILEGROUP filegroup_name [ CONTAINS FILESTREAM ] [ DEFAULT ]
    <filespec> [ ,...n ]
]
[
    [ LOG ON { <filespec> [ ,...n ] } ] ]
```

The syntax arguments are detailed in Table 22-3.

Table 22-3. *CREATE DATABASE Arguments*

Argument	Description
database_name	Defines the name of the database.
FILEGROUP filegroup_name [CONTAINS FILESTREAM] [DEFAULT]	Designates the logical name of the filegroup. If followed by the DEFAULT keyword, this filegroup will be the default filegroup of the database (meaning all objects will by default be created there); otherwise, if CONTAINS FILESTREAM is designated, this will point to the directory where filestream attribute files will be located.
<filespec> [,...n]	Designates one or more explicitly defined data files for the database.
[LOG ON { <filespec> [,...n] }]	Designates one or more explicitly defined transaction log files for the database.

This recipe creates a new database called BookStoreInternational, which uses two filegroups. One is the required primary filegroup and the other, the new user-defined FG2 filegroup, is created in the CREATE DATABASE command:

```
USE master
GO

CREATE DATABASE BookStoreInternational
ON  PRIMARY
(   NAME = 'BookStoreInternational',
    FILENAME = 'C:\Apress\BookStoreInternational.mdf',
    SIZE = 3MB ,
    MAXSIZE = UNLIMITED,
    FILEGROWTH = 5MB ),
FILEGROUP FG2 DEFAULT
(   NAME = 'BookStoreInternational2',
    FILENAME = 'C:\Apress\BookStoreInternational2.ndf',
    SIZE = 1MB ,
    MAXSIZE = UNLIMITED,
    FILEGROWTH = 1MB )
 LOG ON
(   NAME = 'BookStoreInternational_log',
    FILENAME = 'C:\Apress\BookStoreInternational.ldf',
    SIZE = 504KB ,
    MAXSIZE = 100MB ,
    FILEGROWTH = 10%)
GO
```

How It Works

In this recipe, a new database was created with two data files and one transaction log file. The first data file was created on the PRIMARY filegroup. The second database data file was created in a new user-defined filegroup called FG2, using the FILEGROUP keyword. This filegroup was marked as the default filegroup, so that any new database objects created in the database will be created in this filegroup:

```
...
FILEGROUP FG2 DEFAULT
(   NAME = 'BookStoreInternational2',
    FILENAME = 'C:\Apress\BookStoreInternational2.ndf',
    SIZE = 1MB ,
    MAXSIZE = UNLIMITED,
    FILEGROWTH = 1MB )
...
```

Since transaction logs are not placed in filegroups, the LOG ON keywords were used with the standard filespec definition.

In this recipe, a single file was placed in the FG2 filegroup, though you can put multiple files in a single filegroup. With multiple files in a filegroup, SQL Server will fill each in a proportional manner, instead of filling up a single file before moving on to the next.

Setting Database User Access

SQL Server provides three database user access modes that affect which users (and how many) can access a database: SINGLE_USER, RESTRICTED_USER, and MULTI_USER. The SINGLE_USER and RESTRICTED_USER options are methods used to "shut the door" on other users performing activities in the database. This is often useful if you need to perform database configuration changes that do not allow other users to be in the database at the same time. These options are also used when you need to undo a data change, or force users out prior to a cutover to a new system or application upgrade. The upcoming table describes each option in more detail.

The abridged syntax for modifying user access is as follows:

```
ALTER DATABASE database_name
SET { SINGLE_USER | RESTRICTED_USER | MULTI_USER }
[WITH { ROLLBACK AFTER integer [ SECONDS ]
  | ROLLBACK IMMEDIATE
  | NO_WAIT
}]
```

The arguments of this syntax are described in Table 22-4.

Table 22-4. *ALTER DATABASE Arguments*

Argument	Description
database_name	This defines the name of the existing database to modify user access for.
SINGLE_USER | RESTRICTED_USER | MULTI_USER	When SINGLE_USER is selected, only one user is allowed to access the database at a time. When this option is selected, unless the termination options are used (see the next row for a description of termination options), the modification is blocked until all other users disconnect from the database. With RESTRICTED_USER selected, only members of the sysadmin, dbcreator, or db_owner roles can access the database. With MULTI_USER, all users with permissions to the database are allowed access.
ROLLBACK AFTER integer [SECONDS] | ROLLBACK IMMEDIATE | NO_WAIT	These termination options allow you to roll back incomplete transactions for the database during the ALTER DATABASE statement. If you don't use a termination option, your ALTER DATABASE may have to wait for however long the locking connection needs to complete its task. Termination options can actually be used with any SET clause; however, they are most often used when changing a database to SINGLE_USER or RESTRICTED_USER modes. ROLLBACK AFTER integer [SECONDS] specifies that open database transactions be rolled back after a specified number of seconds. ROLLBACK IMMEDIATE rolls back open transactions immediately. NO_WAIT, when specified, causes the statement to fail if it cannot complete immediately (using this option requires that there are no open transactions in the database in order to succeed).

This recipe demonstrates taking the AdventureWorks database into a SINGLE_USER mode, rolling back any open transactions, and then putting the database back into MULTI_USER mode:

```
-- Turn off row count messages
SET NOCOUNT ON

SELECT user_access_desc
FROM sys.databases
WHERE name = 'AdventureWorks'
```

```
ALTER DATABASE AdventureWorks
SET  SINGLE_USER
WITH ROLLBACK IMMEDIATE

SELECT user_access_desc
FROM sys.databases
WHERE name = 'AdventureWorks'

ALTER DATABASE AdventureWorks
SET  MULTI_USER

SELECT user_access_desc
FROM sys.databases
WHERE name = 'AdventureWorks'
```

This returns

```
user_access_desc
MULTI_USER

user_access_desc
SINGLE_USER

user_access_desc
MULTI_USER
```

How It Works

In this recipe, the system catalog view sys.databases was queried to check the current user access mode. The database was then changed to SINGLE_USER mode and included a termination of all open transactions in other database user sessions:

```
ALTER DATABASE AdventureWorks
SET  SINGLE_USER
WITH ROLLBACK IMMEDIATE
```

The user access mode was then checked again via sys.databases, and the database was changed back to MULTI_USER:

```
ALTER DATABASE AdventureWorks
SET  MULTI_USER
```

After that, the access mode was checked again via sys.databases:

```
SELECT user_access_desc
FROM sys.databases
WHERE name = 'AdventureWorks'
```

It is important to note that canceling open transactions in this manner may cause issues in your application, depending on how your application handles incomplete processes. When possible, try to change user access during periods of inactivity or when no transactions are active. You need to set the database to SINGLE_USER for certain operations, such as for the READ_ONLY and READ_WRITE options. Another reason to close all current user connections may be, for example, to put in an emergency object fix without having to deal with blocking or errors from the calling application.

Renaming a Database

In this recipe, I demonstrate how to change the name of an existing database using `ALTER DATABASE`.

The syntax is as follows:

```
ALTER DATABASE database_name
MODIFY NAME = new_database_name
```

The two arguments for this command include the original database name and the new database name.

This recipe demonstrates changing the name of the `BookWarehouse` database to the `BookMart` database. `ALTER DATABASE...SET SINGLE USER` is also executed in order to clear out any other concurrent connections to the database:

```
USE master
GO

-- Create demo database
CREATE DATABASE BookWarehouse
GO

ALTER DATABASE BookWarehouse
SET SINGLE_USER
WITH ROLLBACK IMMEDIATE
GO

ALTER DATABASE  BookWarehouse
MODIFY NAME = BookMart
GO

ALTER DATABASE BookMart
SET MULTI_USER
GO
```

This returns the following (results may vary depending on activity in the database during the termination of connections):

```
Nonqualified transactions are being rolled back.
Estimated rollback completion: 100%.
The database name 'BookMart' has been set.
```

How It Works

In this recipe, a database was renamed from `BookWarehouse` to `BookMart`. Before doing so, the query session's context was changed to the master database (because you can't change the name of the database using a connection to the database itself):

```
USE master
GO
```

I started off by creating a new database named `BookWarehouse` for demonstration purposes. The new database was placed into single-user mode, and all active transactions against the database were rolled back (except for transactions existing within the current session):

```
ALTER DATABASE BookWarehouse
SET SINGLE_USER
WITH ROLLBACK IMMEDIATE
GO
```

The database name was then changed using ALTER DATABASE and MODIFY NAME:

```
ALTER DATABASE  BookWarehouse
MODIFY NAME = BookMart
GO
```

Even though the database was put in single-user mode under its original name, it will remain in single-user mode until it is explicitly set back to MULTI_USER access:

```
ALTER DATABASE BookMart
SET MULTI_USER
GO
```

Dropping a Database

You can remove a user database from SQL Server using the DROP DATABASE command. DROP DATABASE removes references to the database from SQL Server system tables. If the underlying files are online, it also removes the physical files from the SQL Server machine.

The syntax is as follows:

```
DROP DATABASE database_name
```

In this recipe, the BookStoreArchive_Ukrainian database is dropped:

```
USE master
GO

-- Create demonstration database
CREATE DATABASE BookStoreArchive_Ukrainian
GO

ALTER DATABASE BookStoreArchive_Ukrainian
SET SINGLE_USER
WITH ROLLBACK IMMEDIATE
GO

DROP DATABASE BookStoreArchive_Ukrainian
GO
```

How It Works

In this recipe, I started off by switching the current query session to the master database, because you cannot drop a database while you are also connected to it. The recipe also set the database into single-user mode and forced any open transactions to be rolled back immediately. Finally, within the same query session, the database was dropped using the DROP DATABASE command.

Detaching a Database

When you drop a database, it is removed from the SQL Server instance along with its physical files. If you wish to remove a database from a SQL Server instance, but still retain the physical files (for archiving or to migrate the database to another SQL Server instance), you can *detach* the database instead. You can also move a database from one SQL Server instance to another, by detaching it from one instance and adding it to the other.

In order to detach a database, you use the system stored procedure sp_detach_db, which uses the following syntax:

```
sp_detach_db [ @dbname= ] 'dbname'
    [ , [ @skipchecks= ] 'skipchecks' ]
```

The parameters for the procedure are described in Table 22-5.

Table 22-5. *sp_detach_db Parameters*

Parameter	Description
dbname	This option supplies the name of the database to detach.
skipchecks	This option allows a true or false value. When this option is true, statistics are not updated prior to detaching the database. By default, statistics are updated.

■**Note** This system stored procedure also takes a @keepfulltextindexfile parameter, which I have not included here. It will be removed in a future edition of SQL Server, since full-text index metadata is maintained within the database now.

In this recipe, I will create, and then detach, a database using sp_detach_db:

```
-- Create a default example database to detach
USE master
GO

CREATE DATABASE TestDetach
GO

-- Kick out any users currently in the database

ALTER DATABASE TestDetach
SET SINGLE_USER
WITH ROLLBACK IMMEDIATE

-- Detach the database

EXEC sp_detach_db 'TestDetach',
            'false' -- don't skip checks
```

This returns the following abridged results:

```
Updating [sys].[queue_messages_1977058079]
    [queue_clustered_index], update is not necessary...
    [queue_secondary_index], update is not necessary...
    0 index(es)/statistic(s) have been updated, 2 did not require update.

...

Updating [sys].[syscommittab]
    [ci_commit_ts], update is not necessary...
    [si_xdes_id], update is not necessary...
    0 index(es)/statistic(s) have been updated, 2 did not require update.

Statistics for all tables have been updated.
```

How It Works

In this recipe, a new database called TestDetach was created. After that, I used ALTER DATABASE to set the TestDetach database into single-user mode, while also kicking out any open database connections using the ROLLBACK IMMEDIATE option.

The system stored procedure sp_detach_db was then used to detach the database—but not before updating statistics (designating false in the second parameter). The database has, for all intents and purposes, been dropped. However, the data files still exist on the SQL Server instance's server, and can be re-created on the current or other SQL Server instance if you choose to do so.

Attaching a Database

The previous recipe demonstrated how to detach a database. In this next recipe, I'll demonstrate how to attach a database. Using the detach/attach method is a clean way to migrate a database from one SQL Server instance to another, assuming that a copy of the database needn't remain on both SQL Server instances.

■**Caution** Detaching and attaching a database from one server to the other doesn't also move the SQL Server logins associated to users in the database. You must move logins to the new SQL Server instance as a separate operation.

To attach a database to a SQL Server instance, you use the CREATE DATABASE FOR ATTACH command.

The abridged syntax is as follows:

```
CREATE DATABASE database_name
    ON <filespec> [ ,...n ]
    FOR { ATTACH
        | ATTACH_REBUILD_LOG }
```

The arguments for this command are described in Table 22-6.

Table 22-6. *CREATE DATABASE...FOR ATTACH Parameters*

Parameter	Description
database_name	This specifies the name of the database to attach.
<filespec> [,...n]	This defines the name of the primary data file and any other database files. If the file locations of the originally detached database match the existing file location, you only need to include the primary data file reference. If file locations have changed, however, you should designate the location of each database file.
ATTACH | ATTACH_REBUILD_LOG	The ATTACH option designates that the database is created using all original files that were used in the detached database. When ATTACH_REBUILD_LOG is designated, and if the transaction log file or files are unavailable, SQL Server will rebuild the transaction log file or files.

In this recipe, the TestDetach database detached in the previous recipe will now be reattached to the SQL Server instance using the same files and file paths. The database, however, will be reattached with a new name of TestAttach:

```
CREATE DATABASE TestAttach
    ON (FILENAME = 'C:\Program Files\Microsoft SQL Server\MSSQL10.AUGUSTUS
\MSSQL\DATA\TestDetach.mdf')
    FOR ATTACH
```

How It Works

In this recipe, a database was reattached by using CREATE DATABASE FOR ATTACH. The command referenced the primary data file name, which contained references to the location of the other files (in this case, the transaction log file).

If you detach a database, and then relocate the secondary data files and/or transaction log files, you will also need to explicitly reference the new location of each file in the CREATE DATABASE...FOR ATTACH command. The new path of the files is designated in the filespec. If the transaction log or logs had been unavailable, you could have used the ATTACH_REBUILD_LOG instead of ATTACH to rebuild the transaction log file.

Configuring Database Options

This next set of recipes covers how to configure database options that impact the behavior of activities performed within the database. Specifically, I'll be showing you how to

- View database options currently configured for the database.

- Configure ANSI SQL options.

- Configure automatic options. Automatic database options impact the behavior of the SQL Server database engine, enabling or disabling automatic maintenance or metadata updates.

- Configure external access options, including DB_CHAINING and TRUSTWORTHY.

- Create or modify a database to use a specific collation.

- Configure cursor options.

- Enable date correlation optimization. Two tables that are related by a datetime foreign key reference can benefit from enabling the DATE_CORRELATION_OPTIMIZATION option.

- Modify database parameterization behavior. The PARAMETERIZATION option is used with ALTER DATABASE and controls whether all or some queries against the database are parameterized.

- Enable row versioning. SQL Server has two database options that allow for statement-level and transaction-level read consistency: ALLOW_SNAPSHOT_ISOLATION and READ_COMMITTED_SNAPSHOT.

- Configure database recovery models. SQL Server uses three different recovery models that define whether or not transaction log backups can be made, and if so, what database activities will write to the transaction log.

- Configure page verification. SQL Server has three modes for handling and detecting incomplete I/O transactions caused by disk errors: CHECKSUM, TORN_PAGE_DETECTION, and NONE.

■**Note** Some of the database options have already been demonstrated in other chapters. For a discussion of the ENCRYPTION database option, see Chapter 19. For a discussion on the AUTO_CLEANUP and CHANGE_RETENTION database options, see Chapter 2. Service Broker database options are discussed in Chapter 20.

I'll begin by reviewing how to see the current database options for a database using the `sys.databases` system catalog view.

Viewing Database Options

This recipe demonstrates how to view database options using the `sys.databases` system catalog view for the `AdventureWorks` database:

```
SELECT name, is_read_only, is_auto_close_on, is_auto_shrink_on
FROM sys.databases
WHERE name = 'AdventureWorks'
```

This returns

name	is_read_only	is_auto_close_on	is_auto_shrink_on
AdventureWorks	0	0	0

How It Works

In this recipe, a query was used to view three database options: is_read_only, is_auto_close_on, and is_auto_shrink_on. The sys.databases system catalog view can be used to view many other database options for both user and system databases.

Configuring ANSI SQL Options

This recipe demonstrates how to set ANSI (American National Standards Institute) SQL-compliance defaults for a database. These settings impact a number of behaviors, which are detailed in Table 22-7.

Table 22-7. ANSI SQL Options

Option	Description
ANSI_NULL_DEFAULT	When this option is set to ON, columns not explicitly defined with a NULL or NOT NULL in a CREATE or ALTER table statement will default to allow NULL values. The default is OFF, which means a column will be defined as NOT NULL if not explicitly defined.
ANSI_NULLS	When this option is enabled, a comparison to a null value returns UNKNOWN. The default for this setting is OFF, meaning that comparisons to a null value will evaluate to TRUE when both values are NULL.
ANSI_PADDING	This option pads strings to the same length prior to inserting into a varchar or nvarchar data type column. The default setting is OFF, meaning that strings will not be padded.
ANSI_WARNINGS	This setting impacts a few different behaviors. When ON, any null values used in an aggregate function will raise a warning message. Also, divide-by-zero and arithmetic overflow errors will roll back the statement and return an error message. This setting is OFF by default.
ARITHABORT	When this option is set to ON, a query with an overflow or division by zero will terminate the query and return an error. If this occurs within a transaction, then that transaction gets rolled back. When this option is OFF (the default), a warning is raised, but the statement continues to process.

Option	Description
CONCAT_NULL_YIELDS_NULL	When this option is set to ON, concatenating a null value with a string produces a NULL value. When OFF (the default), a null value is the equivalent of an empty character string.
NUMERIC_ROUNDABORT	When this option is set to ON, an error is produced when a loss of precision occurs in an expression. When OFF (the default), no error message is raised, but the result is rounded to the precision of the destination column or variable.
QUOTED_IDENTIFIER	When this option is set to ON, identifiers can be delimited by double quotation marks and literals with single quotation marks. When OFF (the default), only literals can be delimited with single or double quotation marks.
RECURSIVE_TRIGGERS	When this option is ON, triggers can fire recursively (trigger 1 fires trigger 2, which fires trigger 1 again). When OFF (the default), trigger recursion is not allowed.

The syntax for setting these options is as follows:

```
ALTER DATABASE database_name
SET  <option> { ON | OFF }
```

This statement takes two arguments: the database name you want to modify and the name of the ANSI SQL setting you wish to enable or disable.

■**Note** The default options for any newly created databases will depend on the values in the model database at the time the new database is created. However, out of the box, SQL Server defaults are those that were underlined in the syntax.

In this recipe, ALTER DATABASE is used to set the ANSI_NULLS option to OFF. This means that comparisons to a null value in a query will evaluate to TRUE when both values are NULL:

```
SET NOCOUNT ON

SELECT is_ansi_nulls_on
FROM sys.databases
WHERE name = 'AdventureWorks'

ALTER DATABASE AdventureWorks
SET  ANSI_NULLS  OFF

SELECT is_ansi_nulls_on
FROM sys.databases
WHERE name = 'AdventureWorks'
```

This returns

```
is_ansi_nulls_on
1

is_ansi_nulls_on
0
```

How It Works

This recipe demonstrated using ALTER DATABASE to change an ANSI SQL setting. The recipe started by querying the sys.databases system catalog view to see the current setting of the database. After that, the ANSI_NULLS setting was turned off, using ALTER DATABASE and SET ANSI_NULLS OFF, and then the sys.databases system catalog view was queried again to confirm the change.

It is important to note that database ANSI options *can still be overridden* by SET statement connection-level settings. For example, even though the AdventureWorks database has the ANSI_NULLS setting OFF, using SET ANSI_NULLS ON in a query batch will override the database setting behavior for the query session.

Also, some of the options reviewed here are required to be turned ON before manipulating indexes on computed columns or indexed views. Those options include ARITHABORT, QUOTED_IDENTIFIER, CONCAT_NULL_YIELDS_NULL, ANSI_NULLS, ANSI_WARNINGS, and ANSI_PADDING. The NUMERIC_ROUNDABORT, however, must be OFF.

Configuring Automatic Options

Automatic database options impact the behavior of the SQL Server database engine, enabling or disabling automatic maintenance or metadata updates. Table 22-8 describes each of the automatic options.

Table 22-8. *Automatic Options*

Option	Description
AUTO_CLOSE	When this option is enabled, the database is closed and shut down when the last user connection to the database exits and all processes are completed.
AUTO_CREATE_STATISTICS	When this option is enabled, SQL Server automatically generates statistical information regarding the distribution of values in a column. This information assists the query processor with generating an acceptable query execution plan (the internal plan for returning the result set requested by the query).
AUTO_SHRINK	When this option is enabled, SQL Server shrinks data and log files automatically. Shrinking will only occur when more than 25 percent of the file has unused space. The database is then shrunk to either 25 percent free, or the original data or log file size. For example, if you defined your primary data file to be 100MB, a shrink operation would be unable to decrease the file size smaller than 100MB.
AUTO_UPDATE_STATISTICS	When this option is enabled, statistics already created for your tables are automatically updated.
AUTO_UPDATE_STATISTICS_ASYNC	When this option is ON, if a query initiates an automatic update of old statistics, the query will not wait for the statistics to be updated before compiling. When OFF (the default), a query that initiates statistics updates will wait until the update is finished before compiling a query plan.

The syntax for configuring automatic database options is as follows:

```
ALTER DATABASE database_name
SET  AUTO_CLOSE { ON | OFF }
  | AUTO_CREATE_STATISTICS { ON | OFF }
```

```
| AUTO_SHRINK { ON | OFF }
| AUTO_UPDATE_STATISTICS { ON | OFF }
| AUTO_UPDATE_STATISTICS_ASYNC { ON | OFF }
```

The first argument is the database name you want to modify. The second argument is the name of the option you wish to either enable (ON) or disable (OFF). This recipe will demonstrate enabling the AUTO_UPDATE_STATISTICS_ASYNC automatic database option for the AdventureWorks database:

```
SET NOCOUNT ON

SELECT is_auto_update_stats_async_on
FROM sys.databases
WHERE name = 'AdventureWorks'

ALTER DATABASE AdventureWorks
SET  AUTO_UPDATE_STATISTICS_ASYNC    ON

SELECT is_auto_update_stats_async_on
FROM sys.databases
WHERE name = 'AdventureWorks'
```

This returns

```
is_auto_update_stats_async_on
0

is_auto_update_stats_async_on
1
```

How It Works

This recipe demonstrated using ALTER DATABASE to change the AUTO_UPDATE_STATS_ASYNC automatic database setting. The recipe started by querying the sys.databases system catalog view to see the current setting of the database. After that, the AUTO_UPDATE_STATS_ASYNC setting was turned ON using ALTER DATABASE, and then the sys.databases system catalog view was queried again to confirm the change.

Some automatic settings can have a *negative* impact on performance when set to ON—including AUTO_CLOSE and AUTO_SHRINK. For AUTO_CLOSE, the overhead of opening the database after cleanly shutting down can cause performance issues in a high-traffic database that has moments where no user is currently logged in (the overhead of starting up and shutting down a database repeatedly). For AUTO_SHRINK, SQL Server may initiate a database shrink operation during an inopportune moment, slowing down query performance of regular end users. Also, database size may expand and contract repeatedly when this option is on. AUTO_SHRINK also causes fragmentation, so allowing this option to be enabled after index rebuilds or reorganizations can undo the positive effects of these maintenance activities. When it's possible, let the free space in the database remain, so that SQL Server isn't continually expanding and contracting the same files.

Other options should usually *not* be set OFF without a very good reason, including AUTO_CREATE_STATISTICS and AUTO_UPDATE_STATISTICS. Statistics help SQL Server compile the best query optimization plan, and the overhead of creating and maintaining statistics automatically is usually not significant compared to the benefits they provide to query performance.

Creating or Modifying a Database to Allow External Access

The CREATE DATABASE command provides two external access database options: DB_CHAINING and TRUSTWORTHY. Both of these options are OFF by default. The DB_CHAINING option, when enabled, allows the new database to participate in a cross-database ownership chain. In its simplest form, an ownership chain occurs when one object (such as a view or stored procedure) references another object. If the owner of the schema that contains these objects is the same as the referenced object, permissions on the referenced object are not checked. *Cross-database chaining* means that one object references another object in a different database. Ownership chaining can result in inappropriate or unintended data access—for example, if a dbo-owned schema in a view references a different database's dbo-owned data table, security will not be checked if the DB_CHAINING option is enabled.

The TRUSTWORTHY option is used to specify whether or not SQL Server will "trust" any modules or assemblies within a given database. When this option is OFF, SQL Server will protect against certain malicious EXTERNAL_ACCESS or UNSAFE activities within that database's assemblies, or from malicious code executed under the context of high-privileged users.

The abridged syntax for creating a database with external access options enabled or disabled is as follows:

```
CREATE DATABASE database_name
...
   [ WITH  { DB_CHAINING { ON | OFF }
        |TRUSTWORTHY { ON | OFF }]]
```

Both options appear in the WITH clause following the transaction log LOG ON option. They can be enabled in the same statement, and both are OFF by default.

You can also set these options for an existing database using ALTER DATABASE:

```
ALTER DATABASE database_name
{SET   DB_CHAINING { ON | OFF }
| TRUSTWORTHY { ON | OFF }}
```

This recipe demonstrates how to create a database with the database chaining option enabled, and then modify the new database to also allow external database access within database objects:

```
USE master
GO
-- Create a database with the model database defaults
CREATE DATABASE BookData
WITH DB_CHAINING ON
GO

USE master
GO
-- Now modify the new database to also have the
-- TRUSTWORTHY option ON
ALTER DATABASE BookData
SET TRUSTWORTHY ON
GO
```

How It Works

In this recipe, database ownership chaining was enabled within the CREATE DATABASE statement. The BookData database was created using default options (file name, size, growth) based on the model system database. After that, the WITH clause was used to enable database ownership chaining:

```
WITH DB_CHAINING ON
```

After that, the ALTER DATABASE command was used to enable the TRUSTWORTHY setting. Instead of the WITH keyword, the SET keyword was used, followed by the external access option name and the ON keyword:

```
ALTER DATABASE BookData
SET TRUSTWORTHY ON
GO
```

Creating or Changing a Database to Use a Non-Server Default Collation

In this recipe, I demonstrate how to create or modify a database to use a specific collation. SQL Server collations determine how data is sorted, compared, presented, and stored. The database collation can be different from the server-level collation defined when the SQL Server instance was installed, for those times that you may wish to store data with a differing code page or sort order from the SQL Server instance default.

The syntax for designating the collation using CREATE DATABASE is as follows:

```
CREATE DATABASE database_name
    [ ON
        [ <filespec> [ ,...n ] ]
        [ , <filegroup> [ ,...n ] ] ]
[ [ LOG ON { <filespec> [ ,...n ] } ]
    [ COLLATE collation_name ]]
```

The COLLATE command is used after the transaction log definition to explicitly define the default database collation.

To change the default collation for an existing database, the syntax for ALTER DATABASE is as follows:

```
ALTER DATABASE database_name
{COLLATE collation_name}
```

This recipe demonstrates creating a new database with a default Ukrainian collation, with case- and accent-insensitive settings. After creating the database, the database will then be altered to use a case- and accent-*sensitive* collation instead:

```
CREATE DATABASE BookStoreArchive_Ukrainian
ON  PRIMARY
(   NAME = 'BookStoreArchive_UKR',
    FILENAME = 'C:\Apress\BookStoreArchive_UKR.mdf',
    SIZE = 3MB ,
    MAXSIZE = UNLIMITED,
    FILEGROWTH = 10MB )
 LOG ON
(   NAME = 'BookStoreArchive_UKR_log',
    FILENAME = 'C:\Apress\BookStoreArchive_UKR_log.ldf',
    SIZE = 504KB ,
    MAXSIZE = 100MB ,
    FILEGROWTH = 10%)
COLLATE Ukrainian_CI_AI
GO

ALTER DATABASE BookStoreArchive_Ukrainian
COLLATE Ukrainian_CS_AS
GO
```

How It Works

Both the CREATE DATABASE and ALTER DATABASE examples used the COLLATE statement, followed by the collation name, to designate the default collation of the database:

COLLATE Ukrainian_CI_AI

Once the database default collation is set, new tables containing character data type columns (varchar, nvarchar, char, nchar, text, ntext) will use the database default collation as the column collation.

■**Caution** Creating a user-defined database with a default collation different from the SQL Server instance default (system database) can cause collation conflicts (cross-collation data cannot be converted or joined in a query). For example, the tempdb system database uses the same collation as the model database, which may cause temporary table data operations to fail in conjunction with a different collation. Always test cross-collation operations thoroughly.

Configuring Cursor Options

In Chapter 9, I discussed how to create and use Transact-SQL cursors. SQL Server has two database options that control the behavior of Transact-SQL cursors, as you can see in Table 22-9.

Table 22-9. *Cursor Options*

Option	Description
CURSOR_CLOSE_ON_COMMIT	When CURSOR_CLOSE_ON_COMMIT is enabled, Transact-SQL cursors automatically close once a transaction is committed.
CURSOR_DEFAULT { LOCAL | GLOBAL }	If CURSOR_DEFAULT LOCAL is enabled, cursors created without explicitly setting scope as GLOBAL will default to local access. If CURSOR_DEFAULT GLOBAL is enabled, cursors created without explicitly setting scope as LOCAL will default to GLOBAL access.

The syntax for configuring cursor options is as follows:

```
ALTER DATABASE database_name
SET CURSOR_CLOSE_ON_COMMIT { ON | OFF }
   | CURSOR_DEFAULT { LOCAL | GLOBAL }
```

The statement takes two arguments, the database name you want to modify and the option that you want to configure on and off.

This recipe will demonstrate enabling the CURSOR_CLOSE_ON_COMMIT for the AdventureWorks database:

```
SET NOCOUNT ON

SELECT is_cursor_close_on_commit_on
FROM sys.databases
WHERE name = 'AdventureWorks'

ALTER DATABASE AdventureWorks
SET  CURSOR_CLOSE_ON_COMMIT   ON
```

```
SELECT is_cursor_close_on_commit_on
FROM sys.databases
WHERE name = 'AdventureWorks'
```

This returns

```
is_cursor_close_on_commit_on
0

is_cursor_close_on_commit_on
1
```

How It Works

This recipe demonstrated using ALTER DATABASE to change the CURSOR_CLOSE_ON_COMMIT automatic database setting. The recipe started by querying the sys.databases system catalog view to see the current setting of the database. After that, the CURSOR_CLOSE_ON_COMMIT setting was turned ON using ALTER DATABASE, and then the sys.databases system catalog view was queried again to confirm the change.

Enabling Date Correlation Optimization

Two tables that are related by a datetime foreign key reference can benefit from enabling the DATE_CORRELATION_OPTIMIZATION option. When enabled, SQL Server collects additional statistics, which in turn help improve the performance of queries that use a join between the two datetime data type columns (foreign key and primary key pair).

The syntax for enabling this option is as follows:

```
ALTER DATABASE database_name
SET DATE_CORRELATION_OPTIMIZATION { ON | OFF }
```

The command takes two arguments: the database name you want to modify and whether to set the DATE_CORRELATION_OPTIMIZATION ON or OFF. This option defaults to OFF, as having it ON adds extra overhead for those tables that meet the criteria for date correlation optimization.

This option, when ON, can benefit queries that join two table datetime values, which are related by a foreign key reference. SQL Server will then maintain additional correlation statistics, which may allow, depending on your query, SQL Server to generate more efficient, less I/O intensive query plans.

In order to take advantage of this database setting and for the statistics to be created automatically, at least one of the datetime columns (primary key or foreign key) has to be the first key column in a clustered index or the partitioning column in a partitioned table.

Be aware that there is extra overhead in updating the statistics, so you should monitor performance for databases that have heavy updates to the primary key and foreign key datetime-related tables, as the benefits of the query optimization may not outweigh the overhead of the statistics updates.

In this recipe, the AdventureWorks database will have this option turned ON:

```
SET NOCOUNT ON

SELECT is_date_correlation_on
FROM sys.databases
WHERE name = 'AdventureWorks'
```

```
ALTER DATABASE AdventureWorks
SET DATE_CORRELATION_OPTIMIZATION ON

SELECT is_date_correlation_on
FROM sys.databases
WHERE name = 'AdventureWorks'
```

This returns

```
is_date_correlation_on
0

is_date_correlation_on
1
```

How It Works

In this recipe, the sys.databases system catalog view was used to check the state of date correlation of the AdventureWorks database. After that, ALTER DATABASE and SET DATE_CORRELATION_OPTIMIZATION ON was issued. The sys.databases system catalog view was checked again, confirming the new setting.

Modifying Database Parameterization Behavior

The PARAMETERIZATION option is used with ALTER DATABASE and controls whether all or just some queries against the database are parameterized.

Parameterization occurs when a query is submitted to SQL Server. SQL Server looks at literal values in a SELECT, INSERT, UPDATE, and DELETE statement and seeks to parameterize them (make a placeholder) so that query execution plans can be reused when similar queries are executed, instead of a new plan being made for each query. Execution plans are created for the parameterized query at the statement level, so that each statement in a batch of statements can be individually parameterized.

The syntax for enabling this option is as follows:

```
ALTER DATABASE database_name
SET PARAMETERIZATION { SIMPLE | FORCED }
```

The command takes two arguments: the database name and the parameterization option. You have two choices with parameterization, SIMPLE (the default) or FORCED. With SIMPLE parameterization (the default value), SQL statements are parameterized for a smaller population of queries (at SQL Server's discretion). Setting parameterization to FORCED increases the population of queries that become parameterized, which can benefit query performance as more query execution plans are created and potentially reused.

This recipe demonstrates how to enable this option using ALTER DATABASE, check the value in sys.databases, and then show the results of parameterization using the sys.dm_exec_cached_plans system catalog view and the sys.dm_exec_cached_plans Dynamic Management Function. First, the AdventureWorks database is checked to see whether the parameterization option is set to forced:

```
SELECT is_parameterization_forced
FROM sys.databases
WHERE name = 'AdventureWorks'
```

The results of this query confirm that this option is *not* enabled:

is_parameterization_forced
0

Next, the parameterization option is changed to FORCED using ALTER DATABASE:

```
ALTER DATABASE AdventureWorks
SET PARAMETERIZATION FORCED
```

The change is then confirmed by querying sys.databases:

```
SELECT is_parameterization_forced
FROM sys.databases
WHERE name = 'AdventureWorks'
```

This returns

is_parameterization_forced

1

Next, I'll use the DBCC FREEPROCCACHE command to clear out the procedure cache, in order to demonstrate the use of the FORCED option:

```
-- CAUTION!  Don't run this on a production SQL Server instance.
-- This clears out the procedure cache and will cause all
-- new queries to recompile.
DBCC FREEPROCCACHE
```

I then execute the following query:

```
-- CAUTION!  Don't run this on a production SQL Server instance.
-- This clears out the procedure cache and will cause all
-- new queries to recompile.
DBCC FREEPROCCACHE

USE AdventureWorks
GO

SELECT BirthDate
FROM HumanResources.Employee
WHERE BusinessEntityID IN
    (SELECT TOP 3 BusinessEntityID
     FROM Sales.SalesPersonQuotaHistory
     WHERE SalesQuota = 263000.00)
```

This returns

```
BirthDate
1941-11-17 00:00:00.000
```

Now I'll query the sys.dm_exec_cached_plans system catalog view. This view returns information about the query execution plans cached in the SQL Server instance. The view column plan_handle contains an identifier that references the query plan in memory. To view this plan in memory, the query uses the sys.dm_exec_query_plan Dynamic Management Function, which takes the plan_handle as a parameter and returns the execution plan in XML format. This next query searches for any reference to EmployeeID from the previous query, for prepared, cached plans:

```
SELECT query_plan
FROM sys.dm_exec_cached_plans p
CROSS APPLY sys.dm_exec_query_plan(p.plan_handle)
WHERE CAST(query_plan as varchar(max))
    LIKE '%TOP 3 BusinessEntityID%' AND
    objtype = 'Prepared'
```

This returns the following abridged results (I'm showing a small fragment of the XML formatted plan):

```
<StmtSimple StatementText="(@0 numeric(38,2))select BirthDate from HumanResources .
 Employee
where BusinessEntityID in ( select top 3 BusinessEntityID from Sales .
SalesPersonQuotaHistory where
SalesQuota = @0 )" StatementId="1" StatementCompId="1" StatementType="SELECT"
StatementSubTreeCost="0.00756866" StatementEstRows="1" StatementOptmLevel="FULL"
StatementOptmEarlyAbortReason="GoodEnoughPlanFound">
```

■**Tip** As an alternative to `sys.dm_exec_query_plan`, you can also use `sys.dm_exec_text_query_plan`, which returns the query plan in text format. This DMV doesn't have the output size limitations of `sys.dm_exec_query_plan`, and it also lets you narrow down the specific statements you would like to evaluate.

This example of parameterization could have also occurred in the `SIMPLE` parameterization setting; however, only the `FORCED` setting increases the chances that the parameterization *will* occur.

To set the database option back to `SIMPLE`, `ALTER DATABASE` is used again:

```
ALTER DATABASE AdventureWorks
SET PARAMETERIZATION SIMPLE
GO
```

How It Works

This recipe demonstrated how to change a database to use forced parameterization and then go back again to simple parameterization. I began the recipe by checking the parameterization state of the `AdventureWorks` database using the `sys.databases` system catalog view. After that, `ALTER DATABASE` and `SET PARAMETERIZATION FORCED` was used. The `sys.databases` system catalog view was checked again to confirm that the option was changed. After that, `DBCC FREEPROCCACHE` was used to clear out the procedure cache.

■**Caution** Only use `DBCC FREEPROCCACHE` on a test, non-production SQL instance, as it removes all plans from the procedure cache, which can negatively impact performance.

Next, a query was executed against the `HumanResources.Employee` table, using a subquery against the `Sales.SalesPersonQuotaHistory` table. I then executed a query against the `sys.dm_exec_cached_plans` system catalog view and the `sys.dm_exec_query_plan` Dynamic Management Function. The results showed an XML-formatted SQL plan (your results may vary) with parameter placeholders for use in the `WHERE` clause:

```
where SalesQuota = @0
```

Tip For more on looking at a SQL execution plan, see Chapter 28.

Enabling Read Consistency for a Transaction

SQL Server provides two database options that allow for statement-level and transaction-level read consistency: ALLOW_SNAPSHOT_ISOLATION and READ_COMMITTED_SNAPSHOT (which will be demonstrated after this recipe).

Note Both of the database options are discussed in the same recipe because they both impact read consistency. They do not, however, need to be used together; they are independent options. Use ALLOW_SNAPSHOT_ISOLATION if you want *transaction-level* read consistency and READ_COMMITTED_SNAPSHOT if you are looking for *statement-level* read consistency.

The ALLOW_SNAPSHOT_ISOLATION database option enables a snapshot of data at the transaction level. When ALLOW_SNAPSHOT_ISOLATION is enabled, you can use the snapshot transaction isolation level to read a transactional consistent version of the data as it existed *at the beginning* of a transaction. Using this option, data reads don't block data modifications. If data was changed while reading the snapshot data and an attempt was made within the snapshot transaction to change the data, the change attempt will *not* be allowed, and you will see a warning from SQL Server's update conflict detection support. Once this database setting is enabled, snapshot isolation is initiated when SET TRANSACTION ISOLATION LEVEL with SNAPSHOT isolation is specified before the start of the transaction.

Note For an example of ALLOW_SNAPSHOT_ISOLATION in action, see Chapter 3's recipe "Configuring a Session's Transaction Locking Behavior."

The READ_COMMITTED_SNAPSHOT setting enables row versioning at the *individual statement level*. Row versioning retains the original copy of a row in tempdb whenever the row is modified, storing the latest version of the row in the current database. For databases with a large amount of transactional activity, you'll want to make sure tempdb has enough space in order to hold row versions. The READ_COMMITTED_SNAPSHOT setting enables row versioning at the individual statement level for the query session. When enabling READ_COMMITTED_SNAPSHOT, locks are not held on the data. Row versioning is used to return the statement's data as it existed at the beginning of the statement execution. Data being read during the statement execution still allows updates by others, and unlike snapshot isolation, there is no mandatory update conflict detection to warn you that the data has been modified during the read. Once this database option is enabled, row versioning is then initiated when executing a query in the default read-committed isolation level or when SET TRANSACTION ISOLATION LEVEL with READ COMMITTED is used before the statement executes.

The main benefit of using these options is the reduction in locks for read operations. If your application requires real-time data values, these two options *are not* the best choice. However, if snapshots of data are acceptable to your application, setting these options may be appropriate.

The syntax for enabling these options is as follows:

```
ALTER DATABASE database_name
    SET ALLOW_SNAPSHOT_ISOLATION {ON | OFF }
    | READ_COMMITTED_SNAPSHOT {ON | OFF }
```

The command takes two arguments: the database name and the snapshot option of enabling or disabling. This recipe will demonstrate enabling both row versioning options for the AdventureWorks database. First, the current database settings are validated by querying sys.databases:

```
SELECT snapshot_isolation_state_desc,
       is_read_committed_snapshot_on
FROM sys.databases
WHERE name = 'AdventureWorks'
```

This returns

snapshot_isolation_state_desc	is_read_committed_snapshot_on
OFF	0

Next, ALTER DATABASE is used to enable both options (although both options needn't be chosen, because you can choose to enable one type of read consistency option and not another):

```
ALTER DATABASE AdventureWorks
SET ALLOW_SNAPSHOT_ISOLATION ON

ALTER DATABASE AdventureWorks
SET READ_COMMITTED_SNAPSHOT ON
```

Next, the database settings are validated again, post-change:

```
SELECT snapshot_isolation_state_desc,
       is_read_committed_snapshot_on
FROM sys.databases
WHERE name = 'AdventureWorks'
```

This returns

snapshot_isolation_state_desc	is_read_committed_snapshot_on
ON	1

To turn these options off again, I execute the following:

```
ALTER DATABASE AdventureWorks
SET ALLOW_SNAPSHOT_ISOLATION OFF

ALTER DATABASE AdventureWorks
SET READ_COMMITTED_SNAPSHOT OFF
```

How It Works

This recipe started off by checking the current state of row versioning in the AdventureWorks database by querying sys.databases. After that, two separate ALTER DATABASE commands were executed to enable snapshot isolation and read-committed isolation levels in the database. The system catalog view sys.databases was queried again to confirm the changes. Keep in mind that both options do not need to be enabled—you can pick and choose whether or not you want statement- or transaction-level read consistency, both, or neither.

Configuring Database Recovery Models

A full database backup is a full copy of your database. Transaction log backups, on the other hand, only back up the transaction log from the latest full backup or latest transaction log backup. When the backup completes, SQL Server truncates the inactive portion of the log. Aside from allowing a restore from the point that the transaction log backup completed, transaction log backups also allow point-in-time and transaction mark recovery. Point-in-time recovery allows you to restore the database as of a specific time period, for example, restoring a database prior to a database modification or failure. *Transaction mark recovery* recovers to the first instance of a "marked" transaction and includes the updates made within this transaction.

■Note For more information on transaction log backups, see Chapter 29.

SQL Server provides three different recovery models that define whether or not transaction log backups can be made, and if so, what database activities will write to the transaction log. The three recovery models are FULL, BULK_LOGGED, and SIMPLE:

- When using SIMPLE recovery, the transaction log is automatically truncated after a database backup, removing the ability to perform transaction log backups. In this recovery mode, the risk of data loss is dependent on your full or differential backup schedule—and you will not be able to perform the point-in-time recovery that a transaction log backup offers.

- The BULK_LOGGED recovery model allows you to perform full, differential, and transaction log backups; however, there is minimal logging to the transaction log for bulk operations. The benefit of this recovery mode is reduced log space usage during bulk operations, but the trade-off is that transaction log backups can only be used to recover from the end of the transaction log backup (no point-in-time recovery or marked transactions allowed).

- The FULL recovery model fully logs all transaction activity, bulk operations included. In this safest model, all restore options are available, including point-in-time transaction log restores, differential backups, and full database backups.

The syntax for changing the database recovery mode is as follows:

```
ALTER DATABASE database_name
SET RECOVERY { FULL | BULK_LOGGED | SIMPLE }
```

In this recipe, the AdventureWorks database will be set to the FULL recovery model:

```
SELECT recovery_model_desc
FROM sys.databases
WHERE name = 'AdventureWorks'
GO

ALTER DATABASE AdventureWorks
SET RECOVERY FULL
GO

SELECT recovery_model_desc
FROM sys.databases
WHERE name = 'AdventureWorks'
```

This returns

```
recovery_model_desc
SIMPLE


recovery_model_desc
FULL
```

How It Works

The initial recovery model when a database is created depends on the recovery mode of the model database. After creating a database, you can always modify the recovery model using ALTER DATABASE and SET RECOVERY.

In this recipe, the sys.databases system catalog view was used to check on the recovery model of the AdventureWorks database. Once it was confirmed that it was currently using a SIMPLE model, ALTER DATABASE and SET RECOVERY were used to change the database to FULL mode.

■**Tip**   After changing a database's recovery model, it is a good practice to perform a full backup of your database.

Configuring Page Verification

Disk errors can occur when a data page write to the physical disk is interrupted due to a power failure or other physical issue. SQL Server has three modes for handling and detecting incomplete I/O transactions caused by disk errors: CHECKSUM, TORN_PAGE_DETECTION, and NONE.

- The CHECKSUM option (the model database default) writes a checksum value to the data page header based on the contents of the entire data page. If a page is corrupted or partially written, SQL Server will detect a difference between the header and the actual page contents. This option offers the most protection.

- The TORN_PAGE_DETECTION option (the main option used in previous versions of SQL Server) detects data page issues by reversing a bit for each 512-byte sector of the data page. When a bit is in the incorrect state when read by SQL Server, a "torn" page is identified.

- When NONE is selected, neither CHECKSUM nor TORN_PAGE_DETECTION handling is used in allocating new data pages or identified by SQL Server during a read.

Unless you have a good reason for doing so (such as a requirement for unfettered query performance for a benchmark test, for example), keeping the default option of CHECKSUM is a good idea. Although CHECKSUM has more overhead than TORN_PAGE_DETECTION, it is also more comprehensive in its ability to identify data page errors. The syntax for setting the page verification mode is as follows:

```
ALTER DATABASE database_name
SET PAGE_VERIFY { CHECKSUM | TORN_PAGE_DETECTION | NONE }
```

In this recipe, the AdventureWorks database is modified to *not* perform page verification:

```
SELECT page_verify_option_desc
FROM sys.databases
WHERE name = 'AdventureWorks'
GO
```

```
ALTER DATABASE AdventureWorks
SET PAGE_VERIFY NONE
GO

SELECT page_verify_option_desc
FROM sys.databases
WHERE name = 'AdventureWorks'
GO
```

This returns

```
page_verify_option_desc
CHECKSUM
```

```
page_verify_option_desc
NONE
```

(1 row(s) affected)

Now it will be added back:

```
ALTER DATABASE AdventureWorks
SET PAGE_VERIFY CHECKSUM
GO

SELECT page_verify_option_desc
FROM sys.databases
WHERE name = 'AdventureWorks'
GO
```

This returns

```
page_verify_option_desc
```

```
CHECKSUM
```

How It Works

This recipe started off by validating the current page verification state in the AdventureWorks database by querying the sys.databases system catalog view. After that, ALTER DATABASE and SET PAGE_VERIFY were executed to disable page verification. The sys.databases system catalog view was queried again, validating the change.

Controlling Database Access and Ownership

In these next two recipes, I'll cover how to control the access and ownership of user databases. First off, I'll show you how to change a database's accessibility using three different states: online, offline, or emergency. The recipe after that demonstrates how to change the owner of the database using the sp_changedbowner system stored procedure.

Changing a Database State to Online, Offline, or Emergency

A database can be in one of three states: online, offline, or emergency.

The *online state* is the default, meaning that the database is open and available to be used. When in *offline status*, the database is "closed" and cannot be modified or queried by any user. You may wish to take a database offline in situations where you need to move the data files to a new physical location, and then use ALTER DATABASE to modify the metadata for that file's new location (demonstrated later in the chapter). Unlike detaching the database, the database is still kept in the metadata of the SQL Server instance, and can then be taken back online later on.

Lastly, if the database is corrupted, setting a database to an emergency state allows read-only access to the database for sysadmin server role logins, allowing you to query any database objects that are still accessible (depending on the nature of the problem).

The syntax for configuring the database state is as follows:

```
ALTER DATABASE database_name
SET { ONLINE | OFFLINE | EMERGENCY }
```

This recipe demonstrates how to bring the database offline, attempt a read, and then bring it online again. Keep in mind that if active connections are in the AdventureWorks database, your command will have to wait for them to disconnect unless you force them out (using techniques discussed previously in the "Setting Database User Access" recipe):

```
USE master
GO

ALTER DATABASE AdventureWorks
SET OFFLINE
GO

-- Attempt a read against a table
SELECT COUNT(*)
FROM AdventureWorks.HumanResources.Department
GO
```

This returns

```
Msg 942, Level 14, State 4, Line 3
Database 'AdventureWorks' cannot be opened because it is offline.
```

Now to bring the database back online again:

```
ALTER DATABASE AdventureWorks
SET ONLINE
GO
```

How It Works

In this recipe, the AdventureWorks database was taken offline by using ALTER DATABASE and the SET OFFLINE command. After taking the database offline, a query against a table in the database was attempted, causing an error to be raised. The database was then brought back online using ALTER DATABASE and the SET ONLINE option.

Changing a Database Owner

In this recipe, I demonstrate how to change the owner of an existing database using the sp_changedbowner system stored procedure.

The syntax for this system stored procedure is as follows:

```
sp_changedbowner [ @loginame = ] 'login'
        [ , [ @map= ] remap_alias_flag ]
```

The parameters for the procedure are described briefly in Table 22-10.

Table 22-10. *sp_changedbowner Parameters*

Parameter	Description
'login'	This specifies the new SQL Server login that will own the database. This login cannot already be mapped to an existing database user (without dropping this user first).
remap_alias_flag	The optional flag references alias functionality, which was used in previous versions of SQL Server and allowed you to map users to a database. Alias functionality is going to be removed in a future version of SQL Server, so don't use it.

This recipe creates a new login and then makes the new login the database owner of the BookWarehouse database:

```
CREATE LOGIN NewBossInTown WITH PASSWORD = 'HereGoesTheNeighborhood10'
GO

USE BookData
GO

EXEC sp_changedbowner 'NewBossInTown'
GO

SELECT p.name
FROM sys.databases d
INNER JOIN sys.server_principals p ON
   d.owner_sid = p.sid
WHERE d.name = 'BookData'
```

This returns

```
name
NewBossInTown
```

How It Works

An owner is mapped from an existing SQL Server login to the dbo user in the database. Once this happens, the new owner has permissions to perform all database-specific operations (for example, creating tables, granting object permissions, deleting data, and so on).

In this recipe, a new login was created, and the database context was switched to the BookWarehouse database. The sp_changedbowner system stored procedure was used to set the new login as the owner:

```
EXEC sp_changedbowner 'NewBossInTown'
```

The new owner was then mapped to the dbo database user. Once set, the sys.databases and sys.server_principals system catalog views were queried in order to confirm that the owner was actually changed.

Managing Database Files and Filegroups

This next set of recipes covers how to manage database files and filegroups. Specifically, I'll be showing you how to

- Add a data or log file to an existing database.
- Remove a data or log file from a database.
- Relocate a data or transaction log file on the operating system.
- Change a file's logical name.
- Increase a database file size and modify growth options.
- Add a filegroup to an existing database.
- Set the default filegroup for a database.
- Remove a filegroup from a database.
- Make a database or filegroup read-only.

This next recipe demonstrates how to use ALTER DATABASE to add a data or log file to an existing database.

Adding a Data File or Log File to an Existing Database

Once a database is created, assuming that you have available disk space, you can add additional data or transaction logs to it as needed. This allows you to expand to new drives if the current physical drive/array is close to filled up, or if you are looking to improve performance by spreading I/O across multiple drives. It usually only makes sense to add additional data and log files to a database if you plan on putting these files on a separate drive/array. Putting multiple files on the same drive/array doesn't improve performance, and may only benefit you if you plan on performing separate file or filegroup backups for a very large database.

Adding files doesn't require you to bring the database offline. The syntax for ALTER DATABASE in order to add a data or transaction log file is as follows:

```
ALTER DATABASE database_name
{ADD FILE <filespec> [ ,...n ]
        [ TO FILEGROUP { filegroup_name | DEFAULT } ]
  | ADD LOG FILE <filespec> [ ,...n ] }
```

The syntax arguments are described in Table 22-11.

Table 22-11. *ALTER DATABASE...ADD FILE Arguments*

Argument	Description
database_name	Defines the name of the existing database.
<filespec> [,...n]	Designates one or more explicitly defined data files to add to the database.

Argument	Description
`filegroup_name | DEFAULT`	Designates the logical name of the filegroup. If followed by the `DEFAULT` keyword, this filegroup will be the default filegroup of the database (meaning all objects will by default be created there).
`[ LOG ON { <filespec> [ ,...n ] } ]`	Designates one or more explicitly defined transaction log files for the database.

In this recipe, a new data and transaction log file will be added to the `BookData` database:

```
ALTER DATABASE BookData
ADD FILE
(   NAME = 'BookData2',
    FILENAME = 'C:\Apress\BD2.NDF' ,
    SIZE = 1MB ,
    MAXSIZE = 10MB,
    FILEGROWTH = 1MB )
TO FILEGROUP [PRIMARY]
GO

ALTER DATABASE BookData
ADD LOG FILE
(   NAME = 'BookData2Log',
    FILENAME = 'C:\Apress\BD2.LDF' ,
    SIZE = 1MB ,
    MAXSIZE = 5MB,
    FILEGROWTH = 1MB )
GO
```

How It Works

In this recipe, a new data and transaction log file were added to the `BookData` database. To add the data file, `ALTER DATABASE` was used with the `ADD FILE` command, followed by the file specification:

```
ALTER DATABASE BookData
ADD FILE
...
```

The filegroup where the new file was added was specified using the `TO FILEGROUP` clause, followed by the filegroup name in brackets:

```
TO FILEGROUP [PRIMARY]
GO
```

In the second query in the recipe, a new transaction log file was added using `ALTER DATABASE` and the `ADD LOG FILE` command:

```
ALTER DATABASE BookData
ADD LOG FILE
...
```

Neither file addition required the database to be offline.

Removing a Data or Log File from a Database

This recipe demonstrates how to remove a data or transaction log file from an existing database. You may wish to do this if you need to relocate files from one drive/array to a different drive/array by creating a file on one drive and then dropping the old one.

The syntax for removing a file (data or transaction log) is as follows:

```
ALTER DATABASE database_name
REMOVE FILE logical_file_name
```

The syntax arguments are described in Table 22-12.

Table 22-12. *ALTER DATABASE...REMOVE FILE Arguments*

Argument	Description
database_name	The name of the existing database
logical_file_name	The logical file name of the file to be removed from the database

This recipe will first check for the logical file names for the BookData database, empty the contents of the file (which moves the data to the remaining data files), and, finally, drop the file from the database:

```
USE BookData
GO

SELECT name
FROM sys.database_files

DBCC SHRINKFILE(BookData2, EMPTYFILE)

ALTER DATABASE BookData
REMOVE FILE BookData2
```

This returns

```
name
BookData
BookData_log
BookData2
BookData2Log

DbId   FileId   CurrentSize   MinimumSize   UsedPages   EstimatedPages
11     3        128           128           0           0

DBCC execution completed. If DBCC printed error messages,
contact your system administrator.
The file 'BookData2' has been removed.
```

How It Works

The recipe started by switching to the BookData database so that the query against sys.database_files would return all logical file names from the current connection's database.

You can't remove the primary data or primary transaction log file from the database, nor can you remove a file that contains data or active transactions logging within it.

`DBCC SHRINKFILE` was used to remove existing data from the file to be dropped. This was done by using the `EMPTYFILE` parameter (see later on in the chapter for a review of this command).

After that, `ALTER DATABASE` was used with the `REMOVE FILE` command to remove the file from the database. Removing the file from the database also removes the underlying file from the file system.

Relocating a Data or Transaction Log File

Sometimes you may find it necessary to relocate a database file for an existing database. Your reasons for doing this may vary—you might need to do this because a physical drive is running out of space or to improve performance (placing files on separate RAID arrays).

This recipe demonstrates how to move a database file's location using the `ALTER DATABASE` command. The syntax for changing the file's location is as follows:

```
ALTER DATABASE database_name
MODIFY FILE
{NAME = logical_file_name , FILENAME = 'new_physical_file_name_and_path')
```

The arguments of this syntax are described in Table 22-13.

Table 22-13. *ALTER DATABASE...MODIFY FILE Arguments*

Argument	Description
database_name	The name of the existing database
logical_file_name	The logical file name of the physical file to be relocated
new_physical_file_name_and_path	The new file path and location

In this recipe, I'll create a new database called `BookWarehouse` using the default settings. After that, the database will be taken offline and then copied to the new location on the server. Once moved, the file will be relocated using `ALTER DATABASE`:

```
USE master
GO

-- Create a default database for this example
CREATE DATABASE BookTransferHouse
GO

ALTER DATABASE BookTransferHouse
SET OFFLINE
GO
```

Next, I'll manually move the file `C:\Program Files\Microsoft SQL Server\MSSQL10.AUGUSTUS\MSSQL\DATA\BookTransferHouse.mdf` to the `C:\Apress` directory. After that, I'll execute the following:

```
ALTER DATABASE BookTransferHouse
MODIFY FILE
(NAME = 'BookTransferHouse', FILENAME = 'C:\Apress\BookTransferHouse.mdf')
GO
```

This returns

```
The file "BookTransferHouse" has been modified in the system catalog.
The new path will be used the next time the database is started.
```

The database can then be brought back online:

```
ALTER DATABASE BookTransferHouse
SET ONLINE
GO
```

How It Works

The recipe started by creating a new database with default options. The database was then taken offline. Once offline, the data file was copied manually to the new location.

Once the file was moved, SQL Server was informed of the change by using the ALTER DATABASE and the MODIFY FILE statement. After that, the database was brought back online by using ALTER DATABASE and SET ONLINE.

Changing a File's Logical Name

You can change a database file's logical name without having to bring the database offline. The logical name of a database doesn't affect the functionality of the database itself, allowing you to change the name for consistency and naming convention purposes. For example, if you restore a database from backup using a new database name, you may wish for the logical name to match the new database name.

The syntax for changing a logical file name is as follows:

```
ALTER DATABASE database_name
{NAME = logical_file_name
    [ , NEWNAME = new_logical_name ] }
```

The arguments of this syntax are briefly described in Table 22-14.

Table 22-14. *ALTER DATABASE...NEWNAME Arguments*

Argument	Description
database_name	The name of the existing database
logical_file_name	The logical file name to be renamed
new_logical_name	The new logical file name

This recipe changes the logical data file name of the BookWarehouse data file in the BookWarehouse database:

```
ALTER DATABASE BookTransferHouse
MODIFY FILE
(NAME = 'BookTransferHouse', NEWNAME = 'BookTransferHouse_DataFile1')
GO
```

This returns

```
The file name 'BookTransferHouse_DataFile1' has been set.
```

How It Works

This recipe modified the BookTransferHouse logical file name to BookTransferHouse_DataFile1 by using ALTER DATABASE with the MODIFY FILE command. The command used the original NAME value and the NEWNAME value in order to make the change.

Increasing a Database's File Size and Modifying Its Growth Options

The previous recipe demonstrated how to change the logical file name using ALTER DATABASE and MODIFY FILE. With the MODIFY FILE command, you can also change the file sizing settings.

The syntax is as follows:

```
ALTER DATABASE database_name
MODIFY FILE
(
NAME = logical_file_name
[ , SIZE = size [ KB | MB | GB | TB ] ]
[ , MAXSIZE = { max_size [ KB | MB | GB | TB ] |
UNLIMITED } ]
[ , FILEGROWTH = growth_increment [ KB | MB | % ] ]
)
```

The arguments of this syntax are briefly described in Table 22-15.

Table 22-15. *ALTER DATABASE...MODIFY FILE Arguments*

Argument	Description
database_name	The name of the existing database.
logical_file_name	The logical file name to change size or growth options for.
size [KB	MB	GB	TB]	The new size (must be larger than the existing size) of the file based on the sizing attribute of choice (kilobytes, megabytes, gigabytes, terabytes).
{ max_size [KB	MB	GB	TB]	UNLIMITED }]	The new maximum allowable size of the file based on the chosen sizing attributes. If UNLIMITED is chosen, the file can grow to the available space of the physical drive.
growth_increment [KB	MB	%]]	The new amount that the file size increases when space is required. You can designate either the number of kilobytes or megabytes or the percentage of existing file size to grow. If you select 0, file growth will not occur.

In this recipe, a file is increased to 6MB in size and given a maximum allowable size of 10MB:

```
ALTER DATABASE BookTransferHouse
MODIFY FILE
(NAME='BookTransferHouse_DataFile1', SIZE=6MB, MAXSIZE=10MB)
```

How It Works

This recipe used ALTER DATABASE and MODIFY FILE to change a specific file's existing size as well as its maximum allowable size. The NAME option was referenced to specify which file was to be modified. The other two options, SIZE and MAXSIZE, were used to configure the new file size and maximum file size values.

Adding a Filegroup to an Existing Database

This recipe demonstrates how to add a filegroup to an existing database using ALTER DATABASE. Once the filegroup is created, you can then add a file or files to it.

The syntax is as follows:

```
ALTER DATABASE database_name
ADD FILEGROUP filegroup_name
```

The arguments of this syntax are described in Table 22-16.

Table 22-16. *ALTER DATABASE...ADD FILEGROUP Arguments*

Argument	Description
database_name	The name of the existing database
filegroup_name	The name of the new filegroup

This recipe adds a new filegroup to the BookWarehouse database:

```
ALTER DATABASE BookTransferHouse
ADD FILEGROUP FG2
GO

ALTER DATABASE BookTransferHouse
ADD FILE
(   NAME = 'BW2',
    FILENAME = 'C:\Apress\BW2.NDF' ,
    SIZE = 1MB ,
    MAXSIZE = 50MB,
    FILEGROWTH = 5MB )
TO FILEGROUP [FG2]
GO
```

How It Works

This recipe used ALTER DATABASE and ADD FILEGROUP to add a new filegroup called FG2 to an existing database. A new file was then added to the filegroup using ALTER DATABASE, ADD FILE, and the TO FILEGROUP command.

Setting the Default Filegroup

This recipe demonstrates how to change a filegroup into the default filegroup, meaning that the filegroup will contain all newly created database objects by default (unless database objects are explicitly put in a different filegroup during their creation).

The syntax for setting a filegroup to the database default is as follows:

```
ALTER DATABASE database_name
MODIFY FILEGROUP filegroup_name
DEFAULT
```

This recipe sets the FG2 filegroup in the BookWarehouse database to the default filegroup:

```
ALTER DATABASE BookTransferHouse
MODIFY FILEGROUP FG2 DEFAULT
```

This returns

```
The filegroup property 'DEFAULT' has been set.
```

How It Works

This recipe used ALTER DATABASE and MODIFY FILEGROUP to change an existing filegroup to the default filegroup. The DEFAULT keyword was used after the name of the new default filegroup.

Removing a Filegroup

This recipe demonstrates how to remove a user-defined filegroup. You can remove an empty filegroup using the following syntax:

```
ALTER DATABASE database_name
REMOVE FILEGROUP filegroup_name
```

The arguments of this syntax are briefly described in Table 22-17.

Table 22-17. *ALTER DATABASE...REMOVE FILEGROUP Arguments*

Argument	Description
database_name	The name of the database to drop the user-defined filegroup from
filegroup_name	The name of the user-defined filegroup to drop

In this recipe, I'll add a new filegroup called FG3 to the BookTransferHouse database. A new file will then be created within the filegroup. After that, the file will be removed, and then the user-defined filegroup will be removed:

```
ALTER DATABASE BookTransferHouse
ADD FILEGROUP FG3
GO

ALTER DATABASE BookTransferHouse
ADD FILE
(   NAME = 'BW3',
    FILENAME = 'C:\Apress\BW3.NDF' ,
    SIZE = 1MB ,
    MAXSIZE = 10MB,
    FILEGROWTH = 5MB )
TO FILEGROUP [FG3]
GO

-- Now, the file in the filegroup is removed
ALTER DATABASE BookTransferHouse
REMOVE FILE BW3
GO

-- Then the filegroup
ALTER DATABASE BookTransferHouse
REMOVE FILEGROUP FG3
GO
```

This returns

```
The file 'BW3' has been removed.
The filegroup 'FG3' has been removed.
```

How It Works

A user-defined filegroup can be removed once it is empty. In this recipe, ALTER DATABASE and REMOVE FILE were used to first empty the FG3 user-defined filegroup of files. Once empty of files, ALTER DATABASE and REMOVE FILEGROUP were used to remove the filegroup from the database.

Making a Database or Filegroup Read-Only

You can use ALTER DATABASE to set the database or specific user-defined filegroup to read-only access. Making a database or filegroup read-only prevents data modifications from taking place and is often used for static reporting databases. Using read-only options can improve query performance, because SQL Server no longer needs to lock objects queried within the database due to the fact that data and object modification in the database or user-defined filegroup is *not* allowed (although this isn't a replacement for setting up appropriate security permissions for data and object modifications).

The syntax for changing a database's updateability is as follows:

```
ALTER DATABASE database_name
SET { READ_ONLY | READ_WRITE }
```

The arguments for this statement only require the database name and the updateability option to be set.

The syntax for changing a filegroup's updateability is as follows:

```
ALTER DATABASE database_name
MODIFY FILEGROUP filegroup_name
{ READ_ONLY | READ_WRITE }
```

All that is needed in this syntax block is the database name, filegroup, and updateability option.

This recipe demonstrates setting the entire BookTransferHouse to read-only mode, and then setting it back to read-write mode (where modifications can then be made again). After this, the recipe demonstrates setting the updateability of a specific filegroup:

```
USE master
GO

-- Make the database read only
ALTER DATABASE BookTransferHouse
SET READ_ONLY
GO

-- Allow updates again
ALTER DATABASE BookTransferHouse
SET READ_WRITE
GO
```

```
-- Add a new filegroup
ALTER DATABASE BookTransferHouse
ADD FILEGROUP FG4
GO

-- Add a file to the filegroup
ALTER DATABASE BookTransferHouse
ADD FILE
(   NAME = 'BW4',
    FILENAME = 'C:\Apress\BW4.NDF' ,
    SIZE = 1MB ,
    MAXSIZE = 50MB,
    FILEGROWTH = 5MB )
TO FILEGROUP [FG4]
GO

-- Make a specific filegroup read-only
ALTER DATABASE BookTransferHouse
MODIFY FILEGROUP FG4 READ_ONLY
GO

-- Allow updates again
ALTER DATABASE BookTransferHouse
MODIFY FILEGROUP FG4 READ_WRITE
GO
```

How It Works

This recipe demonstrated changing the updateability of both a database and a specific filegroup. To modify the database, ALTER DATABASE and SET READ_ONLY were used. SET READ_WRITE was used to allow updates again. The last two queries in the recipe updated a specific filegroup, using ALTER DATABASE and MODIFY FILEGROUP to change updateability.

Viewing and Managing Database Space Usage

The last set of recipes in this chapter covers how to manage and view database disk storage usage. You'll learn how to shrink an entire database, or just the individual files within, depending on your needs. This next recipe demonstrates how to view space usage with the sp_spaceused system stored procedure.

Viewing Database Space Usage

This recipe demonstrates how to display database data disk space usage using the sp_spaceused system stored procedure. To view transaction log usage, I'll also demonstrate the DBCC SQLPERF command.

The syntax for sp_spaceused is as follows:

```
sp_spaceused [[ @objname = ] 'objname' ]
[,[ @updateusage = ] 'updateusage' ]
```

The parameters of this procedure are briefly described in Table 22-18.

Table 22-18. *sp_spaceused Parameters*

Parameter	Description
'objname'	This parameter defines the optional object name (table, for example) to view space usage. If not designated, the entire database's space usage information is returned.
'updateusage'	This parameter is used with a specific object, and accepts either true or false. If true, DBCC UPDATEUSAGE is used to update space usage information in the system tables.

The syntax for DBCC SQLPERF is as follows:

```
DBCC SQLPERF ( LOGSPACE )
[WITH NO_INFOMSGS ]
```

This DBCC command's arguments are briefly described in Table 22-19.

Table 22-19. *DBCC SQLPERF Arguments*

Parameter	Description
LOGSPACE	This is the only documented parameter allowed, and when designated, it returns transaction log space information for the entire SQL Server instance.
WITH NO_INFOMSGS	When included in the command, WITH NO_INFOMSGS suppresses informational messages from the DBCC output.

In this recipe, database and transaction log space will be viewed for the AdventureWorks database:

```
USE AdventureWorks
GO

EXEC sp_spaceused
```

This returns

```
database_name    database_size    unallocated space
AdventureWorks   181.94 MB          48.32 MB

reserved     data        index_size    unused
134776 KB    83872 KB    44912 KB      5992 KB
```

Next, transaction log information is displayed for the entire SQL Server instance:

```
DBCC SQLPERF ( LOGSPACE )
```

This returns the following (your results may vary):

```
Database Name           Log Size (MB)    Log Space Used (%)    Status
master                  0.7421875        47.36842              0
tempdb                  0.7421875        60.85526              0
model                   0.4921875        81.74603              0
msdb                    0.4921875        82.53968              0
AdventureWorks          1.992188         18.97059              0
BookStore               0.484375         44.75806              0
```

BookStoreArchive	0.4921875	46.9246	0
BookStoreInternational	0.4921875	49.80159	0
BookMart	0.484375	45.66532	0
TestAttach	0.484375	48.18548	0
BookData	1.476563	43.02249	0
BookStoreArchive_Ukrainian	0.9921875	53.98622	0
BookTransferHouse	0.484375	87.70161	0

How It Works

In this recipe, space usage for the AdventureWorks database was returned using the system stored procedure sp_spaceused and the DBCC SQLPERF command.

In the results of sp_spaceused, the database_size column showed the current size of the database (including both the data and log files). The unallocated space column showed unused space in the database, and the reserved column the amount of space used by database objects. The data column showed the amount of space used by the object data, and index_size the amount of space used by indexes.

The output of DBCC SQLPERF returned data for all databases on the SQL Server instance, showing the log size in megabytes and the percentage of the log file currently being used with active or inactive log information.

Shrinking the Database or a Database File

In this recipe, I demonstrate how to shrink an entire database using DBCC SHRINKDATABASE or a specific database file using DBCC SHRINKFILE. When following this recipe, keep in mind that shrinking databases and database files is a relatively expensive operation, introduces fragmentation, and should only be performed when necessary.

Database files, when auto-growth is enabled, can expand due to index rebuilds or data modification activity. You may have extra space in the database due to data modifications and index rebuilds. If you don't need to free up the unused space, you should allow the database to keep it reserved. However, if you do need the unused space and want to free it up, use DBCC SHRINKDATABASE or DBCC SHRINKFILE.

The DBCC SHRINKDATABASE command is use to shrink data and log files in a database.

■**Note** This command will shrink data files (MDF, NDF) on an individual basis; however, it will shrink the transaction log file or files (LDF) as if the multiple transaction log files were one continuous file.

The syntax is as follows:

```
DBCC SHRINKDATABASE
( 'database_name' | database_id | 0
    [ ,target_percent ]
    [ , { NOTRUNCATE | TRUNCATEONLY } ]
)
[ WITH NO_INFOMSGS ]
```

The arguments for this command are described in Table 22-20.

Table 22-20. *DBCC SHRINKDATABASE Arguments*

Argument	Description
`'database_name'` | `database_id` | `0`	You can designate a specific database name to shrink the system database ID, or if `0` is specified, the current database your query session is connected to.
`target_percent`	The target percentage designates the free space remaining in the database file after the shrinking event.
`NOTRUNCATE` | `TRUNCATEONLY`	`NOTRUNCATE` performs the data movements needed to create free space, but retains the freed space in the file without releasing it to the operating system. If `NOTRUNCATE` is not designated, the free file space is released to the operating system. `TRUNCATEONLY` frees up space without relocating data within the files. If not designated, data pages are reallocated within the files to free up space, which can lead to extensive I/O.
`WITH NO_INFOMSGS`	This argument prevents informational messages from being returned from the `DBCC` command.

The `DBCC SHRINKFILE` command is use to shrink a specific database file in a database. The syntax is as follows:

```
DBCC SHRINKFILE
(
    { ' file_name ' | file_id }
    { [ , EMPTYFILE]
    | [ [ , target_size ] [ , { NOTRUNCATE | TRUNCATEONLY } ] ]
    }
)
[ WITH NO_INFOMSGS ]
```

The arguments for this command are described in Table 22-21.

Table 22-21. *DBCC SHRINKFILE Arguments*

Argument	Description
`' file_name '` | `file_id`	This option defines the specific logical file name or file ID to shrink.
`EMPTYFILE`	This argument moves all data off the file so that it can be dropped using `ALTER DATABASE` and `REMOVE FILE`.
`target_size`	This option specifies the free space to be left in the database file (in megabytes). Leaving this blank instructs SQL Server to free up space to the default file size.
`NOTRUNCATE` | `TRUNCATEONLY`	`NOTRUNCATE` relocates allocated pages from within the file to the front of the file, but does not free the space to the operating system. Target size is ignored when used with `NOTRUNCATE`. `TRUNCATEONLY` causes unused space in the file to be released to the operating system, but only does so with free space found at the end of the file. No pages are rearranged or relocated. Target size is also ignored with the `TRUNCATEONLY` option. Use this option if you must free up space on the database file with minimal impact on database performance (rearranging pages on an actively utilized production database can cause performance issues, such as slow query response time).
`WITH NO_INFOMSGS`	This argument prevents informational messages from being returned from the `DBCC` command.

In this recipe, the AdventureWorks database will have its files expanded by allocating additional space using ALTER DATABASE...MODIFY FILE and then shrunk using the two DBCC file and database shrinking commands. In the first example, the AdventureWorks data and transaction log file are both expanded to larger sizes and then shrunk using a single DBCC operation:

```
ALTER DATABASE AdventureWorks
MODIFY FILE (NAME = AdventureWorks2008_Data , SIZE= 250MB)
GO

ALTER DATABASE AdventureWorks
MODIFY FILE (NAME = AdventureWorks2008_Log , SIZE= 500MB)
GO
```

The sp_spaceused system stored procedure is then used to return the space usage for the AdventureWorks database:

```
USE AdventureWorks
GO

EXEC sp_spaceused
GO
```

This returns

database_name	database_size	unallocated space	
AdventureWorks	750.00 MB	118.38 MB	

reserved	data	index_size	unused
134776 KB	83872 KB	44912 KB	5992 KB

Next, the size is reduced using DBCC SHRINKDATABASE:

```
DBCC SHRINKDATABASE  ('AdventureWorks', 10)
```

This returns the following (results may vary):

DbId	FileId	CurrentSize	MinimumSize	UsedPages	EstimatedPages
5	1	18664	15360	16752	16752
5	2	8224	256	8224	256

In the second example of this recipe, only the transaction log file is expanded, and then shrunk using DBCC SHRINKFILE:

```
ALTER DATABASE AdventureWorks
MODIFY FILE (NAME = AdventureWorks2008_Log , SIZE= 150MB)
GO
```

The sp_spaceused system stored procedure is then used to return the space usage for the AdventureWorks database:

```
USE AdventureWorks
GO

EXEC sp_spaceused
GO
```

This returns

```
database_name     database_size     unallocated space
AdventureWorks    295.81 MB         14.52 MB

reserved    data        index_size     unused
134440 KB   83864 KB    44912 KB       5664 KB
```

Next, the size is reduced using DBCC SHRINKDATABASE:

```
DBCC SHRINKFILE ('AdventureWorks2008_Log', 100)
```

This returns

```
DbId    FileId    CurrentSize    MinimumSize    UsedPages    EstimatedPages
5       2         13696          256            13696        256
```

How It Works

DBCC SHRINKDATABASE shrinks the data and log files in your database. In this recipe, the AdventureWorks data and log files were both increased to a larger size. After that, the DBCC SHRINKDATABASE command was used to reduce it down to a target free-space size of 10%:

```
DBCC SHRINKDATABASE ('AdventureWorks', 10)
```

After execution, the command returned a result set showing the current size (in 8KB pages), minimum size (in 8KB pages), currently used 8KB pages, and estimated 8KB pages that SQL Server could shrink the file down to.

In the second part of the recipe, DBCC SHRINKFILE was demonstrated. DBCC SHRINKFILE is very similar to DBCC SHRINKDATABASE, only it allows you to shrink the size of individual data and log files instead of all files in the database. In this recipe, the AdventureWorks transaction log file was expanded, and then shrunk down to a specific size (in megabytes):

```
DBCC SHRINKFILE ('AdventureWorks_Log', 100)
```

This command shrinks the physical file by removing inactive virtual log files. *Virtual log files (VLFs)*, which range in size from a minimum 256 kilobytes and larger, are the unit of truncation for a transaction log and are created as records are written to the transaction log.

Within the transaction log is the "active" logical portion of the log. This is the area of the transaction log containing active transactions. This active portion does not usually match the physical bounds of the file, but will instead "round-robin" from VLF to VLF. Once a VLF no longer contains active transactions, it can be truncated through a BACKUP LOG operation or automated system truncation. This truncation doesn't reduce the size of the transaction log file; it only makes the VLFs available for new log records.

DBCC SHRINKFILE or DBCC SHRINKDATABASE will make its best effort to remove inactive VLFs from the end of the physical file. SQL Server will also attempt to add "dummy" rows to push the active logical log toward the beginning of the physical file—so sometimes issuing a BACKUP LOG after the first execution of the DBCC SHRINKFILE command, and then issuing the DBCC SHRINKFILE command again, will allow you to free up the originally requested space.

Database Integrity and Optimization

In the previous chapter, I showed you how to create, configure, modify, and drop a database. In this chapter, I'll show you how to maintain your database using the Transact-SQL language, including ways to use the ALTER INDEX command for rebuilding or defragmenting indexes and DBCC commands for helping identify database integrity problems. I'll also demonstrate a new technique introduced in SQL Server 2008 for rebuilding a heap (a table without a clustered index).

In previous versions of SQL Server, DBCC commands such as DBCC CHECKDB were resource-intensive and could adversely affect performance if executed on a busy SQL Server instance. Microsoft has enhanced several of the DBCC commands to use internal database snapshots of target data instead of using table or database locks. Several of the commands are also more thorough in their checking routines than in previous versions of SQL Server.

■**Caution** Several of the DBCC commands reviewed in this chapter have REPAIR options. Microsoft recommends that you solve data integrity issues by restoring the database from the last good backup rather than resorting to a REPAIR option. If restoring from backup is not an option, the REPAIR option should be used only as a last resort. Depending on the REPAIR option selected, data loss can occur, and the problem may still not be resolved.

This chapter contains recipes that you can run periodically to check for database integrity issues. Running periodic checks (daily, weekly, and so on) will allow you to identify internal errors that can occur in various areas of the database.

As data is modified in your databases, the tables and indexes can become fragmented. The more fragmented a clustered or nonclustered index becomes, the more potential pages are required to be returned by the database engine in order to fulfill the same query request. The last two recipes in this chapter will address how to rebuild or defragment these indexes on a periodic basis using Transact-SQL.

Database Integrity Checking

Database integrity errors are rare, but do occur. The next two recipes will review the commands used to validate and check for issues within a database. You'll learn how to check page usage and allocation in the database by using DBCC CHECKALLOC. You'll also learn how to check the integrity of database objects using DBCC CHECKDB.

Checking Consistency of the Disk Space Allocation Structures with DBCC CHECKALLOC

DBCC CHECKALLOC checks page usage and allocation in the database, and will report on any errors that are found (this command is automatically included in the execution of DBCC CHECKDB too—so you if you are already running CHECKDB periodically, there is no need to also run CHECKALLOC).

The syntax is as follows:

```
DBCC CHECKALLOC
(
    [ 'database_name' | database_id | 0 ]
        [ , NOINDEX
    |
    { REPAIR_ALLOW_DATA_LOSS
    | REPAIR_FAST
    | REPAIR_REBUILD
    } ]
)
    [ WITH { [ ALL_ERRORMSGS ]
             [ , NO_INFOMSGS ]
             [ , TABLOCK ]
             [ , ESTIMATEONLY ]
           }
    ]
```

The arguments of this command are described in Table 23-1.

Table 23-1. *DBCC CHECKALLOC Arguments*

Argument	Description
'database_name' | database_id | 0	This defines the database name or database ID that you want to check for errors. When 0 is selected, the current database is used.
NOINDEX	When NOINDEX used, nonclustered indexes are not included in the checks. This is a backward-compatible option that has no effect on DBCC CHECKALLOC.
REPAIR_ALLOW_DATA_LOSS | REPAIR_FAST | REPAIR_REBUILD	See the beginning of the chapter regarding a warning on using repair options. REPAIR_ALLOW_DATA_LOSS attempts a repair of the table or indexed view, with the risk of losing data in the process. REPAIR_FAST and REPAIR_REBUILD are maintained for backward compatibility only.
ALL_ERRORMSGS	When ALL_ERRORMSGS is chosen, every error found will be displayed. If this option isn't designated, a maximum of 200 error messages can be displayed.
NO_INFOMSGS	NO_INFOMSGS represses all informational messages from the DBCC output.
TABLOCK	When TABLOCK selected, an exclusive table lock is placed on the table instead of using an internal database snapshot, thus potentially decreasing query concurrency in the database.
ESTIMATEONLY	This provides the estimated space needed by the tempdb database to execute the command.

In this brief recipe, data page usage and allocation will be checked for errors in the AdventureWorks database:

```
DBCC CHECKALLOC ('AdventureWorks')
```

This returns the following results (abridged). It includes information about pages used and extents for each index. The key piece of information is in the final line, where you can see the reporting of the number of allocation errors and consistency errors encountered:

```
DBCC results for 'AdventureWorks'.
**************************************************************
Table sys.sysrscols              Object ID 3.
Index ID 1, partition ID 196608, alloc unit ID 196608 (type In-row data).
FirstIAM (1:86). Root (1:87). Dpages 0.
Index ID 1, partition ID 196608, alloc unit ID 196608 (type In-row data).
19 pages used in 2 dedicated extents.
Total number of extents is 2.
**************************************************************
Table sys.sysrowsets             Object ID 5.
Index ID 1, partition ID 327680, alloc unit ID 327680 (type In-row data).
FirstIAM (1:131). Root (1:234). Dpages 0.
Index ID 1, partition ID 327680, alloc unit ID 327680 (type In-row data).
5 pages used in 0 dedicated extents.
Total number of extents is 0.
...
    Object ID 2105058535, index ID 0, partition ID 72057594038779904,
alloc unit ID 72057594039697408 (type In-row data), data extents 98,
 pages 787, mixed extent pages 9.
    Object ID 2105058535, index ID 2, partition ID 72057594044547072,
alloc unit ID 72057594046709760 (type In-row data), index extents 0,
pages 5, mixed extent pages 5.
    Object ID 2117582582, index ID 1, partition ID 72057594045857792,
alloc unit ID 72057594048151552 (type In-row data), data extents 0, pages 2,
 mixed extent pages 2.
The total number of extents = 2864, used pages = 22190, and reserved pages = 22904
 in this database.
        (number of mixed extents = 91, mixed pages = 720) in this database.
CHECKALLOC found 0 allocation errors and 0 consistency errors
in database 'AdventureWorks'.
DBCC execution completed. If DBCC printed error messages,
contact your system administrator.
```

How It Works

In this brief recipe, the DBCC CHECKALLOC command was used to verify the allocation of all database pages and internal structures in the AdventureWorks database with the exception of FILESTREAM data. Informational data was returned, including the internal page information, number of extents, and pages. At the end of the command, any allocation or consistency errors were reported (in this case, none were found).

When DBCC CHECKALLOC is executed, an internal database snapshot is created to maintain transactional consistency during the operation. If for some reason a database snapshot can't be created, or if TABLOCK is specified, an exclusive database lock is acquired during the execution of the command (thus potentially hurting database query concurrency). Unless you have a good reason not to, you should allow SQL Server to issue an internal database snapshot, so that concurrency in your database is not impacted.

Checking Allocation and Structural Integrity with DBCC CHECKDB

The DBCC CHECKDB command checks the integrity of objects in a database. Running DBCC CHECKDB periodically against your databases is a good maintenance practice. Weekly execution is usually sufficient; however, the optimal frequency all depends on the activity and size of the database in question. If possible, DBCC CHECKDB should be executed during periods of light or no database activity. Doing it this way will allow DBCC CHECKDB to finish faster and keep other processes from being slowed down by its overhead.

Like the other commands I've described in this chapter, an internal database snapshot is created to maintain transactional consistency during the operation when this command is executed. If for some reason a database snapshot cannot be created (or the TABLOCK option was specified), shared table locks are held for table checks and exclusive database locks for allocation checks.

As part of its execution, DBCC CHECKDB executes other DBCC commands that are discussed elsewhere in this chapter, including DBCC CHECKTABLE, DBCC CHECKALLOC, and DBCC CHECKCATALOG. In addition to this, CHECKDB verifies the integrity of Service Broker data indexed views and FILESTREAM link consistency for table and file system directories.

The syntax for DBCC CHECKDB is as follows:

```
DBCC CHECKDB
(
        'database_name' | database_id | 0
    [ , NOINDEX
    | { REPAIR_ALLOW_DATA_LOSS
    | REPAIR_FAST
    | REPAIR_REBUILD
    } ]
)
    [ WITH        {
            [ ALL_ERRORMSGS ]
            [ , [EXTENDED_LOGICAL_CHECKS] ]
            [ , [ NO_INFOMSGS ] ]
            [ , [ TABLOCK ] ]
            [ , [ ESTIMATEONLY ] ]
            [ , { PHYSICAL_ONLY | DATA_PURITY } ]
        }
    ]
```

The arguments of this command, which will look familiar based on previous commands reviewed in this chapter, are described in Table 23-2.

Table 23-2. *DBCC CHECKDB Arguments*

Argument	Description
'database_name' | database_id | 0	This defines the database name or database ID that you want to check for errors. When 0 is selected, the current database is used.
NOINDEX	Nonclustered indexes are not included in the integrity checks when this option is selected.

Argument	Description
REPAIR_ALLOW_DATA_LOSS | REPAIR_FAST | REPAIR_REBUILD	See the beginning of the chapter regarding a warning on using repair options. REPAIR_ALLOW_DATA_LOSS attempts a repair of the table or indexed view, with the risk of losing data in the process. REPAIR_FAST is maintained for backward compatibility only, and REPAIR_REBUILD performs fixes without risk of data loss.
ALL_ERRORMSGS	When ALL_ERRORMSGS is chosen, every error found will be displayed (instead of just the default 200 error message limit).
EXTENDED_LOGICAL_CHECKS	When EXTENDED_LOGICAL_CHECKS is chosen, it enables logical consistency checks on spatial and XML indexes, as well as indexed views. This option can impact performance significantly and should be used sparingly.
NO_INFOMSGS	NO_INFOMSGS represses all informational messages from the DBCC output.
TABLOCK	When TABLOCK is selected, an exclusive database lock is used instead of an internal database snapshot. Using this option decreases concurrency with other queries being executed against objects in the database.
ESTIMATEONLY	This argument provides the estimated space needed by the tempdb database to execute the command.
PHYSICAL_ONLY | DATA_PURITY	The PHYSICAL_ONLY argument limits the integrity checks to physical issues only, skipping logical checks. If DATA_PURITY is selected, this is for use on upgraded databases (pre–SQL Server 2005 databases); this instructs DBCC CHECKDB to detect column values that do not conform to the data type (for example, if an integer value has a bigint-sized value stored in it). Once all bad values in the upgraded database are cleaned up, SQL Server maintains the column-value integrity moving forward.

Despite all of these syntax options, the common form of executing this command is also most likely the simplest. This brief recipe executes DBCC CHECKDB against the AdventureWorks database. For thorough integrity and data checking of your database, the default is often suitable:

```
DBCC CHECKDB('AdventureWorks')
```

This returns the following informational results detailing the database objects evaluated within the database, including the number of rows, pages, and—most importantly at the end—number of allocation or consistency errors found:

```
DBCC results for 'AdventureWorks'.
Service Broker Msg 9675, State 1: Message Types analyzed: 14.
Service Broker Msg 9676, State 1: Service Contracts analyzed: 6.
...
DBCC results for 'sys.sysrowsetcolumns'.
There are 1301 rows in 9 pages for object "sys.sysrowsetcolumns".
DBCC results for 'sys.sysrowsets'.
```

```
...
There are 6 rows in 1 pages for object "Person.AddressType".
DBCC results for 'Production.ProductSubcategory'.
There are 37 rows in 1 pages for object "Production.ProductSubcategory".
DBCC results for 'AWBuildVersion'.
There are 1 rows in 1 pages for object "AWBuildVersion".
DBCC results for 'Production.TransactionHistoryArchive'.
There are 89253 rows in 620 pages for object "Production.TransactionHistoryArchive".
...
CHECKDB found 0 allocation errors and 0 consistency errors
in database 'AdventureWorks'.
DBCC execution completed. If DBCC printed error messages,
contact your system administrator.
```

How It Works

In this recipe, a thorough integrity check was performed against the AdventureWorks database using DBCC CHECKDB, including the name of the database within parentheses:

```
DBCC CHECKDB('AdventureWorks')
```

This command returned several hundred lines of information, including the final information about the number of allocation or consistency errors.

■Caution As I warned in the beginning of this chapter, you should be aware that if DBCC encounters errors, Microsoft now recommends that you solve data integrity issues by restoring the database from the last good backup rather than resorting to REPAIR options. If restoring from backup is not an option, the REPAIR options should be used only as a last resort. Depending on the REPAIR options selected, data loss can occur, and the problem may still not be resolved.

Tables and Constraints

The next set of recipes demonstrates DBCC commands used to validate integrity at the constraint and table level. Specifically, I'll be demonstrating how to use the following:

- DBCC CHECKFILEGROUP, which is very similar to DBCC CHECKDB, but limits integrity and allocation checking to objects within a specified filegroup

- DBCC CHECKTABLE, which is used to identify any integrity issues for a specific table or indexed view

- DBCC CHECKCONSTRAINTS, which alerts you to any CHECK or constraint violations found in a specific table or constraint

Lastly, I'll review how to check for consistency in and between system tables using the DBCC CHECKCATALOG command.

Checking Allocation and Structural Integrity of All Tables in a Filegroup Using DBCC CHECKFILEGROUP

The DBCC CHECKFILEGROUP command is very similar to DBCC CHECKDB, only it limits its integrity and allocation checking to objects within a single filegroup. For very large databases (VLDB), performing a DBCC CHECKDB operation may be time prohibitive. If you use user-defined filegroups in your database, you can employ DBCC CHECKFILEGROUP to perform your weekly (or periodic) checks instead—spreading out filegroup checks across different days.

When this command is executed, an internal database snapshot is created to maintain transactional consistency during the operation. If for some reason a database snapshot can't be created (or the TABLOCK option was specified), shared table locks are created by the command for table checks, as well as an exclusive database lock for the allocation checks.

Again, if errors are found by DBCC CHECKDB, Microsoft recommends that you solve any discovered issues by restoring from the last good database backup. Unlike other DBCC commands in this chapter, DBCC CHECKFILEGROUP doesn't have repair options (although repair options are no longer recommended by Microsoft anyhow).

The syntax is as follows:

```
DBCC CHECKFILEGROUP
(
[ { 'filegroup' | filegroup_id | 0 } ]
[ , NOINDEX ]
)
    [ WITH
        {
            [ ALL_ERRORMSGS | NO_INFOMSGS ]
            [ , [ TABLOCK ] ]
            [ , [ ESTIMATEONLY ] ]
        }
        ]
```

The arguments of this command are described in Table 23-3.

Table 23-3. *DBCC CHECKFILEGROUP Arguments*

Argument	Description
'filegroup' | filegroup_id | 0	This defines the filegroup name or filegroup ID that you want to check. If 0 is designated, the primary filegroup is used.
NOINDEX	When NOINDEX is designated, nonclustered indexes are not included in the integrity checks.
ALL_ERRORMSGS	When ALL_ERRORMSGS is chosen, all errors are displayed in the output, instead of the default 200 message limit.
NO_INFOMSGS	NO_INFOMSGS represses all informational messages from the DBCC output.
TABLOCK	When TABLOCK is selected, an exclusive database lock is used instead of using an internal database snapshot (using this option decreases concurrency with other database queries, but speeds up the DBCC command execution).
ESTIMATEONLY	ESTIMATEONLY provides the estimated space needed by the tempdb database to execute the command.

In this recipe, the primary filegroup integrity will be checked in the AdventureWorks database:

```
USE AdventureWorks
GO
DBCC CHECKFILEGROUP('PRIMARY')
```

This returns the following abridged results:

```
DBCC results for 'AdventureWorks'.
DBCC results for 'sys.sysrowsetcolumns'.
There are 1301 rows in 9 pages for object "sys.sysrowsetcolumns".
DBCC results for 'sys.sysrowsets'.
There are 248 rows in 2 pages for object "sys.sysrowsets".
DBCC results for 'sysallocunits'.
...
There are 10 rows in 1 pages for object "Sales.SalesReason".
DBCC results for 'Sales.Individual'.
There are 18484 rows in 3082 pages for object "Sales.Individual".
DBCC results for 'Sales.SalesTaxRate'.
...
CHECKFILEGROUP found 0 allocation errors and 0 consistency
errors in database 'AdventureWorks'.
DBCC execution completed. If DBCC printed error messages,
contact your system administrator.
```

How It Works

In this recipe, allocation and structural integrity were checked for all objects in the PRIMARY file-group in the AdventureWorks database. The resulting output showed row and page counts for filegroup objects and a sum total of the number of allocation and consistency errors found (reported at the end). Like the other DBCC commands, the second-to-last line was most critical for determining if there are any issues:

```
CHECKFILEGROUP found 0 allocation errors and 0 consistency errors
in database 'AdventureWorks'.
```

Checking Data Integrity for Tables and Indexed Views Using DBCC CHECKTABLE

In order to identify issues in a specific table or indexed view, you can use the DBCC CHECKTABLE com-mand. (If you want to run it for all tables and indexed views in the database, use DBCC CHECKDB instead, which performs DBCC CHECKTABLE for each table in your database.)

When DBCC CHECKTABLE is executed, an internal database snapshot is created to maintain trans-actional consistency during the operation. If for some reason a database snapshot can't be created, a shared table lock is applied to the target table or indexed view instead (thus potentially hurting database query concurrency against the target objects).

The syntax is as follows:

```
DBCC CHECKTABLE
(
        table_name | view_name
    [ , { NOINDEX | index_id }
```

```
    |, { REPAIR_ALLOW_DATA_LOSS | REPAIR_FAST | REPAIR_REBUILD }
    ]
)
    [ WITH
        { ALL_ERRORMSGS ]
          [ , EXTENDED_LOGICAL_CHECKS ]
          [ , NO_INFOMSGS ]
          [ , TABLOCK ]
          [ , ESTIMATEONLY ]
          [ , { PHYSICAL_ONLY | DATA_PURITY } ]
        }
    ]
```

The arguments of this command are described in Table 23-4.

Table 23-4. *DBCC CHECKTABLE Arguments*

Argument	Description
`'table_name'` | `'view_name'`	This defines the table or indexed view you want to check.
`NOINDEX`	This keyword instructs the command not to check nonclustered indexes.
`index_id`	This specifies the specific ID of the index to be checked (if you are checking a specific index).
`REPAIR_ALLOW_DATA_LOSS` | `REPAIR_FAST` | `REPAIR_REBUILD`	See the warning at the beginning of the chapter regarding the use of `REPAIR` options. `REPAIR_ALLOW_DATA_LOSS` attempts a repair of the table or indexed view, with the risk of losing data in the process. `REPAIR_FAST` is no longer used, and is kept for backward compatibility only. `REPAIR_REBUILD` does repairs and index rebuilds without any risk of data loss.
`ALL_ERRORMSGS`	When `ALL_ERRORMSGS` is chosen, every error found during the command execution will be displayed.
`EXTENDED_LOGICAL_CHECKS`	When `EXTENDED_LOGICAL_CHECKS` is designated, it enables logical consistency checks on spatial and XML indexes, as well as indexed views. This option can impact performance significantly and should be used sparingly.
`NO_INFOMSGS`	`NO_INFOMSGS` represses all informational messages from the `DBCC` output.
`TABLOCK`	When `TABLOCK` is selected, a shared table lock is placed on the table instead of using an internal database snapshot. Using this option decreases concurrency with other database queries accessing the table or indexed view.
`ESTIMATEONLY`	`ESTIMATEONLY` provides the estimated space needed by the `tempdb` database to execute the command (but doesn't actually execute the integrity checking).
`PHYSICAL_ONLY`	`PHYSICAL_ONLY` limits the integrity checks to physical issues only, skipping logical checks.

Continued

Table 23-4. *Continued*

Argument	Description
DATA_PURITY	This argument is used on upgraded databases (pre–SQL Server 2005 databases); this instructs DBCC CHECKTABLE to detect column values that do not conform to the data type (for example, if an integer value has a bigint-sized value stored in it). Once all bad values in the upgraded database are cleaned up, SQL Server maintains the column-value integrity moving forward.

This recipe provides a few examples of using the command. In the first example, the integrity of the Production.Product table will be checked in the AdventureWorks database:

```
DBCC CHECKTABLE ('Production.Product')
WITH ALL_ERRORMSGS
```

This returns the following (results vary based on your environment):

```
DBCC results for 'Production.Product'.
There are 504 rows in 13 pages for object "Production.Product".
DBCC execution completed. If DBCC printed error messages,
contact your system administrator.
```

In the next example in the recipe, we return an estimate of tempdb space required for a check on the Sales.SalesOrderDetail table. This allows you to know ahead of time if a specific CHECKTABLE operation requires more space than you have available:

```
DBCC CHECKTABLE ('Sales.SalesOrderDetail')
WITH ESTIMATEONLY
```

This returns the following (these results may differ from yours, since they are based in part on the local environment):

```
Estimated TEMPDB space needed for CHECKTABLES (KB)
897

(1 row(s) affected)

DBCC execution completed. If DBCC printed error messages,
contact your system administrator.
```

This last example executes DBCC CHECKTABLE for a specific index, checking for physical errors only (no logical). First, however, the index ID needs to be determined:

```
SELECT index_id
FROM   sys.indexes
WHERE  object_id = OBJECT_ID('Sales.SalesOrderDetail')
AND name = 'IX_SalesOrderDetail_ProductID'
```

This returns

```
index_id
3
```

Next, the index_id will be used in the command:

```
DBCC CHECKTABLE ('Sales.SalesOrderDetail', 3)
WITH PHYSICAL_ONLY
```

This returns

```
DBCC execution completed. If DBCC printed error messages,
contact your system administrator.
```

How It Works

In this recipe, the first example demonstrated how to check the integrity of a single table, showing all error messages if they exist (instead of the 200 message maximum default). The name of the table to check was included as the first argument:

```
DBCC CHECKTABLE ('Production.Product')
```

The second argument, ALL_ERRORMSGS, designated that any and all error messages found would be returned:

```
WITH ALL_ERRORMSGS
```

DBCC CHECKTABLE checks for errors regarding data page linkages, pointers, verification that rows in a partition are actually in the correct partition, and more.

In the second example, a tempdb size requirement estimate was returned for the Sales.SalesOrderDetail table by designating the WITH ESTIMATEONLY argument:

```
DBCC CHECKTABLE ('Sales.SalesOrderDetail')
WITH ESTIMATEONLY
```

In the last example, the index ID of the IX_SalesOrderDetail_ProductID index on the Sales.SalesOrderDetail table was retrieved from the sys.indexes system catalog view. After retrieving the index ID, it was used in the DBCC CHECKTABLE command along with the PHYSICAL_ONLY argument, which was used to skip logical integrity checks against that index.

Checking Table Integrity with DBCC CHECKCONSTRAINTS

DBCC CHECKCONSTRAINTS alerts you to any CHECK or foreign key constraint violations found in a specific table or constraint. This command allows you to return the violating data so that you can correct the constraint violation accordingly (although this command does not catch constraints that have been disabled using NOCHECK).

The syntax is as follows:

```
DBCC CHECKCONSTRAINTS
[( 'table_name' | table_id | 'constraint_name' |
constraint_id )]
[ WITH
{ ALL_CONSTRAINTS | ALL_ERRORMSGS } [ , NO_INFOMSGS ] ]
```

The arguments of this command are described in Table 23-5.

Table 23-5. *DBCC CHECKCONSTRAINTS Arguments*

Argument	Description
`'table_name'` | `table_id` | `'constraint_name'` | `constraint_id`	This defines the table name, table ID, constraint name, or constraint ID that you want to validate. If a specific object isn't designated, all the objects in the database will be evaluated.
`ALL_CONSTRAINTS` | `ALL_ERRORMSGS`	When `ALL_CONSTRAINTS` is selected, all constraints (enabled or disabled) are checked. When `ALL_ERRORMSGS` is selected, all rows that violate constraints are returned in the result set (instead of the default maximum of 200 rows).
`NO_INFOMSGS`	`NO_INFOMSGS` represses all informational messages from the DBCC output.

In this recipe, I demonstrate how to check the constraints of a table after a CHECK constraint has been violated:

```
ALTER TABLE Production.WorkOrder  NOCHECK CONSTRAINT CK_WorkOrder_EndDate
GO

-- Set an EndDate to earlier than a StartDate
UPDATE Production.WorkOrder
SET EndDate = '1/1/2001'
WHERE WorkOrderID = 1
GO

ALTER TABLE Production.WorkOrder  CHECK CONSTRAINT CK_WorkOrder_EndDate
GO

DBCC CHECKCONSTRAINTS ('Production.WorkOrder')
```

This returns the following results:

```
Table                       Constraint                Where
[Production].[WorkOrder]    [CK_WorkOrder_EndDate]    [StartDate] = '2001-07-04
                                                      00:00:00.000' AND [EndDate] =
                                                      '2001-01-01 00:00:00.000'
```

How It Works

In this recipe, the check constraint called CK_WorkOrder on the Production.WorkOrder table was disabled, using the ALTER TABLE...NOCHECK CONSTRAINT command:

```
ALTER TABLE Production.WorkOrder  NOCHECK CONSTRAINT CK_WorkOrder_EndDate
GO
```

This disabled constraint restricted values in the EndDate column from being less than the date in the StartDate column.

After disabling the constraint, a row was updated to violate this check constraint's rule:

```
UPDATE Production.WorkOrder
SET EndDate = '1/1/2001'
WHERE WorkOrderID = 1
GO
```

The constraint was then reenabled:

```
ALTER TABLE Production.WorkOrder
CHECK CONSTRAINT CK_WorkOrder_EndDate
GO
```

The DBCC CHECKCONSTRAINTS command was then executed against the table:

```
DBCC CHECKCONSTRAINTS('Production.WorkOrder')
```

The command returned the table name, constraint violated, and the reason why the constraint was violated:

```
Table                        Constraint               Where
[Production].[WorkOrder]     [CK_WorkOrder_EndDate]   [StartDate] = '2001-07-04
                                                      00:00:00.000' AND [EndDate] =
                                                      '2001-01-01 00:00:00.000'
```

■**Note** Unlike several other database integrity DBCC commands, DBCC CHECKCONSTRAINTS is *not* run within DBCC CHECKDB, so you must execute it as a stand-alone process if you need to identify data constraint violations in the database.

Checking System Table Consistency with DBCC CHECKCATALOG

DBCC CHECKCATALOG checks for consistency in and between system tables (this is another command that is automatically included in the execution of DBCC CHECKDB).

The syntax is as follows:

```
DBCC CHECKCATALOG
[ ( 'database_name' | database_id | 0)]
    [ WITH NO_INFOMSGS ]
```

The arguments of this command are described in Table 23-6.

Table 23-6. DBCC CHECKCATALOG Arguments

Argument	Description
'database_name'	database_id	0	This defines the database name or database ID to be checked for errors. When 0 is selected, the current database is used.
NO_INFOMSGS	NO_INFOMSGS represses all informational messages from the DBCC output.

In this brief recipe, system table consistency checks are performed for the entire Adventure-Works database:

```
DBCC CHECKCATALOG ('AdventureWorks')
```

This returns the following (assuming no errors found):

```
DBCC execution completed. If DBCC printed error messages,
contact your system administrator.
```

How It Works

In this recipe, the system catalog data was checked in the AdventureWorks database. Had errors been identified, they would have been returned in the command output. If errors are found, DBCC CHECKCATALOG doesn't have repair options, and a restore from the last good database backup may be your only repair option.

Like the other commands I've described in this chapter, when DBCC CHECKCATALOG is executed, an internal database snapshot is created to maintain transactional consistency during the operation. If for some reason a database snapshot cannot be created, an exclusive database lock is acquired during the execution of the command (thus potentially hurting database query concurrency).

■**Note** CHECKCATALOG is already executed automatically within a DBCC CHECKDB command, so a separate execution is not necessary unless you wish to investigate only system table consistency issues.

Index Maintenance

Fragmentation is the natural byproduct of data modifications to a table. When data is updated in the database, the logical order of indexes (based on the index key) gets out of sync with the actual physical order of the data pages. As data pages become further and further out of order, more I/O operations are required in order to return results requested by a query. Rebuilding or reorganizing an index allows you to defragment the index by synchronizing the logical index order and reordering the physical data pages to match the logical index order. In the next two recipes, I'll demonstrate two methods you can use to defragment your indexes.

■**Tip** See Chapter 28 to learn how to display index fragmentation. It is important that you rebuild only indexes that require it. The rebuild process is resource intensive and has minimal impact if fragmentation is low, or if querying is primarily for singleton lookups and not range scans.

Rebuilding Indexes

If you've used previous versions of SQL Server, you may be searching this chapter for the DBCC DBREINDEX or DBCC INDEXDEFRAG commands, which were used to rebuild indexes and defragment indexes, respectively. DBCC DBREINDEX has been deprecated in place of the ALTER INDEX REBUILD command. DBCC INDEXDEFRAG, used to defragment an index while allowing access to the data, has been deprecated in place of ALTER INDEX REORGANIZE (covered in the next recipe).

Rebuilding an index serves many purposes, the most popular being the removal of fragmentation that occurs as data modifications are made to a table over time. As fragmentation increases, query performance can slow. Rebuilding an index removes fragmentation of the index rows and frees up physical disk space.

Large indexes that are quite fragmented can reduce query speed. The frequency of how often you rebuild your indexes depends on your database size, how much data modification occurs, how much activity occurs against your tables, and whether or not your queries typically perform ordered scans or singleton lookups.

The syntax for `ALTER INDEX` in order to rebuild an index is as follows:

```
ALTER INDEX { index_name | ALL }
    ON <object>
    { REBUILD
    [ [ WITH ( <rebuild_index_option> [ ,...n ] ) ]
    | [ PARTITION = partition_number
[ WITH ( <single_partition_rebuild_index_option>
                    [ ,...n ] )
        ]
      ]
    ]
    }
```

The arguments of this command are described in Table 23-7.

Table 23-7. *ALTER INDEX...REBUILD Arguments*

Argument	Description
index_name	ALL	This defines the name of the index to rebuild. If `ALL` is chosen, all indexes for the specified table or view will be rebuilt.
<object>	This specifies the name of the table or view that the index is built on.
<rebuild_index_option>	One or more index options can be applied during a rebuild, including `FILLFACTOR`, `PAD_INDEX`, `SORT_IN_TEMPDB`, `IGNORE_DUP_KEY`, `STATISTICS_NORECOMPUTE`, `ONLINE`, `ALLOW_ROW_LOCKS`, `ALLOW_PAGE_LOCKS`, `DATA_COMPRESSION`, and `MAXDOP`.
partition_number	If using a partitioned index, `partition_number` designates that only one partition of the index is rebuilt.
<single_partition_rebuild_index_option>	If designating a partition rebuild, you are limited to using the following index options in the `WITH` clause: `SORT_IN_TEMPDB`, `DATA_COMPRESSION`, and `MAXDOP`.

This recipe demonstrates `ALTER INDEX REBUILD`, which drops and re-creates an existing index. It demonstrates a few variations for rebuilding an index in the `AdventureWorks` database:

```
-- Rebuild a specific index

ALTER INDEX PK_ShipMethod_ShipMethodID
ON Purchasing.ShipMethod  REBUILD

-- Rebuild all indexes on a specific table

ALTER INDEX ALL
ON Purchasing.PurchaseOrderHeader REBUILD
```

```
-- Rebuild an index, while keeping it available
-- for queries (requires Enterprise Edition)

ALTER INDEX PK_ProductReview_ProductReviewID
ON Production.ProductReview REBUILD
WITH (ONLINE = ON)

-- Rebuild an index, using a new fill factor and
-- sorting in tempdb

ALTER INDEX PK_TransactionHistory_TransactionID
ON Production.TransactionHistory REBUILD
WITH (FILLFACTOR = 75,
SORT_IN_TEMPDB = ON)

-- Rebuild an index with page-level data compression enabled
ALTER INDEX PK_ShipMethod_ShipMethodID
ON Purchasing.ShipMethod  REBUILD
WITH (DATA_COMPRESSION = PAGE)
```

How It Works

In this recipe, the first ALTER INDEX was used to rebuild the primary key index on the Purchasing.ShipMethod table (rebuilding a clustered index does not cause the rebuild of any nonclustered indexes for the table):

```
ALTER INDEX PK_ShipMethod_ShipMethodID
ON Purchasing.ShipMethod  REBUILD
```

In the second example, the ALL keyword was used, which means that any indexes, whether nonclustered or clustered (remember, only one clustered index exists on a table) will be rebuilt:

```
ALTER INDEX ALL
ON Purchasing.PurchaseOrderHeader REBUILD
```

The third example in the recipe rebuilt an index *online*, which means that user queries can continue to access the data of the PK_ProductReview_ProductReviewID index while it's being rebuilt:

```
WITH (ONLINE = ON)
```

The ONLINE option requires SQL Server Enterprise Edition, and it can't be used with XML indexes, disabled indexes, or partitioned indexes. Also, indexes using large object data types or indexes made on temporary tables can't take advantage of this option.

In the fourth example, two index options were modified for an index—the fill factor and a directive to sort the temporary index results in tempdb:

```
WITH (FILLFACTOR = 75,
SORT_IN_TEMPDB = ON)
```

In the last example, an uncompressed index was rebuilt using page-level data compression:

```
WITH (DATA_COMPRESSION = PAGE)
```

■**Tip** You can validate whether an index/partition is compressed by looking at the data_compression_desc column in sys.partitions.

Defragmenting Indexes

ALTER INDEX REORGANIZE reduces fragmentation in the leaf level of an index (clustered and nonclustered), causing the physical order of the database pages to match the logical order. During this reorganization process, the indexes are also compacted based on the fill factor, resulting in freed space and a smaller index. ALTER TABLE REORGANIZE is automatically an online operation, meaning that you can continue to query the target data during the reorganization process.

The syntax is as follows:

```
ALTER INDEX { index_name | ALL }
    ON <object>
    { REORGANIZE
        [ PARTITION = partition_number ]
        [ WITH ( LOB_COMPACTION = { ON | OFF } ) ]
    }
```

The arguments of this command are described in Table 23-8.

Table 23-8. *ALTER INDEX...REORGANIZE Arguments*

Argument	Description
index_name | ALL	This defines the name of the index that you want to rebuild. If ALL is chosen, all indexes for the table or view will be rebuilt.
<object>	This specifies the name of the table or view that you want to build the index on.
partition_number	If using a partitioned index, the partition_number designates that partition to reorganize.
LOB_COMPACTION = { ON | OFF }	When this argument is enabled, large object data types (varchar(max), navarchar(max), varbinary(max), xml, text, ntext, and image data) are compacted.

This recipe demonstrates how to defragment a single index, as well as all indexes on a single table:

```
-- Reorganize a specific index
ALTER INDEX PK_TransactionHistory_TransactionID
ON Production.TransactionHistory
REORGANIZE

-- Reorganize all indexes for a table
-- Compact large object data types
ALTER INDEX ALL
ON HumanResources.JobCandidate
REORGANIZE
WITH (LOB_COMPACTION=ON)
```

How It Works

In the first example of this recipe, the primary key index of the Production.TransactionHistory table was reorganized (defragmented). The syntax was very similar to rebuilding an index, only instead of REBUILD, the REORGANIZE keyword was used.

In the second example, all indexes (using the ALL keyword) were defragmented for the HumanResources.Jobcandidate column. Using the WITH clause, large object data type columns were also compacted.

Use ALTER INDEX REORGANIZE if you cannot afford to take the index offline during an index rebuild (and if you cannot use the ONLINE option in ALTER INDEX REBUILD because you aren't running SQL Server Enterprise Edition). Reorganization is always an online operation, meaning that an ALTER INDEX REORGANIZE operation doesn't block database traffic for significant periods of time, although it may be a slower process than a REBUILD.

Rebuilding a Heap

In SQL Server 2008, you can now rebuild a heap (a table without a clustered index) using the ALTER TABLE command. In previous versions, rebuilding a heap required adding and removing a temporary clustered index, or performing a data migration or table re-creation.

In this example, I will create a heap table (using SELECT INTO) and then rebuild it:

```
USE AdventureWorks
GO

-- Create an unindexed table based on another table
SELECT ShiftID, Name, StartTime, EndTime, ModifiedDate
INTO dbo.Heap_Shift
FROM HumanResources.Shift
```

I can validate whether the new table is a heap by querying sys.indexes:

```
SELECT type_desc
FROM sys.indexes
WHERE object_id = OBJECT_ID('Heap_Shift')
```

This returns

```
type_desc
HEAP
```

If I wish to rebuild the heap, I can issue the following ALTER TABLE command:

```
ALTER TABLE dbo.Heap_Shift REBUILD
```

How It Works

In this recipe, I created a heap table, and then rebuilt it using ALTER TABLE...REBUILD. Using ALTER TABLE...REBUILD, you can rebuild a table, even if it does not have a clustered index (heap). If the table is partitioned, this command also rebuilds all partitions on a table and rebuilds the clustered index if one exists.

■ ■ ■

Maintaining Database Objects and Object Dependencies

This chapter contains a few recipes that you can use to maintain database objects and view object dependencies. You'll see recipes used to

- Change the name of user-created database objects.
- Change an object's schema.
- Display information about object dependencies via the new SQL Server 2008 sys.sql_expression_dependencies view and Dynamic Management Views sys.dm_sql_referenced_entities and sys.dm_sql_referencing_entities.

Tip Object dependency tracking is much more robust in SQL Server 2008, allowing you to reliably track both cross-database and cross-server dependencies. Dependencies are now tracked by object name instead of by ID, allowing for dependency tracking for deferred name resolution scenarios.

Database Object Maintenance

In these next two recipes, I'll show you how to change the name of an existing user-created database object using the sp_rename system stored procedure and how to transfer an existing object from its existing schema to a different schema using ALTER SCHEMA.

Changing the Name of a User-Created Database Object

This recipe demonstrates how to rename objects using the sp_rename system stored procedure. Using this procedure, you can rename table columns, indexes, tables, constraints, and other database objects.

The syntax for sp_rename is as follows:

```
sp_rename [ @objname = ] 'object_name' , [ @newname = ] 'new_name'
    [ , [ @objtype = ] 'object_type' ]
```

The arguments of this system stored procedure are described in Table 24-1.

Table 24-1. *sp_rename Parameters*

Argument	Description
object_name	The name of the object to be renamed
new_name	The new name of the object
object_type	The type of object to rename: column, database, index, object, and userdatatype

This recipe demonstrates how to rename a table, column, and index:

```
USE AdventureWorks
GO

-- Add example objects

CREATE TABLE HumanResources.InsuranceProvider
(InsuranceProviderID int NOT NULL,
 InsuranceProviderNM varchar(50) NOT NULL
)
GO

CREATE INDEX ni_InsuranceProvider_InsuranceProviderID
ON HumanResources.InsuranceProvider (InsuranceProviderID)

-- Rename the table
EXEC sys.sp_rename 'HumanResources.InsuranceProvider',
          'Provider',
          'Object'

-- Rename a column
EXEC sys.sp_rename 'HumanResources.Provider.InsuranceProviderID',
          'ProviderID',
          'Column'

-- Rename the primary key constraint
EXEC sys.sp_rename 'HumanResources.Provider.ni_InsuranceProvider_
InsuranceProviderID',
          'ni_Provider_ProviderID',
          'Index'
```

This returns the following message for each sp_rename execution:

```
Caution: Changing any part of an object name could
break scripts and stored procedures.
```

How It Works

This recipe began with you creating a new table called HumanResources.InsuranceProvider with an index on the new table called InsuranceProviderID. After that, the system stored procedure sp_rename was used to rename the table:

```
EXEC sys.sp_rename 'HumanResources.InsuranceProvider',
          'Provider',
          'Object'
```

Notice that the first parameter uses the fully qualified object name (`schema.table_name`), whereas the second parameter just uses the new `table_name`. The third parameter used the object type of `object`.

Next, `sp_rename` was used to change the column name:

```
EXEC sys.sp_rename 'HumanResources.Provider.InsuranceProviderID',
            'ProviderID',
            'Column'
```

The first parameter used the `schema.table_name.column_name` to be renamed and the second parameter the new name of the column. The third parameter used the object type of `column`.

In the last part of the recipe, the index was renamed:

```
EXEC sys.sp_rename 'HumanResources.Provider.ni_InsuranceProvider_
InsuranceProviderID',
            'ni_Provider_ProviderID',
            'Index'
```

The first parameter used the `schema.table_name.index_name` parameter. The second parameter used the name of the new index. The third used the object type of `index`.

This recipe returned a warning that "changing any part of an object name could break scripts and stored procedures." In a real-life scenario, before you rename an object, you'll also want to `ALTER` any view, stored procedure, function, or other programmatic object that contains a reference to the original object name. I demonstrate how to find out which objects reference an object later on in this chapter in the "Identifying Object Dependencies" recipe.

Changing an Object's Schema

In SQL Server 2000, before the concept of schemas, an object's owner was changed using the `sp_changeobjectowner` system stored procedure. Now in SQL Server 2005 and 2008, users (owners) and schemas are separate, and to change an object's schema, you use the `ALTER SCHEMA` command instead.

The syntax is as follows:

```
ALTER SCHEMA schema_name TRANSFER object_name
```

The command takes two arguments: the first being the schema name you want to transfer the object to, and the second the object name that you want to transfer.

This recipe demonstrates transferring a table from the `Sales` to the `HumanResources` schema:

```
Use AdventureWorks
GO

CREATE TABLE Sales.TerminationReason
(TerminationReasonID int NOT NULL PRIMARY KEY,
TerminationReasonDESC varchar(100) NOT NULL)
GO

ALTER SCHEMA HumanResources TRANSFER Sales.TerminationReason
GO
```

How It Works

In this recipe, a new table was created in the `Sales` schema. An object is not *owned* by a specific user, but is instead contained within a schema. After creating the table, it was then transferred to the `HumanResources` schema using the `ALTER SCHEMA TRANSFER` command.

■**Caution** Permissions granted to the original `schema.object` will be dropped after the transfer (for example, `SELECT` permissions for USER1). If these permissions need to be maintained in the new schema, be sure to script them out prior to using `ALTER SCHEMA`.

Object Dependencies

SQL Server 2008 has introduced more reliable methods of tracking object dependencies, as the next few recipes will demonstrate.

■**Caution** The `sp_depends` system stored procedure and the `sys.sql_dependencies` catalog view have been deprecated in this edition of SQL Server. Moving forward, use the views demonstrated in this chapter for tracking object dependencies.

Identifying Object Dependencies

SQL Server 2008 provides new methods for identifying object dependencies within the database, across databases, and across servers (using linked server four-part names). This recipe will demonstrate the use of the `sys.sql_expression_dependencies` object catalog view to identify dependencies in several scenarios.

I'll begin by creating two new databases and some new objects within them in order to demonstrate the functionality:

```
USE master
GO

-- Create two new databases
CREATE DATABASE TSQLRecipe_A
GO

CREATE DATABASE TSQLRecipe_B
GO

-- Create a new table in the first database
USE TSQLRecipe_A
GO

CREATE TABLE dbo.Book
   (BookID int NOT NULL PRIMARY KEY,
    BookNM varchar(50) NOT NULL)
GO

-- Create a procedure referencing an object
-- in the second database
USE TSQLRecipe_B
GO

CREATE PROCEDURE dbo.usp_SEL_Book
AS
```

```
SELECT BookID, BookNM
FROM TSQLRecipe_A.dbo.Book
GO
```

I've created a stored procedure that references a table in another database. Now if I wish to view all objects that the stored procedure depends on, I can execute the following query against sys.sql_expression_dependencies (I'll elaborate on what the columns mean in the "How It Works" section):

```
SELECT referenced_server_name, referenced_database_name,
   referenced_schema_name, referenced_entity_name, is_caller_dependent
FROM sys.sql_expression_dependencies
WHERE OBJECT_NAME(referencing_id) = 'usp_SEL_Book'
```

This query returns one row (abridged for formatting):

referenced_server_name	NULL
referenced_database_name	TSQLRecipe_A
referenced_schema_name	dbo
referenced_entity_name	Book
is_caller_dependent	0

Now let's say I create another stored procedure that references an object that doesn't yet exist (this is an allowable scenario for a stored procedure and is a common practice). For example:

```
-- Create a procedure referencing an object
-- in the second database
USE TSQLRecipe_B
GO

CREATE PROCEDURE dbo.usp_SEL_Contract
AS

SELECT ContractID, ContractNM
FROM TSQLRecipe_A.dbo.Contract
GO
```

In previous versions of SQL Server, dependencies on non-existent objects weren't tracked. In SQL Server 2008, this behavior is now corrected. You can issue the following query to check dependencies of usp_SEL_contract:

```
USE TSQLRecipe_B
GO

SELECT referenced_server_name, referenced_database_name,
   referenced_schema_name, referenced_entity_name, is_caller_dependent
FROM sys.sql_expression_dependencies
WHERE OBJECT_NAME(referencing_id) = 'usp_SEL_Contract'
```

This query returns one row (abridged for formatting):

referenced_server_name	NULL
referenced_database_name	TSQLRecipe_A
referenced_schema_name	dbo
referenced_entity_name	Contract
is_caller_dependent	0

Even though the object TSQLRecipe_A.dbo.Contract does not exist, the dependency between the referencing stored procedure and the referenced table is still represented.

How It Works

This recipe demonstrated how to determine object dependencies using the sys.sql_expression_ dependencies catalog view. In the SELECT clause, I referenced five columns. The first column, referenced_server_name, referenced the four-part linked server name (when applicable). The referenced_database_name returned a non-null value if the three-part database, schema, and object name were used. The referenced_schema_name was available if a two-part schema and object name were used in the referencing module. The referenced_entity_name was the object name being refer- enced. Finally, the is_caller_dependent column indicated whether the object reference depends on the person executing the module. For example, if the object name was not fully qualified, and an object named T1 existed under two different schemas, the actual object referenced would depend on the person calling the module and the execution context.

Identifying Referencing and Referenced Entities

SQL Server 2008 includes two new Dynamic Management Views that are used to identify referenced and referencing objects, as this recipe will demonstrate. The sys.dm_sql_referenced_entities Dynamic Management View, provided with the referencing object name, returns a result set of objects being referenced. The sys.dm_sql_referencing_entities Dynamic Management View, when provided the name of the object being referenced, returns a result set of objects referencing it.

In this first example, I will create a table with two references to it, one reference from a stored procedure and another from a view:

```
USE TSQLRecipe_A
GO

CREATE TABLE dbo.BookPublisher
    (BookPublisherID int NOT NULL PRIMARY KEY,
     BookPublisherNM varchar(30) NOT NULL)
GO

CREATE VIEW dbo.vw_BookPublisher
AS

SELECT BookPublisherID, BookPublisherNM
FROM dbo.BookPublisher
GO

CREATE PROCEDURE dbo.usp_INS_BookPublisher
    @BookPublisherNM varchar(30)
AS

INSERT dbo.BookPublisher
(BookPublisherNM)
VALUES (@BookPublisherNM)

GO
```

Next, I'll use the sys.dm_sql_referenced_entities Dynamic Management View to show all objects that the view itself references:

```
SELECT referenced_entity_name, referenced_minor_name
FROM sys.dm_sql_referenced_entities ('dbo.vw_BookPublisher', 'OBJECT')
```

This returns

referenced_entity_name	referenced_minor_name
BookPublisher	NULL
BookPublisher	BookPublisherID
BookPublisher	BookPublisherNM

(3 row(s) affected)

Notice that this function shows one row for the table referenced in the view, as well as two rows for each column referenced within the view. I'll discuss the parameters in the "How It Works" section.

Next, I'll query sys.dm_sql_referencing_entities to determine all objects that reference the dbo.BookPublisher table (the Dynamic Management Views are similarly named, so notice that I am using "referencing" and not "referenced"):

```
SELECT referencing_schema_name, referencing_entity_name
FROM sys.dm_sql_referencing_entities ('dbo.BookPublisher', 'OBJECT')
```

This returns

referencing_schema_name	referencing_entity_name
dbo	usp_INS_BookPublisher
dbo	vw_BookPublisher

(2 row(s) affected)

How It Works

This recipe demonstrated two methods for identifying object dependencies. I created a table and then referenced it within a view and a stored procedure. The sys.dm_sql_referenced_entities Dynamic Management View was used to return a list of entities referenced within the specified object.

```
sys.dm_sql_referenced_entities ('dbo.vw_BookPublisher', 'OBJECT')
```

The first parameter was the name of the object that is referencing other objects. The second parameter designates the type of entities to list. The choices were OBJECT, DATABASE_DDL_TRIGGER, and SERVER_DDL_TRIGGER. I chose OBJECT, and the result was the name of the referenced table and specific columns in the SELECT clause of the view.

The second example in the recipe demonstrated showing all references to a specific object, in this case, the table that was created at the beginning of the recipe:

```
FROM sys.dm_sql_referencing_entities ('dbo.BookPublisher', 'OBJECT')
```

The first parameter takes the name of the object that I wanted to identify references to. The second parameter designated the class of the object I wanted to identify. The choices include OBJECT, TYPE, XML_SCHEMA_COLLECTION, and PARTITION_FUNCTION. I chose OBJECT, which resulted in a list of the view and stored procedure that referenced the table designated in the first parameter.

Viewing an Object's Definition

Once you've identified dependencies regarding a module that you need to modify, you can have a look at its definition using the OBJECT_DEFINITION function. This function can be used to return the Transact-SQL definition of user-defined and system-based constraints, defaults, stored procedures, functions, rules, schema-scoped DML and DDL triggers, and views.

The syntax is as follows:

```
OBJECT_DEFINITION ( object_id )
```

The only argument for this command is the object ID, which is the unique object identifier (each object identifier uniquely identifies a database object within a database).

In this example recipe, the Transact-SQL definition is returned for an AdventureWorks database's user-defined function, and the OBJECT_ID function is used within the OBJECT_DEFINITION function to get that user-defined function's identifier:

```
USE AdventureWorks
GO

SELECT OBJECT_DEFINITION
(OBJECT_ID('dbo.ufnGetAccountingEndDate'))
GO
```

This returns the Transact-SQL definition:

```
CREATE FUNCTION [dbo].[ufnGetAccountingEndDate]()
RETURNS [datetime]
AS
BEGIN
    RETURN DATEADD(millisecond, -2, CONVERT(datetime, '20040701', 112));
END;
```

If you're curious about how Microsoft programs its own system objects, you can also use OBJECT_DEFINITION to peek at its Transact-SQL definition. In this example, the system stored procedure code for the sp_depends stored procedure is revealed:

```
USE AdventureWorks
GO

SELECT OBJECT_DEFINITION(OBJECT_ID('sys.sp_depends'))
GO
```

This returns the following abridged results:

```
create procedure sys.sp_depends
--- 1996/08/09 16:51  @objname nvarchar(776)
...
select @dbname = parsename(@objname,3)

if @dbname is not null and @dbname <> db_name()
begin    raiserror(15250,-1,-1)
return (1)
end
...
```

How It Works

In this recipe, I demonstrated using OBJECT_DEFINITION to return the Transact-SQL code for a user-defined function and for a system stored procedure. In both cases, the OBJECT_ID function was nested within the function in order to pass the object ID as an argument:

```
OBJECT_DEFINITION
(OBJECT_ID('dbo.ufnGetAccountingEndDate'))
```

The object name was fully qualified using the schema.object_name format.

Both examples returned the Transact-SQL code definition for the database objects. Had those objects been encrypted, you would have gotten a NULL result set instead.

■■■

Database Mirroring

Database mirroring provides high availability at the user database level. High availability in this case refers to the SQL Server databases being available to end users to query with little or no unplanned downtime. Database mirroring allows database redundancy, by synchronizing a primary (principal) database on one server with a second copy of a database on a second server. This second copy can be used as a hot standby, allowing for fast failover in the event you need to take your primary copy offline for any reason. Unlike failover clustering (described in the next section), database mirroring doesn't require expensive hardware such as shared disk arrays or SAN. At a minimum, all you need are two SQL Server instances on the same network.

■**Caution** Unlike failover clustering, database mirroring operates at the *user* database level. You cannot mirror system databases (master, msdb, tempdb).

In this chapter, I'll review how to set up, configure, monitor, and remove database mirroring. Before I get into the specifics of database mirroring in the next section, I'll first talk about database mirroring in the context of other SQL Server high-availability options.

■**Tip** Although the core functionality of database mirroring has not changed, SQL Server 2008 does introduce data stream compression and automatic page recovery. These improvements don't require changes to the existing syntax.

Database Mirroring in Context

Database mirroring is provided as one of a set of high-availability technologies included with SQL Server:

- *Failover clustering*: Available in previous versions of SQL Server, failover clustering allows you to maintain high availability at the SQL Server instance level, using two or more nodes that are connected to shared disks. When you install a SQL Server instance on a failover cluster, the user and system database files are installed on the shared disk, and the regular binary install files are written to all nodes (servers) participating in the cluster. One physical node "controls" the SQL Server instance at a time, and if something happens to that node that makes it unavailable, a second node in the cluster can take over the duties of serving that SQL Server instance. Depending on the settings of the SQL Server instance, a failover from one server to another can take just a few seconds.

- *Log shipping*: Also available in previous versions, log shipping is the most similar to database mirroring functionality. Log shipping enables high availability at the database level, and involves keeping a primary online database on one SQL Server instance and a continuously recovering database on a second SQL Server instance. As transaction log backups are performed on the primary database, the transaction log backups are copied to the second SQL Server instance and continuously applied to the database copy. In the event of a failure, either on the primary database or on the server where it resides, the second database copy can be brought online by applying the last of the transferred transaction log backups.

- *Replication*: Also available in previous versions, replication allows you to move data and object definitions (tables, views, and more) to a second database copy on one or more SQL Server instances. Depending on the type of replication you've chosen, you can push data changes on a specific schedule, migrate data as changes are made, or synchronize data changes across multiple data sources. Replication provides high availability in a lesser form, focusing on specific objects and data, but not allowing you to automate the transfer of all database object types. This means that you cannot depend on it to produce an identical copy of your database (something that database mirroring *can* do).

There are several ways in which database mirroring differentiates itself from other high-availability options:

- Database mirroring doesn't require shared disks or special hardware required by failover clustering. Failover clustering protects the entire SQL Server instance, but database mirroring only allows high availability at the user database scope. System databases cannot be mirrored.

- Unlike log shipping, setup of a database mirror can be performed entirely with Transact-SQL. Log shipping requires manual configurations and is considered to be a warm standby solution. Database mirroring is integrated into the database engine and allows for a hot database standby, allowing failover within seconds.

■**Note** A *hot* standby server is one that receives frequent updates from a production server and is immediately available for use in the event of a failure on the production server. A *warm* standby server is one that receives updates, but may require adjustments or a few minutes of transition before taking over in the event of a failure on the production server.

- Replication allows you to push or pull specific database objects, but doesn't allow you to pull *all* database objects. Database mirroring, however, creates an exact copy of the database.

In the next section I'll discuss the architecture of database mirroring.

Database Mirroring Architecture

Database mirroring involves a principal server role, a mirroring server role, and an optional witness server (shown in Figure 25-1). The database on the principal server is actively used, and as transactions are applied to the principal server's database, they are also submitted to the mirror server's database. The mirror server database is left in a recovering state, where it receives changes made on the principal copy, but it cannot be used while the principal mirror database is still available.

Principal Server Role
1. Has the active database
2. Allows user updates and reads
3. Pushes all modifications to mirror copy

Principal Mirror Server
1. Has the recovering copy of the principal database
2. Receives updates as they are made
3. If the principal database becomes unavailable, the mirror database can switch roles and become the principal

Witness Server Role
1. Is required for automatic failover
2. Helps make the decision that the principal database is unavailable.
3. Doesn't contain a copy of the database.

Figure 25-1. *Database mirroring basic architecture*

If an issue occurs on the principal server database that makes the database unavailable, the mirror server can take on the role of the primary database. When the other database (the original principal) comes back online, the former primary database takes on the mirrored server database role, receiving transactions from the principal server.

Failover from principal to mirror databases can be initiated manually or automatically, depending on the database mirroring mode. If automatic failover is required, a third server must join the mirroring session as a witness server. The *witness server* monitors the principal and mirror servers. In a database mirroring session that consists of these three servers (principal, mirror, and witness), two of the three connected servers can make the decision (called a *quorum*) as to whether or not an automatic failover should occur.

Database mirroring sessions can run in a synchronous or asynchronous mode. When in synchronous mode, transactions written to the principal server database must also be written to the mirror server database before any containing transaction can be committed. This option guarantees data redundancy, but has a trade-off of potential performance degradation.

Asynchronous mode allows transactions to commit on the principal database mirroring session before actually writing the transaction to the mirror server database. This option allows for faster transaction completion on the principal database, but also poses the risk of lost transactions if a failure occurs on the principal server before updates can be reflected on the mirror database.

■**Tip** SQL Server 2008 Enterprise Edition provides automatic data page repair on the principal and mirror databases if page corruption has occurred. For example, if a page is corrupted on the principal database, an attempt will be made to retrieve the non-corrupted page from the mirror database. If available, the mirror copy of the page will be used to overlay the bad page on the principal database. Such fixes are also available if a page is corrupted on the mirror database but not the principal.

With regards to application and client connectivity to the principal database, SQL Server maintains metadata that allows .NET application redirection in the event of a failover. Specifically, you can use the SQL Native Client in your .NET code to connect to the mirrored database and the code can be configured such as to be aware of the locations of the mirrored databases. With the SQL Native Client, you can designate both the principal and mirroring SQL Server instances in the connection string, allowing the application connection to be transparently redirected to the newly active principal when the primary database is unavailable.

Setting Up Database Mirroring

In this chapter, I'll demonstrate one scenario across several smaller recipes, much like I did in Chapter 20. In this scenario, I'll be setting up a database mirroring session on the BookStore database. One SQL Server instance will house the principal database, another will house the mirrored database, and another will act as the witness (no database needed).

The following is a general list of steps used to enable database mirroring:

1. *Create endpoints*: You should create mirroring endpoints, which will allow the SQL Server instances (principal, mirror, and witness) to communicate with each other. You have your choice regarding which authentication method is used, and I'll discuss that issue in the upcoming recipe.

2. *Create the database mirror copy*: Before doing this, though, you need to make sure the principal database is in FULL recovery mode, because transaction log backups are applied to the mirror database from the principal database, in order to propagate principal database modifications. To make the mirror database copy, a full database backup is made to the principal database and is then restored to the mirror SQL Server instance WITH NORECOVERY (this option also leaves the database in a state to receive additional transaction log restores). After the full database backup is made on the principal, a transaction log backup must also be made, and then restored on the database mirror copy.

3. *Initialize the database mirroring session*: These last steps involve designating the role of each database using ALTER DATABASE. This command tells SQL Server which SQL Server endpoints connect to the partners and which connect to the witness. *Partner databases* have the principal and/or mirror database, and can also change roles if the principal database becomes unavailable.

The first recipe in this scenario will show you how to create mirroring endpoints that can be used to define which SQL Server instances participate in which actions within the database mirroring session.

Creating Mirroring Endpoints

In order to establish a mirroring session, the participant servers must be able to communicate with one another on their own dedicated TCP port. These endpoint ports will be dedicated to listening for mirroring messages and operations.

In getting ready to set up a new database mirroring session, the mirroring server is the first to have an endpoint created, followed by the primary server, and then the optional witness server (designated if you wish to have automatic failover).

The CREATE ENDPOINT command is used to create the mirroring endpoints. Recall from the previous chapters in this book that CREATE ENDPOINT is also used to create HTTP endpoints and to enable Service Broker cross-server communication. The syntax as it applies to database mirroring is as follows:

```
CREATE ENDPOINT endPointName [ AUTHORIZATION login ]
STATE = { STARTED | STOPPED | DISABLED }
AS TCP (LISTENER_PORT = listenerPort )
FOR DATABASE_MIRRORING (
   [ AUTHENTICATION = {
            WINDOWS [ { NTLM | KERBEROS | NEGOTIATE } ]
      | CERTIFICATE certificate_name
   } ]
   [ [ , ] ENCRYPTION = { DISABLED |SUPPORTED | REQUIRED }
      [ ALGORITHM { RC4 | AES | AES RC4 | RC4 AES } ]
]
   [,] ROLE = { WITNESS | PARTNER | ALL }
)
```

The arguments of this command are described in Table 25-1.

Table 25-1. *CREATE ENDPOINT...FOR DATABASE MIRRORING Arguments*

Argument	Description
endPointName	This argument defines the name of the new server endpoint.
login	This option specifies the owning SQL Server or Windows login of the endpoint. When not designated, the default owner is the creator of the new endpoint.
STATE = { STARTED	STOPPED	DISABLED }	This argument defines what state the endpoint is created in. STARTED means the endpoint will immediately be active. DISABLED means that the endpoint will not listen or respond to requests. STOPPED means that the endpoint listens to requests, but returns errors back to the caller.
listenerPort	This argument specifies the free TCP port on which the mirroring session will listen for incoming communications.
WINDOWS [{ NTLM	KERBEROS	NEGOTIATE }]	This option designates the authentication method of connection to the endpoint, using NTLM, KERBEROS, or NEGOTIATE (which allows the Windows negotiation protocol to choose from NTLM or Kerberos). If not designated, NEGOTIATE is the default authentication option.
CERTIFICATE certificate_name	The CERTIFICATE option allows a certificate to be used for authentication, requiring the calling endpoint.
ENCRYPTION = { DISABLED	SUPPORTED	REQUIRED }	This option applies encryption to a mirroring process. When DISABLED is selected, data sent between mirroring sessions isn't encrypted. When SUPPORTED is selected, if both communicating endpoints support encryption, encryption is used (otherwise it is not). REQUIRED designates that communicating endpoints must support encryption.

Continued

Table 25-1. *Continued*

Argument	Description
ALGORITHM { RC4 | AES | RC4 | RC4 AES }	This option designates the encryption algorithm used in encrypted data transmission.
WITNESS | PARTNER | ALL	These options designate the database mirroring server role. When PARTNER is designated, the created endpoint can be used for either primary or mirrored session communications. If WITNESS is selected, the endpoint is used for the witness role in a mirroring session. The ALL session allows the endpoint to be used for the primary, mirroring, and witness mirroring session roles.

Before starting with the recipe, I need to first discuss authentication options that are required in order for the three SQL Server instances to communicate with one another. First of all, as long as each of the SQL Server instances is running under the same domain service account, and if you use the WINDOWS option to create your endpoint, your SQL Server instances will automatically have access to one another for the database mirroring session. If, however, these SQL Server instances are *not* running under the same domain user account, you'll need to create the Windows login of the remote SQL Server instance on each participating SQL Server instance. For example, let's say the SQL Server instance that is housing the principal database has a startup service account [JOEPROD\ SQLAdmin]. Assume also that the SQL Server instance that is going to house the mirror database copy uses a startup service account of [JOEPROD\Node2Admin]. In order to allow the mirror SQL Server access to the principal SQL Server, the [JOEPROD\Node2Admin] must be added to the principal database. For example:

```
USE master
GO
CREATE LOGIN [JOEPROD\Node2Admin]
FROM WINDOWS
GO
```

The same thing must be done on the mirror SQL Server instance, in order to allow access to the principal and witness SQL Server instances. If these new accounts are also in the Windows administrator groups on the other SQL Server servers, those logins will automatically have access to connect to the database mirroring endpoint. If they are not members of this group, however, you must also explicitly grant the remote login access to the endpoint. For example:

```
GRANT CONNECT ON ENDPOINT::JOEPROD_Mirror
TO [JOEPROD\Node2Admin]
GO
```

In this chapter's scenario, I'll be using three SQL Server instances that run under the same Windows service account. In the first part of this example, a new endpoint is created on the SQL Server instance that will hold the mirrored copy of the database:

```
-- Create an endpoint on the mirror SQL server instance

CREATE ENDPOINT JOEPROD_Mirror
    STATE = STARTED
    AS TCP ( LISTENER_PORT = 5022 )
    FOR DATABASE_MIRRORING (
```

```
    AUTHENTICATION = WINDOWS NEGOTIATE,
    ENCRYPTION = SUPPORTED,
    ROLE=PARTNER)
GO
```

This next step is to create a new endpoint on the SQL Server instance that will hold the principal database:

```
-- Create an endpoint on the primary SQL server instance

CREATE ENDPOINT JOEPROD_Mirror
    STATE = STARTED
    AS TCP ( LISTENER_PORT = 5022 )
    FOR DATABASE_MIRRORING (
        AUTHENTICATION = WINDOWS NEGOTIATE,
        ENCRYPTION = SUPPORTED,
        ROLE=PARTNER)
GO
```

In the third step, a new endpoint is created on the SQL Server instance that will act as the witness in the mirrored database session:

```
-- Create an endpoint on the witness SQL server instance

CREATE ENDPOINT JOEPROD_Witness
    STATE = STARTED
    AS TCP ( LISTENER_PORT = 5022 )
    FOR DATABASE_MIRRORING (
        AUTHENTICATION = WINDOWS NEGOTIATE,
        ENCRYPTION = SUPPORTED,
        ROLE=WITNESS)
GO
```

After creating the endpoints, you can verify the endpoint settings by querying the sys.database_mirroring_endpoints system catalog view.

On the SQL Server instance that will eventually house the database mirror copy, the following query confirms the name of the endpoint, the state (meaning, whether it is started), and its mirroring role:

```
SELECT name, state_desc, role_desc
FROM sys.database_mirroring_endpoints
```

This returns

name	state_desc	role_desc
JOEPROD_Mirror	STARTED	PARTNER

This query is then executed on the SQL Server instance that will house the principal database:

```
SELECT name, state_desc, role_desc
FROM sys.database_mirroring_endpoints
```

This returns

name	state_desc	role_desc
JOEPROD_Mirror	STARTED	PARTNER

Next, the SQL Server instance that will assume the witness role is queried:

```
SELECT name, state_desc, role_desc
FROM sys.database_mirroring_endpoints
```

This returns

name	state_desc	role_desc
JOEPROD_Witness	STARTED	WITNESS

How It Works

Before you can set up a database mirroring session, you must add endpoints to the participating SQL Server instances. These endpoints use the TCP/IP protocol to listen in on a designated port.

In this recipe, an endpoint called JOEPROD_Mirror was first created on the mirroring SQL Server instance:

```
CREATE ENDPOINT JOEPROD_Mirror
```

The initial state was set to STARTED, meaning that the endpoint was created in a state that can be used right away:

```
STATE = STARTED
```

The TCP listening port was set to 5022. This is the port that the endpoint will listen on for database mirroring communication:

```
AS TCP ( LISTENER_PORT = 5022 )
```

The port number choice was arbitrary; just make sure the port is available. If your SQL Server instances communicate over a firewall, the designated mirroring ports must be opened for those machines in order to allow communication.

For the authentication, WINDOWS NEGOTIATE was chosen, which means that Windows authentication will be used to communicate between the participating SQL Server instances:

```
FOR DATABASE_MIRRORING (
   AUTHENTICATION = WINDOWS NEGOTIATE,
```

For encryption, SUPPORTED was designated, meaning that if both communicating sessions support encryption, encryption will be used in the data transmission:

```
   ENCRYPTION = SUPPORTED,
```

The ROLE for the mirrored server was PARTNER, which means that the endpoint can be used for principal database or the mirror:

```
   ROLE=PARTNER)
```

In exactly the same fashion, CREATE ENDPOINT was then executed on the principal SQL Server instance (again, using PARTNER) and then executed on the witness SQL Server instance with a role of WITNESS.

Finally, I queried the system catalog view, sys.database_mirroring_endpoints, which contains information on any database mirroring endpoints that may exist on each SQL Server instance. (In this scenario, there was one endpoint per SQL Server instance.)

Backing Up and Restoring Principal Databases

Once the endpoints are created, the next step in creating a database mirroring session is to create a database backup of the principal database and then restore it to the mirrored SQL Server instance. After restoring a full database backup, a transaction log backup should be made and then applied to the database mirror copy.

■**Note** This chapter demonstrates BACKUP and RECOVERY techniques. These commands are reviewed in more detail in Chapter 29.

Prior to backing up the database, and in order to use database mirroring, the database needs to use the FULL recovery model. In this example, I demonstrate making this change on the principal database SQL Server instance:

```
-- This is executing on the principal database SQL Server instance
USE master
GO

IF NOT EXISTS (SELECT name
                  FROM sys.databases
                  WHERE name = 'BookStore')

CREATE DATABASE BookStore
GO

-- Make sure the database is using FULL recovery

ALTER DATABASE BookStore
SET RECOVERY FULL
GO
```

Next, I perform a full database backup:

```
-- Backing up the BookStore DATABASE

BACKUP DATABASE BookStore
TO DISK =
'C:\Apress\Recipes\Mirror\principalbackup_BookStore.bak'
WITH INIT
```

Once the database backup is complete on the primary SQL Server instance, the .bak file is then manually copied to the *mirroring* SQL Server instance, where it will be restored using NORECOVERY. NORECOVERY mode leaves the database in a state where additional transaction logs can be applied to it:

```
RESTORE DATABASE BookStore
FROM  DISK = 'C:\Apress\Recipes\Mirror\principalbackup_BookStore.bak'
WITH MOVE 'BookStore' TO 'C:\Apress\Recipes\Mirror\BookStore.mdf',
    MOVE 'BookStore_log' TO 'C:\Apress\Recipes\Mirror\BookStore_log.ldf',
    NORECOVERY
GO
```

Keep in mind that the database that you restore must use the same name as the principal database in order for database mirroring to work.

If any transaction log backups occur *after* you perform a full backup on the principal SQL Server instance and *before* you perform the restore on the mirrored server, you must also apply those transaction log backups (using RESTORE) to the mirrored server database. Before enabling mirroring, you also must perform one more transaction log backups on the principal database and then restore it to the mirrored copy.

This example demonstrates backing up the transaction log of the *principal* database:

```
BACKUP LOG BookStore
TO DISK =
'C:\Apress\Recipes\Mirror\BookStore_tlog.trn'
WITH INIT
```

Once the transaction log backup is complete on the primary SQL Server instance, the .trn file is then manually copied to the mirroring SQL Server instance, where it is restored using NORECOVERY:

```
RESTORE LOG BookStore
FROM DISK = 'C:\Apress\Recipes\Mirror\BookStore_tlog.trn'
WITH FILE = 1, NORECOVERY
```

■**Tip** Restoring a user database doesn't bring along the necessary SQL or Windows logins to the server containing the mirrored database. Any SQL or Windows logins mapped to database users in the principal database should also be created on the mirrored SQL Server instance. These logins should be ready in the event of a failover, when the mirror database must take over the role as the principal. If the logins are not on the mirror database SQL Server instance, the database users within the mirrored database will be orphaned (the database users, without any associated logins, will not be able to be accessed).

How It Works

In this recipe, the principal database was first modified to a FULL recovery mode so that it could participate in a database mirroring session:

```
ALTER DATABASE BookStore
SET RECOVERY FULL
```

After that, a full database backup was made of the BookStore database. The INIT option was used to entirely overlay the database file with just the most recent full backup (in case an older backup already existed on the specified file):

```
BACKUP DATABASE BookStore
TO DISK =
'C:\Apress\Recipes\Mirror\principalbackup_BookStore.bak'
WITH INIT
```

The backup file was then manually copied to the second SQL Server instance, which would house the mirrored copy of the database. A new database was then restored using the MOVE and NORECOVERY option. You should use the MOVE option when you want to relocate *where* the database files are restored, versus *how* they were stored when the original backup was created:

```
RESTORE DATABASE BookStore
FROM  DISK = 'C:\Apress\Recipes\Mirror\principalbackup_BookStore.bak'
WITH MOVE 'BookStore' TO 'C:\Apress\Recipes\Mirror\BookStore.mdf',
    MOVE 'BookStore_log' TO 'C:\Apress\Recipes\Mirror\BookStore_log.ldf',
    NORECOVERY
GO
```

After that, back on the principal database server, a transaction log backup was created:

```
BACKUP LOG BookStore
TO DISK =
'C:\Apress\Recipes\Mirror\BookStore_tlog.trn'
WITH INIT
```

The transaction log backup file was then manually copied to the second SQL Server instance prior to restoring it on the mirrored copy of the database (again using the NORECOVERY option):

```
RESTORE LOG BookStore
FROM DISK = 'C:\Apress\Recipes\Mirror\BookStore_tlog.trn'
WITH FILE = 1, NORECOVERY
```

Now you have a second copy of the database in a NORECOVERY state, and you are ready to proceed to the next step in this example scenario, which involves creating the database mirroring session.

Creating a Database Mirroring Session

Once the database is restored and in recovery mode on the mirror server, the mirroring session can then be started using the ALTER DATABASE command. This is achieved in two steps (three, if you are using a witness SQL Server instance, which in this scenario you are). First, ALTER DATABASE will be executed on the mirror SQL Server instance to set it as a partner with the principal server endpoint. After that, ALTER DATABASE will be executed on the principal SQL Server instance to set the mirroring partner and witness endpoint locations.

The specified syntax for using ALTER DATABASE to enable database mirroring is as follows:

```
ALTER DATABASE database_name
[PARTNER { = 'partner_server'
 | FAILOVER
 | FORCE_SERVICE_ALLOW_DATA_LOSS
 | OFF
 | RESUME
 | SAFETY { FULL | OFF }
 | SUSPEND
| TIMEOUT integer
           } |
   WITNESS { = 'witness_server'
           | OFF
           }]
```

The arguments of this command are described in Table 25-2. Keep in mind that several of these options touch on the functionality demonstrated later on in the chapter.

Table 25-2. *ALTER DATABASE Arguments*

Argument	Description
database_name	This defines the name of the database participating in the mirror session (the name must be the same on both the principal and mirror servers).
partner_server	This specifies the name of the partner server, which expects the following format: TCP://fully_qualified_domain_ name:port.

Continued

Table 25-2. *Continued*

Argument	Description
FAILOVER	The FAILOVER option manually fails over the principal database to the mirror database. This option requires that the SAFETY option be FULL.
FORCE_SERVICE_ALLOW_DATA_LOSS	FORCE_SERVICE_ALLOW_DATA_LOSS forces the failover to the mirrored database without fully synchronizing the latest transactions (thus potentially losing data). This operation requires that the principal server database be unavailable, the SAFETY option OFF, and no witness designated.
OFF	The OFF option stops the database mirroring session.
RESUME	The RESUME option starts back up a suspended database mirroring session.
SAFETY { FULL | OFF }	The SAFETY setting has two values, FULL or OFF. When SAFETY is FULL, the database mirroring session works in synchronous mode, requiring transactions on the principal database to be written to the mirror database before the transaction is allowed to commit. When SAFETY is OFF, the mirroring session is asynchronous, meaning that transactions at the principal don't wait to be applied at the mirror before committing (which introduces the potential for data loss).
SUSPEND	The SUSPEND mode suspends the database mirroring session.
TIMEOUT integer	The TIMEOUT option designates how long a server instance will wait to receive a PING message back (the heartbeat method between the partner servers) from the other partner before deeming that connection to be unavailable (thus causing a failover). The minimum wait time is five seconds, with a default value of ten seconds.
witness_server	This is the name of the witness server, which expects the following format: TCP://fully_qualified_domain_name:port.
OFF	OFF removes the witness from the database mirroring session.

Continuing with the example scenario, on the *mirrored* SQL Server instance, the following command is executed to begin the mirroring process by referencing the principal SQL Server instance and TCP port number (where the endpoint listens):

```
-- Set on the mirrored SQL Server instance
-- Default SAFETY is FULL - synchronous mode
ALTER DATABASE BookStore
    SET PARTNER = 'TCP://NODE2.JOEPROD.COM:5022'
GO
```

Next, ALTER DATABASE is executed on the *principal* SQL Server instance, designating the mirror server's name and TCP port number:

```
-- Enable the mirroring session on the principal SQL Server instance
-- Default SAFETY is FULL - synchronous mode
ALTER DATABASE BookStore
    SET PARTNER = 'TCP://NODE1.JOEPROD.COM:5022'
GO
```

After setting up both the mirror and principal, you can then optionally add a witness server, which is configured on the *principal* SQL Server instance, as this example demonstrates:

```
-- Enable the witness on the principal SQL Server instance
-- Default SAFETY is FULL - synchronous mode
ALTER DATABASE BookStore
    SET WITNESS = 'TCP://NODE3.JOEPROD.COM:5022'
GO
```

Mirroring is now configured in this example with the optional witness server. Any data modifications or schema changes made on the principal database will be logged to the mirror database. The mirror database will *not* be available for activity, unless it becomes the principal database either by an automatic or manual failover (discussed and demonstrated later in the chapter).

How It Works

In this example, the ALTER DATABASE command was used to start a database mirroring session. You started off on the mirrored SQL Server instance. ALTER DATABASE was executed using SET PARTNER:

```
ALTER DATABASE BookStore
    SET PARTNER = 'TCP://NODE2.JOEPROD.COM:5022'
GO
```

The PARTNER of this command pointed to the principal database SQL Server server name and the listening endpoint port of that SQL Server instance. Recall earlier that the endpoint was configured to listen on port 5022 in a partner (not witness) capacity.

Next, on the principal database SQL Server instance, the ALTER DATABASE command was used to set the database mirroring partner, this time pointing to the mirrored database node and listening to the TCP port:

```
ALTER DATABASE BookStore
    SET PARTNER = 'TCP://NODE1.JOEPROD.COM:5022'
GO
```

The SQL Server instance containing the principal database is also where you need to configure the witness for the database mirroring session. Recall from the earlier recipe that I created a database mirroring endpoint on the witness SQL Server instance. When you use ALTER DATABASE and SET WITNESS, the name of the witness machine and listening TCP port are designated (from the principal database SQL Server instance):

```
ALTER DATABASE BookStore
    SET WITNESS = 'TCP://NODE3.JOEPROD.COM:5022'
GO
```

The database mirroring session has now been configured. Any database objects that have been added or modifications that have been made in the BookStore database will be transferred to the mirror copy. If the principal database becomes unavailable, a failover can occur, changing the mirrored database's role to the principal role. Before you get into these tasks, however, I'll quickly recap what was accomplished in these last few recipes.

Setup Summary

The general steps for setting up database mirroring spanned the last three recipes, so here is a step-by-step review of how it was done:

1. First, on the mirror SQL Server instance, an endpoint was created using `CREATE ENDPOINT` and designating the role of `PARTNER`, employing the TCP port of 5022.

2. On the principal SQL Server instance, an endpoint was created using a role of `PARTNER` and a listener port of 5022 (because these are separate servers, you can use the same TCP port on each, so long as the port is available for use).

3. Next, on the witness SQL Server instance, an endpoint was created with a role of `WITNESS`, using a listener port of 5022.

4. Back on the principal SQL Server instance, the `BookStore` database (the database to be mirrored) was set to `FULL` recovery mode using `ALTER DATABASE` (if it was already using `FULL`, this step wouldn't have been necessary).

5. Still on the principal SQL Server instance, a full database backup was performed on the `BookStore` database.

6. On the mirror SQL Server instance, the database was then restored using the `NORECOVERY` option, leaving it in a state to receive transactions from the mirroring process. Had additional transaction log backups been made on the principal database after the last full backup, those transaction log backups would need to be applied to the mirrored, restored copy too.

7. On the principal SQL Server instance, a transaction log backup was performed on the `BookStore` database.

8. On the mirror SQL Server instance, the transaction log backup was then restored using the `NORECOVERY` option, leaving it in a state to receive transactions from the mirroring process.

9. Still on the mirror SQL Server instance, the `ALTER DATABASE...SET PARTNER` command was executed, pointing to the fully qualified *principal* server name and TCP port that the *principal* SQL Server instance endpoint listens on.

10. On the principal SQL Server instance, `ALTER DATABASE...SET PARTNER` was executed, pointing to the fully qualified name of the *mirrored* server and TCP port that the *mirror* SQL Server instance endpoint listens on.

11. Lastly, still from the principal SQL Server instance, `ALTER DATABASE...SET WITNESS` was executed, pointing to the fully qualified name of the *witness* server and TCP port that the *witness* SQL Server instance endpoint listens on.

After all of this, the database mirror session begins. Modifications to the principal database will be logged to the awaiting mirror database. The witness server will be keeping an eye on the connection between the principal and mirror databases, making sure that if there are any problems, the appropriate actions are taken (such as automatic failovers). Before I discuss failovers, however, in the next section I'll discuss the various operating modes of a mirroring session, and how they can be both modified and controlled.

Operating Database Mirroring

Database mirroring sessions operate in three modes; high availability (used in the previous example), high protection, or high performance.

High-availability mode means that transactions committed on the principal database require the availability of both the principal and mirror databases before the transaction can commit. This mode also requires a witness server, which allows automatic failover to occur. The owner of the principal database is determined by a quorum, which is the presence of at least two servers that can communicate with each other. If the witness loses contact with the mirror, but keeps contact with the principal, the principal database will remain in its role. If the witness loses contact with the principal, however, but can still see the mirror, in high-availability mode the mirror assumes the role of principal. If the witness becomes unavailable for whatever reason, the principal and mirror form the quorum, and remain in their present roles. In short—it takes two to make a quorum, and a quorum decides which partner controls the principal database.

High-protection mode, just like high-availability mode, means that transactions committed on the principal database require the availability of both the principal and mirror databases before the transaction can commit. Unlike high-availability mode, however, there isn't a witness server in the mix. This means that while a manual failover can occur, an automatic failover can't. High-protection mode still forms a quorum (of just the two partner servers) with the mirror database; however, if the mirror database becomes unavailable, SQL Server will make the database unavailable (meaning take it out of service). This is because high-protection mode requires the mirror in order to commit transactions.

Both of the aforementioned modes suggest data protection and availability as the primary emphasis. With this functionality, however, comes performance overhead. If your mirrored database has significant update activity, each transaction on the principal database must wait for an acceptance from the mirrored copy before a commit can happen.

Enter *high-performance mode*, which allows asynchronous updates on the principal database (no waiting for the mirror before committing the transaction) and no witness server. This mode emphasizes transaction speed, but not data availability (because of the lack of manual or automatic failover) and minimal data recoverability (asynchronous modifications allow for the potential of lost transactions on the mirror database).

■**Note** In SQL Server 2008, database mirroring has been optimized to take automatic advantage of data stream compression and log send buffer optimizations.

In this next recipe, I'll demonstrate how to use ALTER DATABASE to configure the high-availability, high-protection, and high-performance modes.

Changing Operating Modes

Both high-availability and high-protection modes use the FULL safety mode (which is the default mode when you start a mirroring session). You can, however, turn this setting off by using ALTER DATABASE...SET SAFETY. This command takes two options: OFF or FULL.

In this first example, the safety of a specific mirrored session is turned OFF for a database (putting it in high-performance mode) by executing the command on the principal SQL Server instance:

```
ALTER DATABASE BookStore SET SAFETY OFF
```

This second example demonstrates turning safety back on again, and changing from high-performance to high-availability mode:

```
ALTER DATABASE BookStore SET SAFETY FULL
```

High-protection mode was not demonstrated here, as it also has FULL safety mode enabled, only without the use of a witness in the database mirroring session.

How It Works

In this example, the mirroring session safety was turned off and then on again by referencing the database name, followed by the new safety mode (either OFF or FULL). With the presence of a witness and the safety on FULL, your database mirroring session will operate in high-availability mode. If you aren't using a witness, but safety is still FULL, the database mirroring session is operating in high-protection mode. With safety OFF, the database is in asynchronous, high-performance mode. See Table 25-3 for a summary of these different modes.

Table 25-3. *Database Mirroring Operating Modes*

Mode	Safety Configuration	Witness?
High availability	FULL	Yes
High protection	FULL	No
High performance	OFF	No

■**Tip** As a best practice, use synchronous high-availability mode for mission-critical databases. Only use asynchronous high-performance mode for databases where you can easily recover the lost data through other mechanisms or sources. Of the synchronous choices, use a witness server whenever possible (high availability) in order to take advantage of automatic failover.

Performing Failovers

A failover involves switching the roles of the principal and mirror database, with the mirror copy becoming the principal and the principal becoming the mirror. Existing database connections are broken during the failover, and the connecting application must then connect to the new principal database (and with .NET functionality, the connection string can be database-mirror aware).

You can manually set databases participating in a mirroring session to failover in synchronous high-performance or high-availability modes using the ALTER DATABASE...SET PARTNER FAILOVER command.

In this example, a failover is initiated from the *principal* server (which becomes the mirror server after the operation):

```
USE master
GO
ALTER DATABASE BookStore SET PARTNER FAILOVER
```

How long the actual failover operation takes depends on the time it takes to roll forward the logged transactions on the mirrored copy.

If the database session is running in asynchronous, high-performance mode, you cannot initiate a manual failover. Instead, if the principal becomes unavailable, you can either wait for the database to become available again or force the service on the mirror copy. To force the service, use the ALTER DATABASE...SET PARTNER FORCE_SERVICE_ALLOW_DATA_LOSS command. After forcing the service, the mirrored database will roll forward logged transactions (and in asynchronous mode, the principal could have lost some of the transactions in transit prior to the outage). The mirrored database then takes over as the principal.

■**Caution** Force service on a mirrored database only if absolutely necessary, as data can be lost from the unavailable principal database.

In this example, the mirrored database in a database session using asynchronous high-performance mode is forced into service (this requires that the actual principal database be unavailable to the mirroring session):

```
ALTER DATABASE ReportCentralDB SET PARTNER FORCE_SERVICE_ALLOW_DATA_LOSS
```

How It Works

These examples demonstrated failover options, which depend on the database mirroring session mode. You may decide to perform a manual failover, for example, in order to perform maintenance activities on the principal database server.

For asynchronous high-performance mode, however, if the principal database becomes unavailable, you'll only want to force service on the mirror session when absolutely necessary, as data can be lost from any unsent transactions on the unavailable principal database.

Pausing or Resuming a Mirroring Session

If your mirrored principal database is undergoing a significant number of updates, which are then being bottlenecked by the synchronous updates to the mirror, you can temporarily pause the mirroring session using ALTER DATABASE...SET PARTNER SUSPEND. This option keeps the principal database available and preserves changes in the log, which will then be sent to the mirroring database once it's resumed. The database mirroring session should only be paused for a short period of time, as the transaction log will continue to grow, causing it to fill up if the transaction log file size is fixed or expand until the drive is full (if the transaction log file size is not fixed).

In this example, the BookStore database mirroring session is paused from the principal server:

```
ALTER DATABASE BookStore SET PARTNER SUSPEND
```

The state is then confirmed by querying the sys.database_mirroring system catalog view on the principal server:

```
SELECT mirroring_state_desc
FROM sys.database_mirroring
WHERE database_id = DB_ID('BookStore')
```

This returns

```
mirroring_state_desc
SUSPENDED
```

This next example demonstrates resuming the database mirroring session, causing the mirror database to synchronize with the pending log transactions:

```
ALTER DATABASE BookStore SET PARTNER RESUME
```

How It Works

You can pause or resume a database mirroring session without removing it entirely. Use the techniques demonstrated in this recipe to allow the removal of performance bottlenecks that may appear on high-activity databases. Be mindful, however, of the transaction log size, and don't keep the mirroring session disabled longer than is strictly necessary.

Stopping Mirroring Sessions and Removing Endpoints

The previous example demonstrated briefly pausing and resuming a mirroring session; however, if you wish to remove it altogether, you can use the ALTER DATABASE...SET PARTNER OFF command.

In this example, the BookStore database mirror is stopped and removed (mirroring metadata is removed):

```
ALTER DATABASE BookStore SET PARTNER OFF
```

You can remove the mirroring endpoints on each SQL Server instance using the DROP ENDPOINT command, for example:

```
-- Executed on the witness server
DROP ENDPOINT JOEPROD_Witness

-- Executed on the mirror server
DROP ENDPOINT JOEPROD_Mirror

-- Executed on the principal server
DROP ENDPOINT JOEPROD_Mirror
```

How It Works

Use ALTER DATABASE...SET PARTNER OFF to stop and remove the database mirroring session. Connections will be broken in the principal database, but allowed back in again for regular activity after the mirroring session is removed. The mirrored copy is left in a restoring state, where you can either recover or drop it. If you wish to reinstate mirroring, you have to follow the steps of setting up the principal, mirror, and witness from scratch.

If you remove mirroring, it's best to also remove the endpoints using DROP ENDPOINT, so that you don't forget that they are there holding onto the TCP port (which you may decide to use for other things).

Monitoring and Configuring Options

The last batch of recipes in this chapter will show you how to

- Monitor the status of the database mirror using the sys.database_mirroring system catalog view.
- Configure the connection timeout period using the ALTER DATABASE...SET PARTNER TIMEOUT command.

You'll begin with learning how to monitor a database mirroring session's current status.

Monitoring Mirror Status

You can confirm the status of your mirroring session by querying the sys.database_mirroring system catalog view.

For example, this view is executed on the principal and shows the state of the mirror, the role of the current database, the safety level (described in the next recipe), and the state of the witness connection to the principal:

```
SELECT mirroring_state_desc, mirroring_role_desc, mirroring_safety_level_desc,
mirroring_witness_state_desc
FROM sys.database_mirroring
WHERE database_id = DB_ID('BookStore')
```

This returns

mirroring_state_desc	mirroring_role_desc	mirroring_safety level_desc	mirroring_witness_state_desc
SYNCHRONIZED	PRINCIPAL	FULL	CONNECTED

How It Works

The SYNCHRONIZED state, when seen for the default FULL safety mode, means that the principal and mirrored database contain the same data. Other states you can see in this view include the following:

- SYNCHRONIZING, which means that the principal is sending log records that the mirror is still in the process of applying.
- SUSPENDED, which means that either the mirrored copy of the database is unavailable, errors have occurred, or the database has been manually put in this state. In a SUSPENDED state, the principal database runs without sending log records to the mirror.
- PENDING_FAILOVER, which is seen when a manual failover request has been made, but not yet executed.
- DISCONNECTED, which means that the partner has lost communication with the other partner and witness.

Configuring the Connection Timeout Period

Database mirroring uses a default connection timeout period of 10 seconds. If a connection cannot be made after 10 seconds, a failure occurs, and depending on the role of the database (principal, mirror, or witness) or the mirroring session mode (synchronous, asynchronous), a failover or mirroring shutdown can occur.

If your network latency causes premature failures in the database mirroring session, you can configure the connection timeout period using the ALTER DATABASE...SET PARTNER TIMEOUT command. This command configures the timeout period in seconds (with a minimum of 5 seconds allowed).

In this example, the connection timeout period is increased to 15 seconds on the principal server:

```
ALTER DATABASE BookStore SET PARTNER TIMEOUT 15
```

You can confirm the new setting by querying the sys.database_mirroring system catalog view:

```
SELECT mirroring_connection_timeout
FROM sys.database_mirroring
WHERE database_id = DB_ID('BookStore')
```

This returns

```
mirroring_connection_timeout
15
```

How It Works

In this recipe, the connection timeout period was modified using the `ALTER DATABASE...SET PARTNER TIMEOUT` command:

```
ALTER DATABASE BookStore SET PARTNER TIMEOUT 15
```

When a mirroring session is active, `PING` communication messages are sent between the participating servers. When a server instance has to wait longer than the configured timeout, a failure occurs. The reaction to the failure depends on the role of the server, how quorum is defined (which two servers still see one another), and the database mirroring mode (high availability, high protection, or high performance).

■ ■ ■

Database Snapshots

Database snapshots are read-only, static copies of a database, representative of a specific point in time. You can connect to these snapshots just as you would any other database, allowing you to use them for reporting, testing, training, or data recovery purposes. Before you conduct large or potentially hazardous database updates, you can use database snapshots as a just-in-case precaution when you may need to undo your work.

In this chapter, I demonstrate how to create, query, and drop database snapshots, as well as how to use database snapshots for data recovery purposes.

Snapshot Basics

Database snapshots can be created from user databases, providing a read-only view of the data, from the specific point in time when the snapshot was generated. Multiple snapshots can be created for a single database, allowing you, for example, to create a snapshot of a database at the end of each day or week, or at month's end.

Database snapshots are also space efficient, because they use sparse files. A *sparse file* is a file that contains no user data when first created. Snapshots reserve a minimum amount of space in order to maintain the original snapshot's data. When first created, a database snapshot does *not* produce an extra copy of all data in the source database, but as database changes occur over time in the source, a copy of the pre-changed data is placed in the sparse file. The snapshot will then contain the contents of the database as it appeared the moment the snapshot was created.

Queries against the snapshot will return data from the snapshot, the database, or both. Unchanged source database data will still be retrieved from the source database. But, if the data has been changed on the source database since the snapshot database was created, it will be retrieved from the snapshot.

As the percentage of changed data in the database source approaches 100%, the database snapshot will approach the size of the original database at the time the snapshot was originally created. Keep in mind that if the same data is modified on the source database multiple times, no additional updates are made to the database snapshot. Once a data page is updated on the source, the pre-changed data page is only moved a single time to the snapshot database.

There are a few limitations to be aware of when deciding whether to use snapshots. For example, snapshots can't be created for the system databases. And, database snapshots can't be backed up, restored over, attached, or detached like regular databases. Also, snapshots do add performance overhead to the source database. This is because you'll see increased I/O activity for each modification that causes a data page to be moved to the snapshot file. If you have multiple snapshots on the same source database, the I/O activity will increase for each snapshot that requires page updates.

Limitations aside, database snapshots offer an excellent means of preserving point-in-time data, separating out reporting queries from the source database, and allowing quick data recovery.

The next set of recipes will demonstrate database snapshots in action.

Creating and Querying Database Snapshots

You create a database snapshot using the CREATE DATABASE command.

The syntax for this command is as follows:

```
CREATE DATABASE database_snapshot_name
    ON
        (NAME = logical_file_name,
         FILENAME = 'os_file_name' ) [ ,...n ]
    AS SNAPSHOT OF source_database_name
```

The arguments for this command are described in Table 26-1.

Table 26-1. *CREATE DATABASE...AS SNAPSHOT Arguments*

Argument	Description
database_snapshot_name	This specifies the name of the database snapshot that you want to create.
(NAME = logical_file_name,FILENAME = 'os_file_name') [,...n]	logical_file_name is the logical file name of the source database data files. os_file_name is the physical file name to be created for the snapshot file. For each source database data file, there must be a snapshot file defined.
source_database_name	This defines the source database that the snapshot is based on.

In this recipe's example, a snapshot is generated for the AdventureWorks database:

```
CREATE DATABASE AdventureWorks_Snapshot_Oct_08_2008
ON
(  NAME = AdventureWorks2008_Data,
   FILENAME =
'C:\Apress\Recipes\AdventureWorks_Snapshot_Oct_08_2008.mdf')
AS SNAPSHOT OF AdventureWorks

GO
```

Next, I'll perform an update in the AdventureWorks database in order to demonstrate the database snapshot's functionality:

```
USE AdventureWorks
GO

UPDATE HumanResources.Department
SET GroupName = 'Materials'
WHERE Name='Production'
GO
```

Now I'll query the HumanResources.Department table in the AdventureWorks source database to confirm my change:

```
SELECT GroupName
FROM AdventureWorks.HumanResources.Department
WHERE Name='Production'
```

This returns

GroupName
Materials

Next, I'll query the snapshot:

```
SELECT GroupName
FROM AdventureWorks_Snapshot_Oct_08_2008.HumanResources.Department
WHERE Name='Production'
```

The snapshot returns the original value of the GroupName *prior* to the change and as of when the snapshot was created:

GroupName
Manufacturing

How It Works

In this recipe, a database snapshot was created using the CREATE DATABASE command:

```
CREATE DATABASE AdventureWorks_Snapshot_Oct_08_2008
```

The ON clause included the logical name of the data file from the AdventureWorks database, followed by the physical path and file name of the new database snapshot data file (since the snapshot is read-only, no transaction log file is needed):

```
ON
(   NAME = AdventureWorks_Data,
    FILENAME = 'C:\Apress\Recipes\AdventureWorks_Snapshot_Oct_08_2008.mdf')
```

The AS clause designated which database the snapshot would be based on:

```
AS SNAPSHOT OF AdventureWorks
```

Once the snapshot was created, an update was performed in the AdventureWorks database. Behind the scenes, SQL Server copied the pre-changed data pages to the database snapshot file.

Queries against the snapshot that require data that has changed in the source database since the snapshot was created will be read from the snapshot database. This copy-on-write functionality allows the size of the snapshot file to remain relatively small, meaning that only the data affected by any changes would need to be stored in the snapshot data file.

Removing a Database Snapshot

To remove a database snapshot, use the DROP DATABASE command.

The syntax is as follows:

```
DROP DATABASE database_snapshot_name
```

This command uses just one argument: the name of the database snapshot.

In this next example, I demonstrate dropping the database snapshot created in the previous recipe:

```
DROP DATABASE AdventureWorks_Snapshot_Oct_08_2008
```

How It Works

The snapshot was removed in this recipe using DROP DATABASE. This removed the snapshot from the SQL Server instance, along with the removal of the underlying physical snapshot file.

Recovering Data with a Database Snapshot

Consider this not-so-uncommon scenario: you get a call from a database end user telling you that he has accidentally updated a column's value for all rows in a table. The database he modified is very large, and restoring the data from backup will first require that you retrieve the backup file from tape. Once retrieved, you'll have to restore the database under a separate database name, and then INSERT...SELECT out the missing data into the production database. In addition to the pain of doing all of this, you may also find that you don't have the required disk space to store both the backup file and additional restored copy of the database.

Now imagine that you had created periodic snapshots of your database prior to significant data update events. Depending on the volatility of the data in your source database, database snapshots may only consume a fraction of the space required for a full database restore. With a snapshot, you can restore/update the data affected by the previous example by updating the source database with data from the snapshot database.

Or, if you can afford to do so, you can overlay the existing source database, recovering data as of the last snapshot using the RESTORE...FROM DATABASE_SNAPSHOT command. Using RESTORE...FROM DATABASE_SNAPSHOT, SQL Server will copy over the existing source database with the database snapshot. The RESTORE...FROM DATABASE_SNAPSHOT command is only used in conjunction with snapshots.

■**Note** For other uses of the RESTORE command, see Chapter 29.

The syntax for reverting from a database snapshot is as follows:

```
RESTORE DATABASE <database_name>
FROM DATABASE_SNAPSHOT = <database_snapshot_name>
```

This command takes two arguments: the name of the source database that you want to restore over, and the name of the database snapshot that you want to revert from.

Using RESTORE...FROM DATABASE_SNAPSHOT, you'll lose any data modifications made to the source database since the last snapshot, only recovering your data as of the point in time when the snapshot was created. But, with only having to update information that was modified since the snapshot was created, RESTORE...FROM DATABASE_SNAPSHOT operations can take significantly less time than regular database restores. You are achieving similar results to those in a regular database restore, in that your database state is reverted to the contents as they were when the snapshot was created.

■**Caution** Only revert to a snapshot if you can afford to lose all the changes you made in the source database since the last snapshot! This method is most useful for "scratch" databases, such as the ones used for training or testing. Also, although database snapshots are a convenient means of recovering data, database snapshots should not be considered a replacement for a good data recovery plan.

If you plan on using database snapshots to recover data in your SQL Server instance, note that other database snapshots (snapshots you are not recovering from) must be deleted prior to the

RESTORE...FROM DATABASE_SNAPSHOT operation. Otherwise, you will receive an error message similar to this:

```
Msg 3137, Level 16, State 4, Line 2
Database cannot be reverted. Either the primary or the snapshot names are improperly
specified, all other snapshots have not been dropped, or there are missing files.
Msg 3013, Level 16, State 1, Line 2
RESTORE DATABASE is terminating abnormally.
```

In addition to database snapshots, any full-text catalogs in the database must be removed prior to a database snapshot RESTORE...FROM DATABASE_SNAPSHOT operation, and your source database can't contain read-only or offline filegroups.

■**Note** Since a restore from a snapshot file breaks the transaction log backup sequence (see Chapter 29), it is a good idea to perform a full database backup after performing the RESTORE operation.

For this next recipe, I'll create a new database and then populate a table using data from the AdventureWorks database:

```
IF NOT EXISTS (SELECT name
                 FROM sys.databases
                 WHERE name = 'TSQL_AW')
BEGIN
   CREATE DATABASE TSQL_AW
END
GO

USE TSQL_AW
GO

SELECT BusinessEntityID, CreditCardID, ModifiedDate
INTO dbo.PersonCreditCard
FROM AdventureWorks.Sales.PersonCreditCard
```

Next, I'll create a new database snapshot on the TSQL_AW database:

```
CREATE DATABASE TSQL_AW_Oct_09_2008
ON
(   NAME = TSQL_AW,
    FILENAME = 'C:\Apress\Recipes\TSQL_AW_Oct_09_2008.mdf')
AS SNAPSHOT OF TSQL_AW
GO
```

Next, all rows from the dbo.PersonCreditCard table are accidentally deleted (no WHERE clause was used):

```
USE TSQL_AW
GO
DELETE dbo.PersonCreditCard
```

This returns

```
(19118 row(s) affected)
```

A query is executed to validate what happened in the TSQL_AW database:

```
SELECT COUNT(*)
FROM dbo.PersonCreditCard
```

This returns

0

Next, I'll revert the TSQL_AW database to the state it was in as of the database snapshot. Keep in mind that no sessions can be connected to the source database during the RESTORE, so this example changes the database context to the master database. The TSQL_AW database is offline during the operation:

```
USE master
GO

RESTORE DATABASE TSQL_AW
FROM DATABASE_SNAPSHOT = 'TSQL_AW_Oct_09_2008'
```

The validation query is executed again to see if the rows are restored:

```
USE TSQL_AW
GO

SELECT COUNT(*)
FROM dbo.PersonCreditCard
```

This returns

19118

How It Works

The RESTORE...FROM DATABASE_SNAPSHOT command allows you to undo any changes you made to the source database after the date and time of the creation of the designated database snapshot. This operation can also take less time to perform than a regular restore operation (for more on this topic, see Chapter 29).

In this recipe, all rows from a table were accidentally deleted. A database snapshot was then used to revert to the data as of the point when the database snapshot was created. During the RESTORE...FROM DATABASE_SNAPSHOT operation, the database was offline and unavailable for use. After the operation completed, any changes made to TSQL_AW since the database snapshot were lost.

■ ■ ■

Linked Servers and Distributed Queries

Linked servers provide SQL Server with access to data from remote data sources. Using linked servers, you can issue queries, perform data modifications, and execute remote procedure calls. Remote data sources can be *homogeneous* (meaning that a source is another SQL Server instance) or *heterogeneous* (from other relational database products and data sources such as DB2, Access, Oracle, Excel, and text files). A query that joins or retrieves data across multiple platforms is a *cross-platform query*. Using a cross-platform query, you can access legacy database systems without the cost of merging or migrating existing data sources.

The remote data sources are connected to via an OLE DB provider. *OLE DB*, created by Microsoft, is a set of component object model (COM) interfaces used to provide consistent access to varying data sources. To establish access from a SQL Server instance to another data source requires that you choose the correct OLE DB provider. How the OLE DB provider was designed determines what kind of distributed query operations can be implemented through a distributed query.

So in a nutshell, a linked server is a means of establishing a connection to a remote data source. Depending on the OLE DB driver used to set up the linked server, you can execute distributed queries to retrieve data or perform operations on the remote data source.

Distributed queries can also be run without having to define linked servers, for example, by using the Transact-SQL function OPENROWSET. In addition to querying a remote data source without a linked server, OPENROWSET allows BULK reads of ASCII, Unicode, and binary files. Using OPENROWSET and BULK, you can read tabular data from a text file, or use it to import an ASCII, Unicode, or binary type file into a single large data type column and single row (such as varchar(max), nvarchar(max), or varbinary(max)).

SQL Server also provides the SYNONYM object, which allows you to reference an object that has a long name with a shorter name. This can be useful for long identifiers in general, but particularly for distributed queries that reference a four-part linked server name, using a shorter name for the data source instead.

This chapter contains recipes for creating linked servers, executing distributed queries, reading from a text file using OPENROWSET and BULK, and using the new SYNONYM object.

Linked Server Basics

This next set of recipes will demonstrate how to use linked servers. Specifically, I'll be demonstrating how to

- Create a linked server connection to another SQL Server instance.
- Configure the properties of a linked server.

- View information about configured linked servers on the SQL Server instance.

- Drop a linked server.

I'll start off by discussing how to use the system stored procedure sp_addlinkedserver to create a new linked server.

Creating a Linked Server to Another SQL Server Instance

Linked servers allow you to query external data sources from within a SQL Server instance. The external data source can be either a different SQL Server instance or a non-SQL Server data source such as Oracle, MS Access, DB2, or MS Excel.

To create the linked server, use the system stored procedure sp_addlinkedserver. The syntax is as follows:

```
sp_addlinkedserver
    [ @server= ] 'server' [ ,
    [ @srvproduct= ] 'product_name' ]
    [ , [ @provider= ] 'provider_name' ]
    [ , [ @datasrc= ] 'data_source' ]
    [ , [ @location= ] 'location' ]
    [ , [ @provstr= ] 'provider_string' ]
    [ , [ @catalog= ] 'catalog' ]
```

The parameters of this system stored procedure are described in Table 27-1.

Table 27-1. *sp_addlinkedserver Arguments*

Argument	Description
server	This is the local name used for the linked server. Instance names are also allowed, for example, MYSERVER\SQL1.
product_name	This is the product name of the OLE DB data source. For SQL Server instances, the product_name is 'SQL Server'.
provider_name	This is the unique programmatic identifier for the OLE DB provider. When not specified, the provider name is the SQL Server data source. The explicit provider_name for SQL Server is SQLNCLI (for Microsoft SQL Native Client OLE DB Provider). MSDAORA is used for Oracle, OraOLEDB.Oracle for Oracle versions 8 and higher, Microsoft.Jet.OLEDB.4.0 for MS Access and MS Excel, DB2OLEDB for IBM DB2, and MSDASQL for an ODBC data source.
data_source	This is the data source as interpreted by the specified OLE DB provider. For SQL Server, this is the network name of the SQL Server (servername or servername\instancename). For Oracle, this is the SQL*Net alias. For MS Access and MS Excel, this is the full path and name of the file. For an ODBC data source, this is the system DSN name.
location	This is the location as interpreted by the specified OLE DB provider.
provider_string	This is the connection string specific to the OLE DB provider. For an ODBC connection, this is the ODBC connection string. For MS Excel, this is Excel 5.0.
catalog	The catalog definition varies based on the OLE DB provider implementation. For SQL Server, this is the optional database name. For DB2, this catalog is the name of the database.

In a network environment with multiple SQL Server instances, linked servers provide a convenient method for sharing SQL Server data without having to physically push or pull the data and replicate the schema.

■**Tip** In this chapter, I cover examples of communication between SQL Server instances. For heterogeneous data sources such as DB2, Access, and Oracle, parameters will vary substantially. For an extensive table of required sp_addlinkedserver options, see the SQL Server Books Online topic "sp_addlinkedserver (Transact-SQL)."

The configurations used to connect to heterogeneous data sources vary, based on the OLE DB provider. If you're just connecting to a different SQL Server instance, however, Microsoft makes it easy for you. In this recipe, I demonstrate creating a linked server connection to another SQL Server instance:

```
EXEC  sp_addlinkedserver
            @server=  'JOEPROD',
            @srvproduct=  'SQL Server'
```

You can also create linked servers to connect to SQL Server named instances, for example:

```
EXEC  sp_addlinkedserver
            @server=  'JOEPROD\NODE2',
            @srvproduct=  'SQL Server'
```

How It Works

Adding a linked server to an external data source allows you to perform distributed queries (distributed queries are reviewed later in this chapter in the "Executing Distributed Queries" section). When adding a SQL Server linked server to a SQL Server instance, whether it's a default or named instance, Microsoft makes it easy for you by requiring just the server and product_name values.

Regarding security methods for connecting to the SQL Server instance, when creating a new linked server, the current user's login security credentials (SQL or Windows) will be used to connect to the linked server. You can also create explicit remote login mapping for the linked server, which you'll see discussed in the "Adding a Linked Server Login Mapping" recipe.

Configuring Linked Server Properties

There are a number of different settings you can use to configure a linked server after it has been created. These settings are described in Table 27-2.

Table 27-2. *Linked Server Properties*

Setting	Description
collation compatible	Enable this setting if you are certain that the SQL Server instance has the same collation as the remote SQL Server instance. Doing so can improve performance, as SQL Server will no longer have to perform comparisons of character columns between the data sources, because the same collation is assumed.
collation name	If use remote collation is enabled and the linked server is for a non–SQL Server data source, collation name specifies the name of the remote server collation. The collation name must be one supported by SQL Server.

Continued

Table 27-2. *Continued*

Setting	Description
connect timeout	This designates the number of seconds a connection attempt will be made to the linked server before a timeout occurs. If the value is 0, the sp_configure server value of remote query timeout is used as a default.
data access	If this option is enabled, distributed query access is allowed.
lazy schema validation	If this option is set to true, schema is not checked on remote tables at the beginning of the query. Although this reduces overhead for the remote query, if the schema has changed and you are not schema-checking, the query may raise an error if the referenced objects used by the query no longer correspond with the query command.
query timeout	This determines the number of seconds it takes for a waiting query to time out. If this value is 0, then the sp_configure value configured for the query wait option will be used instead.
rpc	This enables remote procedure calls from the server.
rpc out	This enables remote procedure calls to the server.
remote proc transaction promotion	When this option is enabled (which it is by default), remote procedure calls start a distributed transaction that is managed via MS DTC.
use remote collation	This determines whether remote server collation is used (true) instead of the local server collation (false).

To change linked server properties, use the sp_serveroption system stored procedure. The syntax is as follows:

```
sp_serveroption [@server =] 'server'
    ,[@optname =] 'option_name'
    ,[@optvalue =] 'option_value'
```

The arguments of this system stored procedure are described in Table 27-3.

Table 27-3. sp_serveroption Arguments

Argument	Description
server	The name of the linked server to configure properties for
option_name	The option to configure
option_value	The new value of the option

In this recipe, the query timeout setting for the JOEPROD\NODE2 linked server will be changed to 60 seconds:

```
EXEC sp_serveroption
    @server = 'JOEPROD\NODE2' ,
    @optname = 'query timeout',
    @optvalue = 60
```

How It Works

In this recipe, the linked server JOEPROD\NODE2 was modified to a query timeout limit of 60 seconds. The first parameter, called server, designated the linked server name. The second parameter, option_name, designated the option to configure, and the third parameter, option_value, configured the new value.

Viewing Linked Server Information

You can use the sys.servers system catalog view to view linked servers defined on a SQL Server instance. For example:

```
SELECT name, query_timeout, lazy_schema_validation
FROM sys.servers
WHERE is_linked = 1
```

This returns

name	query_timeout	lazy_schema_validation
JOEPROD\NODE2	60	1

How It Works

The system catalog view sys.servers can be used to retrieve information about linked servers defined on your SQL Server instance. Other options you can view from sys.servers include product, provider, data_source, location, provider_string, catalog, is_linked, is_remote_login_enabled, is_rpc_out_enabled, is_data_access_enabled, is_collation_compatible, use_remote_collation, and collation_name. The is_linked column was qualified in the query to return only linked servers (excluding the local SQL Server instance settings).

Dropping a Linked Server

The sp_dropserver system stored procedure is used to drop a linked server. The syntax for sp_dropserver is as follows:

```
sp_dropserver [ @server= ] 'server'
    [ , [ @droplogins= ] { 'droplogins' | NULL} ]
```

The parameters of this system stored procedure are described in Table 27-4.

Table 27-4. *sp_dropserver Arguments*

Argument	Description
server	This defines the name of the linked server to remove from the SQL Server instance.
droplogins	If droplogins is specified, login mappings are removed prior to dropping the linked server.

This recipe demonstrates dropping a linked server:

```
EXEC sp_dropserver
    @server= 'JOEPROD',
@droplogins= 'droplogins'
```

How It Works

This recipe demonstrated removing a linked server from your SQL Server instance using the system stored procedure sp_dropserver. The droplogins option was designated in the second parameter to drop any existing login mappings (I'll review linked server logins in the next block of recipes) prior to removing the linked server. If you try to drop a linked server before removing logins, you'll get the following message:

```
There are still remote logins for the server.
```

Linked Server Logins

In the next three recipes, I'll demonstrate how to work with linked server login mappings. Specifically, I'll cover how to

- Create a linked server login mapping.
- View linked server login mappings configured on the SQL server instance.
- Drop a linked server login mapping.

I'll start off by discussing how to use the system stored procedure sp_addlinkedsrvlogin to create a login mapping.

Adding a Linked Server Login Mapping

When executing a distributed query against a linked server, SQL Server maps your local login and credentials to the linked server. Based on the security on the remote data source, your credentials are either accepted or rejected. When sp_addlinkedserver is executed and a linked server is created, the default behavior is to use your local login credentials (either SQL or Windows) to access data on the linked server. Even if you don't have the proper permissions to connect to a linked server, security on the linked server is not checked until you attempt a distributed query. Since security configurations, logins, and database users vary by SQL Server instance, you may need to set up a different mapping from your local login to a different remote login.

The login mapping information is stored on the SQL Server instance where the linked server is defined. To create a login mapping, you use the sp_addlinkedsrvlogin system stored procedure.

The syntax is as follows:

```
sp_addlinkedsrvlogin [ @rmtsrvname = ] 'rmtsrvname'
     [ , [ @useself = ] 'TRUE' | 'FALSE' | 'NULL']
     [ , [ @locallogin = ] 'locallogin' ]
     [ , [ @rmtuser = ] 'rmtuser' ]
     [ , [ @rmtpassword = ] 'rmtpassword' ]
```

The parameters of this system stored procedure are described in Table 27-5.

Table 27-5. *sp_addlinkedsrvlogin Arguments*

Argument	Description
rmtsrvname	This defines the local linked server that you want to add the login mapping to.
Useself	When the value true is used for this option, the local SQL or Windows login is used to connect to the remote server name. If false, the locallogin, rmtuser, and rmtpassword parameters of the sp_addlinkedsrvlogin stored procedure will apply to the new mapping.

Argument	Description
localllogin	This is the name of the SQL Server login or Windows user to map to a remote login. If this parameter is left NULL, the mapping applies to all local logins on the SQL Server instance.
rmtuser	This is the name of the user/login used to connect to the linked server.
rmtpassword	This defines the password of the login/user used to connect to the linked server.

In this recipe, a login mapping is created for all local users—mapping to a login named test on the JOEPROD\NODE2 linked server:

```
EXEC sp_addlinkedsrvlogin
    @rmtsrvname = 'JOEPROD\NODE2',
    @useself = 'false' ,
    @locallogin =  NULL,  -- Applies to all local logins
    @rmtuser =  'test',
    @rmtpassword =  'test1!'
```

How It Works

In this recipe, a login mapping was explicitly created using the sp_addlinkedsrvlogin system stored procedure. The first parameter, @rmtsrvname, contained the name of the linked server you are connecting to. The second parameter, @useself, was a false value, so that the defined login and password in @rmtuser and @rmtpassword on the remote server will be used. The @locallogin was set to NULL, meaning that the test login will be used to map from any login on the local SQL Server connection. Now when a query is executed against the TESTSRV linked server, those queries will run under the test remote user.

Viewing Linked Logins

To see explicit local login mappings to remote logins, you can query the sys.server_principals, sys.linked_logins, and sys.servers system catalog views, as this query demonstrates:

```
SELECT s.name LinkedServerName, ll.remote_name, p.name LocalLoginName
FROM sys.linked_logins ll
INNER JOIN sys.servers s ON
   s.server_id = ll.server_id
LEFT OUTER JOIN sys.server_principals p ON
   p.principal_id = ll.local_principal_id
WHERE s.is_linked = 1
```

This returns

LinkedServerName	remote_name	LocalLoginName
JOEPROD\NODE2	test	NULL

How It Works

This recipe retrieved explicit login mappings to remote logins by querying the sys.linked_logins, sys.servers, and sys.server_principals system catalog views. The query returned the name of the linked server, the remote login on the remote data source, and the local login that was mapped to it.

In this case, the results returned the remote login name of `test` and `NULL` for the local login name (meaning that all local connections will map to the remote `test` login).

Dropping a Linked Server Login Mapping

Use the `sp_droplinkedsrvlogin` system stored procedure to drop a linked server login mapping. The syntax for `sp_droplinkedsrvlogin` is as follows:

```
sp_droplinkedsrvlogin [ @rmtsrvname= ] 'rmtsrvname' ,
    [ @locallogin= ] 'locallogin'
```

The parameters of this system stored procedure are described in Table 27-6.

Table 27-6. *sp_droplinkedsrvlogin Arguments*

Argument	Description
rmtsrvname	The linked server name of the login mapping
locallogin	The name of the SQL Server login or Windows user mapping to drop from the linked server

This recipe demonstrates dropping the login mapping created in an earlier recipe:

```
EXEC sp_droplinkedsrvlogin
    @rmtsrvname= 'JOEPROD\NODE2' ,
    @locallogin=  NULL
```

How It Works

In this recipe, the default login mapping for all local users was removed by sending the linked server name in the first parameter and a `NULL` value in the second `@locallogin` parameter.

Executing Distributed Queries

So far in this chapter, I've demonstrated how to create and configure linked servers. In this next set of recipes, you'll learn how to execute distributed queries against the linked server remote data source. You aren't limited to using a linked server to connect to a remote data source, however, and the next few recipes will also demonstrate how to access external data using commands such as `OPENQUERY` and `OPENROWSET`. You'll also learn how to create and use an alias to a linked server name.

Executing Distributed Queries Against a Linked Server

Distributed queries are queries that reference one or more linked servers, performing either read or modification operations against remote tables, views, or stored procedures. The types of queries (`SELECT`, `INSERT`, `UPDATE`, `DELETE`, `EXEC`) that are supported against linked servers depend on the level of support for transactions present in the OLE DB providers. You can run a distributed query referencing a linked server by using either a four-part name of the remote object in the `FROM` clause or the `OPENQUERY` Transact-SQL command (`OPENQUERY` is reviewed later in the chapter in the "Executing Distributed Queries Using OPENQUERY" recipe).

The basic syntax for referencing a linked server using a four-part name is as follows:

```
linked_server_name.catalog.schema.object_name
```

The parts of the four-part name are described in Table 27-7.

Table 27-7. *Linked Server Four-Part Name*

Part	Description
linked_server_name	The linked server name
catalog	The catalog (database) name
schema	The schema container of the data source object
object_name	The database object (for example the view, table, data source, or stored procedure)

This distributed query selects the performance counter value from the sys.dm_os_performance_counters Dynamic Management View on the linked server:

```
SELECT object_name, counter_name, instance_name,
cntr_value, cntr_type
FROM JOEPROD.master.sys.dm_os_performance_counters
WHERE counter_name = 'Active Transactions' AND
  instance_name = '_Total'
```

This returns

object_name	counter_name	instance_name	cntr_value	cntr_type
SQLServer:Databases	Active Transactions	Total	0	65792

This next query demonstrates executing a system stored procedure on the linked server (for a SQL Server named instance). The linked server is a named instance, so the full name is put in square brackets:

```
EXEC [JOEPROD\NODE2].master.dbo.sp_monitor
```

This returns various statistics and result sets about the remote SQL Server instance:

last_run	current_run	seconds	
2005-09-02 22:47:26.770	2005-10-09 10:52:27.007	3153901	
cpu_busy	io_busy	idle	
53(53)-0%	22(21)-0%	10433(10192)-0%	
packets_received	packets_sent	packet_errors	
182(154)	377(349)	0(0)	
total_read	total_write	total_errors	connections
693(693)	201(201)	0(0)	8091(8079)

How It Works

As you can see, executing a distributed query simply involves referencing the database object using the four-part name. If you need to reference a linked server that is a SQL Server named instance, use square brackets around the linked server name.

Creating and Using an Alias to Reference Four-Part Linked Server Names

You can create an alias for a database object (including stored procedures, functions, tables, and views) that can then be referenced in your code, allowing you to shorten a long name or obscure changes to the underlying object source (switching from a development to production linked server name, for example).

This functionality is performed using CREATE SYNONYM, which uses the following abridged syntax:

```
CREATE SYNONYM [ schema_name. ] synonym_name
FOR < object >
```

The arguments for this command are detailed in Table 27-8.

Table 27-8. *CREATE SYNONYM Arguments*

Argument	Description
[schema_name.] synonym_name	The optional schema name and required synonym name.
object	The object that will be aliased. This can be of the format server_name.database_name.schema_name.object_name, database_name.schema_name.object_name, or schema_name. object_name.

Also, to drop a synonym, use the DROP SYNONYM command. The syntax is as follows:

```
DROP SYNONYM [ schema. ] synonym_name
```

The command takes the optional schema of the synonym and the required synonym name. In this recipe, a synonym is created on a linked server:

```
CREATE SYNONYM dbo.PerfInfo
FOR JOEPROD.master.sys.dm_os_performance_counters
```

Next, the linked server synonym is referenced in the FROM clause of the query using the new synonym name:

```
SELECT  cntr_value
FROM dbo.PerfInfo
WHERE counter_name = 'Active Transactions' AND
instance_name = '_Total'
```

After that, the synonym is dropped from the database:

```
DROP SYNONYM dbo.PerfInfo
```

Lastly, I create a new synonym with the same name as before, but this time pointing to a different SQL Server instance:

```
CREATE SYNONYM dbo.PerfInfo
FOR [JOEPROD\NODE2].master.sys.dm_os_performance_counters
```

How It Works

In this recipe, a synonym called PerfInfo was created to represent a four-part linked server table name. Synonyms can reduce keystrokes by allowing you to use a shorter name to represent a linked server four-part name. The PerfInfo synonym was then used in the FROM clause in order to query the underlying linked server table. After that, the synonym was dropped (although in real life you would have kept the synonym around for future use). Lastly, a new synonym was created with the previous name, referencing a new data source. This means the original query against dbo.PerfInfo will now access a different SQL Server instance. Synonyms can give you the ability to change underlying data sources without changing the referencing synonym name.

Executing Distributed Queries Using OPENQUERY

SQL Server provides a different method for executing distributed queries other than using the four-part naming method.

OPENQUERY is a function that issues a pass-through query against an existing linked server and is referenced in the FROM clause of a query just like a table. The syntax is as follows:

```
OPENQUERY ( linked_server ,'query' )
```

The parameters for this command are described in Table 27-9.

Table 27-9. *OPENQUERY Arguments*

Argument	Description
linked_server_name	The linked server name that you want to query
Catalog	The actual query to issue against the linked server connection

The OPENQUERY command queries a linked server by sending it as a pass-through query instead of referencing the four-part name. A pass-through query executes entirely on the remote server and then returns the results back to the calling query.

Why use one over the other? Some OLE DB providers that you can use to create a linked server may have varying abilities to be referenced using the four-part name in the FROM clause. OPENQUERY is an alternative method for retrieving distributed data, and may work correctly where a four-part name query does not. Using the OPENQUERY command may also remove the potential for cross-platform joining performance issues, allowing the query to execute fully on the remote server.

This recipe demonstrates querying a linked server with the same query as the previous recipe, only this time the actual query in the second parameter of the OPENQUERY command uses the three-part, not four-part, name in the FROM clause:

```
SELECT cntr_value
FROM OPENQUERY ( [JOEPROD] ,
'SELECT object_name, counter_name, instance_name, cntr_value, cntr_type
FROM master.sys.dm_os_performance_counters
WHERE counter_name = ''Active Transactions'' AND
instance_name = ''_Total''' )
```

How It Works

In this recipe, the first parameter of the OPENQUERY command was the name of the linked server. The second parameter was the query itself. Notice that the WHERE clause contains double-ticked values, which serve as delimited single ticks.

Executing Ad Hoc Queries Using OPENROWSET

Like OPENQUERY, the OPENROWSET command is referenced in the FROM clause and acts like a table in a SELECT statement. Unlike OPENQUERY, however, OPENROWSET creates an ad hoc connection to the data source. It does *not* use an existing linked server connection to query the remote data source. This is a useful function if you don't wish to retain a linked server for a remote data source on the SQL Server instance.

The syntax for OPENROWSET is as follows:

```
OPENROWSET
( { 'provider_name' ,
{ 'datasource' ; 'user_id' ; 'password' | 'provider_string' }
, { [ catalog. ] [ schema. ] object | 'query' }
```

The parameters for this command are described in Table 27-10.

Table 27-10. *OPENROWSET Arguments*

Argument	Description
provider_name	The unique programmatic identifier for the OLE DB provider.
datasource ; user_id ; password | provider_string	The connection string expected by the OLE DB provider. You designate either the datasource, user_id, and password *or* the provider string.
catalog.schema.object| query	The object name to return results for or the query to execute.

In this recipe, a query is issued against a SQL Server named instance:

```
SELECT *
FROM OPENROWSET
('SQLNCLI','TESTSRV\NODE2';'test';'test1!',
'SELECT * FROM AdventureWorks.HumanResources.Department
WHERE GroupName = ''Research and Development''')
```

This returns

DepartmentID	Name	GroupName	ModifiedDate
1	Engineering	Research and Development	1998-06-01 00:00:00.000
2	Tool Design	Research and Development	1998-06-01 00:00:00.000
6	Research and Development	Research and Development	1998-06-01 00:00:00.000
18	Misc	Research and Development	2005-09-20 19:20:25.570

How It Works

In this recipe, I used OPENROWSET to query a remote data source without having to define a linked server. The first parameter of the command designated SQLNCLI, which is the provider name for the Microsoft SQL Native Client OLE DB Provider. The second parameter included three semicolon-delimited values—the SQL Server instance name, login, and password. The last parameter for the command included a query against the AdventureWorks database on the remote SQL Server instance.

Tip Remote access requires the Ad Hoc Distributed Queries sp_configure option to be enabled and the provider Disallow Adhoc Access registry option set to 0.

OPENROWSET can be used in the FROM clause of a SELECT and can also be used as the target table of an INSERT, UPDATE, or DELETE operation—depending on the update support of the OLE DB provider.

Reading Data from a File Using OPENROWSET BULK Options

As demonstrated in Chapter 2's recipe, "Inserting or Updating an Image File Using OPENROWSET and BULK," you can query data from an ASCII, Unicode, or binary file using the new BULK options in the OPENROWSET command. With this functionality, you can query a file and also use the result set in a data modification statement—all without having to first physically import the data from the file into a SQL Server table.

The syntax for the BULK options in OPENROWSET is as follows:

```
OPENROWSET
( { BULK 'data_file' ,
      { FORMATFILE = 'format_file_path' [ <bulk_options> ]
      | SINGLE_BLOB | SINGLE_CLOB | SINGLE_NCLOB }
} )
```

The parameters for this command are described in Table 27-11.

Table 27-11. *OPENROWSET...BULK Arguments*

Argument	Description
data_file	This defines the name and path of the file to read.
format_file_path	This specifies the name and path of the format file—which lays out the column definitions in the data file. You have a choice of two format file layouts—XML or non-XML.
bulk_options	These options define how the data is read, as well as which rows are retrieved. See Table 27-12 for details.
SINGLE_BLOB | SINGLE_CLOB | SINGLE_NCLOB	When designated, the format file parameter is ignored. Instead, the data file is imported as a single-row, single-column value. For example, if you wish to import a document or image file into a large data type column, you would designate one of these flags. Designate the SINGLE_BLOB object for importing into a varbinary(max) data type, SINGLE_CLOB for ASCII data into a varchar(max) data type, and SINGLE_NCLOB for importing into a nvarchar(max) Unicode data type.

The BULK options syntax is as follows:

```
<bulk_options> ::=
    [ , CODEPAGE = { 'ACP' | 'OEM' | 'RAW' | 'code_page' }]
    [ , ERRORFILE = 'file_name' ]
    [ , FIRSTROW = first_row ]
    [ , LASTROW = last_row ]
    [ , MAXERRORS = maximum_errors ]
    [ , ROWS_PER_BATCH = rows_per_batch ]
```

These options are described in Table 27-12.

Table 27-12. *BULK Options*

Option	Description
`'ACP'` | `'OEM'` | `'RAW'` | `'code_page'`	This defines the chosen source data code page of character data to be converted to the destination SQL Server code page. `OEM` is the default. `ACP` is the ISO 1252 code page, `RAW` implies no conversion, and `code_page` is a specific encoded code page number.
`file_name`	This defines the error file name used to hold any reject rows from the `BULK` process.
`first_row`	This specifies the first row in the result set to load (default is 1). If the first row includes column names, you can designate a `first_row` of 2 to skip the first column.
`last_row`	This defines the last row in the result set to load (default is 0, the last row of the result set).
`maximum_errors`	This gives the maximum number of errors in the load process before the load fails (default is 10).
`rows_per_batch`	This value indicates the number of rows to import per batch; however, `OPENROWSET` should always import the data as a single batch. Specifying a number here may help the query processor allocate appropriate resources. However, in most cases, this option can be ignored or set to 0.

In this recipe, I'll demonstrate two examples of reading from an external text file.

The first example demonstrates using a `SELECT` statement to read data from a text file. The text file has the following comma-delimited data in a text file called `ContactType.txt`:

```
21,Sales Phone Rep,2005-06-01 00:00:00
20,Sales Phone Manager,2005-06-01 00:00:00
```

The columns in this file will be defined using a format file called `ContactTypeFormat.Fmt`, which contains the following format file definition (SQL Server allows both XML format and regular text format files):

```
10.0
3
1 SQLCHAR 0 2 "," 1 ContactTypeID ""
2 SQLCHAR 0 20 "," 2 Name SQL_Latin1_General_CP1_CI_AS
3 SQLCHAR 0 19 "\r\n" 3 ModifiedDate ""
```

This query reads from the `ContactType.txt` file in a `SELECT` query:

```
SELECT ContactTypeID, Name, ModifiedDate
FROM OPENROWSET( BULK 'C:\Apress\Recipes\ContactType.txt',
            FORMATFILE = 'C:\Apress\Recipes\ContactTypeFormat.Fmt',
            FIRSTROW = 1,
            MAXERRORS = 5,
            ERRORFILE = 'C:\Apress\Recipes\ImportErrors.txt' )
            AS ContactType
```

This returns

ContactTypeID	Name	ModifiedDate
21	Sales Phone Rep	2005-06-01 00:00:00
20	Sales Phone Manager	2005-06-01 00:00:00

The second example in this recipe will import the `ContactType.txt` file into a single column and single row (instead of breaking it out into a tabular result set as was done in the previous query). First, a table is created to hold the imported document:

```
-- Create a table to hold import documents
CREATE TABLE dbo.ImportRepository
   (ImportHistoryID int IDENTITY(1,1) NOT NULL PRIMARY KEY,
    ImportFile varchar(max) NOT NULL)
GO
```

Next, the value is imported into a new row using `OPENROWSET...BULK`:

```
INSERT dbo.ImportRepository
(ImportFile)
SELECT BulkColumn
FROM OPENROWSET( BULK 'C:\Apress\Recipes\ContactType.txt',
           SINGLE_CLOB) as ContactTypeFile
```

Now to confirm the contents:

```
SELECT ImportFile
FROM dbo.ImportRepository
```

This returns

```
ImportFile
21,Sales Phone Rep,2005-06-01 00:00:00   20,Sales Phone Manager,2005-06-01 00:00:00
```

How It Works

In the first example in this recipe, a data file was queried using the `OPENROWSET BULK` option. The `SELECT` clause included the columns from the data file, as defined by the format file:

```
SELECT ContactTypeID, Name, ModifiedDate
```

The `OPENROWSET` command was then included in the `FROM` clause. The `BULK` option was the first parameter in the command, followed by the data and data format file:

```
FROM OPENROWSET( BULK 'C:\Apress\Recipes\ContactType.txt',
FORMATFILE = 'C:\Apress\Recipes\ContactTypeFormat.Fmt',
```

Three options were also included, designating the first row of the data file to be imported:

```
        FIRSTROW = 1,
```

The number of allowable errors for the import before failure was also designated, along with an error file to contain the rejected rows:

```
        MAXERRORS = 5,
        ERRORFILE = 'C:\Apress\Recipes\ImportErrors.txt' )
```

After the closed parenthesis, a table name alias was required in order to be used in the `SELECT` query:

```
        AS ContactType
```

The second example used `OPENROWSET` to insert the entire contents of a single file into a single column and single row. After creating a table to store the results, an `INSERT SELECT` was used:

```
INSERT dbo.ImportRepository
(ImportFile)
```

The SELECT referenced the BulkColumn system column name, which is returned from OPEN-ROWSET when using any of the SINGLE_ options (BLOB, CLOB, NCLOB):

```
SELECT BulkColumn
```

The OPENROWSET is held in the FROM clause of the SELECT statement, followed by the name of the file and the SINGLE_CLOB option (which imports the data as ASCII text):

```
FROM OPENROWSET( BULK 'C:\Apress\Recipes\ContactType.txt',
           SINGLE_CLOB) as ContactTypeFile
```

This is a much easier method of importing files (ASCII, Unicode, or binary) using Transact-SQL than was available prior to SQL Server 2005. A query is executed against the table, and the results of the raw file format are displayed in a single column/row (with delimiting commas intact).

CHAPTER 28

■ ■ ■

Query Performance Tuning

SQL Server query performance tuning and optimization requires a multi-layered approach. Following are a few key factors that impact SQL Server query performance:

- *Database design*: Probably one of the most important factors influencing both query performance and data integrity, design decisions impact both read and modification performance. Standard designs include OLTP-normalized databases, which focus on data integrity, removal of redundancy, and the establishment of relationships between multiple entities. This is a design most appropriate for quick transaction processing. You'll usually see more tables in a normalized OLTP design, which means more table joins in your queries. Data warehouse designs, on the other hand, often use a more denormalized Star or Snowflake design. These designs use a central fact table, which is joined to two or more description dimension tables. For Snowflake designs, the dimension tables can also have related tables associated to it. The focus of this design is on query speed, not on fast updates to transactions.

- *Appropriate indexing*: Your table indexes should be based on your high-priority or frequently executed queries. If a query is executing thousands of times a day and is completing in 2 seconds, but could be running in less than 1 second with the proper index, adding this index could reduce the I/O pressure on your SQL Server instance significantly. You should create indexes as needed and remove indexes that aren't being used (this chapter shows you how to do this). As with most changes, there is a trade-off. Each index on your table adds overhead to data modification operations and can even slow down SELECT queries if SQL Server decides to use the less efficient index. When you're initially designing your database, it is better for you to keep the indexes at a minimum (having at least a clustered index and non-clustered indexes for your foreign keys). Add indexes once you have a better idea about the actual queries that will be executed against the database. Indexing requirements are organic, particularly on volatile, frequently updated databases, so your approach to adding and removing indexes should be flexible and iterative.

- *Index fragmentation*: As data modifications are made over time, your indexes will become fragmented. As fragmentation increases, index data will become spread out over more data pages. The more data pages your query needs to retrieve, the higher the I/O requirements and the slower the query.

- *Configurations*: This category includes databases, the SQL instance, and operating system configurations. Poor choices in configurations (like enabling automatic shrinking and automatic closing of a database) can lead to performance issues for a busy application.

- *Up-to-date statistics*: As I discussed in Chapter 22, the AUTO_CREATE_STATISTICS database option enables SQL Server to automatically generate statistical information regarding the distribution of values in a column. If you disable this behavior, statistics can get out of date. Since SQL Server depends on statistics to decide how to best execute the query, SQL Server may choose a less-than-optimal plan if it is basing its execution decisions on stale statistics.

- *Hardware*: I once spent a day trying to get a 3-second query down to 1 second. No matter which indexes I tried to add or query modifications I made, I couldn't get its duration lowered. This was because there were simply too many rows required in the result set. The limiting factor was I/O. A few months later, I migrated the database to the higher-powered production server. After that, the query executed consistently in less than 1 second. This underscores the fact that well-chosen hardware *does* matter. Your choice of processor architecture, available memory, and disk subsystem can have a significant impact on query performance.

- *Network throughput*: The time it takes to obtain query results can be impacted by a slow or unstable network connection. This doesn't mean that you should be quick to blame the network engineers whenever a query executes slowly—but do keep this potential cause on your list of areas to investigate.

In this chapter, I'll demonstrate the T-SQL commands and techniques you can use to help evaluate and troubleshoot your query performance. You'll also learn how to address fragmented indexes and out-of-date statistics, and evaluate the usage of indexes in the database.

■**Note** Since this is a T-SQL–focused book, I don't review the graphical interface tools that also assist with performance tuning such as SQL Server Profiler, graphical execution plans, System Monitor, and the Database Engine Tuning Advisor. These are all extremely useful tools—so I still encourage you to use them as part of your overall performance tuning strategy in addition to the T-SQL commands and techniques you'll learn about in this chapter.

As for new SQL Server 2008 functionality, in this chapter I'll demonstrate how to

- Control workloads and associated CPU and memory resources using Resource Governor.

- Create statistics on a subset of data using the new filtered statistics improvement.

- Display query statistics aggregated across near-identical queries (queries that are identical with the exception of non-parameterized literal values) or queries with identical query execution plans.

- Create plan guides based on *existing* query plans in the query plan cache using the sp_create_plan_guide_from_handle system stored procedure.

This chapter will also review a few miscellaneous query performance topics, including how to use sp_executesql as an alternative to dynamic SQL, how to apply query hints to a query without changing the query itself, and how to force a query to use a specific query execution plan.

Query Performance Tips

Before I start the discussion of the commands and tools you can use to evaluate query performance, I'd first like to briefly review a few basic query performance tuning guidelines. Query performance is a vast topic, and in many of the chapters I've tried to include small tips along with the various content areas. Since this is a chapter that discusses query performance independently of specific objects, the following list details a few query performance best practices to be aware of when constructing SQL Server queries (note that indexing tips are reviewed later in the chapter):

- In your SELECT query, only return the columns that you need. Fewer columns in your query translate to less I/O and network bandwidth.

- Along with fewer columns, you should also be thinking about fewer rows. Use a WHERE clause to help reduce the rows returned by your query. Don't let the application return 20,000 rows when you only need to display the first 10.

- Keep the FROM clause under control. Each table you JOIN to in a single query can add additional overhead. I can't give you an exact number to watch out for, as it depends on your database's design, size, and columns used to join a query. However, over the years, I've seen enormous queries that are functionally correct, but take far too long to execute. Although it is convenient to use a single query to perform a complex operation, don't underestimate the power of smaller queries. If I have a very large query in a stored procedure that is taking too long to execute, I'll usually try breaking that query down into smaller intermediate result sets. This usually results in a significantly faster generation of the final desired result set.

- Use ORDER BY only if you *need* ordered results. Sorting operations of larger result sets can incur additional overhead. If it isn't necessary for your query, remove it.

- Avoid implicit data type conversions in your FROM, WHERE, and HAVING clauses. Implicit data type conversions happen when the underlying data types in your predicates don't match and are automatically converted by SQL Server. One example is a Java application sending Unicode text to a non-Unicode column. For applications processing hundreds of transactions per second, these implicit conversions can really add up.

- Don't use DISTINCT or UNION (instead of UNION ALL) if the unique rows aren't necessary.

- Beware of testing in a vacuum. When developing your database on a test SQL Server instance, it is very important that you populate the tables with a representative data set. This means that you should populate the table with the estimated number of rows you would actually see in production, as well as a representative set of values. Don't use dummy data in your development database and then expect the query to execute with similar performance in production. SQL Server performance is highly dependent on indexes and statistics, and SQL Server will make decisions based on the actual values contained within a table. If your test data isn't representative of "real life" data, you'll be in for a surprise when queries in production don't perform as you saw them perform on the test database.

- When choosing between cursors and set-based approaches, always favor the latter. If you must use cursors, be sure to close and deallocate them as soon as possible.

- Query hints can sometimes be necessary in more complex database-driven applications; however, they often outlast their usefulness once the underlying data volume or distribution changes. Avoid overriding SQL Server's decision process by using hints sparingly.

- Avoid nesting views. I've often seen views created that reference other views, which in turn reference objects that are already referenced in the calling view! This overlap and redundancy can often result in non-optimal query plans due to the resulting query complexity.

- I pushed this point hard in Chapter 10, and I think it is worth repeating here: stored procedures often yield excellent performance gains over regular ad hoc query calls. Stored procedures also promote query execution stability (reusing existing query execution plans). If you have a query that executes with unpredictable durations, consider encapsulating the query in a stored procedure.

When reading about SQL Server performance tuning (like you are now), be careful about the words "never" and "always." Instead, get comfortable with the answer "it depends." When it comes to query tuning, results may vary. Keep your options open and feel free to experiment (in a test environment, of course). Ask questions and don't accept conventional wisdom at face value.

Capturing and Evaluating Query Performance

In this next set of recipes, I'll demonstrate how to capture and evaluate query performance and activity. I'll also demonstrate several other Transact-SQL commands, which can be used to return detailed information about the query execution plan.

Capturing Executing Queries Using sys.dm_exec_requests

In addition to capturing queries in SQL Server Profiler, you can also capture the SQL for currently executing queries by querying the sys.dm_exec_requests Dynamic Management View, as this recipe demonstrates:

```
SELECT r.session_id, r.status, r.start_time, r.command, s.text
FROM sys.dm_exec_requests r
CROSS APPLY sys.dm_exec_sql_text(r.sql_handle) s
WHERE r.status = 'running'
```

This captures any queries that are currently being executed—even the current query used to capture those queries:

session_id	status	start_time	command	text
55	running	2008-10-16 13:53:52.670	SELECT	SELECT r.session_id, r.status, r.start_time, r.command, s.text FROM sys.dm_exec_requests r CROSS APPLY sys.dm_exec_sql_text(r.sql_handl e) s WHERE r.status = 'running'

How It Works

The sys.dm_exec_requests Dynamic Management View returns information about all requests executing on a SQL Server instance.

The first line of the query selected the session ID, status of the query, start time, command type (for example, SELECT, INSERT, UPDATE, DELETE), and actual SQL text:

```
SELECT r.session_id, r.status, r.start_time, r.command, s.text
```

In the FROM clause, the sys.dm_exec_requests Dynamic Management View was cross-applied against the sys.dm_exec_sql_text Dynamic Management Function. This function takes the sql_handle from the sys.dm_exec_requests Dynamic Management View and returns the associated SQL text:

```
FROM sys.dm_exec_requests r
CROSS APPLY sys.dm_exec_sql_text(r.sql_handle) s
```

The WHERE clause then designated that currently running processes be returned:

```
WHERE r.status = 'running'
```

Viewing Estimated Query Execution Plans Using Transact-SQL Commands

Knowing how SQL Server executes a query can help you determine how best to fix a poorly performing query. Details you can identify by viewing a query's execution plan (graphical or command based) include the following:

- Highest cost queries within a batch and highest cost operators within a query
- Index or table scans (accessing all the pages in a heap or index) versus using seeks (only accessing selected rows)
- Missing statistics or other warnings
- Costly sort or calculation activities
- Lookup operations where a nonclustered index is used to access a row, but then needs to access the clustered index to retrieve columns not covered by the nonclustered index
- High row counts being passed from operator to operator
- Discrepancies between the estimated and actual row counts
- Implicit data type conversions (identified in an XML plan where the `Implicit` attribute of the Convert element is equal to 1)

In SQL Server, there are three commands that can be used to view detailed information about a query execution plan for a SQL statement or batch: SET SHOWPLAN_ALL, SET SHOWPLAN_TEXT, and SET SHOWPLAN_XML. The output of these commands helps you understand how SQL Server plans to process and execute your query, identifying information such as table join types used and the indexes accessed. For example, using the output from these commands, you can see whether SQL Server is using a specific index in a query, and if so, whether it is retrieving the data using an index seek (nonclustered index is used to retrieve selected rows for the operation) or index scan (all index rows are retrieved for the operation).

When enabled, the SET SHOWPLAN_ALL, SET SHOWPLAN_TEXT, and SET SHOWPLAN_XML commands provide you with the plan information without executing the query, allowing you to adjust the query or indexes on the referenced tables before actually executing it.

Each of these commands returns information in a different way. SET SHOWPLAN_ALL returns the estimated query plan in a tabular format, with multiple columns and rows. The output includes information such as the estimated IO or CPU of each operation, estimated rows involved in the operation, operation cost (relative to itself and variations of the query), and the physical and logical operators used.

■**Note** Logical operators describe the conceptual operation SQL Server must perform in the query execution. Physical operators are the actual implementation of that logical operation. For example, a logical operation in a query, INNER JOIN, could be translated into the physical operation of a nested loop in the actual query execution.

The SET SHOWPLAN_TEXT command returns the data in a single column, with multiple rows for each operation. You can also return a query execution plan in XML format using the SET SHOWPLAN_XML command.

The syntax for each of these commands is very similar. Each command is enabled when set to ON, and disabled when set to OFF:

```
SET SHOWPLAN_ALL  { ON | OFF }
SET SHOWPLAN_TEXT { ON | OFF}
SET SHOWPLAN_XML  { ON | OFF }
```

This recipe's example demonstrates returning the estimated query execution plan of a query in the AdventureWorks database using SET SHOWPLAN_TEXT and then SET SHOWPLAN_XML:

```
SET SHOWPLAN_TEXT ON
GO

SELECT p.Name, p.ProductNumber, r.ReviewerName
FROM Production.Product p
INNER JOIN Production.ProductReview r ON
    p.ProductID = r.ProductID
WHERE r.Rating > 2
GO

SET SHOWPLAN_TEXT OFF
GO
```

This returns the following estimated query execution plan output:

```
StmtText

SELECT p.Name, p.ProductNumber, r.ReviewerName
FROM Production.Product p
INNER JOIN Production.ProductReview r ON
    p.ProductID = r.ProductID
WHERE r.Rating > 2

(1 row(s) affected)

StmtText
  |--Nested Loops(Inner Join, OUTER REFERENCES:([r].[ProductID]))
       |--Clustered Index Scan (OBJECT:(
          [AdventureWorks].[Production].[ProductReview].
          [PK_ProductReview_ProductReviewID] AS [r]),
          WHERE:([AdventureWorks].[Production].[ProductReview].[Rating]
          as [r].[Rating]>(2)))
       |--Clustered Index Seek
          (OBJECT:([AdventureWorks].[Production].[Product].
          [PK_Product_ProductID] AS [p]),
          SEEK:([p].[ProductID]=[AdventureWorks].[Production].
          [ProductReview].[ProductID] as [r].[ProductID]) ORDERED FORWARD)

(3 row(s) affected)
```

The next example returns estimated query plan results in XML format:

```
SET SHOWPLAN_XML ON
GO

SELECT p.Name, p.ProductNumber, r.ReviewerName
FROM Production.Product p
INNER JOIN Production.ProductReview r ON
    p.ProductID = r.ProductID
WHERE r.Rating > 2
GO

SET SHOWPLAN_XML OFF
GO
```

This returns the following (this is an abridged snippet, because the actual output is more than a page long):

```
<ShowPlanXML xmlns="http://schemas.microsoft.com/sqlserver/2004/07/showplan"
Version="1.1" Build="10.0.1424.2">
  <BatchSequence>
    <Batch>
      <Statements>
...
  <RelOp NodeId="0" PhysicalOp="Nested Loops" LogicalOp="Inner Join" EstimateRows="3"
  EstimateIO="0" EstimateCPU="1.254e-005" AvgRowSize="105"
  EstimatedTotalSubtreeCost="0.00996111" Parallel="0" EstimateRebinds="0"
  EstimateRewinds="0">
              <OutputList>
                <ColumnReference Database="[AdventureWorks]" Schema="[Production]"
                Table="[Product]" Alias="[p]" Column="Name" />
                <ColumnReference Database="[AdventureWorks]" Schema="[Production]"
                Table="[Product]" Alias="[p]" Column="ProductNumber" />
                <ColumnReference Database="[AdventureWorks]" Schema="[Production]"
                Table="[ProductReview]" Alias="[r]" Column="ReviewerName" />
              </OutputList>
...
```

How It Works

You can use SHOWPLAN_ALL, SHOWPLAN_TEXT, or SHOWPLAN_XML to tune your Transact-SQL queries and batches. These commands show you the estimated execution plan without actually executing the query. You can use the information returned in the command output to take action toward improving the query performance (for example, adding indexes to columns being using in search or join conditions). Looking at the output, you can determine whether SQL Server is using the expected indexes, and if so, whether SQL Server is using an index seek, index scan, or table scan operation.

In this recipe, the SET SHOWPLAN for both TEXT and XML was set to ON, and then followed by GO:

```
SET SHOWPLAN_TEXT ON
GO
```

A query referencing the Production.Product and Production.ProductReview was then evaluated. The two tables were joined using an INNER join on the ProductID column, and only those products with a product rating of 2 or higher would be returned:

```
SELECT p.Name, p.ProductNumber, r.ReviewerName
FROM Production.Product p
INNER JOIN Production.ProductReview r ON
   p.ProductID = r.ProductID
WHERE r.Rating > 2
```

The SHOWPLAN was set OFF at the end of the query, so as not to keep executing SHOWPLAN for subsequent queries for that connection.

Looking at snippets from the output, you can see that a nested loop join (physical operation) was used to perform the INNER JOIN (logical operation):

```
|--Nested Loops(Inner Join, OUTER REFERENCES:([r].[ProductID]))
```

You can also see from this output that a clustered index scan was performed using the PK_ProductReview_ProductReviewID primary key clustered index to retrieve data from the ProductReview table:

```
|--Clustered Index Scan (OBJECT:([AdventureWorks].[Production].[ProductReview].
[PK_ProductReview_ProductReviewID] AS [r]),
```

A clustered index *seek*, however, was used to retrieve data from the Product table:

```
|--Clustered Index Seek(OBJECT:([AdventureWorks].[Production].[Product].
[PK_Product_ProductID] AS [p]),
```

The SET SHOWPLAN_XML command returned the estimated query plan in an XML document format, displaying similar data as SHOWPLAN_TEXT. The XML data is formatted using attributes and elements.

For example, the attributes of the RelOp element show a physical operation of Nested Loops and a logical operation of Inner Join—along with other statistics such as estimated rows impacted by the operation:

```
<RelOp NodeId="0" PhysicalOp="Nested Loops" LogicalOp="Inner Join" EstimateRows="3"
EstimateIO="0" EstimateCPU="1.254e-005" AvgRowSize="105"
EstimatedTotalSubtreeCost="0.00996111" Parallel="0" EstimateRebinds="0"
EstimateRewinds="0">
```

The XML document follows a specific schema definition format that defines the returned XML elements, attributes, and data types. This schema can be viewed at the following URL: http://schemas.microsoft.com/sqlserver/2004/07/showplan/showplanxml.xsd.

Viewing Execution Runtime Information

SQL Server provides four commands that are used to return query and batch execution statistics and information: SET STATISTICS IO, SET STATISTICS TIME, SET STATISTICS PROFILE, and SET STATISTICS XML.

Unlike the SHOWPLAN commands, STATISTICS commands return information for queries that have actually executed in SQL Server. The SET STATISTICS IO command is used to return disk activity (hence I/O) generated by the executed statement. The SET STATISTICS TIME command returns the number of milliseconds taken to parse, compile, and execute each statement executed in the batch.

SET STATISTICS PROFILE and SET STATISTICS XML are the equivalents of SET SHOWPLAN_ALL and SET SHOWPLAN_XML, only the actual (*not* estimated) execution plan information is returned along with the actual results of the query.

The syntax of each of these commands is similar, with ON enabling the statistics and OFF disabling them:

```
SET STATISTICS IO { ON | OFF }

SET STATISTICS TIME { ON | OFF }

SET STATISTICS PROFILE { ON | OFF }

SET STATISTICS XML { ON | OFF }
```

In the first example, STATISTICS IO is enabled prior to executing a query that totals the amount due by territory from the Sales.SalesOrderHeader and Sales.SalesTerritory tables:

```
SET STATISTICS IO ON
GO

SELECT  t.name TerritoryNM,
       SUM(TotalDue) TotalDue
FROM Sales.SalesOrderHeader h
INNER JOIN Sales.SalesTerritory t ON
   h.TerritoryID = t.TerritoryID
WHERE OrderDate BETWEEN '1/1/2003' AND '12/31/2003'
GROUP BY t.name
ORDER BY t.name

SET STATISTICS IO OFF
GO
```

This returns the following (abridged) results:

```
TerritoryNM      TotalDue
Australia        4547123.2777
Canada           8186021.9178
...
Southwest        11523237.5187
United Kingdom   4365879.4375

Table 'Worktable'. Scan count 1, logical reads 39, physical reads 0, read-ahead
reads 0, lob logical reads 0, lob physical reads 0, lob read-ahead reads 0.

Table 'SalesOrderHeader'. Scan count 1, logical reads 686, physical reads 0,
read-ahead reads 0, lob logical reads 0, lob physical reads 0, lob read-ahead
 reads 0.

Table 'SalesTerritory'. Scan count 1, logical reads 2, physical reads 1, read-
ahead reads 0, lob logical reads 0, lob physical reads 0, lob read-ahead reads
0.
```

Substituting SET STATISTICS TIME with SET STATISTICS IO would have returned the following (abridged) results for that same query:

```
TerritoryNM      TotalDue
Australia        4547123.2777
...
Southeast        3261402.9982
Southwest        11523237.5187
United Kingdom   4365879.4375

SQL Server parse and compile time:
   CPU time = 20 ms, elapsed time = 21 ms.

(10 row(s) affected)

 SQL Server Execution Times:
   CPU time = 30 ms,  elapsed time = 24 ms.
```

How It Works

The SET STATISTICS commands return information about the actual execution of a query or batch of queries. In this recipe, SET STATISTICS IO returned information about logical, physical, and large object read events for tables referenced in the query. For a query that is having performance issues (based on your business requirements and definition of "issues"), you can use SET STATISTICS IO to see where the I/O hot spots are occurring. For example, in this recipe's result set, you can see that the SalesOrderHeader had the highest number of logical reads:

```
...
Table 'SalesOrderHeader'. Scan count 1, logical reads 686, physical reads 0,
read-ahead reads 0, lob logical reads 0, lob physical reads 0, lob read-ahead
 reads 0.
...
```

Pay attention to high physical (reads from disk) or logical read values (reads from the data cache)—even if the physical read is zero and the logical read is a high value. Also look for worktables (which were also seen in this recipe):

```
Table 'Worktable'. Scan count 1, logical reads 39, physical reads 0, read-ahead
reads 0, lob logical reads 0, lob physical reads 0, lob read-ahead reads 0.
```

Worktables are usually seen in conjunction with GROUP BY, ORDER BY, hash joins, and UNION operations in the query. Worktables are created in tempdb for the duration of the query, and are removed automatically when SQL Server has finished the operation.

In the second example in this recipe, SET STATISTICS TIME was used to show the parse and compile time of the query (shown before the actual query results), and then the actual execution time (displayed after the query results). This command is useful for measuring the amount of time a query takes to execute from end to end, allowing you to see whether precompiling is taking longer than you realized, or if the slowdown occurs during the actual query execution.

The two other STATISTICS commands, SET STATISTICS PROFILE and SET STATISTICS XML, return information similar to SET SHOWPLAN_ALL and SET SHOWPLAN_XML, only the results are based on the *actual*, rather than the estimated, execution plan.

Viewing Performance Statistics for Cached Query Plans

In this recipe, I demonstrate using SQL Server Dynamic Management Views and Functions to view performance statistics for cached query plans.

> **■Tip** SQL Server 2008 introduces various improvements for managed collection and analysis of performance statistics. For example, the new Data Collector uses stored procedures, SQL Server Integration Services, and SQL Server Agent jobs to collect data and load it into the Management Data Warehouse.

In this example, a simple query that returns all rows from the Sales.SalesPerson table is executed against the AdventureWorks database. Prior to executing it, you'll clear the procedure cache so that you can identify the query more easily in this demonstration (remember that you should only clear out the procedure cache on test SQL Server instances):

```
DBCC FREEPROCCACHE
GO

SELECT BusinessEntityID, TerritoryID, SalesQuota
FROM Sales.SalesPerson
```

Now, I'll query the sys.dm_exec_query_stats Dynamic Management View, which contains statistical information regarding queries cached on the SQL Server instance. This view contains a sql_handle, which I'll use as an input to the sys.dm_exec_sql_text Dynamic Management Function. This function is used to return the text of a Transact-SQL statement:

```
SELECT   t.text,
         st.total_logical_reads,
         st.total_physical_reads,
         st.total_elapsed_time/1000000 Total_Time_Secs,
         st.total_logical_writes
FROM sys.dm_exec_query_stats st
CROSS APPLY sys.dm_exec_sql_text(st.sql_handle) t
```

This returns the following abridged results:

text	total_logical_ reads	total_physical_ reads	Total_Time_ Secs	total_logical_ writes
SELECT BusinessEntityID...	2	0	0	0

How It Works

This recipe demonstrated clearing the procedure cache, and then executing a query that took a few seconds to finish executing. After that, the sys.dm_exec_query_stats Dynamic Management View was queried to return statistics about the cached execution plan.

The SELECT clause retrieved information on the Transact-SQL text of the query, number of logical and physical reads, total time elapsed in seconds, and logical writes (if any):

```
SELECT   t.text,
         st.total_logical_reads,
         st.total_physical_reads,
         st.total_elapsed_time/1000000 Total_Time_Secs,
         st.total_logical_writes
```

The total elapsed time column was in microseconds, so it was divided by 1000000 in order to return the number of full seconds.

In the FROM clause, the sys.dm_exec_query_stats Dynamic Management View was cross-applied against the sys.dm_exec_sql_text Dynamic Management Function in order to retrieve the SQL text of the cached query:

```
FROM sys.dm_exec_query_stats st
CROSS APPLY sys.dm_exec_sql_text(st.sql_handle) t
```

This information is useful for identifying read- and/or write-intensive queries, helping you determine which queries should be optimized. Keep in mind that this recipe's query can only retrieve information on queries still in the cache. This query returned the totals, but the sys.dm_exec_query_stats also includes columns that track the minimum, maximum, and last measurements for reads and writes. Also note that the sys.dm_exec_query_stats has other useful columns that can measure CPU time (total_worker_time, last_worker_time, min_worker_time, and max_worker_time) and .NET CLR object execution time (total_clr_time, last_clr_time, min_clr_time, max_clr_time).

Viewing Aggregated Performance Statistics Based on Query or Plan Patterns

The previous recipe demonstrated viewing query statistics using the sys.dm_exec_query_stats Dynamic Management View. Statistics in this Dynamic Management View are displayed as long as the query plan remains in the cache. For applications that make use of stored procedures or pre- pared plans, sys.dm_exec_query_stats can give an accurate picture of overall aggregated statistics and resource utilization. However, if the application sends unprepared query text and does not properly parameterize literal values, individual statistic rows will be generated for each variation of an almost identical query, making the statistics difficult to correlate and aggregate.

For example, assume that the application sends the following three individual SELECT state- ments:

```
SELECT BusinessEntityID
FROM Purchasing.vVendorWithContacts
WHERE EmailAddress = 'cheryl1@adventure-works.com'

SELECT BusinessEntityID
FROM Purchasing.vVendorWithContacts
WHERE EmailAddress = 'stuart2@adventure-works.com'

SELECT BusinessEntityID
FROM Purchasing.vVendorWithContacts
WHERE EmailAddress = 'eunice0@adventure-works.com'
```

After executing each query, I execute the following query:

```
SELECT   t.text,
     st.total_logical_reads
FROM sys.dm_exec_query_stats st
CROSS APPLY sys.dm_exec_sql_text(st.sql_handle) t
WHERE text LIKE '%Purchasing.vVendorWithContacts%'
```

This returns

text	total_logical_reads
SELECT BusinessEntityID FROM Purchasing.vVendorWithContacts WHERE EmailAddress = 'stuart2@adventure-works.com'	12
SELECT BusinessEntityID FROM Purchasing.vVendorWithContacts WHERE EmailAddress = 'cheryl1@adventure-works.com'	12
SELECT BusinessEntityID FROM Purchasing.vVendorWithContacts WHERE EmailAddress = 'eunice0@adventure-works.com'	12

Notice that a statistics row was created for each query, even though each query against Purchasing.vVendorWithContacts was identical with the exception of the EmailAddress literal value. This is an issue you'll see for applications that do not prepare the query text.

To address this issue, SQL Server 2008 introduces two new columns into the sys.dm_exec_ query_stats Dynamic Management View: query_hash and query_plan_hash. Both of these columns contain a binary hash value. The query_hash binary value is the same for those queries that are identical with the exception of literal values (in this example, differing e-mail addresses). The gener- ated query_plan_hash binary value is the same for those queries that use identical query plans.

These two columns add the ability to aggregate overall statistics across identical queries or query execution plans. For example:

```
SELECT  st.query_hash,
        COUNT(t.text) query_count,
        SUM(st.total_logical_reads) total_logical_reads
FROM sys.dm_exec_query_stats st
CROSS APPLY sys.dm_exec_sql_text(st.sql_handle) t
WHERE text LIKE '%Purchasing.vVendorWithContacts%'
GROUP BY st.query_hash
```

This returns

query_ hash	query_count	total_logical_reads
0x5C4B94191341266A	3	36

How It Works

I started off the recipe by executing three queries that were identical with the exception of the literal values defined for the EmailAddress column in the WHERE clause. After that, I demonstrated querying the sys.dm_exec_query_stats Dynamic Management View to view the logical read statistics for each query. Three separate rows were generated for each query against Purchasing.vVendorWithContacts, instead of showing an aggregated single row. This can be problematic if you are trying to capture the TOP X number of high-resource-usage queries because your result may not reflect the numerous variations of the same query that exists in the query plan cache.

To address this problem, I demonstrated using the new query_hash column introduced to the sys.dm_exec_query_stats Dynamic Management View in SQL Server 2008.

Walking through the query, the SELECT clause of the query referenced this new query_hash column and produced a COUNT of the distinct queries using different literal values and a SUM of the logical reads across these queries:

```
SELECT  st.query_hash,
        COUNT(t.text) query_count,
        SUM(st.total_logical_reads) total_logical_reads
```

The FROM clause referenced the sys.dm_exec_query_stats Dynamic Management View and used CROSS APPLY to access the query text based on the sql_handle:

```
FROM sys.dm_exec_query_stats st
CROSS APPLY sys.dm_exec_sql_text(st.sql_handle) t
```

I narrowed down the result set to those queries referencing the Purchasing.vVendorWithContacts view:

```
WHERE text LIKE '%Purchasing.vVendorWithContacts%'
```

Lastly, since I was aggregating the statistics by the query_hash, I used a GROUP BY clause with the query_hash column:

```
GROUP BY st.query_hash
```

The query_hash value of 0x5C4B94191341266A was identical across all three queries, allowing me to aggregate each of the individual rows into a single row and properly summing up the statistic columns I was interested in. Aggregating by the query_hash or query_plan_hash improves visibility to specific query or plan patterns and their associated resource costs.

Identifying the Top Bottleneck

Have you ever been approached by a customer or coworker who reports that "SQL Server is running slow"? When you ask for more details, that person may not be able to properly articulate the performance issue or may attribute the issue to some random change or event without having any real evidence to back it up.

In this situation, your number one tool for identifying and narrowing down the field of possible explanations is the sys.dm_os_wait_stats Dynamic Management View. This DMV provides a running total of all waits encountered by executing threads in the SQL Server instance. Each time SQL Server is restarted, or if you manually clear the statistics, the data is reset to zero and accumulates over the uptime of the SQL Server instance.

SQL Server categorizes these waits across several different types. Some of these types only indicate quiet periods on the instance where threads lay in waiting, whereas other wait types indicate external or internal contention on specific resources.

■**Tip** The technique described here is part of the Waits and Queues methodology. An in-depth discussion of this methodology can be found under the Technical White Papers section of http://technet.microsoft.com/en-us/sqlserver/bb331794.aspx.

The following recipe shows the top two wait types that have accumulated for the SQL Server instance since it was last cleared or since the instance started:

```
SELECT   TOP 2
    wait_type, wait_time_ms
FROM sys.dm_os_wait_stats
WHERE wait_type NOT IN
    ('LAZYWRITER_SLEEP', 'SQLTRACE_BUFFER_FLUSH',
     'REQUEST_FOR_DEADLOCK_SEARCH', 'LOGMGR_QUEUE',
     'CHECKPOINT_QUEUE', 'CLR_AUTO_EVENT','WAITFOR',
     'BROKER_TASK_STOP', 'SLEEP_TASK', 'BROKER_TO_FLUSH')
ORDER BY wait_time_ms DESC
```

This returns the following (your results will vary based on your SQL Server activity):

wait_type	wait_time_ms
LCK_M_U	31989
LCK_M_S	12133

In this case, the top two waits for the SQL Server instance are related to requests waiting to acquire update and shared locks. You can interpret these wait types by looking them up in SQL Server Books Online or in the Waits and Queues white papers published by Microsoft. In this recipe's case, the top two wait types are often associated with long-running blocks. This is then the indication that if an application is having performance issues, you would be wise to start looking at additional evidence of long-running blocks using more granular tools (Dynamic Management Views, SQL Profiler). The key purpose of looking at sys.dm_os_wait_stats is that you troubleshoot the predominant issue, and not just the root cause of an unrelated issue or something that isn't a lower priority issue.

If you wish to clear the currently accumulated wait type statistics, you can then run the following query:

```
DBCC SQLPERF ('sys.dm_os_wait_stats', CLEAR)
```

Clearing the wait type statistics allows you to provide a delta later on of accumulated wait statistics based on a defined period of time.

How It Works

This recipe demonstrated using the sys.dm_os_wait_stats Dynamic Management View to help determine what the predominant wait stats were for the SQL Server instance.

The SELECT clause chose the wait type and wait time (in milliseconds) columns:

```
SELECT    TOP 2
   wait_type, wait_time_ms
FROM sys.dm_os_wait_stats
```

Since not all wait types are necessarily indicators of real issues, the WHERE clause was used to filter out non-external or non-resource waits (although this isn't a definitive list of those wait types you would need to filter out):

```
WHERE wait_type NOT IN
   ('LAZYWRITER_SLEEP', 'SQLTRACE_BUFFER_FLUSH',
    'REQUEST_FOR_DEADLOCK_SEARCH', 'LOGMGR_QUEUE',
    'CHECKPOINT_QUEUE', 'CLR_AUTO_EVENT','WAITFOR',
    'BROKER_TASK_STOP', 'SLEEP_TASK', 'BROKER_TO_FLUSH')
ORDER BY wait_time_ms DESC
```

The Dynamic Management View's data is grouped at the instance level, not at the database level, so it is a good first step in your performance troubleshooting mission. It is *not* your end-all-be-all solution, but rather a very useful tool for helping point you in the right direction when troubleshooting a poorly defined performance issue. This Dynamic Management View also comes in handy for establishing trends over time. If a new wait type arises, this may be a leading indicator of a new performance issue.

Identifying I/O Contention by Database and File

Assume for a moment that you queried sys.dm_os_wait_stats and found that most of your waits are attributed to I/O. Since the wait stats are scoped at the SQL Server instance level, your next step would be to identify which databases are experiencing the highest amount of I/O contention.

One method you can use to determine which databases have the highest number of read, write, and I/O stall behavior is the sys.dm_io_virtual_file_stats Dynamic Management View (this DMV shows data equivalent to the fn_virtualfilestats function).

This recipe demonstrates viewing database I/O statistics, ordered by I/O stalls. I/O stalls are measured in milliseconds and represent the total time users had to wait for read or write I/O operations to complete on a file since the instance was last restarted or the database created:

```
SELECT DB_NAME(database_id) DatabaseNM,
       file_id FileID,
       io_stall IOStallsMs,
       size_on_disk_bytes FileBytes,
       num_of_bytes_written BytesWritten,
       num_of_bytes_read BytesRead
FROM sys.dm_io_virtual_file_stats(NULL, NULL)
ORDER BY io_stall DESC
```

This returns

DatabaseNM	FileID	IOStallsMs	FileBytes	BytesWritten	BytesRead
tempdb	1	3729468	92602368	216678400	78725120
AdventureWorks	1	520481	405536768	234594304	328687616
AdventureWorks	2	54145	18874368	279374848	409600
master	1	9927	4194304	2998272	22315008
msdb	1	4435	12124160	843776	20725760
tempdb	2	2095	1048576	4382720	663552
master	2	997	786432	1622016	458752
model	1	456	1310720	57344	4431872
msdb	2	182	524288	262144	450560
AdventureWorks	3	150	1048576	139264	196608
AdventureWorks	7	96	1048576	90112	131072
AdventureWorks	4	93	1048576	139264	196608
model	2	66	524288	61440	450560
AdventureWorks	5	24	1048576	139264	196608
AdventureWorks	6	17	1048576	139264	131072

How It Works

This recipe demonstrated using the sys.dm_io_virtual_file_stats Dynamic Management View to return statistics about each database and file on the SQL Server instance. This DMV takes two input parameters: the first is the database ID, and the second is the file ID. Designating NULL for the database ID shows results for all databases. Designating NULL for the file ID results in showing all files for the database.

In this recipe, I designated that all databases and associated files be returned:

```
FROM sys.dm_io_virtual_file_stats(NULL, NULL)
```

I also ordered the I/O stalls in descending order, in order to see the files with the most I/O delay activity first:

```
ORDER BY io_stall DESC
```

These results identified that the highest number of stalls were seen on file ID 2 for the AdventureWorks database, which in this example is the log file. If you have identified that I/O is the predominant performance issue, using sys.dm_io_virtual_file_stats is an efficient method for narrowing down which databases and files should be the focus of your troubleshooting efforts.

Index Tuning

This next batch of recipes demonstrates techniques for managing indexes. Specifically, I'll be covering how to

- Identify index fragmentation, so you can figure out which indexes should be rebuilt or reorganized.

- Display index usage, so you can determine which indexes *aren't* being used by SQL Server.

Before getting into the recipes, I'd like to take a moment to discuss some general indexing best practices. When considering these best practices, always remember that, like query tuning, there are few hard and fast "always" or "never" rules. Index usage by SQL Server depends on a number of factors, including, but not limited to, the query construction, referenced tables in the query, referenced columns, number of rows in the table, and uniqueness of the index column(s) data. Following are some basic guidelines to keep in mind when building your index strategy:

- Add indexes based on your high-priority and high-execution count queries. Determine ahead of time what acceptable query execution durations might be based on your business requirements.

- Don't add too many indexes at the same time. Instead, add an index and test the query to see that the new index is used. If it is not used, remove it. If it is used, test to make sure there are no negative side effects to other queries. Remember that each additional index adds extra overhead to data modifications to the base table.

- Unless you have a very good reason *not* to do so, always add a clustered index to each table. A table without a clustered index is a heap, meaning that the data is stored in no particular order. Clustered indexes are ordered according to the clustered key and its data pages reordered during an index rebuild or reorganization. Heaps, however, are not rebuilt during an index rebuild or reorganization process, and therefore can grow out of control, taking up many more data pages than necessary.

- Monitor query performance over time. As your data and application activity changes, so too will the performance and effectiveness of your indexes.

- Fragmented indexes can slow down query performance, since more I/O operations are required in order to return results for a query. Keep index fragmentation to a minimum by rebuilding and/or reorganizing your indexes on a scheduled or as-needed basis.

- Select clustered index keys that are rarely modified, highly unique, and narrow in data type width. Width is particularly important because each nonclustered index also contains within it the clustered index key. Clustered indexes are useful when applied to columns used in range queries. This includes queries that use the operators BETWEEN, >, >=, <, and <=. Clustered index keys also help reduce execution time for queries that return large result sets or depend heavily on ORDER BY and GROUP BY clauses. With all these factors in mind, remember that you can only have a single clustered index for your table, so choose carefully.

- Nonclustered indexes are ideal for small or one-row result sets. Again, columns should be chosen based on their use in a query, specifically in the JOIN or WHERE clause. Nonclustered indexes should be made on columns containing highly unique data. As discussed in Chapter 5, don't forget to consider using covering queries and the INCLUDE functionality for non-key columns.

- Use a 100% fill factor for those indexes that are located within read-only filegroups or databases. This reduces I/O and can improve query performance because fewer data pages are required to fulfill a query's result set.

- Avoid wide index keys. Always test narrower composite keys in favor of larger indexes.

- Try to anticipate which indexes will be needed based on the queries you perform—but also don't be afraid to make frequent use of the Database Engine Tuning Advisor tool. Using the Database Engine Tuning Advisor, SQL Server can evaluate your query or batch of queries and determine what indexes could be added (or removed) in order to help the query run faster. I'll demonstrate this later on.

The next recipe will now demonstrate how to display index fragmentation.

Displaying Index Fragmentation

Fragmentation is the natural byproduct of data modifications to a table. When data is updated in the database, the logical order of indexes (based on the index key) gets out of sync with the actual physical order of the data pages. As data pages become further and further out of order, more I/O operations are required in order to return results requested by a query. Rebuilding or reorganizing an index allows you to defragment the index by synchronizing the logical index order, reordering the physical data pages to match the logical index order.

■**Note** See Chapter 5 for a review of index management and Chapter 23 for a review of index defragmentation and reorganization.

The sys.dm_db_index_physical_stats Dynamic Management Function returns information that allows you to determine an index's level of fragmentation.

The syntax for sys.dm_db_index_physical_stats is as follows:

```
sys.dm_db_index_physical_stats (
    { database_id | NULL }
    , { object_id | NULL }
    , { index_id | NULL | 0 }
    , { partition_number | NULL }
    , { mode | NULL | DEFAULT }
)
```

The arguments of this command are described in Table 28-1.

Table 28-1. *sys.dm_db_index_physical_stats Arguments*

Argument	Description
database_id | NULL	This defines the database ID of the indexes to evaluate. If NULL, all databases for the SQL Server instance are returned.
object_id | NULL	This specifies the object ID of the table and views (*indexed views*) to evaluate. If NULL, all tables are returned.
index_id | NULL | 0	This gives the specific index ID of the index to evaluate. If NULL, all indexes are returned for the table(s).
partition_number | NULL	This defines the specific partition number of the partition to evaluate. If NULL, all partitions are returned based on the defined database/table/indexes selected.
LIMITED | SAMPLED | DETAILED | NULL | DEFAULT	These modes impact how the fragmentation data is collected. The LIMITED mode scans all pages for a heap and the pages above the leaf level. SAMPLED collects data based on a 1% sampling of pages in the heap or index. The DETAILED mode scans all pages (heap or index). DETAILED is the slowest, but most accurate, option. Designating NULL or DEFAULT is the equivalent of the LIMITED mode.

In this example, the sys.dm_db_index_physical_stats Dynamic Management View is queried for all objects in the AdventureWorks database with an average fragmentation percent greater than 30:

```
USE AdventureWorks
GO

SELECT OBJECT_NAME(object_id) ObjectName,
       index_id,
       index_type_desc,
       avg_fragmentation_in_percent
FROM sys.dm_db_index_physical_stats
(DB_ID('AdventureWorks'),NULL, NULL, NULL, 'LIMITED')
WHERE avg_fragmentation_in_percent > 30
ORDER BY OBJECT_NAME(object_id)
```

This returns the following (abridged) results:

ObjectName	index_id	index_type_desc	avg_fragmentation_in_percent
BillOfMaterials	2	NONCLUSTERED INDEX	33.3333333333333
BusinessEntityContact	1	CLUSTERED INDEX	50
BusinessEntityContact	2	NONCLUSTERED INDEX	50
BusinessEntityContac t	3	NONCLUSTERED INDEX	50
BusinessEntityContact	4	NONCLUSTERED INDEX	50
CountryRegion	1	CLUSTERED INDEX	50
DatabaseLog	0	HEAP	32.6732673267327
...			

This second example returns fragmentation for a specific database, table, and index:

```
SELECT OBJECT_NAME(f.object_id) ObjectName,
       i.name IndexName,
       f.index_type_desc,
       f.avg_fragmentation_in_percent
FROM sys.dm_db_index_physical_stats
       (DB_ID('AdventureWorks'),
        OBJECT_ID('Production.ProductDescription'),
        2,
        NULL,
        'LIMITED')  f
INNER JOIN sys.indexes i ON
   i.object_id = f.object_id AND
   i.index_id = f.index_id
```

This returns

ObjectName	IndexName	index_type_desc	avg_fragmentationin_percent
ProductDescription	AK_ProductDescription_rowguid	NONCLUSTERED INDEX	66.6666666666667

How It Works

The first example started off by changing the database context to the AdventureWorks database:

```
USE AdventureWorks
GO
```

Since the OBJECT_NAME function is database-context sensitive, changing the database context ensures that you are viewing the proper object name.

Next, the SELECT clause displayed the object name, index ID, description, and average fragmentation percent:

```
SELECT OBJECT_NAME(object_id) ObjectName,
       index_id, index_type_desc,
       avg_fragmentation_in_percent
```

The index_type_desc column tells you if the index is a heap, clustered index, nonclustered index, primary XML index, or secondary XML index.

Next, the FROM clause referenced the sys.dm_db_index_physical_stats catalog function. The parameters, which were put in parentheses, included the database name and NULL for all other parameters except the scan mode:

```
FROM sys.dm_db_index_physical_stats
(DB_ID('AdventureWorks'),NULL, NULL, NULL, 'LIMITED')
```

Since sys.dm_db_index_physical_stats is referenced like a table (unlike 2000's DBCC SHOWCONTIG), the WHERE clause was used to qualify that only rows with a fragmentation percentage of 31% or greater be returned in the results:

```
WHERE avg_fragmentation_in_percent > 30
```

The query returned several rows for objects in the AdventureWorks database with a fragmentation greater than 30%. The avg_fragmentation_in_percent column shows logical fragmentation of nonclustered or clustered indexes, returning the percentage of disordered pages at the leaf level of the index. For heaps, avg_fragmentation_in_percent shows extent-level fragmentation. Regarding extents, recall that SQL Server reads and writes data at the page level. Pages are stored in blocks called *extents*, which consist of eight contiguous 8KB pages. Using the avg_fragmentation_in_percent, you can determine whether the specific indexes need to be rebuilt or reorganized using ALTER INDEX.

In the second example, fragmentation was displayed for a specific database, table, and index. The SELECT clause included a reference to the index name (instead of index number):

```
SELECT OBJECT_NAME(f.object_id) ObjectName,
       i.name IndexName,
       f.index_type_desc,
       f.avg_fragmentation_in_percent
```

The FROM clause included the specific table name, which was converted to an ID using the OBJECT_ID function. The third parameter included the index number of the index to be evaluated for fragmentation:

```
FROM sys.dm_db_index_physical_stats
(DB_ID('AdventureWorks'),
OBJECT_ID('Production.ProductDescription'),
2,
NULL,
'LIMITED')  f
```

The sys.indexes system catalog view was joined to the sys.dm_db_index_physical_stats function based on the object_id and index_id.

```
INNER JOIN sys.indexes i ON
   i.object_id = f.object_id AND
   i.index_id = f.index_id
```

The query returned the fragmentation results just for that specific index.

Displaying Index Usage

Creating useful indexes in your database is a balancing act between read and write performance. Indexes can slow down data modifications while at the same time speeding up SELECT queries. You must balance the cost/benefit of index overhead with read activity versus data modification activity. Every additional index added to a table may improve query performance at the expense of data modification speed. On top of this, index effectiveness changes as the data changes, so an index that was useful a few weeks ago may no longer be useful today. If you're going to have indexes on a table, they should be put to good use on high-priority queries.

To identify disused indexes, you can query the sys.dm_db_index_usage_stats Dynamic Management View. This view returns statistics on the number of index seeks, scans, updates, or lookups since the SQL Server instance was last restarted. It also returns the last dates the index was referenced.

In this example, the sys.dm_db_index_usage_stats Dynamic Management View is queried to see whether the indexes on the Sales.Customer table are being used. Prior to referencing sys.dm_db_index_usage_stats, two queries will be executed against the Sales.Customer table: one returning all rows and columns, and the second returning the AccountNumber column for a specific TerritoryID:

```
SELECT *
FROM Sales.Customer

SELECT AccountNumber
FROM Sales.Customer
WHERE TerritoryID = 4
```

After executing the queries, the sys.dm_db_index_usage_stats Dynamic Management View is queried:

```
SELECT i.name IndexName, user_seeks, user_scans,
last_user_seek, last_user_scan
FROM sys.dm_db_index_usage_stats s
INNER JOIN sys.indexes i ON
    s.object_id = i.object_id AND
    s.index_id = i.index_id
WHERE database_id = DB_ID('AdventureWorks') AND
    s.object_id = OBJECT_ID('Sales.Customer')
```

This returns

IndexName	user_seeks	user_scans	last_user_seek	last_user_scan
IX_Customer_TerritoryID	1	0	2008-10-15 17:13:35.487	NULL
PK_Customer_CustomerID	0	1	NULL	2008-10-15 17:13:34.237

How It Works

The sys.dm_db_index_usage_stats Dynamic Management View allows you to see what indexes are being used in your SQL Server instance. The statistics are valid since the last SQL Server restart.

In this recipe, two queries were executed against the Sales.Customer table. After executing the queries, the sys.dm_db_index_usage_stats Dynamic Management View was queried.

The SELECT clause displayed the name of the index, the number of user seeks and user scans, and the dates of the last user seeks and user scans:

```
SELECT i.name IndexName, user_seeks, user_scans,
last_user_seek, last_user_scan
```

The FROM clause joined the sys.dm_db_index_usage_stats Dynamic Management View to the sys.indexes system catalog view (so the index name could be displayed in the results) on the object_id and index_id:

```
FROM sys.dm_db_index_usage_stats s
INNER JOIN sys.indexes i ON
    s.object_id = i.object_id AND
    s.index_id = i.index_id
```

The WHERE clause qualified that only indexes for the AdventureWorks database be displayed, and of those indexes, only those for the Sales.Customer table. The DB_ID function was used to get the database system ID, and the OBJECT_ID function was used to get the table's object ID:

```
WHERE database_id = DB_ID('AdventureWorks') AND
      s.object_id = OBJECT_ID('Sales.Customer')
```

The query returned two rows, showing that the PK_Customer_CustomerID clustered index of the Sales.Customer table had indeed been scanned recently (most likely by the first SELECT * query) and the IX_Customer_TerritoryID nonclustered index had been used in the second query (which qualified TerritoryID = 4).

Indexes assist with query performance, but also add disk space and data modification overhead. Using the sys.dm_db_index_usage_stats Dynamic Management View, you can monitor whether indexes are actually being used, and if not, replace them with more effective indexes.

Statistics

As I discussed in Chapter 22, the AUTO_CREATE_STATISTICS database option enables SQL Server to automatically generate statistical information regarding the distribution of values in a column. The AUTO_UPDATE_STATISTICS database option automatically updates existing statistics on your table or indexed view. Unless you have a *very* good reason for doing so, these options should never be disabled in your database, as they are critical for good query performance.

Statistics are critical for efficient query processing and performance, allowing SQL Server to choose the correct physical operations when generating an execution plan. Table and indexed view statistics, which can be created manually or generated automatically by SQL Server, collect information that is used by SQL Server to generate efficient query execution plans.

The next few recipes will demonstrate how to work directly with statistics. When reading these recipes, remember to let SQL Server manage the automatic creation and update of statistics in your databases whenever possible. Save most of these commands for special troubleshooting circumstances or when you've made significant data changes (for example, executing sp_updatestats right after a large data load).

Manually Creating Statistics

SQL Server will usually generate the statistics it needs based on query activity. However, if you still wish to explicitly create statistics on a column or columns, you can use the CREATE STATISTICS command.

The syntax is as follows:

```
CREATE STATISTICS statistics_name
ON { table | view } ( column [ ,...n ] )
    [ WITH
        [ [ FULLSCAN
          | SAMPLE number { PERCENT | ROWS }
          | STATS_STREAM = stats_stream ] [ , ] ]
```

```
    [ NORECOMPUTE ]
]
```

The arguments of this command are described in Table 28-2.

Table 28-2. *CREATE STATISTICS Arguments*

Argument	Description
statistics_name	This defines the name of the new statistics.
table | view	This specifies the table or indexed view off of which the statistics are based.
column [,...n]	This specifies one or more columns used for generating statistics.
FULLSCAN| SAMPLE number { PERCENT | ROWS }	FULLSCAN, when specified, reads all rows when generating the statistics. SAMPLE reads either a defined number of rows or a defined percentage of rows.
STATS_STREAM = stats_stream	This is reserved for Microsoft's internal use.
NORECOMPUTE	This option designates that once the statistics are created, they should not be updated—even when data changes occur afterward. This option should rarely, if ever, be used. Fresh statistics allow SQL Server to generate good query plans.

In this example, new statistics are created on the Sales.Customer AccountNumber column:

```
CREATE STATISTICS Stats_Customer_AccountNumber
ON Sales.Customer (AccountNumber)
WITH FULLSCAN
```

How It Works

This recipe demonstrated manually creating statistics on the Sales.Customer table. The first line of code designated the statistics name:

```
CREATE STATISTICS Stats_Customer_AccountNumber
```

The second line of code designated the table to create statistics on, followed by the column name used to generate the statistics:

```
ON Sales.Customer (AccountNumber)
```

The last line of code designated that all rows in the table would be read in order to generate the statistics:

```
WITH FULLSCAN
```

Creating Statistics on a Subset of Rows

In Chapter 5, in the "Indexing a Subset of Rows" recipe, I demonstrated the ability to create filtered, nonclustered indexes that cover a small percentage of rows. Doing this reduced the index size and improved the performance of queries that only needed to read a fraction of the index entries that they would otherwise have to process. Creating the filtered index also creates associated statistics.

These statistics use the same filter predicate and can result in more accurate results because the sampling is against a smaller rowset.

You can also explicitly create filtered statistics using the CREATE STATISTICS command. Similar to creating a filtered index, filtered statistics also support filter predicates for several comparison operators to be used, including IS, IS NOT, =, <>, >, <, and more.

The following query demonstrates creating filtered statistics on a range of values for the UnitPrice column in the Sales.SalesOrderDetail table:

```
CREATE STATISTICS Stats_SalesOrderDetail_UnitPrice_Filtered
ON Sales.SalesOrderDetail (UnitPrice)
WHERE UnitPrice >= 1000.00 AND
      UnitPrice <= 1500.00
WITH FULLSCAN
```

How It Works

This recipe demonstrated creating filtered statistics. Similar to filtered indexes, I just added a WHERE clause within the definition of the CREATE STATISTICS call and defined a range of allowed values for the UnitPrice column. Creating statistics on a column creates a histogram with up to 200 interval values designating how many rows are at each interval value, as well as how many rows are smaller than the current key but less than the previous key. The query optimization process depends on highly accurate statistics. Filtered statistics allow you to specify the key range of values your application focuses on, resulting in even more accurate statistics for that subset of data.

Updating Statistics

After you create statistics, if you wish to manually update statistics, you can use the UPDATE STATISTICS command.

The syntax is as follows:

```
UPDATE STATISTICS table | view
    [
        {
            { index | statistics_name }
          | ( { index |statistics_name } [ ,...n ] )
                }
    ]
    [    WITH
        [
            [ FULLSCAN ]
            | SAMPLE number { PERCENT | ROWS }
            | RESAMPLE
        ]
        [ , ] [ ALL | COLUMNS | INDEX ]
        [ [ , ] NORECOMPUTE ]
    ]
```

The arguments of this command are described in Table 28-3.

Table 28-3. *UPDATE STATISTICS Arguments*

Argument	Description
table | view	This defines the table name or indexed view for which to update statistics.
{ index | statistics_name}|	This specifies the name of the index or named statistics to update.
FULLSCAN| SAMPLE number { PERCENT | ROWS } |RESAMPLE	FULLSCAN, when specified, reads all rows when generating the statistics. SAMPLE reads either a defined number of rows or a percentage. RESAMPLE updates statistics based on the original sampling method.
[ALL | COLUMNS | INDEX]	When ALL is designated, all existing statistics are updated. When COLUMN is designated, only column statistics are updated. When INDEX is designated, only index statistics are updated.
NORECOMPUTE	This option designates that once the statistics are created, they should not be updated—even when data changes occur. Again, this option should rarely, if ever, be used. Fresh statistics allow SQL Server to generate good query plans.

This example updates all the statistics for the Sales.Customer table, populating statistics based on the latest data:

```
UPDATE STATISTICS Sales.Customer
WITH FULLSCAN
```

How It Works

This example updated all the statistics for the Sales.Customer table, refreshing them with the latest data. The first line of code designated the table name containing the statistics to be updated:

```
UPDATE STATISTICS Sales.Customer
```

The last line of code designated that all rows in the table would be read in order to update the statistics:

```
WITH FULLSCAN
```

Generating and Updating Statistics Across All Tables

You can also automatically generate statistics across all tables in a database for those columns that don't already have statistics associated to them, by using the system stored procedure sp_createstats.

The syntax is as follows:

```
sp_createstats [ [ @indexonly = ] 'indexonly' ]
      [ , [ @fullscan = ] 'fullscan' ]
    [ , [ @norecompute = ] 'norecompute' ]
```

The arguments of this command are described in Table 28-4.

Table 28-4. *sp_createstats Arguments*

Argument	Description
indexonly	When indexonly is designated, only columns used in indexes will be considered for statistics creation.
fullscan	When fullscan is designated, all rows will be evaluated for the generated statistics. If not designated, the default behavior is to extract statistics via sampling.
norecompute	The norecompute option designates that once the statistics are created, they should not be updated—even when data changes occur. Like with CREATE STATISTICS and UPDATE STATISTICS, this option should rarely, if ever, be used. Fresh statistics allow SQL Server to generate good query plans.

This example demonstrates creating new statistics on columns in the database that don't already have statistics created for them:

```
EXEC sp_createstats
GO
```

This returns the following (abridged) result set:

```
Table 'AdventureWorks.Production.ProductProductPhoto':
Creating statistics for the following columns:
    Primary
    ModifiedDate
Table 'AdventureWorks.Sales.StoreContact':
Creating statistics for the following columns:
    ModifiedDate
Table 'AdventureWorks.Person.Address':
Creating statistics for the following columns:
    AddressLine2
    City
    PostalCode
    ModifiedDate
...
```

If you wish to update all statistics in the current database, you can use the system stored procedure sp_updatestats. This stored procedure only updates statistics when necessary (when data changes have occurred). Statistics on unchanged data will not be updated.

This next example automatically updates all statistics in the current database:

```
EXEC sp_updatestats
GO
```

This returns the following (abridged) results. Notice the informational message of "update is not necessary." The results you see may differ based on the state of your table statistics:

```
Updating [Production].[ProductProductPhoto]
    [PK_ProductProductPhoto_ProductID_ProductPhotoID], update is not necessary...
    [AK_ProductProductPhoto_ProductID_ProductPhotoID], update is not necessary...
    [_WA_Sys_00000002_01142BA1], update is not necessary...
    [Primary], update is not necessary...
    [ModifiedDate], update is not necessary...
    0 index(es)/statistic(s) have been updated, 5 did not require update.
...
```

Viewing Statistics Details

To view detailed information about column statistics, you can use the DBCC SHOW STATISTICS command.

The syntax is as follows:

```
DBCC SHOW_STATISTICS ( 'table_name' | 'view_name' , target )
[ WITH [ NO_INFOMSGS ]
< STAT_HEADER | DENSITY_VECTOR | HISTOGRAM > [ , n ] ]
```

The arguments of this command are described in Table 28-5.

Table 28-5. *DBCC SHOW_STATISTICS Arguments*

Argument	Description
'table_name' | 'view_name'	This defines the table or indexed view to evaluate.
target	This specifies the name of the index or named statistics to evaluate.
NO_INFOMSGS	When designated, NO_INFOMSGS suppresses informational messages.
STAT_HEADER | DENSITY_VECTOR | HISTOGRAM [, n]	Specifying STAT_HEADER, DENSITY_VECTOR, or HISTOGRAM designates which result sets will be returned by the command (you can display one or more). Not designating any of these means that all three result sets will be returned.

This example demonstrates how to view the statistics information on the Sales.Customer Stats_Customer_CustomerType statistics:

```
DBCC SHOW_STATISTICS ( 'Sales.Customer' , Stats_Customer_AccountNumber)
```

This returns the following result sets:

Name	Updated	Rows	Rows Sampled	Steps	Density	Average key length	String Index	Filter Expression	Unfiltered Rows
Stats_Customer_ AccountNumber	Mar 30 2008 12:49PM	19820	19820	152	1	10	YES	NULL	19820

All density	Average Length	Columns
5.045409E-05	10	AccountNumber

RANGE_HI_KEY	RANGE_ROWS	EQ_ROWS	DISTINCT_RANGE_ROWS	AVG_RANGE_ROWS
AW00000001	0	1	0	1
...				
AW00027042	127	1	127	1
AW00027298	255	1	255	1
AW00027426	127	1	127	1
...				
AW00030118	0	1	0	1

How It Works

This recipe demonstrated how to get more specific information about column statistics. In the results of this recipe's example, the `All density` column pointed to the selectivity of a column. *Selectivity* refers to the percentage of rows that will be returned given a specific column's value. Columns with a low density and high selectivity often make for useful indexes (useful to the query optimization process).

In this recipe's example, the `All density` value was 5.045409E–05 (float), which equates to a decimal value of 0.00005045409. This is the result of dividing 1 by the number of rows, in this case 19,820.

If you had a column with a high density of similar values and low selectivity (one value is likely to return many rows), you can make an educated assumption that an index on this particular column is unlikely to be very useful to SQL Server in generating a query execution plan.

Removing Statistics

To remove statistics, use the `DROP STATISTICS` command.

The syntax is as follows:

```
DROP STATISTICS table.statistics_name | view.statistics_name [ ,...n ]
```

This command allows you to drop one or more statistics, prefixed with the table or indexed view name.

In this example, the `Sales.Customer Stats_Customer_AccountNumber` statistics are dropped from the database:

```
DROP STATISTICS Sales.Customer.Stats_Customer_AccountNumber
```

How It Works

This recipe dropped user-created statistics using `DROP STATISTICS`. The statistics were dropped using the three-part name of `schema.table.statistics_name`.

Miscellaneous Techniques

The next several recipes detail techniques that don't cleanly fall under any of the previous sections in this chapter. These recipes will demonstrate how to

- Employ an alternative to dynamic SQL and stored procedures using the `sp_executesql` system stored procedure.

- Force a query to use a specified query plan.

- Apply query hints to an existing query without having to actually modify the application's SQL code using plan guides.

- Create a plan guide based on a pointer to the cached plan.

- Check the validity of a plan guide (in case reference objects have rendered the plan invalid).

- Force parameterization of a non-parameterized query.

- Use the new SQL Server 2008 Resource Governor feature to limit query resource consumption (for both CPU and memory).

I'll start this section off by describing an alternative to using dynamic SQL.

Using an Alternative to Dynamic SQL

Using the EXECUTE command, you can execute the contents of a character string within a batch, procedure, or function. You can also abbreviate EXECUTE to EXEC.

For example, the following statement performs a SELECT from the Sales.Currency table:

```
EXEC ('SELECT CurrencyCode FROM Sales.Currency')
```

Although this technique allows you to dynamically formulate strings that can then be executed, this technique comes with some major hazards. The first and most important hazard is the risk of SQL injection. SQL injection occurs when harmful code is inserted into an existing SQL string prior to being executed on the SQL Server instance. Allowing user input into variables that are concatenated to a SQL string and then executed can cause all sorts of damage to your database (not to mention the potential privacy issues). The malicious code, if executed under a context with sufficient permissions, can drop tables, read sensitive data, or even shut down the SQL Server process.

The second issue with character string execution techniques is in their performance. Although performance of dynamically generated SQL may sometimes be fast, the query performance can also be unreliable. Unlike stored procedures, dynamically generated and regular ad hoc SQL batches and statements will cause SQL Server to generate a new execution plan each time they are run.

If stored procedures are not an option for your application, an alternative, the sp_executesql system stored procedure, addresses the dynamic SQL performance issue by allowing you to create and use a reusable query execution plan where the only items that change are the query parameters. Parameters are also type safe, meaning that you cannot use them to hold unintended data types. This is a worthy solution, when given a choice between ad hoc statements and stored procedures.

■**Caution** sp_executesql addresses some performance issues, but does not entirely address the SQL injection issue. Beware of allowing user-passed parameters that are concatenated into a SQL string! Stick with the parameter functionality described next.

The syntax for sp_executesql is as follows:

```
sp_executesql [ @stmt = ] stmt
[
    {, [@params=] N'@parameter_name data_type [ OUT | OUTPUT ][,...n]' }
    {, [ @param1 = ] 'value1' [ ,...n ] }
]
```

The arguments of this command are described in Table 28-6.

Table 28-6. *sp_executesql Arguments*

Argument	Description
stmt	The string to be executed.
@parameter_name data_type [[OUTPUT][,...n]	One or more parameters that are embedded in the string statement. OUTPUT is used similarly to a stored procedure OUTPUT parameter.
'value1' [,...n]	The actual values passed to the parameters.

In this example, the Production.TransactionHistoryArchive table is queried based on a specific ProductID, TransactionType, and minimum Quantity values:

```
EXECUTE sp_executesql
N'SELECT TransactionID, ProductID,
        TransactionType, Quantity
FROM    Production.TransactionHistoryArchive
WHERE   ProductID = @ProductID AND
        TransactionType = @TransactionType AND
        Quantity > @Quantity',
        N'@ProductID int,
          @TransactionType char(1),
          @Quantity int',
            @ProductID =813,
            @TransactionType = 'S',
              @Quantity = 5
```

This returns the following results:

TransactionID	ProductID	TransactionType	Quantity
28345	813	S	7
31177	813	S	9
35796	813	S	6
36112	813	S	7
40765	813	S	6
47843	813	S	7
69114	813	S	6
73432	813	S	6

How It Works

The sp_executesql allows you to execute a dynamically generated Unicode string. This system procedure allows parameters, which in turn allow SQL Server to reuse the query execution plan generated by its execution.

Notice in the recipe that the first parameter was preceded with the N' Unicode prefix, as sp_executesql requires a Unicode statement string. The first parameter also included the SELECT query itself, including the parameters embedded in the WHERE clause:

```
EXECUTE sp_executesql
N'SELECT TransactionID, ProductID,
TransactionType, Quantity
FROM Production.TransactionHistoryArchive
WHERE ProductID = @ProductID AND
            TransactionType = @TransactionType AND
            Quantity > @Quantity',
```

The second argument further defined the data type of each parameter that was embedded in the first parameter's SQL statement. Each parameter is separated by a comma:

```
N'@ProductID int,
@TransactionType char(1),
@Quantity int',
```

The last argument assigned each embedded parameter a value, which was put into the query dynamically during execution.

```
@ProductID =813,
@TransactionType = 'S',
@Quantity = 5
```

The query returned eight rows based on the three parameters provided. If the query is executed again, only with different parameter values, it is likely that the original query execution plan will be used by SQL Server (instead of creating a new execution plan).

Forcing SQL Server to Use a Query Plan

The USE PLAN command allows you to force the query optimizer to use an existing, specific query plan for a SELECT query. You can use this functionality to override SQL Server's choice, in those rare circumstances when SQL Server chooses a less efficient query plan over one that is more efficient. Like plan guides (covered later), this option should only be used by an experienced SQL Server professional, as SQL Server's query optimizer usually makes good decisions when deciding whether or not to reuse or create new query execution plans.

The syntax for USE PLAN is as follows:

```
USE PLAN N'xml_plan'
```

The xml_plan parameter is the XML data type representation of the stored query execution plan. The specific XML query plan can be derived using several methods, including SET SHOWPLAN_XML, SET STATISTICS XML, the sys.dm_exec_query_plan Dynamic Management View, sys.dm_exec_text_query_plan, and via SQL Server Profiler's Showplan XML events.

In this example, SET STATISTICS XML is used to extract the XML-formatted query plan for use in the USE PLAN command:

```
SET STATISTICS XML ON

SELECT TOP 10 Rate
FROM HumanResources.EmployeePayHistory
ORDER BY Rate DESC

SET STATISTICS XML OFF
```

The XMLDocument results returned from SET STATISTICS XML are then copied to the next query. Note that all the single quotes (') in the XML document have to be escaped with an additional single quote (except for the quotes used for USE PLAN):

```
SELECT TOP 10 Rate
FROM HumanResources.EmployeePayHistory
ORDER BY Rate DESC
OPTION (USE PLAN
'<ShowPlanXML xmlns="http://schemas.microsoft.com/sqlserver/2004/07/showplan"
Version="1.1" Build="10.0.1424.2">
  <BatchSequence>
    <Batch>
      <Statements>
        <StmtSimple StatementText="SELECT TOP 10 Rate&#xD;&#xA;FROM
HumanResources.EmployeePayHistory&#xD;&#xA;ORDER BY Rate DESC&#xD;&#xA;&#xD;"
StatementId="1" StatementCompId="2" StatementType="SELECT"
StatementSubTreeCost="0.019825" StatementEstRows="10" StatementOptmLevel="TRIVIAL">
          <StatementSetOptions QUOTED_IDENTIFIER="false" ARITHABORT="true"
CONCAT_NULL_YIELDS_NULL="false" ANSI_NULLS="false" ANSI_PADDING="false"
ANSI_WARNINGS="false" NUMERIC_ROUNDABORT="false" />
          <QueryPlan DegreeOfParallelism="0" MemoryGrant="1024" CachedPlanSize="8"
CompileTime="20" CompileCPU="3" CompileMemory="72">
```

```xml
            <RelOp NodeId="0" PhysicalOp="Sort" LogicalOp="TopN Sort"
EstimateRows="10" EstimateIO="0.0112613" EstimateCPU="0.00419345" AvgRowSize="15"
EstimatedTotalSubtreeCost="0.019825" Parallel="0" EstimateRebinds="0"
EstimateRewinds="0">
                <OutputList>
                  <ColumnReference Database="[AdventureWorks]"
Schema="[HumanResources]" Table="[EmployeePayHistory]" Column="Rate" />
                </OutputList>
                <MemoryFractions Input="1" Output="1" />
                <RunTimeInformation>
                  <RunTimeCountersPerThread Thread="0" ActualRows="10"
ActualRebinds="1" ActualRewinds="0" ActualEndOfScans="1" ActualExecutions="1" />
                </RunTimeInformation>
                <TopSort Distinct="0" Rows="10">
                  <OrderBy>
                    <OrderByColumn Ascending="0">
                      <ColumnReference Database="[AdventureWorks]"
Schema="[HumanResources]" Table="[EmployeePayHistory]" Column="Rate" />
                    </OrderByColumn>
                  </OrderBy>
                  <RelOp NodeId="1" PhysicalOp="Clustered Index Scan"
LogicalOp="Clustered Index Scan" EstimateRows="316" EstimateIO="0.00386574"
EstimateCPU="0.0005046" AvgRowSize="15" EstimatedTotalSubtreeCost="0.00437034"
TableCardinality="316" Parallel="0" EstimateRebinds="0" EstimateRewinds="0">
                    <OutputList>
                      <ColumnReference Database="[AdventureWorks]"
Schema="[HumanResources]" Table="[EmployeePayHistory]" Column="Rate" />
                    </OutputList>
                    <RunTimeInformation>
                      <RunTimeCountersPerThread Thread="0" ActualRows="316"
ActualEndOfScans="1" ActualExecutions="1" />
                    </RunTimeInformation>
                    <IndexScan Ordered="0" ForcedIndex="0" NoExpandHint="0">
                      <DefinedValues>
                        <DefinedValue>
                          <ColumnReference Database="[AdventureWorks]"
Schema="[HumanResources]" Table="[EmployeePayHistory]" Column="Rate" />
                        </DefinedValue>
                      </DefinedValues>
                      <Object Database="[AdventureWorks]" Schema="[HumanResources]"
Table="[EmployeePayHistory]"
Index="[PK_EmployeePayHistory_BusinessEntityID_RateChangeDate]"
IndexKind="Clustered" />
                    </IndexScan>
                  </RelOp>
                </TopSort>
              </RelOp>
            </QueryPlan>
          </StmtSimple>
        </Statements>
      </Batch>
    </BatchSequence>
  </ShowPlanXML>')
```

How It Works

USE PLAN allows you to capture the XML format of a query's execution plan and then force the query to use it on subsequent executions. In this recipe, I used SET STATISTICS XML ON to capture the query's XML execution plan definition. That definition was then copied into the OPTION clause. The USE PLAN hint requires a Unicode format, so the XML document text was prefixed with an N'.

Both USE PLAN and plan guides should be used only as a *last resort*—after you have thoroughly explored other possibilities such as query design, indexing, database design, index fragmentation, and out-of-date statistics. USE PLAN may have short-term effectiveness, but as data changes, so too will the needs of the query execution plan. In the end, the odds are that, over time, SQL Server will be better able to dynamically decide on the correct SQL plan than you. Nevertheless, Microsoft provided this option for those advanced troubleshooting cases when SQL Server doesn't choose a query execution plan that's good enough.

Applying Hints Without Modifying Application SQL

As was discussed at the beginning of the chapter, troubleshooting poor query performance involves reviewing many areas such as database design, indexing, and query construction. You can make modifications to your code, but what if the problem is with code that you *cannot* change?

If you are encountering issues with a database and/or queries that are not your own to change (in shrink-wrapped software, for example), then your options become more limited. Usually in the case of third-party software, you are restricted to adding new indexes or archiving off data from large tables. Making changes to the vendor's actual database objects or queries is usually off limits.

SQL Server provides a solution to this common issue using plan guides. Plan guides allow you to apply hints to a query without having to change the actual query text sent from the application.

■**Tip** In SQL Server 2008, you can designate both query and table hints within plan guides.

Plan guides can be applied to specific queries embedded within database objects (stored procedures, functions, triggers) or specific stand-alone SQL statements.

A plan guide is created using the sp_create_plan_guide system stored procedure:

```
sp_create_plan_guide [ @name = ] N'plan_guide_name'
 , [ @stmt = ] N'statement_text'
 , [ @type = ] N' { OBJECT | SQL | TEMPLATE }'
 , [ @module_or_batch = ]
     {
       N'[ schema_name.]object_name'
       | N'batch_text'
       | NULL
     }
 , [ @params = ] { N'@parameter_name data_type [,...n ]' | NULL }
 , [ @hints = ] { N'OPTION ( query_hint [,...n ] ) ' | N'XML_showplan' | NULL }
```

The arguments of this command are described in Table 28-7.

Table 28-7. *sp_create_plan_guide Arguments*

Argument	Description
plan_guide_name	This defines the name of the new plan guide.
statement_text	This specifies the SQL text identified for optimization.

Continued

Table 28-7. *Continued*

Argument	Description
OBJECT | SQL | TEMPLATE	When OBJECT is selected, the plan guide will apply to the statement text found within a specific stored procedure, function, or DML trigger. When SQL is selected, the plan guide will apply to statement text found in a stand-alone statement or batch. The TEMPLATE option is used to either enable or disable parameterization for a SQL statement. Recall from Chapter 22, in the topic "Modifying Database Parameterization Behavior," that the PARAMETERIZATION option, when set to FORCED, increases the chance that a query will become parameterized, allowing it to form a reusable query execution plan. SIMPLE parameterization, however, affects a smaller number of queries (at SQL Server's discretion). The TEMPLATE option is used to override either a database's SIMPLE or FORCED parameterization option. If a database is using SIMPLE parameterization, you can force a specific query statement to be parameterized. If a database is using FORCED parameterization, you can force a specific query statement to *not* be parameterized.
N'[schema_name.]object_name' | N'batch_text' | NULL	This specifies either the name of the object the SQL text will be in, the batch text, or NULL, when TEMPLATE is selected.
N'@parameter_name data_type [,...n]' | NULL	This defines the name of the parameters to be used for either SQL or TEMPLATE type plan guides.
N'OPTION (query_hint [,...n])' | N'XML_showplan' | NULL	This defines the hint or hints to be applied to the statement, the XML query plan to be applied, or NULL, used to indicate that the OPTION clause will not be employed for a query.

Note In SQL Server 2008, the @hints argument now accepts XML Showplan output as direct input.

To remove or disable a plan guide, use the sp_control_plan_guide system stored procedure:

```
sp_control_plan_guide [ @operation = ] N'<control_option>'
   [ , [ @name = ] N'plan_guide_name' ]

<control_option>::=
{
    DROP
  | DROP ALL
  | DISABLE
  | DISABLE ALL
  | ENABLE
  | ENABLE ALL
}
```

The arguments of this command are described in Table 28-8.

Table 28-8. *sp_control_plan_guide Arguments*

Argument	Description
DROP	The DROP operation removes the plan guide from the database.
DROP ALL	DROP ALL drops all plan guides from the database.
DISABLE	DISABLE disables the plan guide, but doesn't remove it from the database.
DISABLE ALL	DISABLE ALL disables all plan guides in the database.
ENABLE	ENABLE enables a disabled plan guide.
ENABLE ALL	ENABLE ALL does so for all disabled plan guides in the database.
plan_guide_name	plan_guide_name defines the name of the plan guide to perform the operation on.

In this recipe's example, I'll create a plan guide in order to change the table join type method for a stand-alone query. In this scenario, assume the third-party software package is sending a query that is causing a LOOP join. In this scenario, I want the query to use a MERGE join instead.

■**Caution** SQL Server should almost always be left to make its own decisions regarding how a query is processed. Only under special circumstances, and administered by an experienced SQL Server professional, should plan guides be created in your SQL Server environment.

In this example, the following query is executed using sp_executesql:

```
EXEC sp_executeSQL
N'SELECT v.Name ,a.City
FROM Purchasing.Vendor v
INNER JOIN [Person].BusinessEntityAddress bea
    ON bea.BusinessEntityID = v.BusinessEntityID
INNER JOIN Person.Address a
    ON a.AddressID = bea.AddressID'
```

Looking at a snippet of this query's execution plan using SET STATISTICS XML ON shows that the Vendor and BusinessEntityAddress table are joined together using a nested loop operator:

```
<RelOp NodeId="0" PhysicalOp="Nested Loops" LogicalOp="Inner Join"
EstimateRows="105.447" EstimateIO="0" EstimateCPU="0.000440767"
AvgRowSize="93" EstimatedTotalSubtreeCost="0.322517"
Parallel="0" EstimateRebinds="0" EstimateRewinds="0">
```

If, for example, I want SQL Server to use a different join method, but without having to change the actual query sent by the application, I can enforce this change by creating a plan guide. The following plan guide is created to apply a join hint onto the query being sent from the application:

```
EXEC sp_create_plan_guide
    @name = N'Vendor_Query_Loop_to_Merge',
    @stmt = N'SELECT v.Name ,a.City
FROM Purchasing.Vendor v
INNER JOIN [Person].BusinessEntityAddress bea
    ON bea.BusinessEntityID = v.BusinessEntityID
INNER JOIN Person.Address a
    ON a.AddressID = bea.AddressID',
```

```
@type = N'SQL',
@module_or_batch = NULL,
@params = NULL,
@hints = N'OPTION (MERGE JOIN)'
```

■Tip In SQL Server 2008, you can now also designate *table* hints in the plan guide @hints parameter.

I can confirm that the plan guide was created (as well as confirm the settings) by querying the sys.plan_guides catalog view:

```
SELECT name, is_disabled, scope_type_desc, hints
FROM sys.plan_guides
```

This returns

name	is_disabled	scope_type_desc	hints
Vendor_Query_Loop_to_Merge	0	SQL	OPTION (MERGE JOIN)

After creating the plan guide, I execute the query again using sp_executesql. Looking at the XML execution plan, I now see that the nested loop joins have changed into merge join operators instead—all without changing the actual query being sent from the application to SQL Server:

```
<RelOp NodeId="0" PhysicalOp="Merge Join" LogicalOp="Inner Join"
EstimateRows="105.447" EstimateIO="0" EstimateCPU="0.0470214"
AvgRowSize="93" EstimatedTotalSubtreeCost="0.491476" Parallel="0"
EstimateRebinds="0" EstimateRewinds="0">
```

In fact, all joins in the query were converted from loops to a merge join, which may not be a desired effect of designating the hint for a multi-join statement! If it is decided that this merge join is no longer more effective than a nested loop join, you can drop the plan guide using the sp_control_plan_guide system stored procedure:

```
EXEC sp_control_plan_guide N'DROP', N'Vendor_Query_Loop_to_Merge'
```

How It Works

Plan guides allow you to add query hints to a query being sent from an application without having to change the application itself. In this example, a particular SQL statement was performing nested loop joins. Without changing the actual query itself, SQL Server "sees" the plan guide and matches the incoming query to the query in the plan guide. When matched, the hints in the plan guide are applied to the incoming query.

The sp_create_plan_guide allows you to create plans for stand-alone SQL statements, SQL statements within objects (procedures, functions, DML triggers), and SQL statements that are either being parameterized or not, due to the database's PARAMETERIZATION setting.

In this recipe, the first parameter sent to sp_create_plan_guide was the name of the new plan guide:

```
EXEC sp_create_plan_guide
   @name = N'Vendor_Query_Loop_to_Merge',
```

The second parameter was the SQL statement to apply the plan guide to (whitespace characters, comments, and semicolons will be ignored):

```
   @stmt = N'SELECT v.Name ,a.City
FROM Purchasing.Vendor v
INNER JOIN [Person].BusinessEntityAddress bea
    ON bea.BusinessEntityID = v.BusinessEntityID
INNER JOIN Person.Address a
    ON a.AddressID = bea.AddressID',
@type = N'SQL',
```

The third parameter was the type of plan guide, which in this case was stand-alone SQL:

```
@type = N'SQL',
```

For the fourth parameter, since it was not for a stored procedure, function, or trigger, the `@module_or_batch` parameter was NULL:

```
@module_or_batch = NULL,
```

The `@params` parameter was also sent NULL since this was not a TEMPLATE plan guide:

```
@params = NULL,
```

The last parameter contained the actual hint to apply to the incoming query—in this case forcing all joins in the query to use a MERGE operation:

```
@hints = N'OPTION (MERGE JOIN)'
```

Finally, the `sp_control_plan_guide` system stored procedure was used to drop the plan guide from the database, designating the operation of DROP in the first parameter and the plan guide name in the second parameter.

Creating Plan Guides from Cache

SQL Server 2008 introduces the ability to create plan guides based on existing query plans in a query plan cache using the `sp_create_plan_guide_from_handle` system stored procedure.

Consider using this functionality under the following circumstances:

- You need a query plan (or plans) to remain stable after an upgrade or database migration.
- You have a specific query that uses a "bad" plan, and you want it to use a known "good" plan.
- Your application has mission-critical queries that have service-level agreements regarding specific response times, and you wish to keep that time stable.
- You need to reproduce the exact query execution plan on another SQL Server instance (test, QA, for example).
- You have a query that needs to execute predictably, but not necessarily perform as optimally as it always could.

■**Caution** You should almost always let SQL Server compile and recompile plans as needed instead of relying on plan guides. SQL Server can adapt to any new changes in the data distribution and objects referenced in the query by recompiling an existing plan when appropriate.

The syntax for the `sp_create_plan_guide_from_handle` system stored procedure is as follows:

```
sp_create_plan_guide_from_handle [ @name = ] N'plan_guide_name'
    , [ @plan_handle = ] plan_handle
    , [ [ @statement_start_offset = ] { statement_start_offset | NULL } ]
```

The arguments of this command are described in Table 28-9.

Table 28-9. *sp_create_plan_guide_from_handle Arguments*

Argument	Description
plan_guide_name	This defines the name of the new plan guide.
plan_handle	This designates the plan handle from the sys.dm_exec_query_stats DMV.
statement_start_offset | NULL	The statement start offset designates the starting position within the query batch. If NULL, the query plan for each statement in the batch will have a plan guide created for it.

This functionality allows you to preserve desired query plans for future reuse on the SQL Server instance. In this recipe, I'll demonstrate creating a plan guide from the cache for the following query (which I will execute first, in order to get a plan created in cache):

```
SELECT
    p.Title,
    p.FirstName,
    p.MiddleName,
    p.LastName
FROM HumanResources.Employee e
INNER JOIN Person.Person p
    ON p.BusinessEntityID = e.BusinessEntityID
WHERE Title = 'Ms.'
```

After executing the query, I can retrieve the plan handle pointing to the query plan in the cache by executing the following query:

```
SELECT plan_handle
FROM sys.dm_exec_query_stats qs
CROSS APPLY sys.dm_exec_sql_text(plan_handle) t
WHERE t.text LIKE 'SELECT%p.Title%' AND
    t.text LIKE '%Ms%'
```

This returns

```
plan_handle
0x060005006E48752FB080940B0000000000000000000000000
```

Next, I will create a plan guide based on the plan handle using the `sp_create_plan_guide_from_handle` system stored procedure:

```
EXEC sp_create_plan_guide_from_handle 'PlanGuide_EmployeeContact',
@plan_handle = 0x060005006E48752FB080940B0000000000000000000000000,
@statement_start_offset = NULL
```

Querying the `sys.plan_handles` system catalog view, I can confirm that the plan guide was created properly (results not displayed, as the query plan and text display issues on the printed page):

```
SELECT name, query_text, hints
FROM sys.plan_guides
```

The hints column from sys.plan_guides actually contains the query execution plan in XML format.

■**Tip** You can confirm whether your plan guide is being successfully used by tracking the SQL Server Profiler events "Plan Guide Successful" and "Plan Guide Unsuccessful".

How It Works

This recipe demonstrated how to preserve an existing cached plan as a plan guide. This is the execution plan that will be used for the query matching the query text of the plan guide. Even after a SQL Server instance restart, or flushing of the procedure cache, the associated plan guide query plan will still be used.

I started off the recipe by executing the SELECT query so that a query plan would be cached on the SQL Server instance. After doing that, I can search for the plan handle of the cached plan by querying sys.dm_exec_query_stats. I also used CROSS APPLY with sys.dm_exec_sql_text, so that I could search for text that contained the start and end of my query.

Once I had the plan handle, I executed the sp_create_plan_guide_from_handle system stored procedure. The first parameter was the name of the plan guide:

```
EXEC sp_create_plan_guide_from_handle 'PlanGuide_EmployeeContact',
```

The second parameter contains the plan handle (note that I could have placed the plan handle in a local variable and then fed it to the stored procedure in a single batch with the sys.dm_exec_query_stats query).

Lastly, I designated the statement start offset as NULL. This is because the cached plan contained only a single statement. If this were a multi-statement batch, I could have used this parameter to designate the statement start offset number:

```
@statement_start_offset = NULL
```

Once the plan guide is created, any matching SQL that is executed will use the query execution plan designated in the plan guide (look at the hints column of the sys.plan_guides system catalog view to confirm). This allows you to keep a plan stable across several scenarios—for example, after a database migration to a new SQL Server instance, service pack upgrade, or version upgrade. Highly volatile query execution plans (recompiled often with varying execution plan performance impacts) can benefit from the "freezing" of the most efficient or performing plan for the associated query.

Checking the Validity of a Plan Guide

SQL Server 2008 introduces the new system function sys.fn_validate_plan_guide, which allows you to check the validity of existing plan guides. SQL Server typically does a great job of compiling and recompiling query execution plans based on changes to objects referenced within a query. Plan guides, on the other hand, are not automatically modified based on changing circumstances.

The sys.fn_validate_plan_guide is a table-valued function that takes a single argument, the plan_guide_id. In this recipe, I demonstrate validating all plan guides within the database context I am interested in (for example, AdventureWorks):

```
SELECT pg.plan_guide_id, pg.name, v.msgnum,
       v.severity, v.state, v.message
FROM sys.plan_guides pg
CROSS APPLY sys.fn_validate_plan_guide(pg.plan_guide_id) v
```

If this query returns no rows, this means that there are no errors with existing plan guides. If rows are generated, you will need to re-create a valid plan guide based on the changed circumstances.

How It Works

This recipe demonstrated how to check the validity of each plan guide in a specific database. The SELECT statement referenced the plan guide ID and name, along with the message number, severity, state, and message if errors exist:

```
SELECT pg.plan_guide_id, pg.name, v.msgnum,
       v.severity, v.state, v.message
```

The FROM clause included sys.plan_guides, which returns all plan guides for the database context:

```
FROM sys.plan_guides pg
```

Since this is a table-valued function expecting an input argument, I used CROSS APPLY against sys.fn_validate_plan_guide, and used the plan guide from sys.plan_guides as input:

```
CROSS APPLY sys.fn_validate_plan_guide(pg.plan_guide_id) v
```

This query returns rows for any plan guides invalidated by changes due to underlying object changes.

Parameterizing a Non-parameterized Query Using Plan Guides

When I am evaluating the overall performance of a SQL Server instance, I like to take a look at the sys.dm_exec_cached_plans Dynamic Management View to see what kind of plans are cached on the SQL Server instance. In particular, I'm interested in the objtype column, seeing whether or not the applications using the SQL Server instance are using mostly prepared statements, stored procedures, or ad hoc queries.

For applications that make heavy use of ad hoc queries, I'll often see a very large query cache filled with nearly identical queries. For example, the following query shows the object type and associated query text:

```
SELECT cp.objtype, st.text
FROM sys.dm_exec_cached_plans cp
CROSS APPLY sys.dm_exec_sql_text(cp.plan_handle) st
WHERE st.text LIKE 'SELECT BusinessEntityID%'
GO
```

In my database, I see three rows returned:

objtype	text
Adhoc	SELECT BusinessEntityID
	FROMHumanResources.Employee
	WHERE NationalIDNumber = 509647174

```
Adhoc        SELECT BusinessEntityID
             FROM HumanResources.Employee
             WHERE NationalIDNumber = 245797967

Adhoc        SELECT BusinessEntityID
             FROM HumanResources.Employee
             WHERE NationalIDNumber = 295847284
```

Notice that each row is almost identical—except that the NationalIDNumber value is different. Ideally, this form of query should be encapsulated in a stored procedure or called using sp_executesql in order to prevent identical plans in the cache and encourage plan reuse.

If you cannot control the form in which queries are called by the execution, one option you have is to use a plan guide to force parameterization of the query, which I will demonstrate in this recipe.

In the "Applying Hints Without Modifying Application SQL" recipe, I introduced the sp_create_plan_guide system stored procedure. The TEMPLATE option in that procedure is used to override either a database's SIMPLE or FORCED parameterization option. If a database is using SIMPLE parameterization, you can force a specific query statement to be parameterized. If a database is using FORCED parameterization, you can force a specific query statement to not be parameterized.

The sp_get_query_template system stored procedure makes deploying template plan guides a little easier by taking a query and outputting the parameterized form of it for use by sp_create_plan_guide. The syntax for this procedure is as follows:

```
sp_get_query_template
    [ @querytext = ] N'query_text'
    , @templatetext OUTPUT
    , @parameters OUTPUT
```

The arguments of this command are described in Table 28-10.

Table 28-10. *sp_get_query_template Arguments*

Argument	Description
querytext	The query you wish to parameterize
templatetext	The output parameter containing the parameterized form of the query
parameters	The output parameter containing the list of parameter names and data types

In this recipe, I'll start by populating the template SQL and parameters using sp_get_query_template, and then sending these values to sp_create_plan_guide (I'll walk through the code step by step in the "How It Works" section):

```
DECLARE @sql nvarchar(max)
DECLARE @parms nvarchar(max)

EXEC sp_get_query_template
    N'SELECT BusinessEntityID
FROM HumanResources.Employee
WHERE NationalIDNumber = 295847284',
    @sql OUTPUT,
    @parms OUTPUT
```

```
EXEC sp_create_plan_guide N'PG_Employee_Contact_Query',
    @sql,
    N'TEMPLATE',
    NULL,
    @parms,
    N'OPTION(PARAMETERIZATION FORCED)'
```

After the plan guide is created, I can execute three different versions of the same query (three different values for NationalIDNumber—each executed separately and not part of the same batch):

```
SELECT BusinessEntityID
FROM HumanResources.Employee
WHERE NationalIDNumber = 295847284

SELECT BusinessEntityID
FROM HumanResources.Employee
WHERE NationalIDNumber = 245797967

SELECT BusinessEntityID
FROM HumanResources.Employee
WHERE NationalIDNumber = 509647174
```

After executing these queries, I will now check the cache to see whether there is a prepared plan for this query:

```
SELECT usecounts,objtype,text
FROM sys.dm_exec_cached_plans cp
CROSS APPLY sys.dm_exec_sql_text(cp.plan_handle) st
WHERE st.text LIKE '%(@0 int)SELECT BusinessEntityID%' AND
    objtype = 'Prepared'
```

This returns the number of times the prepared plan has been used (three times since the plan guide was created), the object type, and parameterized SQL text:

usecounts	objtype	text
3	Prepared	(@0 int)select BusinessEntityID from HumanResources . Employee where NationalIDNumber = @0

How It Works

In this recipe, I demonstrated how to force parameterization for a single query. Near-identical queries such as the one I demonstrated can unnecessarily expand the cache, consuming memory and creating excessive compilation operations. By reducing compilation and encouraging the use of prepared plans, you can improve performance of the query itself and reduce resource consumption on the SQL server instance.

Walking through the code, I started off by declaring two local variables that would be used to hold the template SQL and associated parameters:

```
DECLARE @sql nvarchar(max)
DECLARE @parms nvarchar(max)
```

I then executed a call against the sp_get_query_template system stored procedure:

```
EXEC sp_get_query_template
```

The first parameter of this procedure expects the SQL to be converted to template format:

```
N'SELECT BusinessEntityID
FROM HumanResources.Employee
WHERE NationalIDNumber = 295847284',
```

The second parameter is used for the output parameter that will contain the template SQL:

```
@sql OUTPUT,
```

The third parameter is used for the output parameter that will contain the parameters used in association with the template SQL:

```
@parms OUTPUT
```

Next, I called `sp_create_plan_guide` to create a plan guide:

```
EXEC sp_create_plan_guide
```

The first parameter of this procedure took the name of the new plan guide:

```
N'PG_Employee_Contact_Query',
```

The second parameter took the value of the template SQL:

```
@sql,
```

The third parameter designated that this would be a `TEMPLATE` plan guide:

```
N'TEMPLATE',
```

The `@module_or_batch` parameter was given a `NULL` value, which is the required value for `TEMPLATE` plan guides:

```
NULL,
```

The next parameter contained the definition of all parameters associated with the template SQL:

```
@parms,
```

The last parameter designated the hints to attach to the query. In this case, I asked that the query use forced parameterization:

```
N'OPTION(PARAMETERIZATION FORCED)'
```

Once the plan guide was created, I executed the query in three different forms, each with a different `NationalIDNumber` literal value. I then checked `sys.dm_exec_cached_plans` to see whether there was a new row for a prepared plan. I confirmed that the `usecounts` column had a value of 3 (one for each query execution I had just performed)—which helped me confirm that the newly parameterized prepared plan was being reused.

Limiting Competing Query Resource Consumption

SQL Server 2008 introduces the ability to constrain resource consumption for workloads using Resource Governor. Resource Governor allows you to define resource pools that constrain the minimum and maximum CPU task scheduling bandwidth and memory reserved.

■**Tip** CPU task scheduling is only limited when there is CPU contention across all available schedulers.

SQL Server provides two resource pools out of the box: *default* and *internal*. The internal resource pool, which cannot be modified, uses unrestricted resources for SQL Server ongoing process activity. The default resource pool is used for connections and requests prior to Resource Governor being configured and by default has no limitations on resources (although you can change this later).

You can create your own resource pools using the CREATE RESOURCE POOL command. The syntax for this command is as follows:

```
CREATE RESOURCE POOL pool_name
[ WITH
        ( [ MIN_CPU_PERCENT = value ]
    [ [ , ] MAX_CPU_PERCENT = value ]
    [ [ , ] MIN_MEMORY_PERCENT = value ]
    [ [ , ] MAX_MEMORY_PERCENT = value ] )]
```

The arguments of this command are described in Table 28-11.

Table 28-11. *CREATE RESOURCE POOL Arguments*

Argument	Description
Pool_name	This defines the name of the resource pool.
MIN_CPU_PERCENT = value	When there is query contention, this defines minimum guaranteed average CPU task scheduling percentage from 0 to 100.
MAX_CPU_PERCENT = value	When there is query contention, this defines the maximum CPU task scheduling percentage for all query requests in the resource pool.
MIN_MEMORY_PERCENT = value	This specifies the minimum percent of reserved memory for the resource pool.
MAX_MEMORY_PERCENT = value	This specifies the maximum percent of server memory that can be used for query requests in the pool.

Once you create one or more resource pools, you can then associate them with workload groups. One or more workload groups can be bound to a single resource pool. Workload groups allow you to define the importance of requests within the pool, the maximum memory grant percentage, maximum CPU time in seconds, maximum memory grant time out, maximum degree of parallelism, and maximum number of concurrently executing requests. You can create resource pools using the CREATE WORKLOAD GROUP command. The syntax for this command is as follows:

```
CREATE WORKLOAD GROUP group_name
[ WITH
    ( [ IMPORTANCE = { LOW | MEDIUM | HIGH } ]
            [ [ , ] REQUEST_MAX_MEMORY_GRANT_PERCENT = value ]
            [ [ , ] REQUEST_MAX_CPU_TIME_SEC = value ]
            [ [ , ] REQUEST_MEMORY_GRANT_TIMEOUT_SEC = value ]
            [ [ , ] MAX_DOP = value ]
            [ [ , ] GROUP_MAX_REQUESTS = value ] )]
[ USING { pool_name | "default" } ]
```

The arguments of this command are described in Table 28-12.

Table 28-12. *CREATE WORKLOAD GROUP Arguments*

Argument	Description
group_name	Defines the name of the workload group.
IMPORTANCE = {LOW | MEDIUM | HIGH}	Defines the importance of requests within the workload group. If two workloads share the same resource pool, the importance of each workload can determine which requests have a higher priority.
REQUEST_MAX_MEMORY_GRANT_PERCENT = value	Caps maximum memory a request can use from the resource pool.
REQUEST_MAX_CPU_TIME_SEC = value	Caps maximum CPU time (seconds) a single request can use from the resource pool.
REQUEST_MEMORY_GRANT_TIMEOUT_SEC = value	Caps maximum seconds a request will wait for memory before failing.
MAX_DOP = value	Defines maximum degree of parallelism allowed for requests in the workload group.
GROUP_MAX_REQUESTS = value	Caps concurrently executing requests in the workload group.
USING { pool_name | "default" }	Designates which pool the workload group will be bound to.

■**Note** Multiple workload *groups* can be associated with a single resource *pool*, but a workload group cannot be associated with multiple resource pools.

Just as there are the internal and default resource pools, there are also the internal and default workload groups. The default workload group is used for any requests that are not covered by the classifier user-defined function (a function that determines which workload groups incoming connections are assigned to—demonstrated later in this recipe).

After creating user-defined workload groups and their binding to resource pools, you can then create a single classifier user-defined function that will help determine which workload group an incoming SQL Server connection and request belongs to.

For example, if you have a SQL login named Sue, you can assign that login in the classifier function to belong to a specific workload group that is associated with a specific resource pool.

The classifier user-defined function is created in the master database and returns the workload group name that the incoming SQL Server connection will use. In order to activate the classifier for incoming connections, the ALTER RESOURCE GOVERNOR command is used—which I'll demonstrate later on in this recipe.

Beginning the recipe, let's assume that I have a SQL Server instance that is used by an application with two general types of activity. The first type of activity relates to the application itself. The application uses ongoing automated processes with specific connection qualities and must run reliably. The second type of activity comes from ad hoc query users. These are users who require periodic information about transactional activity, but getting that information must never hamper the performance of the main application. Granted, the best practice would be to separate this activity onto two SQL Server instances; however, if this isn't possible, I can use Resource Governor to constrain resources instead.

I'll start by creating two separate user-defined resource pools for the SQL Server instance. The first pool will be used for the high-priority application. I will make sure that this pool reserves at least 25% of CPU and memory during times of query contention:

```
CREATE RESOURCE POOL priority_app_queries
WITH ( MIN_CPU_PERCENT = 25,
       MAX_CPU_PERCENT = 75,
       MIN_MEMORY_PERCENT = 25,
       MAX_MEMORY_PERCENT = 75)
GO
```

Next, I will create a second resource pool that will be reserved for ad hoc queries. I will cap the maximum CPU and memory of these pools at 25% during times of high query contention, in order to preserve resources for the previously created resource pool:

```
CREATE RESOURCE POOL ad_hoc_queries
WITH ( MIN_CPU_PERCENT = 5,
       MAX_CPU_PERCENT = 25,
       MIN_MEMORY_PERCENT = 5,
       MAX_MEMORY_PERCENT = 25)
GO
```

I can change the values of the resource pools using the ALTER RESOURCE POOL command. For example, I am now going to change the minimum memory for the ad hoc query pool to 10% and maximum memory to 50%:

```
ALTER RESOURCE POOL ad_hoc_queries
WITH ( MIN_MEMORY_PERCENT = 10,
       MAX_MEMORY_PERCENT = 50)
GO
```

Once I have created the pools, I can now confirm the settings using the sys.resource_governor_resource_pools catalog view:

```
SELECT pool_id,name,min_cpu_percent,max_cpu_percent,
       min_memory_percent,max_memory_percent
FROM sys.resource_governor_resource_pools
```

This returns

pool_id	name	min_cpu_percent	max_cpu_percent	min_memory_percent	max_memory_percent
1	internal	0	100	0	100
2	default	0	100	0	100
258	ad_hoc_queries	5	25	10	50
259	priority_app_queries	25	75	25	75

Now that I have created the resource pools, I can bind workload groups to them. In this case, I will start by creating a workload group for my highest priority application connections. I will set this workload group to a high importance, and be generous with the maximum memory grant percentage and other arguments:

```
CREATE WORKLOAD GROUP application_alpha
WITH
    ( IMPORTANCE =  HIGH,
      REQUEST_MAX_MEMORY_GRANT_PERCENT = 75,
      REQUEST_MAX_CPU_TIME_SEC = 75,
      REQUEST_MEMORY_GRANT_TIMEOUT_SEC = 120,
      MAX_DOP = 8,
      GROUP_MAX_REQUESTS = 8 )
USING priority_app_queries
GO
```

Next, I will create another workload group that will share the same resource pool as application_alpha, but with a lower importance and less generous resource consumption capabilities:

```
CREATE WORKLOAD GROUP application_beta
WITH
    ( IMPORTANCE =  LOW,
      REQUEST_MAX_MEMORY_GRANT_PERCENT = 50,
      REQUEST_MAX_CPU_TIME_SEC = 50,
      REQUEST_MEMORY_GRANT_TIMEOUT_SEC = 360,
      MAX_DOP = 1,
      GROUP_MAX_REQUESTS = 4 )
USING priority_app_queries
GO
```

I can modify the various limits of the workload group by using ALTER WORKLOAD GROUP. For example:

```
ALTER WORKLOAD GROUP application_beta
WITH ( IMPORTANCE =  MEDIUM)
```

The prior two workload groups will share the same resource pool. I will now create one more workload group that will bind to the ad hoc resource pool I created earlier. This workload group will be able to use the maximum memory available to the ad hoc pool:

```
CREATE WORKLOAD GROUP adhoc_users
WITH
    ( IMPORTANCE =  LOW,
      REQUEST_MAX_MEMORY_GRANT_PERCENT = 100,
      REQUEST_MAX_CPU_TIME_SEC = 120,
      REQUEST_MEMORY_GRANT_TIMEOUT_SEC = 360,
      MAX_DOP = 1,
      GROUP_MAX_REQUESTS = 5 )
USING ad_hoc_queries
GO
```

Once finished, I can confirm the configurations of the workload groups by querying the sys.resource_governor_workload_groups catalog view:

```
SELECT name,
       Importance impt,
       request_max_memory_grant_percent max_m_g,
       request_max_cpu_time_sec max_cpu_sec,
       request_memory_grant_timeout_sec m_g_to,
       max_dop,
       group_max_requests max_req,
       pool_id
FROM sys.resource_governor_workload_groups
```

This returns

name	impt	max_m_g	max_cpu_sec	m_g_to	max_dop	max_req	pool_id
internal	Medium	25	0	0	0	0	1
default	Medium	25	0	0	0	0	2
application_alpha	High	75	75	120	8	8	256
application_beta	Medium	50	50	360	1	4	256
adhoc_users	Low	100	120	360	1	5	257

Now I am ready to create the classifier function. This function will be called for each new connection. The logic of this function will return the workload group where all connection requests will be sent. The classifier function can use several different connection-related functions for use in the logic, including HOST_NAME, APP_NAME, SUSER_NAME, SUSER_SNAME, IS_SRVROLEMEMBER, and IS_MEMBER.

■**Caution** Make sure this function is tuned properly and executes quickly.

I create the following function that looks at the SQL Server login name and connection host name in order to determine which workload group the new connection should be assigned to:

```
USE master
GO

CREATE FUNCTION dbo.JOEPROD_classifier()
RETURNS sysname
WITH SCHEMABINDING
AS
BEGIN
   DECLARE @resource_group_name sysname

   IF  SUSER_SNAME() IN ('AppLogin1', 'AppLogin2')
   SET @resource_group_name = 'application_alpha'

   IF  SUSER_SNAME() IN ('AppLogin3', 'AppLogin4')
   SET @resource_group_name = 'application_beta'

   IF  HOST_NAME() IN ('Workstation1234', 'Workstation4235')
   SET @resource_group_name = 'adhoc_users'

   -- If the resource group is still unassigned, use default
   IF  @resource_group_name IS NULL
   SET @resource_group_name = 'default'

   RETURN @resource_group_name

END
GO
```

Now that I've created the classifier function, I can activate it using ALTER RESOURCE GOVERNOR and the CLASSIFIER_FUNCTION argument:

```
-- Assign the classifier function
ALTER RESOURCE GOVERNOR
WITH (CLASSIFIER_FUNCTION = dbo.JOEPROD_classifier)
GO
```

To enable the configuration, I must also execute ALTER RESOURCE GOVERNOR with the RECONFIGURE option:

```
ALTER RESOURCE GOVERNOR RECONFIGURE
GO
```

I'll validate the settings using the sys.resource_governor_configuration catalog view:

```
SELECT OBJECT_NAME(classifier_function_id,DB_ID('master')) Fn_Name,
      is_enabled
FROM sys.resource_governor_configuration
```

This returns

```
Fn_Name                is_enabled
JOEPROD_classifier     1
```

Now incoming activity for new connections will be routed to the appropriate workload groups and will use resources from their associated resource pools.

Tip You can monitor the incoming request statistics for resource pools and workload groups using the sys.dm_resource_governor_resource_pools and sys.dm_resource_governor_workload_groups Dynamic Management Views.

To disable the settings, I can execute the ALTER RESOURCE GOVERNOR with the DISABLE argument:

```
ALTER RESOURCE GOVERNOR DISABLE
```

I can remove the user-defined workload groups and resource pools by executing DROP WORKLOAD GROUP and DROP RESOURCE POOL:

```
USE master
GO

DROP WORKLOAD GROUP application_alpha
DROP WORKLOAD GROUP application_beta
DROP WORKLOAD GROUP adhoc_users

DROP RESOURCE POOL ad_hoc_queries
DROP RESOURCE POOL priority_app_queries
```

I can also drop the classifier function once it is no longer being used:

```
ALTER RESOURCE GOVERNOR
WITH (CLASSIFIER_FUNCTION = NULL)

DROP FUNCTION dbo.JOEPROD_classifier
```

How It Works

This recipe demonstrated how to use Resource Governor to allocate memory and CPU resources into separate, user-defined resource pools. Once the resource pools were defined, I created workload groups, which in turn had associated limits within the confines of their assigned user-defined resource pool. I then created a classifier user-defined function, which was used to assign workload groups to incoming connection requests. This allowed me to confine lower priority requests to fewer resources than higher priority requests.

This new functionality allows you to maintain significant control over SQL Server instances that have varying workload requirements and limited system resources. Even on systems with generous system resources, you can use Resource Governor to protect higher priority workloads from being negatively impacted by lower priority requests.

Backup and Recovery

One of the most critical responsibilities of a SQL Server professional is to protect data. This chapter contains various recipes for backing up your database, be it a full, file, filegroup, transaction log, or differential backup (all of these backups will be described in more detail).

I'll also review how to use the new compression improvement added to SQL Server 2008 Enterprise Edition, and you'll also learn methods for using these backup types to recover (restore) your database.

Creating a Backup and Recovery Plan

Before getting too far into the details of *how* to perform backups and restores for your SQL Server databases, I'd first like to discuss how to generate a database recovery plan. In general, you should think about answering the following questions:

- Which of your databases are important? If a database is important, that is, used for non-trivial purposes, it should be backed up.

- How much data can you lose? In other words, what is your recovery point objective (RPO)? Can you lose a day's worth of data? An hour's worth? A minute's? The less data you can afford to lose, the more often you should be backing up your databases.

- Do you have an off-site storage facility? Disasters happen. Equipment can be destroyed or catch on fire. If the data is important to you, you need to be moving it to a separate, offsite location via tape or over the network.

- What is your recovery time objective (RTO)? How much downtime can your business handle? How much time would it currently take you to get everything up and running after a loss of all your databases? If your databases are large, and your downtime allowance very small, you may need to consider duplication of your existing databases (database mirroring, log shipping, replication, SAN technologies).

Recovery plans are based on the value your company places on the SQL Server instance and its databases. The business value placed on an individual instance can range from trivial ("crash-and-burn") to mission critical ("can't lose any data at all"). It almost goes without saying that business-critical databases must be backed up. If you cannot afford to lose or reproduce the data within a database, you should be backing it up. This chapter will review how to use Transact-SQL to perform backups and will discuss the various types of backups that can be performed.

Another consideration with backups is the backup frequency. If you can afford to lose 24 hours' worth of data, then, depending on the database size, a full database backup scheduled to run once a day may be acceptable. If you cannot lose more than 30 minutes' worth of modifications, you should consider executing transaction log backups every 30 minutes as well. If you cannot afford to lose any data at all, then you should investigate such solutions as log shipping, database mirroring,

RAID mirroring, or vendor solutions offered with storage area networks (SAN) and split-mirror software. The implication being, of course, that the closer you want to get to a no-data-loss guarantee, the more money you will have to spend.

Along with backups, you should also be thinking about archiving the files generated from the backup to another server on the network or to tape. If your SQL Server instance machine is destroyed, you will definitely need backups from an off-server and offsite source.

The last major point to consider is the maximum allowable downtime for the SQL Server instance and databases. Aside from the data that is lost, how much time can you afford to spend before everything is up and running again? How much money does your business lose for each hour of database downtime? If the number is high, you need to invest in redundancy to offset this outage. If a database restore operation for a single database takes 8 hours, you may need to reevaluate whether restoring from backup is appropriate or cost effective. In this situation, you may choose to use replication, log shipping, database mirroring, or other third-party solutions that involve making copies of the data available across two or more SQL Server instances. Failover clustering can also help you with your SQL Server instance's availability by eliminating many different single points of failure (except for shared disks). If your hardware goes bad, do you have replacement parts on site? Or, do you need to run to the nearest store to buy them? For high-availability requirements, you need to think about any single points of failure, and address them with redundant parts and processes.

As a DBA, you should consider and act upon all the questions raised in this section in order to create a SQL Server backup and recovery plan. At a lower level, you should also know the details of who to contact in the event of a disaster. The following is a list of items that you should document along with your backup and recovery strategy:

- Do you have a "run book"? You will need to know the primary contact or contacts for each application connecting to a database. Who handles the communication with end users? If a database is corrupted, who makes the decision to restore from a backup (and potentially lose some recent data updates) rather than work with Microsoft to potentially save the corrupted data?

- If you have a standby server, who on your IT staff needs to be involved to get the standby server up and running? Who installs the OS, moves files, swaps DSN names, and so on? Do you have a list of these people and their pager/e-mail/contact info?

- Do you have a support plan with your hardware and software vendors? Do you have a central document listing license keys, service codes, and phone numbers?

- Do you have spare parts or an available spare parts server?

- If your entire site is down, do you have an alternative site? Do you have a documented process for moving to this alternate site?

If you lose an entire server and must rebuild it from scratch, you should have even more information available to you. Your company should have the following information documented and available:

- Who on your team needs to be involved in a server rebuild? Can he be available at 2 a.m.? Will he be available when you need him?

- Where do you keep your SQL Server backup files? What types of backups were you performing and how often were they run?

- Were there any other applications installed or configured on the SQL Server server? (Remember, aside from performance improvements, making your SQL Server machine a dedicated server reduces the complexity of reinstalling third-party or home-grown applications.)

- What operating system version were you running on? Do you have the CDs needed to reinstall the OS or reinstall SQL Server? Do you have all necessary license keys?

- Did you document the steps used to install SQL Server? What collation did you choose? Did you install all available components (Integration Services, Analysis Services, Reporting Services, for example) or just the database engine?

The more databases and applications you have running on the SQL Server instance, the more documentation you'll need to keep in order to be prepared for the worst. The important thing is to prioritize accordingly, first forming plans for your organization's most critical databases and then enlisting the help of business partners to help keep your backup and recovery plan both updated and useful.

Making Backups

In this next set of recipes, I'll show you different methods for backing up SQL Server databases. Specifically, I'll be showing you how to perform full, transaction log, and differential backups. I'll also demonstrate the new compression improvement introduced in SQL Server 2008 Enterprise Edition.

A *full backup* makes a full copy of your database. While the database backup is executed, the database remains available for database activity (since this is an online activity). Of all the database backup options, full database backups are the most time-consuming. The full backup includes all changes and log file entries as of the point in time when the backup operation completes. Once created, a full database backup allows you to restore your entire database. A full backup is the core of your data recovery plan, and it's a prerequisite for taking advantage of transaction log or differential backups (as you'll see later). When creating a backup, you have the option of creating a file on a disk drive or writing directly to tape. In general, SQL Server backups execute and complete more quickly when written directly to disk. Once the backup has been created, you can then copy it to tape or to a network drive.

A SQL Server database requires a transaction log file. A transaction log tracks transactions that have committed, or those that are still open and not yet committed. This file contains a record of ongoing transactions and modifications in the database. *Transaction log backups* back up the transaction log's activity that has occurred since the last full or transaction log backup. When the backup completes, SQL Server truncates the inactive portion of the log (the part not containing open transaction activity). Transaction log backups have low resource overhead and can be run frequently (every 15 minutes, for example).

Transaction log backups can only be performed on databases using a FULL or BULK_LOGGED recovery model. Recall from Chapter 22 that the three database recovery models are FULL, BULK_LOGGED, and SIMPLE:

- When using SIMPLE recovery, the transaction log is automatically truncated by SQL Server, removing the ability to perform transaction log backups. In this recovery mode, the risk of data loss is dependent on your full or differential backup schedule, and you will not be able to perform point-in-time recovery that a transaction log backup offers.

- The BULK_LOGGED recovery model allows you to perform full, differential, and transaction log backups—however, there is minimal logging to the transaction log for bulk operations. The benefit of this recovery mode is reduced log space usage during bulk operations; however, the trade-off is that transaction log backups can only be used to recover to the time the last transaction log backup was completed (no point-in-time recovery or marked transactions allowed).

- The FULL recovery model fully logs all transaction activity, bulk operations included. In this safest model, all restore options are available, including point-in-time transaction log restores, differential backups, and full database backups.

Aside from allowing a restore from the point that the transaction log backup completed, transaction log backups also allow for point-in-time and transaction mark recovery. Point-in-time recovery is useful for restoring a database prior to a database modification or failure. Transaction marking allows you to recover to the first instance of a marked transaction (using BEGIN TRAN...WITH MARK) and includes the updates made within this transaction.

The size of the transaction log backup file depends on the level of database activity and whether or not you are using a FULL or BULK_LOGGED recovery model. Again, the SIMPLE recovery model does not allow transaction log backups.

To recover from transaction logs backups, you must first restore from the full backup, and then apply the transaction log backups. Transaction logs are cumulative, meaning each backup is part of a sequential line of transaction log backups and must be restored sequentially in the same order. You cannot, for example, restore a full database backup and then restore the third transaction log backup, skipping the first two transaction log backups.

A database also should not be recovered (meaning brought online and made available for use) until you are finished applying all the transaction logs that you wish to apply in order chronologically by backup date and time. Recovery is handled by the RECOVERY and NORECOVERY keywords of the RESTORE command, reviewed later in the chapter.

You must understand the backups that have been made, what is contained in them, and when they were performed before you can restore them. Later on in the chapter, I'll demonstrate the various commands that you can use to view this information. The following list details a typical backup sequence:

```
Time     Backup Type
8AM      Full database backup
10AM     Transaction log backup
1PM      Transaction log backup
```

If you wanted to recover the database as of 1 p.m., you would need to restore the 8 a.m. full backup first, the 10 a.m. transaction log backup next, and finally the 1 p.m. transaction log backup. If using differential backups, you must restore the full backup first, the differential backup next, and then transaction log backups created after the differential backup. *Differential backups* copy all the data and log pages that have changed since the last full backup. Since the database is online when it's being backed up, the differential backup includes changes and log file entries from the point the backup began to when the backup completes. The files generated by differential backups are usually smaller than full database backups, and are created more quickly too.

Differential backups, unlike transaction log backups, are self-contained and only require the latest full backup from which to restore. Transaction log backups, however, are sequential files that don't include data from previous transaction log backups. For example, if you run a full backup at 8 a.m., a differential backup at 10 a.m., and an additional differential backup at 1 p.m., the 1 p.m. differential backup will still include all changes since the 8 a.m. full backup:

```
Time     Backup Type
8AM      Full database backup
10AM     Differential backup (captures changes from 8am - 10am)
1PM      Differential backup (captures changes from 8am - 1pm)
```

Differential backups can still work side-by-side with transaction log backups, although transaction log backups can't be restored until any full and differential backups have been restored first.

The first recipe in this set of backup recipes will demonstrate how to perform a *full* backup in its simplest form.

Performing a Basic Full Backup

To perform a full backup, you use the BACKUP DATABASE command. The simplified syntax for performing a full backup to disk is as follows:

```
BACKUP DATABASE { database_name | @database_name_var }
TO DISK  = { 'physical_backup_device_name' | @physical_backup_device_name_var }
[ ,...n ]
```

The arguments of this command are described in Table 29-1.

Table 29-1. *BACKUP DATABASE Arguments*

Argument	Description
database_name | @database_name_var	This defines the database name to be backed up (either designated as a string or local variable).
'physical_backup_device_name' | @physical_backup_device_name_var	This specifies the physical path and file name, or a local variable containing the physical path and file name.
[,...n]	You can designate up to 64 backup device names for a single BACKUP DATABASE command.

The BACKUP command also includes several options, many of which I'll demonstrate in this chapter:

```
[ WITH ] [Option Name ] [,...n]
```

■**Tip** For a full list of options, see SQL Server 2008 Books Online. I'll demonstrate the more common options in this chapter.

In this recipe, I'll perform a simple, full database backup of the TestDB database to a disk device (file). Used for demonstrating BACKUP DATABASE, I'll first create a new scratch database that is also populated with a few objects from the AdventureWorks database:

```
USE master
GO

IF NOT EXISTS (SELECT name
               FROM sys.databases
               WHERE name = 'TestDB')
BEGIN
    CREATE DATABASE TestDB
END
GO

USE TestDB
GO
```

```
SELECT *
INTO dbo.SalesOrderDetail
FROM AdventureWorks.Sales.SalesOrderDetail
GO

SELECT *
INTO dbo.SalesOrderHeader
FROM AdventureWorks.Sales.SalesOrderHeader
GO
```

Now, the new database will be backed up:

```
BACKUP DATABASE TestDB
TO DISK  = 'C:\Apress\Recipes\TestDB_Oct_14_2008_1617.BAK'
```

This returns

```
Processed 2456 pages for database 'TestDB', file 'TestDB' on file 1.
Processed 5 pages for database 'TestDB', file 'TestDB_log' on file 1.
BACKUP DATABASE successfully processed 2461 pages in 4.210 seconds (4.788 MB/sec).
```

How It Works

In this simple recipe, a full database backup was created for the TestDB database. The first line of code designated the name of the database to be backed up:

```
BACKUP DATABASE TestDB
```

The second line of code designated the file to back up the database to:

```
TO DISK  = 'C:\Apress\Recipes\TestDB_Oct_14_2008_1617.BAK'
```

A backup file was created with a *.bak file extension. The name of the backup showed the date and military time. Although including a timestamp in the file name helps you identify the time the backup was created, it isn't a requirement. After executing, information was returned regarding the number of data pages processed and the amount of time the backup process took.

Compressing Your Backups

SQL Server 2008 introduces native backup compression for Enterprise Edition and Developer Edition. This functionality allows you to more quickly back up your databases and consume less disk space. The amount of compression gained depends on the data within the database. For example, databases with character data with repeating values will result in higher compression ratios than databases containing mostly numeric or encrypted data.

In this recipe, I'll demonstrate first how to enable compression for the SQL Server instance by default. After doing this, I'll show you how to explicitly *not* compress a backup or compress a backup regardless of the server-level option.

In this first query, I will configure the server-instance default (again, this requires Enterprise Edition or Developer Edition to use):

```
USE master
GO

EXEC sp_configure 'backup compression default', '1'
RECONFIGURE WITH OVERRIDE
GO
```

Executing the following query, I can confirm that the setting is active:

```
SELECT description,value_in_use
FROM sys.configurations
WHERE name = 'backup compression default'
```

This returns

description	value_in_use
Enable compression of backups by default	1

Now I run a simple backup against the AdventureWorks database:

```
BACKUP DATABASE AdventureWorks
TO DISK = 'C:\Apress\AW_compressed.bak'
```

The operation statistics are as follows:

```
Processed 24056 pages for database 'AdventureWorks',
file 'AdventureWorks2008_Data' on file 1.
Processed 36 pages for database 'AdventureWorks',
file 'FileStreamDocuments' on file 1.
Processed 5 pages for database 'AdventureWorks',
file 'AdventureWorks2008_Log' on file 1.
BACKUP DATABASE successfully processed 24112 pages
in 6.318 seconds (29.814 MB/sec).
```

If I do not wish to compress the backup, I can use the NO_COMPRESSION argument (similarly, I can designate COMPRESSION to override the server option if it is disabled):

```
BACKUP DATABASE AdventureWorks
TO DISK = 'C:\Apress\AW_uncompressed.bak'
WITH NO_COMPRESSION
```

The operations statistics are as follows (notice that the compressed backup runs in 6.318 seconds versus the uncompressed 11.863 seconds—but that isn't the only distinction, as you'll find out):

```
Processed 24056 pages for database 'AdventureWorks',
file 'AdventureWorks2008_Data' on file 1.
Processed 16 pages for database 'AdventureWorks',
file 'AW2' on file 1.
Processed 36 pages for database 'AdventureWorks',
file 'FileStreamDocuments' on file 1.
Processed 1 pages for database 'AdventureWorks',
file 'AdventureWorks2008_Log' on file 1.
BACKUP DATABASE successfully processed 24109 pages
in 11.863 seconds (15.876 MB/sec).
```

I can query the statistics about both backups by looking at msdb..backupset:

```
SELECT TOP 2 database_name, backup_size, compressed_backup_size
FROM msdb..backupset
ORDER BY backup_finish_date DESC
```

Looking at the resulting space taken up by the backups, the compressed backup of the AdventureWorks database takes up 45MB versus the uncompressed backup, which takes up 191MB (the following data is in bytes):

```
database_name      backup_size    compressed_backup_size
AdventureWorks     200365056      200365056
AdventureWorks     200365056      47361034
```

How It Works

Backup compression allows you to create database backups that run faster and take up less disk space. The counterbalancing cost can be CPU, so you should evaluate the overhead given your concurrent query traffic and system resource needs.

Using compression by default is accomplished by enabling the backup compression default server option using sp_configure or by simply designating COMPRESSION in the WITH clause of the BACKUP operation. If you wish to not compress a specific backup when the server option is enabled, you only need to designate NO_COMPRESSION, as was demonstrated in this recipe.

To view the compressed size of the resulting backup, I queried the msdb..backupset table, looking at the compressed_backup_size column. If the database backup was not compressed, this value would be the same size as the backup_size column.

Naming and Describing Your Backups and Media

Considering industry regulation of information and retention laws, your company policies may require that you keep database backups for a long period of time. With longer retention periods, backup set metadata becomes more important. Naming your database backup file with the database name and timestamp is usually sufficient; however, SQL Server includes other options you can take advantage of as well for describing and naming your backups. These options include

```
[ WITH
    [ [ , ] DESCRIPTION = { 'text' | @text_variable } ]
    [ [ , ] MEDIADESCRIPTION = { 'text' | @text_variable } ]
    [ [ , ] MEDIANAME = { media_name | @media_name_variable } ]
    [ [ , ] NAME = { backup_set_name | @backup_set_name_var } ]
]
```

Table 29-2 describes these options.

Table 29-2. *Backup Media Options*

Argument	Description
DESCRIPTION	Free-form text description of the backup set, helping identify the contents of the backup device
MEDIADESCRIPTION	Free-form text description of the media set, helping identify the contents of the media
MEDIANAME	Name of the entire backup media set, limited to 128 characters
NAME	Name of the backup set

Two terms related to SQL Server backups are used in Table 29-2: backup set and media set. A *backup set* is simply the result of a database backup operation. The backup set can span one or more backup devices (disk or tape). The *media set* is the collection of one or more backup devices that the backup set is written to.

The following example demonstrates the designating of a description and name for both the backup and media sets:

```
BACKUP DATABASE TestDB
TO DISK  = 'C:\Apress\Recipes\TestDB.bak'
WITH   DESCRIPTION = 'My second recipe backup, TestDB',
   NAME = 'TestDB Backup October 14th',
   MEDIADESCRIPTION = 'Backups for October 2008, Week 2',
   MEDIANAME = 'TestDB_October_2008_Week2'
```

This returns

```
Processed 2440 pages for database 'TestDB', file 'TestDB' on file 1.
Processed 1 pages for database 'TestDB', file 'TestDB_log' on file 1.
BACKUP DATABASE successfully processed 2441 pages in
0.815 seconds (23.399 MB/sec).
```

How It Works

This recipe has demonstrated how to add more descriptive information with your database backup. The additional options were added to the BACKUP DATABASE command using the WITH clause. The DESCRIPTION described the backup set:

```
WITH DESCRIPTION = 'My second recipe backup, TestDB',
```

The NAME identified the backup set name:

```
NAME = 'TestDB Backup October 14th',
```

The MEDIADESCRIPTION designated the description of the media set:

```
MEDIADESCRIPTION = 'Backups for October 2008, Week 2',
```

The MEDIANAME designated the name of the entire backup media set:

```
MEDIANAME = 'TestDB_October_2008_Week2'
```

This information can be retrieved using RESTORE commands (such as RESTORE HEADERONLY), which will be covered later on in the chapter in the "Viewing Backup Metadata" recipe.

Configuring Backup Retention

In the first recipe of this chapter, if the backup file (device) hadn't already existed before the backup, it would be created during execution of the BACKUP command. If the file *did* already exist, the default behavior of the backup process would be to append the backup to the existing backup file (retaining any other backups on the file).

There are several BACKUP options that impact the backup set retention:

```
[ WITH
     [ [ , ] EXPIREDATE = { date | @date_var }
     | RETAINDAYS = { days | @days_var } ]
     [ [ , ] { FORMAT | NOFORMAT } ]
     [ [ , ] { INIT | NOINIT } ]
     [ [ , ] { NOSKIP | SKIP } ]
]
```

These options are described in Table 29-3.

Table 29-3. *Backup Retention Options*

Argument	Description
EXPIREDATE | RETAINDAYS	EXPIREDATE indicates the date the backup set expires and can be overwritten. RETAINDAYS specifies the days before the backup media set can be overwritten.
FORMAT | NOFORMAT	FORMAT generates a media header to all volumes used for the backup. Existing headers are overwritten. This renders a backup set unusable if a stripe exists on the device. NOFORMAT indicates that a media header should not be written on all volumes.
INIT | NOINIT	INIT overwrites existing backup sets, but preserves the media header. Backup sets are not overwritten if they have not expired yet or the name set in the BACKUP statement doesn't match the name on the backup media. NOINIT appends the backup set to the disk or tape device. NOINIT is the default option.
NOSKIP | SKIP	SKIP does not check expiration and name verification. NOSKIP checks the date and name, and is an extra safeguard to ensure the backup is not overwritten improperly.

This recipe demonstrates performing a full database backup while setting a backup set retention period of 30 days, after which it can be overwritten:

```
BACKUP DATABASE TestDB
TO DISK  = 'C:\Apress\Recipes\TestDB_Oct.bak'
WITH RETAINDAYS = 30
```

Now an attempt will be made to overwrite existing backups on the TestDB_June.bak file:

```
BACKUP DATABASE TestDB
TO DISK  = 'C:\Apress\Recipes\TestDB_Oct.bak'
WITH INIT
```

This returns

```
Msg 4030, Level 16, State 1, Line 1
The medium on device 'C:\Apress\Recipes\TestDB_Oct.bak'
expires on Apr 14 2008  2:35:42:000PM and cannot be overwritten.
Msg 3013, Level 16, State 1, Line 1
BACKUP DATABASE is terminating abnormally.
```

How It Works

In this recipe, a new database backup was created with a backup set retention of 30 days. After the backup was created, another backup was executed, this time using the INIT switch (which overwrites existing backup sets). This attempt failed with an error warning that the backup set hasn't expired yet, and therefore cannot be overwritten.

Striping Backup Sets

Striping backups involves using more than one device (disk or tape) for a single backup set operation. In fact, when performing a database backup, you can use up to 64 devices (disk or backup) in your backup operation. This is particularly useful for very large databases, because you can improve backup performance by striping the backup files across separate drives/arrays. Striping the backup files means each file is written to proportionately and simultaneously. Striped backups use parallel write operations and can significantly speed up backup operations.

This recipe demonstrates striping a backup across three disk devices:

```
BACKUP DATABASE TestDB
TO DISK  = 'C:\Apress\Recipes\TestDB_Stripe1.bak',
   DISK  = 'D:\Apress\Recipes\TestDB_Stripe2.bak',
   DISK  = 'E:\Apress\Recipes\TestDB_Stripe3.bak'
```

This backup creates three files that are each used to store one third of the backup information needed to restore the database. If you try to use any one of the devices independently for a backup, you'll get an error message, as this next example demonstrates:

```
BACKUP DATABASE TestDB
TO DISK  = 'C:\Apress\Recipes\TestDB_Stripe1.bak'
```

This returns

```
Msg 3132, Level 16, State 1, Line 1
The media set has 3 media families but only 1 are provided.
All members must be provided.
Msg 3013, Level 16, State 1, Line 1
BACKUP DATABASE is terminating abnormally.
```

How It Works

In this recipe, a backup was created using three devices, which are also called *media families*. The three media families are used as a single *media set,* which can contain one or more *backup sets.* After creating the media set made up of three media families, the second part of the recipe attempted a backup using one of the existing media families. An error occurred because until that file or files are formatted (using WITH FORMAT), they must be used together and not separately in a backup operation.

Using a Named Backup Device

You can define a logical name for a tape or disk device that can be used in your BACKUP or RESTORE command. Defining a device adds it to the sys.backup_devices catalog view and saves you from having to type in a disk's path and file or tape name.

To add a new backup device definition, use the sp_addumpdevice system-stored procedure:

```
sp_addumpdevice [ @devtype = ] 'device_type'
      , [ @logicalname = ] 'logical_name'
      , [ @physicalname = ] 'physical_name'
   [ , { [ @cntrltype = ] controller_type |
        [ @devstatus = ] 'device_status' }
   ]
```

The arguments of this command are described in Table 29-4.

Table 29-4. *sp_addumpdevice Arguments*

Argument	Description
device_type	This argument is used to specify the device type: disk or tape.
logical_name	This option defines the name of the backup device that will be used in the BACKUP and RESTORE syntax.
physical_name	This argument defines the operating system file name, universal naming convention name (UNC), or tape path.
controller_type	This argument is ignored (backward compatible).
device_status	This argument is ignored (backward compatible).

To view the definition of a backup device, use the sp_helpdevice system-stored procedure, which only takes the logical_name as a parameter:

```
sp_helpdevice [ [ @devname = ] 'name' ]
```

To delete a backup device, use sp_dropdevice:

```
sp_dropdevice [ @logicalname = ] 'device'
    [ , [ @delfile = ] 'delfile' ]
```

The first parameter is the name of the backup device, and when DELFILE is designated in the second parameter, the actual backup device file is deleted. In the first part of the recipe, a backup device is created called TestDBBackup, which is mapped to the C:\Apress\Recipes\TestDB_Device. bak file:

```
USE master
GO

EXEC sp_addumpdevice 'disk', 'TestDBBackup', 'C:\Apress\Recipes\TestDB_Device.bak'
```

This returns

```
Command(s) completed successfully.
```

Next, information regarding the device is queried using sp_helpdevice:

```
EXEC sp_helpdevice 'TestDBBackup'
```

This returns the following (abridged columns):

```
device_name      physical_name                        description
TestDBBackup     C:\Apress\Recipes\TestDB_Device.bak  disk, backup device
```

Next, a backup is performed against the device:

```
BACKUP DATABASE TestDB
TO TestDBBackup
```

This returns

```
Processed 2440 pages for database 'TestDB', file 'TestDB' on file 1.
Processed 1 pages for database 'TestDB', file 'TestDB_log' on file 1.
BACKUP DATABASE successfully processed 2441 pages in
0.858 seconds (22.226 MB/sec).
```

Lastly, the device is dropped using sp_dropdevice (since the second DELFILE option is not designated, the physical backup file will remain on the operating system):

```
EXEC sp_dropdevice 'TestDBBackup'
```

This returns

```
Device dropped.
```

How It Works

In this recipe, I demonstrated how to create a named backup device, allowing you to skip the keystrokes you would need to designate a full disk or tape name in your BACKUP or RESTORE commands.

The first example in the recipe created a device using sp_addumpdevice. The first parameter of the stored procedure took the device type disk. The second parameter was the logical name of the device, and the third parameter was the actual physical file path and name. The second query in the recipe demonstrated returning information about the device using sp_helpdevice. The status field relates to the description of the device, and the cntrltype column designates the device type (2 for disk device, 5 for tape). The third query in the recipe demonstrated using the device in a backup, which involved simply designating the device name instead of using the DISK or TAPE option. In the last query of the recipe, the device was dropped using sp_dropdevice.

Mirroring Backup Sets

You can mirror a database, log, file, or filegroup backup. Mirroring creates backup redundancy by creating two, three, or four copies of a media set. This redundancy can come in handy if one of the media sets is corrupted or invalid, because you can use any of the other valid mirrored media sets instead.

The syntax is as follows:

```
BACKUP DATABASE { database_name | @database_name_var }
TO < backup_device > [ ,...n ]
[ [ MIRROR TO < backup_device > [ ,...n ] ] [ ...next-mirror ] ]
```

The MIRROR TO command is used in conjunction with a list of one or more backup devices, and up to three mirrors. In this example, a backup is mirrored to three different copies. Unlike the previous striping example, only one of these generated backup files will actually be needed for a database restore operation. However, if one of the files is invalid, there are three other copies to attempt a restore from instead:

```
BACKUP DATABASE TestDB
TO DISK = 'C:\Apress\Recipes\TestDB_Original.bak'
MIRROR TO DISK = 'D:\Apress\Recipes\TestDB_Mirror_1.bak'
MIRROR TO DISK = 'E:\Apress\Recipes\TestDB_Mirror_2.bak'
MIRROR TO DISK = 'F:\Apress\Recipes\TestDB_Mirror_3.bak'
WITH FORMAT
```

This returns

```
Processed 2456 pages for database 'TestDB', file 'TestDB' on file 1.
Processed 1 pages for database 'TestDB', file 'TestDB_log' on file 1.
BACKUP DATABASE successfully processed 2457 pages in 11.460 seconds (1.756 MB/sec).
```

This second example demonstrates mirroring a striped backup:

```
BACKUP DATABASE TestDB
TO DISK = 'C:\Apress\Recipes\TestDB_Stripe_1_Original.bak',
DISK = 'D:\Apress\Recipes\TestDB_Stripe_2_Original.bak'
MIRROR TO DISK = 'E:\Apress\Recipes\TestDB_Stripe_1_Mirror_1.bak',
DISK = 'F:\Apress\Recipes\TestDB_Stripe_2_Mirror_1.bak'
WITH FORMAT
```

This returns

```
Processed 2456 pages for database 'TestDB', file 'TestDB' on file 1.
Processed 1 pages for database 'TestDB', file 'TestDB_log' on file 1.
BACKUP DATABASE successfully processed 2457 pages in 7.883 seconds (2.553 MB/sec).
```

How It Works

In the first example of this recipe, a backup was executed with three mirrors, which resulted in four backup files for the TestDB database. The first line of code designated the database to back up:

```
BACKUP DATABASE TestDB
```

The second line designated the location of the main (non-mirrored) backup file:

```
TO DISK = 'C:\Apress\Recipes\TestDB_Original.bak'
```

The next three lines designated the three mirrored copies of the backup:

```
MIRROR TO DISK = 'D:\Apress\Recipes\TestDB_Mirror_1.bak'
MIRROR TO DISK = 'E:\Apress\Recipes\TestDB_Mirror_2.bak'
MIRROR TO DISK = 'F:\Apress\Recipes\TestDB_Mirror_3.bak'
WITH FORMAT
```

Note that WITH FORMAT is required the first time a mirrored backup set is created. The original backup was placed on the C:\ drive, and then each mirrored copy placed on its own drive (D:\, E:\, F:\). Any single .bak file in this example can then be used to restore the TestDB database, thus providing redundancy in the event of a backup file corruption.

The second example in the recipe demonstrated mirroring a striped backup (two media families in a media set). This time, TO DISK included the two files used to stripe the original backup:

```
BACKUP DATABASE TestDB
TO DISK = 'C:\Apress\Recipes\TestDB_Stripe_1_Original.bak',
DISK = 'D:\Apress\Recipes\TestDB_Stripe_2_Original.bak'
```

The MIRROR TO DISK also designated two files that will be the mirror copy of the original striped backup:

```
MIRROR TO DISK = 'E:\Apress\Recipes\TestDB_Stripe_1_Mirror_1.bak',
DISK = 'F:\Apress\Recipes\TestDB_Stripe_2_Mirror_1.bak'
WITH FORMAT
```

Notice that MIRROR TO DISK was only designated once, followed by the two devices to mirror to.

Performing a Transaction Log Backup

The BACKUP LOG command is used to perform a transaction log backup. The following is the basic syntax for performing a transaction log backup:

```
BACKUP LOG { database_name | @database_name_var }
{
    TO <backup_device> [ ,...n ]
[ [ MIRROR TO <backup_device> [ ,...n ] ] [ ...next-mirror ] ]
    [ WITH ] [Option Name ] [,...n]
}
```

BACKUP LOG shares many of the same options and functionality as the BACKUP DATABASE command. Options not yet demonstrated in this chapter that are specific only to transaction log backups are described in Table 29-5.

Table 29-5. *BACKUP LOG Options*

Argument	Description
NO_TRUNCATE	If the database is damaged, NO_TRUNCATE allows you to back up the transaction log without truncating the inactive portion (the inactive portion contains committed transaction entries). This is often used for emergency transaction log backups, capturing activity prior to a RESTORE operation. Don't run this on a long-term basis, because your log file size will keep expanding.
NORECOVERY | STANDBY =	NORECOVERY backs up the tail of the transaction log and then leaves the database in a RESTORING state (which is a state from which additional RESTORE commands can be issued). STANDBY also backs up the tail of the transaction log, but instead of leaving it in a RESTORING state, puts it into a read-only STANDBY state (used for log shipping). This option requires a file to be designated to hold changes that will be rolled back if log restores are applied.

In the first query of this recipe, a transaction log backup will be executed on the TestDB database:

```
BACKUP LOG TestDB
TO DISK = 'C:\Apress\Recipes\TestDB_Oct_14_2008_1819.trn'
```

This returns

```
Processed 13 pages for database 'TestDB', file 'TestDB_log' on file 1.
BACKUP LOG successfully processed 13 pages in 0.448 seconds (0.230 MB/sec).
```

The second example in this recipe demonstrates making a transaction log backup on the tail of the transaction log. This assumes that there has been a database corruption issue—taking a backup of the "tail" means that you are backing up the latest transactions in the database without truncating the inactive portion of the transaction log:

```
BACKUP LOG TestDB
TO DISK = 'C:\Apress\Recipes\TestDB_Oct_14_2008_1820_Emergency.trn'
WITH NO_TRUNCATE
```

How It Works

In this recipe, I demonstrated two examples of transaction log backups. Note that BACKUP LOG can't be performed unless the database has had a full database backup in the past. Also, in both examples, the database had to be using either a FULL or BULK_LOGGED recovery model. The first example was a standard transaction log backup to disk. The first line of code designated the name of the database to back up:

```
BACKUP LOG TestDB
```

The second line of code designated the device to back up to:

```
TO DISK = 'C:\Apress\Recipes\TestDB_Oct_14_2008_1819.trn'
```

After the backup was completed, a file is generated, and the inactive portion of the transaction log is truncated automatically. In the second query, the WITH NO_TRUNCATE option was designated, allowing you to back up the active portion of the transaction log without truncating the inactive portion of the transaction log.

Later on in the chapter, you'll learn how to restore data from a transaction log file, including how to use point-in-time recovery.

Create Backups Without Breaking the Backup Sequence

Database and transaction log backups can use the COPY_ONLY option to create backups that don't impact the backup sequence. As you'll see in future recipes in this chapter, both differential and transaction log backups depend on a full backup being performed first. Whenever other full database backups are created, the sequence restarts again. This means that previous differential or log backups cannot use the later-generated full database backups. Only those differential or transaction log backups that are created after the full database backup can be used.

When you use the COPY_ONLY option, however, a full backup does not disrupt the sequence of backups. This is useful for creating ad hoc backups prior to major database changes, where you don't want to disrupt the standard backup schedule, but might like to have a "just-in-case" full backup available to RESTORE from. This example demonstrates how to use COPY_ONLY with a full database backup:

```
BACKUP DATABASE TestDB
TO DISK = 'C:\Apress\Recipes\TestDB_Copy.bak'
WITH COPY_ONLY
```

When you're using COPY_ONLY with transaction log backups, the transaction log is not truncated after the backup is created (leaving an unbroken chain of transaction log backups). This example demonstrates how to use COPY_ONLY with a transaction log backup:

```
BACKUP LOG TestDB
TO DISK = 'C:\Apress\Recipes\TestDB_Copy.trn'
WITH COPY_ONLY
```

How It Works

This recipe demonstrated using COPY_ONLY to create both full and transaction log backups. The syntax was similar to previous recipes, with the difference being that COPY_ONLY was included in the WITH clause. Full database backups using this option will not break the sequence of restores required for previous transaction log or differential backups. Transaction log backups using the COPY_ONLY option will also not break the chronological order of the other transaction log backups.

Performing a Differential Backup

In this next recipe, I demonstrate how to create a differential backup. Recall from earlier in the chapter that differential backups are used to back up all data and log pages that have changed since the last full backup. This differs from transaction log backups, which only capture changes made since the last transaction log and/or full database backup.

Differential backups are performed using BACKUP DATABASE and use the same syntax and functionality as regular full database backups—only the DIFFERENTIAL keyword is included. This recipe demonstrates creating a differential backup on the TestDB database:

```
BACKUP DATABASE TestDB
TO DISK = N'C:\Apress\Recipes\TestDB.diff'
WITH DIFFERENTIAL, NOINIT, STATS = 25
```

This returns

```
58 percent processed.
78 percent processed.
Processed 40 pages for database 'TestDB', file 'TestDB' on file 1.
100 percent processed.
Processed 1 pages for database 'TestDB', file 'TestDB_log' on file 1.
BACKUP DATABASE WITH DIFFERENTIAL successfully
processed 41 pages in 0.339 seconds (0.989 MB/sec).
```

How It Works

In this recipe, a differential backup was created on the TestDB database. The command usage was similar to previous recipes, only this time the DIFFERENTIAL keyword was included in the WITH clause. Two other options (both available when using different backup types) were used: NOINIT, which appends the backup set to an existing disk or tape device, and STATS, which returns feedback to the client on backup progress. Differential backups can only be executed after a full database backup, so for a new database, a differential backup can't be the initial backup method.

Backing Up Individual Files or Filegroups

For very large databases, if the time required for a full backup exceeds your backup time window, another option is to back up specific filegroups or files at varying schedules. This option allows recovery in the event of lost files or filegroups. In order to perform file or filegroup backups for read-write enabled databases, the database must be using either the full or bulk-logged recovery models, as transaction log backups must be applied after restoring a file or filegroup backup.

Backing up a file or filegroup uses virtually the same syntax as a full database backup, except you use the FILEGROUP or FILE keywords, and you can specify more than one filegroup or file by separating each by a comma.

To demonstrate backing up a filegroup, you'll create a new database that uses a secondary filegroup called FG2:

```
USE master
GO

CREATE DATABASE VLTestDB
ON  PRIMARY
( NAME = N'VLTestDB',
FILENAME =
N'c:\Apress\Recipes\VLTestDB.mdf' ,
```

```
SIZE = 3048KB ,
FILEGROWTH = 1024KB ),
 FILEGROUP FG2
( NAME = N'VLTestDB2',
FILENAME =
N'c:\Apress\Recipes\VLTestDB2.ndf' ,
SIZE = 3048KB ,
FILEGROWTH = 1024KB ),
( NAME = N'VLTestDB3',
FILENAME =
N'c:\Apress\Recipes\VLTestDB3.ndf' ,
SIZE = 3048KB ,
FILEGROWTH = 1024KB )
 LOG ON
( NAME = N'VLTestDB_log',
FILENAME =
N'c:\Apress\Recipes\VLTestDB_log.ldf' ,
SIZE = 1024KB ,
FILEGROWTH = 10%)
GO
```

This first example creates a single filegroup backup:

```
BACKUP DATABASE VLTestDB
FILEGROUP = 'FG2'
TO DISK = 'C:\Apress\Recipes\VLTestDB_FG2.bak'
```

This returns the following results:

```
Processed 8 pages for database 'VLTestDB', file 'VLTestDB2' on file 1.
Processed 8 pages for database 'VLTestDB', file 'VLTestDB3' on file 1.
Processed 3 pages for database 'VLTestDB', file 'VLTestDB_log' on file 1.
BACKUP DATABASE...FILE=<name> successfully
processed 19 pages in 0.082 seconds (1.756 MB/sec).
```

This second example demonstrates backing up two specific files for this database. To get a list of file names first, execute sp_helpfile:

```
USE VLTestDB
GO

EXEC sp_helpfile
```

This returns the following (abridged) results:

name	fileid	filename
VLTestDB	1	c:\Apress\Recipes\VLTestDB.mdf
VLTestDB_log	2	c:\Apress\Recipes\VLTestDB_log.ldf
VLTestDB2	3	c:\Apress\Recipes\VLTestDB2.ndf
VLTestDB3	4	c:\Apress\Recipes\VLTestDB3.ndf

Using the logical file name from the sp_helpfile results, this example demonstrates backing up the TestDB3 file in the TestDB database:

```
BACKUP DATABASE VLTestDB
FILE = 'VLTestDB2',
FILE = 'VLTestDB3'
TO DISK = 'C:\apress\Recipes\VLTestDB_DB2_DB3.bak'
```

This returns

```
Processed 8 pages for database 'VLTestDB', file 'VLTestDB2' on file 1.
Processed 8 pages for database 'VLTestDB', file 'VLTestDB3' on file 1.
Processed 2 pages for database 'VLTestDB', file 'VLTestDB_log' on file 1.
BACKUP DATABASE...FILE=<name> successfully processed
17 pages in 0.278 seconds (0.499 MB/sec).
```

How It Works

This recipe started out by demonstrating backing up a specific filegroup. The syntax is almost identical to a regular full database backup, only the FILEGROUP is specified:

```
...
FILEGROUP = 'FG2'
...
```

The second example demonstrated backing up two specific files using the FILE option, in this case backing up two database files:

```
...
FILE = 'VLTestDB2',
FILE = 'VLTestDB3'
...
```

Restoring from a filegroup or file backup will be demonstrated later in the chapter.

Performing a Partial Backup

A partial backup automatically creates a backup of the primary filegroup and any read-write filegroups in the database. This option is ideal for those very large databases with read-only filegroups that needn't be backed up as frequently as the writable filegroups. The syntax for performing a partial backup is almost the same as a full backup, except that with a partial backup you need to designate the READ_WRITE_FILEGROUPS option. If there are read-only files or filegroups you also want to back up, you can explicitly designate them too.

To prep for this example, the VLTestDB's FG2 filegroup will be set to READONLY:

```
USE master
GO
ALTER DATABASE VLTestDB
MODIFY FILEGROUP FG2 READONLY
GO
```

This returns

```
The filegroup property 'READONLY' has been set.
```

Now, performing a backup with the READ_WRITE_FILEGROUPS option means that only read-write filegroups and files will be included in the backup:

```
BACKUP DATABASE VLTestDB
READ_WRITE_FILEGROUPS
TO DISK = 'C:\Apress\Recipes\TestDB_Partial_include_FG3.bak'
```

This returns

```
Processed 152 pages for database 'VLTestDB', file 'VLTestDB' on file 2.
Processed 1 pages for database 'VLTestDB', file 'VLTestDB_log' on file 2.
BACKUP DATABASE...FILE=<name> successfully
processed 153 pages in 0.120 seconds (9.960 MB/sec).
```

How It Works

A read-only filegroup contains files that cannot be written to. Since read-only data doesn't change, it only needs to be backed up periodically (as in when it's changed to read-write for updates). For very large databases, unnecessary backups of read-only filegroups can eat up time and disk space. The new partial database backup option allows you to back up just the primary filegroup and any writable filegroups and files, without having to explicitly list each filegroup. If you wish to include a read-only filegroup in the backup, you can still do so.

In this recipe, I modified the FG2 filegroup to be read-only. I then backed up the database using the READ_WRITE_FILEGROUPS option, meaning that the files in the FG2 filegroup were not included in the backup.

A database restore from a partial backup also assumes that you have a filegroup/file backup for the skipped-over files. A restore from a partial backup is demonstrated later on in this chapter.

Viewing Backup Metadata

Once a backup is created, you can view the contents of the media set by using various RESTORE functions, including RESTORE LABELONLY, RESTORE HEADERONLY, RESTORE FILELISTONLY, and RESTORE VERIFYONLY:

- RESTORE LABELONLY is used to return information about backup media on a specific backup device.

- RESTORE HEADERONLY returns a row for each backup set created on a specific device.

- RESTORE FILELISTONLY goes a level deeper by showing the database file names (logical, physical) and other information of the backed-up database.

- RESTORE VERIFYONLY prevalidates the backup device to report whether a RESTORE operation would succeed without errors.

The syntax is very similar across all four commands, and I'll demonstrate the common usages of these commands in this recipe.

In most cases, you'll use these RESTORE commands to identify the contents of the device prior to writing your actual RESTORE DATABASE operation. In this first example in the recipe, the media set information is returned for the TestDB.bak device:

```
RESTORE LABELONLY
FROM DISK = 'C:\apress\Recipes\TestDB.bak'
```

This returns the following (abridged) results:

```
MediaName                MediaDate
TestDB_October_2008_Week2   2008-10-14 16:23:30.000
```

In this second query, the same device is evaluated to see what backup sets exist on it:

```
RESTORE HEADERONLY
FROM DISK = 'C:\Apress\Recipes\TestDB.bak'
```

This returns the following (abridged) results:

Position	DatabaseName	DatabaseCreation	DateBackupTypeDescription
1	TestDB	2008-10-14 16:15:03.000	Database

In the third example of this recipe, the individual files backed up in the backup sets of a device are validated:

```
RESTORE FILELISTONLY
FROM DISK = 'C:\Apress\Recipes\TestDB.bak'
```

This returns the following (abridged) results:

LogicalName	PhysicalName	Type
TestDB	C:\Apress\Recipes\TestDB.mdf	D
TestDB_log	C:\Apress\Recipes\TestDB_log.LDF	L

In the last example of this recipe, the backup device's RESTORE validity is checked:

```
RESTORE VERIFYONLY
FROM DISK = 'C:\Apress\Recipes\TestDB.bak'
WITH FILE = 1,
LOADHISTORY
```

This returns

```
The backup set on file 1 is valid.
```

How It Works

The four commands discussed in this recipe, RESTORE FILELISTONLY, RESTORE HEADERONLY, RESTORE VERIFYONLY, and RESTORE LABELONLY, are each useful for gathering the information that you'll need prior to performing a RESTORE operation. In the first example in this recipe, RESTORE LABELONLY was used to return information on the media set of a specific backup device.

The second example used RESTORE HEADERONLY to see what backup sets actually existed on the device, so that when you restore, you can specify the backup set file number to restore from (also making sure you are restoring from the correct date and backup type).

The third example in the recipe used RESTORE FILELISTONLY to return the actual database files that were backed up in the device's backup sets. This is particularly useful information if you want to restore a database to a different server, because the drive and folder structures could be different on the new server versus the old. In later recipes in this chapter, you'll learn how to move the location of database files during a restore.

The last example checked the backup device to make sure it was valid for the RESTORE DATABASE operation. The backup set was designated using FILE = 1. Also, history regarding the backup set was saved to the msdb system database using the LOADHISTORY option.

Restoring a Database

The first part of this chapter was dedicated to reviewing how to back up a database, including how to perform a full, transaction log, differential, file, and filegroup backup. The second part of this chapter will discuss how to restore a database from a backup file. A restore operation copies all data, log, and index pages from the backup media set to the destination database. The destination database can be an existing database (which will be overlaid) or a new database (where new files will be created based on the backup). After the restore operation, a "redo" phase ensues, rolling forward committed transactions that were happening at the end of the database backup. After that, the "undo" phase rolls back uncommitted transactions.

This next set of recipes will demonstrate database restores in action.

Restoring a Database from a Full Backup

In this recipe, I demonstrate how to use the RESTORE command to restore a database from a full database backup. Unlike a BACKUP operation, a RESTORE is not always an online operation—for a full database restore, user connections must be disconnected from the database prior to restoring over the database. Other restore types (such as filegroup, file, or page) can allow online activity in the database in other areas aside, from the elements being restored. For example, if filegroup FG2 is getting restored, FG3 can still be accessed during the operation.

■**Note** Online restores are a SQL Server Enterprise Edition feature.

In general, you may need to restore a database after data loss due to user error or file corruption, or if you need a second copy of a database or are moving a database to a new SQL Server instance.

The following is simplified syntax for the RESTORE command:

```
RESTORE DATABASE { database_name | @database_name_var }
[ FROM <backup_device> [ ,...n ] ]
[ WITH ] [Option Name ] [,...n]
```

The RESTORE DATABASE command also includes several options, many of which I'll demonstrate in this chapter.

The first example in this recipe is a simple RESTORE from the latest backup set on the device (in this example, two backup sets exist on the device for the TestDB database, and you want the second one). For the demonstration, I'll start by creating two full backups on a single device:

```
BACKUP DATABASE TestDB
TO DISK  = 'C:\Apress\Recipes\TestDB_Oct_15_2008.BAK'
GO

-- Time passes, we make another backup to the same device

BACKUP DATABASE TestDB
TO DISK  = 'C:\Apress\Recipes\TestDB_Oct_15_2008.BAK'
GO
```

Now the database is restored using the second backup from the device (notice that the REPLACE argument is used to tell SQL Server to overlay the existing TestDB database):

```
USE master
GO

RESTORE DATABASE TestDB
FROM  DISK = 'C:\Apress\Recipes\TestDB_Oct_15_2008.bak'
WITH  FILE = 2, REPLACE
```

This returns the following output:

```
Processed 2456 pages for database 'TestDB', file 'TestDB' on file 2.
Processed 1 pages for database 'TestDB', file 'TestDB_log' on file 2.
RESTORE DATABASE successfully processed 2457 pages in 5.578 seconds (3.607 MB/sec).
```

In this second example, a *new* database is created by restoring from the TestDB backup, creating a new database called TrainingDB1. Notice that the MOVE argument is used to designate the location of the new database files:

```
USE master
GO

RESTORE DATABASE TrainingDB1
FROM  DISK = 'C:\Apress\Recipes\TestDB_Oct_15_2008.BAK'
WITH  FILE = 2,
MOVE 'TestDB' TO 'C:\Apress\Recipes\TrainingDB1.mdf',
MOVE 'TestDB_log' TO 'C:\Apress\Recipes\TrainingDB1_log.LDF'
```

This returns

```
Processed 2456 pages for database 'TrainingDB1', file 'TestDB' on file 2.
Processed 1 pages for database 'TrainingDB1', file 'TestDB_log' on file 2.
RESTORE DATABASE successfully processed 2457 pages in 4.799 seconds (4.193 MB/sec).
```

In the last example for this recipe, the TestDB database is restored from a striped backup set (based on the striped set created earlier in the chapter):

```
USE master
GO

RESTORE DATABASE TestDB
FROM DISK = 'C:\Apress\Recipes\TestDB_Stripe1.bak',
DISK = 'D:\Apress\Recipes\TestDB_Stripe2.bak',
DISK = 'E:\Apress\Recipes\TestDB_Stripe3.bak'
WITH FILE = 1, REPLACE
```

This returns

```
Processed 152 pages for database 'TestDB', file 'TestDB' on file 1.
Processed 1 pages for database 'TestDB', file 'TestDB_log' on file 1.
RESTORE DATABASE successfully processed 153 pages in 0.657 seconds (1.907 MB/sec).
```

How It Works

In the first example, the query began by setting the database to the `master` database. This is because a full `RESTORE` is not an online operation, and requires that there be no active connections to the database that is being restored in order to run.

The `RESTORE` was for the `TestDB` database, and it overlaid the current database with the data as it existed at the end of the second backup set on the `TestDB_Oct_15_2008.bak` backup device. The first line of the command detailed the database to `RESTORE` over:

```
RESTORE DATABASE TestDB
```

The second line of this example designated the location of the backup device:

```
FROM  DISK = 'C:\Apress\Recipes\TestDB_Oct_15_2008.bak'
```

The last line of this example designated which backup set from the backup device should be used to `RESTORE` from (recall from earlier in this chapter that you can use `RESTORE HEADERONLY` to see what backup sets exist on a backup device):

```
WITH  FILE = 2, REPLACE
```

Any data that was updated since the last backup will be lost, so it is assumed in this example that data loss is acceptable, and that data as of the last backup is desired. In the second example, a new database was created based on a `RESTORE` from another database. The example is similar to the previous query, only this time the `MOVE` command is used to designate where the new database files should be located (and the new database name is used as well):

```
MOVE 'TestDB' TO 'C:\apress\Recipes\TrainingDB1.mdf',
MOVE 'TestDB_log' TO 'C:\apress\Recipes\TrainingDB1_log.LDF'
```

`RESTORE FILELISTONLY` (demonstrated earlier) can be used to retrieve the logical name and physical path of the backed-up database.

▪**Tip** The `RESTORE...MOVE` command is often used in conjunction with database migrations to different SQL Server instances that use different drive letters and directories.

In the last example of the recipe, the `TestDB` was restored from a striped backup set. `FROM DISK` was repeated for each disk device in the set:

```
RESTORE DATABASE TestDB
FROM DISK = 'C:\apress\Recipes\TestDB_Stripe1.bak',
DISK = 'C:\apress\Recipes\TestDB_Stripe2.bak',
DISK = 'C:\apress\Recipes\TestDB_Stripe3.bak'
WITH FILE = 1, REPLACE
```

In each of these examples, the database was restored to a recovered state, meaning that it was online and available for users to query after the redo phase (and during/after the undo phase). In the next few recipes, you'll see that the database is often *not* recovered until a differential or transaction log backup can be restored.

Restoring a Database from a Transaction Log Backup

Transaction log restores require an initial full database restore, and if you're applying multiple transaction logs, they must be applied in chronological order (based on when the transaction log backups were generated). Applying transaction logs out of order, or with gaps between backups, isn't allowed. The syntax for restoring transaction logs is RESTORE LOG instead of RESTORE DATABASE; however, the syntax and options are the same.

To set up this demonstration, a new database is created called TrainingDB:

```
IF NOT EXISTS (SELECT name
                FROM sys.databases
                WHERE name = 'TrainingDB')
BEGIN
    CREATE DATABASE TrainingDB
END
GO

-- Add a table and some data to it
USE TrainingDB
GO

SELECT *
INTO dbo.SalesOrderDetail
FROM AdventureWorks.Sales.SalesOrderDetail
GO
```

This database will be given a full backup and two consecutive transaction log backups:

```
BACKUP DATABASE TrainingDB
TO DISK = 'C:\Apress\Recipes\TrainingDB.bak'
GO

BACKUP LOG TrainingDB
TO DISK = 'C:\Apress\Recipes\TrainingDB_Oct_14_2008_8AM.trn'
GO

-- Two hours pass, another transaction log backup is made

BACKUP LOG TrainingDB
TO DISK = 'C:\Apress\Recipes\TrainingDB_Oct_14_2008_10AM.trn'
GO
```

The previous RESTORE examples have assumed that there were no existing connections in the database to be restored over. However, in this example, I demonstrate how to kick out any connections to the database prior to performing the RESTORE:

```
USE master
GO

-- Kicking out all other connections
ALTER DATABASE TrainingDB
SET SINGLE_USER
WITH ROLLBACK IMMEDIATE
```

Next, a database backup and two transaction log backups are restored from backup:

```
RESTORE DATABASE TrainingDB
FROM DISK = 'C:\Apress\Recipes\TrainingDB.bak'
WITH NORECOVERY, REPLACE

RESTORE LOG TrainingDB
FROM DISK = 'C:\Apress\Recipes\TrainingDB_Oct_14_2008_8AM.trn'
WITH NORECOVERY, REPLACE
```

```
RESTORE LOG TrainingDB
FROM DISK = 'C:\Apress\Recipes\TrainingDB_Oct_14_2008_10AM.trn'
WITH RECOVERY, REPLACE
```

This returns

```
Processed 1656 pages for database 'TrainingDB', file 'TrainingDB' on file 1.
Processed 2 pages for database 'TrainingDB', file 'TrainingDB_log' on file 1.
RESTORE DATABASE successfully processed 1658 pages in 4.164 seconds (3.260 MB/sec).
Processed 0 pages for database 'TrainingDB', file 'TrainingDB' on file 1.
Processed 2 pages for database 'TrainingDB', file 'TrainingDB_log' on file 1.
RESTORE LOG successfully processed 2 pages in 0.066 seconds (0.186 MB/sec).
RESTORE LOG successfully processed 0 pages in 0.072 seconds (0.000 MB/sec).
```

In this second example, I'll use STOPAT to restore the database and transaction log as of a specific point in time. To demonstrate, first a full backup will be taken of the TrainingDB database:

```
BACKUP DATABASE TrainingDB
TO DISK  = 'C:\Apress\Recipes\TrainingDB_Oct_14_2008.bak'
```

Next, rows will be deleted out of the table, and the current time after the change will be queried:

```
USE TrainingDB
GO

DELETE dbo.SalesOrderDetail
WHERE ProductID = 776
GO

SELECT GETDATE()
GO
```

This returns

```
2008-10-14 20:20:56.583
```

Next, a transaction log backup is performed:

```
BACKUP LOG TrainingDB
TO DISK = 'C:\Apress\Recipes\TrainingDB_Oct_14_2008_2022.trn'
```

This returns

```
Processed 18 pages for database 'TrainingDB', file 'TrainingDB_log' on file 1.
BACKUP LOG successfully processed 18 pages in 0.163 seconds (0.876 MB/sec).
```

The database is restored from backup, leaving it in NORECOVERY so that the transaction log backup can also be restored:

```
USE master
GO

RESTORE DATABASE TrainingDB
FROM  DISK = 'C:\Apress\Recipes\TrainingDB_Oct_14_2008.bak'
WITH  FILE = 1,  NORECOVERY,
STOPAT = '2008-10-14 20:18:56.583'
GO
```

Next, the transaction log is restored, also designating the time prior to the data deletion:

```
RESTORE LOG TrainingDB
FROM  DISK = 'C:\Apress\Recipes\TrainingDB_Oct_14_2008_2022.trn'
WITH  RECOVERY,
STOPAT = '2008-10-14 20:18:56.583'
GO
```

The following query confirms that you have restored just prior to the data deletion:

```
USE TrainingDB
GO

SELECT COUNT(*)
FROM dbo.SalesOrderDetail
WHERE ProductID = 776
GO
```

This returns

228

How It Works

In the first example for this recipe, the `TrainingDB` database was restored from a full database backup and left in `NORECOVERY` mode. Being in `NORECOVERY` mode allows other transaction log or differential backups to be applied. In this example, two transaction log backups were applied in chronological order, with the second using the `RECOVERY` option to bring the database online.

The second example in the recipe demonstrated restoring a database as of a specific point in time. Point-in-time recovery is useful for restoring a database prior to a database modification or failure. The syntax was similar to the first example, only the `STOPAT` was used for both the `RESTORE DATABASE` and `RESTORE LOG`. Including the `STOPAT` for each `RESTORE` statement makes sure that the restore doesn't recover past the designated date.

Restoring a Database from a Differential Backup

The syntax for differential database restores is identical to full database restores, only full database restores must be performed *prior* to applying differential backups. When restoring the full database backup, the database must be left in `NORECOVERY` mode. Also, any transaction logs you wish to restore must be done *after* the differential backup is applied, as this example demonstrates.

First, however, I'll set up the example by performing a full, differential, and transaction log backup on the `TrainingDB` database:

```
USE master
GO

BACKUP DATABASE TrainingDB
TO DISK = 'C:\Apress\Recipes\TrainingDB_DiffExample.bak'

-- Time passes

BACKUP DATABASE TrainingDB
TO DISK = 'C:\Apress\Recipes\TrainingDB_DiffExample.diff'
WITH DIFFERENTIAL
```

```
-- More time passes

BACKUP LOG TrainingDB
TO DISK = 'C:\Apress\Recipes\TrainingDB_DiffExample_tlog.trn'
```

Now, I'll demonstrate performing a RESTORE, bringing the database back to the completion of the last transaction log backup:

```
USE master
GO

-- Full database restore
RESTORE DATABASE TrainingDB
FROM DISK = 'C:\Apress\Recipes\TrainingDB_DiffExample.bak'
WITH NORECOVERY, REPLACE

-- Differential
RESTORE DATABASE TrainingDB
FROM DISK = 'C:\Apress\Recipes\TrainingDB_DiffExample.diff'
WITH NORECOVERY

-- Transaction log
RESTORE LOG TrainingDB
FROM DISK = 'C:\Apress\Recipes\TrainingDB_DiffExample_tlog.trn'
WITH RECOVERY
```

This returns

```
Processed 152 pages for database 'TrainingDB', file 'TrainingDB' on file 1.
Processed 2 pages for database 'TrainingDB', file 'TrainingDB_log' on file 1.
RESTORE DATABASE successfully processed 154 pages in 0.443 seconds (2.831 MB/sec).
Processed 40 pages for database 'TrainingDB', file 'TrainingDB' on file 1.
Processed 1 pages for database 'TrainingDB', file 'TrainingDB_log' on file 1.
RESTORE DATABASE successfully processed 41 pages in 0.069 seconds (4.860 MB/sec).
RESTORE LOG successfully processed 0 pages in 0.070 seconds (0.000 MB/sec).
```

How It Works

Differential backups capture database changes that have occurred since the last full database backup. Differential restores use the same syntax as full database restores, only they must always follow a full database restore (with NORECOVERY) first. In this recipe, the database was initially restored from a full database backup, then followed by a restore from a differential backup, and then lastly a restore from a transaction log backup. The differential RESTORE command was formed similarly to previous RESTORE examples, only it referenced the differential backup file. On the last restore, the RECOVERY option was designated to make the database available for use.

Restoring a File or Filegroup

Restoring a file or filegroup uses virtually the same syntax as a full database restore, except you also use the FILEGROUP or FILE keyword. To perform a restore of a specific read-write file or filegroup, your database must use either a full or bulk-logged recovery model. This is required because transaction log backups must be applied after restoring a file or filegroup backup. In SQL Server, if your database is using a simple recovery model, only read-only files or read-only filegroups can have file/filegroup backups and restores.

To set up this recipe's example, a filegroup backup is taken for the VLTestDB database:

```
USE master
GO

BACKUP DATABASE VLTestDB
FILEGROUP = 'FG2'
TO  DISK = 'C:\Apress\Recipes\VLTestDB_FG2.bak'
WITH NAME = N'VLTestDB-Full Filegroup Backup',
SKIP, STATS = 20
GO
```

Time passes, and then a transaction log backup is taken for the database:

```
BACKUP LOG VLTestDB
TO DISK = 'C:\Apress\Recipes\VLTestDB_FG_Example.trn'
```

Next, the database filegroup FG2 is restored from backup, followed by the restore of a transaction log backup:

```
USE master
GO

RESTORE DATABASE VLTestDB
FILEGROUP = 'FG2'
FROM  DISK = 'C:\Apress\Recipes\VLTestDB_FG2.bak'
WITH  FILE = 1, NORECOVERY, REPLACE

RESTORE LOG VLTestDB
FROM DISK  = 'C:\Apress\Recipes\VLTestDB_FG_Example.trn'
WITH  FILE = 1, RECOVERY
```

This returns

```
Processed 8 pages for database 'VLTestDB', file 'VLTestDB2' on file 1.
Processed 8 pages for database 'VLTestDB', file 'VLTestDB3' on file 1.
RESTORE DATABASE ... FILE=<name> successfully processed
16 pages in 0.119 seconds (1.101 MB/sec).
Processed 0 pages for database 'VLTestDB', file 'VLTestDB2' on file 1.
Processed 0 pages for database 'VLTestDB', file 'VLTestDB3' on file 1.
RESTORE LOG successfully processed 0 pages in 0.062 seconds (0.000 MB/sec).
```

How It Works

Filegroup or file backups are most often used in very large databases, where full database backups may take too long to execute. With filegroup or file backups comes greater administrative complexity, because you'll have to potentially recover from disaster using multiple backup sets (one per filegroup, for example).

In this recipe, the VLTestDB database filegroup named FG2 was restored from a backup device and left in NORECOVERY mode so that a transaction log restore could be applied. The RECOVERY keyword was used in the transaction log restore operation in order to bring the filegroup back online. In SQL Server Enterprise Edition, filegroups other than the primary filegroup can be taken off-line for restores while leaving the other active filegroups available for use (this is called an ONLINE restore).

Performing a Piecemeal (PARTIAL) Restore

The PARTIAL command can be used with the RESTORE DATABASE command to restore secondary filegroups in a piecemeal fashion. This variation of RESTORE brings the primary filegroup online, letting you then restore other filegroups as needed later on. If you're using a database with a full or bulk-logged recovery model, you can use this command with read-write filegroups. If the database is using a simple recovery model, you can only use PARTIAL in conjunction with read-only secondary filegroups.

In this example, the VLTestDB is restored from a full database backup using the PARTIAL keyword and designating that only the PRIMARY filegroup be brought online (and with filegroups FG2 and FG3 staying offline and unrestored).

First, to set up this example, the primary and FG2 filegroups in the VLTestDB are backed up:

```
USE master
GO

BACKUP DATABASE VLTestDB
FILEGROUP = 'PRIMARY'
TO  DISK = 'C:\Apress\Recipes\VLTestDB_Primary_PieceExmp.bak'
GO

BACKUP DATABASE VLTestDB
FILEGROUP = 'FG2'
TO  DISK = 'C:\Apress\Recipes\VLTestDB_FG2_PieceExmp.bak'
GO
```

After that, a transaction log backup is performed:

```
BACKUP LOG VLTestDB
TO DISK = 'C:\Apress\Recipes\VLTestDB_PieceExmp.trn'
GO
```

Next, a piecemeal RESTORE is performed, recovering just the PRIMARY filegroup:

```
RESTORE DATABASE VLTestDB
FILEGROUP = 'PRIMARY'
FROM DISK = 'C:\Apress\Recipes\VLTestDB_Primary_PieceExmp.bak'
WITH PARTIAL, NORECOVERY, REPLACE

RESTORE LOG VLTestDB
FROM DISK = 'C:\Apress\Recipes\VLTestDB_PieceExmp.trn'
WITH RECOVERY
```

The other filegroup, FG2, now contains unavailable files. You can view the file status by querying sys.database_files from the VLTestDB database:

```
USE VLTestDB
GO

SELECT name,
   state_desc
FROM sys.database_files
```

This returns

```
Name              state_desc
VLTestDB          ONLINE
VLTestDB_log      ONLINE
VLTestDB2         RECOVERY_PENDING
VLTestDB3         RECOVERY_PENDING
```

How It Works

In this recipe, the VLTestDB was restored from a full backup, restoring just the PRIMARY filegroup. The WITH clause included the PARTIAL keyword and NORECOVERY, so that transaction log backups can be restored. After the transaction log restore, any objects in the PRIMARY filegroup will be available, and objects in the secondary filegroups are unavailable until you restore them at a later time.

For very large databases, using the PARTIAL keyword during a RESTORE operation allows you to prioritize and load filegroups that have a higher priority, making them available sooner.

Restoring a Page

SQL Server provides the ability to restore specific data pages in a database using a FULL or BULK_LOGGED recovery model. In the rare event that a small number of data pages become corrupted in a database, it may be more efficient to restore individual data pages than the entire file, filegroup, or database.

The syntax for restoring specific pages is similar to restoring a filegroup or database, only you use the PAGE keyword coupled with the page ID. Bad pages can be identified in the msdb.dbo. suspect_pages system table, in the SQL error log, or returned in the output of a DBCC command.

To set up this example, a full database backup is created for the TestDB database:

```
BACKUP DATABASE TestDB
TO DISK = 'C:\Apress\Recipes\TestDB_PageExample.bak'
GO
```

Next, a restore is performed using the PAGE argument:

```
RESTORE DATABASE TestDB
PAGE='1:8'
FROM DISK = 'C:\Apress\Recipes\TestDB_PageExample.bak'
WITH NORECOVERY, REPLACE
GO
```

This returns

```
Processed 1 pages for database 'TestDB', file 'TestDB' on file 1.
RESTORE DATABASE ... FILE=<name> successfully processed 1 pages
in 1.107 seconds (0.007 MB/sec).
```

At this point, any differential or transaction log backups taken after the last full backup should also be restored. Since there were none in this example, no further backups are restored.

Next, and this is something that departs from previous examples, a new transaction log backup must be created that captures the restored page:

```
BACKUP LOG TestDB
TO DISK  = 'C:\Apress\Recipes\TestDB_PageExample_tlog.trn'
GO
```

This returns

```
Processed 2 pages for database 'TestDB', file 'TestDB_log' on file 1.
BACKUP LOG successfully processed 2 pages in 0.840 seconds (0.014 MB/sec).
```

To finish the page restore process, the latest transaction log taken after the RESTORE...PAGE must be executed with RECOVERY:

```
RESTORE LOG TestDB
FROM DISK = 'C:\Apress\Recipes\TestDB_PageExample_tlog.trn'
WITH RECOVERY
```

How It Works

In this recipe, a single data page was restored from a full database backup using the PAGE option in the RESTORE DATABASE command. Like restoring from a FILE or FILEGROUP, the first RESTORE leaves the database in a NORECOVERY state, allowing additional transaction log backups to be applied prior to recovery.

Identifying Databases with Multiple Recovery Paths

Multiple recovery paths are created when you recover a database from backup using point-in-time recovery, or when you recover a database without recovering the latest differential or chain of log backups. When there are backups created that you do not use in your RESTORE process, you create a fork in the recovery path.

This recipe demonstrates how to use the sys.database_recovery_status catalog view to get information about a database with more than one recovery path. In the first step, I will create a new database and give it a full database backup, create a table and some rows, and finish up with a transaction log backup:

```
USE master
GO

IF NOT EXISTS (SELECT name
                FROM sys.databases
                WHERE name = 'RomanHistory')
BEGIN
     CREATE DATABASE RomanHistory
END
GO

BACKUP DATABASE RomanHistory
TO DISK = 'C:\Apress\RomanHistory_A.bak'
GO

USE RomanHistory
GO

CREATE TABLE EmperorTitle
   (EmperorTitleID int NOT NULL PRIMARY KEY IDENTITY(1,1),
    TitleNM varchar(255))
GO
```

```
INSERT EmperorTitle (TitleNM)
VALUES ('Aulus'), ('Imperator'), ('Pius Felix'), ('Quintus')

BACKUP LOG RomanHistory
TO DISK = 'C:\Apress\RomanHistory_A.trn'
GO
```

Next, I'll query the sys.database_recovery_status catalog view to get information about the database at this point (column aliases are used to shorten the names for presentation in this book):

```
SELECT last_log_backup_lsn LastLSN, recovery_fork_guid Rec_Fork,
first_recovery_fork_guid Frst_Fork, fork_point_lsn Fork_LSN
FROM sys.database_recovery_status
WHERE database_id = DB_ID('RomanHistory')
```

This query returns the following (your values will vary):

LastLSN	Rec_Fork	Frst_Fork	Fork_LSN
18000000010900001	D020752F-1085-49F6-A848-21C9EDBFF290	NULL	NULL

Notice that the first_recovery_fork_guid and fork_point_lsn columns are NULL. This is because I have not created a fork yet in my recovery path. The last_log_backup_lsn tells me the LSN of the most recent log backup, and the recovery_fork_guid shows the current recovery path in which the database is active.

▌**Tip** A log sequence number (LSN) uniquely identifies each record in a database transaction log.

Next, I will perform a few more data modifications and another transaction log backup:

```
INSERT EmperorTitle (TitleNM)
VALUES ('Germanicus'), ('Lucius'), ('Maximus'), ('Titus')

BACKUP LOG RomanHistory
TO DISK = 'C:\Apress\RomanHistory_B.trn'
GO
```

I'll now go ahead and RESTORE the database to a prior state (but not to the latest state):

```
USE master
GO

RESTORE DATABASE RomanHistory
FROM DISK = 'C:\Apress\RomanHistory_A.bak'
WITH NORECOVERY

RESTORE DATABASE RomanHistory
FROM DISK = 'C:\Apress\RomanHistory_A.trn'
WITH RECOVERY
```

Now if I reissue the previous query against sys.database_recovery_status, I will see that both the fork_point_lsn and first_recovery_fork_guid columns are no longer NULL:

```
SELECT last_log_backup_lsn LastLSN, recovery_fork_guid Rec_Fork,
first_recovery_fork_guid Frst_Fork, fork_point_lsn Fork_LSN
FROM sys.database_recovery_status
WHERE database_id = DB_ID('RomanHistory')
```

This query returns

LastLSN	Rec_Fork	Frst_Fork	Fork_LSN
18000000010900001	F18522D8-6FDB-40BE-AB99-047DE4280F40	D020752F-1085-49F6-A848-21C9EDBFF290	18000000010900001

How It Works

The sys.database_recovery_status catalog view allows you to see whether multiple recovery forks have been created for a database.

In this recipe, I made one full database backup and two transaction log backups. If I restored the database using all three of the backups, I would have remained in the same recovery path. However, instead, I only restored the first full backup and first transaction log backup, putting the database into recovery before restoring the second transaction log. By recovering prematurely, I brought the database online into a second recovery path.

Index

■Symbols

@ prefix, 13, 328
@@ prefix, 293
%= modulo, assign operator, 84
&= bitwise &, assign operator, 84
^= bitwise exclusive OR, assign operator, 84
|= bitwise |, assign operator, 84
*.bak files, 794
*= multiply, assign operator, 84
+= add, assign operator, 84
-= subtract, assign operator, 84
/= divide, assign operator, 84
= equality operator, 84
; semicolon, 59
[ ] wildcard, 11
[^] wildcard, 11
!< operator, 8
!> operator, 8
!= operator, 8
sign, prefixing local temporary tables, 176
sign, prefixing global temporary tables, 176
% wildcard, 11
< operator, 8
< > operator, 8
<= operator, 8
> operator, 8
+ operator, 24
= operator, 8
_ wildcard, 11

■A

ABS function, 261
accent sensitivity, 218
ACID test (Atomicity, Consistency, Isolation (or Independence), and Durability), 115
ACOS function, 261
ad hoc queries, executing via OPENROWSET command, 733
add, assign (+=) operator, 84
ADD FILE command, 654
ADD FILEGROUP command, 660
ADD LOG FILE command, 655
AdventureWorks sample database, downloading, 1
AFTER DML triggers, 375
AFTER triggers, 374
aggregate functions, 22, 257–261
aggregated performance statistics, viewing, 750
alias data types. *See* user-defined types
aliases, 732
    column, 15, 22
    table, 29
ALL operator, 8

allocated unit lock resource, 124
ALLOW_SNAPSHOT_ISOLATION database option, 647, 648
ALTER APPLICATION ROLE command, 498
ALTER ASSEMBLY command, 417
ALTER ASYMMETRIC KEY command, 557
ALTER BROKER PRIORITY command, 597
ALTER CERTIFICATE command, 570
ALTER COLUMN command, 149
ALTER DATABASE AUDIT SPECIFICATION command, 543
ALTER DATABASE command, 213, 393, 397, 581, 629, 631
    ANSI SQL options and, 637
    changing recovery mode and, 649
    cursor options and, 642
    database compatibility level and, 623
    database mirroring and, 700, 707
    database state and, 652
    external access and, 640
    files/filegroups and, 654–663
    operating modes, configuring via, 711
    page verification and, 651
    parameterization and, 644
    read-consistency options and, 648
    shrinking databases/database files and, 667
    Transparent Data Encryption and, 575
ALTER DATABASE...SET PARTNER FAILOVER command, 712
ALTER DATABASE...SET PARTNER FORCE_SERVICE_ALLOW_DATA_LOSS command, 712
ALTER DATABASE...SET PARTNER OFF command, 714
ALTER DATABASE...SET PARTNER SUSPEND command, 713
ALTER DATABASE...SET PARTNER TIMEOUT command, 714
ALTER FULLTEXT CATALOG command, 221
ALTER FULLTEXT INDEX command, 222
ALTER FULLTEXT STOPLIST command, 227, 229
ALTER FUNCTION, 354
ALTER INDEX command, 200, 205, 215, 429
ALTER INDEX REBUILD command, 682
ALTER INDEX REORGANIZE command, 682, 685
ALTER LOGIN command, 483, 612
ALTER MASTER KEY command, 552, 554
ALTER OWNERSHIP command, 527
ALTER PARTITION FUNCTION command, 186
ALTER PARTITION SCHEME command, 186
ALTER PROCEDURE command, 332
ALTER QUEUE command, 598
ALTER RESOURCE GOVERNOR command, 786
ALTER RESOURCE POOL command, 784

You Need the Companion eBook